D0409232

UCD WOMEN'S CENTER

PLAYING *Nice*

PLAYING *Nice*

Politics and
Apologies
in
Women's Sports

Mary Jo Festle

Columbia University Press   *New York*

Columbia University Press
Publishers Since 1893
New York Chichester, West Sussex
Copyright © 1996 Columbia University Press

Library of Congress Cataloging-in-Publication Data

Festle, Mary Jo
    Playing nice : politics and apologies in women's sports / Mary Jo Festle.
        p.   cm.
    Includes bibliographical references and index.
    ISBN 0–231–10162–7(cloth : alk. paper)
    1. Sports for women—United States—History. 2. Sex differences
    (Psychology) 3. Women athletes—United States—History. 4. Sports and
    state—United States. I. Title.
GV709.F37   1996
796'.0194—dc20   96–4739

Casebound editions of Columbia University Press books are printed on permanent and
durable acid-free paper.

Printed in the United States of America
c 10 9 8 7 6 5 4 3 2 1
p 10 9 8 7 6 5 4 3 2 1

To Bob

and Jill,

for their courage and love

CONTENTS

ABBREVIATIONS

AAHPER	American Alliance for Health, Physical Education, and Recreation (*before 1975:* American Association for Health, Physical Education, and Recreation)
AAU	Amateur Athletic Union
AIAW	Association for Intercollegiate Athletics for Women
ATA	American Tennis Association
CIAW	Commission on Intercollegiate Athletics for Women
DGWS	Division for Girls' and Women's Sports
ILTF	International Lawn Tennis Federation
NAGWS	National Association for Girls' and Women's Sports
NAIA	National Association of Intercollegiate Athletes
NAPECW	National Association for the Physical Education of College Women
NCAA	National Collegiate Athletic Association
NSGWS	National Section for Girls' and Women's Sports
NSWA	National Section on Women's Athletics
PCPF	President's Council on Physical Fitness
PCYF	President's Council on Youth Fitness
SAPECW	Southern Association for Physical Education of College Women
USLTA	United States Lawn Tennis Association
USOC	United States Olympic Committee
USODC	United States Olympic Development Committee
WAA	Women's Athletic Association
WBL	Women's Basketball League
WTA	Women's Tennis Association

PREFACE

"The personal is political" insisted feminists in the late 1960s. By that, they meant that power relations have an impact on the fabric of individuals' daily lives, and that, conversely, an individual's personal experiences help shape her political beliefs. There's no doubt that the political, intellectual, social, and personal arenas have been intertwined in my life. In particular, many of my sports-related experiences influenced my thinking in this book.

Both my mother and my father were talented athletes, meeting as physical education (PE) majors at DePaul University in Chicago. They passed along their interest (and a bit of coordination) to my brothers and myself, encouraging us to both play and compete. My mother displayed a matter-of-fact competence and skill, thereby serving as an important role model for me. At our mother-daughter volleyball and softball games in grammar school, other girls were embarrassed because their mothers didn't even know the rules and moved so clumsily. Not me—mine excelled. Through Mom, I also became aware that females used to play by different rules than males (a concept I found incredibly stupid). She had grown up with a rule prohibiting her from dribbling a basketball more than two times. Despite that limitation, she could drive powerfully to the basket from beyond the top of the key, and I was impressed.

My father occasionally had time summer evenings to play out in the alley with the neighborhood children, and there he began to mold me as an athlete. I learned how to catch and throw the proper way, how to execute a perfect rundown, how to hit the ball to all fields. I imbibed his philosophy, too: always play smart; don't swing for a home-run when the team needs a single; second place is virtually worthless; and winning requires "killer instinct." Dad's suggestion that I (like most of my female teammates) did not possess killer instinct both angered and troubled me. On the one hand, I knew that I was more competitive and intense than almost anyone I knew. I liked that, because I wanted to be an athlete my dad would be proud of. On the other hand, there were times mercy felt more appropriate than killer instinct and when winning did not feel worth the cost. I wasn't sure I wanted to throw at the head of runners who didn't slide, or bowl over a fielder who got in the way. In fact, I feared that I (or others) would lose control of those competitive instincts and actually hurt someone. As early as high school, then, I felt some ambivalence about the established model of sports that my Dad so ably conveyed.

Still, I'll never forget the hours of almost pure pleasure I spent in my youth playing a wide variety of sports—passing a volleyball for hours on end, fielding ground ball after ground ball in the mid-afternoon sun, staking out an early morning tennis court, playing "running bases" in the twilight in the alley. I loved the companionship of the girls and boys who hung out with me, I loved the competition and the excitement, and I loved the comforting sense of belonging to a place and to a team. I loved the constant repetition of motor patterns and the way it feels to execute a physical skill just right. Strange as it sounds to one who doesn't share the sentiment, I still appreciate the smells of a gymnasium recently used, enjoy sweating from exertion, and thrill at the sight of a ball field.

The summer before I went off to college, I had an experience that foreshadowed one of the themes of this book. A much-loved coach, concerned about my well-being, took me aside for a talk. Be careful in PE departments, she warned, intimating that I knew what she was talking about. Look out for PE majors. Confused, I told her that my college didn't offer a physical education major, so she needn't worry. Frustrated that I didn't get her drift, she made another allusion to the "type" of women who were found in athletic programs—lesbians, I eventually gathered—and suggested I not associate with them. As I look back, my ignorance seems an indication that up to that point I had been competing in a supportive climate. But naïveté did not last much longer. My coach's warning turned out to be merely the first of many signs that while it was considered all right for a girl to be a tomboy playing sports, it was quite a different matter for a woman. The implicit message—that one would be considered weird (and/or lesbian) if one were not careful—became more apparent with each passing year.

After high school, I wanted to exercise my brain and body even further and made a good choice in Knox College. At Knox, an excellent small liberal arts institution, athletes passionate about sports prided themselves on being students first. There I could participate wholeheartedly in a number of varsity sports. (I had what I imagine is a typical experience: intense involvement with teammates, exciting rivalries, fevered competition, caring coaches, seemingly endless van rides, loss of sleep, box lunches, injuries, and excellent memories.) At the same time, at Knox I could drink in an exciting intellectual community, one that fostered critical thinking and my interests in social change and history. Even as I played sports, I questioned some of its unappealing aspects: its potential for violence, authoritarianism, self-destructiveness, inequality, insensitivity, and loss of perspective. I started to think more systematically about whether it was possible to find an alternative model of sports, one that eliminated its more unsavory aspects while keeping the positive ones.

Because I had attended an all-girl high school, I was naive in yet another way: I hadn't experienced sex discrimination. At other high schools, I discovered, girls had endured clearly inferior athletic opportunities, constantly begging for sufficient gym space, coaching, practice time, resources, and cheerleaders. At my school, however, we *were* the basketball team (not just "the girl's team"). We hadn't had to worry about whether fans would stay for our games or think less of us or whether the boys wouldn't like us as much as the other girls. Those issues were irrelevant. Although Knox's athletic department was not nearly as unequal as most of those in other schools, as a college student I now experienced a variety of injustices. Female athletes were squeezed into a very small locker area; they could not use the weight and training rooms (because one had to walk through the men's lockers to get there); they received less money for food on road trips and never got the Saturday steaks the football team enjoyed; they shared nasty uniforms, had to use inferior equipment, and got little or no publicity for their contests. To the athletic department's credit, it did respond fairly quickly to complaints from female athletes and their faculty advocates. However, it distressed me that these inequities even had to be pointed out, that some of the men in charge literally *did not see* the problems until women protested.

While I was at Knox, another event described in this book briefly touched my life. The Association for Intercollegiate Athletics for Women (AIAW), the national governing body for women's sports, was on the brink of folding, and our conference was discussing what to do about it. We had to choose whether to stick with the AIAW while it existed or move to one of the previously all-male organizations, the National Collegiate Athletic Association (NCAA) or the National Association of Intercollegiate Athletes (NAIA). I remember the debate only dimly, but I do recall that most of the conference's faculty athletic representatives favored remaining loyal to the AIAW, and most of the athletic directors (all of whom were male) wanted to switch to the NCAA. Our male athletic administrators did not understand why some of us did not want to join an organization that so strenuously opposed gender equity, and why we felt the NCAA was trying to buy us out of our commitment to principles (such as women having a strong voice in running their own athletic programs). The conflict was both frustrating and ironic, because Knox actually was a place where student-athletes like myself had a voice in their athletic programs. We had joined in long discussions about training rules, what sort of dress to wear on road trips, what defenses to use, and how to balance academic and social interests. Even at a small liberal arts college with sensible athletic values, then, there were difficult battles over how to obtain justice for female athletes. Later, as a historian, I would discover just how common such battles were.

Since undergraduate days, my athletic experiences have been less frequent but quite varied, and my participation has ranged from very competitive to recreational; I have coached an egalitarian, cooperative, feminist softball team as well as taught baseball skills to boys six to eight years old. All these sports experiences have shaped me, as have countless discussions with coaches, feminists, athletes, sports administrators, and friends.

My ideas, values, and experiences unrelated to athletics have further shaped me. My concern for justice, especially in eradicating racism, sexism, heterosexism, classism, and poverty, have influenced this book. So, too, did my early graduate studies in history. While researching the Student Nonviolent Coordinating Committee (SNCC) and the Black Power movement, I came to better understand the difficulty of achieving equality while allowing for difference in the United States. African-Americans during the 1960s understandably wanted the same rights as all other citizens, but at the same time wanted the power to determine their own fate, and to choose to be different from the dominant culture. By deconstructing this dilemma, feminists gave me a paradigm and language critiquing the limits of dualistic thinking. In particular, Joan Scott's description of how women are forced into choosing between equality and difference seems pertinent to the situation of both AIAW leaders and tennis pros.

Feminists (and some Marxist theorists) also convinced me of the extraordinary (hegemonic) power of certain ideas and cultural expectations, such as femininity. A number of writers, ranging from W. E. B. Du Bois to lesbian psychologist JoAnn Loulan, interested me in the psychological toll endured by members of marginal groups. They describe the paradox in which oppressed individuals can both articulate an intellectual critique of prejudice, yet also at times believe and feel ashamed of stereotypes circulated about them. This awareness of "double consciousness" has helped me appreciate the pang of internalized sexism as well as the joy that female athletes have experienced. Finally, studies of past social movements have convinced me that change is an extremely complex phenomenon, possible only in certain circumstances and influenced by ideology, opposition, tactics, internal dynamics, organization, government, economics, timing, and power. This book's interpretation, then, as a product of my own historical, political, and athletic opinions, is my responsibility alone.

I am very grateful to the people who have helped me with this book. In particular, thanks to those who shared many meaningful sports experiences with me, especially my parents and brothers and my fellow athletes. My dissertation committee was equally important—in a very different way. Thanks to Jacquelyn D. Hall, William E. Leuchtenburg, Donald G. Mathews, Nell Painter, and Suzanne Lebsock, for providing historical expertise, timely and helpful suggestions, and enthusiastic encouragement about the project. Peter Filene, my dissertation adviser, listened carefully to what I was trying to do and helped me find ways to do it. His constructive and detailed criticism improved my writing enormously. Peter's fundamental decency has been an inspiration, and his support, both scholarly and personal, has been unflagging.

A number of other people—including Susan Cahn, Dan Hinman-Smith, Edward M. Neal, Penny Gold, Joel Williamson, and Jill Snider—also read and commented on portions of the book. It would be difficult to measure the impact of discussions with my colleagues at the University of North Carolina and Elon College. At Elon, the Research and Development Committee awarded me a travel grant and course release time for writing. The History Department has stood behind me, and the Old Ladies Athletic Adventures crew buoyed me. In addition, Pat Long and Stephanie Henly helped make production of the manuscript possible. Elizabeth Raynor helped me reproduce photographs. Archivists like Anne Turkos and Lauren Brown at the University of Maryland made my life much easier. Charlotte West doggedly tracked down who was who in some old photographs. Jennifer Hamlet copied microfilm for me. At Columbia University Press, Roy E. Thomas's careful eyes caught awkwardness and inconsistencies, and Kate Wittenberg warmly guided me through the process of turning the dissertation into a book. Many people involved in sports willingly let me interview them, some formally, and some not. To all of you, including those who wanted to remain anonymous, please know you have my heartfelt appreciation.

This project outlived some people I loved very much. I especially feel the absence of John, Dad, and Gram. I am grateful to those members of my family who are here to celebrate with me—Mom, Tom, Jim, and Bob, and Jackie, Lisa, Grandma, Uncle Bob, and the Thompsons. They—and Bob most especially— with love and humor have continually supported me in my work and in my life. My Chicago-based family served as only part of my support system, however; my North Carolina family has also sustained me. I hope the members of this nurturing community know how much I value them. No one has meant more than Jill Snider. Her insights about history, politics, and life have taught me more than any years of research. I am awed by her love, friendship, and courage. I treasure our history and look forward to our future.

INTRODUCTION

During the winter of 1993–94, millions of Americans sat glued to their televisions devouring details of a dramatic tale involving figure skaters Nancy Kerrigan and Tonya Harding. Each had been competing at the U.S. Figure Skating Championship in Detroit, hoping to win one of two positions on the U.S. Olympic team. One early January afternoon, as Kerrigan was leaving the ice after practice, a bulky white man suddenly appeared from the shadows and attacked her. Swinging a long metal object as if it were a baseball bat, he hit her above the knee. Kerrigan fell to the ground and, filled with anguish, cried "Why? Why me?" The injury prevented Kerrigan from continuing the contest she had enjoyed a good chance of winning. Nevertheless, outraged skating officials assured Kerrigan a spot on the U.S. team, along with Tonya Harding, who had won the competition more easily in Kerrigan's absence. Police quickly captured the thugs who had performed the attack. When authorities disclosed connections between the assailants and Harding's bodyguard and her ex-husband (with whom she was again involved), suspicion immediately shifted to Harding. Had she known about the attack? Even worse, had she been in on it? Or was she, as she claimed, innocent of any wrongdoing? It would be embarrassing for someone suspected of a crime to represent the United States, but downright scandalous if she had aided and abetted that crime in order to make the Olympic team. Americans debated whether Harding should be removed from the team or presumed innocent unless proven otherwise. As Kerrigan's muscles healed, Harding became the subject of intense scrutiny.

The media fanned the flames of the story. Interest skyrocketed after Harding belatedly admitted that, although she did not report it to police, she found out after the attack that her ex-husband, Jeff Gillooly, had been involved. As evidence mounted against Gillooly, he implicated Harding. Claiming that he was trying to blame her in order to save himself, Harding maintained that she had no role in the conspiracy. Meanwhile, respectable and sensational news organizations competed to tell the public every possible detail about the case and Harding's turbulent life. Interviewing her mother (who had been married five times), father and stepfathers, lawyer, employers, competitors, childhood coaches, friends, and anyone remotely connected to her, the press painted a picture of an ambitious, tough, and talented competitor who had battled poverty, instability, and domestic violence to rise to the top of her field. A mob of reporters shadowed her every move and informed the growing audience that Harding drove a truck and knew how to overhaul its transmission, played pool, hunted deer, and, although asthmatic, smoked cigarettes. By nineteen she had dropped out of high school, married, and requested restraining orders against her husband for abusing her. She worked afternoons at Spud City, a mall fast-food potato restaurant, in order to pay morning ice rink fees. Journalists unearthed details about her stormy on-again, off-again marriage to Gillooly, and even televised a home videotape of her disrobing on their wedding night. Matching the other gossip sensation of the day (in which Lorena Bobbitt had cut off her husband's penis after he raped her), the story displaced other news, distracting Americans from horrific wars in Bosnia and Rwanda, and a major earthquake near Los Angeles.[1]

Some managed to capitalize on the story, of course. Commentators noted it was a soap opera that had everything: "a beautiful heroine, vicious attack, high-stakes competition, a bunch of sleazy thugs, and lots and lots of legs."[2] Almost instantly, biographies of the two athletes hit the bookstores, and three networks began plans for made-for-TV movies. Kerrigan found it a good time to negotiate with the Disney company for a million-dollar endorsement deal including personal appearances, a skating video, a children's book, and ice shows. For her part, Harding sold exclusive interviews to tabloids and threatened to sue American amateur sports officials if they did not allow her to compete. Only after her tearful and controversial performance at the Olympics, and a silver medal victory by Kerrigan, did all the hype subside. CBS, which earned at least $250,000 per thirty-second commercial, reveled in the 126.6 million viewers who watched the Olympic figure skating competition. The controversy had boosted ratings to record-setting levels.[3]

How should people who care about women's sports have responded to this incident? Should they have celebrated the fact that, for once, millions paid attention to women athletes? Should they have rejoiced that media executives finally found them worthy of front-page coverage? Many did. They were pleased that the figure skating finals became the fourth most-watched prime-time TV show in American history, and that along the way millions had discovered the combination of skill, grace, strength, and drive required of top figure skaters.

After years of playing second fiddle, women had good reason to want full inclusion in sport. Measured in virtually any terms—participants, spectators, media attention, economic impact—athletics has played an increasingly important role in the United States during the twentieth century. It constitutes a hugely successful business as well as one of the most prevalent forms of leisure.[4] Culturally, by the 1950s sport had virtually achieved status as a national religion, with its attendant rituals, vestments, holidays, saints, and language. Some observers believe sport is so widely practiced because play and competition are natural human activities; or because it involves body, mind, and spirit symbolically acting out the compelling drama of life and death, ecstasy and disappointment. Others credit the way sport resonates with the needs and values of American capitalism.[5] Regardless of the reason for sport's popularity, it is readily apparent that male athletes reap significant social benefits from it. As celebrities or heroes, stars (even high school and college ones) attract attention and sometimes adulation. Professionals earn enormous financial rewards. Many males—even those who do not become famous—enjoy sport's more intrinsic rewards. Knowing the appropriate movements, language, and symbols gives those who participate camaraderie and a feeling of belonging to an approved-of activity. In addition, athletes can experience a transcendent sensation from being mentally and physically absorbed and challenged. They develop physical skills combining strength and coordination, which contribute to a sense of accomplishment, competence, mastery, and well-being—in sum, to physical and psychological empowerment.[6] Although recently it has been changing, throughout the twentieth century many women have been deprived of opportunities to enjoy these benefits. Some did compete, but mostly in obscurity. Given this history, it is understandable that many celebrated the appearance of female athletes like Kerrigan and Harding in the limelight.

On the other hand, some who care about women's sports found little to celebrate in the Kerrigan-Harding spectacle. Unfortunately, they said, the one time female athletes received so much attention it was because of a negative incident. They bemoaned the fact that all the publicity resulted from off-the-ice behavior rather than the competition itself. (Some interpreted Americans' interest as that of voyeurs watching a "cat fight" between two scantily clad women instead of as fans of accomplished athletes.)[7] In addition, they questioned why people found this particular incident of violence and poor sportsmanship so fascinating. After all, athletes regularly bend the rules, taunt each other, and engage in brawls; in baseball, pitchers throw 90-mile-an-hour fastballs at a batter's head, and football players aim to take out an opponent's knees. Maybe it was surprising that participants in the noncontact, genteel, performance-oriented sport of figure skating could be so fierce. Or maybe it was shocking because the villain was female: perhaps people were surprised that a *woman* would refuse to play nice, that she might cheat and be so competitive as to condone violence in the pursuit of victory, glory, and money. If so, should we be glad that people are shocked when a women's sport exhibits some of the excessive, win-at-all-costs behavior sometimes present in men's sports? Should we be glad that Americans have different expectations of female athletes than male? Perhaps expecting greater integrity is not too harmful, but what if those different expectations include assumptions of inferiority, weakness, and a lack of seriousness and competitive drive?

Even before the clubbing of Kerrigan, one could have raised important questions about fairness in contemporary women's figure skating. Figure skating is different from most other sports; in fact, many say it is more of an artistic performance than a sport.[8] It depends in large part on style and presentation and has a very subjective scoring system. In basketball, for example, a basket counts as two points whether it was lucky, ugly, or the perfect shot, whereas in skating a jump is judged in part on the grace with which it has been exhibited. Nor would one be penalized in football because a team's uniform is deemed in poor taste.[9] Observers of figure skating believe it is impossible for a woman to win a championship if she is "too athletic" or "too muscular" (such as France's Surya Bonaly) or the wrong kind of person. In the politics of women's figure skating, "wrong" might mean from the wrong nation or ethnic group, or, more likely, someone too ambitious, too openly competitive, or too poor and "low-class." Tonya Harding personified "wrong": she crudely admitted that "what I'm really thinking about are dollar signs"; she combatively announced she intended to "whip [Kerrigan's] butt"; and she unapologetically associated with people from the wrong side of the tracks. Harding was seen as "white trash." According to her own coach, "Skating for Tonya [was] her ticket out of the gutter."[10]

Being the "wrong type" meant Tonya Harding could not climb from the gutter all the way to the summit. Harding did not fare as well with judges as the long, lean, classically good looking but less athletic Kerrigan. Even though she was one of only two women in the world who could land a jump called a triple axel, Harding could not land endorsements. Kerrigan, on the other hand, enjoyed contracts with Reebok, Campbell's Soup, Evian, and Northwest Airlines. Kerrigan and Harding had been typecast into two simplistic roles—

those of good girl versus bad girl, or to put it another way, the innocent princess victim and the evil conniving witch.[11] Kerrigan was far more complex than (and certainly not so upper-class as) a princess who had been victimized, and she would have difficulty living up to such a perfect image. But more troubling was Harding's role. Even before the attack, everyone knew Harding, who did not "play nice," had an image problem. As one sportswriter put it, "She was not glamorous. Her costumes reeked of polyester. She was known for mannish habits: shooting pool, cursing, repairing cars, shooting deer."[12] Many speculate that even if she had not crossed the unforgivable line into cheating, Harding had been unfairly prejudged and could not have become world champion in figure skating. The "mannish" Harding had crossed too many other lines. Indeed, sportswriter Robert Lipsyte perceived "a fierce determination to punish this woman [Harding] for not knowing her place, for challenging the establishment, for daring to use muscle and energy to beat sweetness and finesse, for smearing her low-rent, dysfunctional entourage over this crystalline floor."[13] Throughout the months of the saga, the language and images associated with Harding suggested she was bad—not simply for breaking accepted rules of sportsmanship but in a social sense, as low class and unfeminine.

The Kerrigan-Harding spectacle hardly typifies women's sports, yet in some ways it illustrates the legacy with which today's women athletes must contend. As they watched the drama unfold, many sportswomen identified with the plight of its protagonists. Accustomed to the pain of missed opportunities, they empathized with Kerrigan's frustration and anger that someone had tried to cheat her out of her big chance. They knew well the fear that she might not have the strength to overcome all the obstacles in her path. Despite growing suspicions that Harding may have committed a terrible deed, however, many female athletes also empathized with her. They were familiar with the phenomenon of being considered "bad girls" simply for being strong, aggressive, and ambitious. Olympic rower-turned-journalist Anna Seaton, for example, identified with Harding's dream that, even though she could never fit the darling image, if she only worked hard enough, people would judge her on her ability and accept her. To her dismay, she discovered that no matter how good she was at her sport, some would ridicule her as a failed woman. "Like the rowers I know who spit, grimace, blow mucus, wring the sweat out of their shirts in the course of hard practice and are generally considered just too big and powerful to be attractive," wrote Seaton, "Harding doesn't fit into any of the acceptable roles for female athletes."[14] The rejection (or fear of it) that these women endure is shared by many sportswomen, as well as by members of most marginalized groups. So long deprived of cultural acceptance and positive publicity, they worry considerably about the image being presented of anyone from the same group. Because they feel it reflects upon them personally, they cringe when it seems the media focus not on the virtuous and hard-working members of the oppressed group, but on the one exception who happens to fulfill the worst, or most stereotypical, characteristics. And many of them bend over backward to display perfect (in this case modest, feminine, and "nice") behavior—what this book calls "apologetic behavior"—in order to compensate for/counter the image that has been forced upon them.

Understandably, then, Seaton hoped Harding was innocent. But even if she were not, she thought Americans should be clear about which of Harding's characteristics they condemned. In fact, many of the same street-tough, openly ambitious traits Harding displayed would not be criticized in a male athlete (such as Charles Barkley), and might in football or basketball actually enhance his reputation.[15] Just like men, maintained Seaton, women should be given legal and safe outlets to express whatever form their competitive spirit takes. Seaton's reaction to Harding demonstrates that women athletes are still sensitive to the manner in which they are presented and perceived. Not all of them feel they are completely free to perform like a top-notch athlete—at least not if they want to be considered a "nice," normal woman. This book describes the ways women athletes were treated and judged in the past, as well as how they reacted to those circumstances. This history helps explain both the expectations and fears lingering today.

As the "gutter" and "pool-shooting" allusions to Harding suggest, women athletes must contend with more than a straightforward legacy of gender expectations. Socioeconomic class connotations are also crucial. Just as they help explain why Harding received less approval than Kerrigan, they are essential to understanding the historic complexities of women's sports in general. This book argues that gender combines with socioeconomic class as well as with race and sexuality to help determine not only who participates and how but also which sports become socially acceptable for women. For example, figure skating is one of the most televised of women's sports. Many believe its more genteel competition, its subjective scoring, its emphasis on grace and femininity and appearance contribute greatly to its acceptance. Other sports considered especially appropriate for women, such as gymnastics, golf, and tennis, share with figure skating certain characteristics: they are primarily individual, non-contact sports, practiced mostly (in the United States) by white and upper-middle-class females who wear revealing, feminine outfits. Despite their higher numbers of participants (including black and working-class white women), it is much more rare that aggressive team sports, especially those involving physical contact, gain national audiences. Athletes in sports like softball, basketball, and volleyball receive less attention, compensation, and approval than figure skaters. Today's athletes are forced to cope with disadvantages resulting from expectations and prejudices from earlier times.

Each sport has a unique history and development, and each sportswoman—black or white, rich or poor, professional or amateur, heterosexual or lesbian, married or single—reacted to her environment in an individual fashion. Still, over the years women in different sports frequently adopted similar strategies for coping with some recurrent problems. By focusing in detail on a couple of particular areas, this book tries to illuminate some of these shared experiences without masking the actual complexity that existed. It spotlights the history of tennis, one of the traditionally upper-middle-class, white, individual sports, tracing it from its amateur days in the 1950s through the turbulent movement in the 1970s leading to its present status as one of the success stories in women's sports, in which girls can aspire to notoriety and wealth as professionals. Basketball provides an effective contrast to tennis. Drawing on a much broader base of working, middle, and upper-class participants, it is a team sport, which is perceived as more aggressive and less feminine. The book follows basketball's path from the days of restrictive "girls' rules" to recent failed efforts to provide professional opportunities in the United States to women who can dunk.

Like that of many sportswomen before her, Nancy Kerrigan's story is partly one of victimization. Unfortunately, many of the female athletes who received the most media attention during 1993–94 did so precisely because they were victims. Tennis star Monica Seles was stabbed in the back on the court by a crazed "fan." Traumatized as well as physically injured, the talented and vivacious Seles—ranked number one and expected to become the dominant player on the tour—did not return to competition for over two years. Tennis pro Mary Pierce made headlines because her father, who had beaten, harassed, and stalked her, was prohibited from attending her matches. Gymnast Christy Henrich died from anorexia and bulimia. The only women to appear on the cover of *Sports Illustrated* in 1993 besides Seles, Pierce, and Kerrigan were those modeling swimsuits and the widows of baseball players killed in a boating accident.[16]

Although these disturbing events should be taken seriously, it is ironic and unfortunate that the images of female athletes that stick in the popular mind are ones in which they are crying. Female athletes are among the strongest and most capable of women. True, female athletes have frequently been victimized in the last half century, but rarely has it been by blatant physical attacks. Instead, they have been discouraged, ridiculed, discriminated against, and ignored. Although occasionally there have been some outright villains like the thugs who attacked Kerrigan, the biggest oppressor in women's sports has been unnecessarily restrictive gender roles. These roles have warned females not to strive for success and taught them to internalize shame for being athletic. But only a small part of Kerrigan's story is oppression; she has triumphed over numerous obstacles in her career (besides the clubbing) on her way to an Olympic silver medal. In the same way, sportswomen have a long and impressive record of battling limiting gender expectations. They have a history of finding opportunities, fighting for fairness, and of adapting creative strategies for coping with negative cultural messages. Their history is not merely one of suffering and shame but of pride, self-assurance, intense bonding, and of joyful (if often anonymous) victory.

In both the past and present, this highlighting of victims unfairly overlooks the exciting competition and sometimes inspirational achievements of other female athletes and teams. National television networks and local TV stations, national sports magazines and local newspapers alike still tend to allocate a small amount of space to coverage of women's sports. In fact, one study found that articles devoted to men's sports outnumbered women's by twenty-three to one and that 92 percent of all sports photographs are of males.[17] Viewers and readers intermittently receive scores and updates, but they do not become devoted followers of women's sports since the media do not report its day-to-day drama. Potential fans do not discover the personalities of the main characters—the super-talented stars, the hustling overachievers, the dependable role players—nor the plot lines of winning streaks, altered strategies, and upsets.

In reality, victimization played only a small part in women's sports in 1993–94. American speedskater Bonnie Blair exhibited remarkable humility while winning an unmatched fifth Winter Olympic gold medal. And continuing to be one of the most powerful dynasties in any men's or women's sport, the University of North Carolina's soccer team set a record streak for consecutive contests without a defeat, in November 1994 claiming its eleventh national championship in twelve years. Twice as old and not as sharp as some of her opponents, Martina Navratilova capped her historic career by advancing to the finals at Wimbledon. Helen Alfredsson broke a U.S. Open Golf scoring record with an eight-under-par first round, but Patty Sheehan came from behind to win the tourney. Amid charges that Chinese swimmers enhanced their performance with illegal drugs, American Janet Evans beat the world's best in the 800-meter freestyle race. In the Goodwill Games, Shannon Miller brought home a gold medal in all-around gymnastics competition and the U.S. basketball team defeated Russia. There were numerous "firsts": the University of Maryland named Debbie Yow the first female athletic director of the Atlantic Coast Conference; Ila Borders became the first woman to pitch in a college baseball game; females became the public address announcer for a professional baseball team and did play-by-play commentary for an NHL hockey team on radio. Although not a first, the Colorado Silver Bullets, a new professional baseball team, began touring against men's semi-pro teams. Realizing it probably would destroy her hopes of gaining a medal, U.S. speed skater Kristen Talbot donated bone marrow to help save her brother Jason's life.

A winter 1994 game pitting rivals Texas and Texas Tech highlights the distance women's intercollegiate sports has traveled. Outside a light drizzle made it a dreary January night, but inside the UT basketball arena the excitement was tangible. Texas Governor Ann Richards beamed alongside former Congresswoman Barbara Jordan. The chancellor, president, and regents chairman of the University of Texas sat near the team bench. Intent upon victory, Admiral Bob Inman, President Clinton's nominee for Secretary of Defense, served as guest coach. As the lights dimmed, smoke rose, rock music blared, and 12,000 fans loudly and lovingly greeted their team, the Texas Lady Longhorns, as they sprinted to center court.[18] Only twenty years earlier, in the 1973–74 academic year, a couple of physical education (PE) teachers had doubled as the coaches for women's teams at the University of Texas. Though unpaid, they sometimes covered team expenses out of their own pockets, or had players camp out with family on road trips. Attendance at the contests was sparse, consisting of a few friends. Since the entire budget for women's intercollegiate athletics at UT was a mere $9,000, clearly there was no scholarship money for athletes.[19] Just a year later, though, Texas administrators, responding to Title IX—a law prohibiting gender discrimination—slowly began initiating changes that would make the UT women's athletic program a model for the future. In the mid-1990s the university allocated over $4.3 million for seven women's sports; full-time coaches earned respectable salaries; and female athletes competed for seventy-one full scholarships (worth $523,000). They created a tradition of excellence. Since 1982, Texas women can boast of 456 All-Americans, 17 Olympians, 18 national championship trophies, and 61 Southwest Conference (swc) titles. Attendance figures show that many appreciated the efforts. For six years the Lady Longhorns averaged over 8,000 fans per home game, top in the nation.[20] Texas seemed to be a model of governance, too: it is one of the few universities in which the separately administered women's athletic program is run by a female athletic director.

Beneath the surface, however, conflict brewed. In 1992 seven women athletes filed a lawsuit claiming Texas violated Title IX's requirement that women receive athletic opportunities in proportion to their makeup at the school. Even though the university outfitted the same number of teams for women as men, those teams included 326 men and just 93 women. (While women were 47 percent of all undergraduates, then, they made up only 23 percent of the athletes and enjoyed only 32 percent of the athletic scholarships.)[21] Many observers were surprised by the lawsuit. Elsewhere across the country female athletes were fighting to get their teams reinstated after budget cuts. But Texas already had one of the most impressive women's programs. "This is not a defensive legal action where we are trying to hang on to what we have," said the students' lawyer. "This is a major offensive move in the fight for gender equity."[22]

Cognizant of recent court decisions, the university decided to settle out-of-court. It agreed to nearly double the number of female athletes within the next three years (making them 44 percent of the athletes) by permitting more non-scholarship "walk-on" players on women's teams and adding two new varsity sports. In addition, the number of male walk-ons would be decreased somewhat. (All these measures had already been under consideration by the university, but were sped up by the lawsuit.)[23] The changes, including more scholarship aid to women, would cost about $1 million to implement.

The settlement pleased advocates of women's sports everywhere. "The message this sends to other schools is that it is simply time for them to come into compliance with the law," said a representative of the National Women's Law Center.[24] Conversely, the agreement annoyed many sportsmen. "One question left out by the people pushing for [gender equity] is, how do you pay for it?" remarked Texas Tech's athletic director.[25] In the twenty years since Title IX was passed, most universities had found enough money to create solid programs for women. However, almost none meets the part of the regulation demanding athletic opportunities to women in proportion to their numbers as students. Part of the problem has been football teams, which often choose to outfit well over one hundred athletes, significantly increasing the number of opportunities and scholarships solely for males. As a favorite sport of men—and one considered special—suggestions about cutting its numbers cause great resentment, especially among those who feel that men's sports bring in more revenue than women's and therefore deserve to spend more. They are tired of sharing athletic resources with women who are not sufficiently appreciative and seem intent (in one SWC administrator's words) on "emasculating" football.[26] Notre Dame's Rev. Edmund Joyce has denounced women's groups for waging a "strident, irresponsible, and irrational campaign" against football.[27] Congress has responded by holding hearings about changing Title IX requirements.[28] Along with increasing opportunities, then, comes conflict.

Another issue plagued the Texas women's program. The *Austin American-Statesman* printed a story describing the women's basketball team's homosexual reputation. A former player confirmed that when she was considering Texas, "People were saying, 'They're a bunch of dykes up there.'"[29] The newspaper claimed the team was losing players and potential recruits because of its image. "I think a lot . . . do believe [Texas] is a lesbian team," it quoted a high school star. "All my friends believe that's how they are."[30] According to coach Jody Conradt, no recruit has ever said she did not sign with the Lady Longhorns for that reason. However, she acknowledged that the issue now comes up when they visit the school. She also admitted that team chemistry had been a problem. Nevertheless, she has resisted the temptation of denying that lesbianism—she uses the term *diversity*—exists. "The best team I ever had had diversity. When our society learns to embrace diversity, we'll be a lot better society." She strives for inclusiveness. "I would hope everybody who is a member of this team is made to feel welcome."[31]

Coach Conradt faces a problem with long roots. Such allegations can easily hurt recruiting because many female athletes are intimidated by the idea of being called lesbian. In this age the label is still used to smear or intimidate women as unfeminine and abnormal. In one of the most unethical practices in women's sports, rather than combat that stereotype, a few coaches try to use it to their advantage. Down the road from UT, Baylor coach Pam Bowers sent recruits a series of postcards with reasons to choose Baylor. "Coach is outspoken against lesbianism and won't accept it," one read.[32] Penn State's coach appealed to the same phobia by publicly announcing she would not allow lesbians on her team. (Since then, she has been forced by the school to adhere to its nondiscrimination policy, but her message of intolerance already had the desired effect.)[33] Others use the ploy more surreptitiously. Indeed, every single player Conradt recruited received through the mail—anonymously—a copy of the article about the Texas team's homosexual reputation. Because it would have been difficult to obtain such specific information about who was being recruited, many suspect (without proof) that insiders—male boosters or athletic administrators at Texas angry about cuts in men's sports—might have spearheaded it. Some also wonder whether the newspaper story—appearing just a few weeks after the out-of-court settlement—might have been planted to try to discredit Conradt (now women's athletic director). The timing could well be coincidental. However, after hearing about the newspaper article, an unidentified administrator in the men's athletic department told a reporter, "It's about time you nailed them."[34] Apparently, tension is still high over improvements in women's resources, and as Donna Lopiano, the former women's athletic director (who built the program) said, "With Title IX, we have to expect hardball now."[35]

For good and evil, then, the University of Texas mirrors both the changes and continuity in women's intercollegiate sports. The multimillion dollar program with full-time coaches and full-scholarship athletes differs greatly from its earlier invisible, low-budget, sleeping-bag days. The heated contest with Texas Tech, witnessed by dignitaries and 12,000 screaming enthusiasts, attests to the recognition these strong and talented women now receive. Equality of opportunities is a fairly accepted notion today (with a law to enforce it), but as the Texas lawsuit illustrates, there remains great disagreement over how to define and achieve equality. And despite all the new benefits, all is not rosy. "It hurts every time I have to relive those articles," notes Texas coach Conradt, who almost quit over the innuendo.[36] Texas players, too, have suffered abuse, especially at road games, where they have been harassed with nonstop, sexually explicit chants. "It makes you sort of sick to your stomach," said Conradt.[37] Some suggest that such nastiness is part of the price strong, assertive women pay for fighting for equal resources and challenging old stereotypes of femininity. As this book will show, disapproval has long been a companion to female athletes—as much as the excitement of competition.

Contemporary power struggles fit into a long string of discussions about what is appropriate for college women in sports. Today the questions are over how to define and enact equality: Should women do the exact same thing as men? Does equality mean equal opportunities, equal outcomes, self-determination? Will it hurt men's opportunities? These became heated issues when the women's movement and Title IX forever altered the political landscape in the early 1970s. But the debate over the proper form of athletics for women actually began much earlier with basic questions about whether competition should be encouraged, whether athletics should be public, commercialized, and limited to the talented, and how to integrate athletics with education. As the case of Tonya Harding suggests—her future was determined in part by the police, the FBI, figure skating officials, and the U.S. Olympic Committee—the lives of female athletes can be greatly influenced by forces far from the playing field. Both amateur and professional sports are affected not only by their cultural climate but by athletic associations, businesses, and community organizations. Athletes in schools constitute a special group, since education (especially public education) can be regulated by the government. Much more than professional tennis or golf, distance running, or figure skating, intercollegiate athletics has been affected by Congress, federal bureaucrats, and the courts (as well as a men's athletic organization, the NCAA). In addition to describing the development of tennis and basketball, then, this book focuses on college sports. It traces what sorts of programs existed and who decided about them. In this area, too, women have done more than passively accept conditions presented them; though often lacking significant power, they seized the opportunities presented them and made their unique mark on the sporting world.

Like the realities behind the Kerrigan-Harding incident, the year's actual events, and UT's intercollegiate athletics program, the story of women's sports since 1950 is a complex one. It is not one or two stories, but many, stories of self-sacrifice and hard work; excellent performances and rigorous opposition; intense feelings toward arbiters and coaches and teammates and adversaries; notoriety, lack of appreciation, and luck; disappointment, shame, and pride. There have been periods of improvement and backsliding, stagnation and momentum, change and continuity. This book aspires to make known the complex and important history of women's sports because these stories have often been hidden from view, and because this history still affects us today.[38]

PLAYING *Nice*

Part I

Introduction: The 1950s

Conservatism reigned during the 1950s. It makes sense that it did, since periods of widespread change are generally followed by periods when people look backward fondly. During World War II, Americans on the home front (1941–1945) diverged from many norms, especially in the area of gender. A government campaign persuaded patriotic women that they could and should do heavy industrial work, and hundreds of thousands of them heeded the call, stepping into important roles vacated by men. They wore pants, carried lunch pails, developed muscles, and left children elsewhere while they welded, drilled, riveted, and got paid much more than usual. Although generally they enjoyed their work, after the war women were urged (and sometimes forced) to relinquish those jobs and to return to the old ways. A powerful postwar propaganda campaign advocated the resurgence of traditional domestic ideology: a proper (middle-class) woman should again be a housewife. Reality didn't always match the ideology, of course. But in many ways it did: heterosexual couples married in droves, women bore babies at an astonishing rate, nuclear families prodigiously moved to the new suburbs, society discouraged individual rebelliousness, and feminism lay in a deep state of hibernation.

During the 1950s the message from all corners—psychiatrists, educators, best-selling books, magazines, and television—told women to embrace femininity. *Look* magazine, for example, raved about the "wondrous" 1956 woman who "marries younger than ever, bears more babies and looks and acts far more feminine than the emancipated girl of the 1920s or even '30s."[1] Current television shows portrayed women as unpaid, apolitical, and exceedingly happy housewives. The 1950s' definition of femininity hearkened back to an earlier, supposedly simpler and happier age, when women put their families before themselves. The feminine woman found fulfillment through pure dedication to her husband, children, and home. She left initiative, competition, ambition, and achievement to men. Dependent, she got her material needs met by her protective husband. In return, she served as his ideal companion—pleasant, supportive, compliant, and passive. She created for her husband a refuge from the male world; she herself stayed away from that competitive and materialistic arena.[2]

Society expected women in the 1950s to exhibit very different characteristics from men. Masculinity and femininity were seen as two poles of a dichotomy; they were defined by contrast to each other. People were perceived as belonging either to one pole or the other. Thus a person who was not masculine was considered feminine, and a woman who was not feminine was considered masculine. Feminist theorists have described this sort of thinking as bipolar dualism, and have criticized it for being illogical and needlessly restrictive.[3] In practice people rarely exhibit all masculine or feminine characteristics; they fall somewhere along a wide spectrum of behavior. Despite this complex reality, thinking about gender during the 1950s was overly simplistic—it was bipolar. Instead of being considered androgynous, for example, a woman who exhibited some feminine and some masculine characteristics was labeled "masculine." Such so-called masculine women were considered failed women and ridiculed. Freudian psychiatrists postulated that "masculine" women—that is, those who were intelligent, aggressive, and ambitious—became that way due to some sort of warped psychological development. Normal feminine women, they said, repressed their masculine strivings and related to the world outside the home only through their husband and children. They declared that the more women emulated men, the less likely they were to be satisfied. Many educators, even those at women's colleges, agreed that women should study a "distinctively feminine curriculum." Feminists—those women from earlier decades who demanded more opportunities and questioned the traditional gender roles—were often mocked as well. Best-selling books declared that feminism was a "deep illness," a neurotic reaction to male dominance. Normal women, on the other hand, exulted in their natural distinctiveness from and subordination to men.[4]

In another leap in logic, unfeminine or "mannish" women were often considered lesbians. Being unconventional in terms of gender became equated in the popular mind with unconventionality in sexuality. (In reality the two spheres could be related, but were not necessarily so.) The perception that "masculine" women were lesbians had become common earlier in the century as the larger society became increasingly aware of an emerging gay subculture, in which one partner of some "butch-femme" lesbian couples adopted a mannish style. Whether or not they were homosexual, few women wanted to be considered a lesbian in the 1950s. Despite data that showed over 25 percent of Americans had "homosexual tendencies," the heterosexual majority considered lesbians deviant.[5] Hostile toward (merely) independent and unfeminine women, society tyrannized lesbians. Parents panicked if their children did not fit heterosexual norms and sent them off to psychiatric hospitals. Many psychiatrists deemed same-sex love as disturbed sexuality, and women who loved women as "not merely neurotics, but . . . actually borderline or outright psychotics."[6] Meanwhile the government treated homosexuals as "perverts" who were unstable, morally inferior, and detrimental to the country's image. Sen. Joseph McCarthy extended his Communist witch-hunts to include homosexuals, and many lost jobs, friends, or their reputations. Such persecution forced actual lesbians to live secret "closeted" lives in fear that their sexuality might be discovered.[7] For heterosexual women as well, the belief that being not feminine meant masculine (which in turn meant lesbian) intimidated them. It forced them to worry about being too independent, ambitious, or assertive. The "lesbian taboo" also made women increasingly wary about women-only activities, especially sports.

Sports continued in the 1950s to be associated with masculinity. Competing in baseball or basketball or wrestling helped make boys into men; unfortunately, then, it followed (with bipolar logic) that the same activities would also masculinize females. In fact, one man referred to female athletes as "she-males." Where did this notion that sports were more appropriate for males come from? Sport historians date it back to the origins of most organized sports (the late nineteenth century and earlier). Then throughout the twentieth century, many more men participated in sports than women, further reinforcing the idea that sports were a "masculine" activity. But sports also required a whole cluster of characteristics contrary to women's role.

The physical nature of sports was one such characteristic. In the nineteenth century proper women were not expected to be strong, and it was taken for granted that women were weaker than men. In a Darwinian explanation common early in the century, Stone Age women had responsibility for the home and children and did not need the ability to run, strike, or throw. Men, on the other hand, had to hunt and protect their families and thus developed those qualities, which made them superior athletes centuries later. By nature, then, women were "unsuited for prolonged small exertions such as walking[,] . . . long runs and jumping of all kinds," according to a male teacher in 1906.[8] Acting contrary to this nature could be dangerous because female athletes could damage their reproductive organs.[9] It was also inappropriate. To some men in the 1920s, muscles on a woman made her a "monstrosity," and some in the 1950s agreed. "There's nothing feminine or enchanting about a girl with beads of perspiration on her alabaster brow, the result of grotesque contortions in events totally unsuited to female architecture," asserted sportswriter Arthur Daley.[10] Even though working-class women had long successfully performed quite strenuous work and middle-class women had done the same during wartime, during the 1950s still little scientific data existed about women's capabilities. Nor was there consensus about how much physical activity was safe during menstrual periods. The notion persisted that sports, which required strength, naturally lay in the male dominion.

Sports demand quick, aggressive movement, which requires nonrestrictive clothing. As early as the turn of the century, clothing was a problematic issue for female athletes, whether it was for the oddness of bloomers for bicycling or the "unsightly mannish attire" for which athlete Eleanora Sears was criticized.[11] While fashions in the 1950s were far more practical and less binding than the corsets of a half century earlier, designers were lowering the length of skirts again during the postwar period, and normal middle-class women still wore girdles and heels, and rarely wore pants. If women wanted to play comfortably and effectively, then, they had to wear apparel that made them stand out from other women. When sportswriter Paul Gallico complimented Texas sophisticate Peggy Chandler as "one of the few lady golfers I know who knows how to dress," he insulted the other golfers quite clearly. Thus, serious sport participation required enough courage to ignore the norms of ladies' fashion—yet another strike against the female athlete.

Perhaps more important than the physical issues, sport's extreme competitiveness also made it unsuitable for women. Coaches lauded sport for boys because it prepared them for the rough, dog-eat-dog business world, but those same reasons could not justify girls' participation. Females were not imagined to venture into that world. While women were expected to be passive, selfless, pliant, and cooperative, successful athletes were supposed to be aggressive, ambitious, hard-working, and single-mindedly pursuing victory. When star athlete Babe Didrikson displayed those traits, sportswriter Paul Gallico described it as "wholly masculine pugnacity." Further desexing her, he also speculated whether the woman athlete "should be addressed as Miss, Mrs., Mr. or It." Gallico's suggestion that Didrikson was either a man or not quite human corresponded with the spreading notion that women athletes were deviant. In particular, by the 1930s the stereotype of the lesbian athlete or "butch ballplayer" was firmly entrenched in popular culture.[12]

There were many reasons adult women might not compete. In general, women had less leisure time than men. They had less income. Communities offered few programs to entice them, and some athletic organizations banned them outright. Probably the most powerful deterrent, however, was the notion that sports was unfeminine. Illogical (and unfair) though it was, even if female athletes displayed more "feminine" than "masculine" attributes in their dress, style, speech, desires, and work, bipolar thinking meant that their divergence from *some* feminine characteristics was sufficient to get them branded as "masculine." The stigmatized stereotype of women athletes as unfeminine preyed upon their minds—athletics meant risking one's reputation as a normal woman. Not surprisingly, then, the majority of adult women did not participate in any competitive sports. Conservative ideas about gender combined with sports' historic association with masculinity in a powerful one-two punch knocking most women out of sports.

What *is* surprising is that, despite the stigma, so many women did participate in sports. We know that these sportswomen were well aware of the danger to their reputations.[13] Conscious that they were taking part in questionable behavior, then, one is left wondering: How did these women athletes cope with sports' unfeminine reputation? Were they unconcerned about femininity? Were they feminists or defiant women out of sync with their times? Or *did* they worry about their reputation as women and try to find some way to be both feminine and athletic? Did they rationalize or justify their behavior in other ways?

Women had choices about whether or not to participate in sports and about how to cope with the "masculinity" problem. All women, of course, would not make the same decisions. They differed in their backgrounds as well as in their personalities and beliefs. They differed, too, in the particular obstacles they faced (and the support they enjoyed). In part, their fate depended on the sport they played. Even though sports *in general* were considered unfeminine, not all sports were alike, and some sports were considered "worse" for women than others. To thresh out the complexities of the situation, the following three chapters describe different groups of women: college physical educators, elite competitors in basketball, and top amateur tennis players. They describe their experiences and the innovative strategies they developed for competing in a world unwelcoming to women athletes.

CHAPTER 1

Only the Right Kind:

College Women's Sports in the 1950s

"While we do not believe in taking competition out of activity, we believe the ultimate role of women in our culture is [for] cooperation rather than competition."

—National Association for the Physical Education of College Women

Given the conservative tenor of the 1950s, female athletes felt grateful for encouragement wherever they found it. They would have rejoiced, then, if they had heard about a new campaign proposed by the Amateur Athletic Union (AAU) to develop top female athletes. In April 1953, Ada Taylor Sackett, chair of the AAU's Special Women's Committee, wrote athletic directors at colleges and universities across the United States, asking them to appoint someone to stimulate participation and interest in women's sports. "It is not too early to start our Olympic preparation," she said. Besides producing champions, the AAU wanted to support ordinary women, who "find increased zest in living through sports participation."[1]

Surprisingly, though, Sackett's seemingly benign letter distressed women in the physical education profession. Josephine Fiske, chair of the National Section for Girls' and Women's Sports (NSGWS), vowed to write Sackett "a forceful letter" conveying her disapproval. But first she checked with another physical educator, Pauline Hodgson. President of the National Association for the Physical Education of College Women (NAPECW), Hodgson agreed that "the goals of the A.A.U. and also the methods used in reaching them pose a very great and grave problem."[2] She asserted,

"[The] NAPECW is concerned, and prepared to stand firmly for the right kind of athletic program and against the wrong kind."

Why in the world would women physical educators oppose an effort to encourage college women to take up sports? They of all people—women who had dedicated themselves to teaching skills to females—were the most logical group to promote women's competition. Why, then, was there conflict between physical educators and the AAU? Hodgson's language offers a clue—the battle was not over *whether* women should participate in sports, but over precisely *what kind* of sports they should participate in. Sensitive to disapproval, women physical educators espoused a clear ideology about what constituted the "wrong" sorts. Oddly enough, their very love of sport, and a desire to preserve the place in it they had carved out for women like themselves, prompted them to condemn AAU's plan. Physical educators' conservative, limited vision of the "right" sort of athletics illustrates the predicament facing sportswomen during the 1950s.

The National Section for Girls' and Women's Sports (NSGWS) was the women's branch of the American Association for Health, Physical Education, and Recreation. Formed in 1917, it was an umbrella group of individual women who held college degrees in physical education. Most taught PE to females in schools. Members of NAPECW were a subset of physical educators who taught exclusively in colleges. Often the two women-only organizations dedicated to bettering girls' and women's sports stood firmly together. The Amateur Athletic Union, on the other hand, was a predominantly but not exclusively male-run organization. Founded late in the nineteenth century, it provided athletic opportunities to both males and females in a variety of sports, especially basketball, track and field, and swimming. The AAU had no relationship to schools. Instead, both its children's and adult programs were allied with community (and sometimes national) recreation efforts. Sometimes AAU organizers were college-trained experts, and sometimes they were (untrained) volunteers.

In part, AAU's initiative represented a threat to NSGWS's sphere of authority. Women physical educators resented incursions into the schools, which they considered their exclusive jurisdiction. According to Josephine Fiske, the relationship between athletic groups would be better served "if AAU will refrain from suggesting to colleges the type of program they should offer."[3] More specifically, though, NSGWS found fault with both the background and the gender of AAU leaders. "I am distressed," Fiske told Hodgson, "that this organization which is made up of non-trained men should try to direct professionally trained women."[4] Even when Fiske discovered that some of the men running AAU's female events had PE degrees, she was unappeased. Control of girls' and women's programs, she insisted, should be in the hands of women, "by nature better equipped to understand their individual needs than is a man."[5]

As that comment suggests, ideology was more important than jurisdiction. According to women physical educators, AAU representatives (as well as men in general) did not always see matters correctly. When coaching girls, they sometimes used the same techniques, strategies, and philosophy as they did for boys. They did not appreciate the special hazards females faced in intense athletic competition. Nor did they sponsor sports for the right reason, as AAU's Olympic development proposal illustrated. "The one and only goal," complained Fiske, "is to produce star women athletes so that the United States will place first in the 1956 Olympics."[6] Victory should not be the primary goal; such a philosophy flew in the face of NSGWS's credo that sports be conducted for the good of the participant. A proper athletic program should arise from the needs and interests of women, according to the physical educators, "not from some outside pressure with an ulterior motive."[7] Even more objectionable was that AAU would *use* women for such a goal. Though helping America achieve international prestige, AAU was "exploiting our girls."

Women physical educators also disapproved of the particular sports AAU emphasized. Some Olympic events, such as gymnastics, were not commonly practiced in the United States in the 1950s, and PE teachers saw no compelling reason to begin stressing expensive or odd events. They especially disdained track and field, for somewhat vague reasons. "We no longer feel track and field meets the needs, socially or psychologically, of the modern college girl," explained NSGWS leader A. Gwendolyn Drew.[8] Rather than building national champions in Olympic sports, college PE teachers instead emphasized sports that they thought would meet women's leisure needs in their postschool years, such as tennis, swimming, and golf. Not coincidentally, these sports were the ones considered most feminine and appropriate for women during the 1950s. Studies showed that individual sports like swimming, badminton, golf, tennis, and bowling ranked much higher in "acceptability" than team sports like volleyball, basketball, and softball. The more ladylike sports also tended to be those that could be performed at a less frenetic pace, with less exertion and sweat, and with no physical contact between opponents. Although they were not necessarily the ones females enjoyed the most, NSGWS's Josephine Fiske cited interest surveys placing the dashes, hurdling, and shot put of track and field almost at the bottom of the list of female preferences as another reason to oppose AAU's efforts.[9]

At the very heart of NSGWS's disapproval, though, lay the assumption that an excellent woman athlete was unappealing. Women were aware of the stigma, and thus few openly aspired to become Olympians. "Actually, there are very few college students who really want a highly competitive sports program," reported Fiske.[10] A "highly competitive sports program" developed specialists, who were referred to as "champions" or "athletes." Women in PE did not encourage the development of "athletes." Instead, they cultivated "sports-women."[11] The term *sportswoman* connoted a lady casually swinging a golf club or tennis racquet at the country club—a healthy, vibrant, graceful woman familiar with swimming and croquet. An "athlete," on the other hand, had worked with dedication to become an expert in one sport. A strong woman, she loved her sport, competed very seriously, and took pride in her performance.

Once they won medals, American society did not really have a place for female champions. (There were virtually no professional opportunities.) It made no sense, then, for responsible educators to encourage female athletes. Better to concentrate on serving "the many," rather than "the few," and to develop women for whom there was a niche in society. "Sports for girls and women in this country should be conducted toward the complete development of the individual for the place she probably will occupy in American society as a wife, mother or career woman," declared a female PE professor, "and her personal good and her ability to cooperate with others is of far greater importance than any championship she may ever win through competition."[12]

Did physical educators oppose all serious events for women? Did they disapprove of the concept of competition? They claimed they did not. "Any form of competition may be acceptable," asserted NSGWS leader Mabel Locke, "if good leadership is present."[13] An NAPECW leader echoed her sentiments. College women *could* participate in top-level competition, "provided the standards—which we hold inviolate—are maintained."[14] But without proper standards, and in the wrong hands, competition had negative outcomes.

Men's varsity intercollegiate programs sometimes got out of control, and NSGWS and NAPECW leaders would not allow women to imitate them. For one thing, "A few women [would] become specialists while the majority remain spectators." In addition, men's college programs often lost sight of educational values and sportsmanship. In the heat of competition, participants succumbed to the blind pursuit of victory. Both a win-at-all-costs philosophy and a desire to please the fans shifted the focus away from the participants' best interests. Females should not be exposed to coaches who lost perspective, allowing their best players to compete even if they were injured, or pushing athletes beyond what they were capable of. Nor should they yield to the temptations of corruption and commercialism, allowing unscrupulous, ill-bred promoters to use athletes to advertise products or take them on vaudeville-like tours to make a buck. As a number of men's college scandals during the 1950s proved, varsity-type programs were rife with hazards.

Physical educators' stern warnings were not new in the 1950s. They had their roots in the 1920s, when many organized sports flourished. Men's professional (baseball and boxing), amateur (track, swimming, golf, and tennis), college (football), industrial, and Olympic sports experienced a "golden age" when the numbers of players and fans multiplied. Although not as popular as men's, women's sports also grew in the postsuffrage era of the "New Woman." Events spread in school, industrial, municipal, and international settings. Sometimes promoted as novelty or glamour exhibitions and covered by the mass media, women's athletics became sensationalized and commercialized. Many people, especially middle- and upper-class reformers, questioned the propriety of these activities. In particular, they disapproved of using scantily clad female athletes to sell products, and worried about women's health. Especially after the well-publicized "collapse" of a woman after the 800-meter run at the 1928 Olympics, they pointed to the "excesses" and "dangers" of sports. Female athletes did not seem to realize it, but they were being led astray. "The exploitation of oncoming womanhood by international competition is a menace to womanhood, the magnitude of which one can only contemplate with a shudder," wrote a male physical educator in 1924. The National Association of Secondary School Principals also harshly condemned girls' interscholastic sports.

> These evils are so patent that they do not require much discussion. The extremely strenuous physical and mental exertion and strain are a menace. . . . Furthermore, sooner or later, the spectacle of interscholastic contests among girls gives rise to undesirable and even morbid social influences.[15]

The principals demanded their suppression.

Keenly feeling charges of inappropriateness, women physical educators responded. They acknowledged that in certain circumstances sports had serious physical and social dangers for women. Indeed, they expounded in great detail about "lowered vitality," "nerve fatigue," "rowdyism," and "hysterical outbursts" that resulted from overdoing it.[16] But rather than banning women's athletic participation altogether, these 1920s educators proposed strictly regulating it. Females could safely participate in moderation, they claimed, if supervised by people with the appropriate standards. Not surprisingly, the people they believed should control women's sports were professionally trained (that is, college-educated) women physical educators. In contrast to commercialized, sensationalized, and intense events, they proposed a limited, gender-separate, and more private type of competition. In 1929 the precursor to NSGWS passed a resolution outlining its opposition to women's participation in extramural competition and in the Olympics. It condemned the collection of gate receipts at any women's contest, any travel by women to participate in sporting events, and all publicity about women in sports.

Therefore, when NAPECW and NSGWS opposed the AAU's campaign in 1953, they acted consistently with a long conservative tradition. But if male-run AAU-type and varsity intercollegiate sports were "wrong," what was the right kind for sportswomen? To help women PE teachers know, in 1937 NSGWS published (and revised in 1948 and 1953) *Standards in Sports for Girls and Women*, which became the authoritative source of guidelines for proper conduct. According to the 1953 *Standards*, high-quality sports programs had the following "desirable outcomes": the participants came to appreciate companionship, experienced growth in desirable personal traits, admired skill in others, and were satisfied with a game well played, regardless of who won. Undesirable characteristics were low participation levels, poor sportsmanship, commercialism, exhaustion, and sensationalism. At the same time, the *Standards* sympathized with some of a teacher's more difficult responsibilities—having to instruct all students, not just the gifted ones; controlling safety and sanitary features of the playing field; always providing a good example; knowing girls' rules were good for girls—and they underlined the importance of performing them conscientiously. They also specified the proper behavioral traits of a professional teacher. She had good manners, put others at ease, showed consideration for others' feelings, and did not lose her temper. Her hair should be well cared for and becomingly arranged; her dress appropriate, neat, and attractive; and her general appearance well put together and agreeable to others.[17]

The *Standards* of the early 1950s echoed earlier warnings about potential dangers. In particular, physical educators should beware of exploitation. Teachers should be able to distinguish between "educational publicity" and "sensational advertising." Sport was to be played for the joy of playing and should provide fertile ground for the growth of wholesome values, and teachers were advised never to lose sight of the purposes of play. They should remember that the game belonged to the participants, not to the audience, alumni, or business sponsors. Even in the choice of uniforms, a teacher must resist the temptation to appeal to fans. "Costumes designed to attract attention either by their departure from good taste or their conspicuousness are inappropriate," decreed the *Standards*.[18] Nor should the desire to please fans or win games cause teachers to overlook safety and health considerations. Special restrictions on participation during a female's menstrual period must be determined by individual differences, *Standards* advised, "and in the absence of final evidence, conservatism should be the rule."[19] Indeed, conservatism ruled on virtually every issue.

Teachers had some leeway in deciding what sorts of competition could appropriately be held. There were three separate categories from which to choose. *Intramurals* were contests taking place between students within one school. *Extramurals* were contests taking place between students from different schools. These extramural teams did not necessarily practice or have coaches, nor be based on try-outs. *Varsity* was a special type of extramural competition in which formally organized teams, whose members were chosen on the basis of skill, had regular practices, coaching, and contests against similar teams from other schools. The 1953 NSGWS *Standards* gave off mixed signals, declaring that no *one* type of competition was "the approved form." The outcomes of a program were more important than its classification.[20] Elsewhere, however, the *Standards* stated, "Intramurals should take precedence over extramurals in regard to facilities, time, and leadership." In addition, it advised, interscholastic competition "should be limited."[21] In a similar vein, NAPECW's 1954 "Policy Statement on Competition" opposed (varsity-type) competition primarily for the determination of championships at successively high levels (local, regional, national).[22]

Although neither group *expressly prohibited* varsity intercollegiate activities in the fifties, clearly both NSGWS and NAPECW discouraged them. The NAPECW wanted the emphasis to remain on "play days" or "sports days" over varsity competition. The definition of these favored events was vague, and practices differed by region. In general, though, they featured any interested females, not only the most talented ones. They participated in a *one-day* series of contests with similar students from a few other schools. "A play day is a day when girls . . . play with rather than against each other," explained one planner.[23] All the participants were divided into a couple of teams so that they were teammates with people from schools other than their own. That way, cooperation could be stressed instead of intercollegiate rivalry and competition. Typically, at the end of the day's outdoor activities, participants gathered for food, entertainment, and conviviality. In a sports day, on the other hand, girls from one school actually competed together against teams from other schools.[24] Although both days were "extramural," they contrasted sharply with varsity athletics. They were more social and less intense, of shorter duration, and encouraged less exclusive participation.

Neither play days nor sports days were as safe as the preferred form: intramurals. Competitive fires might burn when one sorority was pitted against another, or when the senior class battled the freshmen, but because they took place within the walls of one school, intramurals would not be seen by spectators who might disapprove. In addition, since anyone could participate, whatever her skill level, intramurals tended to develop generalists (sportswomen) rather than experts (athletes). The guidebook noted approvingly that many schools had replaced all extramural competition with intramurals in order to broaden participation.[25]

It is difficult to determine if the NSGWS and NAPECW standards translated into reality. Though they were not unknown, varsity intercollegiate programs in which women undertook a full schedule, intensive training and coaching, travel, and postseason competition were rare.[26] There existed only one national intercollegiate championship (in golf), so for basketball, volleyball, tennis, and every other sport there were no state, regional, or national tournaments run exclusively for college women. But since no national organization sponsored any such activities, no one really kept track of what intercollegiate sports might be occurring locally. Occasionally NAPECW tried to find out, but the data is incomplete, inconclusive, and possibly inaccurate. A study around 1960 showed that between 50 and 60 percent of four-year colleges had some type of extramural competition for women.[27] An earlier one showed that 92 percent of colleges had extramurals, most of which were sport days, although 28 percent were varsity. Even those "varsity" teams probably did not resemble what men meant by the term. For example, Longwood College fielded two varsity intercollegiate teams. They held tryouts, and even occasionally played contests outside the state, but played fewer than seven contests a season.[28] At the University of North Carolina, rules prohibited clubs from participating in more than five contests a year and from traveling over fifty miles.[29] At other schools, extramurals meant the top team or players from intramurals might challenge their counterparts at a neighboring school to a contest or two. Another problem with existing surveys is that schools may have been unwilling to report "improper" activities to PE authorities.[30] What is clear is that most colleges had some type of intramurals for female students, but that the intercollegiate programs suffered from severe limitations.

The women physical educators' sports philosophy produced an alternative to the dominant male form of college sports, one that had some positive attributes. For example, by stressing intramurals over intercollegiate programs, it did avoid the abuses of varsity sports. Believing that "man in competition is not as desirable as man in cooperation," women in PE did not allow athletics to become overly important or overly competitive.[31] Sports did not overshadow students' classwork or encourage cheating. Teams did not become so obsessed with winning that players had to worry about keeping their scholarships and coaches had to bring in enough revenue to protect their jobs. Postgame teas meant that players got to know their opponents instead of seeing them as impersonal enemies. In addition, for female students, there were fewer status distinctions between participants. Girls with average ability did not feel the school considered them less important than "stars," and they enjoyed their opportunities to participate equally with more gifted girls in intramurals.

On the other hand, by stressing opportunities for the many rather than the few, the women's physical education philosophy limited the opportunities available to highly skilled or motivated women. Unless aspiring female athletes knew about the handful of schools that offered top-level sports, colleges did not offer them the chance to reach their potential or quench their competitive desires. In fact, PE professors sometimes actively discouraged their ambitions. One woman remembered that she was threatened with expulsion from her university PE department for participating in a semiprofessional softball league.[32] Typically, when a woman's passion for sports would not disappear, her instructors consciously tried to redirect it. According to NSGWS's Mabel Locke, their duty was to "direct those students with high-level capacity into channels where their ability will be used to serve others first, themselves second." For that highly skilled girl, it was a *responsibility* to "use [her] talent as a service to others rather than bring glory to self or to school."[33] Echoing the message that females heard in many arenas of achievement, physical educators portrayed the desire to compete as a selfish quest far inferior to the goal of serving others. As a result, many ambitious students realized that to keep peace (or to win the approval of their teachers), they should adopt the attitudes of their mentors.

Instead of pushing for intercollegiate programs or joining higher-level non-college sports, many of the highly skilled women formed Women's Athletic Associations (WAAs), which reinforced student leadership with the right kind of values. As leaders, they might be team captains or assume greater responsibility by organizing teams, officiating, or teaching the less skilled. Often, WAAs ran special service projects or raised money for good causes. Placing importance on the social values of sports, WAA sportswomen also sponsored speakers or planned nonathletic events such as dances, films, or carnivals.[34]

A woman physical educator belonged to a small, tightly knit society. She recognized that she was one of the few. As such, she had been instructed in a strict code of values and took seriously her role as a professional. This code had been passed down orally from a few "foremothers" at Eastern women's colleges before the turn of the century.[35] Those women teaching in the fifties had been taught by women who had adopted and defended the conservative NSGWS philosophy of the late twenties. While their instructors commanded little respect on the rest of campus, within the women's PE department they were all-powerful. The chair ran "her department" with an iron hand, and students were expected to conform. The NSGWS leaders of the 1950s, who promoted the "serve, don't compete" philosophy, probably at some point had repressed their own competitive desires in the face of their disapproving mentors. For example, after she had achieved status in the field, Celeste Ulrich could afford to smile over how her teachers had taken her firmly in hand. "I was chastened for improper conduct, inappropriate hair style, lack of decorum, vocabulary which suggested impropriety," she remembered. "I was cuddled and coddled when I did the 'right' things, the things which parroted the lifestyle of my carefully culled mentors."[36]

Ulrich's memories echoed Mabel Lee, who was educated more than a generation earlier. Attending Wellesley in 1909, Lee had been a student of Amy Morris Homans, who considered her very doubtful material for the profession. Homans was famous for her "direct method"—a quiet but incisive and complete declaration of a student's failings, intended to make her grow into a dignified, poised, and meticulous teacher.[37] Lee recalled one day when she received from Miss Homans a reprimand so severe that she ran to her room and wept. Shortly afterward, her roommate returned, equally miserable and angry from a similar encounter. But they did not stay angry at Homans for long, for her roommate suddenly realized, "Lee, she does these things for our best good. That woman is absolutely Magnificent!"[38]

This small sorority of physical educators felt a strong sense of loyalty to their foremothers and their standards. They endured the sting of humiliation and disapproval because they so loved and admired their teachers. They recognized their teachers as a rare breed of women who actually promoted women's sports (albeit a limited brand) and who courageously dedicated their careers to it. Many of those women spoke of the PE world as the love of their lives. Indeed, the group did resemble family in some senses, particularly in its system of passing down values from one generation to another. The elders may have espoused a conservative philosophy and stringently controlled their offspring's behavior, but they won the respect of the next generation. However frustrating the foremothers might have been, they had a firm, demonstrated commitment both to sports and to women. Strong women, they served as role models and created tight bonds between women who loved sports.

Like Lee and Ulrich, most physical educators through the first half of the century gave up certain types of competitive behavior; but in retrospect, to what extent was their philosophy adopted by choice, and to what extent dictated by the necessity of circumstance? Certainly the decision to emphasize intramural competition for the general population over extramurals for the more skilled women made practical sense. Whether at the high school or college level, professional physical educators had too much to do. On top of their full-time teaching, research, and advisory duties, they had sole responsibility for women's extracurricular sports. Sometimes the men's system differed in that a PE department taught classes and a separate athletic department ran extracurriculars. If a male PE teacher did work with intramurals or extramural athletics, he got extra pay or release time from teaching. Women physical educators usually did not. If women PE teachers did not offer extracurricular sports activities for female students, there were none. Despite being unrecognized by the larger institution, they took seriously their responsibility to promote fitness through intramurals in volleyball, basketball, tennis, or field hockey. Often they also served as advisers for WAAs, with their attendant social and service activities. Organizing an occasional sports day was difficult enough. Under the circumstances, taking on the added burden of an intercollegiate athletic program was impossible, unless they curtailed their other duties.[39]

The women's PE department lacked resources besides personnel. They had minuscule budgets, and teaching materials necessarily took precedence over luxuries like travel or uniforms for varsity teams. Women physical educators always struggled to find enough supplies. Often they had to borrow equipment from the men's department, and they could have it only when the men did not need it. Although some schools set aside a tiny space for women's activities, female students commonly had to beg for gym time or the use of fields. Every school had its own horror stories. At the University of North Carolina, women's sports had no outdoor facilities at all and were allowed to use the football stadium only when no men needed it. Even then, they could not store equipment there, could not put marking lines on the field, and could use only the end zones. Once, the women's field hockey team actually had to quit in the middle of an intercollegiate contest when the marching band stormed onto the field for practice.[40] With regard to scheduling facilities, women sat at the bottom of the list. Men's intercollegiate teams received the best times, and men's intramurals got the leftover slots. Since male athletic directors valued intercollegiate activities over intramurals, one can imagine how unimportant women's intramurals seemed to them.[41]

The NSGWS philosophy, then, came partly out of realistic, pragmatic considerations. Although frustrated, physical educators became accustomed to doing without because they felt powerless to change things. One said she felt "helpless before the inadequacy of space."[42] In retrospect, another wished she had complained more, protesting the disparities in pay, resources, and benefits. Yet back then, she said, women just did not do things like that. It would have been rude, inappropriate, and made no difference.[43] Thus, faced with hard choices about how to allocate their resources, instead of diverting them "to a few highly skilled individuals," women's departments chose the more egalitarian strategy of stressing instruction and intramurals. "With our limited facilities, trained women leaders and time," asserted Josephine Fiske, ". . . it is impossible to provide as highly a competitive program as AA[U] wishes and at the same time provide for the rest of the student body."[44]

Clearly women physical educators could not do it all, but was it true that females did not want highly competitive sports? Or was that merely a rationalization to make themselves feel better about not being able to provide intercollegiate sports? Because Gallup never polled young college women, it is hard to know. PE teachers found that some of their female students were reluctant to sweat. According to one teacher, some girls of the 1950s balked at certain demands, declaring, "I won't jump an inch unless it means something vital to me personally."[45] A somewhat more objective indication of attitudes comes from a survey of high school superintendents. Out of 339, only 31 reported that they sensed any pressure for more interschool athletic competition for girls, and 123 said they felt very little pressure; 185 said they felt none at all.[46] While educators may have been projecting their own values onto students, it is possible they could honestly report that the majority of females did not mind being limited to nonvarsity sports. Students did not expect more.

Still, every physical educator knew a few females who would have jumped at the chance to play more competitively. "High school girls are bored to death at Play Days," complained a teacher disgruntled with NSGWS.[47] Indeed, the success of the New York City Police Athletic League, which had 5,000 girls participating in track and field, suggested many females were simply waiting for an invitation. "We find we don't have to 'sell' this interest," claimed a police administrator. "We simply service it."[48] Some women physical educators acknowledged this interest. A 1947 survey of teachers at Western colleges indicated that while two-thirds of them believed intramurals and informal extramurals satisfied their students, over half of them admitted that "a few girls want still more."[49] The stigma attached to the image of the woman athlete acted as a powerful deterrent to serious sport, realized Katherine Ley. "In spite of this, we know girls who would like to compete at a high level."[50] One such coed attended Winthrop College, where she was president of the Women's Athletic Association. When she expressed her desire for more outside competition, she was told by the head of women's PE, "That's not the way we do it at Winthrop."[51] No doubt other women learned from the incident, realizing there was no point in asking for more. PE leaders continued to characterize those women as exceptions, but exceptional or not, they posed a continuing problem. When at a meeting in 1954, someone mentioned she had difficulty justifying the traditional NSGWS rationale, one member remarked, "The problem is old, but the children are new."[52] Educators all knew some women were unhappy, yet they chose not to "champion" them.

In selectively reporting their female students' desires, women in PE were pragmatic. Their assessment of women's interests reflected what the general society found acceptable for women. During the 1950s, educational leaders such as college presidents advocated a "distinctly feminine" overall curriculum for females and took an even more adamant stance for the physical realm.[53] Support for women's sports was rare. For example, the 1955 survey of (mostly male) school superintendents asked them if schools ought to encourage state championships in track and gymnastics because Russian women outshone American women.[54] Fully 97 percent of them said no. "Let the Russians continue to develop their women into Amazons," one answered, "but let us con-

tinue to develop femininity and charm in our women." "Our primary objective
should be to turn out homemakers, not athletes," remarked another. Physical
education would move in an "improper direction," agreed a third, if we encouraged "women of masculine type."[55]

Experts, too, believed in strict limitations on female athletics in order to protect them from physical or social harm. In the late 1940s and mid-1950s,
American Avery Brundage, president of the International Olympic Committee,
recommended a reduction in the number of women's track and field events. He
thought women already had too many events, and wanted to eliminate "events
which are not truly feminine, like putting a shot, or those too strenuous for
most of the opposite sex, such as distance runs."[56] After NSGWS sent him a copy
of their extremely conservative recommendations for the safety and propriety
for Olympic athletes, Brundage expressed himself in full agreement. "No one
with any knowledge of the subject could possibly object to the "Official Stand"
which you sent." Indeed, "I have at times expressed myself vigorously on this
subject and have even advocated more strict measures on occasion."[57] The AAU,
though less restrictive than NSGWS, was hardly permissive. It stipulated that no
woman go to international competition without a female chaperone, and prohibited girls and women from running a distance over two hundred meters.[58]
When NSGWS brought together medical and athletic experts to decide whether
it was safe for girls playing softball to slide into base, their opinions were mixed.
One male coach in the group said in all seriousness that the greatest risk to
females was cuts and scrapes, which were "disfiguring."[59]

Parents exerted more influence on young females than anyone. According to
an officer of the National Congress of Parents and Teachers, sports could serve
a purpose beyond enjoyment for high school girls. Sports and PE could teach
them how to aid a husband in relaxation, participate in activities appropriate
later in life, work with children, enjoy being a spectator, and work successfully
with others.[60] Brown's expectations for daughters contrasted with those for
sons. Athletics inculcated determination, faith in one's self, independence, and
that feeling of strength that spells victory, all of which made a male of greater
service to his family and nation, claimed the AAU wrestling chairman. "Every
boy should be provided with some form of competition.... Every boy is suited
for wrestling (and can compete with those of his own weight). It is just as natural for a boy to wrestle as it is for a duck to swim."[61]

Women in physical education, then, shared with many others the notion that
females' sports participation should be different from that of males. All the special standards were designed to keep women's sports within the appropriate
bounds. Beneath the shared attitudes that females should not compete too
strenuously, should only participate under certain conditions, and should
develop from sports cooperative values lay one key assumption: that men and

women differed from each other. Indeed, NSGWS took that assumption as its very starting point. In 1958 some NSGWS members put on a pageant commemorating their organization's history. It began, "Throughout the years women [who] have known that it is fun for a girl to run and jump and compete 'like a boy' have also known that girls are different from boys." Because they wanted to both cater to girls' desires *and* preserve those important gender differences, "In their wisdom they asked, 'How? What? Where? Under What circumstances is it good for girls to play?' and gradually through the years they formulated [and] reformulated . . . their concepts of 'Desirable Practices in Sports for Girls and Women.'"[62] Women in NSGWS, then, were pro-women's sports, but of a very specific kind. Their model offered a way to give females some of what they desired in an appropriate way. The *Standards* would complement, rather than challenge, gender role differences. "Girls are different from boys!" asserted NSGWS's Katherine Ley. "Thank heaven!—Viva la difference!"[63]

Females were well aware that society did not expect a normal woman to pursue athletic achievement. They knew PE majors did not have positive images. "One of the reasons I didn't go into PE was that they are so mannish—not groomed," explained a sports lover in the 1950s. "You see them at a tea and they are the same as they are at school. . . . [They] don't put any glamour into it."[64] Dr. Belle Mead Holm, who grew up in Texas in the late 1930s, remembered seeing signs posted in high school gyms that warned, "Don't Be a Muscle Moll." She internalized the stigma attached to the female athlete, and in particular the "female bogeywoman" of tough, confident Babe Didrikson. Her mother reinforced the message. She tried to dissuade Holm from attending softball games, begging, "Please, I don't want you to grow up like the Babe, Belle. Just don't be like the Babe, that's all I ask." When she got to college, Holm chose to major in music because it was more acceptable than PE. But she did not do well and got called to the president's office. She remembered, "He asked me what I really wanted to do. I burst out, 'Play ball!' Then I broke down and bawled for half an hour in his office. I felt so guilty for wanting to play ball."[65]

Holm had good reason to worry. Women in PE were portrayed as abnormal, "mannish," and lesbian, as the ridicule in a 1952 University of Minnesota yearbook illustrated. "Believe it or not, members of the Women's Athletic Association are normal. . . . At least one of WAA's 300 members is engaged."[66] Physical educators knew that students could be scared off. "To many girls, being athletic means muscles," acknowledged Katherine Ley. "Having muscles means bulges and being called a tomboy. If so labelled, she believes she will lose social prestige and will rate zero with the boys."[67] Sometimes physical educators shared in society's homophobia. Maria Sexton objected to a rule change proposed by the AAU designed to aid the U.S. women's basketball team in international competition. Sexton used the traditional rationale that it would benefit the few rather than the many, but her characterization of "the few" is telling. If new rules were adopted, she said, standards would be "sacrificed for the development of one super team of amazons who would tour the world as diplomats of questionable value to our country."[68] Sexton explicitly associated the team of highly trained top female athletes with the derogatory term *amazon*, adding (though she hardly needed to) that that image would be poor diplomacy.

It seemed necessary for physical educators to protect themselves from the mannish-lesbian taint. In fact, the continued restrictiveness of the NSGWS philosophy probably resulted in part from the stereotype. "Our fears of being accused of sexual perversion" and "patterns of conduct which hinted at masculinity," postulated PE professor Celeste Ulrich in 1975, had created a fundamentally conservative mindset.[69] Because the majority of college PE professors were unmarried, physical educators felt especially vulnerable, and some wanted to take action to dispel the rumors.[70] Some women's PE departments prohibited staff members from living together, and according to one woman, "Close female friendships were viewed with alarm."[71] They also tried to protect their students—or to prevent them from contributing to the stereotype. They forbade mannish dress or haircuts and required majors to take classes emphasizing proper hygiene and posture. Consistent with the 1950s' "ethic of togetherness," they began promoting co-recreational bowling and table tennis WAA events and stressing sports that could be played later in life with husbands and in couples, such as golf and tennis, over teams of women only. The 1953 *Standards* declared, "Individual sports which have a social and heterosexual significance . . . are highly desirable."[72] Finally, they protested via information. They published a 1950 study of several hundred women physical education majors from the State University of Iowa, which showed that 77 percent of them were married—the same percentage as that for all women graduates of the university.[73] (They also had the same number of children.) Far from challenging the stigma attached to homosexuality or to female athleticism, these efforts were to insure and prove that sportswomen were normal, feminine women.

Besides its heterosexual component, the femininity NSGWS sought to comply with also had certain class and racial characteristics. Their class references were coded rather than explicit. When NSGWS leaders looked at their counterparts in AAU, for example, they saw "untrained" coaches, who were not "professionals."[74] Their antipathy toward them stemmed not simply from their conviction that their standards were higher, but from a sense that they, as women from an educated, elite group could better insure the propriety of sportswomen. Although class lines did not hold absolutely true, the makeup of participants in respective events also tended to confirm that a class-based division existed. While there was no guarantee that NAPECW's competitors came from the higher classes, they were all college women. The AAU's constituency, on the other hand, hailed from church and industrial teams, and if they attended a postsecondary institution, more often than not it was a secretarial school or a junior college.[75]

Class and race were linked in the very segregated 1950s. The AAU sponsored competition for female teams mostly in the sports of basketball and track and field. Sport historians and sociologists have long considered those two sports working-class rather than elite sports. Not surprisingly, it was by excelling in track and field that black athletes became noticed by white Americans during Olympic competition as early as the 1930s. Correspondingly, most studies have shown that those same two sports ranked as "least feminine."[76] Indeed, a black newspaper reported that U.S. Olympic Association chair Avery Brundage was "dead set against track and field for women on an international basis. However, this attitude has only been expressed since our [Negro] girls have dominated the scene from 1937 to the present time."[77] The NSGWS was well aware of track's poor reputation, as evidenced by its discouragement of those events. The preface to one of the first track coaching books written by female physical educators (in the early 1960s) further illustrated that cognizance. "Over the years teachers and leaders have been concerned with the image of the woman athlete in track and field, as exemplified by a very small number of women," they wrote. Unfortunately, the public came to associate track and field with the "same undesirable characteristics." A few sentences later made it clear that those few unidentified women had not exhibited "grace and beauty of movement . . . [and] a feminine appearance."[78] The reasons physical educators gave for disapproving of track were always vague but linked to the social aspects of femininity.

The NSGWS encouraged students to play in the more ladylike events, which not coincidentally were practiced more by the upper and middle classes. One usually played games like tennis and golf at private country clubs, which virtually always practiced racial segregation. While not unheard of, public tennis courts were relatively scarce in the 1950s. Many other activities physical educators approved of (like badminton, riding, and shooting) required expensive equipment and thus were rendered equally inaccessible to poor and black women. Sometimes the exclusion was conscious. Women's PE organizations did not step boldly forward in race relations, although AAHPER (NSGWS's parent organization) did include black members. But the Southern Association for Physical Education of College Women (SAPECW), even in the middle of a drive to gain members in the mid-1950s, decided not to solicit the membership of Negro women. They did not prohibit Negroes, but chose not to invite them.[79] (Some leaders assuaged their consciences by saying they had little to offer black members, since they would not be able to attend SAPECW's conventions in Southern cities.) This barrier only reinforced the informal racial and class segregation already existing. Even when physical educators did not set out to exclude poor women, the sports they thought of as acceptable happened to be class-specific.

It is not surprising that the femininity NSGWS hoped to encourage was the dominant one—white, upper-middle class, and heterosexual. Like everyone else, women in physical education were products of their environment and needed to fit in. But they probably felt a more urgent need than most Americans because they were more suspect. Their very choice of career made them feel vulnerable. As professional women, they belonged to a relatively small group. In addition, their profession promoted behavior that was marginally acceptable for women. Even within higher education, PE had low status.[80] Nor could they always count on their male counterparts for support, because they differed in philosophy. The mannish image of female athleticism persisted, signifying perhaps lesbianism, and at least, oddness, and the 1950s was a bad time to be homosexual.[81] Accordingly, then, women physical educators became extremely sensitive about both the image of women in sports and their profession. Like members of any oppressed group, they were keenly aware of the public perception of anyone who was associated with their group. They felt that the behavior of every administrator of women's sports and every female athlete reflected upon them.[82]

Their tenuous position, and the desire to protect themselves, thus helps to explain the unexpected behavior of some PE leaders. Who would expect physical educators to have resisted a plan to encourage more serious competition for college women? The strenuous opposition to Ada Sackett's AAU proposal only makes sense given NSGWS's philosophy and standards. In turn, NSGWS's entire effort to develop sportswomen rather than athletes must be understood in its cultural context, as a reaction to the negative images of serious female athletes. Instead of competitors, NSGWS tried to mold sportswomen who demonstrated cooperative values, which suited women for their special role as companion to husband and children. While the conservative philosophy of the *Standards* on its face appears paranoid, it was based on a realistic assessment of social attitudes and physical educators' marginal place in society. That philosophy was an almost desperate attempt to keep control of women's sports in their own hands so that only women who projected the proper image played them. The NSGWS's and NAPECW's organizers were woman-centered and pro-women's sports but believed they could only take their advocacy so far. They therefore deemed some events unsuitable to females, promoted intramural over intercollegiate contests, stressed good grooming and feminine values, and emphasized teaching the many rather than the few—all as an accommodation to their society. They sacrificed serious competition in exchange for permission to continue at least some activities in a proscribed, "feminine" form. Women physical educators were victims—scared, relatively powerless actors in a drama already scripted with narrowly feminine roles.

Their conservative philosophy may have grown out of their victimization, but it took a heavy human toll. Among its unintended consequences was its exclusiveness. Their goal of serving the many rather than the few was an admirable ideal, an equitable alternative to the dominant form of college sports. It seems unlikely, though, that the many were in fact better served. The philosophy left out the large group of black and working-class women. Even in the already exclusive college population of college women, it limited behavior. It reinforced dated notions about women's capabilities and left out women who were "overly competitive."

The philosophy was born as an accommodation to prejudice against female athletes; in reality, supposedly focusing on the many meant abandoning the few. The sacrifice of the gifted woman had lasting consequences. It severely limited more than one generation of women who loved athletics, and it taught them to consider their love inappropriate and unfeminine. It forced the women most likely to be their role models to quash their own and their pupils' sporting desires, resulting in confusion or self-hatred (like Belle Mead Holm's). And it sent an effective message to all females, gifted or not, that it was all right to regard the serious female competitor as odd. It fed more fuel to the cycle begun in the late 1920s in which women chose not to aspire athletically because it was unusual; then it remained unusual. The philosophy also perpetuated the notion—upon which much discrimination was based—that women were not only different but weaker and in need of protection. PE teachers allowed and even promoted the notion that females should be careful not to step out too far in sports or they would step right out of their appropriate gender into a "perverse" role.

"Hegemonic" norms are notions so pervasive and taken for granted that even people oppressed by them do not challenge them.[83] The importance of femininity was one such dominant idea. People who violate norms often try to justify their behavior, and paradoxically, they often do so by avowing their loyalty to the norms. Then they try to prove that loyalty by criticizing people who openly or more extensively "break the rules." Women PE leaders felt they needed to compensate for their anomalous behavior by being extra-conservative. And like members of other marginal groups, these women went beyond simply mouthing feminine prescriptions to passing them along. Even when those norms restricted freedom, they went so far as to enforce them on others. Given the prevailing attitudes toward women in sports, it made sense that physical educators saw the AAU's proposal as a threat to the "proper" development of sports. But in choosing to oppose Ada Taylor Sackett and the AAU, women PE leaders in the 1950s fought the wrong enemy. They accepted criticism of female athletes instead of criticizing the restrictive definition of femininity that plagued them. It is possible to understand how hegemony works, and to understand how women in PE could come to espouse such curious ideas, but it does not make it any less tragic.

CHAPTER 2

Girls' Rules:

Championships, Apologies, and Basketball

in the 1950s

Claude Hutcherson piloted his women's basketball team—the Wayland Hutcherson
Flying Queens—to St. Joseph, Missouri, in
late March 1954, hoping to unseat Hanes
Hosiery, defending Amateur Athletic Union
(AAU) national champions. A wealthy Texas
rancher and businessman, Hutcherson found
that flying the team around the country in
small planes made for good advertising, but
he also simply enjoyed outfitting them in
style. He felt especially good about the team's
prospects this year because Wayland had
beaten Hanes earlier in the season. Shortly
after they arrived, his players donned sleek,
shiny blue and white uniforms—one of three
sets they had—before they marched into the
arena for the opening ceremonies. There a
color guard and noisy band ushered them
onto the court, and the mayor and the Junior
Chamber of Commerce welcomed them.
That week, the Queens would attend other
festivities that accompanied the actual tournament—breakfast with the Jaycees, a free
throw contest, a beauty contest, and the naming of an all-American team. But these were
sidelights, mere distractions from the
moment the players nervously anticipated—
the whistle beginning play.[1]

Both Wayland and Hanes had byes in the

first round, and both demolished their second-round opponents. The crowd had sometimes cheered against the favorites and had been rewarded with one surprise, when an unknown Texas team defeated the fourth-ranked Atlanta Tomboys. The boisterous spectators yelled loudly for their favorite players, like the frail-looking but scrappy five-foot, 94-pound Charlotte Fallis, and they booed when a team stalled.[2] Everyone expected the top two seeds to reach the finals, but the Kansas City Dons, led by 6'3" Barbara Sipes and a constant ball-hawking defense, ousted Hanes in the semifinals. Wayland did manage to reach the finals, getting impressive post play from Lometa Odom and Ruth Cannon, whose left- and right-handed hook shots accounted for sixteen points. In the championship game neither team led by more than six points. Finally, with six seconds remaining and a couple of thousand fans on the edge of their seats, Faye Wilson of Wayland made two free throws to eke out a 39–38 victory. When the horn blew ending the game, the players leapt into one another's arms, then tried to compose themselves enough to politely shake hands with their tearful opponents. Pleased also by Ruth Cannon's and Lometa Odom's being named to the All-American team, Wayland's Claude Hutcherson beamed with pride.

The AAU women's national tournament climaxed the basketball season. All through the 1950s it was the annual spring ritual that the top thirty or so teams in the country looked forward to—their chance to go head-to-head to determine the best team in the United States. The competition was fierce, and players remembered it the rest of their lives. Winners like Lometa Odom and losers like Hanes's Lurlyne Greer did not experience very different feelings from the high school boys and college men all over the country participating in their postseason "March Madness." Despite the similarities, though, observers would not have confused the male and female tournaments. Both the game itself and some of the pageantry accompanying it reminded spectators that this was basketball with a feminine twist. This was a game specially adjusted for females, played by athletes who made special adaptations to their world. If it differed from the men's model, it also contrasted with that of physical educators. Players at the AAU women's national tournament belonged to an athletic subculture distinctive not only because it was female but because it was working-class.

The AAU women's tournament represented the antithesis of what physical education leaders wanted. First and foremost, it was a national competition. Quite the opposite of providing opportunities for "the many," it was designed for the few—the best. Its participants also differed from the "sportswomen" NSGWS tried to develop; they were champion athletes. Rather than downplaying the performance of stars, as NSGWS did, the AAU rewarded them (by naming a most valuable player and an All-American team). In addition, physical educators found fault with the environment at the tournament; in contrast to their private, tightly controlled intramurals, the AAU tournament was public. A "mixed" crowd of men, women, and children watched the games, loudly and partisanly enjoying themselves, shouting their opinions about the referees' calls and the players' abilities and looks. In physical educators' eyes, the whole thing was a disturbing spectacle—women in tight-fitting, flashy uniforms putting on an exhibition in an exciting, carnival-like, and even sexualized atmosphere, with the mayor kissing the players and noisy bands creating hoopla, all intended to keep the crowd entertained.[3] None of this would have been surprising to older NSGWS leaders, given the fact that it was men who controlled so many of the activities. Businessmen like those in the Jaycees organized tournaments to reap publicity for their town, and those like sponsor Claude Hutcherson were thought to use women to advertise their products. To physical educators, the outcome was not in good taste.

Criticism along these lines was not new. In fact, almost from the moment women picked up a basketball, some people (not just physical educators) disapproved. Females began playing the game just a year or so after James Naismith invented it in 1891, and they took to it in droves, both at women's colleges and in community recreation centers. Just as quickly, though, some raised concerns about whether basketball was appropriate for females. It was quite strenuous, and "in some cases basketball can make too heavy a demand on the organic vitality of a growing girl," reported a medical journal.[4] Its competitiveness was another problem. Struggling for a loose ball, for example, allowed girls to "become 'scrappy,' lose their tempers, and often go so far as to make a complete spectacle of themselves."[5]

According to the Women's Division of the National Amateur Athletic Federation in 1926, such intensity produced "nervous strain and excitement" which caused females to disregard their physical limits, "to play during their menstrual periods and to play beyond the effort a girl ought to make."[6] Scandalous as it was for frail girls to be sweating and fainting during games, it was equally bad that females were allowing their bodies to be used for publicity. Unscrupulous promoters scouted and recruited the top players, only to dress them in suggestive uniforms and display them in front of mixed audiences "whose attitude and comments were anything but constructive."[7] Sportswriter John Tunis denounced the "leering eyes" that watched women's industrial leagues.[8] Eventually, it seemed, those women would hardly be worth leering at. According to a male doctor in 1931, females in a "combative" game like basketball "develop[ed] ugly muscles and scowling faces and the competitive spirit. As an inevitable consequence your girls who are trained in Physical Education today may find it more difficult to attract the most worthy fathers for their children."[9] The game of basketball had its critics, but they reserved their severest disapproval for when females played it. Fiercely competitive athletics had dangers for men, explained a Wellesley teacher in 1903, but at least males developed from it "manly strength." For women, she explained, "the dangers are greater, and the qualities they tend to develop are not womanly."[10]

To address some of these problems, new rules were developed for the women's game. Striving to make it more suitable to females, recreation administrators during the first few decades of the century limited the game's physical exertion and contact. Their most dramatic alteration was to confine players to separate areas.[11] At first these innovators divided the court into thirds (or even ninths, depending on the size of the gym), but eventually most settled on halves.[12] In the most widely accepted version, the 1921 Spalding Rules, there were six players on a team (which differed from men's five). Three players from each team were assigned to both halves of the court and prohibited from straying outside it, so that essentially the game was three-on-three at each end. The reasons behind this adaptation were twofold: to limit the area in which one woman might run (thereby protecting her more delicate nature), and to prevent players from having too much contact with one another. "Boundaries prevent bunching," physical educator Anne Maude Butner explained, "and bunching is what causes roughness."[13] Other rules also limited touching; for example, when two players trapped an offensive player, it was called "overguarding" and declared illegal; players were granted a certain personal space which could not be invaded by an opponent; and grabbing to try to steal the ball was forbidden. "The fundamental principle of girls' rules is undisputed possession of the ball once possessed," declared a NSWA officer, "and no contact with [another] person at any time."[14]

"Girls' rules" not only assumed that females could not do certain physical things; at the same time they communicated that there were things females *should* not do. In the girls' version of the game, for example, breaking the rules ("fouling") was more severely punished. According to one analyst, the boys' rules were designed to permit fouling, and the girls' to prohibit it. In other words, it was taken for granted males would foul, but females should behave better.[15] Girls' rules also restricted the number of times a player might dribble the ball (to either two or three times), which again limited the distance a player might move. In addition, this measure prevented an individual female from achieving too much by herself. By guaranteeing a passing, team-oriented style of play, the rules suggested it was inappropriate for a woman to stand out. "We have tried desperately to steer clear of allowing our basketball to permit the possibility of one-man star playing such as is possible with the dribble," explained a physical educator.[16] One set of rules, dating from 1911, discouraged passing the ball with two hands because it "tends to cultivate flat chests and round shoulders" and "no woman can afford to be flat-chested."[17] The cumulative effect of these rules was to create a game that was slower, more halting, less physically demanding, and more team-oriented than the male version. Girls' rules reflected a belief that females were weak, and that it was dangerous for them (for either physical or sexual reasons, it was not clear) to touch one another. They implied that while passivity, weakness, and large busts were attractive, muscles and aggression were ugly. Rule makers did not trust that women would behave appropriately; instead they actively tried to discourage strength, physical expression, individual accomplishment, and bodily pride.[18]

Different rules made the game "safer" for females not just physically, but in terms of acceptance. Rule differences acknowledged basic differences in men's and women's natures, thereby keeping the game in line with popular attitudes, the implicit message being, "We're not trying to be like men." Conceding women's weakness made the game more appealing to some people. "There is no argument in the statement women athletes do not have the physical stamina men do," said a male sportswriter who was encouraging people to attend the women's tournament. Indeed, "Many feel one of the attractions in the women's A.A.U. tournament here is the differences between the rules. . . . They think the fans like something different."

Not all players liked the limitations on the women's game, and not everybody played the same way. By the 1950s at least five sets of rules (which differed mostly in the details) were used regularly.[19] While some teams used the five-player boys' version, the vast majority used some six-player version, often with a rover. The rover was one player from each team who was permitted to travel the full court. The AAU adopted the rover during the 1950s to make the game a little faster and a little more like the game played by women in foreign countries. It was in some ways a postwar acknowledgment that *some* women were not so weak that they would suffer if they played full court. However, it was only a small compromise; most of the restrictions developed earlier in the century remained.

In spite of the restrictions put on their game, many females played basketball during the 1950s. They competed in high schools and colleges, industrial leagues, community recreation leagues, the military, church leagues, and even on some professional and semi-pro teams. (There's no way of knowing how many participated, but one survey with a low return in the late 1930s found over 300,000.)[20] In some regions the game was more popular than others—the South and Midwest were the heartland—but there was no formula for predicting which hamlet would be crazy for girls' basketball. A coach who loved the game might teach her students; a parent might chaperone his daughter's team; a company desiring positive public relations might pay for uniforms; a YMCA might see basketball as a way to keep young girls out of dancehalls.

While virtually all female basketball players throughout the first half of the twentieth century were amateurs, off and on a professional team would crop up. In the early 1930s, for example, a promoter wanting to capitalize on her Olympic fame and basketball experience put together "Babe Didrikson's All-Americans," a barnstorming team made up of four men and two or three women who played against amateur men's teams in small towns throughout the Midwest.[21] The All-American Red Heads and Hazel Walker's Arkansas Travelers were all-female teams in the 1940s and 1950s. So was the Chicago-based Refiner's Pride Sugar, a semi-pro team that used boys' rules and competed in tournaments organized by an independent network of male sports promoters.[22]

It was difficult at best to make a living as a female professional athlete. The money varied, depending on the crowds, and the lifestyle was hard. In 1947 seven All-American Red Heads and their manager traveled through thirty-eight states (over thirty thousand miles) packed in a station wagon.[23] A 1950 study showed that of 10,230 professional athletes in the United States, only 540 (about 5 percent) were female.[24] Clearly either the opportunities were scarce or not worth the effort. Those few professional basketball teams that did exist had no league and therefore no home stands. They played constantly on the road, accepting competition wherever they could find it (sometimes that meant an area's women's team, but more often a local group of men).

In many senses, pro basketball tours were exhibitions, and to bring in crowds they had to be good entertainment. To provide that, they often took on a vaude-villian atmosphere.[25] The Red Heads wore red wigs and clowned for small-town audiences. Like the Harlem Globetrotters, they had a routine of horseplay, practical jokes, and slapstick. Unlike the Globetrotters, though, much of their humor focused on gender. They would embarrass their male opponents by being flirtatious, unnerve them by teasing them about sex, and encourage the fans to give the men a hard time. One popular magazine revealed examples of how the Red Heads set up "the age-old contest between male brawn and female guile": in one, the center ran her hands through her opposite number's hair and distracted him during the jump ball; in another, a Red Head convinced a man to put his arm around her, only to have the referee call him for a holding foul.[26] Ruby Perlotte was the only Negro girl playing with a white pro team. Her team, the New York Cover Girls, also played against men's teams. Perlotte, according to *Ebony*, was tricky and had a repertoire of "zany antics."[27] In this style, the players got to earn a living with their athletic ability, but the crowds might not take them seriously as athletes.

Such women professional athletes might be considered colorful, but not exactly in good taste. In the early twentieth-century upper-middle-class view, it was inappropriate to be a professional athlete. However much one loved the game, one should be an amateur—a sportsman or sportswoman—and not make one's living by competing. Avery Brundage, head of the U.S. Olympic

Committee, believed an "amateur code" clearly decreed that sport should be the opposite of work.[28] The only people who made sports a career, then, did so because they needed the money, which further reinforced the perception that professional athletes were not from the upper classes. In addition, professionalism was hampered by the view that ladies did not immodestly display their bodies. In fact, a women's leader in 1926 compared women's basketball to beauty contests. Even if sponsored by a respectable group like a church, a basketball team was "little, if any, better or different from the bathing beauty type of exploitation and there is little question about the stand of sane leaders regarding that!"[29] Barnstorming basketball or baseball players, "lady wrestlers," and boxers were lowbrow.

Babe Didrikson discovered that connotation when she tried to join an exclusive Texas country club. Didrikson enjoyed "unladylike" (flamboyant, earthy, or sexually suggestive) humor. She regularly entertained large galleries with comments like, "Well I'm just gonna have to loosen my girdle and let 'er fly." Club members voted to reject Didrikson's bid for membership. One explained, "We really don't need any truck driver's daughter."[30] Indeed, a survey of middle-class sportswomen in 1958 found basketball, along with track, softball, and wrestling, near the top of the list of disapproved-of sports for women.[31] With such attitudes prevailing, the odds were stacked against professional women basketball players achieving respectability from the larger culture. When added to the difficulty of finding comparable competition, making a decent income, and being taken seriously as athletes, it is remarkable that any women at all went professional.

Since middle-class physical educators thought public, overly competitive basketball was bad for a girl's image, it made sense that they tightly regulated it in schools. To lessen the dangers, NSGWS discouraged interschool contests and those open to the public, and encouraged only intramurals. There would be no risk of exploitation by commercial sponsors or rowdy voyeuristic male spectators; and if things got out of hand, few would find out.[32] Historian Susan Cahn argues that female professional physical educators waged an all-out campaign to suppress women's basketball.[33] Although it seems unlikely that they could have succeeded unless other educators shared their goals, certainly it is true that women PE leaders set out to privatize and control basketball wherever they could, in order to distance themselves from any suggestion of impropriety.

But NSGWS leaders only had so much power. Their jurisdiction was limited to the schools, and there were not enough professionally trained, NSGWS-indoctrinated physical educators to staff high schools in the country, to say nothing of all the community recreation departments. Thus NSGWS had little say in many places that offered girls' or women's basketball, such as inner-city parks, Jewish Community Centers, Catholic Youth Leagues, and industrial leagues.

The participants in those nonschool settings were both working-class and middle-class girls (but when adults, mainly working-class). The AAU's leaders hoped to spread athletic opportunities in general, but sometimes targeted working-class children (to help keep them out of trouble). The AAU's coaches were often whoever was available—they might be former athletes or interested novices, paid or volunteer, male or female. Regardless, these working-class athletic leaders often had different values from middle-class, college-trained physical educators. Organizers of black teams, for example, placed more value upon racial uplift and African-American achievement than white middle-class views of femininity. Companies that sponsored women's teams worried less about ensuring propriety than about providing cheap entertainment and winning the loyalty of their employees. The players, too, often wanted the very things that NSGWS frowned upon: the chance to compete intensely, develop rivalries, become stars, and perform in front of eager audiences.

The AAU consciously offered competition for working-class women and those who wanted something different from the more controlled NSGWS format. Top teams hoped to be invited to the AAU's annual national tournament. Tournament teams were all white until the mid-fifties, and the best ones tended to be coached by men.[34] They came from all over, but often fell into two categories: those associated with schools (usually secretarial colleges), like Nashville Business College, Omaha Commercial Extension, and Davenport American Institute of Commerce; and commercially sponsored groups, like Midland Jewelry, Real Refrigeration, the Peoria Dieselettes, the Dallas Airmaids, the Telephone Belles.[35] The teams backed by businesses might be a collection of the best players from an area who managed to secure corporate patronage, but more often they actually worked for the company. Both groups, then, tended to be made up of women employed outside the home, making the AAU's class constituency different from that of college physical educators—and many of the working-class women found some of NSGWS's assumptions about the need to protect females ridiculous.[36] The modern working woman knew she was not so frail as traditional upper-class notions of femininity pretended.

Roxy Andersen, a former hurdler, was the AAU's women's track and field coordinator and spokesperson on women's sports. Andersen regularly denounced physical educators' "fixation that competitive sport is harmful to women." She said their standards implied women "must be protected from this contamination at all costs."[37] Moreover, "If we're going to wrap our girls in cotton wool, let's pad the pavements, flatten the hills, pull cars off the roads and eliminate the bargain counter! In fact, maybe we better just put our girls in softly padded cells."[38]

Some who played AAU basketball accepted the restrictive rules for females, but others merely put up with them. A North Carolina Hanes Hosiery team member, who proudly reported that her coach wanted them to be "tough as boys," said, "I would have given anything to play men's rules. But the people in Greensboro [women physical educators] said it was too hard on us." Her own experience contradicted physical educators' warnings. Far from being exhausted when they were occasionally allowed to use men's rules, she reported, "We went wild."[39] (Then again, maybe their going wild was what had been feared.) Women within AAU resented the conservatism of PE leaders because this squandered the potential to help female athletes. On the twenty-fifth anniversary of the AAU's national tournament, its head criticized educators at the same time she celebrated. "For a quarter of a century," she wrote, "the A.A.U. has kept alive a women's sport in America that has been kicked all over the place by school organizations in most states."[40]

The AAU's leaders thought physical educators did not understand the needs of young, working-class females. Helen B. Laurence worked for a YMCA for nine years, taking very competitive basketball teams "all over," before going to teach at George Washington University. "Most college and school people do not have any idea what adult play in basketball is really like," she told a (NAPECW) colleague at the University of Illinois. "The games are hard-fought and at times a bit difficult [for the woman in charge] but the . . . girls participating are having a wonderful time."[41] She thought they deserved the opportunities basketball competition opened up. "At one time I was coaching nine teams and I still remember what it did for those girls," Laurence explained. "Some had never been on a train before. Some had never eaten in a public restaurant before. That was twenty years ago and I still get Christmas cards from some of those girls." While less privileged girls broadened their horizons through travel, the larger society benefited too. "All of them learned a great deal about the importance of working as a unit and not as individuals. . . . Where would they be if not playing Basketball[?]"[42] According to Roxy Andersen, it made absolutely no sense to deprive them "of the healthy exercise they crave and the fun and release they long for which can be found only in women's competitive sport."[43]

The AAU's leaders also resented physical educators' criticisms of male coaches. If men were the only ones volunteering to instruct highly skilled and competitive women, then the AAU would hardly turn them down. "[The AAU] not only welcomes but would prefer women coaches," declared a 1960 AAU publication. "Unfortunately, only a mere handful of women physical educators across the country have come forward to coach girl athletes."[44] Various factors explain why not many AAU basketball coaches were women. "Coaches" tended to come from the already small pool of female athletes. The same stereotypes that labeled serious competitors unfeminine applied even more so to women who made coaching a career. In addition, women who studied physical education were usually taught by NSGWS members and took jobs in schools.

So into the void stepped men, many more of whom had been athletes and who had confidence in their ability to coach females. Coaching females earned them less prestige than doing the same for males, but still they enthusiastically joined up. Harley Redin, for example, stretched his family's budget in order to coach at Wayland Baptist. Finally, though, he had to resign to take a more secure job at a bank, saying coaching women was "pretty much a hand to mouth existence."[45] The AAU thought it ridiculous for NSGWS to suggest its coaches were indecent men who were exploiting women athletes, especially when the coaches were making such sacrifices. "Male coaches around the country are married men with families who not only take time away from home to teach other people's children the fundamentals of sport, but often they dig into their own pockets to supply necessary athletic equipment and transportation."[46] Generic charges by NSGWS against male coaches were unfair. A few individual male coaches might have deserved criticism for condescension or exploitation, but on the whole, female players were grateful to those who coached or sponsored them, who took their aspirations seriously and made it possible for them to play national-caliber ball.[47]

Sponsoring a top women's basketball team required a special investment, one that mostly men or male-run institutions (like businesses or schools) could afford. The AAU usually paid the costs of travel and lodging of top teams for the national tournament itself, but supporting a team the rest of the season was expensive. Uniforms, equipment and supplies, a coach, a place to practice and stage home games, travel and housing on the road all added up. A few sponsors, like Claude Hutcherson, provided rather extravagantly. While the Flying Queens attended Wayland Baptist College (one of the first colleges to award basketball scholarships to women), Hutcherson, a Plainview, Texas, businessman, footed most of the bills. He flew the team an average of nine thousand miles a year to play worthy opponents. He provided players with three sets of uniforms plus traveling attire.[48] Although few institutions made such a drastic commitment, plenty of teams managed to survive, and some thrived. By 1961 five (and later ten) of the best U.S. teams formed their own AAU league, the National Girls' Basketball League, so that they might face the best competition in the country on a regular basis prior to the national tournament.[49] What Wayland Baptist College got out of the arrangement was wider recognition and more prospective students. (Each year forty to fifty women came to try out for the team.) Hutcherson's rewards were varied. He received publicity for his business and for himself as a philanthropist. In addition, he and his wife "practically adopted the players," so he got the personal satisfaction that all owners of teams get from controlling them and from being their "patron."[50]

The main difference between business- and school-sponsored teams was that players were usually employees rather than being students. As such, they could settle in an area and a job for the long term and compete for longer than the four years to which a student was limited. A secure spot on an industrial team fulfilled an adult basketballer's dreams. Hanes Hosiery, which won the national championship three years in a row in the early 1950s, played around thirty games a year between Thanksgiving and the end of March. They would often play at home one weekend and away the next, trying not to miss much work time. The company sometimes tried to assign players to different areas of the plant so that when they were absent, the mill would not be too adversely affected.[51] They perennially won the title of the Southern Textile League, a powerhouse in industrial basketball until the mid-fifties. Hanes also fielded a men's basketball and baseball and women's softball teams. These programs were leftovers of efforts from earlier in the century when mills tried to secure the loyalty of their employees by providing such extracurricular benefits. (Other industries followed suit, especially during World War II labor shortages, which caused industrial leagues to boom. However, purely industrial teams like Hanes became rarer with every passing year after the war.)

Industrial teams could be a source of both pride and identification. Friday and Saturday evening basketball games provided weekly entertainment for mill towns along the textile belt. Games were a raucous social event, often followed by dances held in the gym.[52] The mill found this philanthropy worthwhile (at least until 1954), and so did the female players. Six-foot three Eunies Futch, one of the championship team's defensive stars, remembered, "Basketball was my life and back then you just jumped at a job. And to play basketball and work was the treat of all treats." Futch was glad for the opportunity; Hanes gained a dedicated lifelong employee.[53]

Some teams (including the Flying Queens) did not fit exactly either the school or industrial category. At Nashville Business College, players either attended the school or worked in a business owned by the school's president.[54] Other times a group of women who neither worked nor studied together organized themselves and looked for a sponsor. A business like the *Philadelphia Tribune* or the *Chicago Defender*, both African-American newspapers, might back a team to provide a community service. The team might become a source of entertainment, identification, and local or racial pride, all of which reflected well upon the sponsor.[55]

Top industrial teams recruited their players. Although participants in the national tournament were supposed to comply with an AAU oath which said that an amateur did not (monetarily) capitalize on his or her athletic ability, one said she "had to laugh" every time she thought of that clause.[56] Everyone knew instances where someone had been given an education or a job precisely because the team needed an accurate-shooting forward. Unlike some of the top men's AAU teams, though, where the stars were given well-paid "executive" jobs, the females usually held down essential jobs in which they really did work, and performed typical women's work—in the mills or as secretaries.[57] "We worked . . . on the poverty plan," remembered Doris Rogers. When male AAU players asked the women about their salaries, she recalled, "we wouldn't answer because we were ashamed to tell them."[58] At Hanes Hosiery, company president James Weeks decided to do less recruiting and build a championship team from the ground up. Fortunately, a strong North Carolina girls high school basketball tradition guaranteed plenty of homegrown talent. Of the textile belt, Hanes player Eckie Jordan said, "You were bred and grew up teething a basketball in that area back then."[59] Weeks's plan did not prevent him, however, from hiring Arkansas native Lurlyne Greer, a five-time All-American who suddenly applied to work at Hanes after her Tennessee team had folded.[60]

If it took an unusual commitment by sponsors, it required extraordinary determination on the part of the players to become national caliber. Practicing for hours after a full day's work was difficult; probably for that reason, most of the women were single and few had children. But Eckie Jordan recalled with pleasure, "We just lived at the gym."[61] In fact, Harley Redin of Wayland found that females showed much more eagerness than the males he had coached.[62] It was fun, but the players took it very seriously. Otherwise they would not have trained in the off-season, transferred jobs, and moved in order to play. Lurlyne Greer, for example, went to Nashville to play on a prominent team there. When her father had heart trouble, she returned home to Arkansas to help on the farm and earn money at a movie theater. Before she did, though, she had the foresight to play in one game before January 1, so that she would be eligible to compete in the national tournament in March. In the meantime, patrons of the theater heard her jumping rope in the projection booth, and neighbors watched her jog around town in combat boots at 5:30 A.M. to stay in shape. After her Nashville team folded a couple of years later, it was basketball that determined her next move. She called Hanes, and when they said they were interested in her, she happily relocated to North Carolina. Many dedicated team members regularly made career, personal, and financial sacrifices.[63] Some teams, for example, even offered to pay their own expenses to the national tournament. "Eckie and I would have gone to the moon to play in a basketball game," declared Eunies Futch.[64]

The players and coaches did what it took to win. In particular, that meant playing hard, smart, and aggressive basketball. This style and attitude stood in stark contrast to the intent of "girls' rules." They did what they could within the framework of the rules restricting speed, exertion, and physical contact. Even though she still could dribble only a couple of times, AAU rules' "roving" player could run the full length of the court. This made a somewhat faster game possible. Hanes's coach Virgil Yow used the rover to "revolutionize" women's competition with a fast-break style. Yow had coached men at High Point College before he came to Hanes. Inexperienced with females, he claimed his plan was simple: "I'll teach them to play like boys."[65] Indeed, Hanes scrimmaged against male teams during the last two weeks before the national tournament. When he recruited high school graduates to play for Hanes, Yow looked for the same characteristics any basketball coach, male or female, would have: natural ability, speed, robust health, and aggressiveness. His girls were not afraid of contact—they elbowed one another and dove fiercely after loose balls. He wanted his players to abandon their ladylike behavior while competing and harness their aggressiveness. "I want you to be friendly to everyone—until you get on the court," he told the team in his pretournament speech. "Then—if beating them hurts them—I want you to hurt every team we play, badly."[66]

Fortunately, the athletes worked so hard primarily for their own satisfaction, not for fortune and fame. The public reaction to them was mixed at best, depending in part on their location. In small towns, especially textile towns, they met with greater support. Hanes Hosiery, for example, whose gym held two thousand, often played to a packed house. In Plainview, Texas, hundreds met the Wayland Queens at the airport after they won the national championship, and escorted them downtown for a parade in their honor. As he congratulated them, the head of the Chamber of Commerce said, "The Flying Queens have spread the name of Plainview over the nation. We're mighty proud of you."[67] On the other hand, his opinion was not unanimously shared. A few years later, Wayland planned to eliminate the team because its large number of athletic scholarships threatened the college's accreditation. Bob Hilburn, a sportswriter for the *Plainview Daily Herald*, did not mourn the possible loss. The Queens had "outlived their interest from a purely sports standpoint," he maintained. "[They were] basically, a sports oddity, despite many fine accomplishments, . . . [and] no oddity will remain in vogue forever."[68] Although Hilburn and the school were willing to let them die, a number of the town's businessmen disagreed with Hilburn and organized a "King's Club" to provide scholarship aid.

Probably because the players were known locally and the team did not compete with too many other athletic teams for the community's attention, white AAU women's teams got the most attention and press coverage in small towns. A team like Hanes Hosiery received detailed, respectful, and even sometimes prominent sports-page coverage from the nearby paper.[69] There was a sense of "ownership" of the Hanes team, which resulted in its members usually being treated as serious athletes. Coverage of their season resembled that given men's teams; stories reported the statistics, highlights, and turning points of the game in detail. Even the best local coverage still occasionally called attention to the players' gender. Papers used phrases like "the speedy blonde defensive wizard" or the "beauteous brunette forward."[70] Still, this coverage sharply contrasted with that of many teams located in large cities. For the Denver Viners, the Atlanta Tomboys, and the Kansas City Dons, the major dailies paid them little mind. At best, a two-sentence summary hidden on the back pages of the sports section noted how the team performed in the national tournament. Big city sports pages were filled with summaries of nearby professional, college, and even high school male teams.[71]

African-American city newspapers, though, differed from white ones. In a study of the *Chicago Defender* and the *Pittsburgh Courier* in the 1930s and 1940s, Linda Williams found that less than 10 percent of all stories contained negative innuendoes about female athletes. Williams said that although the coverage was never equal to that given men, it was straightforward sports reporting that often disregarded the athlete's gender. Stories about women generally were not relegated to the back pages, and they treated the event seriously. Occasionally they, too, made somewhat sexist reference to a basketball player's family (especially her father or husband) in an attempt to "normalize" the athletes in the eyes of readers.[72] But overall, the quality of this coverage was high, and it resembled that given white basketball players in some small towns.

The common denominator in both situations was the sense of community ownership of the women athletes. Indeed, Williams attributes the respectful treatment of female athletes to the fact that "their performances at local, intercity, national or interracial competitions were more than a personal achievement. It reflected the success of the team, the town, and the desire for all Negroes to succeed when given the opportunity." In fact, Williams asserts that success in athletics was a shared concern of the black middle and working classes.[73] When a community (black or white) sensed that the women athletes shared their aspirations, naturally it treated them better.

National coverage, not surprisingly, was the poorest. It was intermittent at best and usually cursory.[74] When the AAU sent male and female All-Star teams on a tour of the Soviet Union, for example, the women's billing was low indeed. Headlines referred only to men. ("Americans Gain Fourth Victory," declared the *New York Times*—meaning the male team. One paragraph out of the thirteen mentioned the women's game, which had been played the same night, on the same court, in front of the same packed stadium.)[75] *Sports Illustrated*'s story on a U.S.-USSR series of contests at Madison Square Garden literally treated women parenthetically: "As for the Russian men (the ladies of both countries played excellent basketball, if you enjoy watching ladies play basketball), they were expected to have produced . . . a smooth, modern team."[76] Any coverage at all by major papers, one supposes, was surprising to women unaccustomed to wide attention.

The elite players had a different experience when they competed in foreign countries. If they were chosen to represent the United States in one of the rare women's international excursions, they played in front of large, vocal crowds like nothing they'd ever seen before. In one stop in the USSR in 1958, 25,000 fans waited over two hours to see them. In Ecuador there were 7,000; in Lima, 13,000; in Chile, 25,000; and the total attendance for the two-month-long women-only South American tour in 1951 was over 100,000. This was impressive after playing before just a few thousand at the AAU tournament.[77] Many other countries found U.S. women's basketball an interesting sight and gave the women's team the red-carpet treatment—sight-seeing tours, police escorts, crowds eager for autographs. "We were enthusiastically treated as V.I.P.s everywhere we went," said the chaperone of a 1958 tour of the Soviet Union.[78] Players appreciated the unusual opportunity to travel to exotic places, and they felt as though they were serving their country in furthering international goodwill, friendship, and sportsmanship. Tennie McGhee, AAU basketball chair, agreed that it was "personally gratifying," a "thrilling and unforgettable experience."[79]

Mostly, though, being part of a competitive women's basketball team had its intrinsic rewards. It was the satisfaction that came from going all out, hard as one could, becoming totally absorbed, sweating and straining, seeing what you could pull on from deep inside yourself to see how far you could go. The joy of a team sport was that one did not struggle alone. All the shared time and effort created a deep bond between teammates. They practiced, traveled, and competed together as a unit, experiencing together many different situations, which drew upon intense emotions—disappointment, anger, joy, impatience, irritation, exhaustion, satisfaction, loyalty, love. Like the tens of thousands of women and men who played on teams in empty gyms, they played for themselves, their coach, and one another; they made friends and enemies for life; and for some of them, the game (and the subculture) was their life. For some, their jobs were simply a way to finance their play. They were "jocks." Like all athletes, they might only do this for a limited time; and some fondly looked back at those years as the best of their lives. When Hanes stopped sponsoring the team after the 1954 season, Eckie Jordan admitted, "I could have bawled a river."[80] Jordan's basketball career ended there, but a few did what they could to stay connected to the game beyond their performing days by coaching—sometimes because they wanted to vicariously recapture the thrill, sometimes because they wanted to give others the chance to experience it too.

The players' rewarding experiences came at a price, though. While AAU basketball offered adult women something many physical educators could not or would not, the AAU had its own problems. The AAU approved of travel, recognized elite athletes, and allowed male coaches and audiences, but it bowed to gender prescriptions in many other areas. It had special rules for females in

numerous sports and prohibited them from competing in others (such as boxing, wrestling, and tug-of-war). It also decreed that when traveling overnight, a
girls' or women's team had to be accompanied by a female chaperone, and "no
competitor shall permit herself to be massaged."[81] In addition, the predominantly male-run AAU was far from feminist. Articles in the AAU's magazine *The
Amateur Athlete* sometimes assumed AAU volunteers were male, overlooking
the many women who gave years of service. When women *were* recognized, it
was often for getting engaged or married.[82] Not even one vice president, noted
one irritated worker, was female.[83]

The drawback to participation in the AAU, then, was male dominance. Sexist
attitudes at the top necessarily made a difference for female athletic opportunities. Especially in obtaining international competition, women got unequal
treatment. The basketball chairwoman declared that more competition and
money were urgently needed.[84] Even more vocal, track and field rep Roxy
Andersen accused the AAU of "half-hearted efforts" on behalf of women. She
lambasted "an apathetic AAU which goes all out for its boys but treats the struggling group of women athletes under its jurisdiction as something akin to an
unwanted step-child, keeping it barely alive by crumbs from its table."[85]

The problems with amateur basketball in the 1950s, though, ran deeper than
the organization running it. Society's sexism took the real toll. Basketball players could not escape the powerful lingering notion that there was something
unfeminine about participating in sports, something incongruous about being
a woman and an athlete. After surveying attitudes toward women athletes during the mid-fifties, scholar Laura Kratz found that the superior female athlete
was considered "at odds with her culture." In fact, Kratz said that while a few
women champions were "celebrities," often the only women's sport stories
included in the media were bizarre or ridiculing.[86] The AAU's top official, Daniel
Ferris, confirmed Kratz's assessment of male attitudes toward women athletes.
"Many U.S. men do [say]: 'We like our women beautiful and feminine,'" he
wrote. " 'We don't want to marry Amazons.'"[87] With such prevalent messages
about the masculinizing force of certain sports, it is no surprise that females
internalized them. After extensive interviews with 150 women, Kratz listed the
most commonly mentioned reasons they expressed aversion to sports participation: "muscles," masculinity, moral and ethical transgressions, bad taste,
social disapproval, inconvenience, lack of competence, and feelings of inadequacy about their bodies.[88]

Conscious of attitudes about the unfemininity of sports, women in the
1950s had several options. They could choose not to participate at all in sports.
Or they could choose to play more feminine sports, like golf, in the most acceptable fashion (that is, not very strenuously, and only as companions to their husbands). But what about those women who chose to play AAU basketball—a

tough, competitive sport with a somewhat negative reputation for being unla-dylike; how did they deal with that? Did some find traditional notions of femi-ninity unfair or unimportant and reject them? In easily accessible historical sources like the popular press, one finds little mention of women choosing that alternative. Of course, that does not mean such women did not exist—it only means that the larger society did not publicize their behavior. In fact, the expe-riences of women basketball players are hardly documented at all (not surpris-ing given the disadvantages of gender, class, and sometimes race); and even when there were stories about them, the players themselves were rarely quoted. Instead, readers heard from coaches, sponsors, and sportswriters. Those who wrote, edited, and published the news stories were virtually all men. Even if they thought they were being helpful to women, they may well have had a different agenda from the players. Players' voices basically remained silent. So to make too many assumptions from these sources (especially about what women were *not* doing) would be a serious mistake.

The very silence about working-class women's basketball opens the possibil-ity that women *were* doing something unacceptable. They may have been het-erosexual women defying social mores without apology. Or they may have been "objectionable" because they were lesbians. A number of sources suggest that during the 1950s (and after World War II in general), amateur athletic teams became informal meeting places for the growing lesbian-identified subcul-ture.[89] Yvonne Zipter asserts that lesbians have had a long, special relationship with amateur softball.[90] Lesbians were already considered marginal because they did not meet the heterosexual requirement in society's definition of femi-ninity; their sports participation would have been another strike against them in the eyes of the dominant culture. Rather than wringing their hands over being considered unfeminine and undesirable, though, they used the space they found in sports to nurture their own sensibilities. Team sports like softball and basketball gave them a chance to achieve, have control over their bodies, be aggressive as well as cooperative and self-sacrificing; and it gave them a chance to meet, work with and play with other women who shared the same interests and values. Interviews by historian Susan Cahn with women who played com-petitive sports indicate as much.[91]

The relative invisibility of adult women basketball players cut two different ways. On the one hand, the lack of coverage by the press hindered athletic women from finding out about one another. It contributed to athletes' contin-ued marginalization and also meant that women in general were denied evi-dence that some women were challenging traditional definitions of femininity. On the other hand, that very lack of interest by the dominant culture con-tributed to the anonymity that gave women (and lesbians in particular) the safety to do nontraditional activities. Cahn calls athletics a "crucial space for the formation of lesbian identities and communities." The prevalence of homophobia often made it too dangerous for lesbian athletes to openly declare their presence; nevertheless, they articulated a growing collective culture through action, style, and unspoken understandings.[92]

Other basketball players (especially those who occasionally were mentioned in the press) chose the other, probably more prevalent, alternative: that of playing basketball yet also proclaiming femininity to be important. Femininity was a powerful and fundamental social prescription and a building block of identity in the dominant culture—one perceived as being so important, in fact, that generally it was not directly challenged. Almost everyone agreed; whether they thought sports were good or bad for women, they never questioned that femininity was necessary. The task, then, was for players to convince people that women could somehow participate in sports and still be feminine. To do this, they resorted to what sport sociologist Jan Felshin called "apologetic behavior."[93] By that, Felshin meant behavior intended to reinforce the socially acceptable aspects of sports while minimizing the perceived violation of social norms. For example, a basketball enthusiast might emphasize that basketball was valuable because it taught her the traditionally feminine value of cooperation; or she might wear pink ribbons in her hair on the court. Both actions, in effect, proclaimed to her audience "I may be playing basketball, but it's still important to me to be a normal woman." Laura Kratz's observations in 1958 explained the reasoning behind the strategy: "as long as the woman athlete typifies the image of the ideal American woman, she is accepted."[94] Some of the important components of "normal femininity" that basketball players strove to exhibit in the 1950s were paying attention to one's appearance, not appearing too muscular, downplaying one's career, displaying (or at least expressing) the desire for a heterosexual relationship and motherhood, and seeking the approval of men.[95]

In essence, female athletes compensated for their lack of femininity on the court by making up for it in their language, looks, and behavior (often off the court). Presumably they did so because they thought it made their lives easier and because it was expected.[96] Apologetic behavior suggests that role conflict exists—that there is some contradiction between one's role as athlete and as female. While it is important to note this conflict, it is also crucial to recognize that it was never the whole story for female athletes. It may have been the result of a specific moment an athlete felt she was at risk (for example, being interviewed by an unsympathetic journalist), or because of certain circumstances (her parents not liking her involvement). There may have been just as many other moments when she felt very comfortable with her sport and her femininity (as when her father or a male friend complimented her after a game, or when socializing just with athletes). The apologetic might have been done consciously and publicly, or it might have been an automatic reflex. In either instance, it may have been outweighed by an overall certainty about her activities. (Just as Southern blacks adopted a public demeanor of accommodation for their own safety but ridiculed racism at home, female athletes may have had different public and private attitudes.) Historians cannot know the full extent to which stigma constrained a woman athlete. After all, plenty of women played despite it. Still the prevalence of public apologetic behavior among female athletes is a trend that both academics and athletes have long acknowledged.

Males associated with sports often shared the assumption that apologetic behavior was necessary. Harley Redin, coach of Wayland's white hoopsters, let it be known that he recruited females who were ladies as well as basketball players; and Ed Temple, coach of the black women's track team at Tennessee State, constantly stressed that his competitors should be ladies first, then athletes. "We were always aware that we were on display," one Tennessee State runner remembered, "and off the track we dressed and acted like young ladies."[97]

Babe Didrikson provides one of the more famous examples of apologetic behavior. Stung by years of negative press, she decided to change her image from that of a loud, arrogant, raucous "masculine" champion. She altered her dress, her demeanor, even her life history to correspond with a softer, more proper and ladylike image. She grew her hair long, began wearing skirts and makeup on the golf course, and denied she ever was the tomboy everyone remembered. "By the time I met Babe, she was not tough or manly," recalled another golfer on the tour. "Sometimes she overdressed a little—she'd wear frilly blouses that didn't look right."[98] To combat her former image, Didrikson sometimes went a little overboard, but she was less often described as "masculine."

Public treatment cued athletes about how they should behave. "With all of that success in the world of sports, Lurlyne Greer never forgets that she is a woman," declared Hank Schoolfield approvingly in the *Winston-Salem Journal and Sentinel.* "Despite the fact that her 5–11, 167 pounds doesn't sound like Betty Grable, it's distributed well enough to rate some whistles."[99] In Schoolfield's eyes, never forgetting she was a woman was important. From the attention paid to it, it is apparent that looking right was a key attribute of femininity. Gay Talese, a *New York Times* writer, provided readers with details about the appearance of the 1958 women's international team. Its members "generally are small-hipped but not ungainly in street clothes, are as attractive as many nonathletic types."[100] Like Schoolfield, who noted that Lurlyne Greer's tall large physique potentially detracted from her womanliness, Talese simultaneously implied that "athletic types" often were *not* attractive. (Both Talese and Schoolfield probably thought that, by stressing their attractiveness, they were doing the female athletes a favor by making them seem less abnormal.) But the athletes' bodies, while well suited to basketball, signaled immediately that these women did not meet the norm. In popular culture, the ideal fifties woman was not big;[101] she had hourglass proportions and paid attention to her appearance. Nor was she strong—she should even avoid "overexercise" that might develop muscles.[102] Roxy Andersen agreed that athletic women worried about their looks. Behind their anxiety was having heard "all sorts of dreadful prognostications, not the least among which is loss of femininity and personal attractiveness."[103]

The AAU's teams did not ignore the notion that sports detracted from feminine good looks. They combated it with apologetic behavior to show that the organizers of women's sports did care about their players' appearance. For example, the National Girls' Basketball League declared it intended to "upgrade all phases of women's basketball from dress to calibre of competition." A team could be rejected from the league not only for insufficient skill or unsportsmanlike behavior but for "poor personal grooming."[104] Claude Hutcherson, too, recognized the stereotype that deemed women athletes to be unattractive. According to the director of public relations at Wayland, Hutcherson wanted the "Flying Queens to be the best groomed and the best poised AAU team." To that end he supplied the three sets of uniforms that were "among the most attractive" in the AAU, and he periodically hired a "prizewinning hair stylist to help players' appearance on and off the court." Comments from friends and strangers alike, according to the publicity, attested to "the Queens being the picture of wholesome American college girls: stylish, poised and charming."[105] Some teams wore shiny, tight-fitting uniforms that showed a lot of skin and left no doubt that the athletes were indeed biologically female. These satin uniforms had been very risqué when they first appeared in the 1930s, but such forwardness did not challenge notions of being attractive and appealing to men.[106]

When Roxy Andersen launched a campaign to bring more women into AAU activities, one of the things she stressed was that sports did not make women unattractive. She allowed *Parade* magazine to photograph her petite feminine figure in her hurdler's uniform as proof that sports actually *helped* a women's figure. "Foolish notions keep girls out of beauty-making sports," she asserted. As for becoming muscular, Andersen tried to make that sound sexy. "A smooth curve of muscle is something for any woman to be proud of."[107] The *Amateur Athlete* began to print articles assuring readers that athletic women did not develop a masculine appearance, and that in fact they often looked ten years younger than their noncompetitive counterparts.[108] One article told women not to worry about developing muscles because, however much training a normal woman might do, the increase in size in her muscles would be barely noticeable. "Indeed," the author divulged, "a friend of mine who has won several beauty contests . . . did weight training to improve her figure!"[109]

Downplaying the importance of one's athletic achievement also constituted part of the apologetic behavior. Circumstances made it difficult for basketball to be central to a woman's life, since only a few could actually earn a living from it. But financial circumstances only reinforced an attribute already important to femininity—modesty about one's achievements. Even though some male athletes cockily boasted of their accomplishments, arrogant female basketball players were largely unknown.[110] Of course, that too may have been because the press monitored the players' voices. Sportswriters interviewed and quoted the male coaches and sponsors more often than the athletes; and when they spoke to the players, they may have printed what they thought appropriate. When quoted, females tended to downplay what they did, or to credit their coach or teammates; after an international tour, they expressed a humble hope that their small efforts might have helped spread goodwill between countries.[111]

They also actively played into the apologetic with how they edited themselves. "We travel and love to play basketball," said international team member Margaret Holloran. She added apologetically, "We don't want to play forever, however."[112] One should keep basketball in perspective, she implied—it should not be *too* important nor should one do it for too long. Love of basketball was merely a temporary phase through which one might pass. A sportswriter took the same approach when assessing Hanes's Lurlyne Greer. In 1953 he discovered Greer was concentrating on winning a national championship. But, he reassured readers, Greer really was normal—she sometimes thought about having a family of her own. "I want someday to get out of this sports business," he quoted her, "so I can start on that other. I want to. I guess you could say that's the goal of every woman."[113]

Greer's remarks confirm heterosexuality's place as a major factor of the femininity with which female athletes strove to comply. If Greer could be considered odd for hungering for a national championship and jogging around in combat boots, just saying you wanted to get married could help make up for it. The AAU's magazine assumed readers were reassured to know that a young athlete "gets as much fun out of normal social activity as she does from athletics."[114] But using phrases like "normal social activity" implied that sports was not at all normal. Sports achievement was not enough for a female to aspire to—ultimately, marriage was more important. "Like everybody else, we want to get married," Holloran almost protested.[115] The *New York Times*'s Talese implied that Holloran, a striking brunette with brown eyes, was fortunate that she had "found that being a girl athlete is no hindrance to popularity with non-dribbling men."[116] Indeed, Kratz found evidence that some women avoided muscular, aggressive sports because they were thought to lower their potential for marriage.[117] If so, a woman might have to give up AAU basketball unless she had an especially understanding boyfriend or husband. Being a tomboy who loved sports was supposed to be a phase until one grew up and looked to the sexual companionship of males. The AAU's magazine told of a rising young athlete who had excelled in many sports as a girl, including baseball, basketball, and football. "But five years ago," *Amateur Athlete* noted approvingly, "she began to give up tackling boys in favor of snaring them in subtler ways."[118]

Marriage—including family and a happy home life—could be proof that sports did not diminish one's womanliness. In an article entitled "Former Swim Titlists Doing Well," an AAU representative tried to demonstrate that being a champion between 1920 and 1950 did not harm females. As her evidence, she related details of former titlists' current lives, especially to whom they were married and how many children they had. "These girls," she concluded, "far from having shattered nerves, are raising families."[119] Indeed, they were healthy mothers—possibly having had an easier time during childbirth—and they had healthy, normal kids. Pressured by Roxy Andersen, AAU secretary-treasurer Daniel Ferris joined the campaign and expressed surprise at the number of beautiful and feminine women he saw competing. "I was convinced: women's sports, properly selected, *do not produce mannish women*." Further, he asked, "Cannot sports give [girls] the strength needed to raise a happy family today?"[120]

If male sexual companionship lent legitimacy to female athletes, so did male approval in general. Physical educators worried about the impropriety of men being around intense, excited women doing physical activity, but AAU women's basketball catered to men, as father figures, partners, and sexually interested fans. In fact, much of the festive spirit of the games seemed to be directed toward male fans—fans who could help make the game popular, acceptable events, especially in small towns. Approval could be even more obvious when the teams were not simply accompanied, but also controlled, by men.[121] With the patronage of wealthy businessmen like Claude Hutcherson, the sponsorship of the local Jaycees, and coaching by men like Harley Redin, a community could see the teams were in good hands. Nashville Business College's coach John Head "understands the beguiling ways of women," wrote Talese. Head was successful, he observed, "largely because he dominates women with suave diplomacy."[122] Suave perhaps, but dominant nonetheless. From what is known, most of the players did not mind; to have men in authority was familiar.[123] Nor were they unmindful of the males' greater societal influence. An AAU article asserted that when promoting serious athletics for females, the most important opinions to consider were those of parents and adult men.[124]

The AAU's national tournament always included an event that epitomized apologetic behavior. One evening early in the tournament the games would stop, the lights would dim. With trumpets blaring and a spotlight following them, a select group of players would parade around the court in front of the fans. From this group was chosen a Beauty Queen. As she was presented with a crown, robe, roses, and trophy, she and the top runners-up—her attendants, the

Queen's court—were loudly cheered by the fans. She was often escorted by the St. Joseph's Jaycees, lauded by the mayor, and photographed in full regalia (including robes over her uniform and knee pads).[125]

Players differed in how they felt about the beauty contest. Some enjoyed it as much as the fans. "We cheered and carried on as if we were winning a national tournament," recalled one player. Others, though, said it was "not necessary" and "didn't interest us."[126] Whatever the players thought, the pageant continued, and it served well the apologetic purpose of highlighting the female athletes' femininity. Most obviously, it celebrated traditional feminine good looks. It demonstrated that the Queen, whatever her athletic ability, was "as gracious and charming as she was pretty."[127] And it proclaimed that being attractive to men was important—as important as basketball. The pageant also reinforced male control. A man—often the mayor or head of the Chamber of Commerce—usually crowned the queen. As other women remembered, it was "just something to appease the crowd with" or "just a little something extra I think for the sponsors."[128] They accepted the pageant as part of the way the game was played (that is, not the basketball game itself but all the things one had to do to in order to compete).

The style of competition adapted by men and women in AAU women's basketball differed from that of the middle-class DGWS's professional physical educators, but only outwardly. In contrast to private, homosocial, intramural competition, tightly controlled by women leaders, AAU teams had stars, male coaches, plenty of travel, national competition, and played very publicly before mixed crowds in a lively sexualized atmosphere. Despite these external contrasts, both styles shared some important assumptions. As their apologetic behavior illustrates, the AAU's working-class players and male coaches and administrators responded to the same concerns about femininity as NSGWS; both constituencies were well aware of the notion that aggressive sports potentially masculinized females. Both groups were trying to create a space for women's athletics in a world that thought that men and women were and should be fundamentally different—and that sports minimized those differences. The NSGWS's strategy was to develop feminine sportswomen rather than strong, aggressively competitive champion athletes. This was to be accomplished by playing certain—especially individual, upper-class, and less physical—sports. When females did play team sports, professional physical educators privatized and closely regulated them. The volunteer-run, more working-class AAU, on the other hand, did not think women needed as much protection from the physical or emotional dangers of sports and therefore allowed female athletes to travel and compete publicly. While participating in those championships, though, they regularly demonstrated their awareness of the unfemininity of sports by adapting compensatory behavior. They appealed to the male heterosexual tastes of fans and sponsors, de-emphasized the true importance of sports in their lives, voiced a willingness to look feminine and get married and have children, and gave control of their teams to men.

Each class strategy had its advantages. Being in a homosocial PE environment gave women a chance to develop their own norms and style, and to be comfortable around one another (without the presence and approval of men). It also gave female PE leaders power and provided female athletes a chance to see women in positions of authority. The working-class heterosocial one, on the other hand, offered men and women a chance to work together and to see that "jocks" of both genders shared certain values. It allowed men to routinely see women in competitive aggressive situations. In addition, it fit in well with the postwar ethic of togetherness between the genders. If sexualizing the game with short shiny uniforms and beauty pageants made it possible for women to play, then in some ways the AAU's format was useful. If it legitimized them as *otherwise* normal (feminine, heterosexual) women, then it might have given working-class female athletes the chance to be tough, aggressive, competent, and in control of their bodies on the court. If it gave them a chance to meet other jocks who shared their values and to build lifelong friendships, then there was some value to the strategy.

In the long term, however, the beauty contest backfired. Ultimately, the apologetic strategy kept the burden on the female athlete to prove her femininity in order to play. She should not have had to "make a deal" to play; she should have had the right to compete and aspire without worrying about whether it was appropriate for her gender. But the typical athlete was trapped by dichotomous narrow prescriptions of femininity: by being an athlete, she was an exception in one area of femininity, and if she didn't want to be kicked out of the category altogether, she had to be extra careful to conform to its other aspects. No wonder she exhibited apologetic behavior. Still, every time an athlete accentuated her dainty looks, wore high heels, spoke of her dream husband and children, or pooh-poohed her accomplishments, it reminded people that her sports were not a normal feminine activity. "Popular sports promoters who emphasized the feminine beauty and grace of female athletes [with events like beauty pageants]," historian Susan Cahn has pointed out, "also implicitly reinforced the masculinity of sport by reaching outside of the activity to legitimate the womanhood of competitors. 'Proof' [of femininity] rested outside of sport, which retained its ability to masculinize participants."[129] Compensatory behavior left unquestioned the assumption that basketball was inherently unfeminine.

In some senses, the female basketball player in the 1950s could not win. However her game was packaged, it would have been marginalized. The few females who actually played five-person rules could not measure up. They were competing in a game in which they had less training than men and some physical disadvantages as well. A woman who performed with distinction was considered to "play like a man." That was both a compliment and an insult.[130] And for the majority who played "girls' rules," history already had branded them as "other." Theirs was a lesser game, by definition. It was designed that way by twentieth-century authorities who had conventional ideas about what females could and should do—about running, touching, behaving, achieving, and exerting. Thus, their game became a slower, inferior, truncated imitation of the real thing. According to sports pages, coaches, rulebooks, Library of Congress headings, and the popular mind, it was not "basketball"—it was "girls' basketball." The word *basketball* connoted boys' basketball, just as *athlete* referred to a male unless otherwise qualified.[131] This was not merely an issue of language but of norms. For example, after the Iowa Girls State High School Basketball Tournament in 1959, *Life* wrote, "The coaches were faced with an odd basketball problem: how to deal with girls who are skilled basketball players but, at the same time, girls."[132]

Thus AAU female basketball players faced a painful dilemma. They wanted to perform competently in basketball and to be considered normal women. To try to achieve both, they adjusted to their circumstances. In effect, AAU rules—which included the rover—represented a compromise between gender expectations and what the players wanted to do. The rover rule, said one female proponent, "lends itself to a more feminine game than that of the boys, and yet it allows for a much faster and more all-around game than that of the previous two-division game."[133] The distinctive rituals of the AAU girls' national tournament were part of the same process of carving out a unique place for women basketball players. Many of the rituals brought great joy to participants, but nonetheless they were apologetic—it was a strategy of necessity in a world where to be a female basketball player was odd.

CHAPTER 3

Members Only:

Class, Race, and Amateur Tennis
for Women in the 1950s

On a late August day in 1950, thousands of spectators crowded around a tennis court at the West Side Tennis Club in Forest Hills, New York. Those who could not squeeze into the limited seating available tried to watch from under the fence or gratefully accepted standing room. They grumbled about tournament officials' poor scheduling. "The tennis fathers, in their infinite wisdom, must surely have realized that her appearance in the tournament was a matter of considerable interest to many," complained one reporter, "yet they staged her first-round match on the remotest possible court, where not more than three hundred spectators could watch, although about three thousand deserted the stadium and tried to."[1] Who had generated such interest? It was a woman, Althea Gibson, the first "Negro" player to compete in the United States Lawn Tennis Association (USLTA) national outdoor championship. Fans were curious as to how a black player would do in the elite, white, and tradition-bound USLTA tournament.

With bad luck in the draw, in her second match Gibson had to face the reigning Wimbledon champ, Louise Brough, and in the first set Gibson's nerves showed. She settled down, though, and won the second set. Gibson fell behind in the third but rallied again, and according to a seasoned tennis observer, "her powerful service and mannish net attack . . . threaten[ed] the former national champion with defeat."[2] As the match tightened, the sky darkened, and peals of thunder punctuated their shots. Rain was moments away, but hardly anyone left. "Everyone in the stands sensed that a fabulous upset was in the making."[3] Finally, with Gibson leading 7–6 in the third set, the clouds released a deluge and the match was halted. Disappointed fans raced for cover and journalists to their typewriters. That a black woman was playing on the grass courts at Forest Hills was a story in itself, but now she had the white champ on the ropes. As if to confirm the drama, lightning struck one of the stone eagles on top of the stadium, and it toppled to the ground.

Gibson's appearance at Forest Hills indeed toppled a long-standing tradition in a game known for its traditions. But when play resumed the next day, the excitement soon dissipated. Brough made short work of Gibson, defeating her in three straight games to finish the match in just eleven minutes. In the same way, the previous day's impression of dramatic change in the tennis world also proved illusory: despite some challenges like Gibson's, most of tennis's traditions remained intact in the 1950s. The USLTA retained its tight grasp on the game. Forest Hills remained an amateur tournament, and the game still kept its white, clubby, elitist atmosphere. Tennis fathers still wielded enormous power in deciding things like who would be allowed to enter tournaments, how to define amateur, and who played on which courts. And as the Gibson-Brough match illustrated, rarely did women grace the center courts. Still, although tennis authorities often relegated women to the fringes, it is significant that certain women were included at Forest Hills and that fans crowded to see them. Tennis traditions meant female tennis stars enjoyed greater status than other female athletes, but as the description of Gibson's "mannish" game suggests, their acceptance was far from unqualified.

Historically, tennis was considered a genteel sport. Upper-class sportsmen developed the modern game of lawn tennis in England in the late nineteenth century. After seeing it in Bermuda, Mary Outerbridge reportedly introduced the game in the United States in 1874.[4] Tennis became fashionable in elite circles (especially at seaside resorts on the East Coast) and was an expensive luxury—equipment came only from England, and only country estates or clubs could provide the grass courts. "Lawn tennis remained the game of polite society[,] essentially one for ladies and gentlemen," wrote a sportsman in 1886.[5] Clubs formed in Boston, New York, and Philadelphia, and a group of male enthusiasts organized the USLTA in 1881. Power in the USLTA theoretically belonged to individual members and clubs, but as early as 1904 an observer claimed that "its actions are governed by a certain clique of men mostly in

Boston and New York who re-elect themselves or choose their successors each year."[6]

Although tennis at the turn of the century was very exclusive in terms of class, it was less so by gender—women of the upper classes were included. As early as 1889, in fact, the USLTA extended "its protecting wing" to lady players.[7] The game was not played very aggressively by anyone, including men (and certainly it would have been difficult for women to run quickly while wearing corsets, starched skirts, petticoats and shirtwaists, long sleeves, cuff links and high collars).[8] In the early days, all players "padded" around the court, tapping the ball. In fact, a Harvard man claimed in 1878 that the game was only for weak, unathletic men. As a relatively unstrenuous game, then, it was not objectionable for females to play. In 1902, though, over the objections of some women, the USLTA insured that women would not do too much. It passed a new rule limiting women's matches to two out of three sets instead of the customary three out of five.[9] As the game developed and became more strenuous, women had already established the precedent of participating.

The game's setting contributed to its acceptability for women. Country estates, clubs, and resorts were intended as refuge from the cold and crowded urban industrial world. As such, they excluded others on the basis of class, race, and ethnicity, but included the whole upper-class family. Around the turn of the century, claims historian Cynthia Himes, "female athleticism in the leisure class posed no apparent threat to the family unit. The wealth, social prominence and family connections of upper-class women acted as a shield against accusations commonly leveled at female athletes."[10] In 1883 a popular magazine conferred its approval on women playing tennis on the basis of class exclusiveness. It "assured its feminine readers that this was far too refined a game to offer any attractions for the lower orders of society" and that "a lady who took part in a tennis match would find herself in the company of persons in whose society she is accustomed to move."[11]

Upper-middle-class associations of tennis persisted into the 1950s. Although athletic skill could not be determined by class, access to courts could be. With the exception of a few places like California, which had an extensive system of outdoor public courts, most tennis in the United States was taught and played in private clubs, and players from those clubs were most likely to advance up the amateur tennis ladder. At clubs players were introduced to strict tennis etiquette, which included wearing the right clothes (pure white ones) and behaving correctly (e.g., remaining silent during opponents' serves, respecting umpires' decisions, and so on). The *New Yorker* observed in 1952:

> Of all the tight little worlds that have grown up around the popular
> sports of our age, the most civilized by far is the one inhabited by the peo-

> ple who play and follow lawn tennis. . . . This world appears to be an unruf-
> fled and exclusive Eden of green grass, multicolored umbrellas, sunshine,
> crisp white clothes, good breeding, good manners, good bodies, fair
> enough minds, and good credit at the bank.[12]

Consistent with this reputation, one study shows that the parents of top female
players in the 1950s were socioeconomically above average, overwhelmingly
white collar, and among the most highly educated 20 percent of the population.[13] Still, talented but poorer athletes sometimes found their way into tennis
circles through luck or pluck—sweeping courts, retrieving balls, or finding a
generous patron.[14] Whatever their origins, though, females still had to conform
to the manners of upper-middle-class tennis and to continually win the
approval of tennis authorities. Perry Jones, top man in California amateur tennis, believed young ladies should be attired in "correct, demure tennis dresses,"
remembered Maureen Connolly. At one junior tournament, she recalled, "I was
wearing shorts and a t-shirt—all I had—and neither garment was fashionable
or expensive. Jones looked at me in horror. I might have been wearing burlap to
the Royal Ball. He took Mom aside . . . and press[ed] a fifty-dollar bill on Mom
to purchase a suitable outfit."[15]

As with its class connotation, the ladylike reputation of tennis also continued into the 1950s. When in 1958 a scholar asked sportswomen which were the
"sports with the most feminine appeal," tennis ranked second on their list
(swimming came in first, basketball twenty-eighth).[16] A number of respondents elaborated that they hoped their daughters would take up tennis (or golf)
because it afforded social opportunities and was a graceful and ladylike game.
Indeed, Pauline Betz's mother, alarmed by her daughter's tomboyish tendencies, directed her away from other athletic activities and toward tennis.[17] Other
girls remembered the same parental guidance. "When I was growing up, girls
didn't do much of anything [athletically]," explained one, "and tennis was the
only socially acceptable thing to do."[18]

The tradition of amateurism also kept tennis exclusive. In theory, professionals played for money and amateurs played for the love of sport. To protect
the amateur nature of the game, the USLTA's earliest rules prohibited players
from benefiting financially from their talent. They could not earn money from
winning tournaments, teaching, advertising, or even writing about tennis. As a
result, few of those who competed regionally were poor—a player had to be
able to afford to travel to tournaments and to secure room and board. But as the
game became more popular, both players and tournament directors (who
wanted top players to perform at their events) became disgruntled. Therefore
two separate changes occurred. First, the USLTA loosened some of its rules defin-

ing amateurism. (For example, during the 1930s the USLTA began allowing players to receive expense money for a limited number of weeks a year, and slowly that practice expanded.)[19] The other adaptation was that many players and tournament directors simply quietly broke the rules.

By the mid-fifties the distinction between amateur and professional had become almost meaningless for male players. Top "amateur" men on the tour earned a lot of money—much more than their expenses and more than the USLTA allowed. They made tennis their careers and earned a fine living doing so. Since the USLTA did not officially let them do this as a professional career, these men received their payments "under the table." Players disliked this dishonesty (which they called "shamateurism") but felt forced into it by the USLTA. If one *openly* accepted money, one became a professional, and often opportunities actually decreased. A few men had succeeded in an openly professional tour, but it was risky. If the tour failed, pros had nowhere to turn because, once they turned pro, the USLTA barred them from playing against amateurs. Indeed, all the most prominent tournaments, such as the U.S. national indoor and outdoor, French, and Wimbledon championships, were closed to professionals.[20]

Sometimes the USLTA used its authority over amateur games to harshly punish even the *suggestion* of professionalism, as when it suspended Sarah Palfrey and Pauline Betz for simply looking into professional opportunities (and then did not schedule a hearing until after Wimbledon). Other times, however, it looked the other way. Players thought arbitrary tennis authorities not only wanted to preserve traditions but to preserve their *control* of the game.[21] As Pauline Betz recalled, the USLTA "had a stranglehold on tennis."[22]

"All the up and coming tennis amateur needs is a taste for the right clothes, a talent for cocktail party chatter and a superior knack for belting tennis balls," claimed *Time* magazine in 1955. "It is no trick at all to parlay such gifts into a year-round, expenses paid vacation—wives and kids included."[23] But *Time's* hypothetical player was male—"shamateurism" had fewer benefits for women. Amateur rules allowed paying women expense money on certain occasions, but they were rare, and the permitted per diem was insufficient. Nor was this reimbursement very dependable.[24] Under-the-table payments were infrequent for women, and because they were not expected to support a husband or children, tournament officials felt no obligation to pay them as much as men.[25] They did not believe women deserved much, anyway. One of the top draws, Maureen Connolly, claimed she received appearance money under-the-table only twice in her career. As a result, Shirley Fry recalled, "I didn't break even. . . . It cost me money to play. It cost $350 to go to Europe and back on the boat. I'd say it cost $1,000 for a summer in Europe. Trying to make ends meet was an endless job."[26] Realistically, aspiring female players had to have parents or husbands who had money. Many tried to minimize expenses by staying at private homes rather than hotels, but even that required knowing the right people, further ensconcing class exclusiveness.

The traditional code of amateurism intertwined with gender prescriptions to discourage women from making tennis a career. Unable to earn a living at it, most people (including many of the players) viewed it as an avocation for women, or as an "interlude" between schooling and married life.[27] A very few players made tennis their top priority. Doris Hart, for example, dropped out of college to work on her game. "Tennis has meant everything to me," she said at age thirty.[28] But Hart was unusual in that she actually conceived of tennis as a long-term career; for the majority, the structures were not available to make one likely. First was the lack of money. "If Wimbledon and Forest Hills had been professional, I would probably have stayed on as an active player," claimed one player.[29] In addition, social pressure made it difficult to continue for very long. Both those who did not marry and those that did encountered difficulties. After Margaret Osborne duPont married, it was clear her husband was the boss. He refused to stay overnight once a tournament was over and prohibited Margaret (under threat of divorce) from entering certain championships.[30] Things were even more difficult for mothers, given the expectation that mothers should be the primary caregivers for children. "I wanted to be a good wife and good mother and good tennis player and couldn't do it *all*," recalled a player who ended up quitting.[31] By the 1950s the demands of the more serious circuit became so heavy that fewer top players were married. Putting off marriage was permissible for a while, but players felt pressure to get on with a "normal" life. According to one player, her mother repeatedly told her, "When I was your age I was married and had ten kids."[32]

Just as the code of amateurism blended with gender to make tennis more exclusive, so did the code of race. Few blacks in the United States during the 1950s belonged to the most elite level of society; nor did African-Americans often grace—as spectators or players—the same country clubs as whites. It was a segregated game. Exceptions did exist; for example, New York's Cosmopolitan Tennis Club (defunct by 1957) was mixed, and the University of Chicago's varsity tennis team had a black captain in 1929. But no black played in a major USLTA tournament until Reginald Weir did so in 1948.[33] Before then, black Junior Champions had been rejected from the nationals because of their race, just as in the 1920s Helen Wills Moody flatly refused to play Ora Washington, a legendary tennis and basketball star.[34]

Exclusion, it seems, was based as much on tradition as explicit rules; unwritten policies and private decision-making worked effectively to institutionalize racism.[35] When white former champion Alice Marble made informal inquiries to USLTA officials in 1949 about Althea Gibson's chances of entering the U.S. outdoor national championship at Forest Hills, she discovered exactly how the system worked. Marble was not told outright that Gibson would be refused, but that she would have to make a strong showing at the major Eastern grass tournaments preceding the nationals. Unfortunately, though, those tournaments were by invitation only, and a USLTA official informed Marble that Gibson probably would not be invited. Appalled, Marble wrote a guest editorial in *Lawn Tennis* magazine that denounced the ruse. "If she is not invited to participate in them, as my committeeman freely predicts, then she obviously will be unable to prove anything at all, and it will be the reluctant duty of the committee to reject her entry at Forest Hills. . . . Miss Gibson," she concluded, "is over a very cunningly wrought barrel."[36]

Marble had been surprised to learn how the USLTA subtly discriminated, but blacks knew all too well and tried to adjust accordingly. African-Americans started playing tennis shortly after it was introduced in the United States. Often prohibited from playing on public courts, they developed their own clubs in cities like Washington, Baltimore, Philadelphia, New York, and Chicago. The American Tennis Association, a race-separate organization parallel to USLTA, held annual championships for Negro men and women annually beginning in 1917. By 1951, 150 Negro tennis clubs were allied with the ATA.[37] Like the USLTA, the ATA was run by a small group of well-off men, and as in the white community, tennis was an elitist game among blacks. A poor girl often in trouble on the streets of Harlem, Althea Gibson shot pool, gambled at cards, and had crude manners. At first she was uncomfortable with all the rules and proper etiquette that were part of tennis traditions, but she understood their roots.

> The Cosmopolitan [Tennis Club] members were the highest class of Harlem people and they had rigid ideas about what was socially acceptable behavior. They were undoubtedly more strict than white people of similar position, for the obvious reason that they felt they had to be doubly careful in order to overcome the prejudiced attitude that all Negroes lived eight to a room in dirty houses and drank gin all day and settled all their arguments with knives.[38]

The manners and propriety of tennis appealed to some of the wealthy blacks who patronized the game. They wanted a share of tennis's refined reputation and some association with the powerful people who played. Many other blacks supported the upper-middle-class efforts to integrate the white tennis world. *Ebony* described the galleries at USLTA tournaments as being populated by "snobbish people who say 'Who, us? Why we've never discriminated,'" and the magazine's editors applauded when Gibson gained access to this audience. "When she made good in this society, Althea reached over the masses to win the support of the few who frequently influence the masses."[39]

Because they believed that achievement in sports could make a difference in the perception of blacks by the dominant white culture, male black leaders sometimes encouraged female athletes. Physical educator and sport historian Edwin B. Henderson of Washington, D.C., had carefully considered the risk:

> There are those who condemn strenuous athletic contests for women, who fear women will lose some of their charm and possibly what is more important, health. But so long as women of other races and nations engage in these sports with no proven evidence of detriment, our girls have reason and right to compete. Victory in physical contests, as with high rating in mental or spiritual measurements, helped kill off the Nazi-inspired doctrine of inferiority.[40]

In part, Henderson took his cue about what constituted appropriate femininity from "other races and nations." Not surprisingly, then, he worried most about black women's participation in sports like basketball and track, recognizing that most people readily considered individual sports like tennis and golf as very acceptable for women.[41]

Therefore, ATA leaders ignored Gibson's gender and overlooked her class background in order to groom her for the hoped-for opportunity in the white championships. Pygmalion-like, Dr. Walter Johnson of Lynchburg, Virginia, and Dr. Hubert Eaton of Wilmington, North Carolina, took Gibson under their wings. They worked on both her technique and her social skills. Eaton "tried to show Althea how to be a lady on the court" and to accept defeat with grace, and his wife "bought her a few dresses and tried to make her more feminine by getting her straight hair curled and showing her how to use lipstick."[42] Gibson lived with the Eatons while school was in session, and during the summer traveled the ATA circuit as one of Johnson's protégées. She won almost everything on it in 1947, including the ATA women's crown. After Marble's prodding, some chastened white officials invited Gibson to an exclusive grass tournament. After a good showing there, they allowed her to enter the national championship at Forest Hills in 1950, where she created such a stir against Brough.

The better Gibson did (her USLTA ranking rose to ninth in 1952), the more blacks' hopes were raised. "Althea Gibson is to the tennis world what Jackie Robinson was to major league baseball," asserted the *Chicago Defender*.[43] Newspaper coverage of her success encouraged African-Americans all over the country to rally around her, making her aspirations collective. They realized that a black tennis player faced all sorts of extra obstacles to becoming a champion.[44] "Everybody is pulling for you," wired a black sportswriter. In addition to sending prayers, then, Detroit blacks raised $770 toward her Wimbledon costs, and boxer Joe Louis gave her a plane ticket and hotel suite. Even after she lost in 1950 in the finals of the national indoors, she returned to Florida A. & M. University to an overwhelming welcome, in which the president of the college and a marching band greeted her. "Obviously," noted Gibson, "they all felt that what I had done was important not just to me but to all Negroes."[45]

Her image became tarnished, however. On a number of occasions she refused to grant interviews, and after one incident a sportswriter for the *Chicago Defender* lambasted her as "ungracious as a stubborn jackass" and "the most arrogant athlete it has been my displeasure to meet."[46] As her success spread, so did her reputation for being difficult to deal with—sulky, tight-lipped, temperamental, and discourteous. Even her coach acknowledged her "personality problem." Especially worrisome—so much so that controversy over it filled the black press—was the impact her behavior had on the reputation of all blacks. *Ebony* politely suggested she felt out of place in the dainty, feminine world of tennis and that she was not ready to assume the public relations demands of her role. A *Pittsburgh Courier* editorialist insisted that the usually gracious Gibson should not have to be perfect. "Should she grin and show her teeth every time a reporter says, 'Come here, Althea?'" he asked rhetorically. But the *Defender*'s Russ Cowans declared that Gibson was ungrateful for black support and was not fulfilling her responsibilities as a race hero. "Her face is a badge and whether you like it or not, she represents 16 million of her people in the field of tennis. Therefore, she is obligated to act as a goodwill ambassador."[47]

Clearly Gibson struggled with her role as race representative. "It was a strain," she wrote, "always trying to say and do the right thing, so that I wouldn't give people the wrong idea of what Negroes are like."[48] When she lost important matches (as she increasingly did in the mid-1950s), she had to live with not only her own frustration but that of millions. Critics began labeling her "the biggest disappointment in sports" and hinted she did not have what it took.[49] Even when she won, she suspected people wanted things from her. The pressure of "feel[ing] responsibilities to Negroes" was a "burden," and she thought it contributed to her failures in the mid-1950s. So she decided to start playing to please simply herself and not the black community. Unlike Jackie Robinson, then, she shied away from the role of race hero and refused to speak out about racial injustice. She wanted to be appreciated as an individual achiever, not to be a spokesperson or crusader. "I don't consciously beat the drums for any special cause, not even the cause of the Negro in the United States, because I feel that our best chance to advance is to prove ourselves as individuals."[50] Gibson thought the black press turned on her precisely because she did not welcome her role as champion of the race. "A lot of those who disagree with me are members of the Negro press, and they beat my brains out regularly. I have always enjoyed a good press among the regular [white] American newspapers and magazines, but I am uncomfortably close to being Public Enemy No. 1 to some sections of the Negro press."[51]

Thus the sense of community ownership of black athletes could cut a number of ways. For some female athletes, like the track stars from Tennessee State and the *Philadelphia Tribune* basketball team, a sense of racial mission gained them support and acceptance despite their gender. However, as Gibson's experience indicates, the same sense of community ownership could become burdensome. For having different ideas about her role and responsibility, Gibson was viewed by some blacks as ungrateful. In turn, Gibson felt more alienated from the black community that had such aspirations for her. As she looked back years later, Gibson said she would probably do things differently. But "at that time I felt I was just representing myself," she remembered. "My people weren't in that sport anyway."[52] Gibson's use of the phrase "my people" surely implies her identification with African-Americans but might also suggest her sense of class separateness from those elite blacks in the tennis world. Regardless, even before extensive criticism from the press, Gibson's frustration mounted. Tired of disappointments and the pressures of the amateur tour, she decided in 1955 to retire from tennis. "I'm sick of having people support me, taking up collections for me, buying me clothes and airplane tickets and every damn thing I eat or wear. I want to take care of myself for a change."[53] She planned to join the Women's Army Corps.

Suddenly, though, Gibson's luck changed. In the mid-fifties the federal government was aggressively trying to improve its international reputation and win the ideological Cold War. In particular, U.S. leaders wanted to counteract Communist propaganda which painted American freedom and democracy as a sham because of the nation's treatment of African-Americans. As part of this campaign, the State Department invited Gibson to participate in a "goodwill tour" to developing countries in Asia. Instead of joining the WACs, then, in 1956 Gibson traveled with three other athletes throughout the world playing exhibition matches and entering tournaments along the way. Gibson aided the country by providing the image of a successful black American, and at the same time benefited from playing tennis often and inexpensively—the first time a Negro was able to play the international tennis circuit. In some ways, however, this year was difficult.

> Having to contend with crowds hostile to me because of my color, with newspapers demanding twice as much of me as they did of anybody else simply because my color made me more newsworthy, and even with powerful governments seeking to use me as an instrument of national policy

because of my color, seemed to me to be more than anybody should have
to bear.[54]

Still, the "experience did wonders for me."[55] In particular, it helped her game.
Gibson won her first "significant" singles title as well as sixteen of the eighteen
tournaments she entered.[56]

More comfortable and confident, Gibson finally appeared to be reaching her
potential. That year, she made it to the quarterfinals at Wimbledon, and the
next two summers (1957 and 1958) she won the championship. After her first
Wimbledon victory, she came home to 100,000 New Yorkers cheering her at a
ticker tape parade.

Gibson finally managed to "arrive" at the top by the late 1950s, but her success must be put in perspective. Compared to other champions, she had struggled disproportionately to get there. If she had been white and welcomed by the
tennis elite, she probably would have been a U.S. and international champion
all through her twenties. Instead, her rise took much longer. She did not win
Wimbledon and the U.S. national outdoor championships until age twenty-
nine. In addition, Gibson endured "a wicked amount of punishment along the
way."[57] She may have hobnobbed with royalty, but right after winning
Wimbledon she was not allowed to stay in a hotel in a Chicago suburb.[58]

Gibson attributed her success both to her ability to survive abuse and to
people who cared enough to help her. Clearly her courage, the efforts of the
ATA leaders, assistance from blacks all over the country, and the timely support
of some liberal white players made an enormous difference. But Gibson was
also lucky. At least as significant as the fact that she "made it" is that despite her
enormous talent and dedicated friends, she very nearly did not. She was fortunate to come along at a moment when the postwar political climate meant
white tennis authorities would be embarrassed if they excluded her, and lucky
that the State Department entered the picture just before she quit so as to fur-
nish opportunities that a talented and well-off white girl would have had years
earlier.

Nor did Gibson's arrival mean that the racial and class hegemony of the tennis establishment had been overturned. When she published her autobiography
in 1958, Gibson thought USLTA was becoming more open to black competitors.
"U.S.L.T.A. works closely with A.T.A. in examining the qualifications of Negro
players," she said, "and, in effect, any player strongly recommended for a place
in the national championship draw is accepted without question."[59] However,
history proved her hope illusory. Unlike basketball and baseball, where blacks
entered in large numbers once racial barriers were lowered, tennis remained
predominantly white.[60] Tennis's white fathers enjoyed positive publicity from
accepting Gibson into their major tournaments, but proved unwilling to

address the circumstances that continued to limit access to tennis. Besides remaining silent about racial discrimination at most country clubs, they seemed unperturbed by class exclusion.

The combination of class and racial factors proved extremely difficult for an African-American athlete to overcome. Throughout the 1950s USLTA allowed blacks into a few national tournaments but did not let them compete the rest of the year on the same footing. Blacks were not welcomed in the same lead-up tournaments and were evaluated in a different manner from white players. Blacks had "advanced" to the position where they might petition USLTA and expect some response, but USLTA's hegemonic position remained firmly in place. Historian William Chafe describes the "civilities" of race relations in Greensboro, North Carolina, during the 1950s, in which wealthy white "patrons" doled out occasional favors to black leaders as long as blacks remained in their "proper place."[61] The description seems to apply to the USLTA-ATA patron-client relationship as well. "The A.T.A., of course, is careful not to recommend any but the finest players, which is as it should be," explained Gibson.[62] Gibson and ATA leaders displayed gratitude and respect toward their USLTA patrons, but they really had no choice. Clearly they remained entrenched in a supplicating, subordinate, and ultimately submissive role, forced to ask for token favors from the powerful white organization.

Early in their lives, females who loved competition, physical exertion, and aggression learned what behavior they should be careful about. Sports participation was risky, bringing them both benefits and disadvantages. As athletes they felt happy and fulfilled, but also different and criticized. When Althea Gibson played football and baseball with boys as a teenager, she enjoyed feeling talented and expressive but was upset by others' reactions. "It used to hurt me real bad to hear the girls talking about me. . . . 'Look at her throwing that ball just like a man,' they would say, and they looked at me like I was a freak."[63] Gibson's mixed emotions probably typified those of tomboys, who sometimes felt pride but also sometimes self-hatred (wishing they knew how to do girl things comfortably) and anger ("I hated them for it") as well as often feeling different and alone. "It seemed sometimes," she wrote, "as though nobody could understand me." The challenge for these girls was to find ways to minimize disapproval while still doing the loved activities. As noted in the previous chapter, "apologetic behavior" was one strategy for dealing with these dilemmas; another was choosing their athletic activities carefully.

Tennis was a shrewd choice because the game's propriety—associated as it was with elitism—seemed to grant female athletes permission to make gender transgressions. Gibson discovered with glee that tennis provided an acceptable outlet where she could compete and still belong. "After a while I began to understand," she wrote, "that you could walk out on the court like a lady, all dressed up in immaculate white, be polite to everybody, and still play like a tiger and beat the liver and lights out of the ball."[64] One had to conform to the game's etiquette, but that conformity yielded benefits. As a top amateur recalled, "Tennis clothes were very expensive, but . . . [they] projected the image of a well-scrubbed, all-American girl in whites."[65] Sometimes the game conferred on female athletes an image that sharply contrasted with their self-perceptions. At the same time that white tennis star Sarah Palfrey "felt like a tiger out there," sportswriters raved about her "exquisite daintiness" and "eternal femininity."[66]

This greater acceptance of female tennis players also can be seen in their public notice. Publishers during the 1950s never asked a basketball star like Lurlyne Greer to write her autobiography, but they did ask top tennis players like Doris Hart, Maureen Connolly, and Althea Gibson. While national publications never reported on top amateur basketball teams like Hanes Hosiery or Wayland's Flying Queens, periodicals like *Time, Newsweek, Life*, and the *New Yorker* occasionally contained stories on women in tennis. They fairly regularly covered the major tournaments like Wimbledon and Forest Hills and, when discussing tournament results, usually included women.[67] It may well be that women would have been ignored if they had not been paired with men at such prominent events, and that the co-recreational nature of USLTA tennis helps account for the greater attention these female athletes received. At least a couple of times a year, women stars had the amazing experience of performing in front of huge audiences. "And that is a wonderful feeling," remarked Doris Hart, "when you are out on a court with fifteen thousand people watching every move you make."[68] Daily newspapers, too, had intermittent coverage of the top female players, with the result that when a woman made the sports page, it was often a tennis player (or golfer).

The greater acceptance, of course, was relative. Compared to male tennis players, females clearly were disadvantaged. Just as they were usually relegated to the fringe courts of a club, they rarely occupied the center of press coverage. Articles that included both sexes often discussed women in one paragraph compared to men's three. Even when sportswriters acknowledged that the only surprises in a tournament came from women's competition, they spent most of their time discussing the men's rounds.[69] Sportswriters apparently found the women's events less interesting, and they treated the men more seriously. Still, the average typical American sports fan in the 1950s probably had heard of Maureen Connolly, Althea Gibson, and Doris Hart.

Even more likely, sports fans would have heard of Gertrude Moran. Moran's coverage illustrates some of the limits to the respect given female tennis players. Although she never ranked higher than fourth in the United States, Moran probably garnered more publicity around 1950 than all the other players combined. Rarely was Moran mentioned without reference to her appearance, as reflected in her nickname, "Gorgeous Gussie" Moran.[70] After Moran became the talk of London by wearing lace panties underneath her tennis skirt, the public received updates on such nonathletic information as her bust measurements, her apparel, and her male suitors.[71] That Moran got attention solely because of her looks was bad enough; worse was the implicit suggestion that other female players—more talented but not as pretty—deserved less attention. "Although duly impressed with her skill, sportswriters were careful to note that Miss Moran has lovely green eyes, the face and figure of a movie starlet and is the most attractive raw material they have had to write about in some time," reported *Life*.[72] Other players got the message that flirting with the fans and media made more of an impact than winning. "It used to bother me a bit that they didn't write up the tennis," admitted Louise Brough.[73] Moran complained about all the publicity but also benefited; even though she was not ranked very high, she was one of only a few women signed to a professional tour.[74]

During the 1950s most tennis people believed that the general public was not interested in pure athletic competition between top women. Consequently, the few women who did try to turn professional relied not only on skill but also their "novelty value." To a lesser degree, they resorted to the same gimmickry as the barnstorming basketball teams like the All-American Red Heads. During their 1947 national tour, for example, Pauline Betz and Sarah Palfrey Cooke gave comic instructional clinics before the match. Dressing up in sloppy men's size-forty shorts and a rain hat and using a warped racquet, Betz developed a character named "Susie Glutz" who did everything wrong.[75] In the same vein, when Jack Kramer signed Betz and Moran to his 1950–51 tour, he did so because he hoped Moran's reputation would grab headlines. Indeed, although newspapers did pay attention (reporting on the length of Moran's skirt), the strategy backfired.[76] Moran was not as pretty as the hype indicated, nor really all that daring, and Betz regularly and easily defeated her. Unfortunately, besides describing Moran's appearance, the *New York Times* also reported that the women's match was rather tame and uninteresting.

Women's attempts at pro tennis proved disappointing. During the postwar period, female pros only had a couple of choices. They could go out on their own, sometimes traveling four hundred miles a night to sparsely filled arenas, doing exhibitions combined with novelty. This might feel like sacrificing your athletic integrity, especially if, as in the case of Betz, your promoter asked you to play below your ability to keep the matches close and interesting.[77] Or female pros could make up the preliminaries, the "warm-up" on a men's pro tour. Althea Gibson, for example, did a one-year stint of exhibitions during half-time at Harlem Globetrotters basketball games. Neither option gained these women the respect they desired. They earned fairly good money for a female player, but even these opportunities were limited.[78] Not more than one pair of women could succeed at a time, and their tours lasted no more than a year. After that, what? No longer allowed to play against amateurs, they dropped from the limelight. In the long run it did not pay off—in fact, from 1959 to 1967 no women toured as professionals.

Lack of opportunities combined with gender prescriptions to insure that a female tennis player could only go so far. She could be a sportswoman only if she followed certain rules. For one thing, she had to look right. Although shorts were more comfortable and practical, skirts were considered more feminine. A few players, like Helen Jacobs, wore shorts as early as the 1930s, but most opted for traditional skirts or dresses.[79] To the question, "What should a girl wear on the courts?" the young Maureen Connolly replied, "Dresses preferably! They're more feminine, look nicer and give one the feeling of being well groomed. Shorts and t-shirts are fine for practice, but in tournament play dresses are far more attractive."[80] Although top amateurs in the 1950s dressed far less restrictively than their foremothers, they still compromised comfort and ease in order to please their select audience.[81]

The truly feminine tennis player also had to keep the game in perspective. The inability to make tennis a career (and pressure to get married) helped dissuade players from taking the game too seriously. In case they needed reminding, however, journalists reinforced the proper attitude. In praising her tenure, a male sportswriter said of Sarah Palfrey: "Sportsmanship has had no truer exemplar than the slip of a Boston blueblood who fought unrelentingly to win, but never at all costs, and ever mindful that it was a game."[82] Correspondingly, fans found fault with female players who made winning *too* important. "Bent on victory," *Newsweek* observed, "Miss Gibson played with a sullen intensity that annoyed the gallery."[83]

Finally, to be considered feminine, athletes actually had to play a certain way. Except for the decree that women should play a shorter length of time, the game's rules were identical for men and women. But in the popular mind, the play of men and women differed. In tennis two styles predominate: some players use a defensive baseline strategy, others a more aggressive one in which they follow a strong serve to the net. More women—whether because they thought of themselves as weak, never developed a powerful serve, psychologically preferred a defensive game, or thought it more feminine—used the baseline strategy. When a female player did not (such as Althea Gibson and Alice Marble), often her game was described as "mannish."[84] *Time* reported on an Althea Gibson match at Wimbledon: "Right from the start Althea grimly set her lips and set out to play a man's game. Lean and agile (5 ft. 10¾ in., 138 lbs.), she sprinted about the court on tireless legs, belted her serve with unladylike gusto."[85]

It was not simply that Gibson played in a man's style; also problematic was her display of excellence. Such mastery, especially in the athletic world, was equated with masculinity. Male star Tony Trabert "complimented" Gibson. "She hits the ball hard and plays like a man. She runs and covers the court better than any of the women."[86] Performing with such outstanding skill was thought to masculinize women—or at least put them into a different category from the feminine one, a risky proposition for one's identity.[87] A male colleague of Gibson's said, "You had to look two or three times at Althea to convince yourself she was a girl. She played all the games so well. You couldn't tell she was a girl by the way she pitched or the way she shagged fly balls in the outfield."[88] Some spectators were fascinated by the gender bending, while others reacted with hostility. Obviously many women chose to hide or not pursue their talents. Female athletes knew well the danger of becoming experts. When some Ohio sportswomen were asked in 1958 if men were more critical of women who were "too good" or highly proficient athletes, two-thirds of them said yes. Others had had more supportive encounters with men. "[It] depends on his ego," commented one. "The feminine charming girl might carry it off." The investigator thought that most of the women downplayed their own skills. In fact, over one-third affirmed that they would let a male opponent win in some circumstances.[89]

The case of Maureen Connolly illustrates why a woman might choose to downplay her athleticism. When she burst into the public eye at the nationals in 1951, Connolly earned positive headlines. The press portrayed her as a charming, cute, nimble, and normal girl.[90] "She loves tennis, sure, and practices three hours a day. But she also has a great time listening to records, going to movies, swimming, riding and dancing."[91] Reporters raved about "the blonde, blue-eyed and bubbly Little Mo Connolly [who] was a distinct blessing to women's tennis." One predicted, "People are going to love her probably more than they ever loved any other tennis player."[92]

Rather rapidly, though, things changed. Winning mattered to Connolly. She proclaimed her ambition to win a record number of events and started dominating the game. During a three-and-a-half-year stretch she won every major tournament she entered. Correspondingly, observers began noticing Connolly's intensity and lack of emotion on the court, and her serious, methodical, and relentless play.[93] With her increasing success, the tone of the press shifted. *Newsweek* said Connolly played "with a poker-faced preoccupation that had the galleries calling her the mechanical doll.[94] Also noting Connolly's awesome determination, *Time* said she advanced "with machine-like precision." Fans missed the "girlish, hard-playing bobby soxer who wept with joy" the previous year. "Little Mo," it decreed, "had turned into Killer Connolly."[95] Such mechanical metaphors were not typically applied to female athletes—in essence, they desexed Connolly. And fans apparently did not like this desexed female athlete.

"There was an unladylike grimness about Maureen's playing that shocked most proper Britons into a grudging admiration—and a keen wish to see her roundly trounced."[96]

If Connolly's intensity and dominance bothered fans, it also made her uncomfortable. "At times, to my distaste, I had been called a killer in the newspapers," she wrote. "This struck too close to the truth, the truth I wanted no one to know."[97] Connolly feared her consuming passion to win might be an abnormal, "alien" obsession. Shamefully, she admitted to hating her opponents and believed former women champions probably had not felt the same. Although Connolly did not explicitly say she worried about being considered unfeminine, gender formed the backdrop for her concerns. It would have been unheard of for a top male athlete to express the same remorse about overdoing it, or for the press to seize upon it and refer to in gendered terms such as "unladylike abandon."[98] Some psychologists theorize that competition is generally more stressful for women because they personalize it, and because its conflict seems to endanger relationships, which women value more than achievement.[99] Taking competition personally made life difficult for Connolly. She thought she should not hate, but it was the only way she knew how to win. And, at the same time, she acutely needed to do well since she had grown up getting approval for success. "I had to win because I wanted to be liked, and only by winning, I thought, would I be liked."[100] Imagine her confusion when she discovered that in the wider culture people disliked her ambition, that there was such a thing as a woman winning too much.

Connolly struggled to reach some sort of happy medium. She was gratified to report that, with time and a friend's help, she started being able to defeat her opponents without hating them. Theoretically, that way she could still win and not be disliked for it. It is impossible to know whether that adjustment would have resolved her dilemma, and whether she would have become a well-liked winner, because an accident cut short her career.

After the injury, she attempted to come back but was prevented by frustrating, insurmountable pain. In her autobiography, published a few years later, she declared that she had desperately wanted to play again. But her public retirement announcement at the time suggested that tennis was not too important to her. Instead of admitting her personal agony, she adopted a breezy air, saying she had lost her spark and did not enjoy tennis anymore. Further, she implied it was time to get on with a normal sort of life. "There's no use going on like this; might as well tie that hitch and get married."[101]

As Connolly and Gibson's stories illustrate, there were limits to what tennis players could acceptably do. In fact, they shared some of the same difficulties as other female athletes. Any career they could manage was brief. Nor was it taken as seriously as they would have liked. Competing too seriously meant they teetered close to crossing the line into disapproval. Therefore, occasionally tennis players exhibited apologetic behavior in the same areas as basketball players. When tennis players tried to keep up appearances, however, they did so more to *safeguard* rather than to achieve feminine acceptance. Still, they wore extra-feminine attire, downplayed their competitiveness, alluded to their heterosexuality, minimized the importance of the game, and eschewed careers. Like other female athletes, they faced the challenge of competing fiercely but not overstepping the bounds of proper femininity.

Nevertheless, in relative terms, top amateur tennis players had it good. They played the sport with one of the best reputations for women. Associated with a proper elite world, they suffered much less stigma than other female athletes; they tended to get the benefit of the doubt about being acceptable women. With less burden of proving their femininity, they displayed less apologetic behavior. (For example, Doris Hart's autobiography, *Tennis with Hart*, never once assured readers of her romantic interest in men.) In addition, tennis players had other advantages. Unlike many basketballers, most of them did not work forty-hour weeks and have to squeeze sports in afterward. And although they were rarely and poorly paid, they reaped other benefits.[102] Acceptance in elite tennis circles opened doors to perks like free equipment and designer clothes, and access to rich, powerful, or famous people. At the Essex Country Club Invitational, players "would all stay in very elaborate private homes. . . . There was a nice party every night, a clam bake; they could go swimming and horseback riding." They traveled around the world. "I played on cow-dung courts in Durban, South Africa. I rode a camel in Egypt. I saw the Pyramids. What fun it was," remembered Shirley Fry. And there were psychological rewards. Success in any sport brings satisfaction and self-confidence, and even more so when people notice. Their respective hometowns staged impressive ceremonies honoring both Doris Hart and Althea Gibson. "I was deeply moved by all this attention," recalled Hart, and Gibson kept repeating, "It's amazing, wonderful."[103] For females who wanted to pursue sports, tennis was a welcome haven.

Unfortunately, tennis players' enviable position came at a high price—that of exclusiveness. As historian Elsa Barkeley Brown has reminded her colleagues, women of varying classes, races, ethnicities, and sexual orientations are not just "different" but live in relationship to each other. Even without direct contact, individuals' lives are affected by the structures of power undergirding the "categories" they belong to. The leisure of the upper classes, for example, is built upon the service and labor of the working classes. The heightened status of whites comes only with the demeaned status of blacks, that of heterosexuals depends on the stigmatizing of homosexuals. In the same way, the genteel reputation of tennis derived from its class and racial elitism; the existence of working-class, less refined and less white sports helped tennis stand out in stark contrast. So, too, did women's participation in more "masculine" games like basketball, softball, boxing, and roller derby set female tennis players apart. In addition, the relatively "feminine" reputation of tennis probably resulted partly from its being considered something of a "sissy" sport for men.[104]

Tennis's traditional class and racial exclusiveness disadvantaged many but benefited others, specifically those mostly white upper-middle-class women who were "included." But tennis's exclusiveness took its toll even on those women. Their situation was far from ideal. Although the country club atmosphere appeared elegant or charming, many resented it and privately condemned its "snobbery and exclusivity."[105] Although it may have seemed to other female athletes that tennis players "belonged," tennis players themselves understandably felt in a precarious position. They had more to risk than basketball players. Rather than feeling free and secure, they worried about losing what they had. In a world where proper etiquette mattered as much as a proper backhand, they correctly perceived that their success did not depend solely on talent. Even if they behaved correctly, they had no guarantee of inclusion. Almost all players disliked the politics and hypocrisy of amateur tennis, but they felt hopeless about changing it in the face of the powerful and sometimes arbitrary USLTA. Indeed, tennis authorities did not value women highly and were willing to punish transgressions. "We were controlled," recalled one player; "we were told what we could do, when we could do it, and why we should do it. This didn't allow for too much individuality."[106]

Female tennis players were also controlled by a more subtle and pervasive hegemony than the USLTA: that of traditional cultural values. These traditions meant that some women players were accepted into the inner circle of amateur tennis, but only some. And those who were had to conform to genteel feminine expectations. In the 1950s female tennis players used the space allowed them, but a few began to chafe at its limitations. Althea Gibson challenged the game's traditions because of her race, class, and style of play; so did Maureen Connolly because of her intense ambition; and so did tame-looking Doris Hart, who wanted to make a full-time career out of the game. These women loved their sport and achieved notoriety from it. None of them, though, received the opportunities, appreciation, and real freedom she wanted and deserved. At the end of the decade, most tennis traditions for women remained fairly firmly entrenched. The traditions gave them some room to compete, for which they were grateful, but also kept them confined. Perhaps tennis in the 1950s could be compared to a well-off family, where women enjoyed advantages simply from belonging. Unfortunately, the head of the household expected strict obedience from his dependents and only rarely allowed them any real say in the decision-making. As one player put it, in this family, women were still the "little stepchildren."[107]

Part II

Introduction: 1955–1967

Conservatism during the 1950s stemmed from both a postwar desire to return to traditional ways and a new geopolitical climate. Cultural authorities decreed that men should regain their former places and women should forget whatever blurring of gender roles had taken place during World War II. The idealized happy, middle-class, *Father Knows Best*-type nuclear family took up residence in the expanding suburbs and the popular mind. Femininity assumed enormous importance. In the international arena, the dropping of atomic bombs on Japan had ended the war, but tensions with the Soviet Union reached dangerous levels. Political leaders denounced Communism at home and abroad as a fundamental threat to the American way of life. Because red-baiters intimidated leftists and liberals, the range of political debate narrowed. In this "age of consensus," liberals did not differ much from conservatives, criticism of the government abated, and significant social change appeared impossible.

Accurate as the characterization of the 1950s as conservative is, there is more to the story. Generalizations oversimplify and, especially during the late 1950s, reality did not always match the image. While it is true, for example, that the era was generally prosperous, three recessions plagued the nation. While it is true that there was a great deal of political consensus, it is also true the nation divided sharply over racial issues. In fact, despite conservative sentiment and the resurgence of antiblack groups working against change, other circumstances opened the door to it. President Truman integrated the armed forces in 1948, the Supreme Court outlawed segregation in public schools in 1954, and Congress considered civil rights legislation. Some political support for civil rights resulted from the fear that Communist countries would spread propaganda portraying the United States as a hypocritical, unequal society. In the ideological battle to win over nonaligned countries, the existence of racial discrimination in America was an embarrassment. Paradoxically, then, some of the era's Cold War conservatism actually led to some liberal change.

Women also encountered a situation a bit more complicated than the conservative image suggested. Cultural authorities certainly urged women to revert to traditional femininity, but other circumstances allowed some more modern behavior. Despite the push for women to return to the home, for example, an "ethic of togetherness" meant that they enjoyed a bit more power in the home.[1] Husband and wife considered each other partners in the family enterprise—chores were to be distributed, decision-making shared, sex mutually satisfying. Nor was the reversion to the home as universal as supposed. Although women did surrender their well-paying jobs in heavy industry, they did not stop working for pay outside the home. In fact, the percentage of women working actually *increased* steadily throughout the 1950s. By 1960, 35 percent of adult women worked for pay.[2] The numbers of women getting a college education also rose dramatically. Today, observed *Look* magazine in 1956, if a woman "makes an old-fashioned choice and lovingly tends . . . a bumper crop of children, she rates louder hosannas than before. . . . If, by contrast, she chooses to take six to ten years out for family, then returns to the work for which she was educated, no one fusses much about that either."[3] Despite the steady stream of propaganda to become a feminine housewife, many middle-class women—with their husband's approval—did not conform to that image.

How did women explain this gap between actual behavior and conservative ideology? They did not defiantly reject norms. Instead, in an ideological sleight of hand, women synthesized the new behavior with conservative notions of propriety: they justified the behavior with very "feminine" rationales. They said they worked outside jobs for their families (not for themselves), and for very specific goals like that second car or the kids' college education or the family vacation. Mom's income was supplementary to Dad's; she was merely "helping out" temporarily. As *Look* put it, "She works rather casually . . . less toward a big career than as a way of filling a hope chest or buying a new freezer."[4] Thus despite the importance of such work to the women and their families (it helped many achieve middle-class status), it was accepted by society only in a qualified way. It was as though women had made a "deal" that they could work only if they minimized or demeaned their labor. Not all females appreciated such subtle ideological maneuvering. Instead, they felt like they got mixed messages: do well in school but don't do *too* well (so that you scare off a man); work, but only in an appropriate manner.[5] Although a perceptive young woman in the 1950s might realize she actually did have some choices, she might well feel anxious about the conflicting winds swirling around her.

The election of Democrats to national offices increased the chances for progress in the early 1960s. Just as strenuously anti-Communist as Republicans in foreign policy, Democrats were more liberal on some domestic issues. In a movement that shook the nation, black activists seized the moment and pressed authorities hard for change, and the pillars of inequality began to crumble. Although many women joined the black civil rights movement, women were slow to push for an end to their own oppression. Only an exceptional few spoke out before the late 1960s. Still, the seeds for change had been planted by the contradictions between women's lives and expectations for them. Educated but unemployed suburban women stewed, uncertain if their discontent was caused by societal unfairness or personal maladjustment. Employed women chafed at unequal wages or segregation in "women's work." President Kennedy appointed a commission to study the status of women, which compiled data and set in motion a network that gradually raised consciousness of gender issues. No movement exploded yet, as the nation reeled from racial issues. But the rumblings had begun.

The period from 1955 to 1967 was a complex one. In general the spread of Cold War anti-Communism and the resurgence of domestic ideology spelled conservatism. Paradoxically, however, both trends occasionally opened the possibility of very limited opportunities for disadvantaged groups. When it served their interests, the government, families, and cultural authorities sometimes encouraged those groups. Ideology, though, often lagged behind behavior. In sum, then, the period must be seen as a transitional one, bridging the postwar era that desired stability and continuity with a more modern one which recognized that the behavior of women and blacks had already changed. Like black Americans, women noticed not only the backward-looking messages but also these humble opportunities, and quietly they began evaluating their options. Sportswomen, too, had to decide how to cope with the ambiguous new currents. The choices they made laid the foundation for the future and illustrated their principles, hopes, and fears.

CHAPTER 4

Transitional Years:

Physical Educators, the State, the Media, and New Opportunities for Athletes, 1955–1967

In the early 1950s women PE leaders deservedly had a conservative reputation. Their two main organizations—the National Section for Girls' and Women's Sports (NSGWS) and the National Association for the Physical Education of College Women (NAPECW)—both issued warnings about females doing the wrong sorts of sports and competing without proper safeguards. Physical educators frowned upon interschool and Olympic sports and did not lend much support to the serious and talented female athlete. Cognizant of societal disapproval, they promoted a tame, proper program to develop "sportswomen." But by the mid-1960s these conservative women had become much bolder. Between 1955 and 1963 they expanded the definition of proper competition and became energetic advocates for female athletes. This ideological shift did not result from a sudden conversion experience. Instead, it occurred in a complex relationship with other changes taking place among their constituents, in the world arena and government, and in the media. Actors as well as acted upon, physical educators in a dialectical interchange adjusted their traditional ideology to a changing world.

In 1950 it would have been hard to imagine female PE leaders working with the

Amateur Athletic Union (AAU) on any matter, but in the mid-fifties they began doing so. Although they still did not approve of many AAU activities (especially its emphasis on training Olympic stars), they could not stop them. The NAPECW's president, Josephine Fiske, realized this as early as 1953, when the AAU proposed bringing college students into its Olympic development programs. Although outraged, Fiske acknowledged the wisdom of a colleague's advice: "We must not take steps at this time that will antagonize AAU and thereby jeopardize our chances of working with them at some future time."[1] She resisted the urge to publicly denounce AAU. "[The] AAU will undoubtedly continue," Fiske concluded, "so we will probably try to work with them rather than merely condemn."[2]

Working with AAU (on some matters) was a pragmatic decision. Rather than surrendering, Fiske hoped they could get in and "redirect [AAU's] thinking."[3] Female physical educators agreed with Fiske's approach. According to a 1954 NAPECW survey, 77 percent of its membership favored forming a NAPECW-NSGWS-AAU committee to further cooperation between the groups.[4] Thus by the latter half of the decade, physical education representatives communicated with AAU basketball, track and field, and synchronized swimming committees.

After serving on AAU committees, physical educators became all the more convinced that they should be involved. Maria Sexton, for example, was "disgusted" by the AAU-USOC women's basketball committee meeting she attended, in which men outnumbered women and formed a united front pressuring for international rules. Now she realized how important it was to control that committee.[5] Others liked working with AAU because of more positive experiences. When NSGWS's Grace Fox worked with the AAU's track and field chair, for example, she discovered they shared the primary goal of insuring safe and positive experiences for sportswomen. Clearly they could cooperate in certain areas.[6] Indeed, by 1960 representatives of AAU and NSGWS could hold an amazingly amiable meeting, at which they compromised on some provisional basketball rules. "For a few hours everyone was free of all existing rules and ingenuity dominated," reported the NSGWS representative, "and there didn't seem to be any insurmountable barriers to further discussion."[7]

When the National Women's Collegiate Golf Tournament fell into their laps, PE leaders took another step forward. This golf tournament had been started in 1941 by a rebellious physical educator, without NAPECW or NSGWS approval, and had been held annually since then. In 1956, however, the tournament was in danger of folding. Although their organizations had never officially supported the tourney, some women in PE thought it was an excellent example of properly controlled competition. They proposed that representatives of three groups involved with college women's PE discuss the issue. The NSGWS had recently been renamed the Division of Girls' and Women's Sports (DGWS),[8] and the DGWS joined with NAPECW and a student group to form the Tripartite Committee. The committee's task was to choose among three options: should they let the tournament die, find it a temporary home, or perpetuate it?

The Tripartite Committee attended the golf tourney and was "quite favorably" impressed. It enthusiastically recommended that the tournament continue under Tripartite sponsorship. All three organizations endorsed this course, although NAPECW insisted that another joint committee be formed to study the larger implications of such broad high-level extramural competition.[9]

The resulting National Joint Committee on Extramural Sports for College Women revealed sentiment for change within the profession. "People want to talk about competition," reported Anna Espenschade after conducting a nationwide survey of physical educators in 1954. "Many seem to feel that they were taught that it is bad but they cannot always justify this viewpoint from their own observation or experience."[10] Sometimes physical educators were expressing their dissatisfaction hesitantly, suggesting that DGWS standards were ambiguous about interschool competition. Others, however, had quietly begun breaking the rules in this area by holding more competitions.[11] By the late fifties, one DGWS committee acknowledged that "sincere disagreement on basic principles" existed within the organization.[12]

Now the subject of high-level competition came out into the open, and in January 1958 the DGWS's Executive Committee held a lively debate. On one side, a few members feared that if the Joint Committee recommended more extramural opportunities for college women, intramurals would have to be curtailed. Another said it would be wrong to create high school teachers who were *too* skilled and therefore unable to sympathize with their beginner students. Clearly the majority, however, favored giving more attention to the needs of talented female athletes. Just as it would be considered ridiculous to discourage proficiency in math or music, they argued, there was no reason to stigmatize women who sought accomplishment in sports. "We should no longer feel guilty when we do something for the highly skilled," insisted one. While the bolder women argued for more opportunity on principle, others made a more pragmatic case. They pointed to evidence that some college students were not getting the competition they wanted. To keep their constituency, they maintained, conscientious physical educators had already had to develop more extensive programs, and DGWS ought to guide them. Concluded one, "We do need to recognize that Extramurals are going on and we must take steps to control them."[13]

The Joint Committee, then, became a catalyst for change. It decreed that some talented women were not getting what they wanted and deserved. "Every college woman has the right to expect opportunities for participation in sports which test her skill and knowledge and afford her the satisfaction of equal competition."[14] The Joint Committee encouraged schools to offer more opportunities, and went even further, proposing to become actively involved in designing acceptable extramural events. This would go far beyond merely writing standards and hoping schools followed them; instead of just "guiding," they would be "governing" (an entirely new function for DGWS). Some leaders differed over whether they should take that step. But because they wanted unity (and because "people are asking for it"), they ironed out a compromise.[15] Shortly thereafter, all three groups approved a sanctioning procedure whereby colleges holding interschool athletic events could get their plans reviewed and get the Joint Committee's stamp of approval.

"First we are led to believe competition for girls must be kept within the walls of one school. Then suddenly we are asked to send our best golfers across the country to participate in a national golf tourney," wrote Sara Staff Jernigan. "No wonder our teachers are confused."[16] As Jernigan noted, now that the Joint Committee was sanctioning college women's tournaments, DGWS's officially published philosophy was out of date, so the organization moved to clear things up.[17] Instead of its current ambiguous discouragement of advanced competition, the 1963 revised statement on competition clearly encouraged it.

> Sound instructional and well-organized intramural programs will answer the needs and desires of the majority of young women. For the college woman and high school girl who seek and need additional challenges in competition and skills, a sound, carefully planned, and well-directed program of extramural sports is recommended.[18]

For the first time, sports outside a school's walls were actually "recommended"—that is, explicitly advocated in positive terms.

Although a "sound, carefully planned" program hardly seemed objectionable, some women did oppose the change. Jernigan privately referred to them as the "old guard" and "die-hards."[19] Mabel Locke was the most vocal foe of varsity-type sports. She thought the women pushing for change were bitter because they had not gotten the opportunity to reach their own athletic potential. In her opinion, they missed the point. Rather than fostering more competition, women educators should control the human competitive drive.[20] A Minnesota public high school teacher also disliked the change. She thought it would result in low-skilled girls being even further neglected.[21] Another woman vowed to leave the profession before she became a "coach" instead of a "teacher."[22] Katherine Ley found the foot-dragging and dissension frustrating, confessing, "I just hope I miss the [next] time around on competition statements."[23]

Ley and Jernigan skillfully maneuvered, however, to "help to calm the turbulent waters" within the organizations.[24] They used careful language to minimize the conflict, calling their differing colleagues "friends" and their disagreements "misunderstandings."[25] Lobbying behind the scenes to rally their supporters, they also met with their opponents to assuage their fears. In particular, they did so by stressing the continuity of the new statement with their traditional philosophy.[26] In an article for a widely read PE journal, they argued that it had always been "legal" according to DGWS for females to participate in interschool competition, provided certain principles were upheld. The current problem, they asserted, was that many people had been misconstruing DGWS's policy ("No organization has been so frequently misquoted or misinterpreted as DGWS"). According to Jernigan and Ley, the updated statement had only "clarified" the traditional philosophy. "These standards . . . have not changed!"[27]

Intricacies of language aside, the "new guard" actually *was* advocating change, but it was doing so in the manner people often adopt to justify change. The DGWS leaders stepped hesitantly toward the future with one hand firmly clutching the past. They rationalized change with traditional language reflecting values so widely agreed-upon that they appeared moderate and, in fact, not to be changing at all. This was not simply a contrived strategy to convince their opponents. They sincerely believed (with some justification) in their consistency with the philosophy and goals of the past. They thought they were allowing a bit of new behavior, but for old reasons. This belief helped ease the transition. So, too, did the belief that it was the most pragmatic course. Interschool sports were already taking place, and if DGWS did not keep up with the times, they would have lost the chance to affect anything at all. So women in PE okayed the change, somewhat fearfully, but qualified it by attaching lots of conditions. They were true conservatives, approving only slow careful change in order to preserve the ideals of the past.[28]

The NSGWS had spent decades discouraging women from doing the wrong sorts of sports and from too much or too public competition, worrying about society's disapproval of the serious female athlete. What, then, happened to that concern? When NSGWS changed its statement on competition, did women in PE suddenly decide to ignore societal standards? Hardly. They still remained cognizant of and sensitive to the cultural image of women in general and women in sports. But in the late fifties and early sixties, they sensed change occurring around them—and with it, an opening, greater tolerance. In 1958 the Joint Committee referred to sports developments for women "in light of the changing culture," and DGWS and NAPECW called a conference to ponder "the role of women in our changing society and its implications."[29] This theme constantly appeared in physical educators' discussions in the late fifties. In 1959 a convention session addressed "The Role of Women in the Changing Social Scene—How Physical Education Can Help the College Woman Be Prepared to Meet

This Role," and another discussed "The Challenges of Today—Social Change and Sports."[30]

PE leaders perceived an expansion of a woman's acceptable role, and they welcomed it. World War II had shifted employment patterns, they believed, and permitted a typical woman to do more than she used to.[31] "In 1962 a woman no longer seeks to conform to one female personality with one role in life," Katherine Ley asserted. "She has a choice of many roles, including specifically, the acceptable role of a feminine sportswoman."[32] The Joint Committee's "Statement of Belief" brimmed with the same optimism. "In our present-day culture, it is acceptable for a girl or woman to have a high level of skill in sports."[33] Wilma Gimmestad, NAPECW president, was one voice "not certain that women [have] quite the degree of freedom indicated," but Virginia Crafts insisted, "We are on the threshold of a potentially golden era for women in sports."[34] The modern female had more freedom and a new image. "Today the ideal American girl," said a PE teacher from Hawaii, "is strong, healthy and full of vitality."[35]

Physical educators's perceptions were correct. By the mid-1960s the media was portraying sportswomen differently. This shift, which began in the late fifties, corresponded with a new emphasis on sports among U.S. political and cultural authorities. By the mid-1950s sports had become an important forum through which U.S.-Soviet tensions were played out. In the absence of a shooting war, athletic virility and dominance became symbolic of success in the Cold War. Competing for world power as well as influence over other countries, both nations viewed the struggle between socialism and capitalism as largely an ideological one and were concerned about their cultural images. Therefore the American state, like its Soviet counterpart, consciously intervened in the administration and cultural presentation of sport. Top government officials used their influence to bring issues of sports and fitness to national attention.

Both presidents Eisenhower and Kennedy paid unprecedented attention to sports.[36] They made America's physical well-being a prominent issue and created executive agencies that sponsored innovative programs. Eisenhower worried about propaganda victories, especially in "Third World" countries, which the Soviet Union achieved through its commercial, cultural, and athletic appearances. Congress shared his concern and appropriated in 1954 an Emergency Fund for International Affairs. Part of the $5 million fund was used to sponsor tours by outstanding U.S. athletes. The U.S. Information Agency widely publicized these tours and the State Department considered them effective; in fact, over half of U.S. diplomatic posts reported that the United States was viewed in terms of its athletic excellence. Along with similar State Department-sponsored "People to People Sports Committees," these tours represented the first official government use of sport as diplomacy. One congressman claimed athletes were "some of the best salesmen for the American way of life."[37] Eisenhower agreed. After watching the first annual U.S.-USSR track meet, he said such "athletic competition can perhaps, in the end, prove more effective than the most skilled diplomatic maneuver." In this vein, Eisenhower believed the United States needed a strong Olympic showing and told his advisers that he wanted to see a more active fund-raising campaign. Although he hesitated about directly providing federal funds, he threw his weight behind private groups and encouraged formation of the semiofficial United States Olympic Development Committee (USODC).[38]

Perhaps most significantly, Eisenhower launched a campaign on the home front to increase the nation's fitness. In 1956 he established by executive order the President's Council on Youth Fitness (PCYF) declaring, "Our young people must be physically as well as mentally and spiritually prepared for American citizenship."[39] The council reflected increasing concern that, although materially wealthy, Americans were growing physically "soft," and it conducted a massive study of millions of schoolchildren that yielded distressing results. The media was suddenly filled with reports that U.S. children were less fit than their British and Japanese counterparts; in some instances, they reported with alarm, British girls scored higher than American boys! ABC televised a special program on "The Flabby American," and *Reader's Digest* exhorted, "Let's Close the Muscle Gap!"[40] In his State of the Union message in 1960, Eisenhower maintained, "America did not become great through softness and self-indulgence." Fitness, of course, differed from sports, but the PCYF tried to link the two. By encouraging mass fitness participation, council leaders hoped they incidentally might accomplish the goal of creating a greater supply of elite athletes. "Perhaps as we consider the next Olympics, the theme should be not so much 'Win in Rome' as 'Win at Home,'" suggested ex-CIA official and council executive director Shane McCarthy. "For if we succeed in getting our country off its seat and on its feet, the victories in the field of international competition will inevitably follow."[41]

President Kennedy picked up where Eisenhower left off. Shortly after his election, he authored an article in *Sports Illustrated* emphasizing the growing physical softness of Americans and the resulting risk to security. "This is a national problem, and it requires national action."[42] At his first Presidential Conference on Youth Fitness, he urged physical educators to help "change an image of the 'soft American' into a reality of the 'strong American.'"[43] His administration made America's sports "crusade" an even higher priority than Eisenhower's. Kennedy found amateur sports important enough to intervene personally in an AAU-NCAA dispute, create a new sports office in the State Department, and create an executive Inter-Agency Commission on International Athletics. Like Eisenhower, he believed sports brought international prestige and pursued victories, but he also emphasized State Department and Peace Corps exchange programs that used athletes as goodwill ambassadors.[44] The Kennedy administration clearly linked fitness with sports achievement.[45] The President's Council on Physical Fitness (PCPF) sponsored a workshop entitled "Sports for Fitness" and joined with AAHPER (DGWS's parent organization) in "Operation Fitness-USA"—a program to introduce *twenty million* youngsters to track and field events. The choice of track and field was no accident since it was an important Olympic sport but unpopular among Americans. Kennedy himself made the connection between the goals of fitness and sports achievement. He wrote an adviser, "From this greater participation will emerge the calibre of athletics, in all sports, that our position as leader of the free world demands of us."[46]

The emergence of sport as a central ideological tool into the political arena in the 1950s illustrates how the state could alter some of culture's established relations when it seemed important enough.[47] In this case, government leaders believed the Cold War threatened the nation's security and reputation as world leader and used government programs and the power of persuasion to improve athletic performance. Significantly, this goal seemed fundamental enough that the state stepped into areas often perceived as being unrelated to politics— sociocultural arenas in general, and sport in particular. As they promoted foreign policy goals, these decisions also could aid the disadvantaged. Sending a San Francisco-based Chinese-American basketball team on tour to the Far East, and black athletes (such as track stars and Althea Gibson) to Africa, pleased the athletes who got these new opportunities. In addition, the exposure and government legitimation improved the chances for cultural acceptance of those marginalized groups.[48] Theoretically, women as a group could reap benefits from state encouragement.

Given the state's relationship to women in the 1950s, however, intervention on behalf of women athletes seemed unlikely. Government officials might have said there was no official policy concerned with women as a group; in fact, though, the government played an important part in legitimating and propagating the conditions whereby women were subordinate to, dependent upon, and considered weaker than men. Sometimes it did so by *not* intervening in certain areas where the male traditionally held power—like the family, workplace, church—thereby allowing discrimination to continue. Often, though, government policies actively oppressed women. For example, where the state regulated the terms and conditions of employment, it allowed wage differentials and encouraged women's dependence with the notion of a family wage.[49] It permitted "protective legislation" that linked women's physical difference with weakness. Social security, federal welfare policy, and government insurance systems took for granted women's role as nonworking spouses, perpetuating both the image and reality of the dependent, helpless housewife. The tax system massively privileged the nuclear family with male head of household, and other laws permitted banks and businesses to deny credit to independent women.[50] Social service agencies and police treated men and women differently (penalizing women more for sexual crimes, for example) and failed to punish men for many acts of aggression toward women.[51] Blaming women for being raped, calling wife battering a "domestic matter," and ignoring sexual harassment, the male-run state permitted a norm of male power over women's sexuality and further ensconced feminine weakness and subordination.[52] Not guaranteed representation on federal and many state juries, and occupying less than 5 percent of public offices, women had little power to change matters.[53] Within such a system, it was difficult for individual women to achieve a full sense of independence. The restrictiveness of the image made state encouragement of female athletes (who were physically strong, capable, achieving, homosocial women) difficult to imagine.

Sometimes government power was used explicitly to restrict women in the realm of sports. For example, Oregon law, like that of most states, prohibited females from participating in organized wrestling competition. In 1956 police arrested a woman for that very crime. Justice Tooze, who wrote the court's opinion upholding her conviction, empathized with the predominantly male legislative assembly that had passed the law. "Obviously it intended," he explained, "that there should be at least one island on the sea of life reserved for man that would be impregnable to the assault of woman."[54] Oregon representatives had watched women move from their demure ways to worldliness, from needing the protection and chivalry of men to asserting independence. "In these circumstances," he asked, "is it any wonder that the legislative assembly took advantage of the police power of the state . . . to halt this ever-increasing feminine encroachment upon what for ages had been considered strictly as manly arts and privileges?" He thought not and ruled it neither an unjust nor unconstitutional discrimination against women.[55]

Justice Tooze's argument illustrates how the male-dominated justice system could stare discrimination in the face and approve of it. He recognized that the typical middle-class woman regularly did activities previously considered inappropriate, but he believed he had to draw a line somewhere, delineating what behavior went too far. Because he accepted most of the changes in roles, Tooze thought he could enforce the line strictly. If his attitude was any indication, men in power in the 1950s were willing to allow women certain new freedoms in sport, but only up to a point.

In fact, the nation's male athletic leaders in the early 1950s seemed reluctant to expand women's acceptable role any further. Their first attempts to beef up U.S. Olympic performance often ignored women and, at times, consciously excluded them. (For example, early government efforts to improve Olympic performance included giving more aid to athletes in the military—few of which were women.) Even though top U.S. officials knew that American women fared poorly in international games compared to American men, they did nothing to try to improve women's performances. Despite their intense desire to improve U.S. standing, they chose to try to do so while preserving the gender status quo. Indeed, instead of aiding female athletes, U.S. officials strove to keep sport defined as "male sport." In the first annual track and field competition with the Soviet Union, for example, U.S. officials negotiated an agreement so that the scores of men's and women's competition would be tallied separately and not combined into one total. One sportswriter noted that the effort was absurd. "My eye, it's a separate meet. The events for men and women are sandwiched between each other and held on the same field." Everyone knew the real reason the United States wanted scores kept separately by gender: since U.S. men consistently outscored Soviet men, America then could ignore the women's performance and declare that the U.S. team (which was equivalent to men) had defeated the USSR.[56] Many suspected the United States of similarly manipulating the Olympics. Soviets accused the head of the International Olympic Committee—American Avery Brundage—of trying to stack the games against them by eliminating events in which the U.S. did not excel—in particular, women's competitions. The AAU's Roxy Andersen complained, "It is typical of the past attitude of some of our near-sighted sport officials who have made our [female] athletes 'go it alone' that they are now endeavoring to have certain women's events on the Olympic program cancelled." Off to a bad start in the dash to create top female athletes, the United States tried to abolish the race.

But since women's events continued to take place internationally, it was necessary to explain why Eastern bloc female athletes were more successful. The implicit explanation seemed to be: we lost because it was not important for our women to win. "I have yet to hear anyone moan because the Russians will beat us badly in women's track and field," observed a San Francisco sportswriter, "because we simply dismiss women's track and field from important consideration in discussing the Olympic Games."[57] There was also the suggestion that although Eastern bloc stars were more successful athletically, they were failed women. U.S. officials denigrated the femininity of Soviet female athletes and contrasted them unfavorably to models of American womanhood. Like sore losers, U.S. officials implied that they, too, could create female athletic machines if they wanted, but they did not want to. Smearing Soviet women, Avery Brundage explained that the athletes of the Communist bloc were a special, "unfeminine" breed: "They carry bricks, labor in the fields, clean the streets and do hard manual labor in their daily life." He implied their strength, class, and physical labor marred them as women, even suggesting their athleticism made them ugly: "What do these women look like? Get a picture for yourself."[58] Top U.S. representatives suggested that no self-respecting American woman would want to be an athlete like Soviet champions.

As the decade proceeded, however, and Cold War tensions flamed higher, America switched strategies. Soviet women kept beating American women, but then Soviet men began catching up with American men. The attempt to keep men's and women's scores separate failed, and the Soviet Union trumpeted its overall victories in the 1956 and 1960 Olympics. To Americans expecting to be number one, excuses about unfemininity sounded lame. The Eisenhower administration, the usoc, and Congress became troubled that the USSR was winning an increasing number of propaganda triumphs in sports. Since U.S. men already were doing their best in most events, it became clear that unless U.S. women held up their end, it would be extremely difficult ever to beat the Soviet Union.[59] After the 1956 Olympic defeat, a new organization formed to help remedy the situation. The U.S. Olympic Development Committee (usodc) came up with a ten-point program for regaining lost American Olympic supremacy, which included giving incentives for minor sports and increasing the number of instructional clinics and international contests. Significantly, it also created a Women's Advisory Board to address women's perennially weak performance.[60]

Retired rear admiral Thomas J. Hamilton, chair of usodc, quickly concluded that the best way to get more proficient women athletes for the 1960s was to get more girls and women to participate. From previous aau and Olympic officials, he heard laments over the lack of training sites for women, especially compared to other countries. In track, for example, only a handful of clubs and colleges (mostly black) coached women. "High schools and colleges don't go in for women's track," complained the former director of the U.S. Olympic Association. "Women's sports are available mostly in industrial plants."[61] As a result, female Olympic athletes came from a few, very separate sources: upper-class white women competed in elite individual sports like archery and dressage, and working-class women or black college students in track and field. "If we did not have such outstanding Negro athletes," declared Avery Brundage, "the U.S. would have sent a second-rate team to Rome in 1960."[62] Many potential stars never were introduced to sports in which they might have excelled, so America needed to develop a broader base of participation. Including sports like track and field and gymnastics in schools' PE curriculum might be an effective long-term strategy for attracting larger numbers of women. Besides reaching many more potential stars, students in general would come to see such sports as important and approved of for women.

The state moved on a number of fronts to broaden female participation in international competition. The usodc encouraged aau to sponsor more women's track meets, and it tried to convince DGWS not to oppose them. Without the support of women PE teachers, Hamilton believed, his efforts would be stymied.[63] So the U.S. Olympic Association invited DGWS to send an official representative to its Women's Sport Committees and to get involved in the Women's Advisory Board. Government officials complimented the work women in PE had done and asked them to see themselves as allies in the effort to gain further legitimation for women's sports and fitness. The PCYF invited leading educators, including twenty-five female college PE teachers and numerous DGWS officers, to its workshops. At these gatherings, the President's Council solicited their advice about how to achieve the nation's goals, and none-too-subtly linked sports performance (especially in track and field) with fitness goals.

In particular, the PCYF strove to get the nation attuned to fitness issues. In the process, it prominently included girls. It did, however, approach girls and boys somewhat differently. It widely distributed two booklets—*Vim* for girls and *Vigor* for boys. While *Vigor* had sections on weight training and isometrics for "physique development," *Vim* offered exercises to aid female "figure development."[64] *Vim* included a special section for girls offering "a word of reassurance: Don't worry about developing heavy, bulging muscles. You won't. Exercise will slim and smooth the contours of your figure. . . . In short, you will be well on your way to becoming the poised attractive and interesting young lady you would like to be."

Vim's gender-separate approach illustrated a key part of the strategy: females had to be persuaded that it was not unfeminine for them to become more physical and competitive. "Both track and gymnastics need to be glamorized from the girls' viewpoint," declared Hamilton.[65] So the public relations firm hired by the government tried to find ways to appeal to women. Politicians—like Sen. Hubert Humphrey, extolling the virtues of mothers who raised fit children—took part in the encouragement.[66] Robert F. Kennedy wrote in *Sports Illustrated*, "As a world leader in the emancipation of women, and with women playing an increasingly important role in our national life, our country should have more women winning in the Olympics."[67] At a special PCPF forum, print and broadcast media representatives were urged to help persuade children that sports were important, fun, and, significantly, consistent with femininity.[68]

Although the government had begun encouraging competition, it did not exactly adopt a liberating message. While conveying to girls that track would now be an approved activity, cultural authorities chose to stress certain themes and ignore others. They did not tell girls, "You should do track because it will make you big and strong." Nor did they say: "Sports will build good character." Instead, they emphasized traditional femininity—which meant in part cultivating good looks and appealing to males. "It must be something that will make teen-age boys seem heroes to teen-age girls, and will make teen-age girls appear glamorous to teen-age boys," publisher and PCPF speaker Joseph Kingsbury-Smith told his media colleagues.[69] And USODC chair Thomas Hamilton also stressed the issue of appearance. "A look at most of our girl athletes readily disproves the misguided view that bulging muscles and a perspiring brow are the image of the girl athlete." It was possible to participate in Olympic sports *and* be a normal, feminine female, he insisted. "There are numerous examples of beautiful ladylike girl athletes competing in gymnastics and track."[70] Such messages reassured girls that sports would not necessarily detract from their proper efforts to appeal to boys (their heroes).

Whether because persuaded by government officials or because reporters naturally shared dominant values, much of the popular press's coverage of women in sports corresponded with the state's needs. Through the early and mid-fifties, magazines usually treated U.S. women in the Olympics in one of two ways: they ignored them, or they acknowledged their dismal performance but suggested that superior athletes were unfeminine. The *Saturday Evening Post* provided an example of the first approach. When its 1956 Olympic preview issue announced that it "Pick[ed] the Winners in Track," it referred only to men's track.[71] Similarly, *Collier's* Olympic forecast noted that the United States would be crushed in some "unappealing" sports (like women's events), but then made no mention of women at all in its official "prediction" list.[72] Like government officials early in the decade, the press often treated sport as male sport. When magazines *did* cover women's track, they did not conceal how poorly America had fared but rationalized away that lack of success by stressing the unpopularity of the events. They also implied that Olympic sports had a detrimental effect on the anomalous female athletes who performed them.

In fact, in the early 1950s the media appeared to have joined the campaign smearing successful foreign women athletes. According to *U.S. News and World Report*, the red nation singled out well-muscled women for training, gave them illegal incentives, and then capitalized on their brawn.[73] "No alarm was sounded" after losing to the "well-stocked strength and depth" of the "Amazons of the Steppes."[74] Journals printed photos of Soviet champions accompanied by unflattering captions, as with the javelin thrower who "glared," the "Amazonian shot put queen," the "Hefty Heroine," or "Tank-Shaped Tamara."[75] American competitors often were referred to as "girls" while Soviets were "women athletes" who were "ponderous, peasant-types." In the media's presentation, our girls stood little chance against the socialist athletic warriors. Nor did feminine Americans have any reason to emulate them—American women had better things to do. Top U.S. javelinist Karen Anderson, readers were told, had blonde hair, light gray-blue eyes, and a sensible attitude. "I'm not going to roll over and die if I don't win a medal," Anderson admitted. "Life will go on for me." *Sports*

Illustrated approvingly characterized her as the all-American girl.[76] In a similar vein, a male sportswriter stated "Venus Wasn't a Shot-Putter" and deplored the possibility that America might someday brag about having the best-muscled girls in the world.[77]

But later in the decade, coverage of Soviet female athletes began to shift. "They're Tough . . . and Pretty" read a headline that typified the press's less caustic portrayal.[78] In 1963 *Life* not only acknowledged the "superb form" of Russian athletes but said they piled up victories "with the grace of ballet dancers."[79] Indeed, pictures of modern Soviet record holders now "could go up on anybody's wall," claimed Roxy Andersen. The *Amateur Athlete* reprinted a British article that stated that the Russian women, who used to be "so very far from being feminine," now were attractive and wearing lipstick and pretty clothes. "Those formidable Amazons of former years" now were "allowed to be women, not machines."[80] *Sports Illustrated* extended the newfound flattery to outstanding athletes from other countries. A West German sprinter was described as "statuesque and seductive," a Polish competitor as "attractive," and British runners as "swift and svelte." There was even a photoessay on "The World's Loveliest Sportswomen."[81] In some cases, journalists made the shift quite deliberately. *Sports Illustrated* writer John Underwood explained that if he was going to try to encourage American women athletes, it was only consistent that he stop ridiculing foreign ones. "In deference to our own women," he admitted, "we have quit calling the Russians 'muscle molls.'"[82]

This shift in the treatment of foreign athletes corresponded with growing concerns about U.S. women's Olympic performances in the late 1950s and early 1960s. Consistent with other post-Sputnik alarms, a 1963 *Sports Illustrated* article demanded, "Why Can't We Beat This Girl?" The girl in question, featured in a full-page photo, was a "beautiful young [Russian] girl . . . with auburn hair [who] not only looks better than the girl next door, she most certainly can run much faster."[83] The article answered its own question. American girls could not defeat her because "most will not even try." Because of the unpopularity of track, U.S. women were unwilling to do their part. This was not a good reason, it declared. Everyone from the editor of *Vogue* to Helen Gurley Brown now was for women's athletics, and photos from other countries demonstrated that females could do athletics and still be beautiful. "Pretty girls from all over the world are competing in track and field—and having fun," but Americans "are at home, demurely avoiding physical stress and missing out on a very good thing."[84]

Sportswriters continued to use ridicule regarding women's sports, but in a different manner. In a 1964 article, John Underwood contrasted two normal feminine Olympic hopefuls—who ran gracefully and efficiently—with the typical American schoolgirl:

Her thighs move forward in a short, stiff swishing motion. Her knees remain low, as though broken or restricted by a tight skirt; the lower legs describe half circles away from the body, independent of the direction of the thighs. The chest and shoulders make like a washing-machine agitator. . . . The forearms and hands are not communicating and tend to fly up at scary angles. The fingers are splayed, completing a motion excellent for flagging the bus or drying the fingernails. The eyes bat furiously. The head rolls dangerously. It is an altogether lovely exercise in ineptness, an American girl running like a girl.[85]

Instead of criticizing the gender expectations that created inept female runners, Underwood blamed females themselves for not bucking that gender system and becoming competent athletes. Some sportswriters also began to lambaste women physical educators (cruelly characterized as "old maids") for not doing their part in preparing American girl athletes.[86]

Correspondingly, the media began complimenting American women athletes for their ability and highlighting their attractiveness. A *Sports Illustrated* photo of the U.S. track and field team had the caption: "Most of them were pretty young . . . almost all of them were pretty . . . [and] they performed with an attractive maturity."[87] In 1958 *Life* jumped on the beautification bandwagon. "To most Americans," it acknowledged, "gymnastics is an athletic ritual pursued by crackpots, muscle-bound culturists and misguided persons named Ivan. Just how wrong they are is proved by [*Life*'s photographer] who shows in these pictures that a gymnast can be as graceful as a ballerina and as appealing as a model in a perfume ad."[88] A typical description of an Olympic swimmer now read, "some good, tough muscles show on her otherwise ladylike figure."[89] Suddenly U.S. women athletes competing for sports on the Olympic team were "lithe envoys" who had "lyrical grace" and were "strictly feminine."[90]

The press had to make a point of female champions' beauty and normality because no one had forgotten their former image. Rather than ignore that unflattering stereotype, the press acknowledged it and combated it. Regular people reassured readers that these new athletes did not fit the old mold. Her home economics teacher reported that runner Marie Mulder sewed quite well; the men's track team now welcomed the women's team on trips; and parents admitted that they knew the risks but still thought their daughters—who had boyfriends—remained feminine.[91] A women's track team called the "Bouffant Belles" consciously attacked old perceptions. Bouffants may not be aerodynamically sound, *Sports Illustrated* pointed out, but they were a hit at track meets. "I'm trying to change the stereotyped image of the track girls," it quoted their female coach. "Every year we have a good-looking team and good-looking uniforms—none of those bags. I prefer pretty girls. I insist that they wear makeup.

We all go to the beauty shop before each meet, so we can get beautiful and get our minds off the meet."[92] Normality, attractiveness, and femininity seemed to become a prerequisite for talking about females who participated in nontraditional sports. *Sports Illustrated* passed along a male track coach's assessment of his forty-two member team. "Not a dog in the bunch," he announced proudly. "Every one as neat and feminine as you'll find."[93]

As a method for liberating female athletes, this strategy was flawed. Competing in a track meet was now permissible, but it was clear that the newfound approval was conditional. The constant harping on the femininity of the athletes meant they were far from free; it appeared they were acceptable (to the press) only if they were "otherwise ladylike." This did not help the athlete who merely wanted the right to play. And for the athlete for whom being considered feminine was important, it reminded her that her sports activities had once been considered nonfeminine and might still be in some people's minds, so she'd better watch out. It confirmed to her that it was helpful to go to the beauty shop before and after the meet. The press's and government's choice of how to appeal to women was natural, given decades of stereotyping and stigmatizing athletes as unfeminine. It was the same strategy used by the AAU national basketball tournament with its beauty contest. But the main assumption was that females must first of all be feminine—not that females could find joy in sports and deserved to. It did not accept female athletes simply as athletes. In effect, the constant emphasis on the athletes' femininity made apologetic behavior feel necessary.

Despite the continued deference to femininity, however, an important change *had* occurred. Surprisingly, some powerful cultural actors had begun encouraging women to participate in events like track and field: the state, the popular press, and (if the press is to be believed) parents, fashion consultants, and men in general. Even the medical profession agreed. In the mid-1960s the American Medical Association's Committee on the Medical Aspects of Sports laid to rest any remaining belief in women's frailty. It decreed sports were not dangerous and that females were not active enough:

> Whether from culturally imposed restrictions, untenable physiological taboos or from disproportionate allotment of time, facilities, and leadership, many are not receiving the desired experiences from suitable and regular physical recreation. It is *imperative* that all girls be reached and involved.[94]

The AMA completed an impressive lineup of cultural leaders who gave their approval to this shift in the gender roles. "Participation in healthful physical recreation is now accepted, rightfully, as contributing to the feminine image instead of detracting from it."[95]

Unexpectedly, then, physical educators found themselves affected by the Soviet-American conflict. In some senses, they were beneficiaries. They welcomed the attention and validation brought by the president's fitness agenda, especially since they had been worrying about a shortage of female PE majors and about physical education becoming a lower priority in schools. "The President's Conference was naturally a thrilling experience," said Mabel Locke after attending the first conference on youth fitness in 1956. "I believe it could be the biggest boost our profession has had in years."[96] Government officials publicly thanked women PE teachers and reiterated their importance in spreading the word about girls' recreation.[97] This sudden attention had an effect; their inclusion in a government crusade legitimated and flattered them. "We were handsomely entertained and provided for," reported Jane Mott.[98] Impressed, female physical educators continued to attend government-sponsored conferences, and then did just what the conference organizers hoped.[99] Thelma Bishop, DGWS's vice president, told its Executive Council, "Perhaps we should take a look at our services to see if we can contribute more to this national need."[100] And NAPECW president Ruth Wilson assured President Eisenhower that her organization would be pleased to cooperate with whatever he initiated.[101]

But state validation had a price. The government wanted not only fitness but competition; not just sportswomen but female athletes geared toward winning. Female physical educators seemed to be moving toward such high-level competition, but only slowly and carefully. While they had always separated the goals of fitness and achievement, they suspected that the government and the public might care more about international athletic performance than fitness. "More and more pressure may be exerted to develop better women competitors, especially for the Olympics," observed Katherine Ley.[102] At AAU basketball committee meetings, DGWS members heard about State Department displeasure over the country's fourth-place finish in the 1964 World Tournament, and male coaches blamed DGWS for rules that disadvantaged the United States in international games.[103] They heard the Kennedys urge them to teach lesser known Olympic sports. "It is obvious," noted Ley, "that officials of the national government regard excellence in sports as an essential weapon in the Cold War."[104]

Apparently, physical educators were willing to risk paying the price. As with the decision to approve intercollegiate competition for highly skilled women, they decided they could take a new step (encouraging Olympic athletes) without losing sight of traditional goals. Besides, some had tired of criticism directed toward them. "Will we always have to be apologetic for the performance of our girls?" asked Phebe Scott. "Will we always have to listen to the sports writers ... denunciate [*sic*] the efforts of the American female athlete?"[105]

The patriotic appeal was just what some women in PE had wanted but not dared hope for—high-level approval for women's sports. "We must be responsible citizens of the world," declared one.[106] Many clearly appreciated the difference that societal approval made. "For the first time in my life," claimed another physical educator, "competition is no longer a dirty word and even more important, both teachers and students know that it's all right for women to be good in sports and to play to win."[107]

In this context, DGWS took a step in 1963 unthinkable a decade earlier. It joined forces with the Women's Board of the U.S. Olympic Development Committee to cosponsor a number of National Institutes on Girls' Sports. Two-day workshops for teachers from every state, the institutes were designed to help them teach advanced skills in Olympic events. To the USODC they were a necessary step in creating more and better Olympians. Institute organizers recognized that women in PE—general teachers of beginners—lacked specialized knowledge. They hoped that after training these "master teachers," each would go back to her home state and hold similar workshops. That way expertise would trickle down as women shared it with one another and their students, and by "chain-reaction" there would be an increase in the "depth and breadth" of female sports.[108] The first institute, in April 1964, focused on gymnastics and track and field. Subsequent institutes, held at least annually, added canoeing, diving, fencing, and basketball.

Participants appreciated the gatherings both for what they learned and who they met. Because of the strict divisions between AAU and DGWS, women from each group rarely had met, and at the institutes they could see their differences often had been exaggerated. And while the focus remained on training women, it eventually became clear that men who were already coaching Olympians should be invited. In addition, the institutes were interracial, thus serving as yet another bridge in a divided field.[109]

The participation of DGWS in the National Institutes was not a knee-jerk response to the desires of the state. And NAPECW's response to a request from the President's Council on Youth Fitness illustrates that physical educators did not do whatever the state asked. Asked for help in drafting a statement about college sports, NAPECW participated but, displeased with the final result, refused to endorse it.[110] Nor was physical educators' participation in the National Institutes somehow unwilling. As someone who "for years felt like one small voice crying in the wilderness to promote activities for girls," Phebe Scott expressed heartfelt gratitude for the chance to attend the institutes.[111] And Sara Staff Jernigan welcomed it as "one great opportunity."[112]

PE leaders made it clear that they were taking part in the National Institutes for their own reasons. They did not adopt all portions of the USODC's rhetoric. Repeatedly they downplayed the importance of beating the Russians. "The problem is much larger than . . . the United States . . . Olympic team in 1964," insisted Ley.[113] Instead, she emphasized the "softer" goals of the state. "If handled intelligently," Scott told participants at the Third National Institute in January 1966, "international competition can be a positive force for greater understanding between nations and individuals."[114] The DGWS justified its 1969 decision to make major changes in girls' basketball rules with similar language stressing cooperation. "If the present roving player game played by women in the United States is no *better* than the five player game played by every country in the world, should we not reduce friction in the political world?"[115] Women in DGWS expressed a willingness to be "personal resource[s]" of the United States, but preferred the tone of cultural interchanges and Peace Corps sports programs over militaristic and nationalistic events. In fact, far from being passive reflectors of state philosophy, PE leaders hoped that women's increased participation could change the nature of international competition. They wanted to set an example and help shift the emphasis from the outcome of an event to the personal satisfaction individuals derived from it.[116]

PE leaders also tried to use the state's encouragement to promote their own traditional goals. They saw the alliance with the government as a tradeoff—perhaps if they helped meet its Olympic goals, the Olympic crusade could help them, too. Therefore, they did not object to the USODC's goal of training "the few" stars for international competition, but linked it and made it secondary to upgrading the fitness levels and athletic skills of "the many." "Our crucial need is to raise the dynamic fitness of girls and the average performance of girls in all sports," insisted Jernigan at the Third National Institute.[117] Katherine Ley envisioned a sort of synthesis of the new goals with the traditional standards. "Please do more than teach your local leaders how to teach them gymnastics and track and field events," she urged; "teach them the philosophy of more for everyone that goes with it."[118]

Cosponsoring the National Institutes marked the final stage of DGWS's transition from the mindset of the early fifties to one for the mid-sixties. In the immediate postwar years, DGWS mainly had published its *Standards*, discouraged the wrong type of competition, and criticized the way other organizations ran women's sports. Its initial, tentative stride away from that mode had been to accept invitations to sit on committees of organizations like the AAU, a step DGWS's members had taken for pragmatic reasons—so that DGWS might influence the conduct of women's activities run by others and to uphold its standards. After that, DGWS gradually began to give explicit approval to some intercollegiate events for highly skilled athletes, especially if they were run by women in PE (like the National Women's Collegiate Golf Tournament). Next, women physical educators set up a sanctioning body, the National Joint Committee, and changed the wording of their "Statement on Competition" so it would be less prohibitive and more encouraging of serious, interschool contests. The final step of the transition, illustrated by their involvement in the National Institutes, was to go beyond merely approving of such events to actually running them. Women PE leaders took each step—from influencing to encouraging to sponsoring—carefully. They moved thoughtfully, trying to attain consensus, keep societal approval, and most importantly, be consistent with their traditional philosophy.

The DGWS went even further along this path when it created in 1966 the Commission on Intercollegiate Athletics for Women (CIAW). For over four years, physical educators on the Joint Committee had been reviewing requests for approval of intercollegiate tournaments, and writing a set of "how to" guidelines for proper management of them. Now they took the next step of running those events themselves. Considering that a decade earlier they had been wary of any intercollegiate events, sponsoring national tournaments was quite a bold move.[119]

Although bold, forming CIAW also represented a somewhat conservative attempt to keep women's sports unique and woman-defined. Creating their own organization would help maintain women's high-quality standards and also prevent women from "plunging into . . . the pitfalls of men's athletics."[120] These pitfalls included recruiting and gambling scandals, programs that had lost an educational outlook, too much attention given to a few elite athletes, "rampant commercialism," and "the most devitalizing, destructive aspect of sport—the almost insane compulsion to win at any cost."[121]

By 1967 the CIAW had become a primitive but functional organization. Its four commissioners had given it a minimal number of actual rules but instilled it with high standards. Hoping to avoid the NCAA's extensive regulations, they counted upon the common sense, good intentions, and shared values of women physical educators. In matters like eligibility, they mostly depended on self-policing. The rules, for example, allowed only full-time students to compete for up to four years, as long as they made normal academic progress (as defined by the school's rules for any other students). Each college was expected to be responsible for its own student-athletes. In addition, they declared ineligible from CIAW tournament play anyone who had been awarded a scholarship based upon athletic ability. This antischolarship policy constituted a radical departure from the male model. Consistent with DGWS's philosophy, it encouraged participants to be students before athletes and discouraged too much emphasis on developing "stars." It eliminated the problem of coaches spending all their time trying to attract recruits rather than teaching, prevented coaches from harassing or exploiting young players, and diminished the chances for scandals. Prohibiting recruitment altogether also avoided the massive problem of regulating it. In addition, CIAW expected intercollegiate teams to be run by the women's PE department, and therefore it could remain, in DGWS tradition, a hands-off organization. Since most women in PE already were acquainted with such standards, the CIAW could get started relatively quickly. By late 1967 it was soliciting bids, an exciting prospect for those who had been waiting so long. The first tournaments took place in 1969; in a DGWS vice president's opinion, it was a "magnificent birth."[122]

Although it differed from the men's model, the CIAW alternative in no way threatened it. In 1967 women's sports was a small-time venture, hardly noticed by anyone but the participants. Doing things differently from the men was practical and seemed natural. Men did not expect women's sports to aspire to reach the status of their athletic programs—that would have been ridiculous to imagine. So even if women criticized men's programs, it did not matter. No one really listened to women in PE.[123] Because they had so little power, there was no reason the two models could not coexist.

Still, formation of the CIAW represented a significant, new achievement for female athletes. It multiplied the number of athletic opportunities available to college women and made clear beyond a shadow of a doubt that leaders in women's PE favored such competition. It prompted more schools to create varsity intercollegiate teams, spurring the beginnings of a formal system of regular seasons and conferences. Most importantly, CIAW gave more players a chance to compete at high levels of skill, and by doing so further legitimated their desire to do it. Moreover, CIAW events allowed serious female athletes and coaches an opportunity to meet and to see how many they were, which heightened their confidence and furthered the notion that they did not have to apologize for intense competition. Any diminishment of the self-hatred athletic women experienced was valuable.

Despite the change that CIAW represented, women physical educators in the mid-1960s showed some important elements of continuity, not all of which were positive. Even as Katherine Ley declared, "Someone should champion the few [women] who can and will succeed if given a chance," she underlined the equal importance of intramurals and implied that the competent athlete would be a rarity.[124] Many still assumed they must exhibit "model" behavior in order to win acceptance for girls' track and field. A new basketball coaching book told coaches to monitor their own behavior carefully and to "encourage players to be ladies."[125] Another physical educator justified athletic competition on the grounds that "competition for boyfriends, for jobs, for husbands, for advancement will all enter into the future of any girl."[126] They made these claims not only because they felt they should conform to norms of heterosexual appeal but because of the reality of power relations. The approval of husbands and fathers, one noted accurately, could prove essential in gaining tolerance.[127] Katherine

Ley exhibited the same nonfeminist analysis. Rather than attacking the sexist assumptions that portrayed the girl athlete in a bad light, she suggested the girl athlete should change her own image (presumably by looking and acting feminine).[128] These statements illustrated that women still felt they had to request permission to do sports; they still felt marginalized; they still felt vulnerable.

Many women in PE continued to uphold society's traditional gender arrangements. Even as she made the case for women's intercollegiate athletics, one educator denounced "unfeminine" women, declaring "I don't think the world needs [more] highly aggressive, competitive, tough-minded women."[129] In the same vein, DGWS continued stressing the importance of women coaches for girls' teams—not because women had a right to those jobs, but because they had to make sure girls were taught by people who knew the correct behavior for females. Sport had enough "masculinizing" influences without male coaches. As they had during the 1950s, women physical educators continued to insist that sports would enhance, not detract from, femininity. A DGWS pamphlet reassured parents worried about their daughters' reputations,[130] as did Phebe Scott: "We are not interested in promoting sports for women as a way to decrease differences between the sexes, but rather to assist both men and women to discover their own unique sex differences in sport. Sports for women must help them retain their feminine identity, not destroy it."[131]

Not surprisingly, then, women PE leaders went no further than the space cultural authorities allowed them. The physical educators' deference to traditional definitions of femininity mirrored that of the state and the press. In its campaign to persuade women to become more fit, the government, rather than saying this would build character or muscles, had stressed how it would make girls more glamorous to boys. The press, too, had consciously pointed out how normal, feminine, attractive women now were competing in sports. Thus, although they now supported women's participation in certain sports, that support had an important qualification—the expectation that female athletes would adhere to all other aspects of femininity. In effect, the "feminine bargain" granted to women taking part in certain (especially Olympic) sports an exemption from the unflattering stereotypes of female athletes as long as they acknowledged the importance of femininity. Athletic participation had not been conferred on women as a right; it was still not expected of women. Neither the state nor the press ever permitted anyone to forget that these athletes were female and therefore different. They had an uncertain status. Thus, the opening cultural authorities gave to sportswomen in the early 1960s was in reality merely a crack (one that threatened to snap shut at any moment).

That opening certainly had its limits, but it still mattered. Conscious of greater toleration for expanded roles for women and new encouragement for female fitness and Olympic participation, many took advantage of the space.

The gradual liberalization of DGWS and its shift from discouragement to the sponsorship of certain sports corresponded with changes made by the hegemonic authorities.

But to say the state *caused* the changes in women's sports would be an overstatement; it was more of an interactive process. Some female students had wanted more opportunities, some PE leaders wanted to offer it to them, and the state supplied the opening. While there was a connection between physical education and government organizations, the link was not strong. The state did not assume the role of patron of sportswomen—its support was more indirect and symbolic. Nor did the women always do what the state wanted.

In the final analysis, women themselves brought about change. Encouragement from cultural authorities made a difference, but sportswomen were ready to seize the initiative. Women like Jernigan, Ley, Bryant, and Scott, after years of feeling like voices in the wilderness, welcomed the opportunity for change. *They* adopted the golf tournament, chose to work with the AAU, lobbied and discussed with other women what they wanted, organized the National Institutes, and built the CIAW. They had to overcome a legacy of generations of discouragement from those same cultural authorities. Indeed, it took courage for them to advocate new behavior. Change frightened conservative, culturally vulnerable women in PE, and the old guard's caution and resistance made sense. They had good reason to worry whether approval would be lasting, and if there would be a price for doing what had always been considered inappropriate. Still, the combined efforts of an influential state and an energetic vanguard of women in PE won them over. The support of both parties was necessary to achieve the change. The state provided some impetus, and some brave women stepped forward to build the bridges between what the state wanted, what women in PE wanted, and the traditional philosophy of DGWS.

By 1967 DGWS blended the new and the old. It advocated competition without hesitation and now provided new opportunities for serious and highly skilled female athletes, even in Olympic events. Given some external encouragement, women in PE had taken an *active* role in creating those opportunities by using their own rationale for change, by occasionally refusing to give government officials exactly what they wanted, and by insisting upon running things their own way. This approach resulted in CIAW—a uniquely woman-defined alternative to intercollegiate athletics. But this alternative was based on some traditional gender expectations, and—because women's version of sports was different (perceived as being less serious, less competitive, less real)—it was largely ignored. Like special legislation intended to protect weaker female industrial workers in the early twentieth century, it benefited women but also had disadvantages. It kept them defined as "other." Its rationale—that women were different (weaker)—potentially could be used to deny women further opportunities. Finally, as was the case with protective legislation, society generally overlooked the fact that decent treatment designed for women might have helped men too.

Results, then, were mixed. The efforts of physical educators to create a woman-defined alternative were sometimes justified by dangerously negative rationales and had not broken free from the larger culture's constraints. Often they went unnoticed by the rest of society. Still, women's struggles to shape their own destiny made a difference to sportswomen. Within limits, by the mid-1960s athletes experienced greater tolerance and approval, and new opportunities. Significant as these changes were, they were minor compared to those still to come.

Part III

Introduction: 1968–1979

Social movements shook the nation's very core during the mid-1960s and early 1970s. Using nonviolent direct action, the black civil rights movement forced Americans to reexamine their basic institutions and decide if they actually did embody the ideals of liberty and justice for all. Followers of Martin Luther King Jr. battled police dogs, mobs, a centuries-old mindset, and laws that treated black Americans differently than whites. Their primary goals were equality and integration. As the decade progressed, some activists moved beyond the goal of integration, refusing to support it if in practice it worked only one way, with blacks sacrificing their traditional culture and institutions in order to assimilate into white America. Black Power advocates stressed the need to preserve the African-American heritage and demanded not just integration but the power to determine their own destiny. They wanted both equality (equal opportunity and an end to discrimination) *and* difference (the right to make distinctive choices). Whether they agreed with the movement's advocates or opponents, all Americans became more sensitive during the era to issues like discrimination, prejudice, and equality.

Identifying with descriptions of injustice and impressed by the blacks' achievements, other disadvantaged groups borrowed from the civil rights movement's example. Students, the elderly, homosexuals, the handicapped, various ethnic groups, and women began fighting oppression on their own behalf. Beginning in the mid-1960s, women within the civil rights movement applied some of its analysis to gender, noting that "assumptions of male superiority are as wide-spread and deeply rooted to the woman as the assumptions of white superiority are to the Negro."[1] Feminists began criticizing how circumscribed the female gender role was—women were expected to be passive, childlike, emotionally nurturing, and physically and intellectually weak. They asserted that many women had to "give up their souls and stay in their place [in order] to be accepted."[2] In particular, middle-class women continued the comparison with racism, demonstrating how both gender assumptions and discriminatory practices prevented women from enjoying the "equality of opportunity and freedom of choice which is their right as individual Americans, and as human beings."[3]

While one branch of the women's liberation movement concentrated on raising women's consciousness of their oppression and finding ways to empower themselves, new, more formal organizations such as the National Organization for Women (NOW) aimed at eliminating legal barriers. NOW hoped to bring women into the mainstream of society's institutions. Its members pointed out the obvious as a problem: that women as a group lacked voice (and equal opportunities) in arenas of power like business, politics, education, religion, and the media.

Like other American institutions, sport became increasingly politicized because of these social movements. Some Americans looked to sport as an escape from controversy and disturbing headlines. They hoped it could be simple, untainted entertainment and release, a place where the rules and rituals remained constant. But sport never has been and could not be immune to social currents and change. Both its extraordinary cultural influence and its very focus on "fair play" made it a natural arena for concerns about social justice. For decades black Americans had been trying to attain more than a token presence in many sports, including major league baseball, amateur tennis and track, and intercollegiate basketball and football. Their successes accelerated with Supreme Court decisions and new legislation prohibiting discrimination; and as black faces increasingly appeared in uniform and changed the games, no one could continue to believe the myth that sports was untouched by politics. During the late sixties, U.S. Olympic track champions raised clenched fists in the Black Power symbol, many students questioned whether sports should be so important on campuses, boxer Muhammad Ali was stripped of his title after refusing to serve in the war in Vietnam, and athletes clashed with authoritarian coaches over issues like the length of their hair. Then as the women's liberation movement took hold, gender bias emerged as an issue in the sports world as well. Although female athleticism existed as a relatively minor political issue during the Cold War, during the seventies the issue began grabbing headlines.

Females started challenging discrimination in sports everywhere they found it—in community programs like Little League Baseball; in high schools and universities; in clubs, road races, locker rooms and weight rooms. They waged their battles in the media and on school boards as well as in courtrooms and the halls of Congress. Theirs was a "political" struggle not only in the narrow sense (as taking place in the legislative arena), but in the wider meaning of the word, as public negotiations over power and self-determination. Nine-year-old tomboys and their supportive fathers, mothers who wanted their daughters to have chances they hadn't, and strong young college women willing to ask why they shouldn't have decent game uniforms all served as the fairly anonymous foot soldiers in this widely dispersed army. The "lieutenants" were articulate athletes and administrators, some of whom became well known, like tennis star Billie Jean King. Sometimes joining them were feminist organizations. Women physical educators assumed leadership positions in the conflict over a new law, Title IX. Although their effort encountered enormous resistance, the movement continued and picked up speed throughout the 1970s. Despite being difficult to define and harder still to achieve, women in sports focused on an important new goal: equality.

CHAPTER 5

Politicization:

Title IX and the Movement for Equality in Intercollegiate Athletics, 1968–1974

Intercollegiate athletics for women was transformed in the early 1970s. The altered cultural and political climate brought with it opportunities galore for growth and acceptance. But it also brought unanticipated problems, including active resistance and a threat to women's autonomy. A fresh set of actors also entered the drama. Congress, federal bureaucrats, and leaders in men's sports would increasingly help determine the course of women's college sports. Already having begun their own process of change, leaders in women's sports had to adjust even further. Their ideology and tactics shifted considerably in response to the new focus on equality.

Women's intercollegiate sports began to take off during the late 1960s. Through their new organization, the CIAW, women physical educators created athletic opportunities for college women. Their experiment exceeded expectations. In the beginning CIAW sponsored just two national championships, but it grew quickly, adding four more. By 1971 the six annual championships included the relatively small badminton competition as well as women from twenty-seven different states in swimming and diving.[1] Every season brought more events and participants, so handling it all became increasingly difficult. The CIAW's success pleased its commissioners but it also slightly overwhelmed them.

Growth and a couple years' experience exposed a few problems not easily remedied by tinkering. Soon CIAW's commissioners found they had too much to handle, and too few resources. Eager volunteers accustomed to "giving their life blood in various forms of service," they wanted to do the work.[2] But only after they finished teaching, advising, researching, and running women's teams or intramurals at their colleges could they find time for CIAW business. This meant administration was sometimes slow and inefficient.[3] In addition, the organization's popularity caused difficulties. The CIAW had encouraged partic- ipation in its national events by keeping them open to almost all comers, but that policy became unwieldy. Yet regional competition could not be established until there was a permanent, stable constituency. Funds were also scarce. Its careful leaders operated on a shoestring budget of around $5,000, but with those limits they could not accommodate much more expansion.[4] "Either the job must be well done or not at all," Katherine Ley told DGWS in 1967. "To do it well will require considerable money." She warned that the anticipated growth also would require more time and effort than a volunteer group could handle.[5]

"In a sense we have reached a turn in the road," Ley asserted. "We should not make the turn unless we are prepared to complete the job."[6] Convinced that the old structure tied their hands, CIAW's leaders believed a permanent membership organization would solve their problems. Ley sought to convince other physical educators that increasing popularity of their championships and new sympathy toward women's rights signaled that this was an auspicious time to move. However, physical educators had to act quickly if they wanted to keep charting the course of women's intercollegiate athletics. If they did not, others (people without such high standards—like men in athletics) might step in, and then women physical educators might lose the little power they did have. Ley knew from her experience in the early 1960s that her colleagues moved conserva- tively, but "somehow we need to impress upon the good ladies of NAPECW that we must do whatever is necessary (almost) to keep the control in the hands of women and that if we sit idly by we will be trying to pick up the pieces instead of keeping ahead of the game."[7] To Ley's pleasure, in late 1970 the two major women's PE groups agreed. The DGWS and NAPECW directed CIAW commis- sioners to form a new, national membership organization, and they did so, assembling the Association for Intercollegiate Athletics for Women (AIAW).[8]

The AIAW's founders set forth a couple of basic purposes. They would help schools extend their sports programs for women, hoping to encourage excellence in women athletes. At the same time, these programs would be consistent with their member schools' educational aims. So that sports would be part and parcel of education (not contrary to it), athletes would be treated like other students. Finally, they wanted to stimulate leadership among those (mostly women) who were responsible for women's programs. To meet those objectives, AIAW would offer the same services as other athletic governing bodies: publishing the rules for various sports; disseminating scheduling and other information; and representing member colleges on matters relating to women's sports.[9] The most basic function would be conducting national athletic championships for women.

Crucial as it was, the creation of AIAW marked just one of the path-breaking efforts in the early 1970s to create more opportunities for women. In the House of Representatives, Oregon's Edith Green introduced legislation to prohibit discrimination against women in federally assisted educational programs. One law—Title VI of the Civil Rights Act of 1964—already prohibited discrimination in such programs, but only on the basis of race, color, and national origin, not sex.[10] Green's proposed law would close that loophole, adding sex discrimination to the list of prohibitions. When she held hearings on the bill in the summer of 1970, professional women testified about widely used practices that handicapped women in higher education, including higher admissions qualifications, quotas limiting their number, unequal allocation of scholarships, differing pay scales, and refusing to take women's aspirations seriously.[11] Athletic opportunities were mentioned only peripherally in these initial hearings.[12]

By 1971 the House seemed agreeable to Green's proposal and incorporated it into a massive Omnibus Education Bill then under consideration.[13] Apparently assuming that sufficient precedent existed in civil rights laws for how the law would be applied, at no time did representatives discuss the definition of the crucial term "program." That assumption blinded them to the extent of changes that would be required in undergraduate services and activities as well as the vehement opposition that would ensue over such details.[14] Green believed her bill was "probably going to be the most revolutionary thing in higher education in the 1970s," but the other committee members did not dwell much on the sex discrimination provisions.[15]

At first, the Senate's version of the Omnibus Education Bill did not contain any mention of sex discrimination, but Sen. Birch Bayh moved to change that. On August 6, 1971, Bayh introduced an amendment which declared that

> no person . . . shall, on the basis of sex, be excluded from, denied the benefits of, or subject to discrimination under any program or activity conducted by a public institution of higher education, or any school or department of graduate education, which is a recipient of Federal financial assistance for any education program or activity.[16]

Like Green, Bayh intended his legislation to mirror already existing federal prohibitions against racial discrimination.[17] As in Title VI, the bureaucratic agencies that distributed federal financial assistance to schools would issue the regulations implementing the law. If an institution did not comply with regulations and would not do so voluntarily, its government funds could be terminated. Bayh's language differed from Green's in one important way. He directed his bill at *institutions* receiving federal aid (meaning that every program within the institution would be covered); the House wording covered *programs* that received federal aid. Because "program" was not precisely defined, Green's intent is unclear, but Bayh clearly meant the scope of the law to be extremely broad. Unfortunately, when he reintroduced the law into the Senate, Bayh used Green's more restrictive "programmatic" language, believing her bill to have the same intent and scope as his.

Did that mean intercollegiate sports would be covered? The record is a bit vague, especially with regard to Green, but it seems Bayh did expect so. He mentioned sports a number of times, but rather indirectly. Once he said differential treatment (of the sexes) would be permitted only in "very unusual cases where such treatment is absolutely essential to the success of the program—such as in classes for pregnant girls or emotionally disturbed students, in sports facilities or in other instances where privacy must be preserved."[18] At another time, Bayh referred to football in the context of times when "separate but equal" might be preferable instead of total integration of the sexes. It might be, he said, one of the rare exceptions to the general rule of *identical* treatment for men and women in any area of education.[19] Because he realized Congress could not yet envision all the areas that might require change, Bayh proposed that the Commissioner of Education conduct both an immediate and ongoing study of sex discrimination to "finally give us a clear picture of the exact nature of sex discrimination in education, its pervasiveness and its cost to society."[20] The House and Senate engaged in heated debate over certain areas of the education bill (especially over busing to remedy years of racial segregation), but the sex discrimination provision, now named "Title IX" of the bill, sparked little controversy. There were a few compromises in areas unrelated to sports,[21] and unfortunately the Conference Committee decided to delete Bayh's requirement of a study to determine the extent of discrimination.

Title IX of the Omnibus Education Act of 1972 became public law on June 23, 1972. Senator Bayh called it "an important first step in the effort to provide for the women of America something that is rightfully theirs."[22] Bayh correctly predicted that the law signaled only the first step in a long process. Probably even he did not imagine how many battles lay in the years ahead. Like most policy makers with a vision, Bayh and Green had sketched only the broad outlines they desired without getting bogged down in details that might provoke opposition. They left working out those details—including the effect on intercollegiate sports—to the federal bureaucracy. Sponsors Bayh and Green logically would have applied the law's nondiscrimination mandate to female student-athletes just like other female students, but there is little direct evidence they had given thought to the particular effects Title IX would have for women in sports. This oversight proved ironic because Title IX turned out to be, in one person's estimation, "the biggest thing to happen to sports since the invention of the whistle."

Passage of Title IX reflected the feminist tenor of the early 1970s, and the creation of AIAW seemed to as well. The women's liberation movement had begun encouraging women to demand more opportunities, break free of stereotypes, reclaim their bodies, and exercise their strength. The AIAW could help achieve those goals. By giving college women a chance to play intercollegiate sports, it challenged notions that women were not physically or psychologically tough enough to compete. The AIAW provided a vehicle for chipping away at the male domination of sport and for empowering women. But although the goals of physical educators in DGWS and NAPECW overlapped with those of feminists, most probably would not have listed women's rights among the reasons they founded AIAW. Instead, they had been improving upon an existing organization and continuing their duty to encourage the right kind of sports for women. Since the early twentieth century, they would have said, women in PE had been acting on the belief that sports were good for women and had been trying to provide suitable opportunities.

Indeed, although they had always been woman-centered, physical educators traditionally were quite conservative. One feminist who encountered PE leaders in the early 1970s characterized them as Republicans and as the least likely women to be involved in a social movement.[23] Former presidents of AIAW later conceded the point, believing their lack of political activism was rooted in their awareness of societal attitudes toward them.

> I think women physical educators, and those associated with sports have understandably been extremely conservative. And I think part of that is the whole business that for us to be outspoken was to be aggressive, for us to be aggressive was to be masculine, for us to be masculine was to run the whole gamut, having everything including your sexual orientation questioned. I think that kept us quiet and in our corners for far too many years.[24]

Given their tenuous position in a marginally feminine field, their caution made sense. It was pragmatic not to rock the boat. But their passivity might have come not just from a pragmatic decision but from being so sensitive to "this psychological stigma and stereotyping" that they had unconsciously internalized society's attitudes and expectations.[25] They had accepted and promulgated exaggerated notions of difference between the sexes and of proper feminine behavior. Trapped by what one called "psychological oppression," physical educators had grown accustomed to meager resources for women's sports and had not questioned the shabby treatment at their schools.

But the women's liberation movement did affect women physical educators. With the rest of society debating women's rights and whether females deserved access to Little League Baseball and the Boston Marathon, they could not avoid it. The new social context forced them to rethink fundamental issues. In a dialectical sort of process, they meshed traditional attitudes about a woman's sphere with newer ones, yielding an interesting hybrid. Even though probably only a minority of women in physical education would have called themselves feminists, the majority's attitudes and behavior still shifted. Furnished with a new lens through which to view their conditions, most physical educators became less satisfied with them. They saw their efforts to improve women's sports as a continuation of their historical role, but provided in turn with a new, critical language, they began to call some of their treatment unjust.

"We are increasingly aware of discrimination against women's programs and the women leaders of those programs," declared one participant at a 1971 DGWS meeting.[26] Her language illustrates how the women's movement had crept into physical educators' consciousness. This is true of Lucille Magnusson, who asserted a new rationale of rights. "[Women] are entitled to financial support for their programs now and in the future."[27] The DGWS even formed a committee of twenty-three interested individuals to study "Equal Opportunities for Women in Sport."[28] Recognizing that each woman needed assistance in her solitary campus battle for better treatment, they intended to contact government agencies and women's groups and circulate information about grievance procedures, legal options, and resources available. Not surprisingly, they approached the subject cautiously, declaring women should follow proper channels for submitting complaints and not defend unsubstantiated grumbling.[29] Where appropriate, however, they should act. Lucille Magnusson exhorted her colleagues to ask whoever holds the purse strings at their institution for more backing. "We have to get over the idea that women must compromise their programs because of lack of financial support. We have to get away from the idea of bake sales, washing cars, etc."[30] And when you go, she added, go "with head held high, not on bended knee."

The new consciousness about gender issues brought some challenges; it meant physical educators had to reassess some of their basic policies. They strenuously supported greater opportunities for women in sports but were less sure about "equal" opportunities. What exactly, they wondered, constituted equal opportunity? For years black Americans, agreeing with the Supreme Court's decision that separate was inherently unequal, had worked for equality through integration. Should things work the same with sexual as with racial discrimination, meaning women should play on men's teams? Or could separate be equal? Traditionally, DGWS had advocated *separate* competition for males and females, except in a few noncontact activities. It had frowned upon a woman's joining an all-male team, because it was improper and dangerous.[31] But such incidents had been rare. The issue became pressing in 1970, when the Southeast Conference (SEC), an athletic alliance of large universities, decided to allow women on its men's teams. While the instinct of DGWS's members was to denounce the move, they decided to appoint a study group, given the tenor of the times.[32]

After some discussion, DGWS reiterated its former position, but in doing so incorporated more modern reasons. Committee chair Dorothy Harris concluded that some physical and psychological evidence supported the argument for separate teams, since the average male had a physical advantage over the average female in certain athletic events. She believed that opponents should be evenly matched, so that "self-confidence, a positive body image, self-concept, and status have the best opportunity to develop."[33] Usually that would mean females competing against females, but she admitted there were instances in which talented females could perform at their best only by playing against males. The members of DGWS agreed with Harris, and as they renewed their call for separate teams they translated it into a feminist-sounding demand for greater funds, facilities, and staff for those teams. In essence, the group moved from its old-fashioned insistence on sex separation toward encouraging separate *but equal* teams. Now they opposed "integration" not so much for allowing a woman on an all-male team as because schools were not willing to do *more* for women.

> Some of the women's liberation efforts to press for the opportunity for girls to play on boys' teams in non-contact sports may result in fewer opportunities for girls to participate in sports programs. For example, rather than fund a modest program of girls inter-scholastic sports, some school boards are using this escape route as an economy measure.[34]

"Equal opportunity," they asserted, should mean providing comparable teams for a significant number of women, not merely opportunities for a few exceptional tokens.[35] The "separate but equal" decision represented one example of how, faced with the existence of a women's liberation movement, physical educators began to synthesize their traditional attitudes with those of feminists.

The scholarship issue presented a similar challenge. The CIAW had prohibited athletic scholarships because, as men's intercollegiate sports demonstrated, all sorts of unethical practices resulted. Schools relentlessly competing to win scoured the country seeking the best athletes and then wooed, hounded, harassed, and occasionally bribed them. They overlooked academic credentials for scholarship athletes. In the estimation of women physical educators, this wasted an enormous amount of time and money and reflected entirely too much emphasis on winning. Schools that focused on winning wrongly put the well-being of their athletic program before that of the student.[36] Although the public was increasingly aware of these problems, there was little impetus to clean up men's intercollegiate athletics. Women in physical education, then, operated outside the mainstream. Their antirecruitment position may have been sound educational philosophy, but neither fans, male athletic administrators, nor even most feminists shared their view.

But debate over equal rights for women did cause AIAW leaders to waver. Aware that female athletes wanted scholarships and that some said the policy was unfair, they asked DGWS's Executive Committee to reconsider the stand.[37] If a college granted scholarships to its male basketball players, should not the female players also get them? If AIAW rules prevented a school from offering its women athletes scholarships, would not AIAW be blocking equal opportunity? No one in AIAW wanted the organization to perpetuate discrimination against women. On the other hand, "just because the men do it is not justification for giving athletic scholarships to women."[38] If athletic scholarships were a bad idea, why should AIAW allow them? This was a problem that had not surfaced until the societal focus shifted to "equality." The scholarship issue illustrated one of the dilemmas of the modern feminist movement—how to pursue equal opportunity yet not unquestioningly accept sameness.

After much soul-searching, women physical educators in DGWS and AIAW again decided to reaffirm their traditional policy. They told unhappy coaches and athletes that they were sensitive to the argument that athletic scholarships helped poor women and fostered excellence, and that sportswomen desperately needed such encouragement.[39] Despite these considerations, though, the majority of DGWS's leaders voted to continue prohibiting scholarships. Their decision could be seen either as a backward-looking, conservative, almost prudish protection of propriety, or as a progressive, almost radical insistence upon their right to a uniquely woman-defined alternative. Probably it was a little of both. Some physical educators were not quite ready to see female athletes treated like the males in every respect; others rebelled against the notion that they should be forced to do something just because men did it. Scholarships also opened up a "hornets' nest" of complicated regulatory and enforcement problems.[40] Therefore, both for practical and philosophical reasons, old and new, AIAW endorsed its traditional stand.

Women physical educators also encountered another unforeseen, and ultimately more serious, challenge. Throughout the century no one had seriously questioned their authority over college women's sports. With the exception of short-lived attention from the AAU in the 1950s, everyone had ignored college-aged female athletes. With the increasing politicization of sports in the early 1970s, however, that uninterest began changing.

The National Collegiate Athletic Association had been running most of men's intercollegiate sports since 1905.[41] A membership organization serving about six hundred colleges and universities, it wrote and enforced rules for and sponsored national championships in a number of sports. All of these were for men. The NCAA appeared to be in full agreement with the traditional separation in PE and athletics—men ran men's, and women ran women's.[42]

Unexpectedly, however, the NCAA's leadership changed course. The AIAW's leaders found out about this sudden interest in women's sports in January 1971, after plans for the organization were well under way, and as a courtesy they had sent a copy of the AIAW blueprint to the NCAA. Walter Byers, executive director of the NCAA, then informed them that NCAA's lawyers were preparing a legal brief about the problem of women being denied access to NCAA events. "It appears that the NCAA is in a difficult legal position on the basis of its present posture," he wrote, "and I suspect it is quite likely that we will proceed to remove such barriers and, in fact, provide competitive opportunities for women as well as men."

Byers spoke prematurely. For one thing, the NCAA Council had only begun to consider the issue and was far from making any recommendations. In addition, policy changes in the NCAA had to be approved by a vote of the organization's member colleges, which at the time knew nothing of any such proposals. Finally, Byers oversimplified what the lawyers had said. In actuality, they had offered the council four different options:

- do nothing and wait and see if someone sues the NCAA and then find out if the NCAA is violating the law
- adopt the position that the NCAA is willing and able to regulate women's intercollegiate athletics but understands that the women's organization [CIAW-AIAW] is developing programs
- create a division within the NCAA for female intercollegiate competition
- permit individual females to participate in existing competition.[43]

Byers preferred the third option, that of moving right in to take over women's college sports, and perhaps because he wielded so much influence, he thought the organization would take that route.

The possibility of NCAA interest in women's sports, at this late date, disturbed the AIAW's architects.[44] At an April 1971 DGWS meeting, they speculated about why the NCAA would pay attention to women. Rachel Bryant thought it stemmed from the reheating of an old NCAA-AAU jurisdictional battle. Both groups wanted the government to grant them sole authority for U.S. national and Olympic teams. All through 1971 the AAU and the NCAA had made headlines for suspending one another's athletes and excluding them from competitions.[45] The NCAA might have been interested in women's intercollegiate sports because the AAU already ran some female (nonschool) events in track and field, basketball, and swimming, which could make the AAU appear more qualified to be the national governing body. The AIAW's officers could not change this national context, but they could try to persuade the NCAA's leaders not to make the move.[46]

A worried Rachel Bryant wrote newly elected NCAA president Earl Ramer, explaining that women wanted to create their own rivalries and traditions, and to conceive and pilot their own distinctive athletic models.[47] They had already designed the policy handbook, begun developing regional organizations, instituted their transition plan from CIAW, and were inviting schools "with anticipation and a sense of history in the making" to become charter members of AIAW.[48] Politely, she pleaded for continuation of the status quo, with the NCAA running men's sports and DGWS-AIAW running women's—and for a chance to make her case at the April NCAA Council meeting.[49] Ramer left open the possibility of later discussions but declined, saying the NCAA "needed to explore its own thinking on the issue before consulting the women."[50]

Asked by the NCAA Council to update his legal opinion about women's sports, George Gangwere's next brief, dated June 1971, moved beyond his earlier wait-and-see attitude. Now he suggested that the NCAA ought to take some action to prevent legal culpability. Opening up NCAA events to women, he said, might not be sufficient; women probably had the right to events of their own. The NCAA could start up some events, but since the CIAW-AIAW was already running women's championships, he thought it might be easier for the NCAA to make some sort of agreement with them.

> To take full advantage of the great amount of work done heretofore in the field of women's sports, to avoid resentment and hostility from the leading women athletic administrators, and as the best means of locating the necessary additional female administrators, it would appear desirable for the NCAA to seek the affiliation as adjunct of the NCAA of the new National Organization for Intercollegiate Athletics for Women. If such an affiliation is not possible then it will be desirable to ascertain the necessary steps for organizing a separate women's group within the NCAA.[51]

Gangwere wanted to avoid offending DGWS's "well-organized and . . . dedicated professionals," but clearly the NCAA's needs came first. In a menacing forecast of the situation that would be played out for the next decade, he predicted, "There would be strong resentment by many of the leading women athletic administrators if the NCAA attempted to supersede their organization[.] Yet," he added, "it has the power to do so."[52]

The NCAA Council appointed a special Committee on Women's Athletics, which made initial contact with DGWS representatives on July 6, 1971. There NCAA agents explained their organization might conceivably be guilty of sex discrimination and that an affiliation between the NCAA and AIAW might be the solution. Delegates of DGWS-AIAW voiced a willingness to listen to any proposals the NCAA might make, but also stressed, "We will not enter into any arrangement where we are controlled by NCAA."[53] The meeting concluded with promises that the women would send AIAW's operating code and that Gangwere would draft an affiliation agreement for DGWS and AIAW to consider.[54]

The meeting confirmed the AIAW founders' wariness. According to Rachel Bryant,

> [The NCAA's] concerns . . . seemed to center around avoidance of the charge of discriminating against women. They don't want to change their Constitution or their regulation that women may not participate on (men's) teams in the NCAA championships. Verbally, at least, they seemed to be looking for an "out," and were seeking some sort of affiliation with AIAW so they could say, "This is the group officially recognized by the NCAA to conduct intercollegiate athletics for women."[55]

The NCAA's concern centered around avoiding trouble, not doing the right thing. The well-being of female athletes and women's sports appeared to be conspicuously absent from the NCAA's list of priorities.[56]

Anxious about what might come next, AIAW women took the initiative, arranging for another joint meeting in September 1971. To it they also invited the National Association of Intercollegiate Athletes (NAIA), an organization serving men's programs mostly at smaller schools, and the National Junior College Athletic Association (NJCAA). They hoped to gain the support of the men's athletic associations and establish an amicable working relationship with all of them. Naively, they thought that by explaining what they were doing for women's athletics, the men would approve and leave them be.[57] As one AIAW president remembered,

> [AIAW's pioneers] thought that we were going to be able to convince the NCAA, NAIA, NJCAA, that the women were going to be better served through [AIAW] than through [the men's] organizations, without creating any conflict in those organizations. [We] wanted to be in the public eye and gen-

erate a public support for girls' and women's sports. [We] felt that somehow what we had to offer was going to be so obvious to everyone that there
would be a minimum of problems in getting that established.[58]

They discovered, however, that the NCAA had prepared an initiative of its
own in quite a different spirit. George Gangwere had put together a proposal,
in the form of an amendment to the NCAA's constitution, which incorporated
AIAW into NCAA. It established a Women's Division—a separate unit within the
organization—which AIAW women physical educators could run. However, the
division would still be subject to all the principles and provisions of the NCAA's
constitution. The amendment gave the NCAA Council the power to allow some
rule differences for women's sports. It also allocated *two* positions for women
on the sixteen-seat NCAA Council. Privately, Gangwere admitted to Byers,
"Perhaps the representation should be greater than provided," but that would
have involved changing the structure of the council.[59] In essence, the proposal
would force AIAW to cut ties with DGWS and would give the NCAA final authority over women's sports. By adding only a short amendment to the NCAA's constitution, it did not involve drastic changes for men's athletics or the NCAA.

The proposal did not please anyone except the NCAA. The junior college association balked when it heard that any school that wanted to join AIAW would be
required to join the NCAA. Neither did NAIA want to hand an entire new arena
of power to its competitor the NCAA. Most importantly, AIAW did not really want
to ally with only one of the men's organizations. Its leaders wanted to keep all
the college women's programs together, since to divide up such a small, fledgling group would slow the cause. "I . . . am convinced that the gals are not yet
ready to be split into three groups," explained Lucille Magnusson.[60] The AIAW's
leaders did show some interest in the less radical move of becoming an NCAA
"affiliate member" (which involved no NCAA control).[61] In the end, AIAW representatives made no firm commitments and ruled out no options until the organization could discuss it further, but they had shown their reluctance.

The NCAA apparently found the AIAW's independent spirit too troublesome
to continue negotiations. It never even sent the AIAW a copy of its proposal.
Walter Byers, for one, objected to AIAW's insistence upon autonomy and its continued association with DGWS-AAHPER. "You can rest assured," he insisted, "that
the NCAA does not intend to delegate responsibilities and Council-voting positions to an organization over which a third party has veto authority."[62] Assistant
executive director Chuck Neinas also rejected AIAW's counterproposal that it
simply become an "affiliate member." The AIAW could become an affiliate member, "but it would have no meaning or provide no solution to our problem."[63]
Dissatisfied with AIAW's response to the NCAA's legal problem, he wrote, "We
hope[d] that your organization would be the vehicle to fill that need, but if you

feel that you cannot make the adjustment necessary to accomplish that end, then I suppose that we will have to look to some other solution."[64]

Neinas's reference to "some other solution" alarmed the AIAW.[65] Reading Neinas's letter as blackmail, Rachel Bryant retorted, "There is only one inference that can be made from this threat: the AIAW must become the female arm of NCAA, or NCAA will set up a competing program to the AIAW and its member schools."[66] She hoped she was mistaken in her interpretation, but in case she was not, she continued with a warning of her own. "No action the NCAA could take could be a bigger mistake." An organization "for men and controlled by men" had no business "threaten[ing] a group of professional women educators who designed a program according to their accepted philosophy and standards."[67] If it tried to take over women's intercollegiate sports, NCAA would have "a real battle on its hands."

In turn, Byers called Bryant's remarks "intemperate" and asserted that the NCAA had the right to regulate all intercollegiate athletics, including women's. Further, he suggested the NCAA's right took precedence over women physical educators.[68]

The disagreement over women's sports went public at the 1972 NCAA Convention. The NCAA's George Gangwere and AIAW's JoAnne Thorpe took opposing sides at a roundtable discussion. There Gangwere told the audience that women lacked competitive opportunities because the NCAA was not making them available. Schools entrusted their intercollegiate programs to the NCAA, so the NCAA had been charged (under its own constitution) with the responsibility of regulating *all* intercollegiate athletics. Despite this obligation, the NCAA had not offered women the chance to participate and therefore "does have somewhat of a legal problem."[69]

Thorpe strenuously disagreed that the NCAA was required to offer women's sports. "When the [NCAA] Constitution was written," she said, "although you did not write it in, you obviously did plan only to regulate for men."[70] She questioned the curious timing of this "mandate." Courts had not yet addressed what obligation the NCAA or colleges might have, so it seemed premature to say the courts were forcing the NCAA into action. On the other hand, Thorpe posed, if the NCAA had had this obligation since its inception in 1929, why did it wait until now to act on it, only after women had begun to plan their own institutional membership organization? "After our women's programs are initiated, I do not think it is honest to say that you feel you are also charged with regulating competition for women." It did not seem fair. "If women in the United States had no competition provided and had no program and no possibility to have one, the NCAA would be wonderful to help us in that respect."[71] However, AIAW already offered competitive events with policies to which women felt allegiance. When the NCAA's leadership pretended those did not exist, the women felt ignored and trivialized. Thorpe concluded by presuming the NCAA's concern for women's lack of opportunities was sincere. She thanked them for their interest and hoped they would continue to express it—in productive ways. "Any deficiencies which exist in programs for women can best be overcome by members of the NCAA supporting the women's programs which are already in existence and are striving for recognition back home [on campus]."[72]

Few NCAA delegates wanted their organization to enter the field of women's sports. Most seemed content to leave women's sports in AIAW's hands. Discussion at the roundtable was sparse, but it tended to side with Thorpe.[73] After all, even women in physical education were not charging the NCAA with discrimination, so why should the men act? No specific legislation lay on the table concerning women's sports, and no action was taken at the convention. The NCAA's own special Committee on Women's Athletics even agreed with AIAW that it would be inappropriate for the NCAA to enter this new area. Executive director Walter Byers objected, declaring that the legal problem was "acute."[74] But Byers was out of sync with most men in athletics, and he could not persuade the council that the problem was serious enough to start up women's championships. Still, to avoid the trouble Byers predicted, the organization did take a less drastic step. At the next convention, in January 1973, the delegates dropped the regulation barring women from NCAA men's events. By allowing the exceptional token female to compete in NCAA championships, they hoped, this compromise would clear them from potential charges of sex discrimination. Its advantages included that it did not offend AIAW nor involve any real commitment to women.

Meanwhile, AIAW officially had gotten under way. By March 1972 members had voted for a president, Carole Oglesby, and her successor, Carol Gordon, as well as a coordinator of national championships. They organized nine regional structures, each with representation on the Executive Council. The CIAW held its last meeting in June 1972, and there CIAW leaders turned over the reins to the newly elected AIAW officers. Not quite self-supporting yet, they also clarified the AIAW-DGWS relationship.[75] In 1972–73, the first year of real AIAW operation, 386 colleges were members.[76] Female athletes from those schools could participate in national championships in eight sports.[77]

Hardly had the AIAW's officers gotten on their feet when they were struck by a serious blow. In January 1973 eleven students and three teachers from two Florida colleges filed a lawsuit challenging AIAW's scholarship ban. Female tennis players on scholarship at Marymount College and Broward Community College believed it unfair that they could not participate in AIAW events. On the basis of the Fourteenth Amendment's guarantee of equal protection, they asked the court for declaratory relief and an injunction against the discriminatory policy. They felt they had the right not to be treated differently from men at their schools, who could receive grants. Their complaint named not only AIAW but also DGWS and AAHPER as well as the National Education Association (NEA), and local associations that followed the AIAW regulation.[78]

The lawsuit posed a "thorny problem" for AIAW's officers. Although heartsick over the implication that they were not working in the best interests of female students, they still believed in their policy and wanted to defend it.[79] Unfortunately, though, they could not find support. The DGWS deferred to AAHPER, which deferred to the NEA, and the NEA wanted to be dismissed as a defendant from the case.[80] The NEA's lawyers assured Oglesby "they were certainly not dumping AIAW," but they certainly did limit the AIAW's options.[81] If AIAW wanted to settle out of court, the NEA was willing to handle the case for minimal fees; but if AIAW wanted to fight it, the NEA would not help. The AIAW could not cover the costs of a legal battle or find anyone willing and able to help bail them out.[82]

The dilemmas of justice for women appeared in troubling form. Strictly speaking, AIAW did not treat women any differently than it treated men, because it did not treat men any way at all. It was not responsible for a college's athletic policies for men. That fact might get AIAW out of the lawsuit, but PE leaders realized that it would not solve all their problems. Even if this particular case were dropped, surely female athletes would just file another grievance against their colleges. Both the law and basic notions of fairness seemed to require comparable treatment for men and women similarly situated. Schools would not want lawsuits, so if they wanted to keep men's scholarships, they would have to award scholarships to their female athletes. In that case, then, they would have to drop out of AIAW. Thus the policy, even if not technically illegal, could indirectly cause AIAW to lose members. Or the AIAW would be pressured to change the policy so as not to lose those members.[83] Either way, AIAW would lose. The women of AIAW felt they had been put in an unfair position by history and power relations. Unless they somehow could win the right to determine a very different destiny, they would be forced to adopt the men's model simply because that model was established first.

With the cards stacked against them, AIAW's leaders gave in without a fight.[84] Perhaps if they permitted scholarships, they consoled themselves, everything would not be ruined. After all, scholarships were not terrible in and of themselves. Exploitation from recruiting was the real evil, and AIAW still could find ways to regulate that. Carole Oglesby later acknowledged that AIAW might have avoided problems if earlier it had distinguished between scholarships and recruitment. It was understandable, because "AIAW was working so hard to make the DGWS philosophy and policies come to life."[85] Still, "we stuck with [the prohibition of scholarships] beyond the realistic point," she admitted.[86] So AIAW decided to drop the ban.[87]

A special committee tackled the task of rewriting the financial aid policy so that it would cling as firmly as ever to the rest of AIAW's alternative ideology. It recommended to athletic administrators a list of guidelines: (1) the enrichment of the athlete's life should be the focus of athletic programs; (2) adequate funding for a comprehensive athletic program should receive priority over money for financial aid (that is, schools should spend money first to make sure many opportunities for competition existed, and that players had appropriate food, travel, lodging, officials, coaches, equipment, and facilities before they spent money on scholarships); (3) schools should allocate scholarships based on the potential contribution of the educated citizen to society instead of on the contribution a point guard, for example, would make to a basketball team; (4) staff should devote their time to the whole program rather than recruiting; (5) students should be free to choose an institution on the basis of curriculum, not the amount of financial aid offered; (6) participants in certain sports should not be favored over those in other sports; and (7) students should be encouraged to participate in athletic programs for reasons other than financial aid. Interim regulations also stated that athletes should be treated as much as possible like other students, so all grants must go through the college's financial aid office, and entering students must meet the institution's normal admissions standards.[88]

This extraordinary list of guidelines constituted quite a departure from the practices and assumptions of much of men's intercollegiate sports. In men's big-time programs, the needs of revenue-producing teams dominated the athletic department's budget and staff, which largely ignored the other men's "minor" teams. They scoured the country for the best players for a particular spot on a team, stressed sports performance before academic achievement, and often disregarded an athlete after his four years of use to the team—all in the quest for victory. As Maryland's athletic director Jim Kehoe explained unapologetically, "You do anything to win. I believe completely, totally, and absolutely in winning."[89]

The women of AIAW could not embrace such values, so they put forward an alternative vision. This vision was not totally unrealistic because women already ran programs untainted by recruitment and high pressure on athletes, ones that focused on educating women rather than amassing victories. However, these women's programs were small-time; they had never been taken very seriously by anyone outside of them, had not been in the limelight, and had few resources available. Whether AIAW could balance scholarships, larger budgets, greater attention, and high-level national competition with educational values remained to be seen. Their ability to bring older attitudes into the modern context and their capacity to merge idealism with realism would be tested. Most importantly, though, their power would be tested. The male athletic model was firmly entrenched, very popular, and successful. No one knew whether, in an arena men had already staked out as their own, it would be possible for a female-defined alternative to thrive.

The AIAW pulled together tightly after surviving the scholarship crisis. In November 1973 it held its initial Delegate Assembly, the first time representatives from women's athletic programs across the country could meet in person to make policy. Previously, all voting had taken place through the mail. There was a lot to talk about at the two-day gathering. "Everything we did," one officer remembered, "we thought of as setting precedent."[90] Starting from scratch, the women often dealt with the most basic values. "In the Delegate Assembly debate we were constantly testing out our philosophy. Constantly. And we were either changing it or reaffirming it, and there is no way you can have too much debate on that." Grateful for the opportunity to be making their own decisions, AIAW delegates took that task seriously. Even the process used was very important; they wanted to be democratic from top to bottom. Presidents bent over backward to make sure opposing viewpoints were heard, and that discussion was open and fair. Hyperconscious that their ideology differed from the dominant one, they had to spend an inordinate amount of time legitimizing it. They worried that any blemish might undercut their efforts for acceptance. "See we thought . . . that we had to do everything perfectly," another explained. They were trying to create a model organization, one that was above criticism and purer than the men's. They later discovered with amazement that, in their naïveté, they had created an organization with far more input from delegates than the NCAA. With amusement, one woman recalled,

> [The] AIAW did things thinking this is how everybody did it, but it really wasn't, it was how AIAW thought it was. The women had never been involved in an all male organization. You know, when somebody said democratic, there was a literal interpretation. Not a male textbook interpretation.[91]

The annual Delegate Assembly served as more than just a place to make policy. It put similarly situated women together where they could make contacts and trade information. It provided a supportive space in which they could share their concerns and garner strength from one another. "Maybe there was a special camaraderie, an energy, an understanding among women who have associated themselves professionally in sport in an era where that not only was not encouraged, but actively discouraged," one woman postulated. "And so I think the bonds of friendship, admiration, respect may have been uniquely deep with this group of people." Besides cementing ties, they learned together. They became familiar with using parliamentary procedure, writing legislation, lobbying, and generally promoting what they wanted. Doing it together was exciting. One president remembered a "little old lady" who got up her courage to present "a cautious resolution." Sensitive to her timidity, other women wanted to help her overcome it. They introduced her to people who shared her position and persuaded her to make a real motion. "This encouragement of women for other women to become more aggressive, to speak up," she believed, "never would happen in the NCAA."[92]

In many ways that first Delegate Assembly climaxed more than seven years of planning. The women who attended breathed life into AIAW's structure. By the time it met in November 1973, 405 colleges were members, and about half of those had sent official voting delegates. Facing important issues and limited time, they got down to business. They reviewed the AIAW-DGWS relationship and touched up the constitution. "We dotted 'i's' and crossed 't's' and debated detail by detail our first set of Bylaws," delegate Ann Uhlir remembered. "Our Parliamentarian gave up on us at midnight." They did not recess until 2:00 A.M. and then reconvened five hours later. By the end they had confirmed the decision to allow (although discourage) scholarships, and also passed a resolution supporting separate teams for men and women. They weighed various proposals about financial aid and recruiting regulations.[93]

One final, important topic at the assembly was Title IX. Organizers had invited speakers, including Marjorie Blaufarb from the Women's Equity Action League, to educate them about the issue.[94] Delegates asked basic questions: Did equality mean women were entitled to 50 percent of athletic funds in a public university? Would men be allowed to try out for the women's field hockey team? Would women have to adopt NCAA standards, or could colleges could choose to use AIAW guidelines over the men's? "Is it possible," one hoped, "for us to be a new model and challenge the existence of the old one?"[95] Their questions demonstrated both ignorance and ambivalence about this law that was supposed to provide female athletic opportunity.[96]

Blaufarb told AIAW delegates that the precise interpretation of the law was not yet determined, but that they should sit down with their colleges' decision-makers and try to promote their distinctive athletic model. "If individuals or groups consider certain practices to be very harmful, they must try to get their own institution to forbid them for both sexes. We cannot set double standards."[97] Blaufarb, a feminist, optimistically expected Title IX to bring "constructive changes." While women in athletics dreaded the men's antagonism, she saw opportunity for women and men to talk to one another. "True equality," Blaufarb maintained, "will preclude the men from just taking over."[98] Knowing their own campuses, the women coaches were more skeptical. Like many oppressed women who feared that the Equal Rights Amendment would only make matters worse, women in PE worried about changing the rules.

Probably viewing their ambivalence as a sign of conservatism, Blaufarb urged them to stop arguing about the merits of Title IX and start thinking about the best methods for implementation. She said that the Department of Health, Education, and Welfare's (HEW) Office of Civil Rights had been preparing the guidelines for the past eighteen months and would be issuing them soon, and that representatives from men's sports had already been lobbying HEW.[99] Realizing that they had gotten off to a slow start, the delegates told the AIAW's Executive Board to get involved with national politics and Title IX.[100]

Male athletic administrators got a peek at a rough draft of Title IX's regulations in spring 1974, and what they saw alarmed them. Indeed, HEW had declared that athletics was included in the law's coverage. Therefore, HEW planned to make colleges treat women's sports like their men's sports, in areas including scheduling, equipment, facilities, coaching, services, travel, per diem, publicity, and scholarships.[101] Since most colleges gave almost nothing to their women's teams (women's share of athletic budgets averaged under 2 percent), the proposed regulations appeared to mandate radical changes. Already facing a financial crunch in their men's programs, most male athletic directors resented being told to make more of what they viewed as *extra*, unnecessary expenditures.[102] Bear Bryant, Alabama's football coach, did not sympathize with the women's plight and did not want to share with them. "I'm all for women's athletics," he claimed, "but . . . if we had to split our budget, it would bankrupt us."[103] Neither did Maryland's Jim Kehoe give women much reason for optimism. "While I support philosophically the principle of equality," he said, "as a practical matter it just won't work. This department wholly endorses a comprehensive women's athletic program but that does not include athletic scholarships or equal sharing of revenue."[104] (According to female athletes at the University of Maryland, it also did not include equal access to facilities, equipment, or other benefits. Four separate women's teams shared the same "kind of grungy" uniforms. And women got less than 1 percent of the athletic budget.)[105] According to Kehoe, the proposed guidelines were "unfair, unreasonable, and impractical."[106]

Most impractical, in the minds of male athletic directors, was that the regulations did not distinguish between revenue-producing and nonrevenue-producing sports.[107] To athletic directors, "major" sports like football and basketball constituted the heart and soul of the athletic program. Because of their revenue-producing capability, they claimed, these teams should not have to share money with others until football got every penny necessary to field the best possible team. (Ironically, statistics proved that the vast majority of football programs actually operated at a deficit.)[108] Athletic administrators feared that by creating more "minor" sports that would not bring in revenue, Title IX would ravage the budgets of football and basketball, meaning the "possible doom of intercollegiate sports."[109]

To some men, the women's sports movement spelled more than the doom of intercollegiate sports: it heralded an ominous change in sex roles. Sportswriter Furman Bisher, for example, decried the trend of women playing rough, "men's" sports. "After all," he asked readers of the *Sporting News*, "what are we after, a race of Amazons? Do you want to bring home a companion or a broad that chews tobacco?"[110] Besides spoiling their behavior, sports damaged women's bodies. "What do you want for the darling daughter," he demanded, "a boudoir or a locker room full of cussing and bruises? A mother for your grandchildren or a hysterectomy?"[111] For Bisher, women's enjoyment and rights meant less than their ability to procreate. *Washington Post* sports editor William Barry Furlong added his disapproval. Refusing to take their athletic endeavors seriously, he unapologetically insulted and objectified women. "The clean hard sexist fact," he declared, "is that there are at least three other things I'm going to examine about a woman—four, on the chance she has a brain—before I even begin to think about her golf swing." For female athletes, he coined the term "grotesqueries."[112]

In comparison, the opposition of the male intercollegiate athletic establishment seemed moderate. Few athletic directors publicly lambasted the notion of greater opportunities for women in sports; instead, they criticized the means toward reaching it. Arkansas's athletic director Lou Farrell, for example, asserted his neutrality toward women's sports but protested his responsibility for finding money for them. "We, as the athletic department, don't have any strong feelings one way or another [about women's sports]," Farrell explained. "If the women could get a good strong program together that could support itself, why, that's all right with us, you know. But it would quite naturally be real tough on us if we had to finance it."[113] Robert Scannell complained about bureaucrats intruding on his administrative freedom.

> I'm scared to death of Title 9. Now you get some of your hard-driving investigators in here and they come in after a day of looking at the budgets and our athletic program because some gal has brought a complaint—and that's all you need to start an investigation—they're in here pounding on the desk as they're prone to do."[114]

In sum, the NCAA predicted, the regulations would be "frequently disruptive, often destructive, and surely counter-productive."[115]

Still, while the athletic directors' language was more moderate than the sportswriters', it amounted to the same thing—opposition to Title IX and to women's athletic equity. Unaccustomed to taking women's sports seriously, they were astonished by the amazing new demands from women athletes. At Indiana University, for example, they wanted to play in the same huge gymnasium as the men, receive physical examinations and the services of an athletic trainer, get their meals paid for on the road, and sleep two to a hotel room instead of four or more. "These are things you are going to be involved with," warned Indiana's William Orwig. "I didn't think I would, but now I find I am. . . . You had better get ready."[116] At the 1974 NCAA Convention, athletic directors traded strategies for getting themselves "off the hook" and for "getting the women off [the administration's] backs."[117] Fearing that more opportunities for women meant fewer privileges for men, male athletic directors had more reason than the sportswriters to view Title IX as a threat.[118]

A conservative group within the NCAA wanted to fight tooth and nail against the federal mandate for women's athletic equality. Two NCAA committees, the Joint Legislative and Public Relations groups, "began devoting extensive attention to this threat."[119] They alerted NCAA member colleges and the media that the proposed regulations would bring economic disaster to both men's and women's athletic programs. They also lobbied the government on various fronts. They pressured HEW secretary Caspar Weinberger to reconsider certain portions of the drafted Title IX regulations, and hoped two White House contacts would help persuade President Nixon that they should be weakened.[120] On the congressional front, they pushed for an amendment to exempt athletics from Title IX.[121]

A more pragmatic group within the NCAA opposed waging an all-out fight against equal opportunity for women. Although these men would not have chosen to spend larger sums of money on women's sports and strongly disliked being told what to do, they came to believe there was no sense in opposing the principle of equal opportunity because some reform was inevitable. These men, led by executive director Walter Byers and legal counsel George Gangwere, shrewdly guessed that their energies would be more productively spent *limiting* the change that did occur. To Byers and the NCAA Committee on Women's Athletics, Gangwere wrote, "substantially equal athletic opportunities for women is no longer a matter of speculation, but rather the distinct aim of the courts and the federal government. The longer the implementation of this purpose is delayed, *the less likely the* NCAA *will be able to determine the nature and extent of the actions which will be ultimately adopted*" (emphasis added).[122]

For these men, the most sensible way for the NCAA to reassert control over intercollegiate athletics would be to concede publicly the notion of equal opportunity and establish a separate NCAA women's division.[123] Both Byers and Gangwere kept pointing out to other men in the organization that if the government followed through, the rules and regulations for women and men eventually would be the same.[124] Presumably that worried them because men might be forced to adopt some of the women's attitudes and practices. But if the NCAA could offer women's events and take charge of setting the rules for them, it could prevent any significant changes from occurring in the men's rules. At a meeting of the NCAA Committee on Women's Athletics, chair David Swank admitted as much. He acknowledged that the NCAA male athletic directors would prefer *not* to have a women's division, but said that if women and men could not agree on rules, others might take the power right out of the NCAA's hands.[125]

Both Byers and Gangwere always maintained that the NCAA's entering women's sports would be beneficial to women, yet their ultimate concern— NCAA control—showed through the selfless language. "The truth is that the independent women's organization, AIAW, probably cannot do the job on its own soon enough without the investment of money and administrative effort by NCAA," Gangwere wrote. "Yet the NCAA can hardly make such an investment without some *control* over the program" (emphasis added).[126] As is usually the case with paternalism, at its root is an attitude of superiority and the desire to maintain power relations. Gangwere, Byers, and Swank may have genuinely believed that AIAW women were incapable of doing a good job and that the NCAA's taking over women's sports actually would help women. Still, clearly their primary goal was to protect the NCAA's authority and preserve the status quo of men's intercollegiate sports. Neither Byers nor Gangwere explicitly acknowledged this Machiavellian plan (and it is possible they never consciously conceived it as such), but it does explain the NCAA's incongruous interest in offering women's championships while simultaneously trying to block the main effort to upgrade women's sports.

Those conservatives who were not ready to concede the growth of women's sports nevertheless recognized Byers's logic. They realized that if they lost the fight against Title IX, controlling women's sports was a good contingency plan. Therefore, the NCAA seemed to arrive at a two-pronged policy: it would lobby hard to stop the government from mandating equal opportunity in athletics, but in case that failed it would keep the possibility alive of taking over women's sports. Making what appeared on its face to be a contradictory policy credible would be difficult, but the NCAA's leaders tried. They cultivated a working relationship with AIAW and carefully worded their opposition to Title IX. For example, they passed a resolution tenuously distinguishing between Title IX and the concept of increased opportunities for women. The resolution criticized the proposed regulations as unclear and dangerous, yet endorsed—with qualifications—"the development of opportunities for women students to compete in sports programs of excellence."[127] And on the "pro-women's sports" front, the NCAA Council reconstituted its special Committee on Women's Athletics and even invited AIAW president Carol Gordon to serve on it.[128] Amazingly, though, the committee tried to convince Gordon that the proposed regulations were not in women's best interests and might even force AIAW out of existence.[129]

On a different front, NCAA leaders tried to get Congress to short-circuit Title IX as it applied to sports. In May 1974, Sen. John Tower of Texas responded favorably, with an amendment to another massive education bill that would have protected so-called revenue-producing sports. His amendment stated that Title IX prohibitions against sex discrimination "shall not apply to an intercollegiate athletic activity to the extent that such activity does or may produce gross revenues or donations to the institution necessary to support such activity."[130] The intent of the bill, according to Tower, was to protect revenue-producing sports by allowing them to spend the monies they raised on that sport first, and not be forced by HEW to share it with other sports before they got what was "necessary."[131] Like the NCAA, Tower insisted that he was concerned about the well-being of women's sports as well as men's. "I want to emphasize that one of the prime reasons for my wanting to preserve the revenue base of intercollegiate activities is that it will provide the resources for expanding women's activities in intercollegiate sports."[132] The Senate approved Tower's measure by voice vote.

Women's sports advocates were troubled by the Tower bill. Its wording, for example, could be read as exempting from Title IX's scope any sport that produced *any* gross receipts at all, thus virtually rendering Title IX meaningless. In addition, it applied to gross instead of net revenues. If the intention really was to protect money major sports actually earned, then the bill's phrasing was inaccurate. "Personally I think the language goes farther than they intended," commented HEW's Gwen Gregory. "They've exempted athletics instead of the revenue from athletics."[133] A few doubted that the overarching language was accidental, but intentional or not, sportswomen agreed the wording was dangerous in its ambiguity.[134]

Although initially women in PE felt uncertain about Title IX, the more they discovered how strenuously men in sports opposed equality, the more clear it became how important Title IX could be. With increasing stridency, sportsmen complained (especially to HEW) that equality would mean the end of intercollegiate sports. Male athletic directors kept pointing out the problems of their major, revenue-producing sports but were saying nothing about the much more serious problems women faced.[135] In fact, the National Association of Collegiate Directors of Athletics (an all-male organization) annoyed AIAW further by publishing anti-Title IX propaganda that implied women did not want to participate in sports.[136] Interestingly, then, the men's opposition pushed AIAW women into taking a strong position in favor of the regulations sooner than they otherwise might have. True, AIAW feared that a mandate of absolute equality might make it difficult to keep its unique rules for women. But even though Title IX might not be a perfect tool, they reasoned, this law had wonderful potential. It looked as though it would mean more teams, increased funding, better equipment and facilities, and greater encouragement for women. Why should AIAW oppose those opportunities? If the choice was between achieving equality with absolute sameness, or losing the one tool for change but retaining difference, AIAW would pick Title IX. If the choice of allies was between the government (which seemed to advocate equality, soon) and the NCAA (whose leaders said change would be disastrous), they did not doubt which would be better.[137] Smaller matters of implementation mattered less than HEW's general support of equal opportunity and its muscle to back it up. Women in athletics began to realize that they must speak for themselves, loudly and publicly. Educators, declared Carol Gordon, must "insist that the intent of Title IX to end discrimination in all programs, including athletics, is a legitimate goal for educational institutions and must be preserved."[138]

Although unpracticed in the political process, women's athletic leaders now jumped in. In a bold new step, the AIAW's Executive Board committed the organization to a firm public stand against the Tower amendment and to cooperating with some feminist groups. Realizing they had better catch up and learn how to play in the big leagues, AIAW hired a feminist lawyer, Margot Polivy, who knew how to get things done in Washington. Polivy met with representatives from the National Organization for Women, the Women's Equity Action League, the American Association of University Women, and Women's Lobby, Inc., to discuss strategies for getting the Tower bill completely deleted by the Joint House-Senate Conference Committee.[139] They contacted physical educators from the home states of members of the Joint Conference Committee and urged them to telegram their representatives about the danger of the amendment. Coincidentally, a NAGWS meeting was taking place in Washington (NAGWS was the new acronym for DGWS). During a free afternoon, many of those women "went to the Hill" and visited the conferees.[140] On the afternoon the committee was to decide on the Tower amendment, Polivy and two other NAGWS officers went directly to the meeting room and spoke personally with the conference committee members.[141]

They triumphed. The Joint Conference Committee debated the likelihood of athletic directors' claims that the Title IX regulations would harm men's intercollegiate sports, and then dropped Tower's language. Instead, committee members agreed to substitute a compromise phrase offered by Sen. Jacob Javits. Javits acknowledged that certain sports might pose problems requiring special consideration, but thought a blanket exemption for revenue-producing sports went too far. His rather vague new amendment declared that HEW should publish regulations implementing Title IX's sex discrimination prohibition "which shall include with respect to intercollegiate athletics reasonable provisions considering the nature of particular sports."[142] In effect, the Joint Conference Committee reaffirmed that Congress indeed intended for Title IX to apply to intercollegiate sports and again put decision-making power over specific details in HEW's hands. By doing so, it foiled the NCAA's first major attempt to block women's equality.

Smarting from a lack of follow-up on the Tower initiative, NCAA leaders had to admit that sportswomen had beaten them at their own game. The Joint Conference Committee had met earlier than they anticipated, they confessed, and had been misled by false information disseminated by women's groups.[143] They tried to persuade the conferees to reconsider their action or to clarify Javits's wording, but in vain (they wanted the language clarified so that HEW would not have authority over generated and donated funds). The defeat taught NCAA leaders an important lesson: in contests waged in the federal government, no longer could they assume they had the home-field advantage.

Flushed with the satisfaction of standing up for themselves, women athletic leaders began to believe things might actually be changing. New AIAW President Lee Morrison gleefully reported news of the victory to AIAW voting representatives. Her letter contained a moral:

> We have heard many people say they are tired of writing letters, "it really doesn't make any difference, Congress is going to do what they want to anyway." NOT TRUE! I have included a rather detailed report on the Tower amendment to show you how important it is for us to maintain personal contact with our elected Representatives and Senators. We must telephone, telegraph and write letters to let our Congresspersons know how we feel about particular legislation. May I suggest that you go to see your Congressperson during their summer break and express your concern for women's sports. That initial personal contact may come in handy in the future.[144]

Energized by success, she tried to harness the momentum and gear up for future battles.

Morrison's letter reveals how far women in PE had traveled ideologically by the mid-1970s. For so long they had simply accepted their fate as second-class, marginal citizens. Even two years earlier they had been uncertain about Title IX, worried that its implementation might threaten what little they had and feeling they had hardly any control over what was happening. Now they were running their own independent intercollegiate governing body and had weathered more than one challenge from the powerful men's organization. Despite their inexperience, they had even taken the battle to the halls of Congress. While they always had believed that women's participation in athletics was valuable, now they began asserting it publicly and more confidently. Jan Felshin, professor of physical education at East Stroudsburg State College, used a basketball metaphor to describe the change. Sportswomen had begun moving, she said, from "a prevent defense of conciliatory apologetics" to a contemporary, aggressive strategy of "a full court press."[145] Simultaneous with their efforts for change, they began developing a more complex ideology.

As they analyzed the forces holding females back in sports, women PE leaders found both direct limitations and more subtle restraints. They discovered that most women—even physical educators—had internalized many of the attitudes that discouraged them from pursuing competition in a serious, intense fashion. In order to gain real freedom, they would have to fight not only restrictive rules and male opponents but prevailing attitudes.

First they had to counter ideas about women's physical capabilities. For years everyone, including medical authorities, had recommended a less strenuous lifestyle for women than for men. "Traditionally, we have assumed that females should not be strong because they *can* not be strong, and that females consequently have no endurance potential," admitted Celeste Ulrich.[146] In fact, even women physical educators had been skeptical that women could do more until they witnessed the remarkable performances of athletes who ignored the advice to be careful. But now Ulrich and NAGWS research coordinator Dorothy Harris began noticing the dearth of legitimate scientific knowledge about women's physiology, and they criticized as unfounded many accepted notions about what women were capable of. Ulrich and Harris became pioneers doing their own, woman-centered research.

Likewise, leaders in women's sports began criticizing the social barriers females faced. The most inhibiting, of course, was the idea that sports diminished one's femininity.[147] Along with feminists, Dorothy Harris realized that notions of appropriate gender behavior were constructed by society. They had no essential justification. In fact, sport gender prescriptions were largely arbitrary and sometimes silly. "We have decreed that footballs are masculine and that hockey sticks are feminine as long as they are used on the field rather than on ice," Celeste Ulrich observed wryly, "and we have made sure that boys do not play field hockey and girls do not play football."[148] Such gender constructions often served to limit and oppress women. Challenging the usual definitions, Harris asserted that a female is a female no matter what she does, and that *whatever* women do is "feminine." A slowly increasing number of physical educators agreed that women must stop being cowed by feminine prescriptions, and began spreading the word: "What athletics can do for a man, it can do for a women."[149]

PE leaders acknowledged they had been silent about inequality and discrimination, but they decided not to let victim-blaming distract them. True, DGWS had in some ways "perpetuated the myth of women being 'weaker,' 'nonathletic,' 'noncompetitive' creatures" and had not vociferously proclaimed women's interest in sports before the 1970s.[150] Yet there had been little room for such interest; physical educators merely had behaved the way they were expected to act, accommodating themselves to reality. It made as little sense to blame women for their athletic passivity in the 1950s and 1960s as to blame quiescent blacks in the 1930s for racism. Society cannot realistically measure what oppressed groups want, they discovered, until opportunity exists.[151] As Jan Felshin understood it:

> The "second sex," like other socially inferior groups, has had to adopt approval-seeking and humble interpersonal modes. As long as being called "unfeminine" held the terror of social ostracism, women were prohibited from militancy. Women physical educators have always been vulnerable to charges of aggressiveness, and only conciliation with reference to the leftovers of school time, space, and money for their programs has saved them from the vicious attacks presently in evidence.[152]

Felshin suggested that their marginal position had made it seem too risky to speak out, and that they had made a sort of bargain not to speak out against inequity in the hope of preserving what little freedom they had. Now, however, society stood on the threshold of a new era that would be more accepting of an athletic lifestyle for women. According to AIAW officer Joan Hult, opportunity was knocking on gymnasium doors, and "this time we have all the wisdom of the ages before us to give us courage not to 'cop out' in fear."[153] Felshin agreed that drastic change had occurred. "Women in physical education may have been conservative, but [now] consciousness is raised, oppression is obvious, and it is untenable."[154]

Although the women's liberation movement clearly had influenced the thinking of some physical educators, many of them still held back on embracing feminism wholeheartedly. Some believed they differed with organizations like NOW on certain details about sports (such as whether to work for integrated or sex-separate teams).[155] Many coaches were reluctant to identify themselves as "feminist" because of the term's negative connotations. "I think that uses of that label suddenly infers that you're anti-men," one AIAW president explained.[156] Surely many feminists would not have said they were antimale, but the troubling image persisted. Other women considered feminists as louder and more conspicuous than themselves. "I view them as people who go around marching and making a lot of noise about things, and I'm not that sort of person," another AIAW officer remarked. "There are quiet ways you can fight battles."[157] The sociologist who interviewed her observed others in AIAW who similarly confused style with ideology.[158] In addition, some still appeared to be victims of the same social pressures they had begun denouncing; fearful of the stigma, they were unable to exorcise entirely the notion that activism might be construed as unfeminine.

Finally, a few physical educators shied away from feminism because they had not abandoned the conservative assumptions they had lived by for decades. They still considered commercialized sport, especially when it overemphasized winning, harmful to women. They were still wary of women being exploited by men's teams allowing females to play as publicity stunts, or as a way to ridicule women.[159] They still mistrusted colleges that recruited and might take advantage of female stars. They remained protective of female athletes, sometimes because not all the scientific data was in, and sometimes because they—especially their older members—had not entirely given up all their former notions of what was appropriate for women. For example, when a fourteen-year-old girl from Dubuque, Iowa, wrote Katherine Ley about playing football on a boys' school team, Ley clearly felt ambivalent about that sort of opportunity. Ley urged her to look into girls' flag football teams and to think hard (as she herself had done in her youth) about why she wanted to play.

> You see, Mary, the medical people do not know what effects repeated blows to [the] breast area may have on girls. . . . Football uses intentional contact in the form of blocking that will cause frequent blows to this area. Then, too, many football players suffer injuries to the mouth and nose that disfigure the face—something most girls try to avoid.[160]

However she might be read in 1974, Ley had not been conservative. From the late 1950s through the 1960s, she had been in the forefront of DGWS's move to gain more competitive opportunities for females, even helping create CIAW. Yet so much had changed in fifteen years that a new generation of girls had bypassed her once-progressive notions of propriety.

Although they may not have wanted to call it feminism, physical educators' actions often belied their terminology. The vast majority of them welcomed the new opportunities for females in sports. And it only made sense that they would because the simple act of entering the profession had placed them in opposition to accepted gender roles. What they called themselves, then, really did not matter. A high school gym teacher urged her colleagues to realize that they were already involved in the women's movement:

> We teach women to engage in sports, a predominantly male-oriented activity. We wish our students to be aggressive and assertive in play. In our coeducational classes, we wish the girls to play well, not be "meekly femi-

nine." Thus, whether or not we openly confess to believing in women's liberation, we are, in fact, teaching it.[161]

Another woman told a questioner that she did not consider herself a feminist, yet in the same breath described her dedication to putting her female players on the court with pride:

> I felt when my kids put on their basketball uniforms and walked onto the floor of [the arena] that that act in itself said more about their rights as women than any parade or any petition or any kind of political maneuver that could have been used. I felt they were making a statement for their rights and for all the women that would follow them who will put on those uniforms. . . . And I thought my job was to help them make that statement, by making sure they had uniforms to put on, by making sure that they could walk on to [the arena floor] and by making sure that their game was played in an atmosphere that made some sense for them.[162]

While they were not proclaiming the "personal is political," feminist assumptions had worked their way into the physical educators' collective consciousness. Once a timid organization, NAGWS now published books to aid women in gaining opportunity, exhorting coaches to know the law and, if necessary, use the judicial system.[163] Its leaders began recognizing and rejecting tokenism.[164] They demanded that schools do something to promote, rather than just accommodate, women's interest in sports.[165] Some proposed affirmative action to make up for years of discrimination and neglect.[166] Throughout, they remained committed to an ever-growing AIAW. All signs indicated, if not a verbal identification with them, then at least a practical dedication to the principles of feminism.

They still had some problems with the word *equality*, however. The mainstream liberal branch of the women's movement concentrated on achieving equality, and the law (through the Fourteenth Amendment and Title IX) kept the focus there.[167] To many people, equality implied sameness, and there lay the problem. Since for five decades women in PE had criticized much of what men in athletics did, they understandably had reservations about jumping blindly into this movement. "Must the Women's Rights movement demand for our young girls a share in the things that are wrong in sports today as well as a share in the rights in order fully to prove equality?" rhetorically asked one of the foremothers.[168] Better for women to keep their programs small, poor, and obscure, she believed, than to sell out to equality's promises of money, power, and exposure, if that equality were to be tainted by unethical values.

Naturally, the promise of Title IX sorely tempted them. Although women physical educators had been indoctrinated in the alternative values of their subculture, they could not escape living in the larger culture and sharing to some degree in its values. Women wanted their share of spacious lockers, clean uniforms, travel, trainers, and new tennis racquets. But besides that, they wanted the social benefits. They longed for acceptance instead of marginality. And beyond acceptance, they hoped for the rewards—attention and glory—granted male athletes who displayed the talent, single-mindedness, self-sacrifice, and courage it takes to be successful. At the very least, they wanted respect. Now women had to evaluate all over again: how much of that really was appropriate for athletes? It had been easy to criticize something they had no chance to participate in; but if women got some of the benefits of the male athletic model, might they, too, become apologists for it? If they received money to recruit topnotch players, would they come to disregard the individual student's best interest? If boosters bribed student-athletes to attend their schools, would women coaches look the other way? Would they try to have grades altered? Would they give athletes privileges unavailable to other students? The possibility of equality issued a challenge for women in athletics. Besides garnering the courage to fight for acceptance and their rights, they had to struggle with decisions about what *sort* of opportunity they wanted for women.

It would have been easier, or less complicated at least, to ignore those ethical questions. They could simply have rejoiced over the additional resources for women's sports and quietly delighted in a larger slice of the athletic pie. Instead, they rejected a narrow definition of "equality" (one that simply meant "sameness"). They chose to insist upon *both* greater opportunities for women *and* the right to define the nature of those opportunities. They refused to sacrifice their voice for a more equal share in male-defined sports. They wanted to retain their power, their right to choose what seemed best for them. Very likely that would not mean adopting wholesale the norm that was already there. "The athletic model designed and perpetrated by men pervades schools and society; and it is, in part, a repellent one," Jan Felshin declared. "Women cannot, in good conscience, enter a struggle for the prize of brutality, authority, or the exploitation of young athletes."[169]

The educators' insistence upon their right to self-determination was a difficult decision. It would mean facing up to major, as yet unspecified, change. It would mean scrutinizing their own personal attitudes and then negotiating with other women what was desirable among the old attitudes and synthesizing them with the new opportunities. Perhaps most difficult, for women who felt socially stigmatized and vulnerable, it might mean abandoning their traditional quiescence and risking confrontation with leaders of men's sports. Whatever they called themselves—feminist or not—the choice to strive for self-determination was the most radical and feminist one they possibly could have made.

Ultimately, women physical educators kept faith in their ability to create a superior approach to sports. Many believed their alternative would probably combine the strengths of men's and women's programs. "Men's athletics," AIAW president Carole Oglesby explained, "have had a tradition of overemphasis on excellence to the degree that it becomes an end that justifies any means. But here are women's programs that have been very student-oriented, moderately balanced, but kind of mediocre. I think they can come together."[170] Competition should be encouraged, she thought, yet kept in perspective. At a NAGWS coach's convention, Betty Menzie put forward a similarly dialectical vision:

> Sport can be viewed without overemphasis on winning, but with winning being a part of the game. Sport can be a place where all participants can be winners, where losing the contest does not demean or degrade. Sport can maintain its integrity and value for the participant and not be used solely as a show or a spectacle.[171]

According to Menzie, sport designed for the good of the participants still could be entertaining, but more beneficial to individuals. Athletes could feel the joy of play and reap satisfaction from pursuing excellence. They could gain self-knowledge, maturity, and self-discipline.

This ideal would also be less gendered. Women athletic leaders recognized that American sport often glorified being physically strong, hard-nosed, and individualistic, and that many females shied away from it precisely because of those supposedly "masculine" traits. But sport need not be looked at in only that way. Athletic performance also required grace, cooperation, and self-restraint (e.g., "sacrifice bunts"), attributes valued in women. Why could not society redefine what was important about sport so that women need not worry they were doing something wrong? Why not point out to males that with teamwork they were learning to be sensitive and cooperative as well as competitive? And why not reexamine all behavior in sport and see whether it helped teach and develop the type of human beings our society wanted?[172] "We need to look at *human* behavior in sport," argued Dorothy Harris. "I have yet to find anyone who will identify a behavior characteristic that should be reinforced in one half of the human race but not in the other half."[173] With a more humanistic perspective, males and females alike could be comfortable as athletes.

Establishing the humanistic/educational model implied displacing the current one. Women leaders planned to "invite the men to reexamine and redirect their programs," but they suspected that those men in power probably would decline such an invitation.[174] However, women were enjoying a unique historical chance to promote their alternative. Feminism's increasing influence and government backing of Title IX gave women's athletic leaders more potential power than ever before. More clearly than most, Jan Felshin realized that male leaders of intercollegiate sports had begun to worry that women's influence might destroy the status quo. But she made no attempt to assuage their fears: "Men have excluded women from sport because they recognized that it would be changed by them. Let us hope that it will be and that the half of the budget women take will be the half that supported corruption."[175]

While Felshin acknowledged the threat she posed, she believed that women's alternative ultimately would not harm male athletes but instead save them. While she hoped to banish the dominant form of sport, what she would replace it with would be better for all. Joan Hult shared her belief that women physical educators were the most likely party to achieve real change in intercollegiate sports. Women must act, she insisted, "if competitive athletics for boys or girls is going to meet the acid test of an educationally sound experience."[176] She certainly welcomed society's offer of better opportunities for females, but insisted upon helping define those opportunities. Female athletes were entitled to something more than sameness. "The issue is the right of women to full participation in a domain that has the potential for the finest human actualization," Felshin claimed.[177] Like suffragists in the early part of the century, then, many women in PE looked beyond the goal of integration into a male-dominated arena to that of reforming that arena with their purifying vision. At times, their faith in women's power to revitalize the athletic world sounded millennialistic, as when Bonnie Parkhouse exhorted her colleagues, "If we accept the challenge, the competitive sporting world, for us, is the beginning. If we remain reticent, it's the end."[178]

This remarkably optimistic language, with its assumption of entitlement, indicates what a sea change had occurred within just a few years. Many women in PE evolved from quiet, almost invisible advocates of a conservative brand of sports to strenuous promoters of more extensive, woman-defined, competitive opportunities. In part the change resulted from a new social and political context. In the 1950s and 1960s, women physical educators had been the only ones really interested in whether female college students got the chance to compete, and they had labored in anonymity. The one positive aspect of anonymity was that it had allowed them some freedom to run things as they saw fit. Although constrained by extreme resource limitations and by worries about what was feminine, women had been making the decisions for their own programs and tightly controlled them in an alternative from the male model. In the 1960s, deciding to give more attention to gifted athletes and intercollegiate sports, they had formed CIAW. When CIAW's rapid expansion required a new organization, they created AIAW, and that decision had been theirs alone. In the early 1970s, though, the women's movement and Title IX changed everything. New attention to equity and fairness for women made an enormous difference, since it legitimated their efforts. Unfortunately, it also meant new, formidable actors— like the U.S. Congress and the NCAA—entered the arena of college women's sports. Because these actors did not necessarily share women PE leaders' values, power struggles began in earnest. It meant the beginning of a new era.

Women in PE had been cautiously increasing opportunities for college women before Title IX was passed, but the new political context accelerated the changes. The emphasis on equality forced them to reassess whether in matters like scholarships they really wanted to imitate the male model. Clinging to their alternative vision of sports, initially they felt ambivalent about Title IX. They would have embraced the law eventually, but opposition from male athletic leaders forced them into defense of it rather quickly. The more men criticized Title IX and dug in their heels resisting change, the more women realized they must seize this rare chance. They quickly mobilized to counter the twofold attack by the NCAA—on the legislative front, the attempt to cheat female athletes out of the law's promises of equality; on the organizational front, the plan to take over women's sports. These threats to their domain politicized otherwise cowed, conservative women.

The women's liberation movement, whether they liked it or not, had influenced everyone who administered sports. Equality was the new watchword— the goal of Congress and the federal bureaucracy—although no one yet knew what it would mean. Equality worried Walter Byers, so much so that he foresaw the necessity of the NCAA running women's intercollegiate sports. Equality even concerned women in PE, who otherwise would have been thrilled with help for their goal of greater opportunities for women in sport. Ironically, the focus on equality seemed to them a mixed blessing because it potentially endangered their ability to define an alternative model of intercollegiate athletics, and because it brought the possibility of being swallowed whole by the NCAA. Still, equality brought the promise that sportswomen might finally receive the resources and respect male athletes enjoyed, and that hope had to be pursued. Women athletic leaders chose to define the term *equality* in a radical way. Unaccustomed to conflict being played out in the national political arena, they adjusted to the times. Between 1968 and 1974 they had begun, in a difficult and complicated dialectical process, to weave their own traditions of propriety and woman-centeredness into the modern context of equality.

CHAPTER 6

Rebellion:

Women's Pro Tennis, 1968–1975

It's okay for a "girl" to be an athlete (in the proper sports, of course) . . . , but when she becomes a "woman" she'd sure better be ready to get married and return to a "normal" lifestyle, or else. And what follows is that these women shy away from telling other people, like the press, their true feelings about what they're doing because they don't want to risk criticism. I understand that. It's a natural reaction.

I like being a career woman and I love being an athlete. I *love* it. But I'm not the only one. More and more women are proud of themselves for having chosen a tennis career, and I wish some of these other players, especially the younger ones who still say to me, "You tell 'em how you feel, Billie, and we'll follow," would come out and tell 'em themselves.

—Billie Jean King (1974)

No one is more identified with the movement for women's sports opportunities than Billie Jean King.[1] King's battle differed somewhat from women in intercollegiate athletics because she strove to make it possible for women tennis players to succeed as professionals in a particular sport. Yet when she denounced the sexism that made them feel "abnormal" and vulnerable to criticism for wanting an athletic career, King was drawing upon the common experience of adult women in sports. They all were well aware of their reputation as "musclebound, Amazonian jerks."[2] In the early 1970s, however, King found that her culture was changing. She believed she could break the silence and speak unabashedly of her love of sports. King belonged to a transitional generation that still had one foot in the old world where female athletes needed to be apologetic, and the other foot in a modern setting where women influenced by the feminist movement thought they should be treated better. Armed with a new sense of their worth, they began to stand up for themselves. Unlike college athletic leaders, women tennis pros did not wage their battles in Congress and the federal bureaucracy. But like them, King and her associates struggled with notions of equality and difference, grappled with a male-dominated hegemonic organization, and ultimately created their own opportunities.

When she was growing up in the 1950s (she was born in 1943), Billie Jean Moffitt could not have imagined she'd have an illustrious career in tennis. For one thing, she did not play tennis until she was almost eleven. Before then, she played softball with girls and football with boys in her neighborhood. Although possessing terrible eyesight, she was obviously a very gifted and competitive athlete. She dreamed of becoming a professional baseball player until it dawned on her that no women were in the major leagues. As she grew older, her mother forbade her to play football, and her father informed her that the only acceptable sports for girls were swimming, golf, and tennis. Like Alice Marble, Althea Gibson, and countless others before her, then, King chose to direct her athleticism to the relatively feminine arena of tennis. Her family did not belong to any country clubs (her father was a fireman), so Billie Jean Moffitt learned the game in the public parks of Long Beach, California. Once she took up the sport, she loved it. By the time she was fourteen, she was fantasizing about winning Wimbledon. Still, she did not envision much of a career since she did not see any women earning a living at tennis. In her fantasy, she planned on competing internationally for a couple of years, then retiring to settle down with a husband and four children.[3]

In real life she did go on to marry Larry King, but in other respects she defied conventions. Billie Jean King did not quite fit in with the tennis establishment. She was a little too poor, ambitious, and outspoken. As she rose in the ranks in the 1960s, King became disillusioned with the hypocrisy of the "amateur" game, in which the top players were paid under the table. She saw nothing wrong with competing for money and wanted to do so openly. The leaders of USLTA saw such ambition as contradictory to the ideals of the game and, after King publicly criticized the system, threatened her with suspension.[4] Already irritated that the USLTA had denied her a chance to compete overseas (where players made more money), the warning only made her more disgruntled. Why should that group have so much control over her destiny? Adding to her alienation, King thought tennis was too elitist. She wanted to see the game opened up to players from less wealthy backgrounds and for it to become popular with a mass audience. She believed it was in the game's best interests, as well as her own, to "get it away from the club atmosphere and into the public places, the parks, arenas like Madison Square Garden. You've got to get tennis into places where everyone feels welcome."[5]

Fortunately for her, King came along at an opportune moment in tennis history—the system of "shamateurism" was crumbling. In part this was happening because tennis was following the professionalization trend in sports during the twentieth century. The upper-class amateur ethic belonged to a different era; gentlemen athletes rarely existed anymore, and players needed to be paid. More and more top male players refused to go along with the old system, and when a large group of them formed an independent professional tour, the amateur governing bodies read the handwriting on the wall. In 1967 the British Lawn Tennis Association realized that its tournaments soon would be featuring no-names if they did not welcome professionals. Therefore it announced that amateurs and professionals would no longer be barred from competing against each other. The International Lawn Tennis Federation (ILTF), the worldwide governing body of tennis, and the USLTA followed suit, meaning that the tennis establishment no longer upheld the pretense of pure amateurism, and that "professional" would no longer be a dirty word. Money would become a more explicit force in tennis circles, and players had permission to make tennis a career.

"Open tennis" threw the tennis world into disarray. All the stars immediately declared themselves professionals, and the larger tournaments like Wimbledon, the French nationals, and the U.S. nationals began awarding prize money in order to attract them. Some of the smaller clubs were unwilling or unable to pay the purses, and their traditional tournaments vanished. In their wake, however, other opportunities began springing up. Billie Jean King, for example, signed on for two years with three other women and six men to play in something called the National Tennis League.[6] No one knew exactly what other sorts of opportunities the open market would bring, nor who would be the ones offering them. The USLTA had always been the governing body for amateurs in the United States, and country clubs had run the tournaments. Now USLTA's authority was eroding, and players were beginning to shift their loyalties. Agents and promoters began cropping up, promising big payoffs from corporate money.

Although it would take a while for questions of opportunity and authority to be settled, one thing did become clear fairly quickly—that the new system, like the old, would not treat women very well. Now that everyone competed openly for publicized prizes, women found out exactly how little they were valued. In Europe the ratio of men's prize money to women's was two and a half to one, and in the United States it was usually four or five to one. Not too many women grumbled at first, since they were grateful for having any professional opportunities. Their viewpoint changed, however, when in September 1970 the purse for the Pacific Southwest Championship was announced. The winner of the men's competition would receive $12,500, and the women's champ $1,500, a ratio of eight to one. To make matters worse, a female player would receive nothing unless she reached the quarterfinals, not even her expenses.[7]

This relative deprivation catalyzed the players. "If they had given the women half of what they gave men, I think we probably would have accepted it," remembered player Ceci Martinez. "But we felt the men were taking over."[8] The women pros felt they soon might be squeezed out altogether. A few suggested boycotting the tournament, but that seemed too risky. Besides, then they would miss out on one of the few chances to win money. Instead, they aired some of their grievances at a press conference and privately approached Jack Kramer, the director of the Pacific Southwest tourney. They asked him to increase the women's share to one-quarter of the men's.[9]

Kramer was unsympathetic, believing the ratio was exactly as deserved. "This wasn't prejudice," he recalled later, "it was just good business. The only prejudice practiced in tennis against women players is by the fans, who have shown repeatedly that they are prejudiced against having to watch women play tennis when they might be able to watch men." Kramer conceded that there were a few exceptional women who drew spectators, but in general, "people get up and go get a hotdog or go to the bathroom when the women come on." He was not the bad guy, he insisted—the *marketplace* dictated that 75 to 90 percent of a mixed tournament's purse should go to men. "That is fair enough."[10]

Rebuffed by Kramer, female players looked elsewhere. Fortunately, they could turn to Gladys Heldman. As the founder and editor of *World Tennis* magazine, a former player, parent of a top woman player, and longtime wealthy patron of the game, Heldman knew the ins and outs of tennis. She also knew how to make the game pay, and her skill as a promoter came in handy.[11] Heldman decided to help the women by organizing a different tournament— one for women only—to be held in Houston the same week as the Pacific Southwest. This tournament would have a purse of $7,500, part of which would come from ticket sales and from the Houston Racquet Club. Virginia Slims, a subsidiary of the Philip Morris company, which made cigarettes marketed for women, gave $2,500. Joseph Cullman, chairman of the board at Philip Morris, was happy to sponsor a women's tennis tournament. Besides being a friend of Heldman's and a fan of women's tennis, Cullman had been an ardent supporter of black civil rights and sympathized with the women's movement. To the players the Houston tournament seemed like an ideal solution to their problem; it was less dramatic or confrontational than a boycott, gave them a choice of places to compete, and made more money available to all of them. Seven of the world's top ten signed up.[12]

The officials of USLTA were not pleased. A few days before the Houston Virginia Slims Invitational was to begin, they informed Heldman that USLTA would not grant a "sanction" to the tournament because it could not sanction two open tournaments in the same week. (A sanction was permission to hold a tournament.) Heldman protested that there was no such precedent and that the decision arbitrarily singled out the women. Rejecting her appeal, USLTA offered a compromise: it would sanction the Virginia Slims tournament as an *amateur* event. When the players declined that deal, USLTA threatened to suspend the Houston Racquet Club and all the women competitors. Then the players decided to try using a loophole in the rules, but USLTA rejected that effort.[13] As soon as the tournament began, it suspended Heldman's "original nine" contract pros. This meant they were not eligible for USLTA ranking, could not play in USLTA-sanctioned tournaments, and could not compete as U.S. representatives on the prestigious Wightman and Federation Cup teams.[14]

Already suspended, the small band of rebels decided to continue their defiance. After all, being prohibited from USLTA-sanctioned tournaments did not mean much since there were few scheduled for women pros that winter and spring. Therefore the nine agreed to continue their alliance with Heldman. She arranged a number of other tournaments for them to play in—so that, in effect, they were launching their own independent women's pro tour. For these tournaments the players themselves agreed upon how much money was necessary to survive and set up minimum prize money rules (they started with $10,000 for a sixteen-player draw). Their first hurdle was finding sponsors, a task made difficult since the USLTA opposed them and because conventional wisdom said that women alone would not draw spectators. "The process was agonizingly slow," said Heldman. "I got twenty turn-downs before I got my first 'yes.'" But Cullman's Virginia Slims agreed to sign on as a major sponsor, and other companies eventually made limited commitments. Heldman managed to line up fourteen tournaments over winter–spring 1971, offering a total of $200,000 in prize money. Considering that the total had been $2,000 the previous year, this amount was extraordinary.[15]

Getting sixteen players willing to commit themselves to the tour, thereby risking more trouble with the tennis establishment, proved less difficult. "We knew now that [suspension] might happen again any time," remembered King. "I personally didn't give a damn anymore. I'd had it up to here, and it turned out there were a lot of others who had too." King and Rosie Casals were the ringleaders, and Ann Jones of Great Britain, Françoise Durr of France, and Esme Emanuel of South Africa joined the disgruntled Americans. All had at one time had run-ins with their national associations.[16]

The most important remaining task was getting fans to come out and watch. This was not something they were accustomed to doing because the old tennis hierarchy had never even wanted to appeal to the masses. Except for a few major events like Forest Hills and Wimbledon, players had usually performed before small crowds at exclusive clubs, mainly for the benefit of club members. King had a different goal, though—that of selling their game to a larger audience. Now they would have to achieve it if they wanted to survive. Therefore they reached out: players personally handed out tickets at K-Marts, stood on the road with placards, gave instructional clinics, visited with fans in the stands, and attended cocktail parties. They played anywhere that would have them. They gave as many interviews to the media as possible, even if it meant going on the radio at 6:00 A.M. after a late evening match. These new duties could be tiring and annoying but seemed to be paying off. "We've got certain obligations [like compulsory news conferences]," said Tory Fretz, "[but] we're making more money than we ever thought possible."[17]

It was also rewarding to be building something from scratch. Freed from the tennis establishment, they had a chance to tinker with some of the game's traditions. "We tried anything that we thought would make our tournaments fun for the spectators—without interfering with the seriousness of the tennis itself—anything at all to get rid of that stuffy, tedious atmosphere most of us felt had always surrounded tennis tournaments," said King.[18] They experimented with different scoring systems to try to cut short dull matches; paid officials and dressed them up like basketball referees; used yellow balls; created a slush fund to help some black players join the tour; abandoned all-white outfits for wildly colorful ones; and encouraged more spectator involvement. Players also expressed themselves more freely on the court. An emotional Rosie Casals once smashed a ball into the stands at a spectator. King pumped her fists in the air when triumphant, screamed at herself to do better, and slapped her thighs when angry. It seemed to be working. *Newsweek* reported how in the old days the women's game had depended solely on "Gorgeous Gussie" Moran's panties for color. Now the tour had lively, intense, angry, and charming characters; it had not only Casals' blue panties and the "interesting effect of Californian Tory Fretz's on-court braless look" but also "flamboyance from King's witty and outspoken comments, Julie Heldman's cries of 'Right on!'"[19]

The Virginia Slims tour achieved moderate success—enough to continue the rebellion and sufficient to show USLTA that the women would not soon be begging for forgiveness. After a few months, USLTA lifted the players' suspensions, and the two sides agreed that in exchange for paying sanctioning fees, Virginia Slims tournaments could receive USLTA's seal of approval. Moreover, the rebellious players now were permitted to join a new summer Grand Prix tour.[20] For women tennis pros, 1971 proved to be most profitable. Billie Jean King made headlines as the first female athlete to win over $100,000 in prize money, an impressive enough achievement to earn a phone call from President Nixon.[21]

Harmony was short-lived, however. The USLTA resented the continued independence of certain players (who now played only in tournaments that met their standards). In turn, players became convinced that USLTA (whose forty-odd member Executive Board included only one woman) did not have their best interests at heart. Reasserting its dominance seemed to matter most to USLTA, even if it meant blocking better opportunities for the women. Players felt pressured to avoid Virginia Slims events. Disagreements arose over the amount of sanctioning fees, and USLTA raised them higher and higher. In addition, USLTA refused to sanction some of the Slims tournaments. In one instance, it opposed a Houston event offering a $40,000 purse because it conflicted with a USLTA event worth $4,000. Furthermore, USLTA demanded that the Virginia Slims tour end its policy of having minimum prize money standards, stop scheduling tournaments that conflicted with traditional USLTA events, and get rid of Gladys Heldman. When the "Slimsies" refused to comply, they were again suspended. Another agreement was reached, but it did not last long.[22]

By September 1972 it was all-out war, and players were forced to choose sides. Since it could not simply force the Slims women to come to heel, USLTA decided to try to win them back. For the first time ever, it organized and promoted a full-fledged women's tour of its own—with event dates intentionally conflicting with those of the Virginia Slims tour. It held out two carrots to persuade players to opt for the USLTA tour. The first was the approval of the tennis hierarchy. The second was prize money of almost $220,000, with each tournament awarding at least $20,000. (The Virginia Slims circuit offered $800,000, though, and a minimum purse of $35,000.) Both the president and sanctioning chair of USLTA personally appealed to the Slims competitors to disband and join the USLTA tour. They also hinted darkly about the stick they carried. If the women did not disband, not only would they again be suspended but this time they would be prohibited from playing at Wimbledon and the U.S. Open.[23]

Those already on the Virginia Slims tour decided to take their chances. Partly because USLTA did not directly control Wimbledon, and partly because of their previous success, they voted to stick with Virginia Slims. As a result, even though no one used to think a women-only tour could survive, in 1973 there were *two* women's pro circuits. Billie Jean King and Margaret Court, the world's number one and two players, had top billing on the Virginia Slims tour, accompanied by many other highly ranked American and European names. However, USLTA did manage to persuade two stars to participate in some of its tournaments: Australian Evonne Goolagong and England's Virginia Wade. More conservative than the women on the Slims tour, Goolagong and Wade did not want to commit themselves to playing full time on the Slims circuit and did not want to risk being banned from Wimbledon. In addition, USLTA landed up-and-coming teenager Chris Evert, an amateur whose parents feared bucking USLTA. The conflict caused some ill will between players. Those sticking together on the Slims tour resented what they perceived as the scabs' caution and disloyalty.[24]

No one really wanted the conflict to continue. Neither the players, the Philip Morris company, or USLTA thought two separate tours could survive for long. Two tours diluted the talent, and they agreed women as a whole had better chances of success with all the "name" players together. In addition, players were becoming tired of the uncertainty and of being distracted by politics. As summer approached, defiance grew riskier. The ILTF agreed to back USLTA, and in April ILTF issued an ultimatum: women players had one month to sign a statement that they would play only in tournaments approved by their national associations (such as USLTA). If they didn't, they would not be allowed to play in major tournaments like the U.S. Open and Wimbledon.[25] (This was comparable to an entire industry joining together to stop strikers by blacklisting those in the union.) Almost immediately, the two groups started negotiating. An agreement was hammered out in which the Slims tournaments were accepted and incorporated into USLTA's schedule; with the Slims tournaments approved, its players would be back in good standing and could play in the traditional big-name events like Wimbledon. But the players had to pay a price for peace. They lost Gladys Heldman, with whom USLTA refused to work. Equally important, they lost some autonomy.[26]

Although back under USLTA's authority, the "Slimsies" achieved much of what they wanted. Before splitting with USLTA in early 1971, they had had only a few women-only tournaments, and at mixed tournaments their share of the purse had been getting smaller. Considered unappealing to the fans, they were given little respect. By 1973, however, they were drawing fans everywhere they went, and their winnings increased at least fivefold. When they had started in 1971, their minimum purses were set at $10,000. By 1973 these had increased to $35,000 and, for the 1974 unified USLTA-Slims tour, to $50,000.[27]

These dramatic changes would never have occurred without the women's rebellion. With the dawning of open tennis, USLTA did not offer to help women players and only stood idly by as some traditional tournaments folded and others decreased the amounts of the women's prize money. Worse, rather than helping them find new opportunities, USLTA actively opposed the ones they found. Only *after* Heldman and the women pros went out on their own did USLTA offer them an extensive, financially attractive, and well-promoted tour. But USLTA suddenly seemed to realize that it depended upon its "subjects" at least as much as they needed it. When USLTA tried to put together an American team for the Federation Cup, for example, the only two women available who were not suspended were ranked ninth and nineteenth in the United States. Without its constituency, USLTA was nothing. Therefore it used all the tools at its disposal to retain its dominance. In the end, to regain its authority, it had to make significant concessions. Never again would the relationship between USLTA and the women players be the same. Recognizing that their unity and independence were what caused the improvements, late in 1973 Billie Jean King persuaded over sixty of the top female players worldwide to form a union, the Women's Tennis Association (WTA), a tool to insure negotiating power for the future.[28]

By late 1973 women pros seemed confident of what they wanted and deserved, but they had not started out that way. In the beginning stages of the protest in late 1970, they had not set their sights very high. They had not demanded equal prize money—only a better ratio compared with men, something like five to three or even two to one. Even after they summoned the courage to begin their own independent tournaments, they set the minimum prize money as low as possible, doubting their appeal. (At the time women set the minimum for a field of thirty-two at $18,000, men were asking $50,000 plus expenses at their separate tournaments.)[29] Inexperience partly explained why they underestimated their worth. But in addition, many of the women pros still accepted the old arguments about men deserving more money. Custom said that men should be paid more because they were better players— that is, the best men could easily defeat the best women. Other justifications for men's higher salaries were that sometimes they played longer matches (three out of five instead of two out of three sets), and that men tended to be breadwinners.

Male pros did not take up for their female counterparts. Indeed, whenever a promoter tried to close the earnings gap, men protested that they were taking money out of men's pockets. "Men are playing tennis for a living now. They have families, and they don't want to give up money just for girls to play," explained Arthur Ashe. "Only three or four women draw fans anyhow, so why should we have to split our money with them?"[30] Male players did not see that they had much in common with female pros. Even when they had their own trouble with USLTA and ILTF, they rejected the women's offer to stand with them.[31] Creating a women-only tour helped avoid the issue of reducing men's prize money but did not make some of the sexist male players any more sympathetic. Of the separate Virginia Slims tour, male pro Clark Graebner said: "I'm just as happy never to see the girls. They're not very attractive, and I think it's strange for any wife to be away from her husband on a tennis tour for nine weeks at a time. I wouldn't want my daughter playing on the tour."[32]

With time, however, women players grew more confident of their worthiness and discovered how to respond to arguments that they deserved less. A subtle ideological shift had made it possible for them to start asking not merely for a more just distribution of prize money but for an *equal* share. Shrewdly, the women pros shifted the terms of the argument: they asserted women pros were equally capable *entertainers*. "For two years we've outdrawn the men at Forest Hills by whatever criteria they've used," King claimed, "but this year the men's money was 2½ times the women's."[33] She said fans didn't care how hard a player hit or how fast one ran—what counted was the drama. In boxing, for example, a middleweight champ like Sugar Ray Leonard could not defeat a heavyweight, but an evenly matched bout of his was very exciting. Similarly, the

Virginia Slims tour had the best female tennis players in the world—the best in their own category—and were proving their entertainment value. They insisted they were equally professional. "We expend the same amount of energy as the men," declared Rosie Casals. "We practice as much. We play just as hard. We contribute our share to the success of a tournament." As to the issue of men sometimes playing longer matches, they dismissed that issue too. For one thing, it had been USLTA that originally had forced women to play two out of three sets. Besides, the length of the match did not much matter. "Sometimes a shorter opera is much better than a long one," agreed tennis writer Bud Collins. In fact, some women argued that in general women's matches were more interesting to fans precisely because women lacked the strength and booming serves of the men. Their rallies were longer and had more suspense, and women usually depended more upon strategy and a variety of shots to win their points. And, as King claimed, "I can hit any shot in the book that [male champ Rod] Laver can."[34]

These new arguments were a new way for female athletes to address an old problem. Like the leaders of AIAW, women tennis pros were struggling to fashion a way to get comparable treatment even if their situation was not identical to men. The conventional dualistic trap said that men and women were either the same or different; and if they were different, women should not be treated equally. Shifting the grounds of the debate to entertainment avoided or "deconstructed" the dualism. It took women out of their no-win situation in which they either had to be the "same" as men (and lose their femininity) or "different" (and be considered inferior). In this new framework they could be different in some ways yet also deserving of comparable benefits. Their differences need not be considered deficits, nor reason for depriving them.

In some ways, this new emerging stance served a similar function to apologetic behavior. It tried to gain acceptance for their "nonfeminine" behavior while acknowledging women's differences. But compared to athletes in the 1950s, the modern pros postulated fewer differences between men and women. In addition, their stance differed from apologetic behavior in its tone. Instead of timidly hoping for it, they declared that women athletes deserved acceptance. Like feminists, they were moving toward the belief that they had *rights*—in this case, to do sports and still be appreciated and accepted as normal women.

But this new position was only just emerging in the early 1970s; it had not replaced apologetic behavior altogether. Although apparently in decline, traditional methods of trying to be accepted as an athlete *and* a normal woman were still in use. Some (although fewer) players still downplayed the importance of their tennis careers—especially in comparison to becoming wives and mothers. (Evonne Goolagong said she would rather talk about her children than her tennis.) Some still let the public know they did not want masculine-looking bodies. "I would not like to have a big serve because I fear for [the appearance of] my shoulders, and I would never lift weights," explained Françoise Durr. And implying one's heterosexuality remained especially important. The homosocial environment in which women competed and traveled together could be considered detrimental to one's femininity. Virginia Wade protected her own reputation (and cast aspersions on the other athletes) when she shunned the women-only Virginia Slims tour:

> It doesn't do girls any good to be stuck around together all the time. They become desexed, a terrible thing. It's easy to get caught up, not caring how you look, and lose the good points of one's sex. I'd rather win half as much money and enjoy myself completely.[35]

Being "true" to one's sex was sometimes more important to Wade than being the best athlete she could be.

In their conscious choice of how to present themselves, the pros echoed their predecessors and combined elements of the apologetic. They strove to look good—which meant projecting a feminine appearance, which usually meant appealing to men. "I would never wear shorts in a match," said one player. "I would feel like a slob. I think that most women look better in dresses because that compliments their figures better."[36] Wendy Overton agreed. "I think it's important as an athlete to maintain an air of femininity. We should look nice out there. We're entertainers, people are watching our actions."[37] Reportedly appalled by the way some of the women looked, Joseph Cullman hired designer Ted Tinling (who had created "Gorgeous Gussie" Moran's panties) to work for the tour. Not all of Tinling's creations put practicality first. Val Ziegenfuss wore a heavy skirt of white sequins as well as a halter dress whose top was black velvet with a skirt of silver lamé. "Can you imagine sweating and playing tennis in velvet?" she laughed. "But we were putting on a show. We were trying to put people in the stands."[38] Indeed, according to Tinling, women's tennis needed to use sex appeal to survive. "I put sin into tennis," he boasted. "Tennis couldn't finance itself purely as a sport. It had to turn into a spectacle, and you must pay your debts to the spectators who keep it alive."[39] Clearly many players believed him and went along.

No one on the tour displayed more apologetic behavior than Chris Evert. Evert sometimes went out of her way to downplay the importance of the game to her, once declaring, "No point is worth falling down over."[40] She wore very traditionally feminine dresses, hair ribbons, bright nail polish, and a lot of makeup during her matches "because I thought it would make me look more attractive and feminine for . . . the spectators."[41] She believed both she and the game needed her to be feminine:

That's the one thing women's tennis has, is femininity. If women looked like men or played like men it would be boring. I know some women who lift weights. . . . But even if it made me stronger I'd never do it. It's important to look feminine—for your self-confidence.[42]

Evert did everything she could think of to emphasize her girl-next-door, "normal" female image and endorsed only products that reinforced that image. Her heterosexual romances were well-publicized; at age sixteen she knew well the unflattering stereotypes about women jocks and had announced she wanted to be married by age twenty-six. "[Tennis is] fun now but the penalties you must pay in your social life must eventually tell on you." Not surprisingly, she also said, "I'd rather be known in the end as a woman than a tennis player."[43]

Evert did not mind that her remarks made feminists cringe. Nor was she the only one on the tour distancing herself from the women's liberation movement. Of the "original nine" pros, King estimated that maybe half were feminists.[44] Journalist Grace Lichtenstein was keenly disappointed with the players' lack of understanding of the women's movement, discovering they were jocks first and foremost. Even among those who led the rebellion and shared the developing feminist ideology, there was some reluctance to call themselves "feminist." "Most of them would never say they were, because they felt it was a negative connotation," explained King. "Even though a lot of the women lived up to [feminist ideals] and really strived for [them], if push comes to shove, I don't think they liked to be known as feminists."[45] When asked about their fight with USLTA over a sanction for the first Virginia Slims tournament, King wanted it seen simply as a tennis fairness issue. "This is not a women's liberation movement. It's professional tennis. If you get money for a sport, you should be labeled a pro."[46] In 1972 she said, "The crux [of the women's tennis tour] has nothing to do with Women's Lib."[47] Others also downplayed the connection. Gladys Heldman said the women "are just protecting themselves." (But she also joked, "You've heard of women's lib. This is women's lob.")[48]

Only part of the reason for disassociating themselves was ideological. King herself was not sure about the wider political issues. Her first reaction to feminists was that they were too dogmatic and too liberal.[49] Over time, though, King came to support women's lib.[50] But even then, she remained wary about whether to call herself a feminist. Everywhere she went she was asked whether she was a feminist, and before she answered she usually asked people what they meant by the term, because she thought people did not necessarily oppose her positions but had a negative image of a feminist: "She is a bra burner, she doesn't like to take care of herself, she may not wear makeup. . . . If a woman's [a] feminist she is not feminine."[51]

The women pros had good reason to worry about how they came across. Their tour was a new product, and they were dependent on the public's positive feelings. They feared that if they were perceived as too caustic and demanding, no would come to see them. There was some evidence supporting that theory. To her dismay, King discovered that as a "woman's leader" some people expected her to possess no gentleness and to be ugly and a "shrew."[52] Being an aggressive athlete was bad enough, but being a feminist opened her up to even more criticism. When it became known she had had an abortion, she received anonymous letters calling her a killer, and she said that "grim period" was, up to then, the worst of her life. There were "vicious" comparisons between her and Margaret Court, who had recently become a mother.[53] She also was very aware that the more outspoken players were contrasted with the more docile ones like Evert. Even if King tried apologetic behavior, it did not dispel her "tough-broad image." For example, although she always wore jewelry on the court, nobody ever mentioned it because it contradicted preconceptions of her. "But if Chris [Evert] wore earrings, everyone mentioned that."[54]

If players assumed that it was important to fit in with audience's "comfort zone" in order for the tour to survive, the press's treatment sometimes reinforced that belief.[55] Indeed, journalists raved about Chris Evert's femininity, writing about her blonde good looks, her teenage romances, and calling her "Miss America in a tennis dress."[56] In praising and giving so much attention to factors irrelevant to her athleticism, they gave her plenty of reason to continue her apologetic behavior. For example, New York Times sports columnist Dave Anderson spent most of his article about Evert's 1975 semifinal match at the U.S. Open on a detailed description of how she looked. As she "perched prettily on a metal folding chair," he noted, "some queens don't look as good on a throne." He marveled that Evert could look so good—and not after coming from the hairdresser's but from center court at Forest Hills.

> Her long fingernails were polished a pale pink. She wore a small diamond on a gold chain around her neck and silver earrings, pierced. Against her streaked blonde hair and golden tan, her eyelashes were so dark they appeared to have been dipped in an ink well.
>
> "Most women," somebody observed, "would be afraid that sweat would make that eye stuff run."
>
> "But she doesn't sweat," someone else said. "Look at her. Not a drop of perspiration."[57]

Although it was absurd to expect an athlete not to sweat, Anderson praised Evert for exactly that beauty shop appearance. "Part of her appeal is that she always looks like a female."

Male sportswriters demonstrated that old notions died slowly. In *Sports Illustrated* Edwin Shrake expressed surprise that the women on the Virginia Slims tour met with his approval.

> They were an amazingly good-looking group of people, especially when one thought of the stereotype of the woman athlete. Nobody had a beard. Nobody looked or sounded like Ernest Borgnine. The ones who weren't still in sweat suits from a morning of practice were thoughtfully dressed . . . Nobody waddled, not a lumberjack in the group.[58]

Backhanded compliments could be worse than none. Clearly athletes still had the onus of *proving* their normal femininity or else hear the long-standing innuendoes about being masculine and abnormal. After King lost her temper at a tournament, sportswriter Jim Murray of the *Los Angeles Times* suggested she was unnatural. "King has never forgiven Nature," he wrote, "for the dirty trick it played on her in preventing her from being free safety for the Green Bay Packers."[59] There was still a line female athletes could not cross without risking ridicule.

In particular, the association continued that the female athlete—who was not "normal," "natural," or "feminine"—was a lesbian. As if the players were not already aware of the stereotypical equation, reporters reminded them by regularly inquiring about the sexual preferences of those on the tour.[60] This was an issue even more sensitive and complicated than feminism. Players feared that being considered lesbian in a society intolerant of homosexuality could irrevocably harm the budding tour. Theoretically, they could have set out to educate the press and their fans, correcting the various misconceptions behind the athlete=abnormal=unfeminine=lesbian equation: that female athleticism was not abnormal; that female athletes were not necessarily unfeminine; that being unfeminine was not necessarily abnormal; that a so-called unfeminine woman not necessarily lesbian and that lesbians were not necessarily unfeminine; and that lesbianism not abnormal. But female players were in no position to be tackling such entrenched attitudes. They were trying to sell their new tour, and being independent female athletes seemed risky enough.

Instead, women tennis pros hoped to avoid the issue. Understandably, they did not want discussions about homosexuality to distract from their primary work—which was winning acceptance for female pro tennis players. Peripheral issues could undermine the tour, just as red-baiting slowed the civil rights movement and the lesbian question was serving to divide the women's movement. So women on the tour adopted various strategies. Some players let it be known they resented the stereotype and the fact that they had to endure questions about sexuality that male athletes were not subjected to. "When two men share a room at the Gloucester hotel for Wimbledon, it's accepted as the buddy system," protested Evert. "[But let] two women try to defray their expenses the same way and the rumor mill starts grinding."[61] As in the women's movement (or anywhere), of course, there *were* some lesbians on the tour, and absolute denial potentially could backfire in face of the truth. So others acknowledged that there were some lesbians in tennis just as there were in any professional field. Whoever said so never allowed the possibility that she might be one of them, however. Both lesbian and straight players hinted or made explicit reference to their own heterosexual love lives, some true, some not.[62] Some said nothing. Some lesbians lived very closeted lives and carefully avoided allowing any evidence of the truth to surface.

But resenting, denying, implying heterosexuality, and hiding did nothing to address the root of the problem, nor to attack the illogical unfairness of the equation; in effect, women players remained on the defensive. Hoping to keep the issues separate made sense pragmatically in the short-term because they needed to get the tour on solid ground. (But since no lesbians "came out" in the early 1970s it's impossible to know whether they overestimated the fallout.) Ultimately, acceptance as women athletes and acceptance of lesbians could not be separated. The stigmatization of female athletes as lesbians was part and parcel of the same dualistic thinking (and misogyny) that was unwilling to accept women athletes as normal women. The "lesbian" label was a means of social control used against any woman who ventured too far outside strictly defined gender roles.[63] The issue was not how many lesbians actually were on the tour; what was threatening was that *all* the women pros were breaking ground. In order to be truly free, players needed to reject the notion that the lesbian label was an insult. The common cause of women depended on the acceptance of all women, whether they were aggressive, competitive, competent, angry, strong, feminist, lesbian, black, working class, disabled, or any combination. Tennis pros in the early 1970s did not feel secure enough to stand up and assert, "We're everything you most feared we were and we still have the right to be that" or to ask rhetorically, "So what if we were all lesbians?" To claim their rights as athletes yet to be so defensive on this one issue, as though they had something to be ashamed of, was odd (if understandable). But by not challenging the stereotype, a segment of the pros had to conceal their full identity and to sacrifice freedom in one area of their lives in the hope of achieving it in another. In addition, all women on the tour—straight and gay—lived in fear that any lesbians on the tour might be "exposed."

Although there was reason to be cautious, there actually were certain advantages to being a bold woman in the 1970s. One was attention. The women's liberation movement gripped the American public; it raised fundamental issues that almost everyone had to deal with somewhere (in the workplace, school, kitchen, bedroom, church), and it was constantly in the news. Some people loved feminists, and others hated them, but few were indifferent. And if there's one thing a budding professional sport needs, it's interest. Controversy actually could help. If people were curious (and even if they wanted to heckle), at least they might come to watch.

People became fascinated with Billie Jean King. Portrayed as an example of the new liberated woman, magazines interviewed her not only because she was a great athlete but because she had modern views (she had chosen a career, an abortion, and a modern marriage). For her unconventional attitudes, King received some hate mail but many more letters from the sorts of women whom the movement deeply touched. Women who had never told anyone about their abortions; women who were grateful that King, at least, fought for her worth; women who had been forced to give up "unfeminine" activities; and women who had felt ashamed for loving athletics—all wrote her as though they personally knew her.[64] Although crowds loved Evert's nonthreatening style, they might never have noticed her had not King first demanded that female athletes be paid attention to. They may have preferred their children to grow up like Evert, but they also showed interest in the defiant Rosie Casals, who was going to play tennis whether people liked it or not. "If someone says it's not feminine," Casals told a reporter, "I say screw it."[65] Even if the angry young female athletes were perceived as hating men, an enterprising publicist might be able to sell that connotation. A poster for a 1973 Washington D.C. women's tournament grabbed attention with its caption: "Ball Busters." The manufacturers of Virginia Slims cigarettes also believed a market existed out there that identified with the new independent woman. Its slogan was, "You've Come a Long Way, Baby."[66]

Bobby Riggs, for one, discovered that one could profit from all the interest in gender-role conflict. A gifted athlete, Riggs had played both amateur and professional tennis (he won Wimbledon in 1939), and he still competed on a senior circuit. A betting man, he was a ham and a hustler. He boasted of clever subtle tricks he used to get an advantage—things like making an opponent walk far away to pick up balls when he's tired, or hitting balls high when he had to look in the sun. These strategies—known as "gamesmanship"—were not considered good sportsmanship but could make the difference between winning and losing.[67] In 1973 Riggs was trying to drum up interest in men's senior tennis, in part by claiming that senior men were better than the women. Discovering that a lot of people paid attention to him when he lambasted women athletes and feminists, Riggs got the idea of challenging someone on the women's tour to a match, preferably Billie Jean King. "The women only play about 25 percent as good as the men," he declared. "Their best player couldn't even beat an old man like me."[68] A San Diego real estate developer put up $5,000 for the winner, but then a television network raised the payoff to $10,000 plus bonuses for the winner. King declined the offer, thinking no good could come of it, especially for the budding tour. "If we played and I won, so what? I beat someone twenty-five years older than me. If I lost, Bobby would carry that Male Chauvinist Pig thing on forever."[69] Bobby kept looking for takers, though, and when he made a similar offer to Margaret Court, the top-ranked woman player, she thought it sounded like good money and accepted.

Promoters highlighted the drama of pitting man versus woman, and the Riggs-Court match, held on Mother's Day 1973, attracted an unexpectedly large television audience. Unfortunately for Court, it became known as the "Mother's Day Massacre." Court appeared nervous, perhaps flustered by Riggs's theatrics (he kissed her, gave her roses). Riggs thought she succumbed to his gamesmanship. For weeks he had been referring to Court's history of "choking" (folding in tense situations). Afterwards he boasted he had managed to get the match started before Court was in sync.[70] For whatever reason, Court did not play her usual game, looked terrible, and lost 6–2, 6–1. "That was my worst day," she later sorrowfully recalled, "and unfortunately it happened with the whole world watching."[71]

But the matter did not end there. The match made Riggs an instant celebrity, and he received offers for imitation challenges and appearances on sitcoms and talk shows. Promoter Jerry Perenchio, who had staged the George Forman–Muhammad Ali $20 million extravaganza earlier in the year, had been watching the Riggs-Court match on television. "When it came on, the whole town stopped. Everyone was turned on by the match. Women bet on Margaret Court. Men bet on Bobby Riggs. And I said to myself, 'This isn't tennis—it's something bigger.'"[72] Enamored with the possibilities, Perenchio encouraged Riggs to challenge King again. Women on the pro tour had been embarrassed by Court's poor showing, feeling it reflected poorly on all of them. They did not want her performance to be taken as representative. This time when Riggs proposed a Perenchio-promoted $100,000 "winner-take-all" match (plus a share of $300,000 in endorsements), King agreed. Riggs gleefully announced, "We said we had the Match of the Century the last time. But obviously we had the wrong girl. We should have had the women's lib leader, Billie Jean."[73]

The contest pitting Riggs against King became a much bigger spectacle, supposedly representing the age-old struggle of Man versus Woman. Riggs hyped the match by accelerating his antifeminist rhetoric. Statements like "a woman's place is in the bedroom and the kitchen, in that order" got him publicity, so he kept repeating them. Using overblown rhetoric resembling that used to promote boxing matches, Riggs tried to get King's goat, psych her out, and whip up controversy. The press followed the exploits of the self-proclaimed sex symbol as he popped hundreds of vitamin pills and cavorted with young women on his arm. "Men all over the world write me fan letters," Riggs claimed. "They want me to put her in her place. I haven't met a man yet that didn't want me to win." (On another occasion, he showed reporters a shirt with the nipples cut out, which he intended to give King because she'd look better in it.)[74] King went along with some of the hype, pleased that a tennis match was getting so much attention but also extremely nervous because so many women's hopes rested on her performance. She believed she had more to lose. "Bobby's just fighting for money. I'm fighting for a cause." Many females hoped King would quiet the chauvinist and prove what women were capable of. Wherever she went, women rooted for her. Even stopping at a supermarket before the match, the cashier told her, "I hope that you beat his pompous ass."[75]

The match lived up to its spectacular billing. The Houston Astrodome, a gigantic stadium, held a rowdy crowd of 30,472. Its setting could not have differed more from the elite country clubs with small genteel audiences where tennis used to be held. There were balloons, bands, and lots of illegal betting (conventional wisdom had it that an adequate male player would beat a first-class woman, and Jimmy the Greek made Riggs a five-to-two favorite). There was not a neutral fan in the arena. Some men wore buttons proclaiming they were "Pigs for Riggs" or shirts asking, "Who Needs Women?" Women yelled "Right on, Billie Jean!" and their buttons read, "Bobby Riggs–Bleah!" It was the largest crowd ever to attend a tennis match, and the television audience was even more impressive. ABC paid $750,000 for the rights to televise it live in prime time (in contrast, NBC had paid a mere $50,000 that year to show Wimbledon). An estimated thirty-seven million people all over the world tuned in to watch their circuslike, well-choreographed entrance. Riggs came in in a ricksha pulled by five women he called his "bosom buddies" and presented King with a large Sugar Daddy sucker ("for the biggest sucker in the world"). King, carried in on an Egyptian-style litter by four bare-chested men, gave Bobby a live baby pig.[76]

After the prematch hoopla, the serious competition began. Ironically, despite the claims that Riggs would represent men and King women, their styles did not fit the generalizations. King played what was traditionally considered a "man's game" of serve and volley, and Riggs the "women's style" of strategy, dinks, chips, and lobs. This time Riggs never got in sync, and King, who was quicker than he expected, chased down whatever he threw at her. Fitter and stronger, King found it surprisingly easy to overpower him. "I also couldn't believe how slow he was," King remembered thinking after the first few games. "I thought he was faking it." By the end, Riggs looked old and weary. King had proven more difficult to unnerve than Court, and it became evident that while Riggs had cavorted, she had prepared in earnest. She had rested (recovering from a recent bout of hypoglycemia), studied Riggs's strategy, worked on a couple of different game plans, and practiced against men. Although very nervous, she was completely ready for Riggs, and she won in three straight sets, 6–4, 6–3, 6–3.[77]

What did the match prove? Certainly nothing about men's and women's relative capacities. Although King had won, everyone knew that Jimmy Connors could soundly defeat King. Nor did it prove anything about the merits of feminism. But neither did the match harm the cause of women's tennis (as it easily might have if she had lost). In fact, it probably helped it. King's victory was a testimony to her willingness to defy the odds and her ability to concentrate in chaotic conditions as well as to perform under enormous pressure. It showed her as a serious competitor, but also (by giving Riggs the pig, joking and kissing him after the match) as one with a sense of humor about gender conflict. In addition, it showed to a huge audience a sight most of them had probably never seen: an extremely competent, muscular female professional tennis player. Her appearance may have corrected some misconceptions about what women were capable of, and it proved inspiring to many females. (People still come up to her and tell her where they were on the memorable night.)[78] King enjoyed the fact that all over the country women reaped some small benefits from her victory— husbands who had to do the dishes, bosses getting coffee for their secretaries, and women who marched into their superior's office to demand a raise. But ultimately, what King thought most valuable about the match was that it exposed a mass audience to the game. (Indeed, tennis underwent an amazing boom in the early 1970s.)[79] "On that night, I think, the game of tennis finally got kicked out of the country clubs forever and into the world of real sports, where everybody could see it." King thought she had proven not only that a woman could defeat a man but that "tennis can be a bigtime sport in the hands of people who know how to promote it."[80]

The attention King received certainly lent credibility to her claim that female pros were valuable entertainers. Tournament officials were beginning to take note, as reflected in the steady gains for women in prize money at mixed tournaments. In 1972, U.S. Open champions Ilie Nastase and Billie Jean King won $25,000 and $10,000, respectively. But by 1973 the gap had closed completely, because female pros had new advocates. Like the companies who increasingly hired stars like Chris Evert to endorse their products, Bristol-Myers, maker of Ban deodorant, clearly thought aiding women's sports was good advertising. It donated $55,000 so that the women's purse would be the same amount as the men's. Its vice president announced, "We feel that the women's game is equally as exciting and entertaining as the men's."[81]

But two years after USLTA's surrender, Wimbledon still held out. The symbol of tennis traditionalism, Wimbledon was the oldest and most prestigious tournament. Playing there was so enjoyable and important to one's reputation that some players had said they would compete there for nothing.[82] Counting on this attitude, the All-England Club, which ran the tournament, believed it need not make any changes. Realizing that the All-England Club had the upper hand, the women pros had refrained from a public protest, only quietly suggesting their share should be increased. They hoped the gentlemen in authority would appreciate their restraint and move toward more equitable purses without pressure. But their patience grew thin in January 1975, when the All-England Club announced the next summer's prize money. Women would enjoy only a tiny increase in their share. The total women's purse would be 60 percent of the men's, with the first place woman scheduled to receive 70 percent of what the top man would win ($16,800 to $24,000).[83] Now the Women's Tennis Association told reporters it was considering a boycott. In response, the secretary of the All-England Club declared, "The prize money has been settled and there will be no alteration."[84]

The WTA decided to call the All-England Club's bluff. King and WTA executive director Jerry Diamond drafted a plan of attack, and 80 percent of the WTA voted to boycott Wimbledon unless the All-England Club made some adjustment. So that individuals could not back out at the last minute, they signed a legal agreement to that effect. In the meantime, Diamond made tentative plans for a new grass court tournament to be held at the same time as Wimbledon at the Tennis Hall of Fame in Rhode Island. He even had a sponsor lined up, who promised a substantial purse. That done, Diamond and King flew to England to negotiate. As Diamond remembered it, at first the All-England Club doubted the women would follow through with their threatened boycott.

> They snickered and said let's wait and see what happens when the time comes. And I said, "No, you don't seem to understand: It's not an emotional issue anymore. The women have signed a contract to play in another tournament, and if they decide they want to play in your tournament we'll legally prevent them from doing so. They have no choice and you have no choice."[85]

The WTA's strategy paid off. As they suspected, Wimbledon officials very much wanted the women at the tournament (and needed the women in order to comply with terms of their television contract). As a result, the All-England Club made significant, immediate concessions. It raised the women's share to 80 percent of the men's total purse, and the women's champion would receive 90 percent of the top male player's prize.

By 1975 the rebellion of women tennis pros could be considered quite a success. In a manner unthinkable even ten years earlier, women pros were toppling (with relative ease) USLTA and the All-England Club. Although they had not achieved equality in all situations, they had done remarkably well. They were in the limelight more than ever before; Billie Jean King made the cover of *Sports Illustrated* and a number of other players had become household names. Top women players now could choose tennis as a career and be well-compensated. Money made an enormous difference. It brought attention, legitimation, and security. Benefits came not just to the stars; a second level of players could survive in the profession.

For the athletes, the significance of being able to have professional careers cannot be underestimated. They gladly seized the opportunity to become more serious, full-time athletes. They trained much harder and played more often than their amateur predecessors.[86] With more chances to compete against the best players, they honed their skills and had the chance to reach their potential. Perhaps the greatest benefit was personal—the modern players felt freer, as though they had more choices and more possibility of being accepted. They now could throw themselves wholeheartedly into the sport they felt passionate about. Billie Jean King struggled to put into words the satisfaction that came from hitting the perfect shot: "I got chills and goose pimples and my heart was pounding." The competition was thrilling and could be empowering. She occasionally experienced "this fantastic, utterly unself-conscious feeling of invincibility."[87] Players from other eras probably had the same feelings, but King's generation had less cause to hide or feel ashamed about them. King appreciated this new societal permission because tennis was so fundamental to her identity. "Tennis is a personal expression on my part, certainly the most complete and maybe the only way I can express myself."[88]

King was not the only one to find joy, meaning, and satisfaction in professional tennis. In the mid-1970s, conservative, apologetic Chris Evert began reassessing her plans to retire young. "There's nothing that would make me happier than to get married to someone and retire from tennis—but *not now*."[89] Enjoying the opportunities won by her trailblazing associates, Evert did not want to give them up. Although outwardly she appeared less threatening, Evert had a lot in common with Billie Jean King. Like Althea Gibson and Sarah Palfrey in the 1950s, inwardly she was a tiger. The most unlikely woman ever to call herself a feminist began sounding a bit like the new, liberated woman. Growing more confident that Americans still would accept her, she eventually said publicly what she had confided to her diary in 1976:

> I love tennis, I love the competition, the sheer challenge of playing to perfection. Always striving to hit a better shot, to be more aggressive, to hit with more power. I'm playing for myself now. I'm experiencing sensations in tennis I've never experienced before. No pressure or nerves. Loose, aggressive, daring, gutty, confident. On the tennis court, I'm my own per-

son. I'm expressing my inner desires and personality. I love tennis. How can I give it up? It's my life.[90]

The drama and rapidity of these changes is especially remarkable given the inherent problems for any women trying to succeed as professional athletes. Unlike the high school and college athletes desiring equal respect and rewards, female pros did not have the force of law behind them. They had no "right" to make a living from sports, no guarantees from Title IX. For that reason, their efforts for equality were especially risky since professional athletes, like professional entertainers, are dependent upon the interest and approval of the public. Given the long history of discrimination against and stigmatizing of female athletes, it would be difficult for them all of a sudden to be popular with masses of spectators. In effect, the audience was already prejudiced against them—expecting either not very talented athletes or, like the *Sports Illustrated* reporter, women who looked like lumberjacks or talked like Ernest Borgnine. They had to sell themselves to an audience assuming they were inferior athletes or abnormal women or both.

With generations of prejudice making the odds long against any professional women athletes, how, then, did the women tennis pros succeed? For one thing, their timing was opportune. The downfall of "shamateurism" created both a power vacuum and uncertainty about the direction of professional tennis. This unusual crack in the armor of tennis authorities coincided with the increasing popularity of tennis. Thousands of beginners took up the game, and the media paid more attention to it. Success also derived from piggybacking upon the women's liberation movement. Whether they openly embraced it or not, feminism supplied disgruntled players with an ideology and the language and model of women insisting on their worth. The women's movement also meant greater attention was paid to the tennis players' rebellion. The public gobbled up stories about the gender conflict, so the press suddenly listened to the players' claims and published Bobby Riggs's rebuttals. That this interest could be capitalized on was illustrated by the "Battle of the Sexes" spectacle and the sponsorship of Virginia Slims.

The openings provided by the shake-up in tennis and a newly interested public might have meant nothing, however, had it not been for the bold action of the athletes and their allies, and perhaps also their particular personalities. Billie Jean King was the sort of athlete who fascinated Americans. She was an underdog: she was short, wore thick glasses, and did not come from an advantaged family. She seemed to win through sheer determination. Beyond her athletic skill, King was also a woman with a vision, a sort of populist who opposed the tennis establishment and had the guts, shrewdness, dedication, and persuasiveness to lead others in the fight. Following King's lead were other disgruntled athletes willing to take the risks of defying tennis authorities and setting out on an unprecedented endeavor.

Still, they might not have succeeded without Gladys Heldman and her connections. Besides serving as (unpaid) tour director, Heldman gave the tour free advertising in her magazine and donated tens of thousands of dollars to insure the success of certain tournaments.[91] Through Joseph Cullman, she also was the link to corporate sponsorship for the tour. Thus tennis's upper-class patronage still made a difference. Some of the success of professional tennis was probably due to its long history—its being established as an individual, acceptable sport for women. No such professional movement arose in sports like basketball during the early 1970s.

Finally, tennis rebels used shrewd tactics. Breaking away from the tennis hierarchy and creating their own independent tour proved very effective. They broke new ground by really selling women's tennis and seeking out a whole new set of promoters and sponsors and tournaments, which, left to its own devices, USLTA would not have done. The women's initiative forced USLTA to compete and to take them seriously. In addition, setting out on their own was perhaps the only way the women pros could have proven their value at mixed tournaments. They never would have achieved parity without going on the offensive. Ideologically, they also made a good choice by shifting the argument from women's abilities as athletes to their ability as entertainers. This move bypassed the dualistic trap that had forced them to choose between either being equal to or different from men. This strategy did not eliminate all their problems because entertainers remained very vulnerable to an audience's opinions. However, when combined with a defiant new sense of self-worth and fortunate circumstances, it carried women tennis pros to new heights.

Althea Gibson stretches to reach a ball at Wimbledon in 1957. Gibson's aggressive serve and volley style was often characterized as "mannish." *Credit:* Library of Congress (LC-US262-79902)

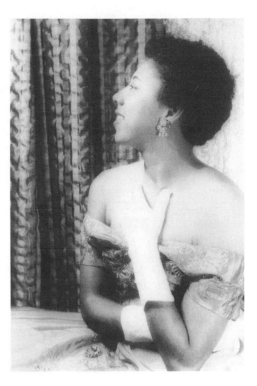

Carl Van Vechten's 1958 portrait demonstrates Althea Gibson's beauty and ability to meet feminine norms. *Credit:* Carl Van Vechten; Library of Congress (LC-US262-105579)

Like Jackie Robinson, Althea Gibson jumped many hurdles keeping African-Americans out of major sports events, and the black press lauded her accomplishments. *Credit:* Bill Curry, *New York Amsterdam News*, July 13, 1957

Maureen Connolly won the U.S. national tennis championship just before reaching age seventeen. At first, the press heralded her girlishness but later criticized her drive, decreeing that "Little Mo" had turned into "Killer Connolly."
Credit: Library of Congress (biographical portrait file)

Long before Nancy Kerrigan and Tonya Harding, figure skating was considered a graceful and feminine sport. Here American Gretchen Merrill practices for the 1948 Olympic Games.
Credit: National Archives (306-NT-811B-4)

Grace Kenworthy was crowned queen in 1951 at the annual beauty contest of the AAU national basketball championship. Runner-up princesses (left to right) were Jeanette Vanderslice, Cora Lou Balding, Joyce Lloyd, and Haydee Gonzales. *Credit:* Amateur Athletic Union (*Amateur Athlete*, June 1951)

Although track and field was not considered feminine, African-American women gained some appreciation for representing the United States' best chance against the Soviet Union during the postwar period. *Credit:* Amateur Athletic Union (*Amateur Athlete*, October 1956)

Mae Faggs of Tennessee State University breaks the finish line to win the 100-meter dash during the 1956 Olympic trials. *Credit:* National Archives (306-PSB-55-15787)

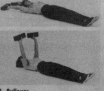

The President's Council on Physical Fitness encouraged both boys and girls but in slightly different ways. Boys were to do weight training to build muscles, and girls worked on "figure development" consistent with attracting boys. *Credit:* President's Council on Physical Fitness ("Vim" and "Vigor," 1964)

Worried about America's poor performance, Cold War-conscious leaders developed pro-grams to encourage both male and female children to take up sports. Here New York City girls race in the "Junior Olympics" in 1957. *Credit:* National Archives (306-PSB-57-9141)

In 1966 physical educators began an organization to sponsor new opportunities for college women. Presented in this photograph of the planning group of the Commission on Intercollegiate Athletics for Women are (from left to right) Rachel Bryant, Alyce Cheska, Maria Sexton, Fran Schaafsma, Ann Stitt, Frances McGill, and Katherine Ley.
Credit: Association for Intercollegiate Athletics for Women (Box 228, AIAW papers, University of Maryland Manuscripts Collection)

Pixielike Olympic gymnast Cathy Rigby helped spark Americans' interest in female
athletes in 1972. Years later, she disclosed her life-threatening eating disorders.
Credit: National Archives (306-PSD-72-527)

Teenager Chris Evert, brandishing a two-handed backhand, All-American looks, apologetic behavior, and a tremendous desire to win, won championships and the love of spectators in the early 1970s. *Credit:* National Archives (306-PSD-72-567)

The fiery and talented Billie Jean King led women pros to break from the male tennis establishment and start their own independent tour. *Credit:* Association for Intercollegiate Athletics (Box 68, AIAW papers, University of Maryland Manuscripts Collection)

The Association for Intercollegiate Athletics for Women (AIAW) began sponsoring championships in 1972 in a variety of sports, including field hockey. *Credit:* Association for Intercollegiate Athletics for Women (Box 73, AIAW papers, University of Maryland Manuscripts Collection)

Portrait of a proud past: AIAW presidents take time out from battles to protect their organization and Title IX. Standing (left to right) are Laurie Mabry, Leotus Morrison, Charlotte West, Christine Grant, Peggy Burke, Carole Oglesby, and Carol Gordon. Sitting (left to right) are Donna Lopiano, Carole Mushier, and Judith Holland. *Credit:* Association for Intercollegiate Athletics for Women (Box 73, AIAW papers, University of Maryland Manuscripts Collection)

Donna Lopiano, formerly director of women's athletics at the University of Texas and president of AIAW, lobbied strenuously for Title IX and helped organize an antitrust lawsuit against the NCAA. *Credit:* Association for Intercollegiate Athletics for Women (Box 73, AIAW papers, University of Maryland Manuscripts Collection)

Nancy Lieberman, Olympian and one of the charismatic stars of the short-lived professional Women's Basketball League, drives to the hoop for Old Dominion University in Norfolk, Virginia. *Credit:* Association for Intercollegiate Athletics for Women (Box 56, AIAW papers, University of Maryland Manuscripts Collection)

Sometimes publicity for the women's pro league sold sex as much as the athletes' abilities. The mascot of the Milwaukee Does (a real doe) here resembles a Playboy Bunny as much as a deer (angering the woman who kept it). *Credit:* Association for Intercollegiate Athletics for Women (Box 56, AIAW papers, University of Maryland Manuscripts Collection)

Despite lacking professional opportunities in the United States, basketball players like Charlotte Smith of the 1994 national champion University of North Carolina Tarheels continue to take the game to a new level. *Credit:* University of North Carolina (Sports Information Department)

As women's sports have gained legitimation, it has become more common for men to coach women's teams. Here Bert Lyle shares the moment with an athlete at the 1979 AIAW Track and Field Championships. *Credit:* Association for Intercollegiate Athletics for Women (Box 73, AIAW papers, University of Maryland Manuscripts Collection)

The diversity of the Queens College 1975–76 championship basketball team helps illustrate the potential of sports to break down barriers such as race and ethnicity between women. *Credit:* Association for Intercollegiate Athletics for Women (Box 73, AIAW papers, University of Maryland Manuscripts Collection)

Martina Navratilova's overwhelming skills and strength, combined with her openness about her sexuality, meant she enjoyed fewer endorsements and less popularity than her rival Chris Evert. Navratilova's superior training ushered in a new era in tennis. *Credit:* WTA Tour

Perhaps if the focus can shift from "playing nice" to "playing fair," women's sports can continue to soar (unidentified high jumper at the 1979 AIAW Track and Field Championships). *Credit:* Association for Intercollegiate Athletics for Women (Box 73, AIAW papers, University of Maryland Manuscripts Collection)

CHAPTER 7

Equality and/or Difference?

AIAW, NCAA, and Intercollegiate Athletics,
1974–1979

After years of being relegated to an insignificant place on campus with little money or power, women's athletics—and its organization—are coming of age.

—a "long-time observer of AIAW"

By the mid-1970s women's sports were highly politicized.[1] Tennis pros had won some contests for respect and fairer compensation, and Billie Jean King had confronted Bobby Riggs in a "Battle of the Sexes." Increasingly aware of gender issues, American society seemed more welcoming than ever of female athletes. In the first half of the decade, Little League Baseball finally accepted the girls who had been begging for entry, women had become able to earn a living as professional golfers, and schools everywhere began providing more chances to compete. At the college level, AIAW spearheaded the drive for equity. Once tentative, its leaders now recognized they had to fight in the political arena if they were to take advantage of this uniquely opportune moment.

The AIAW had already made some impressive strides in organizing championships, lobbying against the NCAA, and developing an alternative ideology. With some justification, however, advocates of college women's sports felt their gains might slip away. They faced three formidable challenges: wrestling within the federal government to protect Title IX; fending off further efforts by the NCAA to control women's sports; and applying constant pressure at individual campuses to obtain the nitty-gritty of equality. Any of these impediments could topple them, and maneuvering around each drained valuable energy. Despite the treacherous terrain, however, the mid-1970s offered the best time yet to be fighting for new opportunities in women's athletics—there were predators but also many allies; the road ahead was steep, but conditions were favorable.

Much of the battle over women's sports would be waged within the federal government. Congress had put the power to interpret its thirty-seven-word prohibition of sex discrimination in the hands of the Department of Health, Education, and Welfare, but HEW officials had never before intervened against sex discrimination in education, much less in athletics. Nor did HEW have clear guidance from Congress (since sports had barely been mentioned in the legislative debate) about even the most basic issues. Did equality mean females must have the right to try out for male teams? Or that females deserved teams of their own? Should HEW take into account physiological differences between the sexes? Should there be affirmative action taken to compensate for girls' historic lack of opportunity? What if women did not want their sports to mirror men's? Bureaucrats saw the sports section as a nightmare and tried to figure out how to avoid controversy, confusion, unfairness, and lawsuits. The regulation-writing process stalled, but on June 19, 1974, almost two years after Congress had passed Title IX, HEW finally published its proposed guidelines.[2]

The first and most important of HEW's decisions was that, although few athletic departments *directly* received federal funding, sports *would* be covered by Title IX. The HEW ruled that federal assistance (through such routes as student financial aid, work-study grants, and building and construction loans) gave to sports indirect benefits. This approach by HEW was based on recent court decisions in racial discrimination cases under Title VI, on which Title IX was modeled.[3] These rulings reinforced the common-sense notion that discrimination should be prohibited across the board—not prohibited in some areas of a school but permitted in others.

With regard to the complicated questions about how equality would be defined, HEW took a middle road. If selection for teams was based on competitive skill, HEW would permit but not mandate sex-separate teams. If a school chose to use sex-separate teams, it could not treat female teams differently from male ones. If an institution did not give female students their own teams, somehow it had to make sure that their athletic interests were being met. Regardless of which route schools chose, they were supposed to make an annual assessment of student interests. And if athletic opportunities for members of one sex had been limited in the past, schools must make "affirmative efforts" to inform them of their new rights. They also had to provide them with support and training to improve their capabilities and expand their interests so they could take advantage of such opportunities. In its final clause, the guidelines declared that nothing in them required equal *aggregate* expenditures for males and females.[4]

Thus, HEW had tried to balance the interests of many groups. Making veiled references to feminists and male athletic directors, HEW secretary Caspar Weinberger announced that the rules "would neither exempt nor disrupt inter-collegiate athletics as some have feared."[5] Indeed, the regulations had something for everyone. Feminists would be happy at the insistence on better treatment for sportswomen, and the AIAW would be pleased that the stress was on "comparable" rather than "identical" opportunities. The NCAA would be pleased that HEW had not demanded equal aggregate expenditures nor included a long list of areas in which equality must be achieved. Colleges would be relieved that HEW wanted to let them solve their own disputes without frequent federal intervention.[6] In fact, eager to cooperate with educational institutions, HEW extended the period for public comment on the regulations to October 15, 1974, and said the proposal might be changed in light of what it heard.[7]

Both AIAW and the NCAA delivered carefully crafted comments on the proposed regulations to HEW. The AIAW expressed strong support for the letter and spirit of Title IX but said the regulations were "hopelessly ambiguous." Because "the proposed guidelines wholly fail to indicate HEW's rationale as to what constitutes equality," AIAW suggested two clear but tough methods for measuring compliance.[8] The first asked HEW to examine an athletic department's per capita expenditures, to make sure that colleges spent the same amount of money on a typical female athlete as a typical male athlete. Women liked this solution because it would guarantee both equity and flexibility.[9] An alternative method was for HEW to specify how to institute fairness in every specific area of athletics (such as number of sports, travel and training budgets, allocation of facilities). But AIAW found this method—which basically guaranteed sameness—less attractive. Finally, AIAW also wanted some protection for women's athletic leaders. Fearing that female employees could lose job security and influence, they hoped HEW would state explicitly that schools did not have to merge men's and women's athletic departments.[10]

The NCAA's criticisms, while agreeing the regulations were "vague, ambiguous, and lacking in specific standards," clearly derived from an opposing point of view.[11] First, the NCAA declared intercollegiate athletic programs should not have to submit to such regulations at all because they received no direct federal financial assistance. Second, the NCAA denied that women were discriminated against. "Historically colleges and universities have provided, within the limits of available resources, athletic opportunities responsive to the demonstrated interests of both male and female students."[12] Besides placing blame for limited opportunities squarely on the shoulders of the victims, the NCAA denied sex discrimination by calling it something else. College athletic departments did not discriminate on account of sex but on other, entirely reasonable and legal, grounds, such as "uniform skill criteria." According to the NCAA, athletic departments awarded their scholarships to those they felt had the most ability (which usually meant only male athletes). The other way they classified teams was by the ability to generate revenue. As the NCAA had said during the Tower hearings, it wanted schools to be able to spend money on teams based on whether those teams could draw fans and earn income. Even if the teams granted special treatment would all be men's teams, the NCAA claimed, "Such differences do not constitute discrimination on the basis of sex." By guaranteeing equality for females, then, Title IX's regulations arbitrarily inhibited what was a fair, nonsexual classification. In addition, the NCAA complained that HEW "would impose a wholly uncertain and potentially endless affirmative obligation [to women]."[13]

Having taken such diametrically opposed positions on the proposed Title IX regulations, it is difficult to imagine the NCAA and AIAW cooperating. However, the organizations had already scheduled a meeting for the autumn of 1974. The two sides entered the October meeting with widely varying expectations and in no mood to compromise. While the NCAA again hoped to convince AIAW to affiliate with it, AIAW merely wanted to form a joint committee that would look into rules variations.[14]

The meeting only confirmed their differences. When an NCAA representative proposed that AIAW join the NCAA in an alliance, AIAW objected to his assumption that the NCAA should absorb AIAW. Why should not both organizations dissolve and form an entirely new governing body? Stanley Marshall cited the NCAA's advantages of a longer history and superior resources. In addition, he assured AIAW leaders that they could retain their leadership of women's sports from within the NCAA. Skeptical, AIAW's Laurie Mabry explained that in any merger, AIAW would want equal representation at all policy-making levels. David Swank, however, admitted women could probably expect only four seats on the eighteen-seat NCAA Council. After that, negotiations stalled—the NCAA's reps were unwilling to give women substantial power and AIAW's reps were unwilling to trade power in their own rapidly growing organization for subordinate status in a new one. Finding no common ground on important issues, they adjourned after agreeing to trade copies of one another's bylaws and to think further on solving their problems.[15]

Stymied, NCAA officials took matters into their own hands. After hearing that chances were slim for "any eventual recommendation that would be . . . acceptable to both organizations," the NCAA Council voted to have NCAA staff look into the legal, financial, and political ramifications of establishing its own women's championships.[16] Then Walter Byers's staff moved quickly. It reported that the NCAA could and should provide competition and services to women.[17] Considering both the imperatives of court decisions and the desire for efficient institutional control of intercollegiate programs, "the only satisfactory approach . . . is to place men's and women's programs under the same administration, the same legislative body and the same eligibility rules."[18] Byers presented this assessment to the council right before the NCAA's convention in January 1975. Although a bit hesitant, the council forwarded two pieces of legislation for consideration at the convention.[19] One authorized the initiation of NCAA "pilot championships" for women in a couple of sports. The other *required* NCAA members to place their women's teams under the NCAA's jurisdiction if the NCAA held championships in those particular sports.

The council's proposal surprised NCAA delegates arriving in Washington, D.C. The report had been so hush-hush that few anticipated it, and several objected to not getting information about the resolutions in advance.[20] Others found the proposals about women's championships odd. After all, many male athletic directors saw the NCAA as their advocate in the fight *against* Title IX and new spending for women's sports. Now the same staff suddenly recommended that the NCAA offer women's championships. Suggesting that "women's athletics are here and we better make the best of it," council members argued that the proposals were in men's best interest.[21] David Swank tried to show delegates that if the NCAA were shrewd enough to let women in, schools could avoid having to choose between men's and women's rules, the men who ran athletic departments would preserve their authority, and the NCAA would avoid competing with the AIAW's more restrictive approach to sports. But upon first hearing it, the NCAA's rank and file did not appreciate the leadership's shrewd strategy.

Meanwhile, two thousand miles to the southwest, women meeting at the AIAW's convention in Houston were stunned to hear of the NCAA's initiative—especially since they had made inquiries to NCAA leaders before the convention. They felt "concern and shock" and betrayed by the secrecy.[22] They also resented the invasion of their territory. "It was because of a lack of a governing body for women's athletics that the AIAW was formed," protested Margot Polivy. "Now that women's athletics are getting attention, the NCAA sees it as another place to set up shop and it happens to be in our home."[23] It seemed unethical for the NCAA to enter women's sports when women did not want it to, especially after the NCAA's leaders had refused to consider giving women an equal voice. Surely, under such circumstances, it was not right for the NCAA to pretend it was motivated by the desire to help women. The AIAW tried to set the record straight, angrily declaring, "That the N.C.A.A. has taken this action under the guise of a Federal law intended to expand opportunities for women cannot hide the fact that N.C.A.A.'s action is nothing more than athletic piracy."[24]

The AIAW's delegates pulled together against the threat. A poll taken at their convention showed 85 percent of them wanted AIAW to remain autonomous; another 14 percent were willing to consider becoming part of the NCAA if an equal voice for women were guaranteed.[25] Outraged, they sprang into action. In droves they wired and phoned Washington, lodging grievances with their male counterparts.

Back in Washington, the majority of men remained cool to Byers's plan. Although trying to act in their best interests, he had misread his constituency. Conservatives did not want the NCAA to be sponsoring women's sports and spending money on them; the NCAA was a men's organization and they wanted it to stay that way. In addition, a few liberal men thought the NCAA should not be intruding in the AIAW's sphere.[26]

Not surprisingly, then, the NCAA's delegates defeated both of the council's bills. However, a new compromise measure was introduced. Resolution 169 acknowledged both the council's concerns about a possible legal obligation to offer women sports and the concerns of those who wanted to deal fairly with the AIAW. It called upon the NCAA Council to prepare a comprehensive report about women's athletics, solicit comments on it from the NCAA's member schools, and then prepare recommendations for the next year's convention. In addition, the report had to be circulated to the AIAW. After getting *both* sets of members' reaction, a joint AIAW-NCAA committee would make recommendations to the council. The delegates approved this compromise by voice vote.[27]

Byers had lost the battle, then, but not the war. After all, Resolution 169 still gave the council the opportunity to recommend women's national championships to the NCAA's membership, and that, in fact, is what it did. Accordingly, a few months later the council adopted with few changes the report already written by the staff.[28] The "new" report reiterated the NCAA's historical mandate to supervise and promote *all forms* of intercollegiate athletics. If it declined to include women's sports, it paternalistically declared, it would be "deny[ing] services to women's intercollegiate athletics, which most needs it."[29] It also implied that through stubborn adherence to its different philosophy, AIAW could injure male athletes. Unless the NCAA acted to make women use the same rules, "NCAA would be *restricted and frustrated in the control of male athletics* by the overlapping and conflicting regulations of others in the field of female athletics" (emphasis added).[30] There beneath the other justifications and official-sounding language lay what was probably the NCAA's main reason for interest in women's sports: the possibility that women's sports leaders might hinder the NCAA's control of men's sports.

The AIAW launched a determined campaign among college presidents and administrators to discredit the report, denouncing the NCAA's secrecy as a "betrayal of AIAW's good faith efforts to work with NCAA."[31] The AIAW also attacked the NCAA's reasoning as illogical and inconsistent. One moment the NCAA said that Title IX did not apply to athletics, and the next it declared Title IX forced it to start women's championships. Besides, female student-athletes were already being well-served by AIAW, and the organization's continuing expansion suggested schools were satisfied. Its membership had grown from 280 in 1971–72 to 659 in 1974–75; it was offering fifteen separate championships for women, and now it could support itself financially.[32] Therefore, the NCAA's plan would unnecessarily duplicate AIAW's program. Finally, according to AIAW, the NCAA's proposal contained a critical weakness: it "d[id] nothing to assure women of real programmatic or administrative equality." Without structural change or guaranteed representation, AIAW believed, women's voice would be muted. The NCAA's voting delegates would remain almost totally male, as would its influential council. In sum, the NCAA's proposal implied "usurpation is preferable to cooperation."[33]

While trying to prevent the NCAA from taking over women's intercollegiate sports, women's athletic leaders had to respond to another urgent situation. Just a month after the NCAA report, HEW released its final regulations for Title IX, and President Ford signed them. Normally, the president's signature on the guidelines would have resulted in their immediately taking effect. However, earlier in the year Congress had passed a law requiring HEW to submit guidelines to Congress before they could be operative.[34] Now HEW had to publish its guidelines in the *Federal Register* and receive more public comment on them. If there was any section that Congress believed inconsistent with its intent, it had forty-five days in which to disapprove it. If Congress did not do so, the regulations would automatically go into effect. That meant one more chance for men in athletics to try to defeat Title IX, and for the women another fervent defense—in effect, another battle over who would gain the government as an ally.

With regard to athletics, HEW's new, final guidelines were more specific than the first version and, in some respects, more lenient. Some of the changes were merely intended to clarify.[35] For example, HEW now delineated the areas in which it expected compliance: equipment, playing facilities, locker rooms, training and dining facilities, coaching, tutoring, medical care, publicity, and the scheduling of games and practice times.[36] Besides clarifying, though, HEW's new guidelines weakened the old ones. For "contact sports," they allowed an exemption to the rule that individual females should be allowed to try out for male teams when there was no female team. If only one or two girls wanted to try out, a school did not have to let them. Only if enough females *to form a team* were interested in a contact sport would the school have to respond to that desire.[37] Altering this rule meant that females might never form teams in sports like football, boxing, wrestling, rugby, and ice hockey.

Moreover, HEW also diluted the original guidelines by dropping two provisions. The first had required schools to survey student interest annually. Although administering such surveys might have been difficult, the deletion meant that if women's interests grew (as their imaginations expanded or as certain gender prescriptions decreased), those interests were not accommodated. Further, HEW also eliminated the proposal that required schools to make "affirmative efforts" to make sure that female students knew about their new opportunities. Sounding a lot like "affirmative action," a concept the Ford administration opposed, the phrase was considered too controversial. This, too, seriously limited the extent colleges would have to reach out to females who were discriminated against.

Two final blows came in the area of enforcement. First, HEW added a new provision just for sports: a three-year grace period. The second alteration made enforcement for female students, even after the three years, more difficult. Instead of investigating individual complaints of discrimination, in the future HEW's Office of Civil Rights (OCR) would wait until a *pattern* of complaints existed before scrutinizing an institution. This was intended to make OCR's job easier, since the number of complaints was expected to skyrocket once the law took effect. A more equitable strategy would have been to increase the number of OCR investigators. Instead, HEW put the burden on women students to organize themselves and make a lot noise before they would be taken seriously.

Congress had until July 20 to consider HEW's regulations, and although hardly had a word been spoken about athletics when Title IX had been passed, now sports took center stage. To its amazement, HEW received 9,700 comments about the proposed regulations; the outcry astonished Caspar Weinberger. "I had not realized until the comment period closed," he quipped, "that the most important issue in the United States today is intercollegiate athletics."[38] Republicans in both houses introduced resolutions to disapprove parts of the regulations.[39] Rep. James O'Hara, chair of the House Subcommittee on Postsecondary Education, held six days of hearings in mid-June to consider the issues. At O'Hara's hearings, twenty-five of the twenty-nine witnesses discussed sports.[40] Those testifying about the athletic regulations fell generally into two groups: male coaches, administrators, and NCAA representatives (about 20 percent); and women involved in athletics and feminist organizations (about 75 percent).[41]

Men's athletic leaders now repeated to congressional representatives the legal arguments they had told HEW. Citing the opinion of an expert in drafting legislation, they argued that if Congress had intended for *every* program of a school to be included in Title IX, it would have stated that intent clearly. Even if colleges received federal funding, athletic programs did not directly receive any, and therefore they should be exempt. They testified that ticket sales, private financial contributions, and media contracts provided the main finances for football teams. "I believe the purpose of Title IX is to take back money if programs are not in accordance with HEW guidelines," said Nebraska's coach Tom Osborne. "If there is no Federal money being given to us, then why should we be regulated by HEW?"[42] In addition, the NCAA's representatives maintained that even the House sponsor of the bill, Edith Green, believed HEW had gone too far.[43]

Quite apart from legislative history, the NCAA repeated its practical argument: Title IX should not apply to them because it would hurt their programs. For HEW to order universities to start spending large amounts on women during a financial crisis was "asinine."[44] Title IX would deplete the budgets of revenue-producing sports like football, which would hurt the quality of teams, which meant fans would quit making donations, which meant the quality of teams would decline again until the vicious cycle damaged all the male and female teams who depended on these revenue-producing sports. Thus, Title IX would be "killing the goose that lays the golden egg."[45]

Male coaches and NCAA representatives denied they were "villains who suppress women's athletics."[46] "I am not personally opposed to women's intercollegiate athletics," insisted the president of the American Football Coaches Association. "So help me, I am not."[47] Yes, male coaches acknowledged, women needed more athletic opportunities, but men should not be blamed for inequality nor hurt by remedies. They hinted that women had no one to blame but themselves for this lack. "Until very recently women leaders in the sports field opposed intercollegiate varsity competition."[48] Now that women *were* showing interest, said NCAA president John Fuzak, male athletic directors were being very helpful.

> Despite what one reads in the popular press, the NCAA and its member institutions have been, and are fully committed within the limits of all available resources, to provide the best possible intercollegiate athletic programs responsive to demonstrated interest of both male and female student athletes. That's not just a pious statement; it is fully supported by the record.[49]

Of course, "the limits of all available resources" had in actuality meant a minimal commitment, but men did not see it that way. They had made some changes and considered them significant. They resented what they saw as Title IX's handing women money on a platter, giving them programs similar to ones men had worked years to develop. "Shouldn't the women have to experience the same growth process we had to struggle through?" asked one athletic director.[50] What they advocated was snail-like change, similar to the attitude of many white Southerners after the Supreme Court's 1954 *Brown* decision, who said they supported gradualism but in practice opposed any plans for desegregation. In particular, male athletic directors resented government coercion. "Women's programs have made substantial progress," said an athletic director, "and will continue to do so without unwarranted Federal regulations."[51]

Not surprisingly, sportswomen and feminists told a very different story to O'Hara's committee. Contradicting the NCAA, they asserted that Congress consciously intended for intercollegiate sports to be covered in Title IX. Sen. Birch Bayh, coauthor of the legislation, testified to that end. "I don't impugn the motives of those involved in these efforts to thwart the thrust of Title IX," Bayh said, "but I must say they read different *Congressional Records* and a different congressional mandate than [I]."[52] In addition, they reminded the committee of the Javits amendment, which said that HEW should write reasonable regulations with regard to intercollegiate athletics—which seemed irrefutable evidence that sports rightfully belonged in the regulations. They also rebutted the NCAA's claim that intercollegiate sports should be exempt from scrutiny because they received no federal help. Here they cited a recent court ruling which said that a program did not have to *directly* receive federal funds to be regulated by HEW, and pointed out that athletic programs indirectly but clearly benefited from federal assistance through tax breaks and building funds.[53] With regard to funding issues, an AIAW representative noted, "Men's programs have grown, in part, because women have contributed financially through state taxes, tuition, and student fees towards men's programs with NO return on the sum paid for women's intercollegiates."[54]

The pro-regulation faction also dispensed with the "alarmist" claim that the regulations would ruin intercollegiate sports. "[A] nation that is as powerful and ingenious as ours" ought to be able to figure out how to give women opportunities "without destroying the major athletic events that we all enjoy," said an exasperated Senator Bayh.[55] "The specter of that sacrosanct institution, bigtime football, dying at the height of its glory, of football heroes in tattered uniforms playing to half-empty stadiums" tugged at one's emotions but was misleading.[56] True, Title IX meant they would probably have to spend more money on women than they had, but athletic departments already possessed the two most expensive ingredients—facilities and equipment. In many cases they would merely have to share them. (And since few schools expected to organize female football teams, they would not have to duplicate the most expensive sport.) Such change might not be easy to swallow, acknowledged the Women's Equity Action League.

> Of course, when boys have had virtually all of the money and the facilities, sharing will be difficult. Going from preferential treatment to equal treatment will be something of a shock. However, this may be an appropriate time for educational institutions to reassess their total athletic program taking into account the goals of education as well as the interests and needs of *all* of its students.[57]

Others dismissed the NCAA's claims as irrelevant to justice. "The test of equity has never been impact on revenues, or even impact on programs we have emotional ties to," reminded a representative from the Federation of Organizations for Professional Women.[58] Indeed, AIAW agreed, "discrimination against women [should not] be permitted to continue because it is profitable to men or institutions."[59]

Perhaps more important, the pro-regulation alliance demonstrated the glaring disparities. Testimony revealed that nationally females received an average of 2 percent of athletic budgets, and at no major university did their share surpass 3.5 percent. For example, the University of Nebraska, a perennial football powerhouse, spent $60,000 for women and $4.1 million for men. At the University of Minnesota the women's track team used the field house only when it was empty and they had the permission of the men's team; women furnished their own uniforms while the men were supplied with free uniforms and daily-laundered practice clothes; the women had to borrow equipment from the physical education department while the men's team owned all it needed. The female swim team, coached by a woman paid less than minimum wage, practiced in a pool much smaller than the men's, which was available at fewer, inconvenient hours, and did not have such necessary equipment as timing clocks and lane ropes. Each male on the team had a locker; thirty-eight women on the team shared two lockers. Other irritations included differences in per diem allowances ($5 for women, $13 for men); travel by car instead of plane; the denial of special privileges (parking spaces, hair dryers, letter jackets, and so on); and the use of none but leftover men's athletic tape.[60] The committee received similar evidence from coaches, feminists, parents, and especially from dissatisfied female athletes. Their letters explained that such everyday discrimination constantly reinforced the feeling that female athletes were considered unimportant.

In sum, feminists and women athletic leaders expressed "reluctant support" of the guidelines. They supported them because they put some women's athletic rights on the books and would force colleges to make changes that otherwise might never occur. Yet they were disappointed because the regulations, and the whole process of writing them, were flawed. Congress's mandate had been vague at best, ignoring most key policy questions. It had been left to bureaucrats in HEW, then, to determine the meaning of equality. And HEW had seemed more concerned with accommodating the interests of different groups than determining what was best for female students. In the end, feminists complained, no one had sufficiently studied what would be the best way to insure that girls achieved equality, whether through coeducational sports or single-sex teams or some combination. Certain alternatives, then, were lost before they had even been considered and tested. Too, no one guaranteed women would have power in the process on campus to help define what equality would be, or to choose an alternative to the male model.[61] Finally, the final regulations were weaker than the first version. They were full of loopholes for "contact sports," did not guarantee affirmative action, and were overly trusting of schools' efforts. It would be too easy for individual victims of discrimination to be ignored, and enforcement had been shamelessly delayed. Forced into choosing between supporting flawed regulations or facing the possibility of no regulations at all, however, women athletic leaders knew which side they were on. At the moment, the political process, though unreliable and problematic, was women athletic leaders' best bet.

Perhaps the most surprising revelation from male athletic leaders at the hearings is that they, too, claimed their stance was reluctant. Whether or not they sincerely hoped women would get equality, they believed they had to say they did. This position was astute. Saying they "reluctantly opposed" the regulations gave men in athletics a certain degree of credibility—they could not be dismissed out of hand as opponents of equality. But if not Title IX, then what? Men in athletics opposed the measures suggested but never spelled out any alternatives. Certainly they wanted slower, less drastic change—nothing that would hurt men's teams, and nothing that would cost much money. And, above all, nothing that gave women much power (e.g., offering them only four seats on the NCAA's eighteen-seat council) or altered male control. Given all the qualifications and delaying and obfuscating, such supposed sympathy with women's goals rings false. In the final analysis, opposition was opposition. But by positing such reluctance, male athletic leaders remained viable actors in the process and kept open the possibility of controlling whatever women's sports developed. With perceptive foresight, NCAA strategists kept their options open, opposing measures for significant changes but maintaining a paternalistic, supposedly gradualist stance.

In the end Congress sided with women's advocates. In a series of close committee votes, the resolution to disapprove the regulations was defeated, meaning the guidelines would take effect.[62] Title IX finally had concrete meaning. More than ever before, the law was on the side of sportswomen, the state somewhat of an ally. Although weaker than they easily might have been, the new guidelines were nonetheless significant. Backed by the power of the federal government, they would require colleges to provide more opportunities for female student-athletes. Although colleges had three years in which to comply (and no one knew how effective enforcement would be), the regulations constituted a qualified political victory for women and laid the foundation for even more change.

Almost immediately after approval of the regulations, sportswomen had to fend off other attacks. In the summer of 1975, Senator Tower reintroduced the bill to provide special treatment to revenue-producing sports.[63] "After a long (and sometimes unpleasant) struggle with the subcommittee staff," Margot Polivy won the right for AIAW sympathizers to testify.[64] Arguments at the hearings echoed those made a year earlier, with supporters claiming that there would be "serious damage to the financial structure of intercollegiate athletics."[65] Opponent Donna Lopiano, on the other hand, complained, "The Tower Amendment is suggesting . . . we should heap all the food on one child's plate and allow the other children to eat only if that child leaves something." Apparently the Senate subcommittee agreed with Lopiano, because it did not report the Tower bill.

Attempts to weaken Title IX having been temporarily thwarted, NCAA staff redoubled its efforts to bring women's sports under the organization's umbrella. With a proposal to apply NCAA rules to women up for consideration at the January 1976 convention, men's and women's athletic leaders spent the six months beforehand presenting their cases. The NCAA asserted that both men and women would be better off if it supervised *all* intercollegiate athletics, and AIAW denounced the proposal as "usurpation." A poll showed that most female *and male* coaches opposed such a move, but Walter Byers dismissed the survey as irrelevant.[66] Delegates to the NCAA Convention still did not agree with Byers, and they voted against the proposal. For the time being, then, AIAW had dodged another bullet.

Just weeks after the convention, however, NCAA Council members launched yet another attack, filing suit against HEW's Title IX regulations.[67] A letter to colleges tried to put a good face on the lawsuit, insisting that "this step is entirely consistent with the NCAA's support of increased athletic opportunities for women." Why, then, was it seeking to destroy the equal opportunity regulations? First, the regulations contained a number of "unreasonable arbitrary standards." Second, universities should be able to determine their own equal opportunity obligations free from illegal federal bureaucratic interference.[68]

When they questioned the scope of the regulations, NCAA leaders were credible because the legislative history of Title IX left room for debate, but their concern for women's athletics sounded hollow.[69] Not surprisingly, AIAW blasted the NCAA's hypocrisy, saying the NCAA was creating "an elaborate legal construct designed to obscure the fact that it seeks this court's intervention to achieve a result it has already sought without success from H.E.W., the President of the United States and the Congress: defeat for the effort to provide equal athletic opportunities for women."[70]

In the meantime, the battle between the NCAA and AIAW continued on yet another front—that of the federal bureaucracy. One might think that all the issues would have been settled with passage of the regulations. However, confusion reigned on campuses about details still undecided, so both sides regularly lobbied HEW officials. The AIAW's counsel Margot Polivy said the first draft of procedural guidelines "could easily have been subtitled '1001 ways to discriminate against women and get away with it.'" After meeting with her, however, HEW revised the guidelines in at least two ways. Polivy planned to continue her efforts at "education" ("We are making real progress in sensitizing HEW," she reported).[71] Almost every directive from HEW to colleges was contested by AIAW and/or the NCAA, but frequent personnel changes within the government often frustrated their efforts.[72]

As they surveyed their prospects in the mid-1970s, supporters of college women's sports had some reason for optimism. Their movement had momentum. They had deflected a number of efforts to defeat Title IX, and Congress had approved the regulations to implement it. Equal opportunity in education was now apparently the law of the land, bringing government legitimation of their goals and the promise of more change. Although enforcement was not scheduled to begin until December 1978, the director of OCR had warned, "The adjustment period is not a waiting period."[73] Colleges had to conduct evaluations of their athletic programs within the next year and begin bringing them in line with Title IX. In addition, AIAW was thriving. It had grown from 280 to 659 member colleges, the number of intercollegiate athletes had increased from 24,000 to 60,000, and the organization had successfully fought off the NCAA's attempts to take over women's sports.[74] All this boded well.

Attitudes, too, were changing. Public opinion data showed greater sympathy for women's rights and equality. (By 1976, for example, 57 percent of those polled favored the controversial Equal Rights Amendment, and the percentage of Americans who would vote for a women running for national political office was at an all-time high.)[75] In addition, Americans in the mid-seventies became caught up in a fitness craze. Many started jogging, lifting weights, playing tennis, or otherwise exercising.[76] These two trends—greater support for women's rights and greater interest in physical well-being—came together to make the mid-seventies a very promising period for women's sports. In fact, according to a 1974 poll, 88 percent of the respondents believed girls' sports in public schools should receive the same financial support as boys' sports.[77]

A small but growing number of men also joined the ranks of supporters of women's sports. Some changed because they saw the handwriting on the wall. "After much soul-searching, we finally decided to [offer women athletic scholarships] . . . without being pressured by society or the courts," explained Penn State's athletic director.[78] Other men had experiences that changed them. Dr.

Charles Crawford coached men's basketball at Queens College, where the top-ranked women's team often grabbed as many rebounds and headlines as his team. At times it had been difficult to share gym time, equipment, and publicity, he confessed, and in the beginning he felt somewhat threatened by women's successes and demands. He still opposed "zealots" who wanted too much for women, but on balance, "it ain't so bad."[79] Previously he had assumed that women were uninterested in or incapable of "real" athletics, but he discovered that women's sports differed from the days of the "powder puff practices and haphazardly scheduled game" that he had scorned.[80] In fact, the female athletes at Queens shared many of his values, joys, and disappointments.

A small group of men supported women's movement into sports because they believed it just. Radicals such as Jack Scott and Harry Edwards were vocal critics of men's intercollegiate athletics. They did not worry about whether women's financial gains would mean reductions for men's programs because they believed those programs were tainted by overspending, misplaced priorities, and exploitation. Some men also welcomed changes in gender roles. Jack Scott, for example, denounced the extent to which sport had become a "masculine obsession."[81] Similarly, in an article entitled "Sissyhood Is Powerful," writer Dan Wakefield sympathized with female athletes who were ridiculed or stigmatized. "Just as the girl who is good at sports is labeled 'unfeminine,'" he pointed out, "so the boy who has no ability at athletics is labeled 'unmasculine.'"[82] Making sport less gendered potentially meant more acceptance for nonathletic males. To these radicals, then, women's entry into athletics provided a chance to reevaluate both sport and gender norms.

Clearly the atmosphere had changed. Now sometimes when women asked for something, they actually had a chance of getting it. Protesting the fact that they had no shower facilities, the women's crew team at Yale burst into an administrator's office with "Title IX" painted on their backs. A week later, they had somewhere to change clothes. At the University of Washington, officials agreed to permit women's teams to use the same training facilities as the men. Colleges also began conferring on women matters of respect. At Harvard, women became eligible to wear the coveted lettermen's "H," and at Yale, females were included in the tradition of team captains' yearbook photos. "We felt real proud," declared field hockey cocaptain Lawrie Mifflin.[83]

"If in 1972 opportunities for women were terrible, now they've improved to bad," reported one feminist in 1976.[84] Significant improvements had been made on campuses almost everywhere, but they were only a drop in the bucket. Along with every bright spot came three disappointments. The number of colleges offering women athletic scholarships increased from 32 in 1973 to 173 in 1975–76, but there were still 670 colleges that gave no athletic aid to females.[85] Feminists celebrated when an independent network carried the first nationally televised women's college game, but felt insulted when the telecast ended with over a minute and a half remaining to be played.[86] Surely women's basketball had achieved respect when a record-breaking 11,969 fans attended a contest at Madison Square Garden. But then at a 1974 game at the University of Cincinnati, officials cleared female hoopsters off the court with five minutes left in a close game because the men's team wanted to warm up.[87] Even the best women's college programs, like that at the University of Texas, fell far short of parity. Texas had increased its women's budget by more than 100 percent for three straight years, so that by 1976 women's sports received $128,000. Still, they needed another $71,000.[88] Two out of three male athletes at Texas received athletic scholarships, and only one out of fifteen women did. Women could not stay in the same quality accommodations, nor were they permitted to use the athletic dining services. Almost all of the twenty-one men's coaches held full-time positions, while the seven women's coaches served part-time. And while an *assistant* football coach earned $20,000 a year, the *head* coach of a women's team made $2,100.[89] Women at Texas did not enjoy equality, but women elsewhere enviously eyed the Texas program.

Although improvements had been made, and more men supported some degree of women's athletic opportunity, plenty of opposition remained. Jim Barnett resigned as athletic director at Oregon State University. "[I] will be the first of several athletic directors throughout the nation to sacrifice himself on the altar of Title IX," he predicted.[90] Few went to Barnett's lengths, but they could find other ways to minimize changes, such as keeping a tight rein on the budget, resisting every important concession, and ridiculing women's requests.[91] They also could ally with other men in athletics in the NCAA, who were stepping up their assault. In its summer 1975 issue, NCAA *News* lambasted the women of AIAW who, "working hand in glove with women lawyers of HEW," joined forces to finance women's athletics by "living on big brother's credit card."[92] The editorial purported to expose the women's hypocrisy: "While decrying the undesirable aspects of income-oriented men's intercollegiate athletics, the women, backed by Federal decree, now demand their share of this tainted money . . . to finance the females in the style to which they feel they should become accustomed."[93] The diatribe demonstrated a hostility toward women usually carefully edited out of the NCAA's public pronouncements. It relied upon dated stereotypes of women—they conspire against men, depend upon men for money and power, and frivolously waste men's hard-earned money.

The tone of the NCAA *News* editorial, combined with intense efforts to discredit and defeat the women, suggest that by the mid-1970s AIAW was perceived as a significant threat. Now that they were backed by Title IX, female athletic leaders were considered to be quite dangerous. Their increasingly successful demands for more money and better treatment were bad enough. Worse, these were coupled with women's stubborn intention to choose their own independent path. "All this in the interest of integration and equality?" continued the NCAA *News*. "Don't believe it. Flushed with its heady victory at HEW, the AIAW . . . continues to urge its campus colleagues to insist upon segregation."[94] Indeed, AIAW's continued insistence upon self-determination—"segregation"— angered NCAA leaders.

In the midst of this turbulent atmosphere, AIAW's leaders struggled to chart their own course. "We never really got to focus our energies on what we were about, which was our program," recalled one AIAW president, "because we were so busy fighting not brush fires but major conflagrations."[95] They would have preferred to concentrate their energy internally, but it was impossible to separate the development of AIAW from the larger political context. Title IX's promises of equality had helped make their organization strong; yet that same concept continued to be problematic. In an ideal world, women's athletic leaders could have selected what they wanted to keep from the cooperative, privatized model of 1950s female physical educators and from the modern, commercialized, extremely competitive men's model. They were not operating in a vacuum, however. As they had discovered in 1973 when they prohibited athletic scholarships, the mandate of equality sometimes limited their choices. Would law and circumstances force them to become a mirror image of men's intercollegiate athletics? Or would they be able to forge a different course? During the late 1970s, there was no clear answer.

In some areas, female athletic leaders had been moving toward the male model. No longer did they disapprove of competitiveness, individual excellence, and exposure as they had in the 1950s. Athletic scholarships and All-American teams recognized individual stars (the AIAW itself named All-American teams and handed out other awards). Moreover, AIAW's directors now did not blink at female athletes being used to advertise products (if they could get the chance), and they actively sought television coverage of women's championships. The AIAW also moved toward the male model with three decisions in recruitment. For years AIAW had discouraged recruiting by not permitting coaches to be paid (or given release time) for it, but in 1978 that changed. Second, in order to avoid harassment and high-pressure tactics, AIAW long had permitted only written communication between coaches and high school players. Gradually, though, it began allowing some telephone and face-to-face communication. Third, rules regarding to on-campus meetings also became more permissive.[96] In each case a combination of two factors influenced the decision: AIAW delegates did not want to deny athletes and coaches benefits that men already had; and they wanted to build the best, which increasingly meant the winningest, team possible.[97]

As coaches embraced more serious competition and colleges invested money in women's programs, there arose more pressure to win. The need to produce victories occasionally caused problems. In the late 1970s, for the first time, rumors of illegal or unethical practices (such as repeated personal sales pitches to families, promises of jobs or under-the-table cash to recruits, and the pirating of stars from other colleges) circulated about *women's* sports.[98] Sometimes male administrators, who found AIAW's strict recruiting rules absurd and who wanted the best for their scholarship dollar, instigated the new practices. "We're going to get the best women's basketball team that money can buy ... within the rules, of course," announced Rev. Oral Roberts in a statement that would have appalled early DGWS women.[99] In many cases, though, it was female coaches who knowingly adopted the practices and philosophy of super-competitive intercollegiate sports. "One coach sees another coach get a player and figures it must've been crooked," observed Vanderbilt's Emily Harsh. "She thinks she's got to do it, too, or she'll get behind."[100] Certainly the problem was not as widespread as in men's programs, but it is impossible to know how frequently the distressing incidents occurred.[101]

In the mid-1970s AIAW stood at a crossroads. One wing wanted a somewhat more competitive version of the old PE programs while the other wanted to jump wholeheartedly into big-business sports.[102] "The AIAW Executive Board is not sure how women feel," admitted an AIAW president.[103] Partly the split reflected the difference between large universities, where men and women alike emphasized winning, and smaller ones, which stressed student-athletes' educational experience. The split also reflected age differences; the younger generation were strictly "coaches," while the old guard were DGWS-loyal physical educators. Katherine Ley, an early founder of CIAW, feared that some female coaches—so long deprived of resources—could be lured by the shiny promises of Title IX and "sameness." "Those women who have scrounged for funds can be won over by adding some money, they can be had with prestige, others can be won over with just politeness and courtesy." She worried that the AIAW was particularly vulnerable in this period because women in athletics no longer shared an identical vision.[104] The AIAW coped with the problem by dividing member schools into three separate divisions with different rules. In addition, at annual conventions delegates spent hour after hour debating basic differences and negotiating compromises.

Although inching closer to the male model, AIAW continued trying to navigate a unique course. In some areas, it failed. In 1977, for example, AIAW approved the radical, forward-looking concept of limiting the amount of athletic scholarships to the cost of tuition and fees. The move would have saved athletic departments millions of dollars during a period of financial crisis. (And it would not have hurt financially disadvantaged students because they would be eligible for government financial aid for their other expenses.) However, when the NCAA refused to approve the same measure, AIAW was forced to reverse the action or else risk depriving female athletes of equal treatment.[105]

In other instances, AIAW did manage to retain differences with the NCAA. The NCAA's eligibility rules stated that a male student-athlete could participate in a sport for four years as long as it was within a five-year period. The AIAW made no such five-year requirement since it believed females were more likely to drop out early in their lives and return to college years later. Transfer rules also differed. Athletes in the NCAA who transferred had to sit out one year before participating on the new intercollegiate team. An AIAW athlete could transfer and play sports immediately at the new school (however, she could not receive an athletic scholarship during that first year). The reasoning behind this decision was that a student-athlete should be treated as much as possible like every other student. For the same reason, AIAW prohibited colleges from paying for an athletic recruit's visit to campus unless the school subsidized the visits of *all* prospective students (this rule held until 1979). Nor were colleges allowed to set more stringent requirements (such as minimum grade point averages) for athletes than they did for students participating in any other extracurricular activities.

The AIAW's officers devoted themselves to shaping a fair, democratic organization that governed lightly. Unlike the NCAA, AIAW invited students to serve on some committees. Another innovation was a student-athlete's bill of rights. The group also tried to minimize the number of intricate rules to enforce. Leaving many regulations to colleges themselves, AIAW sought to make only those necessary to insure fair competition, health and safety, and equal opportunity. Colleges were also expected to turn themselves (and their neighbors) in when they broke the rules. The NCAA's leaders (and as time passed, some AIAW coaches) found AIAW's tradition of self-policing absurd. In fact, as the organization grew, it did have to create a larger and more public enforcement mechanism, but this differed from the NCAA in its more consistent policies and its greater protection of due process and appeal rights.[106]

Neither AIAW nor the NCAA wanted to sacrifice any of its distinctiveness. Fearing that the law would eventually insist on "sameness," a few members of AIAW and the NCAA met and cooperatively drew up a compromise set of concrete, rather minor, rule changes each organization could make to bring them closer to one another. Both organizations, however, refused to enact them.[107] As the NCAA Council put it, there could be no agreement on common rules because "both the NCAA and the AIAW would have to compromise certain of their basic principles."[108] The AIAW's leaders agreed. Although there were some differences of opinion within AIAW on specific issues, on one thing there remained virtual unanimity: whatever the direction of women's intercollegiate sports, it was women who should determine it. It remained to be seen whether they would have the power to do so.

Political and ideological struggles also took place at the local level, where each institution of higher learning had its own unique women's sports saga. Female coaches and administrators—often alone or with a handful of others—found themselves the local advocates for greater opportunities. Their accomplishments differed from campus to campus. A number of interviews done in the mid- and late 1970s illuminate the painful process and the activists' state of mind.[109]

A few did have positive things to report. One student said that although her athletic department was not in compliance with the law, things had come a long way in the last year.[110] (Perhaps coincidentally, sportswomen at her school had recently filed a Title IX complaint with HEW.) "The situation is a million times better since I was a freshman," related another student.[111] A coach said that while one major problem remained, "I haven't fought it because our budget has increased tremendously and we keep adding women's varsity sports. And we've reached parity in terms of the scholarships given in men's non-revenue-producing sports."[112] According to an athletic director from the Southwest, "We are progressing. There is no doubt about it." She did, however, qualify her statement. "But I've never sat down with anybody to lay out a full plan for implementing Title IX, and I don't know of any school in our area that is in total compliance—although they're all better off."[113] Those experiencing improvement felt certain that the law had been the impetus. A representative from a large private school said, "Our affirmative action group studied the problems and decided they'd better come into compliance in order to keep their federal funds. If it weren't for Title IX we'd be in the horse and buggy days. We're lucky."[114]

Many others, however, complained that their colleges were procrastinating. Although the law was official, and it required schools to be making changes, administrators put them off because the government was not yet enforcing the law and had not yet determined some minor policy decisions.

> Our institution has been stalling since 1975 on everything from facility renovation to program improvement. If Title IX policies aren't set and if strong stands on compliance made, we will never get out of the woods. . . . All I hear is "let's wait for the regulations to come out for good."[115]

A women's athletic director had similar experiences:

> It seems that until [our] administrators see specific directives, there is a general reluctance to take necessary steps toward full compliance. . . . The

"foot-dragging" syndrome is certainly apparent at our university. . . . The longer the delay, the greater the morale problem becomes among both our female athletes and our coaching staffs.[116]

Feeling powerless made morale worse. An administrator at a public university felt her hands were tied: "I'm supposedly the women's coordinator but . . . I'm not allowed to meet with the women coaches on anything—especially Title IX. I have absolutely no access to any income information with the exception of student fees. . . . They gave me the women's budget."[117]

Sometimes sportswomen were intentionally kept in the dark. "Our institution submitted a 79-page Title IX comment," reported an employee of a large university. "I didn't even know about it and haven't seen it yet. Our Title IX coordinator is resigning. Neither she nor I had any input in the comments. Every door seems to be closed. . . . It's frustrating."[118] Naturally, the secrecy and opposition caused coaches to fear the worst. "I understand I'm going to be fired," reported another woman. "No one has said exactly why. I think it's because I'm a good administrator and have asked for some things. I haven't even made much noise about Title IX compliance." Many became afraid to speak out. "What about confidentiality? Would you have to mention my name?" asked one student. A coach at a private school revealed, "I can't say this on or off the record. . . . We were told not to submit Title IX comments. I had a friend do it for me on plain white stationary."[119]

Outright hostility and harassment made their fears well-grounded. Horror stories included that of a female teacher in Colorado terminated because she advocated women's rights.[120] Others worked in a threatening environment. "I've personally been told to play it low key or I won't be around if I don't," disclosed a coach at a public university. She had protested about female athletes' "pitiful" conditions—financial inequity, no dressing rooms, no training table, and a facility that "should be condemned." Yet "whenever I ask for anything, they threaten to merge departments so I'd be put under the supervision of the male Athletic Director."[121] She discovered that when real power was at stake, some men played hard ball. They took advantage of the way female athletic leaders traditionally were vulnerable—as not feminine women—and resorted to lesbian-baiting. "Our men's athletic director has even gone so far as to tell our Board of Regents that I was a homosexual."[122] Another southwestern woman, who had already witnessed repercussions after a Title IX complaint, expected more vindictiveness. The university's Title IX coordinator had been intimidated and she herself had experienced a sudden coolness from male colleagues. "Now they treat me like slime." Although angry, she vowed to continue pressing for change because she was less vulnerable than other female coaches. "I can fight because I'm a tenured assistant professor who's married, has two kids, and

nothing to lose. They've even tried that 'queer' stuff on me."[123] Daily functioning in a chilly workplace was difficult enough; fighting for rights in such an
environment required a great deal of courage.[124]

Risky though advocacy was, it was precisely *because* of their lack of power on
campus that individual women needed outside help in the form of Title IX.
"You are probably just as 'swamped' as I am," wrote University of Texas women's
athletic director Donna Lopiano to AIAW coaches, "but we *must* continue to
work for what is right. For most of us, our only hope is a strong federal government position. Hang in there."[125] Without pressure from outside the campus,
Lopiano recognized, sportswomen would be unprotected, in the minority and
dominated by people unsympathetic to their cause. Too, they might forever be
silenced by a practice the NCAA euphemistically called "institutional control."
Under "institutional control," when it came time for a college to take a stand on
an issue—such as comments to HEW about Title IX (or financial aid policies)—
an institution could take only one position. Given that women were in the
minority in athletic departments, that few feminists had power on campus, and
that influential male alumni tended to support football teams, the sportswom-
ens' voice would be missing from official pronouncements. For that reason,
AIAW wanted to keep men's and women's athletic departments separate. That
way, when university administrators asked for input, there would be at least *two*
departmental votes on controversial issues and women would not be stifled
completely. The NCAA, on the other hand, favored the merging of men's and
women's departments (which meant in virtually every case a department
headed by a male athletic director). The NCAA stressed how this arrangement
made "institutional control" more effective, but AIAW members realized that, in
practice, institutional control and one vote meant that on controversial issues
the men always won.[126]

Campus politics became especially heated as July 1978 approached, the date
when colleges were supposed to be in compliance with Title IX. Theoretically,
after that date HEW could investigate schools with complaints against them. In
reality, though, HEW was as reluctant and ill-prepared as universities for
enforcement. Like their predecessors, new officials in the Carter administration
had heard loud complaints from all sides. The NCAA insisted that HEW should
not be regulating intercollegiate athletics at all, so in spring 1978 HEW once
again reconsidered legislative history as to whether revenue-producing sports
deserved to be exempted.[127] Women's groups, on the other hand, demanded
that HEW stop dragging its feet, make a firm policy statement, and begin
enforcement immediately. Colleges and universities—some stalling, some worrying—criticized HEW for its lack of guidance, while HEW kept promising policy directives but did not meet its own deadlines.

Finally, in December 1978, HEW released a "proposed policy interpretation" of the Title IX regulations. These guidelines were *still* not final; during a sixty-day "reading period," interested parties could suggest changes. Like Caspar Weinberger three years before him, HEW director Joseph Califano said the proposal was designed to balance the competing interests involved, and that HEW had considered both the need to encourage more women and the "realistic understanding that men's sports receive more attention and require more money."[128] In Part One, HEW proposed a presumed compliance standard in which it would calculate the schools' *average per capita expenditures* in scholarships, recruitment, equipment, supplies, travel, and publicity. If men's and women's averages were substantially equal, and if benefits in not financially measurable items were comparable, then HEW would presume the school was in compliance. (If the per capita averages were not substantially equal, the institution would have to prove that the disparities were caused by nondiscriminatory factors.) In Part Two, HEW proposed examining an institution's plan for eliminating the effects of discrimination. It would look for more of an affirmative action-type plan to increase the number of women participating and the number of teams, to publicize women's athletic opportunities, and to elevate the scope of women's competition.[129]

Women's leaders worried a bit. Overall, they commended the per capita expenditure standard as a fair and clear policy. But they disliked the language granting exceptions based on nondiscriminatory factors like the "scope of competition" and "nature of the sports."[130] "With the loophole of the 'non-discriminatory' factors," explained one feminist, "they say that because a sport is so advanced—which it is because of the grossest sort of biased spending—then that bias can continue. They justify continued discrimination by the existence of a discriminatory situation."[131] That problem might have been alleviated if the second part of the policy, which required the continued development of women's sports, were enforced strenuously. However, feminists thought that section vague and too dependent on the goodwill of local administrators.[132]

Male athletic leaders praised HEW's acknowledgment of the unique characteristics of football, but still decreed the policy interpretation "grossly inadequate."[133] Calling HEW unrealistic and illogical, an NCAA representative blamed it on the "entrenched thinking of HEW's cadre of young, female lawyers."[134] In particular, they blanched at the average per capita spending test, which the NCAA contended would cost $60 million a year.[135] The second part of the proposal also disturbed many men. "We are supposed to generate more women in athletics—more teams and more sports in the affirmative action aspect," one complained. "Now, where it ends, I don't know."[136]

At the 1979 NCAA convention, some men took action. A couple of Division

III schools proposed that the NCAA start women's championships, but the measure failed again.[137] Delegates agreed, though, on a strongly worded resolution denouncing the proposed policy interpretation and directing the NCAA's leadership to resist it.[138] Notre Dame's Rev. Edmund Joyce took the initiative himself and called a special meeting for those "who feel keenly about this issue."[139] Joyce's followers formed an alliance known as the DeHart Coalition (named after the Washington lobbying firm it had hired) and eventually raised over $100,000 for its sophisticated strategy to lessen the impact of Title IX.[140] Trying to distance itself from the image of angry football coaches dead-set against equality, the DeHart Coalition recruited top administrators of universities, called itself a compromise group, and emphasized a commitment to find ways to eliminate discrimination—just alternative ways.

Terry Sanford, president of Duke University, presented the coalition's case to HEW in a letter signed by officials from fifty universities. "There has been too much confusion, too much debate, too much misunderstanding," wrote Sanford. "We stand ready to join with you, the Office of Civil Rights, with the NCAA and the AIAW to convert this energy to a creative and constructive solution." In particular, Sanford wanted to create something different from the per capita standard, which was "anathema." His alternative solution turned the responsibility for determining methods of compliance over to *individual institutions*, which would have to follow certain procedural safeguards, such as providing representation on a planning group for all affected parties (including women, men, faculty, administrators, alumni, and "institutional supporters"). The planning group would first make a "realistic assessment" of opportunities for men and women on campus. Then it would develop a plan with goals and timetables for numbers of sports, participation levels, financial aid, periodic review, and resolution of complaints. The group would determine what levels of competition should be achieved for each sport, taking into consideration "sex-neutral factors" such as spectator support and the "goals and traditions of the institution." Then HEW could judge a school's compliance based on how well it adhered to its plan, and whether the plan satisfied both women and men on campus.[141]

Despite its relatively conciliatory tone, the DeHart-Sanford plan was designed to produce more lenient standards than HEW's and to give special consideration to revenue-producing sports. It focused on the process of addressing sex discrimination rather than on the effect. It showed no cognizance of the fact that colleges were supposed to have evaluated campus opportunities and developed a plan for meeting Title IX three years earlier. Nor was the DeHart Coalition sensitive to women's complaints about the proposed process. Equal rights advocates would be outnumbered by the inclusion of alumni and fans on those campus committees. As one feminist commented, it was "a little like asking the fox to come up with a plan for guarding the chickens."[142]

"Seems as though Title IX is a lifetime battle," observed an AIAW official, gearing up for another round.[143] Sportswomen's new efforts matched the political sophistication of the hired lobbyists. They joined feminist groups in their own alliance, the National Coalition for Girls and Women in Education.[144] Besides helping supporters critique the Sanford proposal, the women's coalition presented its case to the U.S. Commission on Civil Rights.[145] The commission had taken a compromise position on the proposed regulations, supporting the per capita expenditures standard and proposing more specific affirmative action measures, but suggesting that football expenditures temporarily be excluded from per capita comparisons.[146]

Fighting for the approval of yet another branch of the government, Iowa's Christine Grant made an eloquent plea for justice. Grant argued that the policy interpretation should not be watered down (with an exemption for football) because it already was too weak. As it stood, Title IX would not bring equality; it merely mandated a small step in the right direction. Huge differences in expenditures would still be permissible because nonsexual factors such as event management expenses were excluded from men's costs, and because male athletes still greatly outnumbered females.[147] How could anyone give credence to men's cries of alarm? Under the policy interpretation, Title IX actually allowed the University of Iowa to spend $3.5 million on men's sports, and only $850,000 on women's. " 'Compliance' is not a synonym for 'equality,'" she pointed out. "In reality, compliance could well become a synonym for 'continued discriminatory treatment.'" Although women were due equality, Grant would settle for compliance under the guidelines because they "promise more than we currently have or could achieve by ourselves on our individual campuses." But the commission should realize that this was "the Civil Rights bargain of the century."[148]

The women's coalition also countered other moves by its opponents, such as congressional attacks on the policy interpretation, new bills to exempt revenue-producing sports, and riders to appropriations bills to inhibit HEW's enforcement.[149] It exhorted coaches, administrators, and players to write their congressional representatives, and kept files on how each officeholder stood on the issue. National leaders mailed "Title IX starter kits" to budding local organizers. They drafted a Declaration of Women's Athletic Rights, and volunteers personally delivered copies to members of Congress. They held demonstrations, chanting, "We want to play, don't take it away," and even held a national bake sale in support of Title IX. Prominent female athletes appeared on the news, on talk shows, and in magazines, publicly expressing appreciation for Title IX. "The response from the membership has been phenomenal!" declared AIAW's

Bonnie Slatton. "We may not have financial backing, but we have people—lots of them—who care!"[150]

Once again—as they had throughout the 1970s—sportswomen won a battle in the governmental arena. The U.S. Commission on Civil Rights decided football did not deserve an exemption from the law.[151] The commission also reported it suspected that, despite their claims to the contrary, male athletic leaders seemed to oppose the growth of women's sports. (The commission wrote, "It may be the anticipated growth in the women's program that underlies the opposition of the NCAA and the ad hoc coalition of colleges to equal per capita expenditures.") As for the DeHart-Sanford proposal, "It would be inappropriate . . . to reject equal per capita expenditures in favor of a proposal that declares them to be anathema."[152] On a second front, all congressional efforts to weaken Title IX failed. Third and most important, after months of further delay (while HEW evaluated more comments and underwent another change in personnel), HEW issued a final policy interpretation of Title IX.

Also rejecting the DeHart Coalition's proposal, HEW in its final policy interpretation stood firm on many issues.[153] It dropped the per capita expenditures test (except for the vital area of athletic scholarships). Eliminating the confusing notion of presumed compliance, instead HEW clarified the specific areas that enforcement officers would be examining, providing almost a checklist. With regard to "major" men's sports, it occupied a reasonable middle ground: there would be no exemptions based on whether sports brought in revenue, but special costs for equipment and event management for sports like football and basketball would be permitted as long as they were provided to women as needed. Although it deleted the separate section on future responsibilities, HEW reminded schools that they must continue to accommodate female athletes' interests. They could do this by making sure the same percentage of females participated in athletics as were enrolled in the school. Finally, HEW announced it would begin compliance reviews.[154] Male opponents called the final guidelines "irrational," "intrusive," and "more extensive," and Walter Byers hinted at court challenges. The AIAW's leaders, on the other hand, breathed a sigh of relief. Said Margot Polivy, "We're delighted with the new regulations."[155]

Wisely, women's sports advocates tempered their enthusiasm. Just because the rules were on the books did not mean HEW would crack down on lawbreakers. "Now we'll see if they are enforced," said Margot Polivy, already preparing for the next hurdle. Of course, they had to worry about what the NCAA would do next; it seemed unlikely it would throw in the towel. Its lawsuit was still pending,[156] and there was always the potential threat of its trying to take over women's athletics. Finally, women held back celebrating because the regulations were far from perfect. If universities could spend four times as much on men (UCLA could spend $4,000,000 on men and $700,000 on women) and still be in compliance, clearly the regulations would not bring women's sports up to male levels.[157] The regulations did little to address the lingering discriminatory effects of decades of male preferential treatment; they did not guarantee equality.

Still, preserving the regulations was a tremendous victory. Against more established, wealthy, and powerful opponents, women's sports advocates had kept a relatively strong law on the books. It had taken seven and a half years to reach the point where there was hope for enforcement. Even without government enforcement, however, the threat of the deadline had already resulted in enormous strides. By July 1978 over five hundred colleges awarded athletic scholarships to women (up from sixty in 1974). Four-year institutions in 1978–79 offered women an average of five sports (up from 2.5 in 1973–74). Thirty percent of all intercollegiate athletes were now female, and they enjoyed 16 percent of sports budgets (as opposed to less than 2 percent early in the decade).[158] Significantly, despite the NCAA's dire predictions, the change had not come at the expense of male athletic programs. The number of male teams remained constant, and absolute expenditures for men had actually increased—somehow the money for changes had been found. Considering the obstacles in their path at congressional, bureaucratic, organizational, and campus levels, the women's achievement was impressive. Certainly the climb had taken a toll on women's sports advocates—in the minority and sometimes harassed on their campuses. Exhausted by their accomplishments and frustrated with the price some had paid, most knew they had made only another step toward their ultimate destination. Still, they had reason to feel proud—women's intercollegiate sports programs had reached new heights.

Part IV

Introduction: 1980–1990

Feminists could not have enjoyed a better decade than the 1970s. Their social movement had made an enormous impact on the nation. No one could be unaware of women's rights issues, and this sensitivity stimulated gains in all facets of society. Women now appeared in pulpits, endowed professorships, and as pilots, often with the same salaries as their male counterparts. More people appreciated women's capabilities. Beyond the workplace, the feminist perspective changed how Americans looked at many social issues, like child-rearing, household duties, health care, sexuality, divorce, pornography, and religion. Feminists created new institutions and services such as rape crisis hotlines, battered women's shelters, women's health clinics, lesbian cultural centers, and child care facilities. Congress approved Title IX, which revolutionized school systems, giving females an equal chance to take shop class, be admitted to college, and have their ambitions taken seriously there. Thirty-five states (three short of ratification) had passed an Equal Rights Amendment to the U.S. Constitution. The courts were striking down discriminatory laws and considering the viability of affirmative action programs to remedy years of unfair treatment. In sports, too, women were newly empowered, as the successes of women golf and tennis pros, female Little Leaguers, marathoners, aerobics instructors, and AIAW participants illustrated.

The question for the 1980s was whether women could build upon these gains. Could women become more than tokens in traditionally male fields, break through the "glass ceiling" keeping them from the upper echelons of power, establish an enduring political voice, reach a more equal and secure economic position? Could women move beyond integration to actually change the structure of institutions so that these became truly sensitive to all female and male human beings? Could women and men experience real freedom from restrictive and shame-inducing notions of masculinity and femininity? Sportswomen faced similar issues in the 1980s: now that many clubs, schools, teams, and associations recognized that prohibiting females was wrong, could they take the next step and actually *encourage* large numbers of females? Could male athletic directors give up their battle against Title IX and share more of the wealth (than the 16 percent average of college budgets currently being spent on women's programs)? Could they listen to the voices of women coaches about the meaning of equality? Could male spectators move beyond tolerance of women athletes to actually supporting them, so that women might earn a living as professionals in sports like basketball, baseball, volleyball, and gymnastics? Could a strong, assertive, successful woman athlete be considered a normal, feminine woman and an appropriate hero for little girls?

In 1980 the chances for that progress grew a little dimmer with the election of Ronald Reagan as president. Traditional Republicans—the well-to-do, supporters of big business and a strong national defense, and those who disliked government activism and Communism—contributed to Reagan's success, but he also benefited from the rise of the "New Right." Reacting against the strides made by women, blacks, the poor, gays, and other groups during the sixties and seventies, the New Right favored "old-fashioned morality." At the heart of their program were sexual, gender, reproductive, and family issues. According to Phyllis Schlafly, spokeswoman and head of "Stop ERA," women should accept their naturally ordained differences with men, accept their physical inferiority, and embrace their (subordinate) feminine role as wife and mother. Feminists should stop demanding sexual freedom, challenging male authority, and emulating masculine qualities, because those actions threatened the breakdown of the patriarchal family.[1]

In particular, the New Right targeted abortion laws and the Equal Rights Amendment but also sex education, divorce, married women working and using child care, toleration of homosexuals, affirmative action, and Title IX. (Schlafly sarcastically referred to the "strident demands" of sportswomen, approving instead their realization that beautiful female legs delighted male audiences.)[2] Civil rights laws (like Title IX) were denounced as "overregulation." (Wanting to preserve power where it had traditionally been, the New Right advocated a sort of "corporate privatism" in which government could not intervene in any way in business, private schools, churches, and the patriarchal family.)[3] Indeed, besides cutting funding for abortion, welfare, and other social programs, Reagan weakened enforcement of environmental, health, and safety policies by appointing unsympathetic "nonregulators" to head federal agencies. His civil rights appointees opposed extension of the Voting Rights Act of 1965. As bad in liberal eyes as placing "foxes to guard the chicken coop" was his naming of ultraconservative judges to federal posts. The New Right backlash threatened to reverse the half-century-long trend in which the federal government responded to some of the cries of oppressed groups.

But would all the gains of the 1970s disappear with the blossoming of conservatism during the 1980s? Surely some of the changes would remain. Title IX was on the books, ERA only a few votes from ratification, and many states had passed their own antidiscrimination laws. Married and single women alike worked in large numbers because of career ambitions and/or economic need. Once recognized, could their capabilities be denied? New institutions like AIAW, the National Organization for Women, and the Women's Tennis Association now existed to protect women's interests. Both women's and men's consciousness had been raised—could attitudes reverse so quickly? Older women were growing accustomed to more equal opportunities, and a new generation assumed they could choose from a world of possibilities. Females had developed a sense of entitlement. Strong mentally and physically, they had become more familiar with fierce competition, and it seemed unlikely they would give up their advances without a fight. The question was whether they had the *power* to progress further.

CHAPTER 8

Backsliding:

AIAW, Title IX, and College Sports, 1980–1988

Advocates of women's sports celebrated in December 1979 when HEW issued its final policy interpretation of Title IX. "The impossible has been achieved," rejoiced AIAW president Carole Mushier. "The law of the land in relation to girls' and women's athletics is stronger than anyone could have hoped for in their wildest dreams."[1] Unfortunately, her jubilation did not last long. Saving the Title IX regulations was not the complete victory it had seemed. In fact, the victory may have contained within it the seeds of defeat. This realization hit one AIAW leader "like a ton of bricks" as she was driving into Washington, D.C. Later she recalled, "I said to myself, do you realize that you could win Title IX and as a direct result lose AIAW? I thought . . . that's so logical. If we win Title IX, the only thing [NCAA leaders] can do is to try and get us. That's all they can do. And I took kind of a deep breath."[2] Women's athletic leaders wanted to protect *both* the law and the organization that fought for their self-determination. During the 1970s they had been able to do that, fending off numerous attacks by male opposition. But as the calendar pages flipped into a new decade, AIAW leaders found that their luck had changed.

Just after it became certain that HEW's policy interpretation of the Title IX regulations would be fairly stringent, the NCAA Council appointed a Special Committee (on NCAA Governance, Organization, and Services) to consider incorporating women into the NCAA.[3] The committee met once in December 1980 and issued a preliminary report saying it would be possible financially and administratively to accommodate women's interests and programs into the NCAA.[4] That decision was strictly pro forma since the staff had been saying the same thing for years.[5] The committee report came in time to support yet another proposal to start NCAA women's championships. This year the legislation applied to small and medium-sized schools and would have initiated five championship events each for Divisions II and III. Representatives from a number of colleges cosponsored the legislation.[6]

The AIAW reacted the same way they had to similar proposals in 1975, 1976, 1978, and 1979. Meeting at their annual convention in Washington, D.C., the same time the NCAA convened in New Orleans, AIAW delegates adopted a resolution strenuously opposing NCAA women's championships and telegraphed it to the NCAA Council. The AIAW's leaders also suggested that the NCAA voluntarily put a five-year moratorium on such proposals.[7]

But this year, things turned out differently at the NCAA Convention. There was little debate among delegates about the measures.[8] Perhaps few objected because only 11 out of 886 NCAA delegates were female. However, such disproportionate representation was typical. What was different in 1980 was that Title IX's adjustment period had ended. Now HEW might start enforcing the law and asking why schools in some instances applied different rules to their male and female athletes (and the NCAA's procedures might be put at risk). For whatever reason, this year the proposals passed; in the 1981–82 academic year, then, the NCAA would begin offering to Division II and Division III schools five championships for women.[9]

The AIAW delegates were shocked and outraged. "The preservation of our organization is at stake," one declared.[10] It infuriated them that power was so skewed that another organization could make a decision that might destroy their own. Gary Engstrand, vice president of the University of Minnesota, called the NCAA vote "an act of unsurpassed arrogance . . . in which 600 men decided to be the shepherds for women's programs." At an emotional emergency meeting at the AIAW assembly, former AIAW president Peg Burke agreed. "This is not consent of the governed." To loud applause, she added, "In certain circumstances involving men and women, lack of consent is classified as rape."[11] Despite feeling victimized, delegates tried to brainstorm strategies. Perhaps the championships could be construed as a violation of Title IX, since the NCAA offered colleges only five championships for women, fewer than it offered men. Perhaps members of Congress who had criticized the NCAA's lack of due process could look into the matter. Perhaps AIAW could pursue an antitrust lawsuit. Perhaps the consumer goods of NCAA advertisers could be boycotted. Probably the first step to take, though, was to try to get the NCAA to overturn its vote at the next year's convention. That meant sportswomen would have to persuade the male athletic directors and/or chief executive officers of their universities that the move was unwise. In the atmosphere of panic, past president Charlotte West rallied her forces. "I'm not a quitter and I know you're not. So let's regroup and go get 'em." As they exited the meeting, delegates joined hands and sang, "We shall not be moved."[12]

A year of heated debate followed. The NCAA and AIAW bombarded university officials with information, trying to win their one institutional vote.[13] In January 1980 the NCAA wrote chief executive officers informing them of the championships and of a new governance proposal to bring hundreds of women into the administration of the NCAA by appointing them to its committees. In response to AIAW's criticisms, the NCAA made some alterations in the plan, adding a few more women on committees and eliminating a six-year limit on the period women would be guaranteed positions. The final governance proposal allocated four seats for women on an enlarged twenty-two-seat NCAA Council, two spots for women on the twelve-seat Executive Committee, and an average of 30 percent of the positions on Divisional Steering committees.[14]

The NCAA's leadership maintained that adding women's sports to the organization would be better for its member institutions. Ironically, it argued that the move was necessitated by Title IX. Given the obligation for equal rules for men and women, it would be easier for schools to achieve them "acting in common legislative forum" within the NCAA than through painfully slow negotiations with AIAW. Including women in the NCAA was only natural, part of an evolution toward the "unitary" administration of athletics. It would make the administration of intercollegiate sports more effective, just as the merging of men's and women's athletic departments made "institutional control" easier.[15]

The NCAA also defended its right to be making decisions about women's sports even though it was a predominantly male organization. The chief executive officers of member colleges chose representatives to the NCAA Convention, and those duly authorized delegates had the responsibility to address *any* questions about intercollegiate athletics. The NCAA's leaders went further, suggesting that AIAW's delegates did not have the similar backing of their institutions. They implied AIAW's delegates did not represent official positions but simply women's individual opinions. "Frankly, the extent of institutional control . . . of AIAW is open to question."[16] Having attacked their credibility, the NCAA then dismissed AIAW delegates' vocal opposition. "It is obvious that there are women who are opposed to NCAA involvement in women's athletics. It is equally obvious that there are women strongly urging that same NCAA involvement. Neither of those facts is particularly germane."[17]

Far from stifling women's voice, NCAA officials argued their plan would protect it. The NCAA had demonstrated great care in listening to women while devising their plan and now insured that approximately 215 women would be involved in NCAA committees. Even though women would not have equal voice, the governance plan's allocations reflected the ratios of men and women currently administering intercollegiate athletics and exceeded the percentages of female athletes. To protests that women's interests would not be protected when nearly all voting delegates to the NCAA Convention were men, the NCAA replied, "It is unreasonable to assume that men automatically will vote against women's interests, or that women would vote against men's interests. The majority of men and women in education are neither male chauvinists nor militant feminists."[18]

Finally, the NCAA disputed AIAW's forecasts of doom. How could NCAA championships cause the demise of AIAW? Institutions would not be compelled to enter their women's teams in NCAA events. If they chose to, it presumably would be because the NCAA offered something AIAW did not. If the AIAW were going to be destroyed so easily, perhaps it was not very effective. As for claims that colleges would have far greater expenses, especially in recruiting, if their women's programs adopted the NCAA's more permissive rules, the NCAA disavowed responsibility—those would "be caused by the Department of Education's enforcement of Title IX." As for confusion about eligibility and rules if schools should be playing in either organization's championships, the NCAA promised to be flexible and accommodating and did not anticipate any problems (unless AIAW retaliated in some way). Besides, "if there are ill-advised rules, the best way to affect those rules is to work within the organization to bring about change."[19] The NCAA championships would mean more competition and freedom of choice, which would result in excellence.

The AIAW, on the other hand, argued that the NCAA's plan was unwarranted, dangerous, and unethical. The NCAA women's championships were unwarranted because women's intercollegiate athletic needs were already being served by AIAW, an organization now larger than the NCAA, offering thirty-five championships in seventeen different sports. Even if the NCAA began matching AIAW's full program, there would be needless duplication. The NCAA and NAIA (another men's organization) provided fifty-two championships for all male athletes; for organizations to offer seventy national championships for females, of whom there were half as many athletes, made no sense.[20] The AIAW was proven to be meeting the needs of women in intercollegiate sports. Every poll taken showed sportswomen overwhelmingly preferred that AIAW remain the sole national governing organization for women.

Besides being unnecessary, there would be negative consequences if the NCAA began offering women's championships. First, there would be chaos. If a school could participate in either organization's championships, whose rules would it follow? Whose eligibility standards? Fair competition might well be inhibited—which male athletic directors would never permit if it involved men's sports. Second, recruiting differences could destroy traditional rivalries or force everyone to recruit strenuously. And in the long run, women's sports as a whole could be harmed since the two organizations would be competing for television contracts and neither could promise that its championships would have all the best teams.

The NCAA championships could hurt AIAW because on the surface they looked economically appealing to colleges. The NCAA could woo colleges and universities away with promises of footing the bill for women's championship expenses—benefits AIAW could not yet afford to bestow. (The NCAA's annual operating budget was over $20 million, AIAW's just under $1 million.) Unlike the NCAA, which brought in millions of dollars from men's football and basketball television contracts, AIAW depended largely on membership dues for its survival. If colleges dropped their AIAW membership, AIAW might have to fold. Therefore AIAW tried to suggest that despite the NCAA's apparent financial advantages, there may be hidden costs for schools—such as the increased costs if they had to recruit as strenuously for women as they did for men. The AIAW also suggested the NCAA was not being altogether forthcoming about how the expensive women's championships would be paid for—dues might go up, Division I universities might receive a smaller share of television revenues, and per diem benefits to some men's championships were going to be eliminated. Overall, then, some of the immediate benefits to schools might be outweighed by other costs.[21]

The AIAW's most heartfelt argument, however, was not about practical rules or economic matters but about ethics. For even though AIAW was an institutional membership organization with delegates appointed by chief executive officers, just like the NCAA, AIAW did more than just run sports for institutions of higher education. It provided an alternative philosophy of sport and dedicated itself primarily to women. It was an advocacy group for female coaches, administrators, and student-athletes. Leaders in the AIAW understood the concerns of administrators about different men's and women's rules and were willing to work with the NCAA about compromises; they would even be open to merger talks with the NCAA under certain conditions.[22] But they did not want women's voice to be muffled. Why would women want to trade running their own organization for a "perpetual minority role" in the NCAA? Why should they be satisfied with only 18 percent of the seats on the NCAA Council, and 26 percent of the NCAA general committees seats? And why would they make the change when NCAA initiated it as part of the movement toward unitary administration, which in practice had stolen power from women on campus? How could "the past discrimination represented by departmental mergers legitimize . . . future additional discrimination against women . . . ?" Under such circumstances, it made no sense to trust that the NCAA—whose lawsuit against the Title IX regulations was still pending—was sincerely interested in offering women equal opportunity. There was a fundamental issue of fairness at stake: would those directly involved in women's athletics have the right to develop women's programs, or would a system designed to serve men's athletic programs be forcibly imposed on women?[23]

By the time the NCAA Convention rolled around in January 1981, both sides were prepared. They had to be, because there were at least eighteen complicated, sometimes contradictory, pieces of proposed legislation referring to women. In general, those sponsored by the AIAW's supporters were intended to rescind the Division II and III championships passed the previous year, to delay further championships, or to force the amending of the NCAA's constitution to include women (a process that required a two-thirds vote instead of a simple majority). Opposed by AIAW's supporters were proposals to initiate nine women's championships in Division I, add more sports to those already approved by Divisions II and III, and set aside seats for women onto NCAA committees. This time, there would be many more women present, women who had studied the ins and outs of the NCAA's by-laws and constitution, prepared the arguments they thought most persuasive to male delegates, and mapped strategy for various potential scenarios.[24] Unfortunately, the sponsors of the championships and governance plan were equally prepared.

In fact, the deck was stacked against AIAW supporters. The NCAA's leadership set the order in which business would be taken up, chose the speakers for various roundtables, had the final say about constitutional interpretation, and held the gavel during voting. Although AIAW's sympathizers used every available opportunity to raise questions and spur debate, there were few such occasions. Obviously, most delegates had already made up their minds, and most accepted without question the NCAA leaders' blithe answers about legal interpretations, costs, and unselfish intentions.[25] A number of incidents confirmed women's feeling of being stifled. At the Division II Roundtable, for example, all eighteen motions about women's championships and governance were consolidated into one item, apparently to make use of rules limiting how many speakers could address each item. An AIAW supporter opened the discussion by asking a question. Two Executive Committee members answered, after which a second speaker had the floor, and an Executive Committee member commented. Then in an appallingly undemocratic move, the chair ruled the entire subject closed.[26] At the General Roundtable the delegates heard an extensive presentation by the chair of the Special Committee, lauding the liberality and practicality of the plan.[27] The AIAW delegates tried to point out potential problems with costs and rules and ways the plan used past discrimination to justify unequal representation, but all were denied, deflected, or ignored.

When it came time for the actual business session, AIAW advocates took the initiative, proposing that the agenda be changed so that questions be addressed in an order they thought more logical. The first issue, they thought, was the constitutional one about whether the decision to enter women's sports was properly done by amending a by-law (requiring a two-thirds vote) or by a divisional vote (requiring a simple majority). They suggested that the NCAA was breaking its own rules in order to make it easier for the women's championships to pass.[28] Only after that matter was decided would it be sensible to vote on whether the championships should be delayed in favor of negotiations with AIAW. These larger issues should be debated before minor details of rules, committee assignments, and which particular sports should be added in each division. However, AIAW members were admonished for questioning the established procedure and for their emotion. "I suggest we should return to the mature approach we have always had in this Convention," declared a council member, "[and] approach these matters dispassionately and follow the order as it has been laid out." The AIAW lost that battle, and the agenda remained the way the council had arranged.

The business session was marked by fervent comments and parliamentary maneuvers.[29] One of the first important measures on the floor was the governance proposal putting women on NCAA committees. An amendment to increase the number of seats for women was defeated. An amendment to delay the plan was also defeated. Finally the plan itself was considered, and passed, but barely. On a recount it still passed. Next, delegates considered a measure providing rules flexibility for women's sports until 1985. The NCAA's leadership favored the proposal because it supposedly made it possible for colleges to compete in either the NCAA or AIAW. In a surprising speech, Frank Broyles, the athletic director at Arkansas (and not previously known as a major supporter of women's sports) refuted the NCAA's claim that it was permissive legislation that merely allowed freedom of choice. Everyone knew, he said, that if your neighbor recruits, you have to. "So let's make it clear. When you get back to your campus, there will be no option, you will be recruiting." He protested that the NCAA was forcing women into the male model and generally railroading AIAW. "I have watched a power play I would like to have had when I was playing and coaching football. I have never seen such a blitzkrieg." Despite Broyles' plea, the proposal passed. Only then was the AIAW's legislation—a two-part measure postponing NCAA women's championships and mandating discussions with AIAW—discussed. To make matters worse, the chair ruled the first part of the legislation out of order, saying that altering the constitution by a resolution was an improper procedure. Christine Grant begged that parliamentary rulings not thwart the only chance to vote on this important proposal, but the delegates voted to uphold the chair. There would be no direct vote on AIAW's compromise solution.[30]

Next on the agenda were proposals to add more NCAA women's championships. The first would have instituted nine championships for Division I (large) universities. Alliances on it were confusing. Some Division I delegates opposed women's championships because they sympathized with AIAW; others did so because they thought it would be a larger financial burden for their men's programs. By that time, AIAW supporters did not care who voted with them, as long as the measure was defeated. To their pleasure, on the first vote, the measure failed in a tie (124–124). On the recount, it was again defeated (127–128). It appeared to be the first victory for AIAW, and it was an important one. Immediately, though, NCAA leaders sitting at the council dais emptied out onto the floor to try to convince people to change their minds. Meanwhile, other matters were taken up. Some open-division championships for women, in less popular sports like fencing, golf, and lacrosse, were barely approved. The AIAW lost again when the motion to rescind the championships passed in 1980 was defeated. Then in the last minutes of the session, someone made a motion to reconsider the Division I championships. On this third vote, there was a stunning reversal of ten votes, and the proposal was passed 137–117. The next morning, more women's championships for Divisions II and III were approved, driving more nails into the coffin of AIAW's hopes. Although many votes had been close, AIAW advocates lost on every single issue.

What or who was responsible for that outcome? The AIAW's supporters felt they had been cheated out of justice by NCAA leaders who had maliciously manipulated the convention.[31] Byers denied that the NCAA's leadership was the force behind the championships. He said the impetus came from NCAA members who sponsored the championship and governance plan legislation, and that there was no scheme to "control" women's sports. He did not initiate any such proposals after the membership rebuffed his efforts in 1975 and 1976. Of his staff, he said, "We were willing, but not eager, to take on a whole new area of responsibility."[32]

Technically, Byers's statements were true. The legislation was introduced by member colleges, and as opposition to Title IX suggested, there was not an eagerness on his staff to help women gain equality. Other actions, however, provide a great deal of circumstantial evidence suggesting that the NCAA's leadership did strongly favor the annexing of women's sports and was actively working behind the scenes to attain that objective. First and most obviously, if the NCAA staff had opposed the proposal, everyone would have known, and it could have thrown up roadblocks at many stages of the process. Instead, it helped clear the path. Many of the people who actually sponsored the legislation were NCAA officeholders or had close ties to the upper echelons of the NCAA. The

NCAA's leadership made the appointments to the Special Governance Committee and refused to permit the Committee on Women's Athletics to discuss merger and other alternatives seriously.[33] The Executive Committee had been looking for and finding ways to fund women's championships. Byers made the decision that the championships could be approved by a majority vote, making it easier—and perhaps the only way realistically possible—for the championships to pass.[34] The NCAA *News* printed misleading statements suggesting that HEW would be requiring the same rules for men and women (and that colleges faced trouble unless they applied NCAA rules to women soon).[35] Finally, Byers was negotiating for television rights to women's championships which he obviously felt certain that the NCAA would soon have, even though such Division I championships had not even been officially proposed yet.

The convention experience also undermined the NCAA's protestations of innocence. The choice of speakers, the quashing of discussion at roundtable forums, and the ordering of the agenda all convinced Swarthmore's Thomas Blackburn that NCAA leaders had played "power politics" and had "steamrollered" AIAW.[36] Clearly council members had left the dais to lobby delegates to change their vote after Division I championships had been defeated, and after the last-second reversal, they crowed together.[37] But perhaps noticing these matters was just sour grapes of the part of AIAW supporters, poor losers in a fair fight. Why should NCAA leaders not have been pleased when measures they agreed with passed? It was the tone, AIAW objected, the maliciousness apparent in the way they were treated. More than once they were hissed and booed as they rose to speak on behalf of AIAW. Instead of respectful disagreement, there was "raw hostility in the air." Various AIAW supporters described the atmosphere as "highly frustrating," "adversarial," and "bestial." "That was the most devastating experience of my entire life," an AIAW supporter remembered a few years later.

> I still don't even today like to recall the experience. . . . I had never been in a setting that was comparable to that. . . . There was overt and covert hostility, directed to women because they were women. . . . There's just no way I could be oblivious to it. . . . It wasn't just the fact that a group of men decided the destiny of a larger group of women. I mean, that was hard enough to cope with, but it was the male chauvinism that I've never experienced to that extent, and the absolute powerlessness . . . that is devastating.[38]

Walter Byers may have claimed he was sincere, but he did laugh as he gave a woman a (male chauvinist) pig coin. Another man did not bother to mask his hostility. "Quote me," he said. "Tell them to drop all the damn women's athletics."[39]

It may not be possible to know with certainty whether there was a malicious conspiracy among NCAA leaders to take over women's sports—but that may not be the most important question. Even if nastiness and hostility were present, they were only part of the story. Most people involved in the convention publicly claimed to be concerned with the well-being of women. In fact, among those committed to women's sports, there was some room for disagreement. Judith Holland, for example, a former AIAW president, became one of the few women who agreed to help design the NCAA's championships. She saw the change as inevitable and did not think it would destroy the AIAW.[40] It seems probable that some others who favored NCAA women's championships were well-intentioned. "I would state unequivocally that there is a sincere and honorable commitment," declared James Frank, whose Special Committee designed the governance plan.[41] Furthermore, even if the NCAA's leadership had pulled strings to help bring about the championships, these still had to be approved by a majority of NCAA delegates. What is most important, then, is not what the leadership intended but what the delegates actually did. Those delegates certainly were aware of AIAW protests.

The bottom line is that the odds weighed heavily against AIAW. The battle was taking place on the NCAA's turf, a powerful home court advantage. And not only was the leadership lobbying, but almost all the voting delegates were male. Those delegates had many reasons—malicious or well-intended or paternalistic—for supporting the proposals. Some wanted to save money. Some were concerned about the differing men's and women's rules; they either wanted to protect NCAA men's rules or wanted to simplify matters and avoid further battles over them. Some were probably sick and tired of AIAW women and saw this as a way to silence them and to control women's sports. Some probably wanted to preserve the NCAA's power and position. Some may have believed that the women's championships, if directed by a richer, older organization, really would provide quality opportunities for women. But it is difficult to know if they believed this would benefit women mainly because it was in their own interests to believe it. Regardless of their motives, however, even if they were "sincere," there is one damning fact: men in athletics were using their superior power to overrule the wishes of women. Christine Grant summarized the situation on the final day of the NCAA Convention, as she rose in symbolic opposition to one last proposal:

> Obviously, it was not persuasive to you that by your actions women . . . students and professionals were losing control of their own destinies. Obviously, it was not persuasive to you, but it was a conviction of those most closely associated with women's athletics, that your actions will do untoward damage. . . .

Finally, it was obvious that our appeal to your sense of fair play had little effect upon your action.[42]

There was no way she could convince a group whose leaders believed that
women's strenuous opposition was "not germane." Either NCAA delegates did
not understand the point or they did not care.

Now that it was certain that the NCAA would be offering women's championships the next academic year, AIAW leaders realistically assessed the prospects.
At a "think tank" a month after the convention, they anticipated major problems. There would be defections because AIAW could not come close to matching the $3 million in benefits that the NCAA could afford to offer. "Member insti-
tutions facing critical economic problems would be hard-pressed to refuse cold
cash at no cost," admitted AIAW president Donna Lopiano.[43] To keep winning
programs, many Division I universities would be forced to switch to the NCAA
to take advantage of its less restrictive recruiting rules. Once top Division I
schools began heavily recruiting, others would have to follow in order to keep
up, meaning that the "cream" of Division I would be lost. Since Division I
accounted for half the organization's income, those defections would be very
harmful to AIAW. Lower revenues would force cutbacks in AIAW's offerings for
all divisions, making AIAW less attractive and causing further defections. The
cycle would feed on itself, undermining the chances for attracting television
and other commercial sponsorships. In addition, there would be losses of different kinds of resources—locations for championship events and the women
to run them. Finally, enforcement of AIAW's rules would be hampered since vio-
lators now could simply drop out of the organization. This combination of
problems probably would mean the demise of the organization. Certainly, they
decided, AIAW could not continue for long in its present form.[44]

What, then, were their options? If it was as a common rule-making and governance body that made the NCAA attractive, perhaps AIAW could become a
women's *and men's* athletic organization. Unfortunately, though, it would be
difficult to attract schools away from the NCAA since that organization had
more economic benefits, and men's teams probably would not want to adjust to
the AIAW's more restrictive rules.[45] Another possibility would be for AIAW to
write off Division I championships and concentrate on serving Division II and
Division III colleges. However, it still would be competing with the NCAA for
those institutions as well as with NAIA. Perhaps instead of allowing women's
sports to be split three ways while AIAW died a slow death, it would be best for
women's sports to be handed over intact to the NCAA and NAIA. Women's sports
advocates could dissolve AIAW and try to advance their philosophy within the
NCAA or NAIA. Unfortunately, "that prospect likewise seemed dim" since NAIA

had even fewer women involved in governance than the NCAA, which had a 95 percent male faculty representative system and catered to merged, male-run athletic departments. "What would happen to the voice and vote of student-athletes and female administrators?" lamented Lopiano. "What would happen to our commitment to equal opportunity, to a strong Title IX, . . . to everything we worked so hard to develop and refine over the past decade?" The one remaining option was to seek judicial relief, to claim AIAW had been the victim of illegal acts by a monopolistic NCAA. Having considered these radical options, the AIAW's Executive Committee recommended that the Executive Board either dissolve AIAW or pursue legal action.[46]

The Executive Board decided to wait and see if things turned out as badly as expected. Indeed, membership renewal forms returned in June 1981 made the damage apparent. They showed that, whatever the wishes of women's coaches and administrators might have been, many colleges had read the handwriting on the wall and decided that the NCAA was the way to go. Two hundred schools—20 percent of AIAW's members—dropped out of the organization. An additional 12 percent renewed their memberships but said they would not participate in AIAW championships. In all, then, one-third of the previous year's participants would be gone. The losses were most severe in Division I, where 25 percent of women's programs did not renew their membership and another 23 percent declined to take part in AIAW championships. Division I, AIAW's "financial linchpin," would be half the size of the previous year, and indeed the "cream" of AIAW's Division I colleges had been lured away. Eighteen of the previous year's top twenty basketball teams would be missing, in addition to 90 percent of the best volleyball, 80 percent of swimming and diving, and 70 percent of track and field and gymnastics teams. Obviously, AIAW championships would become second-rate.[47] Things unraveled from there. The NCAA's promised flexibility did not materialize; colleges had to choose between AIAW and the NCAA because the dates of sixteen out of twenty-nine NCAA championships conflicted with AIAW events. ESPN, a sports cable channel, announced it would not televise any of the AIAW events it had options on because the highest quality (teams) could not be assured. In August, NBC announced its coverage also would be limited. Other commercial sponsors, some influenced by the NCAA, became reluctant to support AIAW.

The situation was deteriorating so quickly that AIAW's Executive Board decided to proceed with legal action. Because a typical antitrust case could take from three to five years (by which time the AIAW would be long gone), the organization sought a preliminary injunction against the scheduled NCAA championships. Lawyers for AIAW filed the request on October 9, 1981, and the next day AIAW leaders held a press conference asserting that the NCAA's monopoly power would destroy AIAW. "How long can any collegiate institution refuse NCAA's offer of free programs and cash bonuses?" they asked. The NCAA had earmarked over $3 million to subsidize the women's championships, even though it admitted that the championships would not generate over $500,000. "There is no way AIAW *or any other organization* that supports itself can compete with these inducements." "Obviously it's not fair," said Lopiano. "But our attorneys advise us it's also not legal."[48] Realizing AIAW's limited resources, the presiding judge proposed deferring the request for the injunction and instead recommended holding a speeded-up full antitrust trial. Both the NCAA and AIAW agreed. Unfortunately, by December matters were critical. NBC announced it would not honor its contract to televise AIAW's Division I events unless there was an injunction against the NCAA. It also refused to pay the $191,000 AIAW was counting on. Cutting its budget to the barest bones, AIAW spent its emergency cash reserves and concluded that, without a miracle, operating in 1982 would be "an economic impossibility."[49] Reluctantly, AIAW decided to file for the injunction and recommended to its Delegate Assembly that, unless there was judicial relief by March, they should not solicit memberships for 1983 and should dissolve the organization.

When the delegates met in January 1982, they knew it might be for the last time. The mood of the gathering fluctuated between grief, anger, and determination. The convention discussed the course of events that had led up to the Executive Committee's recommendations, and what to do about rules and regulations if the lawsuit succeeded or failed. They worried about the future of women's sports without the AIAW, and without the special annual ritual of the Delegate Assembly. It was a "marvelous, exciting place to be," recalled one woman. "Even though we debated every issue," related another, "there was still a sense of community and sisterhood."[50] At the same time they mourned their possible loss, they celebrated their accomplishments. "We have created something to be proud of—something that is good for kids—and supremely— something educationally sound and defensible," said Lopiano. In fact, it was because they had succeeded so well that they had been taken over. "Without money, without position, from scratch," recounted Lopiano, "we became too powerful, too threatening for the status quo in intercollegiate athletics to allow us to continue to do our thing."[51] They were tired of the same old story, that once again they were fighting for their very survival. They were angry that, once again, "our destiny lies in large measure upon the decision-making of others, rather than of ourselves."[52] In Lopiano that unfairness provoked a "very stubborn determination" to keep fighting to pursue their ideals, to preserve their rights and legacy. Still, they knew the odds were against them and so used the Delegate Assembly to thank one another for having shared such a unique opportunity, for having supported one another down a difficult yet fruitful path, for the honor of having been a part of the "dream that was AIAW."[53]

The district court rejected AIAW's request for an injunction, as did the U.S. Court of Appeals.[54] As a result, AIAW decided *not* to send out membership renewal applications and suspended its recruiting rules. It was the most responsible course of action. "If we do not get judicial relief, we may not be in business next year," explained new AIAW president Merrily D. Baker, "so we've got to put members in a position to be competitive in recruiting."[55] Meanwhile, the Executive Board laid off the remaining staff, sold the office furniture, and dissolved the organization. The AIAW now existed only in name in order to pursue the lawsuit. It would be reconstituted if it won.[56] As both organizations prepared for a full trial to begin late in the summer, the judge ordered them to try to work out a merger or out-of-court settlement before then.[57] After a series of counterproposals, the two sides met in June 1982, but they could not agree. Final resolution, then, was in the hands of the judicial system.

Hearings began in October 1982, with AIAW asserting that the NCAA was guilty of a number of antitrust violations. First, the NCAA "gave its women's program away free to all subscribers to the NCAA men's program." Such below cost or "predatory pricing" was "a severely anticompetitive tactic frequently engaged in by corporations with significant resources to drive weaker competitors from the field."[58] Economist James Koch testified that unless the NCAA believed women's sports were going to be more lucrative in the future, "one must assume that its recent conduct is designed to drive AIAW out of the market and out of business."[59] The NCAA's proceeds distribution formula created other incentives ("irresistible inducements") so that colleges would transfer their women's programs from AIAW to the NCAA.[60] When the NCAA decreased men's benefits and added women's benefits, it constituted an "unlawful linkage" or "coercive tie" of women's events to the monopolized men's events. Scheduling NCAA championships on dates conflicting with AIAW events, making optional rules, and manipulating and subverting NCAA constitutional procedures all demonstrated NCAA leaders' intent to monopolize. So did the NCAA's secretary-treasurer's acknowledgment that he knew AIAW championships would probably "fade away" as a result of NCAA actions.[61] In addition, the NCAA successfully persuaded corporate sponsors (the Kodak and Broderick companies) to break or modify their contractual arrangements with AIAW. Further, the NCAA used its power as a monopoly seller of men's basketball championships to get its women's championships televised, and marketed them in a manner calculated to deprive AIAW of television revenues. In sum, then, it was the NCAA's leverage (in men's sports)—not the comparative merit of its women's programs—that explained the NCAA's immediate success and AIAW's sudden failure.[62]

The NCAA denied all the charges. There was no malicious interference with AIAW's commercial sponsors. Some conflicting championships were unavoidable and, where possible, the NCAA had avoided the same dates. As for predatory pricing, because of its budget surplus the NCAA could afford to offer some things that AIAW could not. However, a monopoly was not necessary to offer those benefits.[63] Nor did the championship and governance package reveal an attempt to monopolize. The changes came from the NCAA's own membership in a democratic majority vote after extensive public debate in which AIAW actively participated. The AIAW could "not produce a scrap of evidence" that the votes were coerced by the NCAA's leadership.[64] A number of female witnesses testified that colleges had many reasons besides cost to choose NCAA women's championships.[65] They might prefer a single governance organization, a common set of rules, the NCAA's conference and qualifying procedures, and its differing philosophy. "The real controversy at issue here are matters of governance philosophy and educational policy . . . and how schools can best regulate women's intercollegiate athletics and provide equal opportunity on campus," asserted the NCAA's defense. "Such matters are not antitrust concerns."[66] Finally, AIAW was itself a former monopolist simply trying to retain its power, so granting it relief would not be in the public interest. Any losses sustained by AIAW were the result of *competition*, the very thing antitrust laws were intended to protect.

The district court ruled in favor of the NCAA. Justice Thomas P. Jackson said that AIAW had proven the probability of the NCAA succeeding as a monopolist but had not convinced the court that AIAW's devastation was the product of anticompetitive conduct. In particular, AIAW had not proven the specific *intent* necessary to sustain the claim of attempted monopoly. "While the evidence of parliamentary maneuvering may evince the [NCAA] leadership's determination to see the proposal for women's governance adopted," Jackson wrote, "it does not prove that such determination derived from an intent to monopolize."[67] The court believed NCAA leaders' denial that they had been attempting to take over women's athletics. Although there may have been an atmosphere of intimidation at the 1981 NCAA Convention, some institutions testified they had "voted as [they] wished for reasons of conscience, self-interest, or both." As for the claim that the NCAA's dues and distribution formulas constituted "irresistible inducements," the evidence was not persuasive. In fact, two of AIAW's own witnesses, Christine Grant and Donna Lopiano, worked at Division I universities that *had* managed to resist the incentives (when they decided on principle to remain in AIAW). Finally, AIAW failed to prove the NCAA had tied together its men's and women's television rights. The court held to an extremely strict standard of proof, saying that although it was implied, neither television network was *expressly told* that covering women's events was necessary in order to obtain the men's contract. "The evidence may demonstrate, as the AIAW has always contended, that the NCAA is preoccupied with it's men's program and insensitive to the needs of the women," wrote Jackson, "but it does not prove an illegal . . . tying agreement."[68]

The AIAW appealed the decision, arguing that the district court had mistakenly applied some antitrust criteria. The appellate court agreed with AIAW on a minor point, but because it did not find evidence that the district court's other findings were "clearly erroneous," it upheld the decision.[69] The justices reiterated the interpretation that although NBC and CBS felt *obliged* to submit a bid for women's championships, they were not *coerced*. Moreover, AIAW could not make a case of "unlawful monopolization" because the NCAA had not yet become a monopoly when AIAW filed the lawsuit. As for "attempted monopolization," AIAW had not proven specific intent.[70] The NCAA's plan took shape in public view for over a year, a process that was "the antithesis of the conspiratorial plotting of the would-be monopolist to acquire surreptitious control of a market to control prices or destroy competition." Finally, the appellate court was not sure it agreed that leveraging was illegal. Even if it were, however, AIAW could not prove that its economic injury was caused by illegal practices. And AIAW had not convinced the justices that the NCAA' policies "represented anything other than NCAA members' rational judgment of how best and most equitably to promote men's and women's intercollegiate athletics." In fact, the NCAA might simply have been offering a superior product and in that case the shift in membership was a result of "direct competition."[71]

And so, it was over. To AIAW supporters, the decision seemed mistaken because at times the justices agreed with AIAW's arguments but came to a very different conclusion.[72] What was the difference between feeling obliged and being coerced? How could the court acknowledge the NCAA had monopoly power, then say it had not used it? But as after any athletic loss, there was nothing left to do but complain about the outcome (and think what might have been). Backers of AIAW could curse their luck of the draw in getting conservative justices. Or they could criticize the law, which permitted the NCAA to be "preoccupied with its men's programs" while taking over the women's, to manipulate its own rules and be "insensitive to the needs of women." Motives could be mean, and behavior unfair, without being illegal. Or they could question the system of power that meant that, even in a "democratic" vote, women still could not obtain justice.[73]

Its money gone and legal options exhausted, AIAW was dead.[74] The loss was enormous. The organization had been the first and only provider of national women's intercollegiate athletic opportunities. It had started with seven open championships in 1972–73 and expanded to three divisions holding forty-one annual championships in nineteen different sports by 1981–82. It regulated over 42,000 teams in its first nine years, at a very moderate cost. The AIAW's importance went far beyond the events it sponsored, however. Also important was the manner in which it had done things for female athletes. "[The AIAW] cared about kids. Really cared about kids," one member asserted. Its members also cared about one another and the process by which they worked. Further, AIAW's leaders strove to create an organization that was fair, democratic, inclusive, conciliatory, and responsible. This attention to process, as well as their pioneering efforts to create a new model, resulted in an organization very different from the NCAA. There was "encouragement of women for other women to become more aggressive, to speak up"; great efforts toward building consensus; more discussion and questioning of fundamental issues. Women in AIAW took great pleasure in their distinctiveness. "It was the fact that it was different that we were proud [of], because . . . we were not shackled by traditional thinking and traditional structures and traditional approaches."[75] The AIAW was the means through which women could experiment with an alternative to the male model of intercollegiate sports, and which (besides being more sensitive to women) was less commercialized, more student-oriented, less exploitative, more economically prudent, more educationally focused, and more democratic.

In many senses, AIAW was a feminist organization—it was run primarily by women, for women, and it strenuously fought for equal opportunities. "Whatever came up in amateur sport, there was a group that was analogous to the NCAA which everybody knew. Nobody could get our initials straight, but they knew there was an organization that they ought to invite . . . to provide a woman's viewpoint." It had been an extremely effective vehicle for women's self-determination, encouraging female coaches and administrators to meet, discuss, organize, and govern themselves. The AIAW also had made a difference on a more personal level, to hundreds of women who were often isolated and marginalized on their own campuses. In AIAW those nontraditional women were not a minority; they found company, support, and role models. The presidents of AIAW were "strong women," one remembered, "women who have sat down and said, 'This is what I'm going to be and what I'm going to do.' Because they were already in an area that society told them they shouldn't be in, they had to be strong." The acceptance and legitimation for being different could lead to a powerful personal identification with AIAW. "The organization was far more important to me than myself," recalled a former president, "and that's what hurt so much." The death of their collective resulted in profound grief. "There was almost a feeling of family," declared one leader. "We had all grown up together. And I think, too, we took pride in each other. I don't think we realized the degree to which we were helping each other as women. We learned from these positions, and we were supportive of each other."[76]

But was "everything we worked so hard to define and refine over the past decade" lost? In the last Delegate Assembly, AIAW speakers emphasized that no matter what happened to the organization, its founders would be leaving an important, living legacy. They had put women's teams and national intercollegiate competition on a sound footing, and they had nurtured female coaches and administrators so that they practiced their leadership abilities. "Both precedents have been firmly enough established," insisted Merrily Dean Baker, "that neither will disappear from the scene of sport in this country." The goals and dedication of all those women would not perish in the face of adversity. "Curfew never rings for commitment," proclaimed Baker. "Curfew never rings for the pursuit of an ideal."[77] Women's sports leaders had a continuing obligation to student-athletes and to themselves. They should have faith in their values and take heart from the fact that they had succeeded against difficult odds before. After all, women's sports advocates had won decent Title IX regulations and protected the regulations from numerous onslaughts. Although they no longer had their organization, they did have the law on their side. And the law was perhaps the best, more permanent legacy.

Or did they have a secure law? They had definite regulations and an effective interpretation of the policy, but in mid-1980 enforcement had not yet begun. The Office of Civil Rights (OCR) within the newly created Department of Education was still getting ready, preparing a manual and holding a training seminar for investigators. Women's sports advocates kept close watch on the process, calling the first draft of the manual a "debacle." Promises of a second draft appeased them somewhat. "If this all works—(it will be the first time)," wrote Margot Polivy, "[but] it should produce some positive results."[78] With guarded optimism sportswomen lauded the government's announcement that soon it would be enforcing the law "quite vigorously," beginning with eight schools (from among the eighty-four schools with complaints already filed against them). "To the degree that your campuses can show you are actually pursuing equal opportunity for women athletes, you will suffer no penalties," OCR's assistant secretary reassured athletic directors. "But to the degree we ascertain a lack of good faith, we will be there with the full force of the Federal government to compel you . . . to treat women students fairly and justly."[79]

Hardly had enforcement of Title IX begun when disaster struck in November 1980: Jimmy Carter lost his presidential reelection bid to Ronald Reagan. The leaders of the National Coalition for Women and Girls in Education cringed: they had experienced great difficulty trying to persuade a Democratic administration to move quickly on Title IX; now a new administration—especially a Republican one that had promised to dismantle the Department of Education—could only be worse. At a spring 1981 meeting with Terrel Bell, the new Secretary of Education, representatives of the coalition found out that changes were likely. "The clear indication was that the Secretary (like the Reagan Administration) favors a cutback in federal Title IX enforcement," reported Margot Polivy. Bell confirmed that he sympathized with a narrow interpretation of Title IX, similar to the one the NCAA wanted. He also supported a bill that would make enforcement of Title IX very difficult.[80] "The Secretary, while pleasant, left no doubt that 'they' had won the election and felt that the victory gave 'them' the right to reinterpret the law and that this was a 'conservative Republican Administration,'" reported Polivy. "Since he emphasized the point several times, I assume they find it important even if it does represent a novel legal theory that the election, in and of itself, changes the law."[81]

The law may not have been changed by the election, but altering its interpretation and weakening its enforcement could bring about virtually the same result. Indeed, the government's initial investigations disappointed women's sports advocates. Despite finding discrimination in a number of areas, the Department of Education officially decreed the University of Akron to be in compliance with Title IX. "While it is nice to see a [Letter of Finding] on the subject finally released (8 years and 10 months after enactment of the statute)," commented Polivy, "the substance and procedure leave much to be desired."[82] The National Coalition objected to Secretary Bell's policy of "conciliation" and "nonconfrontation," in which there would be negotiations before the department issued its letter of finding. If changes were promised, the schools would be found "in compliance." Feminists protested this new procedure: after all this time, why were institutions given so much flexibility? How quickly would they have to make changes? How would their remedies be evaluated?[83] There were a few victories, though. "Hawaii caved in," celebrated an AIAW representative after the university agreed to double the amount of financial aid to female athletes and hire two new full-time coaches.[84] In general, though, enforcement was not nearly stringent enough for feminists. The letter of finding for the University of Nevada at Reno did "not require any corrective action whatsoever to eliminate major instances of serious deficiency." The coalition requested that the OCR reopen the investigation, declaring, "This constitutes an abdication of OCR's responsibility." After seeing the report on the University of Bridgeport, an AIAW officer noted the OCR had "classif[ied] as negligible differences amazing things."[85]

Suddenly, numerous initiatives to weaken Title IX cropped up. Vice President George Bush took charge of a Presidential Task Force to examine whether the Title IX regulations were among the "burdensome, unnecessary or counterproductive Federal regulations" that should be eliminated.[86] Secretary Bell announced that he wanted to spare small colleges costly paperwork and investigations under Title IX, and accordingly, the Department of Education proposed changing the definition of "federal financial assistance" so that Guaranteed Student Loans and Basic Education Opportunity Grants were not included in it. That would have freed at least 325 colleges from being subject to the law.[87] The Justice Department overruled that suggestion, but as Polivy observed, "The D. of Ed. apparently never sleeps," for it was preparing another proposal to limit Title IX coverage even further, to only those programs or activities that *directly* received federal funds.[88] A split in the Reagan administration temporarily sidetracked that proposal, too. But by late in 1981 women's sports advocates were already becoming "weary of hearing this seemingly never-ending litany" of threats.[89]

While prospects looked increasingly bleak in the federal bureaucracy, in the early 1980s the locus of the battle began shifting to the courts. Two separate types of cases were working their way through the judicial system. Female athletes at a number of institutions had filed suit charging sex discrimination and claiming that Title IX offered them protection.[90] Coming from an entirely different angle, a number of schools directed legal action against the Title IX regulations. The law stated that there should be no sex bias in "any educational program or activity receiving federal financial assistance." Because it received no direct federal funding, the University of Richmond sued the Department of Education, claiming the government had no right to investigate Richmond's athletic programs. Hillsdale and Grove City colleges also challenged Title IX, refusing to sign a form assuring the government they were in compliance. The colleges denied they were subject to Title IX at all because they received no government aid—although some of their students received help under federal financial aid programs. Therefore there were three basic issues at stake. First, what constituted "federal financial assistance"? That is, were grants and loans *to students* considered government aid *to the college* that triggered Title IX coverage, or were colleges that generally avoided federal contact (except student aid) exempt? Second, was the *entire institution* subject to Title IX's rules or were only the specific programs receiving federal dollars covered? Third, how was "program" defined? Did a program have to *directly* receive federal dollars to be covered, or was it sufficient that it had benefited (more indirectly) from federal dollars? The 1975 interpretation ("Nondiscrimination on Basis of Sex . . .") guiding HEW's Title IX regulations—the one generally accepted throughout the remainder of the 1970s—was the broad one: that if a school accepted *any* federal aid (even if just student grants and loans), the *entire institution* had benefited from it and was subject to federal antidiscrimination laws.

Only some courts backed the government's original interpretation. The Third Circuit Court of Appeals ruled that Temple University's intercollegiate athletics program *was* covered by Title IX even if it received no *direct* federal assistance. The court believed that Congress had intended for coverage to be institutional. It also argued that Temple's athletic department should be covered because it clearly benefited from federal aid.[91] In the Hillsdale College case,

however, the Court of Appeals in the Sixth Circuit reached the opposite conclusion. It interpreted "program" very narrowly and declared that, to the extent
they equated "educational program or activity" with the educational institution
itself, the Title IX regulations were invalid.[92] The district court in the University
of Richmond case also ruled that Title IX was strictly "program-specific." That
court went further, enjoining the government from investigating any other athletic departments in its jurisdiction unless they directly received federal aid.[93]
Despite protests from civil rights organizations that this would decimate Title
IX, the Department of Education decided not to appeal the Richmond decision.
"This is a clear retreat," added the National Coalition's chair, "a clear signal that
the Administration is not serious about equity."[94] Harry Singleton, OCR's director, agreed that the Richmond decision went too far, complaining it "contra-
dicts the weight of existing case law, disputes the validity of the department's
regulations and jeopardizes the ability of O.C.R. to effectively perform its statutory duties."[95] Opinion was divided, then, within both the federal bureaucracy
and the judicial system.

The showdown came in the Supreme Court, in the case of *Grove City College
v. [Secretary of Education] Bell.* Grove City College was a small, private,
Presbyterian-related school that prided itself on its independence. The college
refused to sign its compliance form, not because it wanted to discriminate
against women but on principle, because it wanted to remain free of government interference. After the refusal, the government threatened to cut off financial aid to Grove City's students. Grove City sued, arguing that although some
of its students received federal grants, the *school itself* was not a recipient and in
fact had carefully avoided accepting loans or grants from either the state or federal government. Nor should the college have to sign an assurance form covering the whole institution, because Title IX should apply only to programs
receiving direct aid.

It was a unique case, not only because the school's independence was atypical but also because the government's position had changed so radically. The
Nixon and Carter administrations had consistently followed a broad "institutional" interpretation of Title IX, which they believed Congress had intended.
Many people agreed, as indicated by a House vote of 414 to 8 on a resolution
stating Title IX's coverage should not be restricted. But the Reagan administration's heart was hardly in a defense of a strong Title IX. In fact, it was so unen-
thusiastic it considered asking for an outside advocate to defend the government's original position. The National Women's Law Center offered, filing a
brief on behalf of twenty-one civil rights and student organizations and
requesting permission to participate in oral arguments. When the Court denied
the request, that left no one to defend a firm civil rights position. Squaring off
instead were a conservative Reagan administration with tepid support for Title

IX against an even more conservative Grove City College. The Justice Department took the position that Grove City students' basic grants *did* constitute federal aid sufficient to bring the college under coverage of Title IX, but only the student aid office, not the whole institution, had to be in compliance. It argued that "program" should be interpreted very narrowly to mean only the *direct* recipient of money.

In a 6–3 split decision, the Supreme Court approved the government's narrow interpretation. "Although the legislative history contains isolated suggestions that entire institutions are subject to the nondiscrimination provision whenever one of their programs receives federal assistance," wrote Justice Byron White for the majority, "we cannot accept that in the circumstances presented here . . . Grove City [College] itself is a 'program or activity' that may be regulated in its entirety." He ruled that federal financial aid to students did mean Grove City College could be regulated, but *only* its financial aid program. Justice William Brennan spoke for the minority, rejecting the Court's narrow reading because it ignored the legislative history of Title IX, the accepted meaning of the statutory language, and the unique postenactment history of the law, in which Congress had allowed the regulations to stand after examining them in 1975 and repeatedly rejected attempts to narrow their scope. He said the practical effect of the majority's interpretation would be absurd: an institution's financial aid program could not discriminate on the basis of sex, but its admissions, athletics, and even academic departments could. Finally, he criticized the government's about-face on civil rights. "The interpretation of statutes as important as Title IX," he chastised, "should not be subjected so easily to shifts in policy by the executive branch."[96]

Predictably, reaction to the decision sharply differed. Grove City College was not entirely pleased because one part of its institution would be subject to government interference. Many conservatives, however, were ecstatic. The Reagan administration had received approval for its new, narrow interpretation. Many men in athletics celebrated, believing they had finally won the fight against Title IX. One, who had just negotiated a settlement with the OCR to remedy athletics inequities, planned to "tear up our conciliation agreement." His lawyer advised him it was too soon to be certain, just as William Kramer cautioned NCAA members that the Grove City ruling appeared to leave athletic scholarships, at least, under Title IX's jurisdiction. He believed that at some schools, however, the rest of the athletic program would be exempt. Of course, the decision shocked and discouraged women's rights advocates. "Title IX is now like a piece of Swiss cheese," declared Margaret Kohn of the National Women's Law Center. "Instead of being a comprehensive statute, it has holes all over the place."[97]

The Grove City decision had immediate, significant effects. Although few schools made wholesale cuts, some university officials believed they now could get away with doing less for women, and certainly they stopped fearing strict government scrutiny.[98] The OCR informed its officers that in most instances they now would have to trace federal funds to a specific program before they could look into a complaint of discrimination. They could investigate a program that used buildings built with federal aid, for example, and athletic scholarships if students received federal financial aid, but they could not trace funds beyond the specific program unless an institution received the rare instance of "non-earmarked" federal funding.[99] Besides limiting future investigations, the OCR curtailed many currently under way. At the University of Maryland, for example, the OCR had found discrimination against female student-athletes in six different areas. After Grove City, however, it dropped the case because no federal funding had helped finance those activities.[100] At other schools the OCR severely restricted its inquiry. In August 1983 it had informed Auburn University of serious violations of the law in athletic scholarships; travel and per diem allowances; coaching; provision of lockerrooms, practice, and competitive facilities; recruitment; and the accommodation of interests and abilities. But in a March 1984 letter the OCR explained, "It appears that the discrimination found is beyond the jurisdiction of Title IX," and the agency would follow up *only* on the athletic financial aid issue. Legally, the rest of the substantial discrimination could remain.[101] In all, the investigations of the athletic programs of at least twenty-eight institutions of higher education were closed or put on hold.[102]

Civil rights activists moved to halt the bleeding. Not only had sex equality been endangered by the Grove City decision, so were antidiscrimination efforts with regard to age, race, ethnicity, and physical disability. The language that the Court struck down in the Title IX regulations was the same used in Title VI of the Civil Rights Act of 1964, Section 504 of the Rehabilitation Act of 1973, and the Age Discrimination Act of 1975. To prevent those statutes from also being hamstrung, a bipartisan group within Congress introduced legislation to restore the broad interpretation of the laws. It insured that entire institutions were subject to antidiscrimination rules if they received any federal funds. There seemed to be almost unanimous agreement that the Supreme Court's decision was harmful; in fact, over 150 national organizations supported and 56 senators cosponsored the "Civil Rights Restoration" bill. Sen. Bob Packwood, the Republican who introduced the legislation, predicted Congress would speedily and overwhelmingly pass the bill.[103]

A powerful minority, however, opposed the bill, including President Reagan and Attorney General William Bradford Reynolds, who claimed that the language would actually expand the government's authority rather than merely restore it. They contended it would open the way for greater federal intrusion into state and local affairs.[104] Sen. Orrin G. Hatch agreed and vowed to "do anything to stop it." As chair of the committee holding hearings on it, he had many tools available to do so. Although the House passed the measure by a huge majority (375–32), Hatch's allies made parliamentary maneuvers (including pairing it with a controversial appointment and bogging it down with amendments) that contributed to its failure in the Senate. In 1985 and 1986 Hatch and Reynolds again led the fight against the bill, now joined by abortion opponents, who said the Title IX changes would expand abortion rights.[105] For three years in a row the Civil Rights Restoration bill failed, and during that period college athletic departments had little to fear in the way of Title IX enforcement.

By the mid-1980s, then, the cause of women's intercollegiate athletics had sustained some serious blows. Most significantly, Title IX had been riddled with holes. No one knew whether the regulations women had worked so hard to obtain would be restored to their full force. In the short term, that meant that at many schools the expansion of women's programs ground to a halt. No one knew whether matters would get worse—if colleges would actually scale them back. Optimists pointed out that, in some instances, there were other sorts of protections for sportswomen now in place, such as state laws and a college's own nondiscrimination policies. More importantly, notions of equality had taken hold. It was these altered attitudes, they believed—not merely the law— that made the difference. After all, enormous change had taken place even before Title IX became operative.[106] The question remained, though, was it the sincere desire to eliminate discrimination or fear of possible enforcement that had caused the change? "No athletic director would cut women's sports simply because there was no Title IX," asserted an NCAA representative."[107] Bernice Sandler felt less secure, however. Saying that behavior would not change was "like saying because we all have free speech now, we don't need the First Amendment any more. I feel a lot better having the First Amendment. I would also feel a lot better having Title IX back."[108]

Besides no longer having a strong law, AIAW was gone. Women's sports did not suffer terrible setbacks in the NCAA, but neither did they flourish. Competitive opportunities remained about the same, as the number of NCAA women's championships gradually increased to almost as many as AIAW had offered. The NCAA made a few changes to accommodate women, such as making an exception for pregnancy to its five-year eligibility rule. On the other hand, there were some disappointments. Not all the hoped-for economic advantages from the NCAA materialized. The organization substantially increased its dues in 1985 and cut back on the championship transportation benefits for smaller schools in nonrevenue-producing sports.[109] In addition, many men in the organization still resisted equality. A proposal to insure that Division I universities sponsor at least six sports for women (the same minimum as for men) faced significant opposition, and proposals to add Division III women's soccer and lacrosse championships only barely passed.[110] The new championships meant the NCAA offered women only eight fewer championships than men, but the number of male teams and athletes invited to events was almost twice that for women.[111] No affirmative action measures were even considered to equalize participation rates. In fact, skewed priorities remained in evidence. Schools that did not offer enough women's sports received sanctions that penalized only their women's teams, not the men's teams.[112]

The absence of AIAW muted the voice of activist sportswomen. Feminists had difficulty gaining access to NCAA leadership positions and influencing the nominating process.[113] Efforts to obtain a seat on the NCAA Council for conferences that sponsored only women's sports failed. Being a minority within the NCAA meant being outvoted on measures that would have fared quite differently in AIAW. The most important example came when the NCAA submitted a statement to Congress *opposing* the Civil Rights Restoration measure. The official organizational position—consistent with the NCAA's long-standing opposition to the Title IX regulations—made no mention of women's strong support of the bill.[114]

Women's intercollegiate sports also struggled with continuing problems. The NCAA could not be blamed that women's sports were much less popular than men's, but neither did it attempt to alleviate this state of affairs. Some had hoped the NCAA's wealth and history would result in greater attention and legitimation for women. Better advertising capabilities and being associated with the men gave the NCAA an advantage over AIAW. But either the NCAA did not put enough into its women's championships or its greater resources did not make any difference. It is difficult to understand why the entire NCAA women's championship series drew only 73,497 fans in 1984, when *one* women's game at Louisiana State University packed in 22,157.[115] Each year more people watched NCAA women's basketball, but the numbers were still disappointing. Six times as many people attended Division I men's championships as the women's.[116] Was the problem the lack of promotion, the wrong kind of promotion, or the continuing uninterest of American sports fans in women? Probably all three. At many schools women complained that athletic public relations offices did not do enough to sell their teams. Certainly that was true, but besides apathy those offices suffered from ignorance. They did not know how to win essential media exposure for women.[117] They did not know whom to target or how to make women's sports appealing to them. Although the law might force colleges to offer more opportunities to its female students, it could not force people to cheer them on.

Not surprisingly, many believed that spectators were not yet comfortable with female athletes. Americans were more accustomed to the *ideas* of equality and sports for women, but they did not yet embrace the intensely competitive female athlete. As a result, promoters and coaches still sometimes turned to the traditional strategy of apologetic behavior. They tried to assert the "normal" femininity of players in order to reassure fans. For a promotional photo, Louisiana Tech dressed its women's basketball team in the lace gloves and hoop skirts of nineteenth-century Southern Belles. The photo was not an exception to the usual. "We like them to be winners on the court, but nice-looking ladies off it," explained a coach. "You don't wear raggy old jeans to class. There are some things a Lady Techster just can't do." Apologetics continued especially in trying to avoid the "taint" of lesbianism. While recruiting, some coaches subtly (by showing pictures of their husbands and children) or overtly let parents know that they were not lesbians and that they did not condone lesbianism among their players. Anson Dorrance, coach of the repeat national champion UNC soccer team, denounced such gay-bashing as misguided and unethical, but he recognized it as a shrewd recruiting technique. While he asserted that he would never inquire into his players' sexual preferences or recruit on the basis of looks, he admitted he was gratified when his team "looked good getting off the bus." He believed that if they could just combat the old stereotype that female athletes were unfeminine, women's sports would become more popular.[118]

Athletes certainly were not immune to the phenomenon. "A long time ago, women athletes used to be considered men, or manly," explained Cheryl Miller. "But now, at U.S.C., we stress being feminine off the court, [and] being masculine, playing like men, on the court." Like many others, Miller did not realize her coping mechanism was an old and unsuccessful one. And like many other modern athletes, she saw nothing wrong with the expectation that she should emphasize her femininity off the court.[119]

Women's intercollegiate athletics also had a new problem by the mid-eighties. Although the number of participants had been steadily rising, the number of female coaches and administrators had been steadily declining. The drop was dramatic. In 1973 virtually all (92 percent) of women's intercollegiate teams were coached by women. But by 1984 only 53.8 percent were. The numbers were worse in Division I programs, where only 49.9 percent of the coaches were female.[120] The change may have resulted from the greater attractiveness to men of coaching women's teams once Title IX guaranteed decent pay; in addition, men increasingly were doing the hiring for women's programs (and they were probably more comfortable employing men). Women did less hiring because, after most schools merged their men's and women's departments, they had less administrative power. By 1984, 86.5 percent of women's intercollegiate athletic programs operated under the aegis of a male head athletic director. In fact, 38 percent of those programs had *no female at all* involved in their administration.[121] This distressing trend would have serious consequences for the future.

Although there has been little research on the subject, one study suggested male coaches interact differently than female ones with female athletes, and that in many cases the power dynamic becomes abusive as authoritarian coaches dictate players' behavior from hairstyles to diet.[122] Regardless of dynamics, female athletes were injured by the lack of role models. In addition, the prevalence of men in the field created more difficulty for women who wanted to coach. When combined with the loss of AIAW, it further eroded the female voice in the leadership of women's sports.

When Title IX became law in 1972, the leaders of women's intercollegiate athletics started dreaming of a revolution. They hoped that the next generation of female student-athletes would have equal opportunity. They fantasized that the women's program would no longer be a stepchild, hidden away in dimly lit corners of a tiny old building housing the women's physical education department. They longed to share the resources available to men in athletic departments, so they could have bigger and better facilities, longer schedules, new equipment, decent uniforms, more coaches. By equality they did not mean "sameness"— women should not have to adopt all of men's practices or get subsumed into a male-run organization. In effect, they wanted equality *and* difference. They wanted female student-athletes to have the same opportunities for participation and similar resources and benefits as males; but they also wanted self-determination—the right to develop a different model of intercollegiate athletics from the established one. The AIAW was the vehicle through which they pursued both equality and difference—fighting for more teams and bigger budgets but in a less commercialized, less exploitative, less expensive, and more student-centered brand of competition. They hoped that Title IX guaranteed not just sameness but the power to build an alternative so impressive it would eclipse the men's. Colleges and universities then could freely choose whether or not they wanted their male and female athletes to follow the more educational, woman-designed model.

But it had proved difficult to forge a different course. With each year after Title IX passed, women's college sports began to resemble men's a bit more. Sometimes things changed because AIAW leaders thought it unfair to deprive females of the benefits males enjoyed; sometimes, as in the case of athletic scholarships, they were forced by the law to adopt the male practices. By 1980 AIAW differed from the NCAA not so much in kind but in degree. At large universities, winning was the primary goal of most programs; they spent enormous amounts of money to recruit the best female athletes available to help the team; they tried not to break or get caught breaking a myriad of regulations; they played national schedules and vied for commercial rewards. Indeed, many coaches and players of women's teams resented the suggestion that they did anything differently from men's teams. By 1985 there was no AIAW at all, eliminating any remaining differences in rules, regulations, and philosophy. The early AIAW ideals—such as not recruiting, wanting females to pick the school best for them as people, not as athletes, and treating athletes no differently from other students—seemed hopelessly out-of-date. They died out not because they were bad ideas but because the male model was there first, and because women's sports leaders did not have the power to alter it. Undoubtedly, the NCAA forced much more change in the female model than the women's affected the men's. In short, Title IX came to be interpreted as requiring "sameness," and the model adopted was the men's, not the women's.

If women's sports advocates had thought they could have either self-determination without the guarantee of equality or equality without the guarantee of self-determination, probably most would have chosen the latter. In the same vein, if they had to choose between keeping either the law or AIAW, they would have chosen the law. The AIAW leader quoted at the beginning of this chapter realized as she drove into Washington that women probably would not be able to have both:

> I took . . . a deep breath and I said, well, in my book, an organization is just an organization, that's a transient thing. The important thing is the law of the land, the concept. There's no question but that we work for Title IX. And, if the other happens as a direct result, well, we'll do our best. But if that's the case, and we lose AIAW, we still would have gotten what's more important, because AIAW without Title IX, what do you see for the future there? For the young women coming up in this country, they deserved the law . . . a law of the land.[123]

The law—even if it gave only a limited type of equality—was important to preserve. Indeed, for female student-athletes in the 1980s, having the same sorts of opportunities as male athletes was no small matter. A female star at a large university enjoyed a scholarship covering tuition, room and board, outstanding training facilities, free shoes and equipment, nationwide travel, tutoring services, and high-quality coaching. She was much better off than her deprived and virtually invisible compatriot in the 1960s.

Women's sports advocates would have settled for the limited definition, but did the female athlete really have even that sort of equality? She did not have as many teams available to her (Division I schools averaged nine teams for men and seven for women).[124] Although at most institutions her sex put her among a majority of students on campus, she was a minority among athletes: there were twice as many male athletes as female athletes. Her school then used that statistic to justify giving females only 30 percent of athletic scholarships. In addition, women's sports got about 18 percent of the school's athletic budget.[125] Of course, her status did not approximate that of a male star. When she competed, probably only a handful of dedicated fans watched from the stands, and that group probably did not include the school's athletic director. Finally, she experienced pressures about femininity and normality unique to female athletes, which her male coach might not understand.

Hoping to attain the twin goals of self-determination and equality probably was naive. The male model was too popular, too established. Its backers had too much at stake in it and too much power and money (in the NCAA and on campus) to allow it to be destroyed. It seemed more likely that sameness could be achieved because that only required the sharing of resources (not power). But even that proved unattainable. Whether because this was too expensive or required too much commitment to women, it was a rare campus that truly gave its female athletes equality. Therefore, although they deserved and had every right (however unrealistic it might have been) to expect them, women's sports advocates achieved *neither* self-determination nor equality. Still, their efforts had not been in vain. The risks they took by pressing for change in the face of entrenched opposition had made a difference personally and politically, for themselves and their students. No one would mistake the big-time opportunities of the 1980s for the 1960s, but women's sports advocates had reason to be gravely disappointed. Not only had they not reached their goals, but they had lost the tools for future change. The merging of departments and the hiring of men diminished their power on campus. When they had faced barriers on campus in the late 1970s, they were bolstered by AIAW and Title IX; but now AIAW was defunct and the courts and the Reagan administration had cut the heart out of the law. By the late 1980s, then, it was clear they had already reached their peak. That peak was not as high as they had hoped, and chances for going higher were slim. The movement for change had stalled.

CHAPTER 9

A Second Stage:

Pro Tennis in the 1980s

After many strides forward during the 1970s, women's intercollegiate sports suffered two major setbacks during the 1980s. When Title IX was incapacitated and AIAW annexed, college athletes and coaches became more vulnerable to the twin dangers of apathy and antipathy. Would tennis pros also suffer setbacks during the 1980s? Like the collegians, the women pros during the 1970s had argued for equal treatment and had sought better conditions through a separatist strategy. They had made a partial break with the U.S. Lawn Tennis Association (USLTA) and the men's game and built their own tour. Unlike the collegians, however, the tennis pros never had any law to aid them. Thus they were not affected directly by the elections and Supreme Court decisions that weakened Title IX. Still, they were not immune to fallout from shifts in attitudes behind the governmental changes—in fact, as entertainers, the tennis pros depended much more on the goodwill of the public. As seen in the "Battle of the Sexes" matches and the sponsorship by Virginia Slims ("You've Come a Long Way, Baby"), the fledgling tour had capitalized on the fascination with the women's movement. But the 1980s was a postfeminist decade, and the pros were entering a second stage of professionalism. Despite their initial success, they still worried about the burdensome "secret" of lesbianism, were wary of being unfeminine, and had reason to wonder whether winning women would ever be loved.

In the early 1980s it appeared that the women pros were succeeding quite well. After starting small in the early 1970s, each year brought more growth to the circuit. In the mid-1970s there were competitive opportunities available for women pros twenty-six weeks out of the year; by 1982 the total had jumped to forty-nine weeks. Only in a few of the older traditional tournaments like Wimbledon and the U.S. Open did they play at the same locales at the same time as men. At those coed tournaments they often received more national media coverage because of the added attraction of male stars, the long tradition of the tournaments, and network televising. While the women appreciated the greater attention, they were disappointed to share the spotlight unequally with the men. During the rest of the season, however, they had center stage to themselves. At their own tournaments they competed for increasingly large purses, which by 1983 totaled $11 million. Women's prize money had come a long way since 1971, when President Nixon congratulated Billie Jean King for earning $100,000; in 1983 the twentieth-ranked player earned that much, and the top player won over $1 million.[1] Unlike college women, then, tennis pros had arrived at a good balance of independence from and interdependence with men's sports. They still worked under the ruling bodies of the USLTA and the International Lawn Tennis Federation, but they retained self-determination through their union, the Women's Tennis Association. No major decisions about women's tennis—be they about prize money, scheduling, rankings, promotion—were ever made without the WTA's input.

The women pros showed a willingness to be flexible about strategies. Having succeeded on their own in the early 1970s gave them the confidence to demand decent treatment. In the fall of 1980, for example, WTA members felt dissatisfied with USLTA. They believed USLTA should put more resources into junior women's development programs, expand the number of women permitted in the U.S. Open from 96 to 128 (the same number as men), and push for more women's television coverage during the Open. The complaints were not new, and after some footdragging by USLTA, the WTA took action. Its members began discussing a boycott of the Open and the formation of their own rival tournament. Capital Sports, a New York promotional group, promised a tournament for 128 women with almost twice the prize money offered by the Open. If fifteen of the top twenty women agreed to play in the secessionist tournament, NBC promised substantial television coverage. It sounded tempting, but a small and determined minority of top players, including Chris Evert, thought it too risky to break away. Therefore the WTA nixed the deal, but not without having wrung some concessions from USLTA. Increasing the size of the draw to 128, USLTA promised to be more forthcoming about how revenues for the tournament would be used for juniors and agreed to lobby the networks for better television coverage. Most players were satisfied with the outcome because, besides enjoying the occasional major tournaments with the men, they recognized that they benefited from them. "We do realize that 100 years of having a tournament is meaningful," acknowledged King, "and that the hours on television and the growing stature of the tournament are important."[2]

Women's tennis stood on solid ground largely because of corporate sponsors. They supplied the prize money for the tournaments, crucial because gate receipts did not cover expenses. In return, businesses received advertising: their names were included in all tournament publicity, their banners posted all over the courts, and their products were associated with the women (young, usually white, fit, often good-looking) and their very respectable activity. Apparently, sponsors believed the deal worthwhile because there was no shortage of them. When in 1978 Virginia Slims made a less attractive offer than its members desired, the WTA found Avon and Toyota eager to replace them.[3] It had not always been that way. In the late 1960s Billie Jean King had asked the Wilson company to produce another women's racquet. Wilson had refused, saying that its one "Maureen Connolly" model was sufficient until Connolly died.[4] In the early 1980s, however, racquet companies were the ones asking women pros to lend their names to their products. In addition, pros endorsed cosmetics, resorts, cars, shoes, socks, blue jeans, cameras, computers, and watches. As their advertising contracts implied, women tennis pros were in the limelight more than ever before.

Not all the coverage was ideal, of course. Sportswriters still occasionally had difficulty treating the pros strictly as athletes. In particular, they alluded to their gender in ways they did not for male athletes.[5] Of up-and-coming prospect Pam Shriver, *Sports Illustrated*'s Frank Deford declared, "So stylish is she, so unlike the other young women players. Glamorous and leggy as a woman, animated and pouty as a girl."[6] In the course of their descriptions, reporters were more likely to pause over a female players' attire and make observations about their appearance than for a male.[7] For example, *World Tennis* reporter Wayne Kalyn proclaimed Bettina Bunge the second-sexiest player. He liked her intelligent and sensual eyes as well as her manner. She eschewed the "art of coquetry," which made her "all the more flirtatious to her panting audiences." When they pointed out the female pros' attractiveness, reporters believed they were simply calling it the way they saw it (although they did not realize their blind spot with regard to male athletes' bodies and clothes). They also believed they were doing the female pros a favor, adding to their popularity and "normalizing" them. "Pretty, sexy, well-adjusted, happily married ladies have their competitive fires, too," asserted *Sports Illustrated*'s Curry Kirkpatrick. Kirkpatrick was trying to compliment Evert; yet while his adjectives distanced her from traditional stereotypes of female athletes, they did not dismiss the stereotype. Instead, he treated Evert like the exception. And even as he conveyed male approval of her, he diminished her in her own right. "That's Jimmy Evert's daughter and John Lloyd's wife," he wrote. "They think they'll keep her."[8]

Although some of it was flawed, the media coverage of the women pros had improved enormously. By the early 1980s, coverage that highlighted gender as much as athletics was much more rare. Accounts that took the athletes seriously—that narrated the match results and included scores and analysis of turning points and techniques—had become more common.[9] Readers found out not only who Chris Evert and Martina Navratilova were dating (Burt Reynolds and Rita Mae Brown, respectively), but that Evert lacked confidence in her net volley and that Navratilova might be unbeatable if she could master the topspin backhand. Equally important was the quantity of the coverage.[10] As the tour expanded, so did news of it. Women pros graced the pages (if not the cover) of *Sports Illustrated* regularly and could also be found more often in daily sports pages as well. In 1974, for example, the *Washington Post* had had only six stories on women's tennis; by 1980 that number had jumped to forty-four.

For the first time, females could become millionaires through sports, and young girls everywhere began aspiring to do so. By the early 1980s a tennis career had become so appealing that an entire subculture grew up around it. The junior tennis circuit had existed for decades, but its popularity took off when families began single-mindedly pursuing stardom for their daughters. Envisioning the next Chris Evert, parents now handed racquets to children who could barely hold them. Teen success stories did occur—blonde, All-American Tracy Austin won the U.S. Open in 1979, when she was just sixteen. She won $1 million in just twenty months on the tour, and her off-the-court endorsements brought in another $1.5 million annually.[11] Star Andrea Jaeger turned pro at age fourteen. Pursuing the same outcome, parents shuttled their children from school to practice to tournaments; coaches kept their eyes peeled for the next Austin; tennis academies, where would-be prodigies practiced five hours a day, flourished; and pony-tailed girls returned backhand after two-handed backhand. Agents rated the youngsters like cattle, promising cars, fame, and six-figure contracts if they measured up and turned pro at the right time. The best twelve-year-old in the country received free clothing from the French firm Ellesse, free racquets from Wilson, and free trips abroad.[12] Indeed, so willing were corporations to invest in tomorrow's dreams that a junior girl on her way up could get endorsements easier than some of the established pros.[13]

However, the dream most often proved elusive. Very few aspirants—according to one study, only one out of every 12,000 (male or female) high school athletes—could make it to the professional level. Even among those who made it that far, only a few could reach the top. Unfortunately, the payoff for a second-level pro was not so lucrative. In 1983 the fiftieth-ranked player earned $42,256, and almost half of that went toward expenses. Unless she was exceptionally popular and on her way up, she probably had no income from endorsements because those contracts had performance clauses in them. If she got stalled for very long in the lower ranks, a young woman would have difficulty qualifying for the best tournaments, finding practice time, and affording coaching, all of which meant there was little chance of moving up. And what then? She might be able to play professionally for a decade and then become a teaching pro, but if she soured on tennis, she had little to fall back on. Her high school education would have been spotty, and she would have focused all her energy on developing just one skill.[14] Even for the most gifted, there were no guarantees. Tracy Austin made millions quickly, but because of a string of debilitating injuries, retired at age twenty-one. Andrea Jaeger gave up the game by age twenty, the victim of physical and emotional burnout.

Nevertheless, many girls happily traded the normal life of a teenager to pursue their tennis dream. Critics claimed they were too young to make a fully free and informed decision: they were afraid to disappoint their parents; they did not realize what they were giving up. Many teens scoffed at such reasoning, asserting it was their choice and they were doing exactly as they pleased. Thirteen-year-old star Noelle Porter did not care if her days, crammed with tennis and discipline, left little time for socializing. "I feel a lot different from every single student in that whole school," she explained.[15] She hated school, feeling much more comfortable in the tennis world. For many others, though, the junior circuit was filled with tensions. They experienced enormous pressure to succeed from themselves, their coaches, and their parents. Adults pushed them to extremes, theoretically for their own good, or because they were living vicariously through their daughters.[16] "At the Nationals, I saw a little girl lose in the quarterfinals," reported Noelle's mother Madelyn Porter, "and her 250-pound father grabbed her by the ponytail and yanked her off the court and whacked her across the face." Like the infamous parents of Little League boys, mothers and fathers of young tennis hopefuls, too caught up in their children's competition, engaged in fistfights and hair-pulling.[17] Others, having made an enormous financial, physical, and emotional investment, came to view their child as a commodity. Some children may have deemed it worthwhile but, especially when considering that success was so unlikely, the price they paid was high.

The odds of achieving stardom were even longer if a girl did not belong to the right socioeconomic categories. Grooming a junior tennis player required a great deal of money. In 1984 expenses for a ten to twelve-year-old amounted to

they had struggled and socialized together.[23] Billie Jean King said her generation was "protective of each other" and "very family-like with each other." She believed the next generation of players, those in the 1980s, were different. Not having shared the bad old days of empty bleachers, and not having to worry that the tour might fail, they were more focused on individual goals. The new breed stood apart from one another, isolating themselves from their rivals. Players were not close, according to King, because "there's more money . . . more of an entourage. They're more insulated."[24] Younger stars hired professionals to manage every aspect of their careers, from endorsements to investments to training, strategy, diet, and travel. Their parents, coaches, and agents took great care to protect them from harm and distraction. Older players adjusted to this second stage of the tour. Martina Navratilova, for example, hired a coach, manager, and nutritionist. She missed the sense of community, but she also liked the stability of the tour in the 1980s.[25] It gave her the chance to concentrate more fully on her athletic performance and bestowed upon her greater benefits.

Chris Evert serves as a marker for the changes that had taken place. As the press and public began taking women more seriously, Evert began treating herself with more respect. By 1976 she had revised her plan to retire before she ruined her chances of marriage. By 1981 she would not call herself a feminist ("Man is still the breadwinner, no matter what the women's libbers say"), but she informed her husband that she wanted to pursue her career a little longer. Evert made other changes as well. She used to wear makeup "because I thought it would make me look more attractive and feminine." By 1981 she admitted that "makeup runs in about five minutes, and it's ridiculous and impractical to wear." She had also realized that throughout her life she had been trying to win to please the men in her life—first her father, then her boyfriends. In 1980 she could report proudly after her U.S. Open victory, "For the first time . . . I won something for myself."[26] Evert even altered her playing style, becoming more aggressive and taking more risks. These outward modifications evinced a more fundamental transformation in her self-image. Throughout most of her life Evert had performed a fascinating psychological manipulation in order to distance herself from the stigma attached to the female athlete. "I never felt at all like an athlete," she said. "I was just *someone who played tennis matches.*" She admitted that she employed apologetic behavior to counteract not just the disapproval of spectators but her own self-hatred.

> I still thought of women athletes as freaks, and I used to hate myself, thinking I must not be a whole woman. The nail polish, the ruffles on my bloomers, the hair ribbons, not wearing socks—all of that was very important to me, to compensate. I would not be the stereotyped jock.[27]

As she and the women's tour grew up, Evert became more accepting of herself, less ambivalent about her sport, and less afraid of the stereotype. "Now I really love the image that a woman athlete has," she declared. Although skeptics did not think she was as comfortable as she claimed, no doubt she had come a long way. Recalling the days when she had announced she would never fall down for a point, she laughed, "Why, I've been falling down and sweating for a couple years now."[28]

On the other hand, Evert went only so far. The women pros competed for fans, and like the others Evert seemed desperately to want evidence of her acceptance, not just in the form of commercial contracts but in applause from spectators. The women pros frequently interpreted cheering as approval of them as individuals (not simply as athletes). They noticed, and took it personally, when crowds rooted for their opponents instead of them—it meant they were not loved.[29] Speculating about why fans liked certain players more, they hypothesized that the feminine "All-American girl" image paid off because spectators were familiar and comfortable with it. Evert in particular cultivated that image, and when she implicitly denigrated other players, it caused resentment. Rewriting history, Chris Evert began suggesting to journalists that she and Evonne Goolagong were the first players to wear jewelry on the court, and had arrived like saviors finally bringing femininity to women's tennis. "Women's tennis badly needed a young, fresh face," Evert claimed, "someone removed from the stereotyped woman jock."[30] Billie Jean King corrected Evert, pointing out that she wore more jewelry on the court than Evert and that Suzanne Lenglen had been wearing bracelets as early as the 1920s. She also let her know she felt insulted. "I don't like you doing [that]," she told Evert. "I consider myself feminine. I feel like a woman and I am a woman, Chris. . . . I think you're being really unfair to all of us, who, quite frankly, made it possible for you to go out and be as feminine or non-fem or whatever . . . as is possible." King said Evert apologized to her, "but she's continued to do it. I've told her twice and I'm not going to tell her anymore."[31]

The intense concern with a salable, feminine image helps explain the panic that broke out after the disclosure of Billie Jean King's affair with a woman. While estranged from but still married to Larry King, Billie Jean became romantically and sexually involved with Marilyn Barnett, hairdresser to a number of pros. The affair began in 1972 and lasted somewhere between three and six years. During some of that period Barnett served as Billie Jean's salaried personal secretary. Although suspected on the circuit, the affair was not known outside it. When the relationship cooled, a disturbed Barnett tried various ways to continue the connection, including threatening to make it public. Out of a combination of guilt and fear, King allowed Barnett to stay in her Malibu house rent-free and offered her half the proceeds from its sale. Barnett's lawyer argued that scores of love letters were worth more than $125,000, but King refused to give in to either emotional or financial blackmail. In response, Barnett filed suit under California's new community property law, demanding as alimony the house and half of King's earnings for their years together (amounting to over $1 million). King did not know about the suit until early May 1981, when a reporter from the *Los Angeles Times* called her. "I went into shock," she recalled. "I just screamed. I paced back and forth in my bare feet in the apartment holding my racket and I think I wore a trail into the rug." She expected the worst and wanted to run from it. "I've got to get the hell out of here," she said. "This is it. This is going to ruin so many things I've worked for, so many dreams I've had for tennis."[32]

It seemed like disaster. King had poured her heart into building the women's tour, and this seemed to endanger it. A lesbian affair by Billie Jean King, the personification of the game, confirmed the worst stereotype. "Nothing seems to titillate the press and the public more than homosexuality—and particularly if it relates in any form to a female athlete, because we're all supposed to be gay. Right?" wrote King. "I've known well enough about all the slander and innuendo applied to us."[33] King had a number of very specific fears. Mostly, she dreaded public disapproval, and therefore she hid like one ashamed. "I just didn't want to be seen; I didn't want to be anywhere where people could look at me."[34] She also feared she would forever be remembered for the affair instead of everything else she had done. "I fear that, years ahead, when people hear the name of Billie Jean King, they will think of the scandal before the championships," she commented shortly after the disclosure. "And that would hurt, hurt very badly."[35] She worried, too, about her future. Old for an athlete, with many knee operations behind her, she had little time to erase the incident from memory. In addition, she wondered if her friends would now be harassed or become suspect by association. "Does this mean I can never again have a friend who's female?" she lamented. And would a reputation for homosexuality mean she would be discouraged from working with junior players?[36]

Tormented by these fears, King acted appallingly contrite. She followed her first impulse, which was to deny Barnett's story, but after realizing how easily it could be proven, she decided to admit the truth. With Larry and her parents accompanying her, King held a press conference. Head bent and eyes downcast, her tone was sober and apologetic. She called the affair "a mistake." She seemed to be asking forgiveness. "I only hope the fans will have compassion and understanding."[37] In an effort to salvage her career, King joined the public relations circuit, granting interviews to Rona Barrett, Barbara Walters, and *People* magazine. In them she occasionally expressed some resentment at the double standard. She was criticized for entering a loving, long-term relationship at a point when she and Larry were discussing divorce, but no one criticized male athletes who boasted of a string of exploitative one-night stands.[38] More often, though, she looked anguished, her demeanor a far cry from the confident King who had asserted women's rights in the mid-1970s.

As her repentant posture suggests, King accepted many stereotypes of lesbianism. After feminists criticized her for implying that lesbianism was wrong, King clarified that her "mistake" had been having an extramarital affair, not specifically a homosexual one. Few people heard that clarification, however, and the rest of her behavior allowed the perception to continue. Indeed, she strongly resisted being labeled homosexual. Obviously the term did not precisely fit, since she was bisexual, but her objection seemed to be about more than semantics. "I hate being called a homosexual," she told *People*. "It really upsets me." She claimed she resisted the label because "I don't feel homosexual." Like many people during their early nonheterosexual experiences, King had internalized so much homophobia that she would do mental acrobatics in order to avoid applying the term lesbian (with its corresponding stigma) to herself. She thought of the affair (which was hardly a one-night stand) as an "isolated experience" and told herself she had not adopted the homosexual lifestyle (as if there was just one).[39] She shared her rationalizations with the public, hoping they, too, would see that she was not one of those despised lesbians. She asserted that she did not hate men, and that it hurt her feelings when people made that assumption. Clinging to Larry, she said she was closer than ever to him.[40] She emphasized that she really wanted to have children. Distancing herself from stereotypes, King tried to demonstrate that despite the affair she was the same (normal) woman she always had been.[41]

How well did these tactics succeed in disarming public hostility? Press coverage varied. Some tabloids, like the *New York Post*, loudly announced that a lesbian scandal was shaking women's tennis and claimed that parents of young players were so terrified they posted "shower guards" to protect their daughters from lesbian advances. The *National Enquirer* got few bites but offered money to players to expose others and provide sensational stories. *People* magazine was more sympathetic, and mainstream periodicals were generally kinder. Regular tennis reporters, who knew King well and respected her (and had not previously exposed the affair), tended to downplay the incident and be protective of her. Many, like Pete Axthelm of *Newsweek*, simply reported the story and the concerns that it might hurt the tour. George Vecsey of the *New York Times* recounted King's achievements and criticized her only for not being more forthright. *Sports Illustrated*'s Frank Deford helped King write an autobiography diffusing the issue. His magazine's editorial declared that the sex lives of individual athletes were strictly their own business, but that the incident might promote some legitimate inquiry into the issue of homosexuality and athletes.[42]

Although the press discussed the subject more explicitly than ever before, the discussion was short-lived and superficial. *Sport's Illustrated*'s two-page consideration probed more deeply than most. Its editor observed that although homosexuality and bisexuality were more widespread in male sports than usually acknowledged, they had "been far more of a factor in women's sports" because of the image of athletes.[43] No one questioned a male athlete's sexuality because sports confirmed his masculinity, whereas sports called into question a woman's femininity. This unfair stereotyping caused problems for promoters of women's sports. Still, since lesbianism was commonplace on the women's tennis tour (and more so in golf), there should be further study of the phenomenon. In particular, the author wondered about causes. First, was there a biological predisposition toward homosexuality? If so, did this somehow contribute to lesbians participating in sports? Or was the sport-lesbian connection more social in origin? That is, did lesbians gravitate toward traditionally male activities? Or were heterosexual women socialized to avoid certain sports because of their negative image? Was there any truth to the claim that women on the pro tours turned to one another because they were lonely and isolated from men? Were female athletes, as pentathlete Jane Frederick said, more "physical and concerned with our bodies" and therefore more likely to share "an affinity that makes one woman understand the pleasure of another (and . . . draw us to each other)"? Although it raised important questions about a link between sexuality and gender, *Sports Illustrated* could supply no answers. Indeed no one could, since the subject had always been the subject of whispered speculation rather than rational investigation.[44]

Fans' reactions were also mixed. It is difficult to gauge if many people actually changed their opinion of King, because she had almost reached the end of her playing career, and because she had always been someone who evoked strong feelings, both positive and negative, in spectators. Those who never approved of her aggressive play and outspoken feminism probably found the affair one more reason to dislike her. On the other hand, those who rooted for her because of those same characteristics probably did not turn against her. *World Tennis* published only a few letters from readers on the issue, most of which supported her. One man called upon King to promptly resign from her post as president of the Women's Tennis Association because of her "sexual perversion," but another commended her. "The issue of bisexuality has been kept in the tennis closet far too long," he wrote. "Integrity and honesty are all too often compromised in favor of self-gain and deception."[45] Many readers agreed that the incident did not diminish King's outstanding contributions to the game. King reported that "almost all" the letters she received were from people who wanted to tell her "they were for me or they loved me."[46] In fact, she believed that many people who had "thought of me as a tough bitch" now had more sympathy because she had been exposed and was "vulnerable, at last."[47] Just a few weeks after the revelation, King had a match in San Diego. She walked out on the court with trepidation, her mind filled with stories of San Diego conservatism and the spread of the Moral Majority. To her surprise, she was greeted with a long standing ovation. "After that I knew that it wasn't any majority and certainly not a moral one that disapproved of me."[48]

Yet King's short-term assessment of the fallout should not be given too much weight. As she acknowledged, she had "expected the absolute worst and said to myself that anything I got beyond that was fortunate."[49] Years later she saw the matter in a less positive light. "You teach your children to be honest, to be true to yourself, and then . . . [when you are honest about your behavior] everybody doesn't want to hear about it."[50] In fact, there were very real and significant costs because the affair become public, especially from corporate sponsors. Although she did not lose her livelihood or suffer public denunciation, King paid a high price. Negotiations for a Wimbledon clothing line deal worth $500,000, which had virtually been finalized, fell through after news came out. She also lost endorsements with a Charleston hosiery company, a Japanese clothing company, and a blue jeans contract worth $300,000. Her business managers made a conservative estimate that over the next three years she lost at least $1,500,000.[51] She took for granted that many other companies would not renew their contracts with her once they ran out, and doubted new products would sign her. In fact, a year later, she was the only major player in the world without a clothing endorsement contract.[52]

Those associated with King were also affected. Her husband Larry lost over $100,000, as did Team Tennis (which Billie Jean had helped organize), when a backer reneged on a promise of $150,000. Women's circuit organizers feared the incident might hurt all of them. Toyota, one of the tour sponsors, regretted the adverse publicity. One sponsor reported he had only received half a dozen negative letters, which were countered by the same number of supportive ones. Nevertheless, neither Toyota nor Avon categorically reaffirmed their support. "We'd have to take a wait and see attitude," said Avon's director of public relations. "We wouldn't want to do anything to hurt our image."[53]. Then, for reasons not publicized, Avon did not renew its contract when it expired a few months later. Everyone understood advertising realities. "The business community had made itself quite clear," according to one observer; "it liked its players to be happily—overtly—heterosexual." While King lost millions, Tracy Austin, an injured player with a boyfriend, kept collecting huge checks even though she could not compete.[54] At least one woman, on the brink of being hired for a public relations position, was denied it because she was rumored to be lesbian.[55]

Nervous, the pros put aside their usual competition and stood together, realizing that if it were negative enough, the image of one female athlete affected them all. Publicly, they downplayed the extent of lesbianism on the circuit. Homosexuality "is not something that goes on very much," said Pam Shriver.[56] They also made a show of unity and support for King. The WTA, for example, refused to accept her proffered resignation. Chris Evert wrote an editorial in *World Tennis* saying her heart went out to King because her privacy had been invaded. She lauded King's accomplishments and asked, "Who are we to knock it if someone is gay?"[57] King appreciated the support but believed the other pros came to her defense not so much out of loyalty as self-interest, "because all female athletes feel that we are treated unfairly in this regard."[58] Privately, pros (in all sports) worried more than the public stance suggested.[59] Heterosexual pros thought that tour opportunities might be limited because of negative press, and that they might be "unfairly branded." "A lot of people who are straight are scared," admitted golfer Nancy Lopez.[60] Homosexual players, many of whom already lived with the fear of exposure and reprisals, felt Barnett's betrayal of King more intensely. Many people, including some sports psychologists, advised them not to "come out," and indeed, suddenly women presumed to be lesbian were seen in public on the arms of men. Remaining "closeted" took a high toll on a person's energy and self-esteem, but was an understandable response. It was a "lesbian witch hunt," according to an anonymous player, and that served no one's interests.[61]

Only one other player publicly acknowledged being bisexual. Czechoslovakian-born Martina Navratilova, blessed with a forthright nature, had taken no unusual steps to hide her sexuality. It was hardly a secret, and numerous reporters observed, in print, that she was spending her free time with best-selling lesbian novelist Rita Mae Brown.[62] After the King-Barnett incident, however, Navratilova began to worry over further press about the relationship. "The whole tennis world was quaking," she recalled. She had another, more personal reason to be concerned: she had applied for U.S. citizenship and feared her relationships with women could be used against her.[63] Naively, she admitted these fears to a reporter but asked him not to print them. He waited a few months, until Navratilova had been granted citizenship, then published a story in which she explicitly admitted the sexual relationship with Brown. From that point on, the world knew even more of the details of her personal life, from her stormy breakup with Brown to her moving in with basketball star Nancy Lieberman (who declared she was strictly heterosexual), to her taking up with a former beauty queen with two children. Although her roller coaster personal life unquestionably affected her tennis performance, as it would any athlete, rarely had the sports pages seen so much coverage about a pro athlete's love life.

It is difficult to measure the ramifications of Navratilova's disclosure because, besides her sexuality, Navratilova had a number of other "strikes" against her. Her aggressive ("masculine") serve and volley game and her foreign birth all could dampen her popularity. In particular, her number one ranking caused many fans who liked to pull for the underdog to root against her. One sportswriter actually called her an "unlovable champ" because she was so good.[64] It is not uncommon for spectators to dislike dominant champions, but the cheers and jeers for Navratilova sometimes had sexual overtones. Certainly some homosexuals cheered for her because of her sexuality, but more people rooted against her for the same reason. At the U.S. Open match against Chris Evert, a female voice shouted, "Come on, Chris, I want a real woman to win."[65] Navratilova said she only received one "really bad" letter. "I've gotten good letters from women, men, housewives. Mothers haven't been pulling their kids away from me, yelling, 'Get away from her!'"[66] Letters to the editor printed by *World Tennis* varied greatly, but for every one complaining that a story about an "avowed lesbian . . . makes me sick," there were two applauding Navratilova's honesty, courage, grace, and ability.[67] Although the fans usually withheld the outpouring of love and approval that Navratilova desired, on rare occasions she received it.[68] In its place, she had to settle for a grudging respect for her athletic abilities, which was readily acknowledged.

The press and commercial sponsors posed more of a problem than fans. Navratilova had no doubts that sportswriters treated female athletes differently than males. They regularly asked women if their sexual partners were women, but although certainly some well-known male athletes were sleeping with men, no one asked them. "You know that if a reporter asked that question of a man, he'd get a knuckle sandwich," observed Navratilova. "But if a woman smacked a reporter who asked insinuating questions about her sexuality, that would only prove the point, wouldn't it?"[69] Reporters camped out on the WTA pros' hotel doorsteps, salivating for a juicy tidbit of gossip. The tone of the comments about her personal life also bothered Navratilova. "It annoys me," she said, "that you don't see the same level of snideness about male athletes, gay or straight."[70] Because she was bisexual, her acquaintances were subject to rude speculation in print of a sort spared Chris Evert's friends. This intrusive sensational media coverage decreased the chances for commercial ventures. Navratilova knew of only one deal canceled because of her relationship with Brown. (She had contracts with Computerland, Vuarnet, and Porsche as well as tennis equipment companies.)[71] However, there is no way to know how many other companies never considered her because of her sexuality.

Navratilova became very aware of her image and she consciously worked to improve it. In the mid-1970s it was clear she had enormous athletic potential but had not met it yet. A volatile player, she was prone to emotional shifts on court. Nor was she in good shape physically. She weighed 170 pounds and was dubbed "The Great Wide Hope" by commentator Bud Collins. Around 1980, however, Navratilova began to train far more intensely. Besides lengthening her tennis practices and hiring a coach to help with strategy, she began serious off-court workouts. She lifted weights, ran wind sprints, played full-court basketball, trained her reflexes, and paid more careful attention to her diet. She significantly reduced her percentage of body fat and shed thirty-five pounds. Besides the changes to improve her game, Navratilova made some to her appearance. She visited a fashion consultant and changed the style and color of her hair (to blonde), began wearing some makeup, and tried to make sure photographers took pictures only when she was looking good. "I was really concerned about my image," she wrote in her 1985 autobiography, "not so much who I thought I was, not so much what the public thought, but what the gnomes and gremlins in the business world thought."[72] Although unapologetic about her sexuality, Navratilova's autobiography showed some sensitivity about the separate but related issue of femininity. Either for the benefit of promoters, fans, or herself, she pointed out her emotional and sentimental nature, her desire to have children, her new concern for her feminine good looks. "People judge you by appearance," she said while explaining her changes, "and since I was all woman underneath, I finally figured I might as well start dressing the part." She took pleasure in the fact that people began commenting that she was pretty, that *Newsweek* included her photo in a story on the "new femininity."[73]

Given her forthrightness about her sexual "deviance," it seems surprising that she would resort to Evert-like tactics to display her femininity. All her apparent self-esteem seemed to have collapsed into traditional apologetics. However, Navratilova may have felt a stronger need to accentuate her "normal femininity" precisely because of her sexuality. This compensatory behavior, then, may have represented a rational response to negative reactions. One scholar believes that apologetic behavior by athletes in the 1980s was more conscious and calculating than that done by earlier generations of athletes.[74] She suggests that because they grew up in a more supportive environment, they did not experience the same shame and self-doubt. If they displayed apologetic behavior, it was "phoney," that is, not because of some deeper (more authentic) psychological need, but because they were consciously adopting a shrewd strategy. However, this distinction between early and modern athletes' apologies simplifies the truth. For one thing, motives are probably more complicated than being either conscious or unconscious (automatic or calculated). Navratilova's autobiography suggests a combination of pragmatism (awareness of her audience and sponsors) and of emotional need (she recollects her worry and shame about her "masculine" body as a child). And even if modern players adopted the apologetic consciously, it does not change the fact that they are aware of a dissonance between their actual and expected behavior. Regardless of the source, apologetic behavior was a difficult, extra burden that remained on the female athlete.[75]

Despite her new feminine look, Navratilova's success brought its own burdens. Besides becoming thinner, she had become an impressively fit and strong athlete. Her body had been transformed—lean and muscular, a vein stood out in her powerful forearm. As her strength increased, so did her control, speed, and reaction time. As a result, her game took off. She reached her potential and began regularly defeating everyone, including her archrival Chris Evert, putting together an amazing winning streak. In 1982 Navratilova won fifteen of the eighteen tournaments she entered. During one stretch, she won forty-one straight matches; during another, fifty-nine of sixty. She had the highest winning percentage of any player since tennis officials had been keeping records: 96.8 percent.[76] Unfortunately, such dominance led to more negative press. Instead of praising her accomplishments, people treated her as though she and her trainers ("Team Navratilova") were doing something unfair. They began describing her as machinelike, or as Frank Deford put it, "the tip of some scientific fiction iceberg."[77] One reporter, implying that a normal woman could not get so strong simply by training, asked her if she used steroids. Another asked her outright: "Do you think you're just too good for the women?"[78] It dismayed her. "To think I have put in so much work, then to be dismissed as some sort of computer whiz, a programmed wonder woman." It was not fair—the other players could improve by doing the same drills. "If they want to, they can do it. I know I'm blessed with talent and genes, but so are a lot of people. I've put in the work." She resented being painted as an Amazon towering over the other players. Defensively, she pointed out she was only 5'7 ½" tall, 145 pounds, a dress size eight.[79]

Especially after King's and Navratilova's disclosures, the women's tour carefully cultivated a feminine image. "We had a few rough spots," acknowledged WTA executive director Jerry Diamond at the end of 1981, and his organization set out to smooth them. Indeed, Billie Jean King said the decade of the 1980s was characterized by the "feminization of women's tennis."[80] Younger players were indoctrinated on how to behave, especially with regard to the media and promoters. Advertisers, they must realize, were their partners. And image, according to the 1986 WTA *Guide to Playing Professional Tennis*, was extremely important.

> Whether you are glamorous, athletic, businesslike or intellectual, make sure your image is one that the press will latch on to in a positive way. Take time over your appearance. Select tennis clothes carefully and pay attention to what you wear at player functions.... How you conduct yourself *off* the court may have more significance to your career than anything you ever do *on* the court.[81]

Although the guide made it sound as though players could project one of a number of acceptable images (intellectual as well as businesslike), feminine glamour was stressed more than any other. "In the WTA, we try to encourage our players to be as attractive and feminine as possible," admitted King.[82] The subject of lesbian stereotyping also came up at WTA meetings. Trying to bring humor to a difficult situation, one officer sarcastically suggested a rule decreeing that every player bring a boyfriend to WTA dinners, and another added that she should "neck" with him in public.[83] Although they joked, they did make serious efforts to combat the image. Tennis pros were more cautious with the press than were other professional athletes. No reporters were allowed in locker rooms, press conferences were carefully managed, and players had veto power over interviewers.[84] They went further in promoting a collective feminine image in 1984, when the WTA put out a pinup type calendar. Among its photos were Chris Evert Lloyd in a swimsuit and Martina Navratilova in low-backed evening gown. "Everyone wanted to undergo the transformation from world-class athlete to runway model," claimed the calendar's text.[85]

Feminization was a familiar strategy, which history seemed to have proved futile. Apologetic behavior had not really achieved everything Evert had hoped. "[Fans] adored her, briefly, when a 16-year-old schoolgirl who reached the Forest Hills semifinals in 1971," observed *Sports Illustrated*. "But not long after that she came to be perceived as the Ice Maiden, and the romance cooled."[86] *Time* saw the same trend. "Her steely reserve, unblinking will and emotionless court demeanor—together with a seemingly automatic baseline game—left the fans unmoved, then hostile. . . . To the public, she seemed cool and haughty."[87] Evert knew and hated her ice maiden image, but if she had known tennis history, she would not have been surprised. It was a virtual replay of Maureen Connolly's experience in the 1950s—at first she was considered cute, but then, as she began winning all the time, crowds turned on her for being too consistent, unrelenting, unemotional, intense. Only later in their careers, after Connolly was seriously injured and Evert was overtaken by Navratilova, did fans begin warming to them again. Frank Deford believed that the perception of them as being more vulnerable made them more likable and less threatening to men.[88]

If even a blonde, All-American, heterosexual, baseline player lost favor, the women faced a bitter paradox: if they won, they lost. Doing what it took to win, it seemed, was what turned people off. As Deford put it, Evert "won precisely because she was the underside of the iceberg, colder and harder than anyone suspected." When they looked beneath the girl-next-door exterior, they saw (and did not like) a hard woman. If being an intensely competitive winner made female athletes unappealing, there was one encouraging interpretation: disapproval of female athletes may have had less to do with what they wore and who they slept with than they imagined. A much bleaker interpretation is that a truly successfully female athlete (no matter how apologetic) could not win.

Another possibility, however, is that the female pros were hoping for a type of virtually unanimous support that was unrealistic. Perhaps their strong need (as women) for approval made them overlook the fact that no athlete, male or female, could be universally loved, and that the important thing for a professional was not whether fans cheered for or against you, but that they came out to see you. That is, all the attention given to gaining *approval* may have reflected psychological and emotional needs as much as good business sense. Surely it was pragmatic to cultivate a salable image, as Debbie Spence, King, and Navratilova discovered. But the tour *did* survive the public's finding out that two of its stars had had lesbian affairs. And perhaps since, as Evert put it, "The lesbian thing may have always been in the back of peoples' minds," it was helpful to acknowledge that some athletes are lesbians.[89] Trying to keep a "terrible" secret requires a great deal of energy, and often does not work. In addition, revealing the secret is not always as disastrous as anticipated. Certainly there were costs to King's disclosure, but it did not destroy her or women's tennis. Nevertheless, because female athletes had for so long harbored fears and ambivalence about their behavior, they continued believing that femininity was a fundamental precondition to the tour's success. That assumption overlooked some history. Fans had flocked to watch Billie Jean King, not because she was feminine but because she was interesting—she was an exciting, emotional, intense, and talented athlete, full of surprises, occasionally defiant, and very different from the norm. Like male pro John McEnroe, some hated her and some loved her, but everyone knew about her. Perhaps the Women's Tennis Association should have worried less about whether it had enough (teen, blonde, feminine) models and more about whether it had too many.

The continuities—disapproval of winners by fans and apologetic behavior by players—should not overshadow the significant change that had taken place in women's tennis. Although a few of the settings in the mid-eighties were the same as in the fifties and sixties, the game was very different. No longer were women relegated to the back courts at coed tournaments, earning peanuts, if anything. They had their own year-round, first-class tour, of which they were the primary attraction. The most fundamental change was that women's tennis was professional. Exceptionally gifted women could earn hundreds of thousands of dollars in what was not merely play but work, not merely an avocation but a career. Understandably, then, thousands of girls and their families invested a great deal of money and time into pursuing stardom. Like the pros who had made it, they took a businesslike approach to the game. They utilized other professionals (coaches, trainers, managers, agents) to help them along the path. Because the tour had reached such a stable, lucrative point, the atmosphere on the circuit was less friendly and more capitalistic than it had been even during the seventies. Gone was the tightly knit community and its sense of camaraderie characteristic of activists in the building stages of a movement. In their place were professionals and institutions (such as the WTA) aiming to take advantage of, build on, and protect the gains achieved by the pioneers. The benefits and opportunities available in this second stage of professionalism were impressive.

The game and the tour were quite different, and so were the athletes. Besides becoming more businesslike, they became less apologetic. Although they remained concerned with maintaining a feminine image, and were especially nervous about the "taint" of lesbianism, in three significant areas they differed from their counterparts in the fifties and sixties. First, tennis pros in the 1980s did not downplay their competitiveness and their drive. Nor did they minimize the centrality of tennis to their lives; they openly embraced the notion of an athletic career. Finally, they did not eschew muscles. Martina Navratilova had demonstrated how much one's performance improved from intense physical training. After her dominance, no serious contender could go back to the lax practices of earlier years. (Career-ending injuries only confirmed the need to be fit and strong.) By 1985 even Chris Evert was lifting weights—in order to catch up to Navratilova and keep up with the young challengers. Evert had learned from Navratilova the need for greater strength and conditioning, but Navratilova had also learned from Evert how to cultivate greater powers of concentration and mental toughness. The two champions had pushed each other to new heights. In doing so, they had created a prototype for the new woman tennis player—what Billie Jean King called a "brave new athlete." This woman was a finer athlete than the players in the 1950s and 1960s, tougher both mentally and physically.

In historical measure, extraordinary changes had taken place in the blink of an eye. After little more than a decade of professional opportunities, tennis pros enjoyed vastly expanded opportunities and performed at a much higher level of athletic excellence. The brave new athlete—lean, strong, and fiercely competitive—was accepted (if not embraced) and widely known. She was less apologetic and much wealthier. Her success can be attributed to a number of factors. First was the pros' willingness to be flexible.[90] In general, they effectively utilized a separatist strategy, which avoided frequent confrontation over compensation and avoided unflattering contrasts with the men (and gave them a chance to prove themselves capable entertainers). They did not, however, entirely cut ties with the male pros and USLTA, realizing that some association, especially at traditional, well-known, and televised tournaments, benefited them. Yet even when they participated in coed events run by traditionally male organizations, around $9,000 per year. Teens who excelled could begin to receive free equipment, which cut costs to around $6,000, but specialized schools brought the total to between $15,000 and 25,000. Noted one top coach, "Existing in the rarefied air of top junior tennis exacts a high price."[18] Obviously such expenses limited the field to wealthy children, unless somehow one was lucky enough to find excellent public courts, community sponsorship, or one of the rare scholarships to a tennis academy. Not surprisingly, that meant tennis remained mostly upper-class and white. A few black pros—more than in the 1950s and 1960s but still a handful—were ranked in the top one hundred in the early 1980s, and a number of promising black amateurs waited in the wings. But most of the time white stars had had a head start. "What kid wants to play tennis when nobody else is playing?" asked pro Kim Sands. "My mother . . . and my mother's friends didn't know anybody who gave lessons, so I wasn't exposed to it."[19] Besides having picked up a racquet later than white pros, black players often required community assistance to cover their expenses. Leslie Allen got financial help from comedian Bill Cosby; Kim Sands from boxer Leon Spinks; and Andrea Buchanan from Johnson Publishing Company (which put out *Ebony*). Historical factors such as class, race, and cultural traditions conspired to ensure that tennis was not strictly a meritocracy. As Sands put it: "Some things are just never adapted to certain environments."[20]

One's appearance also could play a role in whether one prospered. Debbie Spence was the number one junior girl in the country, but because she had what promoters called a "weight problem" (that is, she constantly battled an extra ten pounds), no agents were knocking on her door. "No matter how great she is," explained one agent, "if she doesn't match a company's needs, they're still not going to sign her up."[21] Companies were looking for talent, but appearance and poise, according to one observer, constituted about one-third of their criteria. Being blonde helped, as did "enthusiastic displays of heterosexuality."[22] While they would not risk signing the more talented Debbie Spence, promoters jumped at the good-looking, well-connected Carling Bassett. She became a minor celebrity (appearing in a movie and numerous glamour magazines), even though she never won a major tour event. Theoretically, only insufficient talent could keep one from the top; in reality, tennis was so expensive that not gaining endorsements could mean not being able to afford the proper coaching and training and not ever reaching one's potential.

Such large financial rewards resulted in a more businesslike approach to the game. In the early and mid-seventies there had been a collective spirit among the tightly knit band of rebels. They had done everything they could to build the tour from scratch, including handing out tickets at K-Mart. Trying to balance working with each other and then competing against one another on the court had caused some tension, but players enjoyed the "sorority" days when they were not powerless. In the WTA they had a vehicle for self-determination that women in intercollegiate sports had not been able to preserve. Tennis pros' experience also differed from college women in that they were not forced by law into such direct competition with the male organizations and model of doing things. Finally, the women pros also owed a debt to corporate sponsors. No matter how well-organized, flexible, or shrewd they might have been, they could not have built such a lucrative tour without subsidization from businesses. Corporations were probably willing to promote women's tennis (more so than other women's sports) because of its respectable—feminine, traditional, and upper-class—image. Certainly that sponsorship had its costs, including unfairness about whose career advanced and constant worry about image, but its benefits were obvious and fundamental. If the pros still felt somewhat vulnerable, that was nothing new. What was extraordinary was how far they had come. Particularly when compared with the declining fortunes of other women in sports, tennis pros were tycoons.

CHAPTER 10

Dreams Deferred:

Professional Basketball in the 1980s

When the fans began pouring onto the court, my whole basketball life flashed before my eyes. I was like a zombie when I realized there would be no more games, no more exciting shots and, I thought, no more friends. This was the end of the world, I thought. I just lay on the locker-room floor and cried.

Despite having scored an unheard-of seventy points in her last Moravia, Iowa, high school game in 1974, "Machine Gun" Molly Van Venthuysen felt devastated.[1] A male athlete with her talent would have had a college scholarship in hand and dreams of a lucrative professional career. But Molly envisioned no such future; in fact, she did not even think she would keep playing basketball. Iowa encouraged youngsters to excel at "girls' basketball," but not women—women were expected to get married and raise a family. To Molly that meant losing excitement, friendship, and a fundamental part of how she defined herself. What was an adult female to do if she wanted to keep playing basketball? If she was intelligent, well-off, and so inclined, she could go to college. By 1974 more colleges had women's teams, but those opportunities were new and unpublicized, and athletic scholarships (only just approved by AIAW) were rare. If she did not go to college, she might find a church or industrial league. True, some really dedicated women had joined the elite AAU subculture, but that path was difficult and atypical. By the 1970s fewer industries gave jobs to women whose main qualification was pinpoint outside shooting. So Molly saw few realistic options. She enrolled in a local college and played one season, but after marrying her high school sweetheart, Dennie Bolin, and giving birth to a son, Molly found herself out of the game of basketball and "going berserk."

What Molly did not realize as she mourned her brief career in 1974 was how rapidly times were changing. Women's basketball began changing in the mid 1960s, when American women embarrassed Cold Warriors by repeatedly losing to Eastern European teams. The U.S. squad had two major disadvantages, the U.S. Olympic Committee realized: first, a lack of support and early training; and second, American females grew up playing "girls' rules" whereas men's rules were used in international competition. The old girls' rules, preventing players from running full-court and limiting the number of times they could dribble, still assumed females were fragile. The top players resented the limitations— after all, they played for the only nation whose females did not play full-court— and their coaches kept pushing for alterations to bring the game up-to-date.[2] In 1969 women physical educators worked out an agreement with AAU leaders, in which the Division for Girls' and Women's Sports (DGWS) would adopt rule changes if the AAU promised to respect other DGWS values (such as trying to hire female officials and coaches).[3] As a result, by the late sixties females in the majority of states (although not Iowa) were permitted to play by the same "real" (and respected) rules as males.

Sparked by the support of physical educators and Title IX, basketball heated up during the late sixties and seventies. As PE leaders gave their stamp of approval to extramural competition, basketball teams were among the first to spring up at colleges. Creation of AIAW championships in the early seventies fueled the expansion. In just a few years AIAW events overtook the AAU's national championships in popularity and prestige. The best young female players started looking to colleges (especially when they began awarding scholarships), and the best college teams were suddenly defeating the old AAU powerhouses. Title IX's guarantees of equal opportunity sped the process along. Almost all high schools and colleges with sports had male basketball teams, and Title IX meant they should add them for females. In 1972 only some 400,000 high school females played basketball, but by 1981 the total had jumped to 4,500,000.[4] The rapid increase in opportunities for such huge numbers of girls raised the level of play. Large universities began pouring money into women's basketball and building quality programs, and the media began noticing. Very quickly women's basketball seemed like a whole new ball game.

The increased popularity of women playing "real" basketball prompted some to begin thinking about forming a professional women's basketball league. After all, women's pro tennis had been a smashing success, and a large pool of players was available. Most importantly, some male investors believed the time was ripe. They may not have shared exactly the same ambition as Molly Bolin, since their concern was profit, but their interests intersected with hers.

Jason Frankfurt, a New York restaurant owner and former stockbroker, envisioned a twelve-team nationwide Women's Basketball Association in which players would be paid at least $10,000 for a sixty-two game schedule. He began putting his blueprint into action in late 1976. Frankfurt hired advertiser Lois Geraci Ernst as commissioner of the league, and she promised "a chance for women basketball players to play out their dreams."[5] Yet despite selling the rights to teams and conducting a player draft, the league collapsed before ever staging a game.

Hope endured. Bill Byrne, a pioneer of the short-lived World Football League, picked up on Frankfurt's idea. Appointing himself president of the Women's Basketball League (wbl) in 1978, he convinced other investors that his three-year plan for the league could succeed where other new professional ventures had failed. From his football experience, Byrne realized the hazards of starting from scratch. "There are three things that will fold a league—players' pay, travel, and arenas," he asserted, "and we're on top of all three."[6] By compensating players meagerly (at an estimated $3,000 to $5,000 for a season), the enterprise would not "be busted by salaries the way some others were."[7] Similarly, the league would have Eastern and Western divisions to minimize transportation costs, and would rent small gymnasiums. Even beginning so modestly, Byrne told investors they should expect only gradual expansion and to lose money at least the first three seasons.[8] If the Women's Basketball League could survive a few years, with some luck it could then capitalize on the publicity given the stars of the U.S. Olympic team in 1980.

Not all the owners of new teams shared Byrne's capabilities. With the exception of Houston's Hugh Sweeney, an Avon tennis promoter, few of the investors had had any professional sports management experience, and fewer still had any with women. Many practiced law, one owned a gymnastics equipment company, and another had just sold his family's undertaking business. Even professional actors owned a team at one point.[9]

The owners' only qualifications were their ability to pay the $50,000 franchise fee and their willingness to risk losing money. The most sensible of the owners hired experts, but others managed by themselves or with the help of wives and friends, enjoying the hands-on power of creating and controlling a team. One man, for example, happily described himself as president, general manager, scout, public relations director, and secretary of his team.[10] John Geraty, a sports promoter hired to be president of the Chicago Hustle, disapproved of the way many of the owners ran their teams. "A lot had never been involved in professional sports before, and consequently they came to run professional teams as they would run a shoe store."[11] In particular, he said, many did not know how to market their product. "We didn't get started with our promotions until late," admitted Tom Brennan of the New Jersey Gems, "and I think that hurt us."[12] Unfortunately, they had little time to overcome their inexperience. "We had only 45 days to prepare," lamented Minnesota's Gordon Nevins.[13] Consequently, in the beginning the league appeared quite unprofessional. In fact, after the WBL's first player draft in July 1978, the league's vice president of marketing felt he had to inform his green owners to phone their potential players immediately, "so at least you'll know the people you've drafted are notified."

The league's draftees came from various backgrounds. The Iowa Cornets signed up "Machine Gun" Molly Bolin and hoped home state fans would remember her high school heroics. The New Jersey Gems also picked a local favorite in "Wicked Wanda" Szeremeta, who had starred at Montclair State (N.J.). Others had to travel much further, like Debbie Waddy-Rossow, who moved with her husband from rural Texas to Chicago. Many had just finished their collegiate careers, but not all of them. Mary Jo Peppler, the league's oldest player at thirty-four, had been on the Olympic volleyball team and recently trained for TV's Superstars competition. Karen Logan had been barnstorming with the All-American Red Heads, the 1970s version of the team of women who mixed basketball and comedy by challenging male teams while wearing red wigs. She had been yearning for more serious competition. Gail Marquis, who had been playing professionally in France, eagerly returned, declaring, "This is what I've been waiting for for three years."[14]

Not everyone, though, was willing or able to join the new league. When Lucy Harris, the first woman chosen in the draft and arguably the best in the country, heard that the first players had signed contracts for less than $5,000, she remarked, "I wouldn't even consider playing for that salary."[15] Houston offered Harris $15,000 for her first season, but it was not enough to persuade her and her husband to leave their home and jobs in Mississippi or to delay starting a family.[16] Others, like Carol Blazejowski, chose to remain amateur so they could go to the 1980 Olympics. Her coach had advised her to wait. "After the Olympics the WBL will be two years old and stronger," he said. "The money and the demand for her will be there in two years."[17] Coaches heeded the same advice. Although there were four female coaches the first season, many others chose not to leave more secure college positions for the fledgling league.[18] Although some women were so excited they would have joined whatever the compensation, clearly not everyone was in a position to do so.

Despite doubts, short-sightedness, and a few missing names, the league managed to get started. Amid much celebration and a mayoral proclamation recognizing the historic moment, on December 9, 1978, the Milwaukee Does hosted the Chicago Hustle in the Milwaukee Arena before 7,824 fans.[19] Within the next week, the other six teams—in New Jersey, New York, Ohio, Iowa, Minnesota, and Texas—also held their opening games. "It was great, I loved it," proclaimed Wanda Szeremeta, despite the New Jersey Gems' defeat in front of only 1,924 fans. "I didn't believe it would happen until I walked out on the court and saw another team."[20]

The WBL's first season showed some promise. Each of the league's eight teams played its full thirty-six game schedule, and the year ended on a high note when almost six thousand fans watched Houston defeat Iowa in the exciting final game of the championship series. "They said we wouldn't get off the ground," boasted Bill Byrne.[21] Indeed, simply having survived exceeded many expectations, but Byrne had other reasons to be pleased. Houston's owner reportedly sold his franchise for a large profit.[22] In addition, the league began to garner some attention. Walter Cronkite did a segment on it during the national evening news, and a local station televised the league's All-Star game.[23] Dannon Yogurt asked New York Stars' twins Kaye and Faye Young to appear in its TV commercials. Best of all, a local station televised ten of the Chicago Hustle's games, and each contest attracted nearly 140,000 viewers (more than the Chicago Black Hawks men's hockey games), providing ratings twice as high as anticipated.[24]

"We didn't have too many bad things happen to us," concluded Byrne, but there had been some serious first-year problems.[25] Dayton's franchise had collapsed in mid-season. The league office rescued it, but lost $96,000 in doing so.[26] Other teams survived on their own at a high price. Team deficits for the year averaged $260,000, and Chicago, the team that lost the least money, still finished the year $150,000 in the red.[27] "No sports league has ever made money in its first season," Byrne assured skeptics, and reminded them of his three-year plan.[28] Consistently low fan turnout proved most worrisome to the owners, since an average of 1,200 people attended each game. Teams in Chicago, Houston, and Iowa succeeded in building some loyalty, but other teams dismally failed, like the New York Stars, who regularly attracted only about eight hundred fans to a high school gym.[29]

Players and coaches tended to be understanding about the discouraging conditions they faced that first season. Mindful of the tenuousness of their pioneering endeavor and grateful for the chance to make a go of it, they rarely complained about low salaries and second-class accommodations. "We want this league to survive so badly that we are willing to play for nothing," claimed Vivian Greene.[30] Financially, Greene and the others gave up any hope of prosperity or security. They also put up with insufficient practice facilities, tiny locker rooms, stalled buses, crowded hotel rooms, and other problems that reflected budgets sometimes resembling those of high school teams. Iowa's Tanya Crevier described that first season: "The travel was the worst, and some of the facilities were atrocious. We usually changed and showered in our motel rooms. In some lockers the floors hadn't been swept in weeks, paint was peeling off the walls and bugs were crawling all over the shower-room floors."[31] Crevier's teammates agreed that in many *material* ways the WBL constituted a step down from college ball. Still, the level of competition was very high, and their sacrifice might be a down payment on a more auspicious future. "We understand," explained a patient Althea Gwyn. "You can't go out and demand things if you want the league to last."[32]

Perhaps more difficult to endure for the players than poor physical conditions was the constant need to prove themselves worthy of being noticed and taken seriously. Initially, every new professional league struggles. It has to establish its legitimacy. It has to attract enough fans (often away from other forms of entertainment), and then it must win their loyalty. To succeed, a new enterprise requires a good product but also effective public relations, lots of media attention, and some luck. Unfortunately, in addition to the hurdles of any new league, the WBL had an additional disadvantage: the gender of its players. Over and over, according to one sportswriter, people would ask, "What are those women doing playing a man's game?" If spectators compared the product to their expectations of the "man's game," the WBL was in trouble. Unquestionably, the female athletes could not match the males in the National Basketball Association in strength, height, and speed. The NBA stars could slam-dunk the ball and play "above the rim"; the WBL's stars could not. Nor could WBL champions make the NBA's rosters. So the women's product differed but, as women's tennis had demonstrated, that should not have doomed it. A player's strength isn't what determines interest in a game; what makes sports exciting is fine athletes in closely matched contests. After all, no one ignored men's college basketball because its athletes were far inferior to the pros. Instead, fans flocked to watch college games, many liking the different style of the intercollegiate game even better. In the same way, the WBL offered a solid product—even if they could not slam-dunk, its players were very highly skilled. They were the best in their classification, and they played a fast-paced, team-oriented, increasingly physical brand of basketball.[33]

Although WBL basketball could be a good product, the players' sex was an enormous hurdle in gaining acceptance for it. Player Kathy DeBoer recognized that "people have to be sold on women's sports," so she spent her free time giving (unpaid) coaching clinics for children and making local appearances. If her teammates could get an audience in the door, they had a chance. "We initially came to ridicule the team," admitted some self-professed superfans, "but now we're coming back because we enjoy the games."[34] Other male observers found to their surprise that they could be interested in the WBL. One journalist favorably contrasted the women's intense efforts over the course of the game with a typical NBA team's lackadaisical first half.[35] And NBA superstar Julius "Dr. J" Erving added his admiration. "These girls can *really* operate."[36] But in general

DeBoer was disappointed with her public relations efforts, because "you don't see the results." "We've spent our lives playing for ourselves because no one much cared," she said. "We're still doing that."[37]

An unsympathetic media compounded the league's problems. Newspapers' male-run sports departments typically did only an occasional feature story on the local team. They withheld the regular coverage they gave other local teams, which promoted loyalty and continued interest. A *Chicago Tribune* columnist admitted that the Hustle players were getting a bum deal. "There hasn't been much coverage of them," he sarcastically noted, "because news space is needed to report on the hangnails of male athletes."[38] Besides being scarce, the stories that were written often treated the league as an odd experiment. Minnesota Fillies owner Gordon Nevins waged a constant battle with the St. Paul and Minneapolis newspapers, which often consciously ignored the league's existence. "Sometimes it seems totally unfair," complained one player. "You're tired and beat up and bruised and you're awake all night because you're still so hyper, and when you open the paper in the morning, there's not even a box score saying what you did the night before."[39] Nevins bitterly criticized the press. "They began by saying we were not going to make it," he said, "and then substantiated their verdict by not writing about us."[40] In a frustrating vicious circle, fans knew little about the league, but the press refused to cover it well unless lots of fans attended.

The sports media shared society's prejudices. When Nevins lined up sponsors and even offered to pay local television stations to try airing just one Minnesota game as an experiment, they resisted. Ignorant about women's sports, reporters asked insulting questions and sometimes ridiculed athletes. Or, like other men, they were interested only in the athlete's sex appeal. "I wish they had a good-looking player, so we could use a picture in the paper," one remarked.[41] A player noted with disgust that the press constantly showed more interest in "pin-ups than lay-ups."[42] When sportswriters did not take the league seriously, it was highly unlikely that fans would. The sports media failed to use its enormous power to confer legitimacy on the league and to elevate its image of female athletes, preferring instead to reinforce traditional notions.

The female players faced a nearly no-win situation. On one hand, men (in particular) denigrated them for not being as big and strong and playing as well as their male counterparts. On the other hand, if men found the quality of play acceptable, they criticized the women's behavior and looks as "masculine." Even in the late 1970s, much of the old equation still remained: playing basketball well meant playing like a man; if women wanted to excel at basketball, surely they must aspire to be men. Male observers expressed their astonishment that a normal woman would want to excel with comments like, "But you don't look like a basketball player." Or they referred to the players as "kids" or "girls" as though they had not yet outgrown childish athletic desires and exchanged them for proper womanhood.[43] More difficult for the players to deal with than surprise was hostility. They were harassed with the taunt: "Why don't you get a sex change?"[44] In Chicago some men in the crowd reacted to the threat the female athletes apparently posed by loudly insisting that the players were still sex objects to them. They wore "Fincher Pincher" T-shirts and yelled "Breathe deeply" while blonde, large-busted guard Janie Fincher prepared to shoot free throws.[45] Even many of their so-called fans, then, exhibited disrespect, continually reminding players that they were women in a male game. In such a difficult situation, perhaps the best WBL hoopsters could hope for was acceptance for "playing like guys" yet "looking like girls."[46]

Acutely aware of the "image issue," WBL management adopted the same strategy used throughout the century—apologetic behavior. It did not portray the female athlete as she was—a strong, aggressive competitor, admirable and worth emulating. Instead, the league's management accepted the popular association of female athleticism with masculinity and allowed the notion to persist that unfeminine athletes were unappealing. The league's owners apparently thought it more likely they could convince the public that female athletes were "otherwise feminine" than that they should look up to unfeminine women. Thus, many owners hearkened back to the days of the AAU beauty pageants. "Talent was still an important consideration, but marketability was a big issue," one player complained, "and as women athletes, how we looked played a big role."[47] The management of the California Dreams confirmed this assessment with a bizarre promotional move. Prior to the second season, it sent its players (under threat of being fined) to a five-week modeling course where they learned how to walk, sit, eat, and talk with poise. The intent was to portray a feminine, heterosexual image.[48] "I wish we had Farrah Fawcett," a general manager remarked in the same vein. "We'd just let her warm up."[49] Profit, ultimately the bottom line, required catering to public desires. Minnesota owner Gordon Nevins admitted as much when asked if a player's so-called femininity entered into her promotional ability. "We'd like to say no, but obviously it does."[50] With many women desperate for a chance to play, management could force its employees to put up with attention-grabbers like charm school and benefit exhibitions against Playboy Bunnies, however demeaning.[51]

Clearly the players also wanted the league to succeed, so as their predecessors had for generations, they made the "feminine bargain." They put up with—sometimes reluctantly, sometimes willingly—the demands of "promotion." Although it was almost unheard of for male pros to be asked about the hair, dress, and general grooming habits of their teammates, articles about the WBL regularly mentioned such details, thereby highlighting the femininity and assumed heterosexuality of those competing. Few players complained openly, and some cheerfully accommodated the press's curiosity about their feminine attributes and interests. For many players such reassurances of "normal femininity" became ingrained, or at least automatic when dealing with the press. One player, for example, admitted that she too made fun of masculine-looking female athletes. In the same breath she assured mothers out there that she and her teammates were good role models for their children, not "freaks."[52] Many lesbian players faked fiancés and otherwise hid their sexual orientations, while sometimes pressuring others to remain in the closet. Feminist players, aware that they were especially suspect, assured men that they were not out to destroy traditional sex roles by playing professionally. "I support the Equal Rights Amendment, but I am not playing basketball to foment feminism," clarified Sharon Farrah. "I am playing because I am an athlete who loves to play basketball."[53]

To pursue their love of basketball, WBL athletes assumed a pragmatic approach toward their audience. "In order for people to accept the WBL, they want to know we are women," Ann Meyers told *Ms.* magazine. "It's not fair, but it's a fact of life."[54] Karen Logan believed her teammates should not imitate Billie Jean King, who loudly demanded respect for women, because they were in a riskier position than King. King played tennis, an accepted sport for women. "But we're in a new sport," she argued, "and we have to play by the rules that will sell that sport."[55] In her opinion, the best ways to sell basketball were to look feminine and to play a style of basketball that, in contrast to the men's power game, would emphasize finesse and grace. A few players went even further. Molly Bolin was named the league's Most Valuable Player in 1980, but her talent alone was not attracting large numbers of spectators. To try to fuel interest, she posed for and financed an 18" x 24" black-and-white poster of herself in a tight-fitting tank top and shorts sitting next to a basketball. Obviously she wanted not just to interest men but to assuage their fears. She said she just wanted to show that women in the WBL were not trying to look like men or be masculine. "It's all about putting people in seats, isn't it?" she rhetorically asked, dismissing suggestions of exploitation. "If you really want to make it when you're new, you've got to grab everything you've got and go with it."[56]

But the line between pragmatism and injustice could be blurry. Players might agree to looking extra-feminine, but doing so allowed stereotypes and sexist assumptions to continue, and forced them to apologize for their behavior instead of insisting there was nothing wrong or abnormal with it. Too, it was difficult to stop compromising once you had begun. A WBL team might draw in an audience by doing something pragmatic, something players felt was only a minor compromise of their dignity, such as wearing tight uniforms. But then management had to keep those fans coming back. Theoretically a club, constantly searching for new ways to please their sexist fans, might let them dictate the lineups and even the style of play. Professional leagues, especially new ones, have always faced the problem of how much power to give fans (their consumers), and the WBL was no different. Chicago's management was considered among those with the most integrity, yet when it traded Janie Fincher and some fans angrily reacted by turning in their tickets, the Hustle responded to fan pressure and reobtained Fincher.[57] And during Chicago's third season, Hustle management openly expressed displeasure with the new coach's more methodical offense, which it felt was less exciting to fans than a fast-break, "run and gun" style.[58]

Smaller promotional ploys intended to sell tickets could snowball if management did not know where to draw the line, and if allowed to, such "democratic innovations" could have disturbing implications. For example, rumors persisted in Chicago that Janie Fincher earned a starting position because of her looks and popularity rather than her playing ability. If true, such criteria were blatantly unfair to the players. Clearly one's physical appearance, arbitrarily judged, had no place in a game whose rules intended that the most skilled won. Nor did one's sexual orientation. But management also had to adhere to the "rules" of entertainment. It was difficult to know where to draw the line. If the league did not make enough compromises to insure survival, the players and the cause of women's sports would be harmed. But catering to the sexist attitudes of their audience also harmed the cause because it delayed real acceptance of women as serious, professional athletes.

Management concerned about pleasing sexist fans might just as easily be willing to accommodate racist ones, particularly in mostly white population areas. Minnesota's Trish Roberts, a black player, did not think her team's roster was designed to please white fans. After all, she said, there really were not enough regular fans to worry about pleasing.[59] So her teammates, black and white, played for themselves, and played to win. But although few players complained publicly, racism was rumored to be present.[60] Blacks constituted 40 percent of players (versus 70 percent in the NBA), but during the first few seasons at least, they seemed to come from predominantly white schools. As in other professional leagues, there were few blacks in front-office positions of power, and the WBL employed a sole black head coach, Dean Meminger. Anonymously, one player told *Ebony,*

> This is a White girls' league. And it's run by White men. The few women coaches they hired last year [four], they got rid of. They [owners] feel that because pro women's basketball is a new product, they can't afford to have it dominated by the Black girls. That's why they're trying to play up the White stars. . . . So you have racism and sexism running things.[61]

Besides being unjust to athletes and insulting their ability, ultimately such pandering—or even rumors of it— could undermine the integrity of the game. Management that used racist, sexist, or homophobic promotions did not seem to realize that by doing so it showed no faith in its product—legitimate professional women's basketball—to gain the loyalty of fans.

After the first season, the league's management still optimistically believed that if it could stay afloat a few years, it could sell the game without "selling out" its integrity. Pleased with the relative success of the first season, the league expanded from its original eight teams to fourteen, hoping to tap the market in Washington, D.C., Dallas, San Francisco, New Orleans, Philadelphia, and St. Louis. Prospects looked good. Each new owner paid $100,000 for a franchise, twice the amount paid by the original group of owners.[62] A number of teams thought they had a chance for cable television contracts, which could significantly boost the chances of solvency. All the teams employed male head coaches, some of them formerly involved with the NBA, hoping to draw fans and lend legitimacy. In the most naively optimistic move, the New York Stars abandoned the suburban New Rochelle area they had promised to grow roots in and contracted to play in Madison Square Garden's Felt Forum, where they hoped to attract and seat more New York City fans.[63]

Perhaps the most important thing to happen in the off-season came when the league acquired, with a great deal of attendant publicity, former UCLA All-American guard Ann Meyers. The NBA's Indiana Pacers had caused a stir when they drafted Meyers and signed her to a $50,000 contract. Meyers tried out for the team but did not make the final cut.[64] Meyers then demanded that the WBL make her an equally attractive offer. The first women's teams with rights to her could not afford to, but the New Jersey Gems took the gamble, signing her to a three-year contract worth $50,000 the first year. New Jersey owner Robert Milo proclaimed hopefully, "Ann Meyers will be to the W.B.L. as other great athletes such as Joe Namath and others were in professional football, hockey, and soccer."[65]

Meyers's attention and big salary ignited some tension within the WBL's ranks. Some players felt Meyers had insulted the female professional league by treating it as her second choice, and they set out to show that Meyers did not possess such superior abilities. Her backcourt partner, Donna Chait Geils, believed the New Jersey management had made a wise move in obtaining the "name" star, but she witnessed the furor it caused: "I had a bird's eye view of all the cheap shots and heard all the epithets thrown her way."[66] The Meyers' signing, like that of Nancy Lieberman for $100,000 the third season, understandably unleashed antagonism between players and with management. Owners hoped the high-priced contracts would pay off with ticket sales from people curious to see if the would-be salvation of the team was as good as the press, hype, and price tag indicated.

Unfortunately, though, exalting the newer players implicitly denigrated the ones already there. The WBL's pioneers had endured low pay and poor conditions because management had told them it was necessary to sacrifice for the good of the league. With owners suddenly shelling out big money, some of them now felt exploited and unappreciated. Veteran Sharon Farrah complained: "I personally resent news organizations' near deifications of certain graduating seniors, who are demanding salaries in excess of many teams' entire payrolls, and who doggedly avoid playing against W.B.L. players until their contracts are in place."[67] Farrah maintained that great players already filled the rosters of the women's pro teams. Management knew that, but they also saw that the very talented "name" players increased attendance everywhere they went, so they were willing to step on some toes to get the all-important publicity. "If [Leiberman is] in the league she'll be good for . . . everybody," one coach acknowledged. On the other hand, he knew he could not afford to sign a Meyers or a Lieberman and pay one player triple his team's average salary. "What would happen to your team? You wouldn't have a team."[68]

The WBL's second season revealed that the league had problems much more difficult than intrateam dynamics. Only a few games into the schedule, the Philadelphia Foxes and the Washington Metros folded. Apparently the D.C. franchise never really had a chance of surviving. Money problems began early, with the team being forced to practice on outdoor courts, even in December, and continued when management could not meet its $2,500 nightly arena rental fee. First the owners canceled a few games, then they gave up.[69] Therefore the league had to consolidate in midseason from fourteen to twelve teams, which caused confusion and bad publicity. Other teams somehow staved off serious troubles. Both the Milwaukee and Dallas clubs neared the brink of disaster, but money from new investors saved them days before collapse. Still, the Milwaukee coach resigned in early February because he had not been paid in two months and was unwilling to agree to coach without pay. His female assistant agreed to take his place.[70]

The human cost of such problems was high. Players received "late paychecks, rubber paychecks and sometimes no paychecks." And their patience was taxed when they lacked the gas money to attend practice.[71] Before the team collapsed, Washington saved money by taking fewer players on road trips. For their part, equally destitute Washington players pooled the food remaining in their apartments for their teammates who stayed behind.[72] When the two clubs folded, it left desperate players unemployed, and it meant that even those wanted by other teams suddenly had to pick up and move to new cities.

Premature expansion had resulted in uneven health. While teams in San Francisco, St. Louis, and New Jersey gradually grew more popular, and already strong organizations like that in Chicago continued to function efficiently, the New York Stars reportedly lost $25,000 a night playing in Madison Square Garden. "It doesn't make sense to have 20,000 seats if you're drawing 2,000 people," co-owner Ed Reisdorf realized too late.[73] The league's average attendance almost doubled over the first season, but one night the Stars played in front of only 389 fans.[74] Ironically, while the Stars consistently beat the best teams in the league, they were cutting their travel budget to pinch pennies: on road trips they left behind an assistant coach, their trainer, and two of their twelve players (including one of the famous Dannon Yogurt twins); they cut the players' daily food allowance from twenty-one to sixteen dollars a day; and they went by bus and van wherever possible. Reisdorf lamented, "Sports requires much more money than anyone understands."[75]

Amazingly, Dean Meminger coached the financially ailing Stars to the league's championship over the Iowa Cornets for that second season. This irony typified the state of the WBL experiment: the level of competition remained high, but financially everything was a mess. Although much about the league hardly seemed professional (one observer said facilities reminded him of a church league), the quality of play was better than could be found anywhere else for these women, even in international amateur or professional competition.[76] The athletes realized the league's fragility and wanted to make the most of each opportunity. "I kept playing," recalled Donna Chait Geils, "and feverishly at that."[77] Unfortunately, despite their winning record and Dean Meminger's being named Coach of the Year, the New York Stars could not pay all of Meminger's salary. In fact, the two most talented teams in the league, Iowa and New York, both suspended operations after their "successful" second season.[78]

The disappointments of the second year brought calls for a massive reorganization of the WBL. Dissatisfied with the disastrous expansion and unhappy with high administrative costs, team owners met during the summer and ousted Bill Byrne as league commissioner. In his place they chose one of the co-owners of the Chicago Hustle, Sherwin Fischer, who moved the league's offices from New York to Chicago and cut the cost of running them by two-thirds. Fischer also instituted strict new guidelines to prevent midseason failures, requiring that each team demonstrate it had $350,000 cash up front. As a result, only eight teams elected to continue operations. To prevent a repeat of the previous year's premature expansion from eight to fourteen teams, he raised the price of a franchise to $500,000; only one new team joined the third season.[79]

The league's restructuring was simply one more episode in the constant change and disarray that affected players' lives and attitudes. Shuttled from team to collapsed team, players after two seasons lived with as much uncertainty as ever. For players from teams that folded, worries about back pay and future trade possibilities occupied them in the off-season.[80] Nor did players on relatively stable teams get guarantees. Since fewer teams would open the coming season, competition for roster positions was tougher than ever. Newly graduated college players further tightened the situation, as did the Olympic boycott, which made other amateur stars eligible.

The situation in Chicago typified the situation players faced. There ten Hustle veterans returning to training camp for their third season found nine rookies and seven newcomers (including three former All-Stars) from other teams, totaling twenty-six women to fight for twelve places. Hustle players also met a new coach, president, and general manager, all of whom emphasized a new style. Gone was the fatherly president so close to his players that he could not bear to make difficult decisions like cutting them. Players now complained, "At training camp, we were treated as if we hadn't played here before." Their hurt feelings were met by the new president's announcement: "The family days are over. This is a business."[81]

For their part, players also adopted a more businesslike attitude. With tighter competition, individuals began to look out for themselves and make demands as they would on any other job. Average salaries had increased, but the same financial stringency continued.[82] "Picture this," related one. "Third-year professional athletes painting and cleaning up their apartments so they can save $100 on their first-month rent."[83] Cognizant that some security was essential, players shed fewer tears after hearing they had been traded. "I was becoming a hardened veteran," explained Donna Chait Geils. "I decided I had to go where I had to go in order to be paid my worth."[84] Others talked of forming a players' association so that they could collectively protect themselves from being taken advantage of.[85] They had tired of sacrificing so much for the chance to play. Mariah Burton Nelson, for example, insisted on being compensated for the costs of moving (and was fired for being "too aggressive off the court"). Chicago players grumbled when they found that "inadvertently" their contracts had left out travel expenses and hospitalization.[86] Similarly, Geils remembered it was after her second season, "I came to realize that my desire to play could not be exploited anymore."[87]

Despite reorganization, renewed realism, and two full seasons under its belt, the wbl seemed to be starting over again in the third season. Most teams had new players, coaches, or management, and two of the most established teams had disappeared. The league had a new commissioner, but he too had to warn investors not to expect profits in the near future. Better players than ever populated the rosters, but many teams still had not developed an identity in the public mind. The press seemed to pay less attention than ever to the wbl, and the hoped-for boon—Olympic gold medal winners to attract new attention—

went bust with the 1980 boycott. To top it all off, according to one observer, "The undercapitalized owners were skimping on the area they least could afford—marketing and public relations."[88]

The league limped through the third season. Then when Commissioner Fischer called for interested owners to prepare for a fourth season, only one responded.[89] No light had appeared at the end of the tunnel to indicate when profits might be made. Still not a major drawing card, teams continued to lose large sums of money, and few of the investors could afford, especially during a recession, to lose hundreds of thousands of dollars a year. Finally they threw in the towel.

Why had the WBL failed? Fundamentally, it did not attract enough spectators. Commissioner Fisher estimated that about one thousand more fans per game were needed to break even, but they never materialized. One reason was the difficulty every new league faced. That was exacerbated by the league's management, which lacked experience and capital. Owners sometimes made unwise decisions about spending (one owner bought a $31,000 bus and produced a basketball movie that flopped), and then often tightened their belts in the most crucial areas, like public relations and treatment of players. Running a league that often appeared second-class made it hard to sell as first-class.[90] In addition, many believed that the market for professional spectator sports in some of the cities chosen was already saturated.

But the primary reason the league failed was gender-related. The kind of comments WBL players heard, the apologetic stance they adopted, and the dilemmas management faced in appealing to sexist audiences all illustrated the continuing lack of interest, the prejudice, the antagonism even, that female basketball players faced. That white men were the sports fans with the most disposable income made the venture more difficult. Women of all races generally had less leisure time, less money, and were much less likely to spend it on spectator sports, so they did not constitute a significant base of support. Young girls were the WBL's most loyal and enthusiastic fans, but clearly they had the least possible means of attending games.[91] The male-dominated sports media—essential to attracting fans and potentially an aid to breaking down stereotypes—did little to help the league's cause. Finally, the league may have begun too soon. After all, the slight (and inconsistent) crowds at intercollegiate women's games indicated that a sufficiently large and enthusiastic foundation spectator base did not yet exist.

But women's professional tennis *had* succeeded; why could not women's professional basketball? The answer probably lies in the differing history and nature of the two sports. When women's tennis shifted from amateur to professional in the late 1960s, it did so accompanied by men. Female tennis players had been playing at mixed-sex tournaments throughout the century, and these tournaments had a sufficiently large and loyal base of fans who came to see both the men and the women. Women's basketball had an equally long history, but rarely had it had the benefit of being linked with the popular men's games. In addition, women's basketball had a much less public tradition. The working-class AAU women's teams—even the nationally ranked ones—played before rel-atively small, local crowds. Upper- and middle-class college teams had been dis-couraged by physical educators in favor of intramurals. Because physical edu-cators wanted to shelter female student-athletes from public disapproval, intercollegiate games that did take place were held in near-private circum-stances. Furthermore, tennis's upper-class associations gave it an added advan-tage. More prosperous tennis players could better afford to cover the costs of competition. Tennis fans generally were wealthier and more able to subsidize players' prize money. Even after the female tennis pros took the risky move of separating from the men during the 1970s, they could count on some wealthy and experienced promoters who had connections at corporations and tennis clubs all over the country.

Nor did basketball enjoy the feminine reputation of tennis. Its elite tradi-tions and participants contributed to its acceptability. In addition, tennis was an individual sport, and individual sports generally were still considered more feminine than team sports. Individual sportswomen were often considered more graceful and less threatening. Tough women supposedly did not travel and bond together in individual sports the way they did on teams. This prox-imity and bond between strong women was threatening because it suggested independence from men and even lesbianism. Moreover, basketball was a much rougher sport—scowling women drenched in sweat elbowed and pushed each other while fiercely fighting for rebounds and loose balls. Tennis, though played by men, did not have the same aggressive image as basketball, and female ten-nis players faced less hostility and astonishment than basketball players. In sum, basketball was still a game much more identified with masculinity. Decades of using separate "girls' rules" underscored the notion that men were the "real" players and females only poor imitations. Actual physiological disadvantages meant WBL players were unfavorably compared with NBA male stars, and their high level of skill went unappreciated. Paradoxically, when it was lauded, that brought its own problems. When they succeeded in playing well—that is, "like men"—its practitioners were viewed as unfeminine.

What were the ramifications of the league's failure? Obviously, the players lost out. Some never got paid what they were promised, and some felt they had been exploited. Trish Roberts remembered it as a "bad experience."[92] "The league dumped on some people," agreed Chicago coach Doug Bruno.[93] But many others felt very grateful for the chance to play. "I've lived the dream of thousands," concluded Donna Geils. "I have no regrets. . . . I'll always be grateful that I got to sign that dotted line. After all, how many people get paid to play?"[94] The league's demise hit hard those players like Molly Bolin, who now had to go through withdrawal all over again. "The end of the league affected me in a bad way," reported Liz Galloway. "It's great to do something you love. And now I don't have it. I miss it something terrible."[95] As they went back to law school or coaching or sales or running a household, they would have to find other ways to satisfy their need. With other basketball "junkies," they would play wherever they could, back to church leagues, 135th Street in Harlem, or in YMCAs. Often they would play against men because the decline of the AAU and the industrial leagues meant that there were very few places where they could find adult women of their own caliber.[96] The Olympics took place only every four years. Nancy Lieberman complained she felt "stifled." Those who had already graduated were not helped by AIAW championships. Nor did the AIAW benefit those unable to attend (or uninterested in attending) college. The mostly white upper-middle-class tennis players could find challenging competition and had professional opportunities, but the many black and working-class women who populated the ranks of basketball were penalized once again by their class and race.[97]

The WBL's demise had repercussions far beyond its relatively small group of players. It harmed the entire cause of women's sports by discouraging further attempts to expand opportunities. The league's failure confirmed—along with the decline of the AIAW and the weakening of Title IX—that the movement for women's sports had stalled. In addition, the league's failure sent out another very clear (and distressing) message to aspiring female athletes: tennis was one thing, but basketball went too far—there was something too masculine about it. Unlike men, women could not make basketball a career. A career means that one is expert in something, and being paid for it means one's ability is valued. Thus, not being able to have a basketball career conveyed a host of negative implications: basketball is all right for girls but not for women; basketball can be play but not work; you can try it but you cannot master it. This was discouraging news for more than just proponents of women's sports. In fact, like the restrictions physical educators had placed on elite athletes during the 1950s, the lack of support for women professional basketballers harmed *all* females. They were still being subjected to the (sometimes not so) subtle signals that women are, and should be, different from men. The absence of professional women suggested to females that they could not achieve the aggressiveness, competitiveness, grace, and skill for which male pros were admired. Indeed, they should not even aspire to those traits because, if they did, they would be at best invisible and, at worst, abnormal. The WBL's demise punctuated a continuing story of unfair limits.

Women's Sports in the 1990s

"Women are handicapped by their boobs," television golf commentator Ben Wright reportedly said in summer 1995. Breasts make it difficult to keep their arms straight, a crucial tenet of hitting a golf ball efficiently. Women on the pro tour are also handicapped by their reputation, he continued. "Lesbians in the sport hurt women's golf." Lesbianism on the LPGA tour today "is not reticent," and "when it gets to the corporate level [where sponsorship comes from], that's not going to fly."[1] After the remarks were widely circulated, Wright denied making them.

Wright's supposed comments illustrate how some matters have hardly changed in forty-five years. Historically, women athletes have battled two perceptions: that their physical differences make them incapable of performing sports competently, and that sports masculinize females and make them abnormal/lesbian women. Of course, there is a grain of truth in these perceptions. The average woman is not as strong or fast as the average man; sports can help make women confident, skilled, and aggressive ("masculine"); and there are lesbian athletes and many lesbian fans of women's sports.[2] Despite these partial truths, however, the perceptions grossly overgeneralize. Individual women may be stronger or faster than individual men; men themselves have certain physiological traits that give them risks and disadvantages in certain sports as well as advantages; sports can help inculcate "feminine" traits like cooperation and self-sacrifice; "masculine" traits like confidence and skill can enhance women; "masculine" does not necessarily mean lesbian; and lesbianism is not a plague. Most dangerously, the partial truths have been warped to make some unjustified conclusions: since women are different and weaker, since sports makes them unfeminine, since there are lesbians in sports, then women athletes do not deserve equal support. That is, those perceptions are twisted to excuse criticism and apathy toward women's sports.

Whether or not Ben Wright made those comments, others have been thinking the same thing. During the late 1980s, the Ladies Professional Golf Association (LPGA) stood at a crossroads. After years of steady growth, in 1988 it lost some sponsors, canceled one tournament, and agreed to a smaller purse in another. Even as men's Senior Golf took off (with former stars now too old to compete on the PGA tour), smaller corporate funding for the women led to less television exposure. *Sports Illustrated* reported that the LPGA faced the two major problems Wright supposedly mentioned: the perception that women cannot play excellent golf and that a large percentage of the pros are lesbians. "The only thing you ever hear about the LPGA is that at least 30 percent of its players are gay," said Terry Kassel, a sports marketing executive.[3] As a result of this second "image problem," the LPGA's leadership adopted the old tried-and-true apologetic strategy of highlighting femininity—in photo poses, Jan Stephenson seductively imitated Marilyn Monroe, Nancy Lopez lovingly fed her two children, and young players modeled revealing swimsuits. According to commissioner Ray Volpe, "Something that was holding the women back financially was the butch image, so we tried to deal with it."[4] In retrospect he believes "we promoted sex too heavily" because, by emphasizing facets other than golf, LPGA marketing did nothing to promote acceptance of women's athleticism and implicitly devalued players who simply played golf exceptionally well. Despite Volpe's lesson, in the 1990s the tour hired an "image consultant," who softens the pros' nails, makeup, skin, and hair. She has noted "a whole new way of thinking. Before, [competitors] were totally focused on being athletes."[5] The next commissioner encouraged players to appear in fashion layouts, declaring, "I'm not at all against marketing our attractiveness."[6]

While golfers' problems sound all-too-familiar, there is another side to the story. Although the LPGA does not have the wealth or notoriety of the PGA or even the Senior men's tours, it is very successful. Since 1990 the tour has enjoyed a 50 percent gain in revenue, prize money has increased (the average purse for an LPGA event was $642,000 in 1995 as compared to $496,000 in 1991), and television coverage has doubled (to twenty-six events, ten on major networks). Corporate sponsors, more aware that women make important consumer decisions, are targeting them as an audience; meanwhile, the female golfing population has been growing steadily.[7] Supporting over a hundred golfers in thirty-eight events, the LPGA represents one of the most reliable opportunities for women to be a professional athlete. (In fact, many golfers admit that golf would not have been their first choice of sports had there been other professional opportunities available.)[8] Another positive aspect is that Ben Wright denied making the comments, and that many people criticized CBS for not chastising Wright in any way.[9] The cultural climate thus has changed, at least to the extent that in the 1990s one does not want to publicly say ignorant things about women or women's sports.

Just as with Ben Wright's comments, the story of women's sports in the years since 1985 is a mixed bag of change and continuity. In the area of sexuality, for example, many heterosexual women continue to be scared off from participating in sports because of the lesbian label. Unfortunately, they never get to discover the benefits (in excitement, skill, companionship, confidence, and joy) athletics can bring. At the same time, lesbian sportswomen also live in fear—both of confirming the stereotype and suffering ramifications for being openly gay (in a homophobic society). For professional athletes, the reasons for concern are obvious. Asked why *not one* of the LPGA's golfers have admitted to being lesbian, an anonymous pro explained impatiently, "Because it would be suicide. Because you'd get cut off from every endorsement opportunity possible. Because there's money and careers at stake." Still, this player was surprised at how explicitly players enforced rules of secrecy on one another. She said they were informed at a mandatory meeting (by a lesbian pro): "Ladies, we do not care what goes on inside your bedroom door. But keep it there."[10]

It is difficult for college coaches, too, who work in a highly competitive field. Added pressure comes from many parents of young female athletes, who worry that their "unfeminine" daughters may turn out to be lesbian. When combined with the unfair stereotype that gays are "predators" luring young people into homosexuality, parents often want to keep their children away from gay coaches. This phobia has led to a number of troubling phenomena—first, coaches hiding integral aspects of their lives in shame and paranoia; second, underhanded lesbian-baiting. In the latter there have been a number of cases in which anonymous people, hoping to smear coaches and ruin their programs, have sent letters to parents of star basketball recruits telling them that certain coaches are lesbians.[11] These rumors—unconfirmed, unjust, and using information that ought to be irrelevant—constitute a sort of 1990s version of McCarthyism in the athletic subculture. And like the enforcement of strict rules against intercollegiate sports by physical educators in the 1950s, this obsessive fear of being considered lesbian within sports circles is tragic. Women who should know better—straight and gay—continue to pass internalized homophobia onto their students and colleagues.[12] In a society where significant numbers of gay youngsters commit suicide, it is cruel to perpetuate the conditions whereby young women feel shame for their sexual and athletic proclivities.

At the same time, however, there is hope that conditions are changing. In 1980 former Olympic decathlete Dr. Tom Waddell conceived of a different type of sporting event, one based on the philosophy that not winning but "doing one's personal best should be the paramount goal."[13] Waddell floated his idea at a gay and lesbian community dinner, combining it with the dream of an athletic event in which any person—regardless of sexual orientation or age, race, ability, sex, or HIV status—could participate. (He hoped to call the event the Gay Olympics, but the U.S. Olympic Committee fought a costly legal battle to keep gays from using the word *Olympics*.) The first "Gay Games" took place in summer 1982, attracting over 1,300 athletes from twelve nations. Since then, the games have taken place every four years, most recently in New York City in 1994, where 11,000 mostly gay athletes competed in thirty-one events. Participants included a slow, chunky, novice runner (applauded by thousands for her effort), a bisexual tennis player, a golfer with AIDS, a blind skier and distance runner, an African-American lesbian grandmother in wrestling, and a multicultural co-gender in-line skating team.[14] These athletes combated stereotypes about homosexuals (including the one that gay males are unathletic sissies) and acted as inspiring role models. The games were welcomed by New York politicians, public and private facilities, and corporate sponsors (who noticed that the revenue generated by the games was estimated at $111 million).[15] The positive coverage, including the phrase "A Gay and Lesbian Tribute" that graced the marquee outside Madison Square Garden, has helped to dispel the notion that disasters necessarily befall athletes who are openly homosexual. A celebration, the games affirmed the spirit of the gay community. Not asking for approval, the athletes and organizers performed the ultimate manifestation of self-esteem—quite the opposite of the secrecy, paranoia, and homophobia present in much of sports. Looking forward to the 1998 Gay Games to be held in Amsterdam, these athletes did their part to make it true that, in executive director Jay Hill's words, "Games really can change the world."[16]

Other alternative athletic events have taken off in the past few decades. Running, biking, triathlon, and swimming competitions regularly compile age-specific scores, so that adults can continue to measure themselves against people their own age. Other events allow people to rank themselves, so they can compete with those of like ability. The Senior Olympics sponsors local, regional, and national events—such as track and field, walking, softball, and horseshoes, so that senior citizens can continue to live healthy, challenging lives. "I feel so good when I do this," declared athlete Betty Wingo.[17] Mentally challenged children, aided by thousands of volunteers worldwide, have made the Special

Olympics a moving celebration of achievement. Increasingly, the physically handicapped are competing in one-legged skiing, blind softball, and wheelchair basketball, tennis, bowling, and racing. Recreation centers and health clubs now regularly sponsor beginner classes for adults in everything from water aerobics to racquetball. Local institutions, often more responsive to community needs than high-level organizations, have even adapted rules so that males and females can more equitably enjoy co-recreational volleyball, softball, and baseball together. Cynics might disdainfully characterize these efforts as "political correctness," but to the participants they represent long-desired opportunities to compete, use their bodies, and test their limits in an environment where they are understood, appreciated, and respected. These opportunities—like those for the most talented young women stars—are long overdue.

Opportunities for women have grown considerably in the decade leading up to the mid-1990s. As the number of females who play amateur sports increases, so does the number of (and rewards for) elite athletes. The number of females playing softball, for example, continues to grow exponentially (from two thousand teams in the mid-1950s to over thirty-five thousand in the mid-1980s), and the International Olympic Committee has responded by including the sport in the games. In bowling, 706,193 women were members of the Women's International Bowling Congress in 1955, with the total climbing to 2.4 million by 1993.[18] In one of the lowest-profile professional tours, a bowling champion can win $100,000 a year.[19] Women can also earn prize money in distance running, triathlons, bicycle racing, and volleyball. Competitions are spreading in relatively new sports for women, such as body building, team handball, rugby, and water polo. As American women succeed on the world scene, communities and schools are adding opportunities for girls and women in soccer. Females are making further inroads in professional car and horse racing. Top track stars usually only earn headlines in the United States every four years, but they are recognized widely and often receive appearance money in international meets. Moreover, women champions in winter Olympic sports gain appreciation for bringing home gold medals (especially since Americans as a group are not bringing home many).[20] The faces of exceptional athletes like speed skater Bonnie Blair become familiar for a few weeks and, if they are lucky, appear on product endorsements. People are no longer surprised that businesses have arisen to teach adult women they can do challenging outdoor sports like kayaking. Women may not be moving mountains—but they *are* climbing them!

Sports and fitness have been "in fashion" for women for almost two decades. A whole industry—including health clubs, sporting goods equipment, athletic apparel, videotapes, and magazines—has grown up around the phenomenon. One of the new and most prevalent images of the modern woman is of a young, fit, woman working out. Hair pulled back, face set in a happy sort of determination, she might be jogging, lifting weights, swinging a softball bat, or doing aerobics. This fitness-conscious woman wears modern workout apparel—skintight spandex designed to feel good (hug the body) and show every muscle and curve. On magazines, of course, she is not sweating, but even off the glossy covers she is considered sexy. The image of beauty in the 1990s is thin with toned muscles.

This trend has decidedly good benefits. Popularizing fitness means more widespread health. Doctors agree that regular exercise helps many of the body's systems—especially circulatory and digestive. People who exercise have less risk of disease and recover better from illnesses. Greater awareness of nutrition and the dangers of drug use and a diet too high in fat and cholesterol clearly complement the physical advantages. A moderate exercise/sports program can give women a physical and social outlet and contribute to mental health as well. Active women who become physically stronger are more likely to feel competent, assertive, and comfortable in and responsive to their bodies. This fitness trend, then, can mean women live longer and healthier lives and feel better in the process.

Unfortunately, the sports and fitness craze for females has a dark side. Among the hundreds of thousands who have participated in order to get healthy are an unknown but high number of girls and women who do so to meet an unrealistic and dangerous image of a perfect—ultrathin—female. Experts believe a silent epidemic of eating disorders is poisoning women's sports. Anorexia nervosa (an addictive pursuit of thinness by drastically limiting food intake) and bulimia (purging food by using laxatives, diuretics, or vomiting) can strike anyone in the population but primarily hits females. Americans in general tend to be unrealistic in their perception of their bodies, but among females the distortion is much more likely to be negative. When they look in the mirror, all they can see is fat—a natural and necessary part of women's bodies—and some become desperate to eliminate it. Girls and women who suffer from depression or low self-esteem (a widespread problem for adolescent females) are particularly susceptible to eating disorders, as are victims of sexual abuse. So, too, it seems, are female athletes in certain sports. The American College of Sports Medicine has estimated that 62 percent of women in "appearance sports"—like gymnastics and figure skating—suffer from these problems.[21] Bulimia and anorexia are "as much a part of competitive gymnastics as leotards and back flips," according to one observer. Cross-country, track, and swimming have equally bad reputations.[22]

Why is this problem so prevalent among female athletes? (Only a small number of male athletes, in sports such as wrestling and distance running, have exhibited a similar problem.) In part, the explanation is that whatever problems touch the female population will hurt female athletes. While one might expect athletes to be stronger and healthier than the other females, many athletes fit the psychological profile of anorexics, which is driven, perfectionist, and practiced in self-control. Some of the explanation also seems to lie in particular sports, however; many of the problem areas are those traditionally considered feminine, in which one's performance is judged in large part by appearance. It *does* make a difference to the success of gymnasts, figure skaters, and divers that they look very thin. A girlish/waif look is absolutely essential now to a gymnast, and signs of maturity—breasts, hips, figure—are disastrous. Indeed, the size of the average Olympic gymnast shrank from 5'3" and 105 pounds in 1976 to 4'9" and eighty-eight pounds in 1992.[23] In the running events, the danger is slightly different; it is a deadly misperception that weight loss necessarily means speed. Unfortunately, its partial truth seduces runners; they can become faster as their weight drops, but one who becomes obsessively compelled to continue losing weight also loses sight of the fact that the body's stores can only last so long. "You'll get results," says a recovering anorexic, "but you'll pay for it."[24] Eventually, the downward spiral of loss of fat, then muscle depletion, then weakness and injuries leads to collapse. Coaches—adults who ought to have better information and perspective (and be concerned about their athletes' well-being)—often ignore the problem. Some actually make it worse, setting unreasonable expectations and holding daily weigh-ins. Anecdotes abound about abusive behavior. Coaches have withheld meals from those who don't meet weight goals, confined them to "fat rooms," and called them "porkers." Humiliation is a common tactic: one coach made girls who were a few pounds overweight wear "Miss Piggy" t-shirts. One woman who finally quit her university track team said coaches gave the wrong message: "It's not like they say 'get strong, work hard,' just 'you've got to be skinny.'"[25]

Despite the extent of the problem, the sports world had been in collective denial until recently. As bulimic and anorexic athletes try to recover, they are spreading the word about the dangers. Anorexic young women can stop menstruating, and the lack of estrogen contributes to an irreversible bone loss (often at the very period in life when they should be gaining bone mass and strength). Doctors report seeing eighteen-year-olds with honey-combed bones similar to those found in seventy-year-olds, who suffer fractures at the slightest contact. Dehydration, low blood pressure, sleep disorders, psychotic behavior, and gland and organ damage are other possible results. Bulimics' teeth are rotted by stomach acids, their lacerated throats swell, their heart rates become erratic.[26] In the 1970s Olympic gymnast Cathy Rigby was told by her coach that she would perform better if she lost weight. She learned from teammates how to purge herself and eventually (especially after the onset of puberty) was throwing up ten times a day. Responding to media stories that celebrated her girlishness (at 4'10" and eighty-five pounds), she tried to maintain it, even pulling her pigtails so tight she got headaches. Anorexic as well as bulimic, Rigby twice went into cardiac arrest.[27] Patti Catalano was a world-class runner, holding records in distances from five miles to the marathon. Her coach-husband wanted her to get thinner, reasoning that it takes less energy to carry something light. By 1981 the 5'5" Catalano weighed only ninety-six pounds and was plagued by an overwhelming need to throw up five times a day. An emotional wreck, she eventually faced her deep dark secret and survived.[28]

Gymnast Christy Henrich was not so lucky. Obsessed by the dream of making the Olympic team (and scared by a judge's comment that she would not unless she lost weight), Henrich tried everything, including running in plastic in ninety-five-degree weather, using laxatives, and stopping eating. She boasted at one point that she could perform her six-hour-a-day training regimen on just three apples. Later she decreased it to a few slices of apple. Some blamed her authoritarian coach for her illness. (He nicknamed her "Extra Tough" and told her to pull in her stomach because she looked "like the Pillsbury Doughboy.") Her parents, however, believe the problem runs deeper than that: "It's the whole system."[29] Parents, coaches, gymnastics officials, feminine expectations, and the girlish mystique of gymnastics all contributed. Finally, increasing paranoia, unsociability, and injuries convinced her coach to force her to retire. Psychologically as well as physically maimed, Henrich was repeatedly hospitalized over the next few years. Lack of fuel meant malnourishment, so that her muscles, cells, and organs could no longer function. At one point her weight dropped to forty-seven pounds. "My life is a horrifying nightmare. It feels like a beast inside me, like a monster," she said. The intensive medical and emotional support helped, so that she came to understand she was a loved and worthwhile human being (apart from gymnastics and regardless of how thin she looked). Unfortunately, it was too late for her body to heal. Slipping into a coma from multiple organ failure, the four-foot, ten-inch, sixty-one-pound, twenty-two-year-old Henrich died. Erica Stokes, a bulimic former teammate, hoped "her death reaches others" with the "message that starving to win is not worth it."[30]

Sports and fitness can clearly be perverted, with dangerous consequences. Eating disorders, like steroid use for male athletes, are a special, sex-based risk. Only recently are women beginning to discuss what may be another particularly female phenomenon: sexual abuse of young athletes by coaches. Through the intense daily interactions in sports, coaches can become very close to their players in what is usually a meaningful, healthy connection. Older, and often admired and needed, coaches have many types of power. Those without appropriate emotional boundaries, perspective, or ethics can easily take advantage of that power. Most frequently in our society it is men who are sexual offenders, but women can as easily abuse their power. "Mostly, coaches molest children because they can. Because no one is stopping them," writes Mariah Burton

Nelson, one of the first women to speak openly of her own victimization (by an older married male coach).[31] Sadly, egotistic coaches sometimes delude themselves and others that such unequal sexual relationships are actually in the athletes' best interests (but one wonders why they are incapable of forming more appropriate attachments with people their own age). Only occasionally is a coach who verbally, physically, or emotionally abuses players stopped, and sexual impropriety is prevented less often. This phenomenon is still only whispered about at schools, but clearly it must be addressed so our daughters can be assured of the supportive and safe environment they deserve. Trustworthy coaches, who put their players' well-being first, are just as crucial to fight for as an equal number of scholarships.

A few other problems have plagued women's sports in the 1990s. As the compensation of coaches of women's teams has increased, so have the number of men in their ranks. In 1972, 90 percent of the coaches of women's college teams were women; in 1992 it was 48 percent. (Only 36 percent of coaches of girls' high school teams were women.)[32] There is nothing inherently wrong with men coaching women. The unfortunate aspect is that women's coaching abilities are not respected; they are not considered capable of coaching males, and lack sufficient opportunities to coach females. In a difficult cycle, then, their shortage of experience only closes more doors to women. In addition, men continue to hold the vast majority of top administrative (hiring) positions.[33] (While women used to run 90 percent of women's programs, the current percentage is 17 percent. It is even more rare for women to be athletic directors at large universities.) Blatant sexism still exists in some areas. Country clubs, for example, often refuse to allow women in general (or unmarried women) to become members, or otherwise restrict their access. During the early 1990s the discriminatory policies (by race, gender, and religion) of some country clubs hosting professional golf tournaments were exposed. A few clubs made token changes, but others gave up tournaments rather than their prejudices. Socioeconomic class still affects the makeup of sports, so that golf, tennis, and triathlons remain more exclusive than games like basketball and softball.[34] The cost of equipment, training, and facilities limits access for children without wealth. Financial barriers blend with historical tradition to push black athletes into certain sports. Eighty-three percent of the black women with athletic scholarships at large universities played on the basketball or track team, and no African-American women have competed on the LPGA golf tour since the mid-seventies. Physically disabled women also find their opportunities extremely scarce.[35] The United States is not egalitarian, and sports still reflect that reality.

For a few minutes at Centre Court at Wimbledon in July 1994, it seemed as if nothing had changed: the grass was green; spectators, including royalty and celebrities, filled the stands. During the championship match, Martina Navratilova served hard, then smoothly charged to the net to put away a winner. But upon closer examination, things were different from the old days: instead of a skimpy pure white dress, Navratilova wore shorts and a red ribbon commemorating AIDS victims. In addition, she was losing; she was thirty-seven years old and a half-step slower. But, perhaps most surprising, she was clearly the sentimental favorite of the crowd.[36] At Wimbledon, as throughout her final year of play, Navratilova met with cheers. Things had not always been this rosy, however; during the 1980s, for example, while even mediocre pros had endorsement contracts, no clothing manufacturer would dress her.[37] Now, as she reached retirement, sportswriters raved she was one of the greatest female athletes ever. She had won 167 singles titles and 164 doubles (more than any player, male or female), fifty-five Grand Slam Crowns, and now respect. An "athletic gem," said *Sporting News*. ("Her intelligence, engaging wit, and newly found elegance make her truly special.")[38] Journalists even applauded her courage—for espousing the rights of women, children, the elderly, and animals. Most controversially, she had become a prominent advocate for gay rights—speaking at a national rally in Washington, helping raise funds for the Gay Games, and joining the ACLU in a lawsuit against Colorado's antihomosexual rights bill. ("If I don't stand up against it, who will?" she asked.)[39] After years of whispers, antagonism, rumor-mongering, and apathy, the press now universally praised her. "She always dared," noted tennis commentator Bud Collins. "She dared to defect [from Czechoslovakia]. She dared to play the way she did. She dared to live the way she did."[40]

Navratilova's retirement marked the end of an era, and unfortunately there was some cause to worry about the coming one. Just when it seemed the tour's worst problem was silly media coverage about grunting, jewelry, and giggling young players, bad news bombarded women's tennis in the mid-1990s.[41] American teen phenomenon Jennifer Capriati's career lapsed after she was arrested for possession of marijuana and entered a drug rehabilitation center. Then WTA officials banished player Mary Pierce's father from attending matches. Accused of battering and stalking his family, he regularly yelled and cursed at competitors from the stands, and assaulted a spectator. In 1993 a deranged German man actually ran onto the court and stabbed Monica Seles, top player in the world, so that his obsession, Steffi Graf, would assume the top ranking. "If this is what it takes to be number one, then forget it," said Seles. "This is too high a price."[42] Increasingly, people questioned whether tennis had lost perspective.[43] Ambitious agents and parents continued to push naive and uneducated children—as young as thirteen—into giving up childhood in order to turn professional. It sometimes led to riches, but more often to injury, burnout, and emotional trauma. At the same time, tennis was losing popularity. The number of Americans who played had declined dramatically since the late 1970s and, with familiar and charismatic stars gone, television ratings were down. The relationship with corporate sponsors also became shakier, as Kraft General Foods and long-time patron Virginia Slims pulled out.[44]

Not all the news about modern women's tennis was bad, however. It is probably more accurate to say that the tour suffered a bruise rather than a career-threatening injury. In 1993 there was a record purse at the U.S. Open (over $9 million), and the women's singles champion won the same amount as the men's champ ($535,000). The WTA tour offered pros sixty-two tournaments in twenty-two countries, and the amount of prize money and television coverage was still high. Indeed, girls and their parents pursue tennis stardom precisely because there are such amazing opportunities. Up-and-coming players can endorse racquets and clothing and cars (even before they are old enough to drive them). However, with so many girls having fallen victim to the dangers of turning pro at fourteen, the WTA has fortunately changed the rules so that now girls under eighteen will be limited to a small number of events. Another hopeful sign on the horizon is that a number of African-American players are rising who may serve as role models.[45] Finally, a movement is under way to renew the tour. Billie Jean King is again pushing tennis authorities and encouraging younger players to learn about the business of entertainment, let fans see their personalities, and give back something to the game. She is joined by Martina Navratilova, new president of the Women's Tennis Association. Their combination of experience, promotional skills, and courage should help the game advance. After all, King helped get it all started, and Navratilova is one of the rare few women athletes who has said, "I have no apologies."[46]

Basketball is advancing, too, but at a slow pace. While the AAU still sponsors some events, clearly the top-level competition is now at the intercollegiate level, where players are bigger, stronger, and more skilled than in the past. And there are more of them. In 1992–93 almost 400,000 girls participated on high school basketball teams, and more great ones graduate each year.[47] They usually proceed to large universities, which now allocate to women's basketball at least ten full scholarships, spend tens of thousands of dollars for recruiting, and compensate their coaches more equitably.[48]

There are discouraging signs, too, though. Apathy means that in many areas players sweat in near-empty gyms (in 1994 the national average attendance at Division 1 universities was just over one thousand). Many apparently agree with the Boston columnist who boasted he would never watch another women's basketball game on TV because the weak and less skilled players made it boring. "At their best," he insisted, "women play like men, in slow motion."[49] And even though the women's Final Four television ratings ranked 14 percent better than an NBA men's regular season game and three times better than an NHL hockey game, they were just a fraction of the number who watch the men's Final Four.[50] Still, ESPN plans to televise a record thirty-one women's NCAA postseason games in 1996 (in part because the previous years' national championships were so exciting). In 1993 Texas Tech's Cheryl Swoopes's forty-seven points against Ohio State so impressed Nike that it named a shoe after her. And in 1994 North Carolina's Charlotte Smith swished a long, three-point shot with .7 seconds remaining to steal the national title. Barely six feet tall, Smith also grabbed headlines with her high-flying dunks.[51] Increasingly, fans showed their appreciation, especially at a couple of powerhouses. Over 13,000 packed the stadium when the University of Tennessee played rivals like Georgia and Vanderbilt, and Tennessee averaged 7,800 fans for home games. In Connecticut, "Husky Mania" meant adoring young boys and girls clamoring for players' autographs hours after the game, students waiting in line the whole weekend for tickets, and stadium speakers blaring Aretha Franklin's "R-E-S-P-E-C-T."[52]

Unfortunately, after starring in college, adult women have few opportunities to use their skills in the United States. All-American or not, they must travel overseas if they want to be paid and challenged. This vacuum in professional opportunities is not for lack of trying. After the Women's Basketball League folded in 1981, the idea survived. Unfortunately, the Ladies Professional Basketball Association (conceived in 1980) never got started; the Women's American Basketball Association (1984) lasted just one season; and coaches were hired for a National Women's Basketball Association (1986), but they never coached a game.[53] The Liberty Basketball Association tried a different route. Believing that fans wanted to see the excitement of dunks, and that women are disadvantaged by their height (on average 8 percent shorter than men), this league's founder lowered the rim to nine feet, two inches. He also dressed the players in skintight unitards. The controversy over the sexy uniforms won some attention, but despite the tens of thousands who attended an exhibition game or watched it on ESPN, the jokingly termed "Spandex League" also collapsed.[54] A short-season, black-owned pro league in Las Vegas lasted a little while in the early 1990s, and the Women's Basketball Association still treaded water in eight midwestern cities in the spring of 1994. One could hardly use the term *professional*, however, to describe its conditions: players held other full-time jobs and often had to cover all their own expenses; and in one seven-week period the Indiana Stars were paid a total of ten dollars. "What we are is a volunteer professional basketball team," remarked player Cassandra Pack. Despite meager support (audiences comprised mainly of relatives), players continued to pay the price. Said an assistant coach hopefully, "I think it'll work itself out if we can stick it out."[55]

Although they, too, make sacrifices, players who truly go professional—that is, who play overseas—clearly do much better. In the mid-1990s top Americans could earn between $200,000 and $300,000 in France, Italy, Japan, Spain, or Hungary. Agents negotiated advantageous, secure deals for them, and besides the money they enjoyed respect. Coaches expect American stars to do the bulk of the scoring, fans know them and crowd arenas, newspapers cover their games. In Italy they get an apartment and a car in addition to their salary. According to one player, expectations differ from the mid-1980s, when women felt a bit reluctant to risk going overseas. "Now it is like [male stars] going to the NBA. It is the alternative."[56] So routine is the move that players often study French and Italian during their college years. There are drawbacks, of course. "You leave your friends. You leave your teammates and most important, you leave your family," explained Portia Hill. Cultural differences sometimes pose difficulty.[57] In Japan coaches often punch and kick their players (Americans now put no-abuse clauses in their contracts); fans can be violent and invasive in Italy; the language is difficult in Hungary. Players often suffer from isolation and loneliness in other countries, and most do not choose to settle permanently. Despite the rewards, then, it isn't home. "It's not the same as being right here in the United States," said Hill. "We just hope to cope with it, and hopefully one day we'll get that chance."[58]

An intense desire to play at home explains why American stars showed up to try out for the U.S. national team in the summer of 1995. "Are you prepared to sit on the bench here when you could be starring overseas for $300,000 a year?" they were asked at interviews. Almost every player invited answered affirmatively. They left high-paying jobs in Europe to sign on for an experiment: for the first time, players on the U.S. women's national team will be professionals. They will be paid $50,000 each to spend fourteen months preparing for the 1996 Olympics. Three million dollars have been budgeted to try to bring home a gold medal, and perhaps in the process to get Americans more excited about women's basketball. The NBA agreed to act as the team's agent and has garnered big-name corporate sponsors and television coverage for ten pre-Olympic games. Clearly, U.S. officials have made an unprecedented commitment to women's basketball, and participants (including coach Tara VanDeveer, who has taken a year's leave from her top-ranked Stanford team) are responding in kind. They are putting their lives on hold, spending a year away from their partners, children, and jobs. They are rescheduling school and even marriages. "Some sacrifices are more financial, others more personal or emotional," says the team's director.[59] Of course, it's no surprise that women basketballers would sacrifice for their game—they always have.

The battle for gender equity in intercollegiate athletics has slowed considerably. Since the rapid expansion during the 1970s, many of the worst abuses have disappeared, but a number of roadblocks have also stalled the movement. First the Supreme Court weakened Title IX's application to athletic programs in the Grove City case in 1984, causing the federal Office of Civil Rights (OCR) to ignore over eight hundred complaints. It took Congress four years to pass (over President Reagan's veto) a Civil Rights Restoration Act. This law put the teeth back into Title IX by making it clear that *every part* of a federally funded institution (not just programs that directly receive funds) must refrain from sex discrimination. The clarified law encouraged sportswomen to file new complaints with the OCR, but under the Reagan and Bush administrations the understaffed agency made enforcing civil rights a low priority. In fact, one study lambasted the OCR for using inconsistent criteria, excusing discriminatory practices, and failing to make sure violations of Title IX were corrected. Indeed, it maintained, the Office of Civil Rights had "become an impediment of gender equity rather than a facilitator and enforcer."[60] Although the Clinton administration pledged greater regulation, understandably many sportswomen with complaints now mistrust the federal bureaucracy and are turning elsewhere for help. Increasingly, they take problems to the judicial system, where Title IX has been more strictly applied. For example, when Oklahoma, Colorado State, Brown, and Cornell eliminated some women's athletic teams, players took their universities to court and won reinstatement of the teams.[61]

In addition to old opponents, limited budgets now appear to be the biggest obstacle to equity. Even before reaching comparable levels of participation as men's teams (not to mention comparable levels in resources, publicity, attendance, and financial aid), women's teams are being scaled back at some colleges in order to save money. Athletic directors insist there is nowhere else to trim other than "minor" nonrevenue-producing sports. These cuts seem unfair, however, given the short history and lack of support shown many women's sports. Title IX rules also make them illegal. The law requires that women and men have opportunities proportional to their overall numbers as students (that is, if women are 50 percent of undergraduates, they should make up 50 percent of athletes); if not, schools must demonstrate they have consistently expanded women's opportunities or satisfied women's interests. While a handful have committed to doing so, almost no schools meet those criteria.[62] In 1990–91, although women comprised 50 percent of undergraduates at Division I schools, they made up only 31 percent of the athletes. They received 30 percent of athletic scholarships, 22.6 percent of operating expenditures, and 17.2 percent of recruiting monies.[63] Athletic directors claimed the numbers were misleading. They said that football teams (which at large universities field around 117 players)[64] skew the numbers. If football were taken out of the equation (as it should be, they say, because it is special and brings in substantial revenue), one would see that men and women already have equal opportunities.

It is just as unethical and illogical to make an exception for one sport in the 1990s as in 1974 when football coaches first made the argument. Even if Title IX permitted discrimination based on the ability to make a profit (which it does not), 93 percent of the NCAA's football programs had deficits.[65] In addition, even when the numbers for football are removed from the calculations, gender inequity still exists. (Even deleting football, Division I schools still had 1.45 male athletes for each female and spent $1.80 on men for each dollar spent on women.)[66] Ultimately, however, it is basically unfair to allow men twice as many athletic opportunities as women. ("If schools designated two-thirds of their academic scholarships for men, we would be outraged. We should have similar outrage with respect to sports," insists Illinois's Rep. Cardiss Collins.)[67] In days of tight budgets, athletic departments must make difficult decisions about how to allocate their resources. Achieving parity without cutting men's opportunities is difficult, but no more difficult than during the recessions of the 1970s. "You either cut costs or you create ways to add revenue," said Georgia Tech's athletic director Homer Rice. "It has been that way for years."[68]

Arguments and resistance to Title IX have not changed much in twenty years. Athletic directors have long insisted that in the zero sum game of athletics, adding opportunities for women means the injustice of taking them from men. While they understandably mourn the loss of opportunities for a few male athletes, those same people do not shed tears over the injustice of depriving large numbers of women opportunities. If there must be one, the real fight over athletic dollars should be taking place *between men* in so-called "minor" sports and "major" ones.[69] Athletic departments choose whether to sponsor a wide variety of sports for men or to allocate the bulk of their opportunities and dollars to football. So far, football coaches have shrewdly managed to shift the grounds of the argument, portraying the battle as one between men and women, and blame women for cuts in men's nonrevenue-producing sports. Meanwhile, as reformers look to expensive and sometimes extravagant football programs for ways to save money, coaches strenuously resist. (They have even denounced efforts to prevent teams from sleeping in hotels the night before home games and to limit squads to ninety-five players, which would permit more than four players at each position). Football coaches continue to characterize their sport as the Golden Goose that pays for other sports (a situation true at only a small minority of large universities), and claim militant feminists in an "irrational attack on football" are out to "emasculate" their programs.[70]

This resentment over equality is old, but it has found a new, powerful, and sympathetic hearing in Washington. The Republican congressional majority elected in 1994 has targeted numerous liberal hallmarks, including civil rights measures, for elimination. Portraying it as an affirmative-action-type "quota," they have targeted the proportionality standard in Title IX. Yet again, conservative sportsmen are lobbying to weaken the law or exempt football from it. What is different from the 1970s is the political climate; their chances are better than ever before to undermine the legal guarantee of equality.

Meanwhile, the NCAA has hardly changed. The organization was embarrassed when its figures showed male athletes outnumbering females two to one and the allocations for recruiting and operating dollars even more disproportionate. Executive director Richard Schultz acknowledged for the first time that some colleges had "dragged their feet" and "done some things to avoid compliance" with the law. Promising leadership on this important "moral issue," he created a special subcommittee.[71] This panel reached agreement on a definition of gender equity but lacked power. Instead of drafting legislation to act on its recommendations, NCAA officers proposed watered-down "guidelines" stating that schools should comply with the law and the NCAA should not adopt measures preventing them from doing so. The organization "chickened out," according to a frustrated Donna Lopiano; positive, specific rules for achieving gender equity never materialized.[72] By merely endorsing a law passed twenty years earlier, the organization remains at best neutral. Indeed, the NCAA's irresolute stance appears even weaker relative to its detailed and stringent enforcement mechanism on other matters. "It is odd that the NCAA would place a school on probation for driving an athlete to class, or providing a loan," observed Illinois's Rep. Cardiss Collins, "but would have no penalty for a school that violates Title IX, a federal law."[73] Instead of championing them, female student-athletes are still viewed by a generation of male leaders as half-invited, troublesome, stepdaughters who are depleting men's resources.

Power relations have changed since the 1970s when the movement for equality had momentum and sportswomen had friends in high places. Feminist organizations and a minority within the NCAA are concerned about sportswomen, but now that AIAW is gone, they have less institutional clout. Lacking an advocate in the NCAA, sportswomen who are discriminated against are mainly left alone, as relatively weak and isolated individuals, to try to change things. They can make a complaint to the Office of Civil Rights and hope something positive happens within a few years. Or if they have the money to afford good legal help, they can file a lawsuit. Many sportswomen will not risk such an action, however.[74] Sometimes they do not have access to budgetary information that would prove their case. Others have heard horror stories about women who complain. For example, even though the Washington D.C. Superior Court awarded Howard University's Sanya J. Tyler $1.1 million in damages for sex discrimination and defamation, hers had been an unpleasant fight. Soon after she started pushing the institution to treat its sportswomen better, a smear campaign spread rumors that she had a poor job evaluation, had stolen money, and was a lesbian.[75] Administrator Marianne Stanley was apparently fired after protesting inequities in her university's system.[76] Other coaches fear harassment less than hurting morale or being labeled a troublemaker.

Nor do sportswomen want to risk losing the gains they have won. While there are not the number of female athletes there ought to be (and they are not appreciated or promoted the way they should be), they do enjoy substantial resources. At large schools, competitive schedules, high-level recruiting, tuition assistance, food, shoes, medical care, housing, effective coaching, and adequate equipment are normal benefits. Women now have a stake in the system. Far from questioning the established male model of intercollegiate athletics, then, many now want to protect it. Happily, thus far women's sports have avoided some of the problems (such as corruption, commercialization, and exploitation of athletes) of men's big-time sports. Female athletes have higher graduation rates than males.[77] Women's sports programs also have much lower rates of rule-breaking. In general, women's sports have a reputation of being more ethical, sensible, and student-centered. "The women's game and the people involved have never as a group been cutthroat and have never based their decisions on pie in the sky or entrepreneurship instead of education," declares Vanderbilt basketball coach Jim Foster. "It is not just an innocence, but a different understanding of what athletics means."[78]

Some worry that this healthy difference cannot last. Christine H. B. Grant, women's athletic director at Iowa and former president of AIAW, fears that as long as there is no major reform movement in the NCAA, women's intercollegiate sports are "just as doomed as the men's are to move further and further away from the academic mission of their colleges."

> None of us wants to take way from the idea of gender equity in any way, but as it now stands, as we move more and more toward equitable treatment for men and women, we move more and more into creating the same kind of environment in terms of pressure to win, to get bonuses, to get recruits, to get fans, to get on television. We have to decide if that's the kind of success for women's sports that we want.[79]

Grant's concerns echo the past, when women physical educators and coaches in the 1950s debated how to regulate athletics without being inappropriate or prudish or lose perspective. In the 1970s they struggled with how to secure for women the goods men enjoyed without being forced to adopt the evils. The future is difficult to predict. Grant may quietly dissent while women's sports comes to more closely mirror men's sports, or she may be a harbinger of reforms to come.

History suggests that change will certainly come in some form—in the political arena, the definition and enforcement of equality may be altered; in the cultural sphere, female athletes may gain or lose acceptance. One thing will probably remain constant, however: sportswomen will face questions about how to properly conduct their competition. Because they have traditionally been considered different, women have been forced to do more than simply accept the male model. Repeatedly, they have had to analyze that model and design alternatives. Although burdensome, this has also been an opportunity to make thoughtful, conscientious decisions. Women may not always have the freedom or power to pursue the direction they wish, but they will always be able to carefully evaluate their activities and roles. That legacy is a benefit that cannot be taken away.

CONCLUSION

Those unversed in women's sports history
tend to assume it is best divided into two basic
periods: the pre-Title IX and post-Title IX
years. In this view, during the so-called dark
ages (the 1950s and 1960s) very few women
competed seriously; then the law with its
guarantees of equality revolutionized
women's sports. This depiction contains
some truth. Female athletes faced enormous
obstacles before 1972, and after politicization
they enjoyed many more opportunities. But
the full story is more complex than oppression suddenly giving way to liberation. In fact,
during the fifties and sixties, some women,
utilizing a variety of strategies, found ways to
compete. Their numbers gradually increased,
even before Congress passed the law. Equality
did not result from Title IX, and indeed
equality has proved to be a problematic goal.
Finally, there are continuities as well as
change between the pre- and post-Title IX
eras. Both the successes and failures contain
lessons for advocates of women's sports.

Women in the 1950s and early 1960s did
participate in sports much less than their
descendants in the 1990s. A lack of opportunities discouraged them, as well as the knowledge that intense athletics were not considered normal for women. "Not feminine" often
translated into "masculine," and "masculine"
often implied "lesbian." Sensitive to the taint,
the majority of adult females did not compete
seriously, and so competing remained abnormal. Despite the aspersion, a minority of
women chose to be athletes anyway. Some of
them did not worry about having unfeminine
reputations. Rarely did the wider world hear

about those women. Although that invisibility meant they remained marginal, it also gave them space to participate happily in the athletic subculture. Many other women, however, did worry about sports' "masculinity." They tried to minimize the dissonance between sports and their proscribed role through apologetic behavior.

In different areas of sports during the 1950s, this strategy took different forms. Tennis enthusiasts, mainly upper-class women, played a not very rough sport and suffered less association with masculinity. Despite their relative advantages, however, Pauline Betz, Maureen Connolly, Althea Gibson, and "Gorgeous Gussie" Moran still engaged in apologetic behavior: they allowed themselves not to be taken seriously, downplayed their careers, wore feminine clothing, did not train very hard, and often quit after they got married. Women in the more working-class, more physical team sport of basketball often rejected upper-class notions of fragility, playing a style that defied the intent of "girls' rules." Still, they adopted some of the same apologetic behaviors as tennis players and added a few of their own. Their "feminine bargain" consisted of submitting to the control of male coaches and sponsors, and catering their more sensationalized game to male audiences with events like the annual AAU beauty pageant. Middle-class physical educators opted for a third strategy. Striving to preserve their tiny arena of authority, they tightly controlled women's college sports—making them private, female-only, safe, and conforming to extremely conservative standards. They encouraged cooperation rather than competition, "sportswomen" instead of athletes. Although their alternative model of college sport had some beneficial features, it was rooted in restrictive notions of femininity and served in practice to discourage and exclude strong assertive women.

Race, class, and choice of sport, then, affected the choice of strategies. Certain groups had advantages—especially white upper-class tennis players—in the degree to which they were deemed acceptable and worthy of notice by the dominant culture. They also enjoyed more leisure opportunities, benefits, and overall status. Occasionally they used these advantages by contrasting themselves to the less feminine and "proper" athletes in working-class and black-dominated sports. But while they made some difference, those racial and class advantages should not be exaggerated. For one thing, they did not always play out as expected. Because women athletes rarely occupied the national spotlight, what was most important to them was the support of their immediate community. Acceptance and legitimation was not forthcoming from *Sports Illustrated* and the *Washington Post*, which made that from families, friends, teachers, employers, and local newspapers even more important. Being identified with some community—be it a school, black neighborhood, textile mill, or group of lesbians—could give a woman the strength to compete despite the stereotypes (and lack of support from the wider culture). This more immediate community encouragement was crucial because, in the long run, even possessing class and racial advantages did not exempt a woman from the possibility of being called unfeminine. No female athlete had complete immunity.

By the mid-1990s, to what extent had the situation for women athletes improved? Significant change had occurred, especially during the 1970s and in the area of opportunities, but not radical change. Equality had not been achieved, and many problems remained. The best tennis players in the 1990s were professionals and, as such, more capable, serious, and wealthy athletes. Modern tennis resembled the 1950s, however, in its exclusivity and in its participants' sense of vulnerability. Likewise, by the 1990s basketball players had thrown off girls' rules and increased their numbers, and as they did so their ability soared. In some senses, though, their prospects worsened. Not only did efforts to establish a professional league fail, but the semipro opportunities of the industrial leagues had disappeared. Finally, in intercollegiate athletics there were three times as many 1990s students participating as in the 1960s, and they enjoyed greater resources, more notice, and better all-around treatment. Still, by the mid-1990s they had not achieved parity. Instead, in what one athletic director called the "civil rights bargain of the century," women's programs received about one-third of men's benefits and their female leaders steadily lost power.

The most important continuity was the fear of disapproval. It is difficult to measure what one coach called "this psychological stigma and stereotyping that most of us were aware of"; cultural and psychological stigma is not easily quantifiable. Still, two things suggest that it had diminished by the 1990s. First, many more athletes competed seriously. Second, certain elements of apologetic behavior declined. Unlike many of their 1950s counterparts, prominent female athletes in the 1990s rarely minimized the personal importance of their sport, or repudiated the notion of an athletic career, or avoided muscles. On the other hand, two basic types of apologetic behavior persisted: trying to project an "otherwise feminine" appearance and asserting a heterosexual image. Both the stereotypical assumption that sport masculinizes women and the actual historical presence of lesbians in sports insured that the lesbian specter continued to frighten athletes and coaches. In order to prevent the fear from deterring them, women required an awareness of how it harmed them. Feminists during the 1970s began pointing out how the threatened taunt of "dyke" served as social control—dividing women from one another and keeping them from being assertive, competitive, and strong. Unfortunately, in a vicious circle, many athletes avoided feminism because they were already engaging in risky behavior as athletes.

The movement achieved reform, not revolution. In the mid-1990s, as during the 1950s, there were times and places in which sports seemed permissible for women and athletes felt safe. But in the 1990s, female athletes received much more public support in terms of money, attention, and encouragement. Significantly, there were fewer ways that sports automatically detracted from one's femininity. Going to the gym, wearing athletic attire, and looking thin and muscular became more acceptable, and even fashionable. This was an incremental improvement. Models having muscle tone hardly constituted liberation, however, if muscles and hyperthinness became simply more requirements demanded by femininity. The women's sports movement decreased the predominance of men in sports but did not lessen the hegemony of femininity. The feminization strategy of the tennis pros, the lesbian-baiting of women coaches, and the failure of pro basketballers to find approval—all of which took place during the 1990s—indicate that there was still a line beyond which female athletes could not cross and still be considered normal women. The "unfeminine" problem still plagued them. The definition of femininity had been expanded during the 1970s to include some athletic participation, but the oppressive concept had not been toppled.

Nor did anything radical occur in the structure or conduct of these women's sports. Where women attempted radical change, as in physical educators' dream of reconstructing intercollegiate sports in a more humanistic and educational vein, they failed. Gradually, women coaches either came to favor or settled for better benefits within the male model. Tennis pros made a partial break from the hegemonic organization that ran tennis, and tried to make the game more professional, popular, and democratic, but it really varied very little from men's tennis.[1] Women's basketball discarded the differing rules and adopted men's practices, seeking legitimation through sameness. There have been grass-roots efforts by other organizations to instill alternative values and methods into sports—some of them similar to the more inclusive, less win-at-all-costs model of early physical educators. But significantly, these values and methods have not come in the areas discussed in this book, which are the most accomplished levels of the older, more established sports.[2] On the whole, the women's movement in tennis and basketball and (eventually) intercollegiate sports was liberal; it sought comparable benefits to and inclusion in the existing male model.[3] Most women did not seek, and they certainly did not achieve, radical change.

Even for the progress that did occur, Title IX deserves only part of the credit. Conditions for college athletes were changing *before* the law was passed in 1972. The first wave of change began in the mid-fifties, when PE leaders slowly responded to a complex set of circumstances. Athletes' interests, greater cultural permissiveness, pressure from the AAU, and the government's Cold War-inspired interest in female champions resulted in physical educators' approving and then sponsoring more intercollegiate athletics. The CIAW (organized in 1966) and AIAW (in 1971) formed a necessary foundation for the second wave of change, which occurred during the 1970s. Title IX helped fuel this more intense, more political stage. As in the fifties and sixties, cause and effect did not operate in only one direction. There was a more subtle, dialectical process in which women and socioeconomic conditions influenced Congress to create an opening, and then women's sports leaders and feminists used that opening to strengthen the law and demand more change. The activism of AIAW members— their complaints, organizing, and pressure—played an essential role in gaining campus opportunities. Although they relied on the threat of the law, the painfully slow bureaucratic process meant that enormous change took place before Title IX officially took effect. And most of the improvements remained even after Title IX was weakened.

That is not to say the law was unimportant. In fact, it had two major effects. First, its presence convinced college and university officials that some change was inevitable. The mere possibility—however remote, as it turned out—that the federal government might cut off funding spurred schools to improve women's conditions. Second, the law made an enormous difference to the women who ran athletic programs. It politicized them. Women physical educators had been a cowed, marginalized minority, pessimistic about the prospects for change. But the federal government shifted the balance of power and dramatically increased their odds. Encouraged by the government's apparent legitimation of their goals and the power to achieve them, they became active both on campus and in the wider political process. In turn, their strenuous advocacy and effective lobbying helped maintain the law and pressure male athletic directors. In the brief period between 1974 and 1979, then, the coupling of state power and women's activism unleashed a chain reaction that caused rapid change.

But the state's intervention proved a mixed blessing. Congress had lacked foresight when it passed Title IX. Without clarifying its intent, it turned over responsibility for writing regulations and enforcement to the federal bureaucracy. Bombarded by protests and unacquainted with intercollegiate sports, HEW wrote regulations that attempted to balance men's and women's interests instead of guaranteeing justice for female student-athletes. Thus, HEW hardly considered many alternatives (such as affirmative action and coeducational sports) and deleted some key protections. Nine years passed before enforcement began. Then, during the Reagan administration, conservatives (with the Supreme Court's approval) seized upon ambiguities in the language of the law to radically narrow its scope. By the time Congress remedied the gray areas, enforcement of the law had slowed to a snail-like pace.

The danger came from more than just the political climate, however—Title IX's very mandate of "equality" was problematic. While it held the potential to lift women's intercollegiate sports out of the dark ages, it also endangered them. Because of the threats Title IX posed to men's sports, it set in motion organized opposition to women. One threat was to men's resources; Title IX demanded that athletic departments give women a larger share. Ultimately more important was the second threat. Because the law required male and female student-athletes to be treated similarly, it meant that either men or women would have to adopt the others' values and practices. The AIAW's supporters believed women should not be forced into the male model, but (after battles on campus and in Congress, and in the federal bureaucracy, the NCAA, and the Supreme Court), they lost the war for self-determination. Casualties included the many individuals who had suffered harassment for their activism, and women in general. As AIAW faltered and men increasingly coached women, women in athletic administration lost their collective voice. Thus the law, embodying the concept of equality through sameness, had a fundamental flaw. It did not insure to women the right of self-determination and did not protect those women who sought (and deserved) change.

Because Title IX applied only to educational institutions, tennis pros experienced neither the disappointments nor the assistance of the law. One must look elsewhere for the causes of their success. Like the intercollegiate women, they capitalized upon favorable circumstances. A weakening amateur tennis empire and the women's liberation movement presented a uniquely opportune moment. Although some pros were reluctant to call themselves feminists, they borrowed from the movement's ideology and example of protest, and they benefited from societal interest in gender conflict. Billie Jean King's associates also made wise tactical decisions. Instead of fighting for a larger share of the pie at coed tournaments, they started an independent women's tour. Their flexible but mainly separatist strategy successfully bypassed the sort of organized male opposition that stymied college women. Their other shrewd move was to shift the grounds of the debate away from the "equality or difference" dualism which said that unless women were the same as men (equally strong athletes), they did not deserve comparable benefits. King short-circuited that argument by demonstrating that women were equally capable *entertainers*.[4]

Professional basketball players also tried to succeed as entertainers. A number of factors seemed to favor them: the enormous grass-roots popularity of the game, the lack of organized male opposition, the willingness of players to sacrifice for the well-being of the league, and the new interest in radical women that tennis capitalized on. Nevertheless, they failed. This outcome suggests that the history and makeup of a sport made a difference—that tennis's more feminine reputation and upper-class connections gave it a distinct advantage over basketball.[5] Whatever the causes, the absence of women's professional basketball has important implications. A glass ceiling blocks the mostly working-class and black women who love basketball. It prevents them and all females from knowing that women can excel and discourages them from aspiring to competitive mastery.

What can an advocate of women's sports conclude from the experience of 1950–1995? One heartening lesson is that activism *made a difference* in bringing about greater opportunities. Activism had a greater chance of succeeding in traditionally more acceptable sports and during favorable circumstances. Shifting attitudes (because of social movements or socioeconomic change) and aid from external sources (such as the government and the media) increased the odds, but without pressure there was no change. Unifying on the basis of sex (that is, overcoming differences in class, race, and sexual orientation) was important. Professional physical educators and tennis players may have benefited in the short run by contrasting themselves to "less feminine" athletes, but in the long run all were hurt by stereotypes of some women athletes as unappealing. Change was also more likely when opposition was handled wisely. Opposition came in the form of people or organizations whose resources, practices, or self-image were threatened. It also came in the less tangible form of cultural prescriptions.

Advocates of women's sports tried many ways to combat the effects of the restrictive definition of femininity. Girls' rules, special private standards, sexualizing the game, and apologetic behavior were creative adaptations to an oppressive situation. They were understandable reactions, but they *did not work*. Generation after generation has tried various forms of apologetic behavior, but these have not made sports more widely accepted for women as a group. Accommodation may help an individual feel somewhat less endangered, but it never brings change. At times, accommodation indicates an acceptance of the stereotypes—and of self-hatred. Without self-acceptance, pride, and a sense of entitlement, athletes did not (and could not) challenge their oppression. Indeed, at times apologetic behavior was counterproductive because it reinforced the idea that female athletes needed to reach *outside* of sports to be considered feminine. At the same time, the compensations further distanced females from "normal" (that is, male) athletes. Thus not only did female athletes remain "other" as women, but they remained "other" as athletes. That "otherness" lent further credibility to the notion that women were different, inferior athletes, and that sports was not a "natural" arena for women.

That is not to say that women should have or should in the future adopt the male model of sports. There has been much to criticize in the dominant model. But the *way* that women rejected men's sports in the 1950s and 1960s—by accepting feminine propriety, embracing difference, bowing to notions of fragility—had serious consequences. Most importantly, it left oppressive assumptions unchallenged. "Difference" has always posed a difficult dilemma. In the past, differences between men and women have been used to justify discriminatory treatment and to suggest female inferiority. Understandably, many activists in the 1970s tried to gain legitimacy by demanding equality and demonstrating women's capacities. They achieved many gains using that strategy, but it has two drawbacks. First, there *are* ways men and women as a group differ physiologically, and arguments that are based on claims of equal capabilities instead of basic justice may be doomed to failure.[6] Second, the emphasis on sameness has blinded people to examining alternative methods of organizing and conceptualizing sports. Perhaps after women have achieved greater power and credibility, women's (and other) alternatives will not be so easily ignored.

There is probably no one viable way to make sports more humanistic and just. As history demonstrates, working for change through established institutions (such as the NCAA) can be difficult, but success can bring notice, legitimacy, and access to greater resources.[7] Bypassing such institutions (as, say, the WTA and WBL did) means less attention and money, but those disadvantages can translate into the freedom to design one's own practices, unopposed.

Whatever the means, the struggle to change sports is well worth attempting. Although the male model of sport is resistant, the changes that occurred between 1950 and 1995 demonstrate that sport is pliable. Sport has been in the past (and has the potential to be) violent, exploitative, elitist, and corrupt. It has perpetuated society's prejudices about race, class, gender, and sexuality.[8] Understandably, it has been an arena that women have avoided, resulting in timidity, weakness, and alienation from their bodies. It has also been a place where women athletes have been socialized to feel self-hatred and shame. On the other hand, sport has been (and has the potential to be) a place where women have experienced joy, comradeship, pride in their bodies, excitement, mastery, strength, and leadership. Sport can be a place where disadvantaged groups build community and pride. It also holds the potential to minimize tensions, to be one of the few cultural spaces in which people from different backgrounds can come together and learn about one another while striving toward common goals. Women's efforts to question, redefine, and not merely integrate into sport are valuable. Americans have choices about how sport can be conducted. We can all benefit if women win.

NOTES

Introduction

1. See, for example, Susan Reed et al., "Judgment Days," *People Weekly*, February 14, 1994, 33–37; Barbara T. Roessner, "Kerrigan: From Coy to Cloying," *Raleigh News and Observer*, February 13, 1994, 1E, 4E.

2. Elizabether Kolbert, "Networks Rush to Adapt Kerrigan-Harding Story," *New York Times* (hereafter, *NYT*), February 10, 1994, C2; Gary Mihoces, "I'm Focused on What I'm Here For," *USA Today*, February 25–27, 1994, 1–2.

3. Richard Sandomir, "Ratings as Powerful as a Big Bodyguard," *NYT*, February 25, 1994, B9; Sandomir, "CBS to Skate Circles Around Rival Shows," *NYT*, February 8, 1994, B14; Rudy Martzke, "CBS Reaps Benefits from Extra Looks," *USA Today*, February 25, 1994, 3E.

4. Television revenues provide one measure of the big business of sports. By 1963 television networks paid $13.9 million to broadcast college and pro football and $3.25 million for pro baseball; by 1975 that number had jumped to $60 million for football and $43 million for baseball. (For all sports combined, television expenditures in 1976 were over $200 million.) The enormity of the commercial enterprise of sports is even clearer if you consider the number of fans buying tickets and the participants who buy sports equipment and how both support other parts of the economy. By the mid-1970s there were seventeen million sports injuries serious enough to require a doctor's attention. See James Michener, *Sport in America*.

5. Marie Hart and Susan Birrell, *Sport in the Sociocultural Process*.

6. See Mihaly Czikszentimihaly, *Beyond Boredom and Anxiety*; Roberta S. Bennett et al., "Changing the Rules of the Game: Reflections Toward a Feminist Analysis of Sport," *Women's Studies International Forum* 10, no. 4 (1987): 370–79.

7. The "cat fight" allusion is in Anna Seaton, "Grace, Sass, and the Many Forms of Competitive Spirit," *NYT*, February 6, 1994, sec. 8, p. 9. A number

of observers suggested voyeurism, including Dick Ebersol, president of NBC Sports, quoted in Sandomir, "Ratings as Powerful as a Big Bodyguard."

8. For some questioning of figure skating as fair or as a sport see, for example, Kate Rounds, "Out of Whack," *Ms.*, May–June 1994, 27–33; Lisa Luciano, "Ice Theater of the Absurd Turns into Russian Fairy Tale," *NYT*, February 27, 1994, sec. 8, p. 11; Robert Lipsyte, "But They're All So, So, You Know, Common," *NYT*, January 28, 1994, B12; George Vecsey, "Skate Junkie Confesses: Axel? Lutz?" *NYT*, February 27, 1994, sec. 8, p. 1.

9. Costumes matter a great deal in figure skating, as Kerrigan's willingness to pay a designer over $10,000 indicates.

10. Richard Sandomir, "Harding's Old Film Newly Valuable," *NYT*, January 16, 1994, B14; Frank Rich, "Tonya Trashed," *NYT*, January 20, 1994, A21.

11. Many feminists have made the same observation, sometimes calling it the madonna-whore dichotomy, or as Barbara Roessner put it, "Mother Teresa on Ice vs. the Skating Slut" (Roessner, "Kerrigan: From Coy to Cloying").

12. Rich, "Tonya Trashed."

13. Robert Lipsyte, "It's Still Strut Your Stuff for the Good Old Boys," *NYT*, February 4, 1994, B10.

14. Seaton, "Grace, Sass, and the Many Forms of Competitive Spirit."

15. This was observed by Anna Quindlen, "The $port$ Report," *NYT*, January 22, 1994, A21.

16. Linda Truman Ryan noted women as victims on the covers of *Sports Illustrated*, cited in "Women as Victims," *NYT*, February 20, 1994, sec. 8, p. 11.

17. This study of four newspapers was conducted by the Amateur Athletic Foundation. Even when football and baseball were eliminated, the articles about men outnumbered those about women eight to one. Cited in William C. Rhoden, "It's Time to Turn the Page," *NYT*, January 23, 1993, 29.

18. Helen Thompson, "A Whole New Ball Game," *Texas Monthly*, March 1994, 92.

19. Rick Cantu, "Legal Equals," *Austin American-Statesman*, July 5, 1992.

20. Cantu, "Legal Equals."

21. Debra E. Blum, "7 Women Sue U. of Texas, Demanding Varsity Teams," *Chronicle of Higher Education* (hereafter, *Chronicle*), July 8, 1992, A32; Debra E. Blum, "U. Of Texas at Austin Settles Sex-Bias Suit by Doubling Women's Sports Opportunities," *Chronicle*, July 28, 1993, A33.

22. Blum, "7 Women Sue U. of Texas."

23. Blum, "U. Of Texas at Austin Settles;" Gene Duffy, "SWC Asks 'Now What?' After UT Settles," *Houston Post*, July 30, 1993, B1, B3.

24. Gardner Selby, "UT Settles Gender Suit in Athletics," *Houston Post*, July 17, 1993, 1, 17.

25. Duffy, "SWC Asks 'Now What?'"

26. Thompson, "A Whole New Ball Game," 145–46.

27. Debra E. Blum, "Officials of Big-Time Colleges See Threat in Moves to Cut Costs and Provide Equity for Women," *Chronicle*, June 16, 1993, A35.

28. "The Third Sex," *Sports Illustrated*, February 6, 1995, 15.

29. "Diversity Creates Dilemma for Lady Horns," *Austin American-Statesman*, August 3, 1993, C1, C3.

30. "Diversity Creates Dilemma for Lady Horns."

31. Thompson, "A Whole New Ball Game," 92.

32. "Diversity Creates Dilemma for Lady Horns."

33. Robert Lipsyte, "Penn State Coach Will Abide by Lesbian Policy, but Won't Discuss It," *NYT*, December 20, 1991, B14.

34. Thompson, "A Whole New Ball Game," 92–94.

35. Lopiano's entire quote was, "I'm really, really upset about the articles. In my seventeen years at UT, I was more aware of problems with men's sports than women's. Did that ever get to press? With Title IX, we have to expect hardball now." Thompson, "A Whole New Ball Game," 145, 94.

36. Thompson, "A Whole New Ball Game," 144.

37. Rick Cantu, "UT Women Targets of Sexually Abusive Remarks," *Austin American-Statesman*, February 22, 1991.

38. Only recently have scholars begun taking sports seriously as a legitimate subject of inquiry, and the study of women's sports is in its infancy. We still have only a handful of historical works on women's sports, and few of them are written by professional historians. A first wave of research, done mostly by physical educators, was published during the 1970s, including Ellen Gerber et al, *The American Woman in Sport*; Carole Oglesby, *Women and Sport: From Myth to Reality*; Stephanie Twin, *Out of the Bleachers* (Old Westbury, N.Y.: Feminist Press, 1979); Reet Howell, ed. *Her Story in Sport: A Historical Anthology of Women in Sports*.

An excellent second wave of books, mostly by historians, includes Susan Cahn, *Coming On Strong: Gender and Sexuality in Twentieth-Century Women's Sport*, and Allen Guttmann, *Women's Sports: A History*. Cahn's analyzes various sports and is especially sensitive to issues of race, class, and sexuality (particularly in the first half of the twentieth century). Cynthia Himes's dissertation, "The Female Athlete in American Society, 1860–1940," likewise deals with class and race.

Many good books about women's sports have been written by sociologists, journalists, and philosophers, including Mariah Burton Nelson, *Are We Winning Yet? How Women Are Changing Sports* and *The Stronger Women Get, the More Men Love Football: Sexism and the American Culture of Sports*; Mary A. Boutillier and Lucinda SanGiovanni, *The Sporting Woman*; Betsy Postow, ed., *Women, Philosophy, and Sport: A Collection of New Essays*; Helen Lenskyj, *Out of Bounds: Women, Sport, and Sexuality*; and Adrianne Blue, *Grace Under Pressure: The Emergence of Women in Sport*. Specialized studies include Larry Engelmann, *The Goddess and the American Girl*; Billie Jean King with Cynthia Starr, *We Have Come a Long Way*; Susan Cayleff, *Babe: The Life and Legend of Babe Didrikson Zaharias*. For a collection of work with a more international perspective, see J. A. Mangan and Robert J. Park, *From "Fair Sex" to Feminism: Sport and the Socialization of Women in the Industrial and Post-Industrial Eras*.

A wide variety of dissertations and theses have been path-breaking. They include Joanna Davenport, "The History and Interpretation of Amateurism in the United States Lawn Tennis Association" (Ph.D. diss., Ohio State University, 1966); Jane Ann Russell, "Tennis and the Woman Player: Why the Changes?" (Ed.D. diss., University of Georgia, 1981); Linda D. Williams, "An Analysis of American Sportswomen in Two Negro Newspapers: The *Pittsburgh Courier*, 1924–1948, and the *Chicago Defender*, 1932–1948" (Ph.D. diss., Ohio State University, 1987); Vivian B. Adkins, "The Development of Negro Female Athletic Talent" (P.E.D. diss,, Indiana University, 1967); Nolan A. Thaxton, "A Documentary Analysis of Competitive Track and Field at Tuskegee Institute and Tennessee State University" (D.P.E. diss., Springfield College, 1970); Sylvia Faye Nadler, "A Developmental History of the Wayland Hutcherson Flying Queens from 1910 to 1979" (Ed.D. diss., East Texas State University, 1980); Elva Elisabeth Bishop, "Amateur Athletic Union Women's Basketball,

1950–1971: The Contributions of Hanes Hosiery, Nashville Business College, and Wayland Baptist College" (master's thesis, University of North Carolina at Chapel Hill, 1984); Kristin L. Burns, "Reconstructing Leadership Experiences: Toward a Feminist Theory of Leadership" (Ph.D. diss., University of Iowa, 1987).

For historiographical essays on sport history, see Nancy Struna, "Beyond Mapping Experience: The Need for Understanding in the History of American Sporting Women," *Journal of Sport History* 11, no. 1 (Spring 1984): 120–33; and Steven A. Riess, "The New Sport History," *Reviews in American History* 18 (1990): 311–25.

My work draws upon the debates articulated by this impressive group of scholars and gives those debates historical specificity—in a period not yet studied by historians. It picks up the story where Cynthia Himes and Susan Cahn left off—in the modern era—but it also breaks new ground by dealing with politicization, professionalization, the active intervention of the state, and organized male opposition. This is the first book-length historical account covering the transformation of intercollegiate sports, including the rise and fall of the Association for Intercollegiate Athletics for Women and Title IX of the Omnibus Education Act of 1972. It is also the first to link the equally dramatic search for equality and fairness in tennis and basketball. In its subject matter, then, it differs from other scholars. In its feminist viewpoint it differs mostly in emphasis.

Part 1. Introduction: The 1950s

1. Quoted in Sara Evans, *Born for Liberty: A History of Women in America*, 249.

2. Nancy Woloch, *Women and the American Experience*, 493–98; William Chafe, *The Paradox of Change: American Women in the 20th Century*, 178–82.

3. Joan Scott, "Gender: A Useful Category of Analysis," *American Historical Review* 91 (December 1986): 1053–75; Joan Scott, "Deconstructing Equality-versus-Difference: Or, The Uses of Poststructuralist Theory for Feminism," *Feminist Studies* 14, no. 1 (Spring 1988): 33–52"; Leslie Wahl Rabine, "A Feminist Politics of Non-Identity," *Feminist Studies* 14, no. 1 (Spring 1988): 11–39;; Josette Feral, "The Powers of Difference," in Hester Eisenstein and Alice Jardine, eds., *The Future of Difference*; Jonathan Culler, *On Deconstruction: Theory and Criticism After Structuralism*.

4. From a 1947 bestseller by Marynia Farnham and Ferdinand Lundberg, quoted in Woloch, *Women and the American Experience*, 497; also the ideas of psychiatrist Helen Deutsch as described in Chafe, *The Paradox of Change*, 178–82.

5. Lillian Faderman, *Odd Girls and Twilight Lovers: A History of Lesbian Life in Twentieth-Century America*, 140, 130–33. The statistic about "homosexual tendencies" comes from the Kinsey Report, as quoted in Faderman, 140.

6. Faderman, *Odd Girls and Twilight Lovers*, 130–33.

7. Faderman, *Odd Girls and Twilight Lovers*, 139–43; John D'Emilio and Estelle B. Freedman, *Intimate Matters: A History of Sexuality in America*; John D'Emilio, *Sexual Politics, Sexual Communities: The Making of a Homosexual Minority in the United States, 1940–1970* (Chicago: University of Chicago Press, 1983), 40–53.

8. Darwinian explanation from Luther Gulick (1906), quoted in Gerber et al., *The American Woman in Sport*, 70–71; "unsuitable" quote in Bishop, "AAU Women's Basketball," 3.

9. "Athletic Strenuosity," *Journal of the American Medical Association* 85 (July 1925); Mabel Lee, "The Case For and Against Intercollegiate Athletics," *Research Quarterly* 2 (May 1931); E.

H. Arnold, "Athletics for Women," *American Physical Education Review* 29 (October 1926); Agnes Wayman, *A Modern Philosophy of Physical Education* (Philadelphia: Saunders, 1938): all cited in Stephen St. Clair, "The Play Day/Sport Day Movement in Selected Colleges of the South" (Ed.D. diss., University of North Carolina-Greensboro, 1984). See also Cahn, "Coming on Strong," 76–84.

10. Quoted in Allen Guttmann, *The Games Must Go On*, 194.

11. Nancy P. Williamson and William O. Johnson quote a California Mother's Club resolution opposing Sears's "unsightly mannish attire" and requesting "that she restrain herself in the future to normal feminine attire" (*"Whatta-Gal!" The Babe Didrickson Story*, 27, 127).

12. By the 1950s the "mannish" athlete had come to be associated with lesbianism. As historian Susan Cahn has demonstrated, it was not always so. Before the 1930s, the mannish female athlete was feared not to be lesbian but to be inappropriate in her *heterosexual* desires. The excitement of sport, it was feared, could cause in women the loss of sexual control and promiscuity. "Muscle moll," for example, was a term typically applied to female athletes. In its only other uses in the early part of the century, "moll" referred to prostitutes or to the female lovers of gangsters, both assumed to be heterosexual "loose" women. By the 1930s, however, those fears of sexual deviance shifted to homosexuality. Journalistic uses of the word *amazon* illustrate the shift. While earlier the term had connoted heterosexual ardor, by the 1930s it referred to failed heterosexuality.

Cahn speculates that the gradual shift occurred as popular culture changed and assertive heterosexuality became an important quality of femininity. By the early decades of the twentieth century, femininity had become increasingly defined as making oneself very different from and attractive to men. If it takes dichotomous thinking to assume the female athlete is mannish, it requires another leap in logic to associate a mannish woman with lesbianism: lesbians had to be considered masculine. This association became more likely after the first few decades of the century as the larger society became increasingly aware of an emerging lesbian and gay subculture. At the same time, doctors and psychologists classified homosexuality and heterosexuality as dichotomous, and provided "scientific" legitimation for a pervasive lesbian taboo. By the 1930s, Cahn believes, the combination of aggressively heterosexual femininity and the lesbian taboo caused increasing wariness about women-only activities, especially sport, since it already had the reputation of mannishness. Susan Cahn, "From the 'Muscle Moll' to the 'Butch Ballplayer': Changing Meanings of 'Mannishness' in U.S. Women's Sport, 1900–1960."

13. In one 1958 study, for example, 150 Ohio sportswomen explained why they felt reluctant to participate in sports. Five of the eight reasons they mentioned over and over—muscles, masculinity, moral and ethical transgressions, bad taste, and social disapproval—demonstrated their sensitivity to sports' unfeminine reputation. (The other three—inconvenience, lack of competence, and feelings of inadequacy about their bodies—might also have been gender-related.) Laura Kratz, "A Study of Sports and the Implications of Women's Participation in Them in Modern Society" (Ph.D. diss., Ohio State University, 1958), 56–60.

1. Only the Right Kind

1. Ada Taylor Sackett (chair Special Woman's AAU Committee) to Athletic Directors, April 6, 1953, ser. 7, National Section on Women's Athletics (NSWA) papers, American Alliance for Health, Physical Education, and Recreation (AAHPER) archives, Reston, Virginia. In the early

1950s, the NSWA changed its name to the National Section for Girls' and Women's Sports (NSGWS), and then around 1960 to the Division for Girls' and Women's Sports (DGWS), and even later to the National Association for Girls' and Women's Sports (NAGWS). For simplicity, in the text of this chapter I refer to the organization all through the 1950s as NSGWS, but in the notes I cite the precise title of the organization as given in the archival files where I found the relevant piece of evidence.

2. Pauline Hodgson to Josephine Fiske, April 16, 1953, ser. 7, NSWA papers.

3. Fiske to Harriet Fitchpatrick, May 27, 1953, "AAU Correspondence" file, ser. 7, NSWA papers.

4. Fiske to Hodgson, April 13, 1953, ser. 7, NSWA papers.

5. National Section for Girls' and Women's Sports, *Standards in Sports for Girls and Women: Guiding Principles in the Organization and Administration of Sports Programs* (1953), 38.

6. Fiske to Hodgson, April 13, 1953.

7. Dudley Ashton to Daniel Ferris, November 24, 1953; A. Gwendolyn Drew to Dudley Ashton, April 24, 1953, ser. 7, NSWA papers.

8. Drew to Ashton, April 24, 1953.

9. Kratz, "A Study of Sports," 129–30; Fiske to Miriam Payne, January 26, 1954, "AAU Correspondence" file, ser. 7, NSWA papers; Fiske to Fitchpatrick, May 27, 1953.

10. Fiske to Fitchpatrick, May 27, 1953.

11. Katherine Ley, address, "Values in Sports and Athletics as They Relate to Personal and Social Value Systems," at Midwest Association for Health, Physical Fitness, and Recreation, April 7, 1963. PE leaders also made a qualitative distinction between being a "coach" and a "teacher." Not only was the coach not professionally trained, somehow he or she was less deserving of respect. Physical educators were concerned after hearing the worrisome news that Wellesley was dropping its program for training PE teachers. Irene Clayton from Bryn Mawr wrote to NAPECW's Pauline Hodgson in 1952 that she feared other schools might follow. The consequence? "What I fear is that we may get into the 'Coach' type of person, actually a woman athlete" (January 16, 1952, file drawer 1, NAPECW papers, Manuscripts Collection, Jackson Library, University of North Carolina at Greensboro).

12. Rosina Koetting, probably spring 1953, "Competition" file, NSWA papers.

13. Mabel Locke, at 1956 AAHPER convention session, "Evaluating Girls' and Women's Sports as Purposeful Activities" (ser. 6, DGWS papers); Edna Willis (Univ. of Colorado) statement, probably spring 1953, copy in ser. 6, NSWA papers.

14. Drew to Ashton, April 24, 1953; Fiske to Hodgson, April 25, 1953, ser. 7, NSWA papers.

15. E. H. Arnold, *American Physical Education Review,* quoted in Bishop, "AAU Women's Basketball," 3; National Association of Secondary School Principals, 1925, quoted in Williamson and Johnson, *"Whatta-Gal!"* 31.

16. Cahn, "Coming on Strong," 76–84, 57–58.

17. NSGWS, *Standards* (1953), 45, 39, 32, 16, 37, 41.

18. Ibid., 23.

19. Ibid., 6, 16, 23, 45.

20. Teachers' criteria for proper outcomes were to be whether the program stimulated increased participation, opportunity for all, and a friendly spirit among competitors. Cited in Virginia Hunt, "Governance of Women's Intercollegiate Athletics: An Historical Perspective" (Ph.D. diss., University of North Carolina at Greensboro, 1976).

21. NSGWS, *Standards* (1953), 36.

22. NAPECW, "Policy Statement on Competition" (1954), cited in Hunt, "Governance," 27.

23. Margaret M. Duncan and Velda P. Cundiff, *Play Days for Girls and Women*, v.

24. St. Clair, "The Play Day/Sport Day Movement," 4–6.

25. NSGWS, *Standards* (1953), 36.

26. Wayland Baptist College proved to be one of these exceptions. It participated in AAU national tournaments against many nonschool teams and will be discussed in the next chapter.

27. NAPECW, *Biennial Record* (1951–1953, 1959–1961), cited in Hunt, "Governance," 25–28.

28. St. Clair, "The Play Day/Sport Day Movement," 110–18.

29. Frances Hogan, interview by author, Chapel Hill, N.C., May 23 and June 3, 1991.

30. In fact, Katherine Ley declared the poll results misleading because many schools regularly violated standards for sports days. Ley, address, December 2–5, 1962, to the National Conference on Secondary School Athletic Administration, in ser. 6, box 1, DGWS papers.

31. Locke, "Evaluating Girls' and Women's Sports" (1956 AAHPER convention session, ser. 6, DGWS papers).

32. Joan Hult, interview by author, College Park, Md., March 29, 1989.

33. Locke, "Evaluating Girls' and Women's Sports," and Mabel Locke to Leona Holbrook, December 17, 1965 (ser. 6, DGWS papers).

34. WAA/WRA file, ser. 8, DGWS papers.

35. In the 1950s Mabel Lee wanted to preserve the history of the foremothers who had led the profession. She mentioned Elizabeth Burchenal, Agnes Wayman, Helen McKinstry, Blanche Trilling, J. Anna Norris, Gertrude Dudley, Margaret Coleman, and Gertrude Moulton. File drawer 1, correspondence 1950–1959, NAPECW papers.

36. Celeste Ulrich, address, "The Woman in Your Life," *The Amy Morris Homans Lecture* (NAPECW, 1975).

37. Elizabeth Halsey, *Women in Physical Education: Their Role in Work, Home, and History*, 149.

38. Mabel Lee, address, "Tribute to Amy Morris Homans," *The Amy Morris Homans Lecture* (1967); Ellen Gerber noted, "The same women who ran the sports programs conducted the teacher education programs and thus indoctrinated the teachers-to-be in the national philosophy" (Gerber, "The Controlled Development of Collegiate Sports for Women," *Journal of Sport History* 2 [Spring 1975]: 10, quoted in St. Clair, "The Play Day/Sport Day Movement").

39. Katherine Ley explained her dilemma about what to curtail in her address to the National Conference on Secondary School Athletic Administration, December 1962.

40. Hogan, interview.

41. Ley, address, December 1962.

42. Comments cited in Margaret L. Barr's survey of fifty-five western colleges, "*Trends in Athletics for Girls and Women*," April 1947 (ser. 6, NSWA papers).

43. Hogan, interview.

44. Fiske to Fitchpatrick, May 27, 1953; Resolution, Central Association for Physical Education for College Women (sent to John Hannah, president of Michigan State, who supported AAU proposal), dated March 24, 1952, but probably actually 1953.

45. Norma Leavitt, "College Physical Education for Women: The Past, the Present, and the Future," *Journal of Health, Physical Education, and Recreation* (October 1960): 78–79.

46. C. C. Cowell, *Survey of Trends and Opinions Concerning Competitive Sports for Girls*, referred to in his address, "Sports Competition for Women: How Much Is Optimum,"

Midwest Association for Health, Physical Education, and Recreation, March 31, 1955 (ser. 8, NSGWS papers).

47. Ruth Weythman to Mrs. Florence Stephenson, March 11, 1953 (file drawer 1, NAPECW papers).

48. Charles J. Setzer, "The P.A.L. Way," *Amateur Athlete* (March 1953): 8.

49. Barr survey, "Trends in Athletics for Girls and Women" (April 1947).

50. Ley, address, December 1962.

51. Julia Post, "The Case Against Intercollegiate Athletics for Women," *The State* (Columbia, S.C.), February 24, 1940, quoted in St. Clair, "The Play Day/Sport Day Movement."

52. Anna Espenschade, Report of Committee on Interpretation of NSGWS Standards on Competition, December 17, 1954 (ser. 8, NSGWS papers).

53. Chafe, *The Paradox of Change*, 178–82.

54. Clifford Lee Brownell's talk at the April 1953 AAHPER Southern District Meeting mentioned that few women belonged to the National Association of Secondary School Principals (Box 4, Southern Association for Physical Education of College Women [SAPECW] papers, Manuscripts Collection, Jackson Library, University of North Carolina at Greensboro).

55. Cowell, *Survey of Trends and Opinions*, in address, March 1955.

56. Quoted in Guttmann, *The Games Must Go On*, 195.

57. Avery Brundage to Elizabeth Beall, May 6, 1948 (ser. 6, NSWA papers).

58. National Track and Field file, 1954 (ser. 8, NSGWS papers).

59. NSGWS Research Committee report, 1954(?) (ser. 8, NSGWS papers).

60. Mrs. Rollin Brown, address, "Evaluating Girls' and Women's Sports—The Parental Viewpoint," AAHPER convention session, 1956 (copy in ser. 6, DGWS papers).

61. Hugo Otopalik, "A Nation Is as Strong as Its Manhood," *Amateur Athlete* (March 1951): 36.

62. Eleanor Metheny, "Women in Action—The Story of DGWS, 1892–1958," pageant at AAHPER convention, March 1958 (script in ser. 6, NSGWS papers).

63. Ley, "Values in Sports," address, April 7, 1963.

64. Kratz, "A Study of Sports," 330.

65. Quoted in Williamson and Johnson. *"Whatta-Gal!"* 132–33.

66. Quoted in Cahn, "Coming on Strong," 316–21.

67. Ley, address, December 1962.

68. Maria Sexton, Report of the AAU and the U.S. Olympic Committee Meeting, November 29–December 5, 1961 (ser. 8, DGWS papers). Sexton's comment echoed PE professor Julia Post a decade earlier, who in making the "Case Against Intercollegiate Athletics for Women" warned that "the flower of Southern womanhood would be lost." She feared developing "athletic types . . . boyish, bold, amazonish, with little of the charm and graciousness or manner of the women for which the South has been famous." Cited in St. Clair, "The Play Day/Sport Day Movement," 58.

69. Ulrich, "The Woman in Your Life."

70. Hult, interview.

71. Ulrich, "The Woman in Your Life."

72. NSGWS, *Standards* (1953), 9.

73. Halsey, *Women in Physical Education*, 58.

74. Fiske to Hodgson, April 13, 1953.

75. This conclusion comes from my examination of AAU basketball tournament entries during the 1950s. Katherine Ley unconsciously demonstrated her attention to an upper-class

constituency when she cited a *Harper's* article about what parents expected of their prep school daughters. Ley, "Values in Sports," address, April 7, 1963.

76. Kratz, "A Study of Sports"; Cahn, "Coming on Strong."

77. "Negro Girls Barred from Competing in Pan American Games in Buenos Aires," *Oklahoma City Black Dispatch*, August 12, 1950, cited in the Tuskegee Institute News Clipping File, 1899–1966 (Division of Behavioral Science Research, Carver Research Foundation, Tuskegee Institute, 1976), microfilm ed., reel 117, frame 600.

78. Phebe M. Scott and Virginia R. Crafts, *Track and Field for Girls and Women*, 12.

79. Accidentally, a membership invitation was sent to a Negro physical educator, and the SAPECW did allow her to become a member. Some members wanted to include Negroes but were outvoted by women who, not surprisingly, were very wary about change. For the racial issue, see *A Fifty-Year History of the SAPECW, 1935–1985*, 106; and correspondence for October 23 and 31, 1951; September 25 and November 13, 1952; August 2, 1954; and January 19, 1955 (Box 4, SAPECW papers).

80. I am indebted to Dr. Joan Hult for delineating all these marginal attributes (Hult, interview).

81. The decade was marked by FBI infiltration of gay groups, police harassment of meeting places, and McCarthy-inspired firings of homosexuals.

82. This extreme sensitivity over and identification with—indeed, a feeling of responsibility for—any other members of an oppressed group is a phenomena I've observed, not something I've seen explicit reference to in scholarly work. African-Americans, Native Americans, homosexuals, and even women sometimes feel that members of the dominant culture use isolated public incidents against the larger group to bolster unflattering stereotypes. (There is, for example, a middle-class black character in Richard Wright's *Native Son* who is embarrassed because of something a poor black says, and wishes he hadn't said it because it reflected poorly on all blacks.) In another example, a female physical educator worried excessively about a new track and field organization she had heard of—for women's track but run by men. Martha Jones complained to Josephine Fiske, "Any action taken by them is certainly a reflection of all of us." This concern may seem excessive (because NAPECW had nothing to do with women's track and field), but it makes sense given the context and reputation of women's sports.

83. Feminist writers have long criticized the extraordinary lasting and pervasive power of cultural expectations like those for gender roles. In addition, I have been influenced by Raymond Williams's use of the term *hegemony*. Williams sees cultural hegemony not merely as political domination bolstered by conscious ideology but as the whole set of cultural practices and expectations constituting the lived dominance and subordination of particular groups. As deep and thorough as cultural hegemony is, Williams points out that it is never total—it is a lived process that has continually to be renewed, recreated, defended, and modified when challenged by oppositional groups. Raymond Williams, *Marxism and Literature* (New York: Oxford University Press, 1977), 108–35.

Even though hegemonic notions (such as the importance of femininity) buttress power relations, they are often accepted to some degree by oppressed groups. As they internalize the constant messages, self-hatred can result. Sometimes individuals realize how dominant ideas oppress them, and they battle these to gain a more positive self-image. But I believe that most members of oppressed groups have what W. E. B. Du Bois described as a double consciousness: at times they are extremely sensitive to the dominant culture's negative view of them, so that their feelings of self-hatred lead them to try to win acceptance; at other times they reject the dominant beliefs and affirm themselves and their own subculture. Some writers have explicitly addressed internalized racism, and I believe it is implicit in W. E. B. Du Bois's famous essay on "twoness" or "double consciousness" (Du Bois, *Souls of Black Folk*, 1903).

This concept of "twoness" helps explain the contradictory finding that female athletes feel inner conflict yet are well-adjusted. See JoAnn Loulan, *Lesbian Passion*, and Loulan, *Lesbian Sex*; Joan Sophie, "Internalized Homophobia and Lesbian Identity," *Journal of Homosexuality* 14, nos. 1–2 (1987): 53–65; Sharon Ruth Guthrie, "Homophobia: Its Impact on Women in Sport and Physical Education"; Boston Lesbian Psychology Collective, ed., *Lesbian Psychologies: Explorations and Challenges.*

2. Girls' Rules

1. "The Flying Queens," *Sports Illustrated*, April 2, 1956, 15; "Wayland Queens Retain AAU Title," *Amateur Athlete* (April 1955): 5–6.

2. *Winston-Salem Journal and Sentinel*, April 3, 1954; April 4, 1954.

3. Cahn, "Coming on Strong," 137–38.

4. Article from the American Medical Association's journal *Hygiea*, quoted in Lenskyj, *Out of Bounds*, 19.

5. Quoted in Himes, "The Female Athlete," 147.

6. Women's Division progress report (1926), quoted in Williamson and Johnson, *"Whatta-Gal!"* 32.

7. Ibid.

8. Himes, "The Female Athlete," 180–82.

9. Quoted in Bishop, "AAU Women's Basketball," 4.

10. Quoted in Gerber et al., *The American Woman in Sport*, 69.

11. At least one physical educator developed the divided court by mistake—Clara Baer misinterpreted a diagram used by basketball's founder James Naismith, thinking he intended the court to be divided. However, this lone incident is probably not a sufficient explanation for "girls' rules" because many others decided to retain the accidental change and further added all sorts of other revisions specifically for females. See Frances H. Ebert and Billye Ann Cheatum, *Basketball*, 5, 10.

12. Gerber et al., *The American Woman in Sport*, 91. See also Margaret Ruth Downing, "Women's Basketball: An Historical Overview of Selected Athletic Organizations Which Influenced Its Ascension Toward Advanced Competition in the United States" (Ph.D. diss., Texas Woman's University, 1983); and Helen B. Laurence and Grace I. Fox, *Basketball for Girls and Women* (New York: McGraw-Hill, 1954), 191–206.

13. Cahn, "Coming on Strong," 140.

14. Quoted in Catherine Snell, ed. DGWS *Official Basketball and Officials Rating Guide for Girls and Women* (September 1957–58); Cahn, "Coming on Strong," 139.

15. Himes, "The Female Athlete," 147.

16. Cahn, "Coming on Strong," 139.

17. Quoted in Himes, "The Female Athlete," 133.

18. For the same interpretation, see Cahn, "Coming on Strong," 140; Himes, "The Female Athlete," 147.

19. Ann Paterson, ed.. *Team Sports for Girls*, 34 and appendix.

20. "Basketball for the Employed Girl," *Recreation* (November 1941), quoted in Cahn, "Coming on Strong," 121.

21. Williamson and Johnson, *"Whatta-Gal!"* 114, 118–19, 126.

22. Cahn, "Coming on Strong," 127; Bishop, "AAU Women's Basketball," 21.

23. John Kord Lagemann, "Red Heads, You Kill Me!" *Collier's*, February 8, 1947, 64–66.

24. Quoted in Kratz, "A Study of Sports," 17.

25. Babe Didrickson, a track and basketball star who gained fame as an Olympic gold medalist in 1928, got one of her best professional offers in the 1930s from vaudeville. She tried a brief stint in Chicago, which blended a demonstration of her running ability, bad jokes, and harmonica-playing. Williamson and Johnson, *"Whatta-Gal!"* 118–19, 126.

26. Lageman, "Red Heads, You Kill Me!" 65.

27. "Speaking of People," *Ebony*, November 1951, 4.

28. Guttmann, *The Games Must Go On*, 116.

29. Williamson and Johnson, *"Whatta-Gal!"* 32.

30. Ibid., 141.

31. Kratz, "A Study of Sports," 132.

32. "Aids for Your Sports Program for Girls," *Recreation* (November 1952): 359.

33. Cahn, "Coming on Strong," 111.

34. Ibid., 126.

35. Names of teams from Alexander M. Wayand, *Cavalcade of Basketball.*

36. See Himes, "The Female Athlete," 124–33.

37. Roxy Andersen, "Don't Blame Our Girls," *Amateur Athlete* (December 1952): 17.

38. Roxy Andersen, "Meet the Opposition," *Amateur Athlete* (August 1952): 15.

39. Elva E. Bishop and Katherine Fulton, "Shooting Stars," *Southern Exposure* 7, no. 2 (Fall 1979): 50–56.

40. Mrs. Irvin Van Blarcom, "Hanes Girls Win 25th National Court Tournament," *Amateur Athlete* (May 1953): 14.

41. Helen B. Laurence to Laura Huelster, December 17, 1954 (NSGWS correspondence), NAPECW papers, file drawer 4, UNC-Greensboro.

42. Laurence to Huelster, December 17, 1954.

43. Andersen, "Meet the Opposition."

44. From 1960 AAU *Study of Effects of Competition on Women*, quoted in Downing, "Women's Basketball," 19.

45. Quoted in Bishop, "AAU Women's Basketball," 42.

46. Downing, "Women's Basketball," 19.

47. Cahn, "Coming on Strong," 138, 123, 135. Female track athletes at Tennessee State thought it made no difference which gender their coach was or even preferred the male because he worked them harder. Thaxton, "A Documentary Analysis."

48. Bishop, "AAU Women's Basketball," 39–40; "The Flying Queens," *Sports Illustrated*, April 2, 1956.

49. George Sherman, "Women's Basketball Round-Up," *Amateur Athlete* (1961).

50. "The Flying Queens," *Sports Illustrated*, 15; Redin, *The Queens Fly High*, 13.

51. Bishop and Fulton, "Shooting Stars," 50–56.

52. Bishop, "AAU Women's Basketball," 9–21; Cahn, "Coming on Strong," 121–25.

53. Eunies Futch and Eckie Jordan were still working there when Bishop interviewed them in the late 1970s. Bishop, "AAU Women's Basketball," 21; Bishop and Fulton, "Shooting Stars," 50–56.

54. Bishop, "AAU Women's Basketball," 30.

55. I have very little information at this point on black women's amateur basketball. Stories about basketball in the *Pittsburgh Courier* and *Chicago Defender* steadily declined in the 1940s and 1950s, while those on track steadily increased. So the years mentioned in this section are uncertain here for black newspaper-sponsored teams; I know those two and the *Philadelphia Tribune* existed in the 1930s and 1940s, but I am not sure about specific years during the 1950s.

56. Bishop, "AAU Women's Basketball," 30–32.

57. Bob Hampton, "Hanes Hosiery Ponders Bid to Mexico's Sports Festival," *Winston-Salem Journal and Sentinel*, March 31, 1952, 13.

58. Bishop, "AAU Women's Basketball," 30–32.

59. Ibid., 9–21.

60. Bob Hampton, "Hanes Girls Style Revolutionizes Basketball," *Winston-Salem Journal and Sentinel*, quoted in the *Amateur Athlete* (April 1953): 17.

61. Bishop and Fulton, "Shooting Stars," 50–56.

62. Bishop, "AAU Women's Basketball," 42.

63. Hank Schoolfield, "Hanes Hosiery All-American Ace Takes Her Sports Play Seriously," *Winston-Salem Journal and Sentinel*, March 22, 1953, B10.

64. Bishop and Fulton, "Shooting Stars"; Lyle M. Foster, "Missouri Coronation," *Amateur Athlete* (May 1959): 16–17.

65. Hampton, "Hanes Girls Style Revolutionizes Basketball."

66. Warner Ragsdale, Jr. "Hanes Team Is More Confident Than Last One," *Winston-Salem Journal and Sentinel*, March 16, 1952, B12.

67. "The Flying Queens," *Sports Illustrated*, April 2, 1956, 15.

68. Quoted in Nadler, "A Developmental History," 79–81.

69. See, for example, the *Winston-Salem Journal and Sentinel*, March 30, 1952; March 22, 1953, B10; April 2, 1953, 24. (In fact, when a male and female were named top amateur athletes in the state, the local woman, Greer, was mentioned in the headline, not the man.)

70. See, for example, *Winston-Salem Journal and Sentinel*, April 3, 1953; April 3, 1954; March 30, 1952.

71. I unscientifically sampled the *Des Moines Register*, the *Denver Post*, the *Houston Post*, the *Atlanta Constitution*, and the *Minneapolis Tribune* for the type of coverage during the AAU national tournament.

72. Williams, "An Analysis of American Sportswomen."

73. Ibid., 116.

74. Major dailies like the *New York Times* sometimes included scores of the AAU national tournament, but not always (apparently if they noticed or there was room).

75. "Americans Gain 4th Victory, 59–41," *NYT*, April 30, 1958, 42. See also *NYT*, April 26, 1958, 12, and April 27, 1958, sec. 5, p. 1.

76. "Rough Night for Yuri and Jack," *Sports Illustrated*, November 19, 1962, 76.

77. Shirley Martin, "U.S. Women's Court Team in USSR," *Amateur Athlete* (June 1958); Mrs. Irvin Blarcom, "Hanes Girls Win 25th National Court Tournament"; Tennie McGhee, "U.S. Girls Capture World Basketball Championship with Comeback Spirit," *Amateur Athlete* (December 1957); Mrs. Irvin Van Blarcom, "Tour of Girl Basketball All Stars," *Amateur Athlete* (September 1951): 16.

78. "Returning Women's Team Hails Soviet 'Red Carpet' Treatment," *NYT*, May 9, 1958, 31.

79. Nadler, "A Developmental History," 90; African-American AAU track stars reported similar experiences, grateful for opportunities to travel places they would not otherwise have gone. One used the exact same language of "thrilling and rewarding." Adkins, "Development of Negro Female Athletic Talent," 185, 195, 203.

80. Bishop and Fulton, "Shooting Stars," 50–56; Cahn, "Coming on Strong," 125.

81. The AAU *Rules of Competition for Women,* cited in Laurence and Fox, *Basketball for Girls and Women,* 245–46.

82. Occasionally assuming that AAU workers were male, it thanked their wives for their patience. I noticed the trend of recognizing women (only) for engagement especially in the *Amateur Athlete*'s "Did You Know?" column off and on during the 1950s. Chauncey W. Ashley, "Just An A.A.U. Man," *Amateur Athlete* (November 1954): 35.

83. Andersen, "Don't Blame Our Girls," 17.

84. Tennie McGhee, "Women's Basketball Highlights," *Amateur Athlete* (October 1956): 9. See also "880 Yards Races for Girls" for an anonymous sexist opinion of when women's events should be offered (*Amateur Athlete* [November 1954]: 35).

85. Andersen, "Don't Blame Our Girls."

86. Kratz, "A Study of Sports," 56–60.

87. Daniel Ferris, "Let's Have More Co-ed Sports," *Parade* magazine, reprinted in *Amateur Athlete* (September 1952).

88. Kratz, "A Study of Sports," 56–60.

89. Faderman, *Odd Girls and Twilight Lovers;* Yvonne Zipter, *Diamonds Are a Dyke's Best Friend: Reflections, Reminiscences, and Reports from the Field on the Lesbian National Pastime.*

90. Zipter, *Diamonds Are a Dyke's Best Friend,* 47–49, 76.

91. Cahn, "From the 'Muscle Moll' to the 'Butch Ballplayer'"; Cahn, "Coming on Strong," 348–50. While there is evidence that some lesbian culture-building did take place, not all serious athletic women were lesbians. Heterosexual women also had reason to value the joys, physical expressiveness, and companionship that came from team sports. A relatively small number of Cahn's interviewees volunteered the fact that they were lesbians. But wanting to preserve their privacy, she did not explicitly ask them about their sexuality, so the actual percentage might be higher.

92. Cahn, "Coming on Strong," 348–50. Lillian Faderman also observes that softball teams during the 1950s and 1960s succeeded in providing legends and heroes for the lesbian subculture, as well as offering participants and viewers some possibilities for making lesbian contacts outside of bars. She also notes that softball networks brought "safety" in a different way—by helping spread the word about military witch-hunts against homosexuals. Faderman, *Odd Girls and Twilight Lovers,* 155, 161–62.

93. Jan Felshin, "The Social View," in Gerber et al., *The American Woman in Sport;* and Felshin, "The Triple Option . . . for Women in Sport," *Quest* 21 (1974): 36–40. Many other authors have used the term, criticizing or adding to it: Lenskyj, *Out of Bounds;* Boutillier and SanGiovanni, *The Sporting Woman;* and Blue, *Grace Under Pressure.*

94. Kratz, "A Study of Sports," 56–60.

95. Athletes tried to comply with society's prescriptions of femininity, but the definition was not absolute. Just as it depended on race and class, historical circumstances could cause compensatory behavior subtly to shift in emphasis. According to Boutillier and SanGiovanni, for example, turn-of-the-century Social Darwinism led upper-middle-class white women sometimes to stress "proper eugenics" and the beneficial role of sports in helping give birth to healthy white children (*The Sporting Woman,* 33–34). Similarly, the authors comment that

during World War II, women tended to point out those characteristics of competition that fit their increasingly important roles as citizen and worker. The particular components of "apologetic behavior," then, provide an illuminating lens through which to view what femininity actually meant to certain groups of women in certain periods. In addition, by isolating the elements of this behavior, it becomes possible to see which things actually changed over time.

96. There has been much criticism of the concept of role conflict and the use of the term "apologetic" along with it. Some early studies found evidence of role conflict, and others, different methodologically, found a high level of psychological adjustment among female athletes (see, e.g., Helen Lenskyj, "Female Sexuality and Women's Sport," *Women's Studies International Forum* 10, no. 4 [1987]: 381–86). Other studies in physical education, according to some critics, assumed role conflict to such a degree that they began blaming the victim. Boutillier and SanGiovanni (*The Sporting Woman*, 110–13) also criticize the term "apologetic" behavior because some studies overlook the relative nature and context of roles. But I believe the term is still useful—there *was* compensatory behavior—and I hope my analysis does not blame the victim, but rather makes it clear that I think prejudice and oppression were what forced athletes into that behavior.

Adrianne Blue believes that during earlier periods athletes sincerely tried to be feminine, but by the 1980s they displayed a "phoney apologetic": "What is new is the fact that at the top sports stars are only apologizing for image purposes. No longer feeling ambivalent about their role as sportswomen, they nonetheless feel the need to pretend to be ambivalent" (Blue, *Grace Under Pressure*, 115). I disagree for two very different reasons. First, we don't know that athletes in the 1950s were not being equally phony, not similarly pretending to be ambivalent publicly for the sake of public relations. Second, I think that apologetic behavior continues to take a toll on modern athletes—that they may play along and think that overemphasizing femininity is ridiculous, but that the prejudice seeps into their subconscious despite their best rational efforts and still becomes internalized (as I believe it tragically does for every stigmatized group in society). But that's a personal belief based on reading sources by women and other oppressed groups; as a historian, not a psychologist, I think it's safest to maintain that we can't make conclusions about athletes' psyches in the 1950s without more evidence.

97. Nadler, "A Developmental History," cites Redin's recruiting goals (originally quoted in the *Plainview Daily Herald*, April 28, 1955); Thaxton, "A Documentary Analysis."

98. Williamson and Johnson, *"Whatta-Gal!"* 161–85.

99. Schoolfield, "Hanes Hosiery All-American Ace Takes Her Sports Play Seriously."

100. Gay Talese, "Tactful Coach Taking Girls Quintet to Russia," *NYT*, April 8, 1958, 30.

101. In fact, *Life* magazine had a story about the terrible travails of being a tall woman ("Trials of a 6'2" Career Girl," *Life*, January 6, 1958, 68).

102. This suggestion came in reference to what should be beautifully slender ankles, according to a "Secrets of Charm" article by John Robert Power. A woman should be fussy about her shoe size. "Slipping heels cause the ankle muscles to work overtime keeping shoes on. This extra activity further develops the muscles that you are trying to reduce," he noted. He also asked, "Is there anything more feminine looking than a slim, well-contoured pair of ankles below a full skirt?" Power, "Do Your Ankles Need Contouring, Slimming?" *Houston Post*, March 27, 1952, 3.

103. Roxy Andersen, "American Women Are Cream Puffs!!!" *Amateur Athlete* (May 1955): 25.

104. Downing, "Women's Basketball," 82.

105. Redin, *The Queens Fly High*, 13; *Sports Illustrated* confirmed tongue-in-cheek the report of hiring the nationally recognized hairstylist "to give the team that look of chic so necessary to feminine morale" ("The Flying Queens," April 2, 1956, 15).

106. Bill Cunningham, "The Colonel's Ladies," *Collier's*, May 23, 1936, 28, 60–62.

107. Roxy Andersen, "Watch This Housewife Jump!" *Parade*, March 16, 1952, reprinted in *Amateur Athlete* (April 1952): 22.

108. Seymour Lieberman, "Statistical Study of Former Women Athletes," *Amateur Athlete* (November 1952): 9; Ernst Jokl, M.D., "The Athletic Status of Women," *Amateur Athlete* (n.d.: circa 1953).

109. Mary Flin, "The Age Old Question—Should Women Do Serious Athletics?" reprinted in *Amateur Athlete* (August 1956): 27–28.

110. Babe Didrikson was actually rather cocky and arrogant, according to Williamson and Johnson, but she was a rare instance;the press would either ignore this characteristic or belittle her for it.

111. Nadler, "A Developmental History," 90.

112. Talese, "Tactful Coach Taking Girls Quintet to Russia."

113. Schoolfield, "Hanes Hosiery All-American Ace Takes Her Sports Play Seriously."

114. Paul Gardner, "Our New Girl Wonder," *Amateur Athlete* (December 1955): 28–29.

115. Talese, "Tactful Coach Taking Girls Quintet to Russia"; for a similar headline about pro golfers see "Next to Marriage, We'll Take Golf," *Saturday Evening Post*, January 23, 1954.

116. Talese, "Tactful Coach Taking Girls Quintet to Russia."

117. Kratz, "A Study of Sports," 52–58.

118. Gardner, "Our New Girl Wonder," 28–29.

119. Beth Kaufman, "Former Swim Titlists Doing Well," *Amateur Athlete* (July 1955): 11.

120. Ferris, "Let's Have More Co-Ed Sports" (emphasis in original).

121. For the role of male promoters in this effort, see Cahn, "Coming on Strong," 141–42. After noting that Wayland's women's basketball team was better known than the men's team, *Sports Illustrated* commented that the men "can comfort themselves by reflecting that a man was the cause of it all" ("Flying Queens," 15).

122. Talese, "Tactful Coach Taking Girls Quintet to Russia."

123. There is not much data on the subject, but in a study of 850 AAU competitors in the mid-1930s, a majority preferred male coaches. See Gerber et al., *The American Woman in Sport*, 43.

124. Flin, "The Age Old Question," 27–28.

125. Bishop and Fulton, "Shooting Stars"; *Winston-Salem Journal and Sentinel*, April 2, 1953, 24; the *Amateur Athlete* gave annual coverage to the tournament.

126. Cahn, "Coming on Strong," 136.

127. Tennie McGhee, "Women's Basketball Won By Wayland Flying Queens," *Amateur Athlete* (May 1956): 23.

128. Quoted in Cahn, "Coming on Strong," 136.

129. Cahn, "Coming on Strong," 145.

130. The male standard assumed that to play the game correctly meant not simply to perform most efficiently (that is, to play "like a man") but also encompassed its opposite—not performing very well was to play "like a girl." For an example, see Ione L. Muir, "As I see It," *Amateur Athlete* (February 1956), who said that the problem with American women swimmers in international competition was they swam like girls. Female athletes really couldn't win, then. Arthur Daley of the *New York Times* criticized the unfemininity "of a girl with

beads of perspiration on her alabaster brow, the results of grotesque contortions in events totally unsuited to female architecture"; but he also criticized those athletes' ability: "It's probably boorish to say it, but any self-respecting schoolboy can achieve superior performance to a woman champion." Arthur Daley, "More Deadly Than the Male," *NYT*, February 8, 1953.

131. Cahn, "Coming on Strong," 39, makes a similar point: "Like 'women drivers' [and] 'lady doctors', the distinction took the form of the generic basketball and 'women's basketball.'"

132. "Hoops, dear, in Iowa," *Life*, March 4, 1957, 97.

133. Patsy Neal, *Basketball Techniques for Women*, 8–9.

3. Members Only

1. P.W.W., Jr. "On the Courts," *New Yorker*, September 16, 1950.

2. Allison Danzig, "Miss Gibson Game from Victory Over Louise Brough as Rain Stops Match," *NYT*, August 30, 1950, 33.

3. David Eisenberg, *New York Journal-American*, quoted in Althea Gibson, *I Always Wanted to Be Somebody*, 74; Danzig, "Miss Gibson Game from Victory."

4. Davenport, "History and Interpretation of Amateurism," 65–69.

5. Ibid., 65.

6. Ibid., 49.

7. Quoted in Davenport, "History and Interpretation of Amateurism," 41.

8. Parke Cummings, *American Tennis: The Story of a Game and Its People*.

9. Angela Lumpkin, *Women's Tennis: A Historical Documentary of the Players and Their Game*, 10.

10. Cynthia Himes, "The Female Athlete in American Society: 1860–1940" (Ph.D. diss., University of Pennsylvania, 1986), 3.

11. "Lawn Tennis in America," *The Wheelman* 2 (September 1883): 468, quoted in Davenport, "History and Interpretation of Amateurism," 65.

12. H. H. Wind, "Profiles," *New Yorker*, August 30, 1952, 31–49.

13. Russell, "Tennis and the Woman Player," ch. 1.

14. See, for example, the experiences of Maureen Connolly and Doris Hart. Maureen Connolly and Tom Gwynne, *Forehand Drive*; "Young Queen," *Time*, September 17, 1951, 52–54.

15. Connolly and Gwynne, *Forehand Drive*, 22. Billie Jean King felt embarrassed and angered by a similar experience in her first-ever tennis tournament at age eleven (in 1954), when Jones excluded her from a group photograph because she was not wearing a tennis dress. Billie Jean King with Kim Chapin, *Billie Jean*, 33.

16. Among the sports they thought men perceived as most appropriate for women, tennis ranked third. Kratz, "A Study of Sports," 129, 299–303.

17. Billie Jean King with Cynthia Starr, *We Have Come a Long Way*, 57–58.

18. Russell, "Tennis and the Woman Player," 55. Billie Jean King was another athlete whose parents urged her toward tennis (and away from other sports like softball).

19. Davenport, "History and Interpretation of Amateurism," 79–127.

20. When one won Wimbledon, he or she automatically became a life member of the Wimbledon Club; if they turned pro, their life memberships were canceled. Gladys

Heldman, "The Women's Pro Circuit in Tennis," address to the NAGWS convention (undated, probably 1975), transcript in the AIAW papers, McKeldin Library, University of Maryland, Box 378.

21. Davenport, "History and Interpretation of Amateurism," 173–78; "They Play for Pay," *Time*, May 30, 1955, 54.

22. King and Starr, *We Have Come a Long Way*, 61–62.

23. "The Road to the Pros," *Time*, March 7, 1955, 76–77.

24. Shirley Fry, for example, remembered making arrangements to go to Egypt, and then when a higher-ranked player changed her mind and became available, the USLTA tried to back out on its promise of paying Fry. Darlene Hard, the best U.S. player in the country from 1960 to 1963, earned only her airfare from New York back to Los Angeles when she won the U.S. national championship at Forest Hills. "Whoopee," she said, remembering the prize decades later. King and Starr, *We Have Come a Long Way*, 80–89.

25. Connolly and Gwynne, *Forehand Drive*, 168–72.

26. King and Starr, *We Have Come a Long Way*, 91–94.

27. Helen Wills, who dominated tennis in the 1920s, said in her autobiography, "I have always thought of tennis as a diversion, and not as a 'career'" (*Fifty-Thirty: The Story of a Tennis Player*, 3). According to Russell, players in the 1950s were more serious but were still affected by the historical circumstances.

28. Doris Hart, *Tennis with Hart*, 11, 192, 62.

29. Quoted in Russell, "Tennis and the Woman Player," 53–54.

30. King and Starr, *We Have Come a Long Way*, 70.

31. Quoted in Russell, "Tennis and the Woman Player," 52.

32. Quoted in ibid., 53. Russell found that many of the 1950s players, when interviewed in 1981, envied the greater options and freedom available to succeeding generations.

33. Marianna W. Davis, ed. *Contributions of Black Women to America*, vol. 1.

34. Edwin B. Henderson, *The Negro in Sports*, ch. 10.

35. Wendell Smith referred to the "ladies and gentlemen's agreement" keeping blacks out of Forest Hills. "Wendell Smith's Sports Beat," *Pittsburgh Courier*, July 29, 1950.

36. Gibson, *I Always Wanted to Be Somebody*, 63–64; "Another Budge," *Time*, July 17, 1950, 74.

37. Edwin B. Henderson, "The Negro in Tennis," *Negro History Bulletin* 15 (December 1951): 54.

38. Gibson, *I Always Wanted to Be Somebody*, 29; description of Gibson's habits and manners from "Gibson Girl," *Time*, August 26, 1957, 44.

39. "Althea Has Finally Arrived," *Ebony*, August 1956, 35–38. And certainly Gibson's working-class neighbors appreciated her achievements by flocking to her apartment to greet and congratulate her after her victories in traditionally white tournaments. George Barner, "Ticker Tape Parade for Althea," *New York Amsterdam News*, July 13, 1957, 1, 35.

40. Edwin B. Henderson, "Negro Women in Sports," *Negro History Bulletin* 15 (December 1951): 55.

41. Henderson, "Negro Women in Sports."

42. "Gibson Girl," *Time*, August 26, 1957, 44–48.

43. Frank A. Young, "Fay Says," *Chicago Defender* (city ed.), July 14, 1956, 17. Another reporter wrote that she "captured the admiration and won the hearts of millions." Chastine Everett, "Althea Gibson Looks Forward to Bid to Compete in Nationals This Summer," *Chicago Defender* (city ed.), June 17, 1950, 16.

44. "Well Done, Althea," *New York Amsterdam News*, July 13, 1957, 8; Frank A. Young, "Fay Says"; Betty Granger, "The Truth About Althea Gibson," *New York Amsterdam News*, July 21, 1956, 14.

45. Gibson, *I Always Wanted to Be Somebody*, 55–61; "Famcee Campus Turns Out for Althea Gibson," *Chicago Defender* (city ed.), April 8, 1950.

46. "Tennis Queen from Harlem," *Ebony*, October 1957; Russ J. Cowans ("Russ' Corner"), "Sports Writers Sour on Althea, But She's Still Champ," *Chicago Defender* (city ed.), July 27, 1957, 1; Russ J. Cowans ("Russ' Corner"), "She Should Be Told," *Chicago Defender* (city ed.), July 27, 1957, 17.

47. Robert M. Ratcliffe, "Althea and the Press," *Pittsburgh Courier*, August 31, 1957; "Tennis Queen from Harlem," *Ebony*, October 1957.

48. Gibson, *I Always Wanted to Be Somebody*, 105.

49. "Tennis Queen from Harlem," *Ebony*, October 1957; "Gibson Girl," *Time*, August 26, 1957, 44.

50. Gibson, *I Always Wanted to Be Somebody*, 61–62, 158. Gibson said, "I am just another tennis player, not a Negro tennis player. Of course, I am a Negro—everybody knows that—but you don't say somebody is a white tennis player, do you?" Kennett Love, "Althea Is at Home Abroad on Tennis Courts," *NYT*, June 24, 1956, 35.

51. Gibson, *I Always Wanted to Be Somebody*, 61–62, 158.

52. Virginia Wade and Jean Rafferty, *Ladies of the Court: A Century of Women at Wimbledon*, 104.

53. King and Starr, *We Have Come a Long Way*, 95.

54. Gibson, *I Always Wanted to Be Somebody*, 118.

55. Ibid., 105–106.

56. "That Gibson Girl," *Newsweek*, May 28, 1956, 62.

57. Gibson, *I Always Wanted to Be Somebody*, 2.

58. Quentin Reynolds, "Long Road to the Center Court," *Saturday Review of Books*, November 29, 1958, 16. Nor would the Ambassador East Hotel's Pump Room hold a luncheon in her honor. See "Gibson Girl," *Nation*, July 20, 1957, 22.

59. Gibson, *I Always Wanted to Be Somebody*, 159.

60. Arthur Ashe became a champion in the mid-1970s, but no other black male has broken into the top ranks since then. And not until the late 1980s did a black woman again win Wimbledon.

61. William Chafe, *Civilities and Civil Rights: Greensboro, North Carolina, and the Black Struggle for Freedom*, 7–9, 32–33, 38–34.

62. Gibson, *I Always Wanted to Be Somebody*, 159.

63. Ibid., 48–49.

64. Ibid., 29.

65. Quoted in Russell, "Tennis and the Woman Player," 55.

66. King and Starr, *We Have Come a Long Way*, 55–56.

67. See, for example, "Top Guy and a Doll," *Newsweek*, July 14, 1952; "Young Queen," *Time*, September 17, 1951; "The Old Men," *Time*, April 3, 1950; "Another Budge," *Time*, July 17, 1950; "On the Courts," *New Yorker*, September 16, 1950; "Wimbledon," *Newsweek*, July 17, 1950; "The Missing X," *Time*, July 10, 1950.

68. Hart, *Tennis with Hart*, 135.

69. "On the Courts," *New Yorker*, September 16, 1950.

70. *Time* unapologetically referred to her as "Curvaceous Gertrude ('Gorgeous Gussie') Moran, 25, the most eye-filling thing in women's tennis." "Heiresses Apparent," *Time*, August 22, 1949, 36.

71. "Miss Moran Gains Final; Mother Surprised at Troth, Quips, 'It's Not the First Time,'" *NYT*, January 22, 1950, sec. 5, p. 1; Gertrude Moran, "Miss Moran Denies Seeking Daring Outfit; Just Wants One That Will Help Her Tennis," *NYT*, March 16, 1950, 44; King and Starr, *We Have Come a Long Way*, 71.

72. "Gorgeous Gussie," *Life*, April 25, 1949, 91–92.

73. King and Starr, *We Have Come a Long Way*, 71.

74. Jack Kramer, with Frank Deford, *The Game: My Forty Years in Tennis*, 94–95; Moran, "Miss Moran Denies Seeking Daring Outfit."

75. King and Starr, *We Have Come a Long Way*, 62; Wade and Rafferty, *Ladies of the Court*, 83.

76. "Miss Moran, who had appeared for the opening singles in a conservative, white, one-piece costume with an abbreviated skirt, was attired more daringly for the mixed doubles and drew whistles and cheers, as did Mrs. [Pauline Betz] Addie, former national champ, with her zebra-striped shorts and white sweater." "Mrs. Addie Routs Miss Moran in Garden Tennis," *NYT*, October 27, 1950, 33.

77. Kramer, *The Game*, 94–95.

78. The amount they made may have been exaggerated by promoters. Moran was said to have signed a contract for $75,000, but more realistic estimates are that the featured male star, Jack Kramer, made $100,000 while Moran earned somewhere between $10,000 and $35,000. In 1947 Betz and Cooke (after her marriage, Sarah Palfrey played under her married name) reportedly got $500 for a weekend match, and $250 for a weekday, which the two of them had to split with their manager. "Sports," *Newsweek*, September 4, 1950, 68; Heldman, "The Women's Pro Circuit in Tennis," address (c. 1975).

79. This attitude had remained virtually unchanged since Helen Wills's heyday in the 1920s. According to Wills, "From an artistic standpoint, the pleated skirt possesses grace and beauty in action. I think that is one of the reasons why women players are often more pleasing to watch upon the court than men. The rhythm of play and the motion of the stroke is carried out by the graceful swing of the skirt." Quoted in Lumpkin, *Women's Tennis*, 24–25.

80. Connolly and Gwynne, *Forehand Drive*, 133.

81. "There were times I wore a skirt because I thought that it would look better to the audience," admitted a 1960s player. Quoted in Russell, "Tennis and the Woman Player."

82. King and Starr, *We Have Come a Long Way*, 55–56. Even players criticized Gibson for being "only interested in her Mission—a ruthless, title-chasing mission." "Althea Gibson Not as Talkative as She Was on 1951 Net Tour," *Chicago Defender*, July 7, 1956.

83. "Triumph of Althea," *Newsweek*, July 15, 1957, 64.

84. See, for example, the quote in the text accompanying note 2, above, at the beginning of this chapter.

85. "The Power Game," *Time*, July 15, 1957, 61.

86. "That Gibson Girl," *Time*, August 26, 1957.

87. Rigidly dualistic notions of gender, which in the popular mind placed *masculine* and *feminine* at two opposite poles, made participating in any "unfeminine" activity dangerous for females who wanted to be considered "normal." Although I believe the concept of bipolar dualism has been extremely helpful to historians—since society only considered these two

categories to be legitimate—in some ways it oversimplifies the actual social categories. Perhaps it would be more accurate to say that culture placed people in at least four categories: "Feminine," "Masculine," "Not-feminine," and "Not-masculine." See Joan Scott, "Deconstructing Equality-versus-Difference" and "Gender: A Useful Category of Analysis,"; Mary Poovey, "Feminism and Deconstruction," *Feminist Studies* 14, no. 1 (Spring 1988): 51–65; Mary Jo Festle, "Billie Jean King's Challenge: Women's Pro Tennis, Gender, and Sexuality in the 1970s" (paper presented at the Berkshire Conference on Women's History, June 1990).

88. Gibson, *I Always Wanted to Be Somebody*, 85.

89. Kratz, "A Study of Sports," 172–77, 282–93.

90. "Young Queen," *Time*, September 17, 1951; "Tennis Gets Some New Champs," *Life*, September 17, 1951, 139.

91. "Mighty Mo," *Senior Scholastic*, April 23, 1952; "Little Moe," *Newsweek*, May 28, 1951, 82.

92. "Sports," *Newsweek*, September 15, 1951.

93. King and Starr, *We Have Come a Long Way*, 82–83.

94. "Top Guy and a Doll," *Newsweek*, July 14, 1952.

95. "Little Mo Grows Up," *Time*, July 14, 1952.

96. Connolly's coach "Teach" Tennant was not apologetic about her attitude: "She's out to kill them. You have to be mean to be a champion. How can you lick someone if you feel friendly toward them?" *Time* described Tennant in unfeminine terms, saying she "snorted scornfully." "Little Mo Grows Up," *Time*, July 14, 1952.

Connolly's reception closely resembled that of Helen Wills twenty-five years earlier. Describing her style, one sportswriter noted that Wills "with a silent deadly earnestness concentrated on her work. That, of course, is the way to win, but it does not please the galleries." She was criticized for having no womanly mercy on her opponents. "It was almost as though a man with a rapier were sending home his vital thrusts against a foeman unarmed." Wills, *Fifty-Thirty*, 153–62.

97. Connolly and Gwynne, *Forehand Drive*, 26.

98. "Sports," *Time*, July 14, 1952.

99. See, for example, the debate surrounding Carol Gilligan's *In a Different Voice: Psychological Theory and Women's Development*.

100. Connolly and Gwynne, *Forehand Drive*, 26.

101. "Road to the Pros," *Time*, March 7, 1955. While the no longer dominant Connolly was accorded sympathy after her injury, she rediscovered how people disliked her ambition. She felt hurt by criticism of her decision to sue the trucking company for damages.

102. King and Starr, *We Have Come a Long Way*, 91, 93.

103. Hart, *Tennis with Hart*, 135; "Ticker Tape Parade on Broadway," *Chicago Defender* (city ed.), July 20, 1957; Barner, "Ticker Tape Parade for Althea," 1.

104. A number of players and commentators have mentioned tennis's sissy reputation, including Angela Lumpkin, *Women's Tennis*; Hart, *Tennis with Hart*, 86; Bobby Riggs with George McGann, *Court Hustler*, 153.

105. Russell, "Tennis and the Woman Player," 74–79.

106. Ironically, this quote came from a woman who did not mind very much all the rules and control. Russell, "Tennis and the Woman Player," 55–60.

107. Quoted in Russell, "Tennis and the Woman Player," 60–63.

Part II. Introduction: 1955–1967

1. Peter G. Filene, *Him/Her/Self: Sex Roles in Modern America*, 172–74. William Chafe believes increased female employment helped prompt a shift in distribution of power in the family. Chafe, *The American Woman: Her Changing Social, Economic, and Political Roles, 1920–1970*, 218–22.

2. Filene, *Him/Her/Self*, 237–38.

3. *Look*, October 16, 1956, 35, 40, quoted in Evans, *Born for Liberty*, 249.

4. Ibid.

5. Evans, *Born for Liberty*, 255. Barnard sociologist Mirra Komarovsky found that college women heard ambiguous messages from authorities about excelling (cited in Chafe, *The American Woman*, 212–13).

4. Transitional Years, 1955–1967

1. Josephine Fiske to Pauline Hodgson, April 25, 1953 (ser. 7, DGWS papers, AAHPER archives).

2. Fiske to Hodgson, April 25, 1953.

3. Ibid. See also Rachel Bryant to Christine White, July 1953 (Basketball Correspondence file, ser. 7, DGWS papers). In a letter Ruth Wilson said substantially the same thing. If NAPECW members could be on AAU committees, "It is very possible that the positive type of influences can be exerted in effecting the proper rules for activity." Ruth Wilson to Laura Huelster, April 22, 1955 (DGWS correspondence, file drawer 4, NAPECW papers).

4. NAPECW Report of Committee on Competition, April 1, 1954 (ser. 8, DGWS papers).

5. Maria Sexton, Report of the AAU and U.S. Olympic Committee Meeting, November 29–December 5, 1961 (ser. 8, DGWS papers); Helen B. Laurence to Laura Huelster, June 6, 1955 (DGWS correspondence, file drawer 4, NAPECW papers).

6. Grace Fox to Mrs. Frances Kaszubski, October 7, 1955 (ser. 7, DGWS papers); minutes of the DGWS Executive Council meeting, January 1–3, 1959 (ser. 1, DGWS papers).

7. Mary Ellen McKee to NAPECW Executive Board, Spring 1960 (NAPECW papers).

8. The new name represented a "promotion" to a higher (divisional) status within AAHPER.

9. Celeste Ulrich to district presidents of NAPECW, "History of NJCESCW," no date (ser. 8, DGWS papers); Hunt, "Governance," 29–37; NSGWS Report of the Chairman, 1955–56 (ser. 8, DGWS papers).

10. Anna Espenschade, Report of Committee on Interpretation of NSGWS Standards on Competition, December 17, 1954 (ser. 8, DGWS papers).

11. DGWS Executive Committee minutes, December 30–31, 1957, and January 1, 1958.

12. Vice President's Report to Legislative Board, December 30–January 1, 1958 (ser. 8, DGWS papers). Another committee referred to "the existing conflict in values about girls' and women's sports programs." Sit and Flit Committee (Dream Committee) report, April 1960 (ser. 8, DGWS papers).

13. Report of the Joint Committee to Study the Larger Implications of Extramural Sports to DGWS Executive Council, minutes, December 30–31, 1957; and Executive Committee meeting January 1–3, 1959.

312   Notes

14. NJCESCW, "Extramural Sports for Women (Statement of Belief)," *Journal of Health, Physical Education, and Recreation* (hereafter *JOHPER*) (December 1960): 63.

15. DGWS Executive Council minutes, March 30–April 3, 1958, and January 1–3, 1959.

16. Sara Staff Jernigan to Betty McCue, Phebe Scott et al., February 9, 1962 (ser. 6, DGWS papers). Katherine Ley to Wilma Gimmestad, May 15, 1962 (Box 4, NAPECW papers); Ley to DGWS Executive Council, May 8, 1962 (ser. 8, DGWS papers).

17. What, then, was the official policy? For a while, no one was sure. As it stood in the early 1950s, the accepted *Standards* "did not state very specifically whether DGWS was in favor or not in favor of interscholastic competition. As a result, many people were interpreting it the way they wished to interpret it." However, everyone agreed that the official statement "had many negative statements." Rachel Bryant to Frances Bragger, October 29, 1963 (ser. 1, DGWS papers).

18. "Statement of Policies for Competition in Girls' and Women's Sports," *JOHPER* (September 1963): 31–33.

19. Sara Staff Jernigan to Leona Holbrook, October 10, 1962 (file drawer 4, NAPECW papers).

20. Mabel Locke to Leona Holbrook, December 17, 1965 (ser. 6, DGWS papers).

21. Helen Starr, letter to the editor, *JOHPER* (May–June 1962): 6–10.

22. Dudley Ashton to Rachel Bryant, March 29, 1957 (file drawer 4, NAPECW papers); Wilma Gimmestad to Sara Staff Jernigan, June 27, 1962 (file drawer 4, NAPECW papers).

23. Katherine Ley to Phebe Scott, January 1963, correspondence on Competition statement (ser. 6, DGWS).

24. Jernigan to Holbrook, October 10, 1962.

25. Jernigan to Holbrook, October 10, 1962; Ley to Gimmestad, May 15, 1962.

26. Jernigan to Holbrook, October 10, 1962; Jernigan to Gimmestad, May 14, 1962 (NAPECW papers); Ley to Gimmestad, May 15, 1962; Jernigan to Ley, April 26, 1962 (ser. 6, DGWS papers).

27. Katherine Ley and Sara Staff Jernigan, "The Roots and the Tree," *JOHPER* (September 1962): 34–36, 57.

28. One DGWS article summarized the moderating attitude with a quotation: "Need not be the first by whom the new is tried, nor yet the last old to lay aside" (quoted in "Extramural Sports for Women," *JOHPER* [December 1960]: 63).

29. National Joint Committee report, June 22, 1958; NSGWS Report of the Chairman, 1955–56 (ser. 8, DGWS papers).

30. From the 1959 convention program of the Southern Association of Physical Education for College Women (Box 4, SAPECW papers), noted in Executive Council minutes, December 1960 (ser. 1, DGWS papers); see also NAPECW-DGWS correspondence, late 1950s (file drawer 4, NAPECW papers).

31. Phebe Scott, "Reflections on Women in Sports," in U.S. Olympic Development Committee and the DGWS, *Proceedings of the Third National Institute on Girls' Sports* (January 1966), 7–13; Virginia Crafts, "Building on Basics," in *Proceedings of the Second National Institute* (September 1965), 79.

32. Ley and Jernigan, "The Roots and the Tree," 35.

33. "Statement of Belief of the National Joint Committee on Extramural Sports for College Women," *JOHPER* (April 1962): 26.

34. Gimmestad to Jernigan, June 27, 1962; Crafts, "Building on Basics," *Second National Institute*, 79.

35. Quoted in *JOHPER* (May–June 1962): 8.

36. According to one historian, they took every step short of direct subsidy to enhance the country's athletic image. Thomas M. Domer, "Sport in Cold War America, 1953–1963: The Diplomatic and Political Use of Sport in the Eisenhower and Kennedy Administrations" (Ph.D. diss., Marquette University, 1976), 23–26.

37. Domer, "Sport in Cold War America," 118–22, 145, 107.

38. Ibid., 154, 206, 58, 179.

39. Quoted in President's Council on Youth Fitness (PCYF) pamphlet, Workshop Reports, nos. 2, 3, 4 (Washington, D.C.: GPO, 1960).

40. Max Eastman, "Let's Close the Muscle Gap," *Reader's Digest*, November 1961. See also *JOHPER* (March 1961): 10; *JOHPER* (January 1961): 75; *JOHPER* (February 1960): 61.

41. State of the Union message quoted in PCYF pamphlet, Workshop Reports, nos. 2, 3, 4 (1960).

42. John F. Kennedy, *Sports Illustrated*, December 26, 1960; press release, *JOHPER* (January 1961): 4. Kennedy said, "Our Olympic teams and athletes play a significant role in preserving our way of life in the world." Domer, "Sport in Cold War America," 228–31.

43. Domer, "Sport in Cold War America," 116–17.

44. Ibid., 263–66, 28–49.

45. At a special PCPF workshop, USODC director Thomas J. Hamilton acknowledged the connection between helping youth with fitness and training elite athletes. "Steps are being taken to enhance future American Olympic success by providing greater participation here at home." PCPF, "Sports for Fitness" (April 13, 1960), Workshop Report, no. 7; Domer, "Sport in Cold War America," 115–16. See also Robert F. Kennedy, "A Bold Proposal for American Sport," *Sports Illustrated*, July 27, 1964, 13–15.

46. John F. Kennedy to Kenneth Wilson, November 30, 1961, quoted in Domer, "Sport in Cold War America," 23–27.

47. Historians and social theorists have debated at length the state's role—what it responds to, who it represents, and whether it is meaningful to speak of "the state" in the United States. It is clear that "the state" can be divided within itself (as will be seen during the 1970s and 1980s), especially between different branches of government. It is also clear that there are different kinds of state power. See Wendy Brown, "Finding the Man in the State," *Feminist Studies* 18, no. 1 (Spring 1992): 7–34.

48. Domer, "Sport in Cold War America," 118–22.

49. Mary McIntosh, "The State and the Oppression of Women," in Annette Kuhn and AnnMarie Wolpe, eds., *Feminism and Materialism: Women and Modes of Production*; Catherine MacKinnon, *Toward A Feminist Theory of the State*, ch. 8; Michelle Barrett, *Women's Oppression Today: Problems in Marxist Feminist Analysis*.

50. Karen Decrow, *Sexist Justice*.

51. Albie Sachs and Joan Hoff Wilson, *Sexism and the Law: A Study of Male Beliefs and Legal Bias in Britain and the United States*, ch. 4.

52. Jane M. Picker, "Law and the Status of Women in the United States," in *Law and the Status of Women: An International Symposium*; McIntosh, "Feminism and Materialism"; Sachs and Wilson, *Sexism and the Law*.

53. Evans, *Born for Liberty*, 247.

54. *State v. Hunter*, 208 Ore. 282, 300 P. 2d 455, quoted in Leo Kanowitz, *Sex Roles in Law and Society: Cases and Materials*.

55. *State v. Hunter*.

56. Domer, "Sport in Cold War America," 153–54.

57. Art Rosenblaum, "If the Russians Win . . . So What?" *San Francisco Chronicle*, reprinted in the *Amateur Athlete* (July 1955): 8.

58. Guttmann, *The Games Must Go On*, 195.

59. Between 1951 and 1960, U.S. women held 6 track and field world records, while Soviet women held 74. In the same period, U.S. men averaged 24 world records per year. Between 1951 and 1954, Soviet men averaged 1.5; but between 1955 and 1960 they increased it to 8 per year. As Soviet men gained on U.S. men (and Soviet women continued to dominate U.S. women), overall the Soviets outdistanced the United States. For example, in 1952 the U.S.-combined men and women's "unofficial" points in the Olympics were 610, and Soviets had 552. But in 1956 the USSR had 722 to America's 593; and in 1960, 807 to America's 564. See Domer, "Sport in Cold War America," 198, 54, 69–70, 202.

60. Domer, "Sport in Cold War America," 222–24.

61. Paula Dee Welch, "The Emergence of American Women in the Summer Olympic Games, 1900–1972" (Ed.D. diss., University of North Carolina at Greensboro, 1975), 122–25; *Proceedings of the First National Institute* (April 1964), 31–32.

62. Domer, "Sport in Cold War America," 201.

63. *Proceedings of the First National Institute*, 31–32; "Women and the Olympics," *JOHPER* (April 1962): 25–26.

64. *JOHPER* (February 1964): 35. See also President's Council on Physical Fitness, *Vim: Complete Exercise Plan for Girls 12 to 18*; President's Council on Physical Fitness, *Vigor: Complete Exercise Program for Boys 12 to 18*.

65. *Proceedings of the First National Institute*.

66. See excerpt of Humphrey's speech in *JOHPER* (June 1964): 14.

67. Domer, "Sport in Cold War America," 218, 43; Robert F. Kennedy, "A Bold Proposal for American Sport," 13–15; see also Charles "Bud" Wilkinson (PCPF consultant), "A Mother's Role in Physical Fitness," YMCA *Magazine* (February 1963).

68. James F. Kelly, "Sports for Fitness" workshop (April 13, 1960); Communications Media Forum, Magazine Forum, Broadcasting Forum (1959–60); PCYF, Workshop Reports, nos. 2, 3, 4 (1960).

69. Communications Media Forum, Magazine Forum, Broadcasting Forum (1959–60); PCYF, Workshop Reports, nos. 2, 3, 4 (1960).

70. *Proceedings of the First National Institute*.

71. H. D. Thoreau, "Olympic Preview," *Saturday Evening Post*, September 22, 1956, 32–33, 94–95.

72. Bob Mathias with Melvin Durslag, "America's Olympic Chances at Melbourne," *Collier's* (n.d.), 96–101. See also Marshall Smith, "What Drives the Olympic Stars," *Life*, December 3, 1956.

73. "Stalin's 'Iron Curtain' for Athletes," *U.S. News and World Report*, July 25, 1952; "How to Win a Track Meet—the Soviet Way," *U.S. News and World Report*, August 8, 1958, 37.

74. Hank Solomon, "It Happened in Philly," *Amateur Athlete* (August 1959): 6–11.

75. "How Reds Mobilized to Win Olympic War," *Life*, July 28, 1952, 15; "Russians Bear Down for Olympics," *Life*, August 6, 1956; Thoreau, "Olympic Preview."

76. Mary Snow, "Can the Soviet Girls Be Stopped?" *Sports Illustrated*, August 27, 1956, 6–11.

77. William Barry Furlong, "Venus Wasn't a Shot-Putter," (subtitled "More and more of

the fair sex are competing in sports, raising a profound question: Do men make passes at athletic lasses?"), *New York Times Magazine*, August 28, 1960, 14, 72–73.

78. Judith Friedberg, "They're Tough . . . and Pretty," *Sports Illustrated*, August 3, 1964, 12–13.

79. "Our Lackadaisical Girls Take a Soviet Shellacking," *Life*, August 2, 1963, 26; *Sports Illustrated*, July 30, 1962, 10–15.

80. From the *London Daily Mail*, reprinted in *Amateur Athlete* (October 1954): 18; Roxy Andersen, "American Women Are Cream Puffs!!!" *Amateur Athlete* (May 1955): 25.

81. "The World's Loveliest Sportswomen," *Sports Illustrated*, December 25, 1961. Other articles highlighted a beautiful Swedish pentathlete and pointed out that, when done properly, the javelin was one of the prettiest of events. "Why Can't We Beat This Girl?" *Sports Illustrated*, September 30, 1963.

82. John Underwood, "This Is the Way the Girls Go," *Sports Illustrated*, May 10, 1965, 34–36.

83. "Why Can't We Beat This Girl?" 54.

84. Ibid.

85. Ibid.

86. Jack Clowser, "Boost the Women," *Amateur Athlete* (September 1959): 37. "Backward" physical educators were also blamed for America's international failures in "Why Can't We Beat This Girl?"

87. John Underwood, "Raves for the Young," *Sports Illustrated*, August 3, 1964, 8–10.

88. "Brace of Balanced Beauties," *Life*, January 13, 1958, 8–10.

89. Barbara Heilman, "Still on Top at 14," *Sports Illustrated*, April 16, 1962, 26.

90. "Lithe Envoys to Our Latin Neighbors," *Sports Illustrated*, May 6, 1963, 28–32; Underwood, "This Is the Way the Girls Go," 34–36; "Olympic Girls—the Classic Grace of U.S. Women Athletes," *Life*, July 31, 1964, 38–47.

91. John Lovesay, "Quick Young Ladies of Quality," *Sports Illustrated*, April 19, 1965, 108–10; Underwood, "This Is the Way the Girls Go."

92. Gilbert Rogin, "Flamin' Mamie's Bouffant Belles," *Sports Illustrated*, April 20, 1964, 30–36.

93. Underwood, "This Is the Way the Girls Go."

94. AMA Committee on Medical Aspects of Sports, May 2–3, 1964, quoted in *JOHPER* (November–December 1964): 46.

95. AMA Committee on Medical Aspects of Sports, May 2–3, 1964.

96. Mabel Locke to Grace Fox, July 20, 1956 (file drawer 4, NAPECW papers).

97. For example, Thomas J. Hamilton lauded AAHPER at the "Sports for Fitness" workshop (April 13, 1960), and government speakers addressed AAHPER conventions (for example, Bud Wilkinson, May 31, 1962) (ser. 8, DGWS papers).

98. Jane Mott, PCPF Report 1958 (ser. 8, DGWS papers).

99. At the very least they attended the 1958 Fitness Conference at the Air Force Academy, the 1956 and 1958 PCPF conferences, the March 1959 President's Fitness Conference, and helped plan the 1960 White House Conference on Children and Youth, and were on the Citizen's Advisory Committee.

100. Thelma Bishop to Executive Council, September 1959 (ser. 7, DGWS papers).

101. Ruth Wilson to Dwight D. Eisenhower, July 20, 1956 (file drawer 4, NAPECW papers).

102. Comments on PCYF college proposal (correspondence 1956–1959, file drawer 1,

NAPECW papers). Ley's statement began, "Many sports organizations and writers are voicing a need to develop bigger and better programs for girls and women." Ley, editorial, "Are You Ready?" *JOHPER* (April 1963): 20.

103. Downing, "Women's Basketball"; Mary Ellen McKee to NAPECW Executive Board, Spring 1960; Maria Sexton, Report of the AAU and USOC Meeting, November 29, 1961; see also minutes of the USODC Women's Advisory Board (Box 4, NAPECW papers).

104. Ley, "Are You Ready?" 20.

105. *Proceedings of the Third National Institute*, 12.

106. *Proceedings of the First National Institute*, 10.

107. Crafts, "Building on Basics," *Second National Institute*, 79.

108. *Proceedings of the Second National Institute*, 115; *Proceedings of the First National Institute*; Sara Staff Jernigan, "Women and the Olympics," *JOHPER* (April 1962): 25.

109. "Fresh Winds Are Stirring," *JOHPER* (March 1967): 27–28.

110. This refusal came even after numerous revisions and personal pleas by the head of the PCYF. In addition, at the "Sports for Fitness" workshops, the recommendations reflected the influence of women from DGWS.

111. *Proceedings of the First National Institute*, 31–32.

112. Jernigan to Holbrook, October 9, 1962 (file drawer 4, NAPECW papers).

113. Ley, "Are You Ready?" 22.

114. *Proceedings of the Third National Institute*, 12–13.

115. Correspondence after Basketball Rules Committee meeting, February 1969 (ser. 5, DGWS papers).

116. The USODC chair, Thomas Hamilton, recognized that the cooperation of women physical educators had been won by careful presentation of the country's goals. He appealed to their concerns when he told participants at the First National Institute (April 1964) that it was important for America not only to display a strong image but also to use athletic talent to "gain friends in other nations." *Proceedings of the First National Institute*, 10.

117. "The Institute Purpose—We Are the Key," *Proceedings of the Third National Institute*, 4.

118. *Proceedings of the First National Institute*, 12–13.

119. Again, DGWS made the move in part because it was clear that college women wanted such competition, because they agreed with it, and because they feared that if DGWS did not run it, others might. Phebe Scott to Celeste Ulrich, November 24, 1965 (file drawer 4, NAPECW papers); Lucille Magnusson to Carl Troester, August 13, 1967 (ser. 4, DGWS papers); Conference Report on Competition for Girls and Women, February 10–12, 1965; Frances McGill to Celeste Ulrich, December 9, 1965 (file drawer 4, NAPECW papers).

120. Charlotte Lambert, "Middle of the Road Position Paper on Women's Intercollegiate Athletics," *JOHPER* (May 1969): 75–77. One of CIAW's first actions was to make sure DGWS would be unopposed by any other group. So among others, Katherine Ley wrote Walter Byers, head of the NCAA (the main organization running men's intercollegiate sports) to confirm it had no interest in conducting women's events. Byers's assistant executive director assured Ley that the NCAA dealt only with men's events. Katherine Ley to Walter Byers, October 6, 1967; Charles Neinas to Richard Larkins, March 8, 1966 (ser. 4, DGWS papers).

121. JoAnne Thorpe to Rachel Bryant, August 3, 1967 (ser. 4, DGWS papers); Lambert, "Middle of the Road Position Paper," 75; *Proceedings of the Third National Institute*, 9; *Proceedings of the Fourth National Institute* (1967); *JOHPER* (March 1967): 28; DGWS Study Committee on Intercollegiate Competition for Women, January 6–7, 1966 (file drawer 4, NAPECW papers).

122. Alyce Cheska to Maria Sexton, December 28, 1967; Lucille Magnusson to Maria Sexton, December 14, 1967 (ser. 4 DGWS papers); 1965 Conference Report, "Competition for Girls and Women" (ser. 2, DGWS papers); "DGWS National Intercollegiate Athletic Championships for Women," *JOHPER* (February 1968): 24–27.

123. Partly it may have been their approach: "Practice expressing your opinions—in a nice way, of course," Ley told her colleagues (*Proceedings of the Second National Institute*, 132). But power relations is the more likely explanation of why no one listened to women physical educators.

124. Katherine Ley to Carol Harding, September 10, 1968 (CIAW file, ser. 4, DGWS papers).

125. *Proceedings of the First National Institute*, 32; Betty Hileman, "Philosophy of Coaching," in Barbara Drinkwater, ed. DGWS *Basketball Guide* (August 1963), 52.

126. *JOHPER* (May–June 1962): 10.

127. *Proceedings of the First National Institute*, 32.

128. Katherine Ley, address, National Conference on Secondary School Athletic Administration, December 1962.

129. Lambert, "Middle of the Road Position Paper," 75.

130. To the question, "Will it detract from her femininity?" the pamphlet answered, "No, with sensitive responsible leadership a program of competitive sport should enhance a woman." "Interpretation of the Policies for Competition in Girls' and Women's Sports," Philosophy and Interpretation Committee Report, October 1963.

131. *Proceedings of the Third National Institute*, 9–11.

Part III. Introduction: 1968–1979

1. Woloch, *Women and the American Experience*, 516. Shirley Chisholm made the same point in "My Views on Women in America," in William White, Jr., ed., *North American Reference Encyclopedia of Women's Liberation*.

2. Mary King, *Freedom Song* (New York: William Morrow, 1987), appendix 2, quoted in Mary Beth Norton, ed., *Major Problems in American Women's History* (Lexington, Mass.: D. C. Heath, 1989), 395.

3. National Organization for Women, "Statement of Purpose" (1966), quoted in Norton, ed., *Major Problems in American Women's History*, 397–400.

5. Politicization, 1968–1974

1. Reports to DGWS, 1971 (ser. 6, CIAW papers).

2. Hunt, "Governance," 86.

3. DGWS Executive Committee minutes, October 22–25, 1970 (AAHPER archives); "1968 Problems at Coaches' meeting which need to be handled by DGWS" (ser. 6, CIAW papers); Reports to DGWS, 1966–1971 (ser. 6, CIAW papers); CIAW Procedures Manual, 1970; Hunt, "Governance," 82, 73–76.

4. They planned to spend $5,425 in 1967–68, $4,600 in 1968–69. CIAW Proposed budget, 1967–68, and Report to DGWS, November 6, 1967 (ser. 6, CIAW papers, AAHPER archives).

5. Report to DGWS, November 6, 1967 (ser. 6, CIAW papers).

6. Ibid.

7. Katherine Ley to Phebe Scott, March 20, 1968 (ser. 5, CIAW papers).

8. DGWS Executive Committee minutes, October 22–25, 1970; Hunt, "Governance," 78–79.

9. Hunt, "Governance," 79–80.

10. Other sections of the Civil Rights Act of 1964 prohibited sex discrimination in employment and prohibited racial discrimination in public education. U.S. Public Law 88–352.

11. House Committee on Education and Labor, *Hearings before the Special Subcommittee on Education on Sec. 805 of H.R. 16098*, 91st Cong., 2d sess., June and July 1970.

12. The blatant manifestations of discrimination described that summer focused mainly on the problems of professors and graduate students. A few people did foresee that any law promoting educational equity would apply to undergraduates' recreational activities. Dr. Peter Muirhead, deputy assistant secretary of the Department of Health, Education, and Welfare's (HEW) Education Office, Frankie Freeman of the U.S. Commission on Civil Rights, and Jerris Leonard, an assistant attorney general in the Civil Rights Division of the Justice Department all warned that there might be problems with Representative Green's proposed bill. No one on the subcommittee followed up on their concerns, however. House Committee on Education and Labor, *Hearings on Sec. 805 of H.R. 16098* (1970), 678, 664, 650.

13. House Committee on Education and Labor, *Hearings before the Special Subcommittee on Education on H.R. 32, H.R. 5191, H.R. 5192, H.R. 5193, and H.R. 7248*, 92d Cong., 1st sess., March, April, and July 1971, 41, 74.

14. No one pressed HEW secretary Elliot Richardson's vague testimony that the legislation would insure that sex "discrimination is prohibited at all levels within the educational institution itself, as applied to students." House Committee on Education and Labor, *Hearings on H.R. 32 et al.* (1971), 381.

15. Ibid., 579–80.

16. *Congressional Record*, 92d Cong., 1st sess., August 6, 1971, 117, pt. 23:30399.

17. In particular, Bayh informed the Senate the bill's enforcement provisions would parallel those of Title VI. *Cong. Rec.*, 92d Cong., 2d sess., February 28, 1972, 118, pt. 5:5803, 5807.

18. Privacy, therefore, seemed to be one factor that could be taken into account when deciding if the sexes might be treated differently. But apparently there were few other factors, because he also said, "in the area of services, once a student is accepted we permit no exceptions." *Cong. Rec.*, February 28, 1972, pp. 5807, 5812.

19. Bayh had made one other reference to sports: "I do not read this as requiring integration of dormitories between the sexes, nor do I feel that it mandates the desegregation of football fields. What we are trying to do is provide equal access to the educational process and the extracurricular activities in a school, where there is not a unique fact such as football involved. We are not requiring that intercollegiate football be desegregated, nor that the men's locker room be desegregated." *Cong. Rec.*, August 6, 1971, p. 30407.

20. *Cong. Rec.*, February 28, 1972, p. 5808.

21. Title IX "was easily accepted by the conference." With regard to Title IX, the Conference Committee agreed to use the Senate language which exempted fewer institutions' admissions policies; kept the House amendment allowing separate living facilities; and allowed an adjustment period for an institution's admissions policy only if it was changing over from single sex to coed. *Cong. Rec.*, 92d Cong., 2d sess., May 23, 1972, 118, pt. 14: 18514, 18437.

22. *Cong. Rec.*, February 28, 1972, p. 5808.

23. Margot Polivy, interview by author, Washington, D.C., March 28, 1989.

24. Burns, "Reconstructing Leadership Experiences," 104.86. For this dissertation Burns conducted interviews with former AIAW presidents. She was trying to arrive at a theory for the leadership style she believed they shared, so her purpose was not to distinguish them as individuals. In addition, since their responses were often quite candid, she wanted to preserve their anonymity. Therefore, when they are quoted in her dissertation, their names are not used; thus when I quote from her work, unfortunately I do not know precisely which of the ten presidents I am quoting. This is somewhat awkward, but the anonymity (an essential component to her research) did result in some extraordinary quotations. For physical educators' reluctance to change, see also Burns, ibid., 104, and Celeste Ulrich, "A Whole New Ball Game," speech reprinted in the *Journal of Health, Physical Education, and Recreation* (hereafter *JOHPER*) (May 1973): 35.

25. Burns, "Reconstructing Leadership Experiences," 59, 99.

26. General Correspondence file, 1970–1975 (ser. 5, DGWS papers).

27. DGWS Executive Committee minutes, October 21–14, 1971.

28. DGWS General Correspondence file, 1970–1975.

29. Ibid.

30. DGWS Executive Committee minutes, October 21–24, 1971.

31. Statement on National Extramural Competition, October 1964, March 1965 (ser. 8, DGWS papers).

32. The DGWS's Rachel Bryant listed the negative results from the SEC experiment: some schools refused to play against teams with women; males who were beaten out of a good position on the team by a woman quit; coaches humiliated male players who performed poorly against teams that fielded a woman; and there were complications with chaperones and accommodations. Rachel Bryant to George Killian (NJCAA), September 11, 1970 (USCS 1970–1972 file, ser. 5, CIAW papers).

33. DGWS Report, Special Committee, "Women on Men's Teams—Clarification of Position Statement," October 20, 1971 (ser. 8, DGWS papers); DGWS Executive Committee minutes, October 21–24, 1971.

34. Report, DGWS activities, 1970–71, General Correspondence file, 1970–1975 (ser. 5, DGWS papers).

35. Report, "Women on Men's Teams," October 20, 1971; JoAnne Thorpe to DGWS Colleagues, October 1971, DGWS General Correspondence file, 1970–1975.

36. DGWS Executive Committee minutes, April 1–6, 1971; Edith Betts to Camille Dorman, Betty Gene Blanton, and Bobbie Knowles, August 7, 1969 (ser. 7, DGWS papers); Hunt, "Governance," 127–30.

37. DGWS Executive Committee minutes, April 1–6, 1971.

38. Ibid.

39. DGWS and AIAW also consulted with a number of lawyers, who told them they did not think AIAW's stand was illegal. DGWS Executive Committee minutes, October 21–24, 1971; Legal Correspondence file, 1967–1972 (ser. 8, DGWS papers).

40. Betts to Dorman, Blanton, and Knowles, August 7, 1969; Hunt, "Governance," 127.

41. The National Association of Intercollegiate Athletes (NAIA) was another men's intercollegiate organization, with many fewer members than the NCAA and primarily serving smaller schools. In the interest of simplicity, I have left that organization out of the narrative except when it seemed crucial.

42. Actually there had been some communication between CIAW-DGWS and the NCAA in

the mid- and late 1960s when CIAW was being formed and a few schools had asked the NCAA if it was going to offer women's sports. Already Walter Byers demonstrated some turf jealousy when he suggested that DGWS was not an institutional membership organization and therefore not as suited as the NCAA to run a national program. But the NCAA did not move to block CIAW, and unofficially Ernie McCoy told Katherine Ley that the NCAA would stick to its "hands-off" policy with regard to women's sports. Officially, the NCAA moved to confine its activities to male student-athletes and at the same time began a Committee on Intercollegiate Competition for Women in 1968. The committee offered DGWS assistance and advice, emphatically stating they were not interested in taking over women's sports. The CIAW's leaders were not sure what to think but were "nonplused" by the experience. See Hunt, "Governance," 193–94; Donna Lopiano Affidavit and Appendix (Box 70, AIAW papers).

43. Walter Byers memo, February 26, 1971 (cited in Lopiano Affidavit).

44. Lucille Magnusson to commissioners and consultants, March 8, 1971 (in Appendix to Lopiano Affidavit).

45. Bryant explained that historically DGWS had tried to maintain a middle-of-the-road position in the long-standing feud between the NCAA and the AAU. But she saw evidence mounting that both sides wanted to provoke DGWS off the fence. DGWS Executive Committee minutes, April 1–6, 1971.

46. DGWS Executive Committee minutes, April 1–6, 1971.

47. Rachel Bryant to Earl Ramer, April 16, 1971.

48. JoAnne Thorpe and Lucille Magnusson, AIAW Introductory Folder, September 15, 1971 (AIAW newsletters, Box 378, AIAW papers); Hunt, "Governance," 89–90.

49. Bryant to Ramer, April 16, 1971.

50. Hunt, "Governance," 197.

51. George H. Gangwere to Walter Byers, June 17, 1971 (in Appendix to Lopiano Affidavit).

52. Gangwere to Byers, June 17, 1971.

53. JoAnne Thorpe to Walter Byers, October 6, 1971 (in Appendix to Lopiano Affidavit).

54. Rachel E. Bryant to Drs. Troester, Anderson, and Merrick (AAHPER), July 15, 1971 (in Appendix to Lopiano Affidavit).

55. Bryant to Troester, Anderson, and Merrick, July 15, 1971.

56. Hunt, "Governance," 197.

57. CIAW report to DGWS, 1966–1971 (ser. 6, CIAW papers).

58. Burns, "Reconstructing Leadership Experiences," 53.

59. George Gangwere to Walter Byers, August 14, 1971 (in Appendix to Lopiano Affidavit).

60. Lucille Magnusson to Chuck Neinas, September 7, 1971 (in Appendix to Lopiano Affidavit).

61. Gene Duffy, an NCAA rep who attended the meeting, heard the women's objections. To Byers, he reported, "Lucille [Magnusson] didn't indicate that the AIAW would not affiliate with the NCAA. Her concern over Gangwere's plan was that the NAIA and the junior colleges would probably not be willing to affiliate with the NCAA. If the women had their choice, they would prefer to have Gangwere determine a way they could operate independently." Gene Duffy to Chuck Neinas, September 8, 1971 (cited in Appendix to Lopiano Affidavit); Magnusson letter to Neinas, September 7, 1971.

62. Walter Byers to Rachel Bryant, October 12, 1971 (in Appendix to Lopiano Affidavit).

63. Chuck Neinas to Lucille Magnusson, September 23, 1971 (in Appendix to Lopiano Affidavit).

64. Neinas to Magnusson, September 23, 1971.

65. A number of AIAW and DGWS leaders responded to Neinas's letter. Lucille Magnusson wrote Neinas that she was "shocked" by his last sentence. How could they make "adjustments," she asked, when they did not even know what adjustments he referred to, and when they had not even received a copy of the NCAA's proposal? JoAnne Thorpe tried to remain diplomatic, stressing her sincere desire to cooperate. "I am sure that we can work out a quite harmonious arrangement if you wish to," she said. But on one point, she remained firm: "We will not enter into any arrangement where we are controlled by NCAA. I stated this to you in the beginning." Thorpe to Byers, October 6, 1971; Lucille Magnusson to Chuck Neinas, October 1, 1971 (in Appendix to Lopiano Affidavit).

66. Rachel Bryant to Walter Byers, October 8, 1971 (in Appendix to Lopiano Affidavit).

67. Bryant to Byers, October 8, 1971.

68. Byers to Bryant, October 12, 1971.

69. General Roundtable comments, NCAA, *Proceedings of the Annual Convention*, January 1972 (cited in Appendix to Lopiano Affidavit).

70. NCAA, *Proceedings*, January 1972.

71. Ibid.

72. Ibid.

73. One delegate in particular maintained Gangwere was shifting the responsibility and exaggerating the NCAA's role. After all, colleges did not provide men's teams because the NCAA told them to; similarly, colleges were the ones responsible for providing the women on their campuses with fair opportunities. In response to this logic, Gangwere was forced to admit, "This is a problem basically of the schools themselves . . . so it is not a divine right that the NCAA do it." 1972 College Division Roundtable, NCAA, *Proceedings*, January 1972.

74. NCAA Council minutes, April 1972 (cited in Lopiano Affidavit).

75. Any changes in AIAW policies were to be consistent with DGWS philosophy and standards and would be referred to the DGWS's Executive Council. The two groups would share publications and have a voting member on one another's boards. The AIAW would use DGWS rules and referees in its national championships, and DGWS-AAHPER would assist with AIAW's budgetary needs. The AIAW currently could cover only half its costs but hoped to grow enough to be self-supporting soon. Hunt, "Governance," 120–25.

76. Larry Van Dyne, "NCAA Writes the Rules, Polices 18 College Sports," *Chronicle of Higher Education* (hereafter, *Chronicle*), November 26, 1973, 6.

77. At first AIAW had championships in golf, gymnastics, track and field, badminton, swimming and diving, volleyball, tennis, and basketball. Lucille Magnusson, "The What and Why of AIAW," *JOHPER* (March 1972): 71.

78. *NEA v. Kellmeyer*, in Southern Florida District Court, No. 73, 21 Civ NCR, papers filed to Carole Oglesby, January 17, 1973 (in "Legal Suit" file, ser. 8, DGWS papers)); Hunt, "Governance," 134.

79. Carole Oglesby to Allan West (NEA's executive director), January 30, 1973 (ser. 8, DGWS papers).

80. Oglesby to West, January 30, 1973.

81. Oglesby's handwritten note to Laurie Mabry on letter from Oglesby to West (ser. 8, DGWS papers).

82. Their lack of money certainly worried AIAW's officers. In the short period of time they had, they could not find anyone who might donate services to the cause. Hunt, "Governance," 136–39.

83. Hunt, "Governance," 134–35.

84. Ibid., 139; Polivy, interview.

85. Hunt, "Governance," 140.

86. Ibid., 147.

87. Mary Rekstad and Betty Hartman, "1972–73 Report to the Division for Girls' and Women's Sports Executive Council," April 2, 1973 ("Legal Suit" file, ser. 8, DGWS papers).

88. AIAW-DGWS Philosophical Statement and New Interim Regulations, reprinted in "Policies on Women Athletes Change," *JOHPER* (September 1973): 51–52.

89. Quoted in Starnes, "Ethical Crisis Gripping Big-Time Intercollegiate Sports," March 10, 1974, 1, 52.

90. Burns, "Reconstructing Leadership Experiences," 54.

91. AIAW presidents quoted (in order of appearance in text) in Burns, "Reconstructing Leadership Experiences," 55, 74 and 85, 87, 85–86. Later Burns asserts: "Any challenging ideology has less direct access to the power of definition. Therefore, women must spend an inordinate amount of time legitimizing that alternative ideology and themselves as leaders" (148).

92. AIAW presidents quoted in Burns, "Reconstructing Leadership Experiences," 54, 81.

93. Executive Director's Report, 1982 AIAW Delegate Assembly (in Appendix to Lopiano Affidavit); Joan Hult, "First AIAW Delegate Assembly," *JOHPER* (March 1974): 79–80.

94. In addition, delegates steadily queried Jack Whitaker, a Kansas City lawyer, who, since HEW had not yet released regulations, rarely could give them a certain answer. Jack Whitaker to AIAW Delegate Assembly (in "Title IX" file, Box 294, AIAW papers).

95. Jack Whitaker to AIAW Delegate Assembly.

96. Edith Betts struggled to articulate the general worry, asking, "If you decide to go a route that is a more educational philosophy rather than a business philosophy, because the men's program is there as a precedent, do we have to be equal to their educationally unsound things as well as their educationally sound things?"

97. Marjorie Blaufarb, speech to AIAW Delegate Assembly, "Solomon's Judgment on Women's Sports," November 4, 1973 ("Title IX—AIAW D.A." file, Box 294, AIAW papers).

98. Blaufarb, "Solomon's Judgment."

99. Ibid.

100. Hunt, "Governance," 172–74.

101. Bart Barnes and Nancy Scannell, "No Sporting Chance," *Washington Post*, May 12, 1974, A1.

102. Robert Scannell, dean of physical education at Penn State, said, "The emergence of women's sport couldn't have come at a worse time. The absolute worst time." Nancy Scannell and Bart Barnes, "Two Schools of Thought on Title 9," *Washington Post*, May 13, 1974, 1.

103. Responding to criticism from the university paper's editor that he should do more for women, Bryant remained unsympathetic, remarking, "If she wants to start a women's program she may have to do what I did when I came here—go out and borrow $100,000." Deane McGovern, "People in Sports," *NYT*, March 14, 1974, 49.

104. Nancy Scannell and Bart Barnes, "The Financial Bind," *Washington Post*, May 14, 1974, 1, 10.

105. Nancy Scannell, "Suit Tests Sex Bias at Maryland U," *Washington Post*, May 22, 1974, E1.

106. Barnes and Scannell, "No Sporting Chance."

107. Per the NCAA's analysis of the draft of proposed guidelines, according to Cheryl Fields, "Fear of Effect on Athletics Delays Sex-Bias Guidelines," *Chronicle*, March 18, 1974, 5.

108. Basketball did indeed, however, bring in enough money at some schools to support some other nonrevenue-producing teams. Joseph Durso, "Athletic Recruiting: A Campus Crisis," *NYT*, March 10, 1974, 1, 10.

109. Barnes and Scannell, "No Sporting Chance."

110. Ibid.

111. Barnes and Scannell, "No Sporting Chance."

112. Ibid.

113. Jay Searcy, "Women Battle for Funds on College Sports Scene," *NYT*, May 19, 1974, 9.

114. Scannell and Barnes, "Two Schools of Thought."

115. Ibid.

116. Minutes of Division I Roundtable, NCAA, *Proceedings*, January 1974.

117. At the Division I Roundtable, Cecil Coleman made the remark that a certain funding strategy would "get the administration off the hook, and the women off their backs." This unintentional double meaning provoked laughter, according to the minutes (NCAA, *Proceedings*, January 1974).

118. Arkansas's athletic director Lou Farrell complained, "You know what happened up at Kansas State, don't you? Women up there have secured some equal rights and poor Jack Hartman can't even get his basketball team on to practice now." Searcy, "Women Battle for Funds on College Sports Scene."

119. Joint Legislative Committee report, NCAA, *Annual Reports*, 1973–74; Public Relations Committee report, NCAA, *Annual Reports*, 1973–74.

120. Carol Gordon to AIAW Executive Board, March 20, 1974. Also the NCAA took credit for causing changes in the proposed regulations in the Joint Legislative Committee report, NCAA, *Annual Reports*, 1973–74.

121. According to an NCAA memo to college athletic directors, cited in "Washington Notes," *Chronicle*, April 22, 1974, 4.

122. George Gangwere to Walter Byers and Swank Committee, March 18, 1974 (in Appendix to Lopiano Affidavit).

123. Gangwere to Byers and Swank Committee.

124. George Gangwere to Walter Byers and Swank Committee; minutes of Executive Committee meeting, August 19–20, 1974 (NCAA, *Annual Reports*, 1973–74).

125. Swank, quoted in Gordon to AIAW Executive Board, March 20, 1974.

126. Walter Byers to David Swank, March 25, 1974 (in Appendix to Lopiano Affidavit).

127. The NCAA Council qualified this "most strong" endorsement by saying that HEW should promote the "orderly growth" of women's sports "consistent with goals developed by the delegated institutional authorities in men's and women's athletics." Presumably by "orderly growth" the NCAA meant at however snail-like a pace the NCAA—a delegated institutional authority—deemed acceptable. Minutes of NCAA Council meeting, May 3–5, 1974 (NCAA, *Annual Reports*, 1973–74).

128. Byers to Swank, March 25, 1974.

129. In part, the committee repeated arguments that drastic changes would cripple athletic budgets and hurt both men's and women's programs. Even more shrewdly, though, they appealed to AIAW's desire to retain its alternative philosophy. They pointed out that Title IX's mandate of equal treatment would probably require that men's and women's programs use the same rules, and HEW might well declare certain AIAW practices illegal. If men and women could not agree upon a similar philosophy (and clearly they did not want to), the government might simply take the power out of their hands. Thus, the drive for equal opportunity might

have the ironic and cruel result of forcing the AIAW right out of existence. The NCAA men hoped Gordon would be equally alarmed by HEW's plans, and that AIAW also would voice its opposition to the regulations—soon. Gordon to AIAW Executive Board, March 20, 1974; Byers to Swank, March 25, 1974.

130. *Cong. Rec.*, Senate Proceedings, 93rd Cong., 2d sess., May 20, 1974, 120, pt. 12:15322–323.

131. "Were HEW, in its laudable zeal to guarantee equal athletic opportunities to women, to promulgate rules which damage the financial base of intercollegiate sports," Tower explained, "it will have thrown out the baby with the bath water." *Cong. Rec.*, Senate Proceedings, May 20, 1974, pp. 15322–323.

132. Ibid., pp. 15322–323.

133. Cheryl M. Fields, "Revenue-Producing Intercollegiate Sports Freed From Sex-Bias Rules by Senate," *Chronicle*, May 28, 1974, 4.

134. The language left wide loopholes in determining what was "necessary" for revenue-producing sports and who would make that determination. Nancy Scannell, "Conferees Compromise on Sex Bias Law," *Washington Post*, June 12, 1974, D4.

135. In fact, no men seemed to consider it might be possible to achieve quality athletic programs for both men and women. Annoyed, AIAW responded, "Our organization is not naive regarding the tremendous problem that revenue-producing sports create, but neither are we naive about the problems that women's programs have faced and are facing on many campuses." Carol Gordon to Presidents of AIAW Member Institutions, March 1974 (Box 294, AIAW papers).

136. Hunt, "Governance," 176.

137. Gordon to AIAW Executive Board, March 20, 1974.

138. After hearing from HEW's Gwen Gregory that there had been effective pressure from men in sports, and that people who had been "got at by the NCAA have tried to make changes," Carol Gordon told her advisers she was troubled that AIAW had not officially discussed the regulations with HEW. Shortly thereafter, she wrote the presidents of all AIAW colleges. Marjorie Blaufarb to Kay Hutchcraft, March 19, 1974 (Box 294, AIAW papers); Gordon to AIAW Executive Board, March 20, 1974; Carol Gordon to Presidents of AIAW Member Institutions, March 1974.

139. Leotus (Lee) Morrison to AIAW Voting Representatives, June 24, 1974 (Box 294, AIAW papers).

140. Polivy, interview.

141. Leotus Morrison to AIAW Voting Representatives, June 27, 1974.

142. Javits's wording of "reasonable provisions" was even vaguer than Tower's had been. The difference was that while Tower's bill had mistrusted HEW and limited its power, Javits's bill assumed that HEW was capable of writing fair guidelines. *Cong. Rec.*, Conference Report, Proceedings of the House of Representatives, 93rd Cong., 2d sess., July 23, 1974, 120, pt. 19:24572.

143. Joint Legislative Committee report to Executive Committee, May 12, 1974, and NCAA Council minutes (interim action reported at August 21–23, 1974, meeting), NCAA, *Annual Reports*, 1973–74.

144. Morrison to AIAW Voting Representatives, June 27, 1974.

145. Jan Felshin, "The Full Court Press for Women in Athletics," in Barbara J. Hoepner, ed., *Women's Athletics: Coping with Controversy*, 89.

146. Ulrich, "A Whole New Ball Game," 35–36.

147. Dorothy V. Harris, "Psychosocial Considerations," *JOHPER* (January 1975): 33.

148. Ulrich, "A Whole New Ball Game."

149. Nancy Scannell and Bill Barnes, "An 'Unfeminine' Stigma," *Washington Post*, May 15, 1974, 1, 10; Joan Hult, "Competitive Athletics for Girls: We Must Act," *JOHPER* (June 1974): 45–46.

150. Dawn E. Evans, letter to the editor, *JOHPER* (May 1974): 6; Ulrich, "A Whole New Ball Game"; Sandra Jean Stutzman and Charles McCullough, "Yes–A Steady Refusal to Change" (part of article, "Did DGWS Fail?"), *JOHPER* (January 1974): 6.

151. Patricia Gold, letter to the editor, *NYT*, June 15, 1974, sec. 5, p. 2; Felshin, "The Full Court Press," 90; Hult, "Competitive Athletics for Girls," 45–46.

152. Felshin, "The Full Court Press," 91.

153. Hult, "Competitive Athletics for Girls," 45.

154. Felshin, "The Full Court Press," 90.

155. For example, while they appreciated NOW's efforts to fight discrimination by opening up the Little League to girls, they disagreed with its belief that coed sports was the way to go. The NAGWS declared that any path besides separate but equal teams would not guarantee extensive enough opportunity for females. They also thought feminists would disagree with NAGWS's priority of choosing women as coaches and referees rather than "the most qualified person for the job." Given the lack of training for women in those areas, NAGWS recognized that a woman had virtually no chance of being the most qualified applicant, so her lack of opportunity would be perpetuated indefinitely by a gender-blind decision. Whether feminists would have disagreed is uncertain, but what matters is that women in PE perceived that they differed from some in the women's movement. Joan Hult, "Separate but Equal Athletics for Women," *JOHPER* (June 1973): 57–58; on NOW's disapproval of the concept of separate but equal see Joseph B. Treaster, "Little League Proving Just a First Step for Girl Athletes," *NYT*, June 23, 1974, 40.

156. Burns, "Reconstructing Leadership Experiences," 102.

157. Ibid., 103.

158. Ibid., 102.

159. William A. Sievert, "NCAA Concerned About Legality of Its Exclusion of Women," *Chronicle*, January 17, 1972.

160. Katherine Ley to Ms. Mary Wynn Ryan, February 13, 1974 (ser. 6, DGWS papers).

161. Pamela Peridier, "What Should Women's Liberation Mean to You?" *JOHPER* (January 1972): 32.

162. Burns, "Reconstructing Leadership Experiences," 103.

163. At PE conventions talks about women's sports assumed prominence rather than being hidden at the bottom of the agenda. See editor Barbara Hoepner's preface in *Women's Athletics*.

164. Hult, "Separate but Equal Athletics for Women."

165. They organized coaching clinics to provide remedial training for themselves and to bring their level of sophistication about the game up to men's. NAGWS, "Service to the Membership," *JOHPER* (May 1974): 53; Hult, "Competitive Athletics for Girls," 45.

166. Felshin, "The Full Court Press," 91–92; Hult, "Competitive Athletics for Girls," 45; NAGWS, "Service to the Membership," 53.

167. Margaret C. Dunkle, "Equal Opportunity for Women in Sports," in Hoepner, ed., *Women's Athletics*.

168. Mabel Locke, letter to the editor, *JOHPER* (May 1974): 6.

169. Felshin, "The Full Court Press," 92.

170. Gordon S. White, Jr., "Women Are a Problem to N.C.A.A.," *NYT*, January 7, 1975, 39.

171. Betty Menzie, "Sociological Aspects of Women in Sports," in Hoepner, ed. *Women's Athletics*, 109.

172. Harris, "Psychosocial Considerations," 35.

173. Ibid., 34.

174. Hult, "Competitive Athletics for Girls," 45.

175. Felshin, "The Full Court Press," 92.

176. Hult, "Competitive Athletics for Girls," 45.

177. Felshin, "The Full Court Press," p. 45.

178. Bonnie Parkhouse, "The Destiny of Women in Sport: Alpha or Omega?" *JOHPER* (January 1975): 54.

6. Rebellion, 1968–1975

1. The quote in the epigraph is from Billie Jean King and Kim Chapin, *Billie Jean*, 144–45.

2. Quoted in Curry Kirkpatrick, "The Ball in Two Different Courts," *Sports Illustrated*, December 25, 1972.

3. King and Chapin, *Billie Jean*, 58, 142, 112; Billie Jean King and Cynthia Starr, *We Have Come a Long Way*, 112.

4. Grace Lichtenstein characterized King as "accepted but not welcomed" by the tennis establishment because she was too hungry, too eager for recognition, and too ready to make tennis a career. Lichtenstein, *A Long Way Baby: Behind the Scenes in Women's Pro Tennis*, 54–56. For "sounding off" and being warned by the USLTA, see King and Chapin, *Billie Jean*, 76.

5. Quoted in Lumpkin, *Women's Tennis*, 81. See also Billie Jean King, "The Millennium Is Just Around the Corner," *World Tennis* (October 1968): 17; King and Starr, *We Have Come a Long Way*, 101.

6. She gave up her freedom to play wherever she wanted, instead committing herself to a rigorous two-year schedule of exhibitions-matches around the world, for which she was guaranteed $20,000 a year plus expenses. King and Chapin, *Billie Jean*, 84.

7. "The Sporting Scene—Tennis Troubles," *New Yorker*, October 2, 1971, 98; King and Starr, *We Have Come a Long Way*, 123; Gladys Heldman, address, "The Women's Pro Circuit in Tennis."

8. King and Starr, *We Have Come a Long Way*, 123.

9. Heldman, address, "The Women's Pro Circuit"; King and Chapin, *Billie Jean*, 100–101.

10. Jack Kramer with Frank Deford, *The Game: My Forty Years in Tennis*, 79–80; Heldman, address, "The Women's Pro Circuit."

11. The USLTA had had serious losses each year at the national indoor championships, but in 1959 Heldman took over and made an $8,000 profit. King and Starr, *We Have Come a Long Way*, 121.

12. "Women Tennis Stars Threaten Boycott Over Unequal Purse," *NYT*, September 8, 1970, 1; King and Starr, *We Have Come a Long Way*, 125; Heldman, address, "The Women's Pro Circuit"; "8 Women to Shun Coast Event," *NYT*, September 9, 1970; "World Tennis Magazine Signs 9 Girls to Pro Contracts," *World Tennis* (November 1970): 14, 48–50.

13. They hoped the loophole would avoid suspension but allow the tournament to pro-

ceed. They declared they were "contract professionals" (that is, under a temporary agreement with Heldman) and that therefore their tournament did not require USLTA sanction.

14. "World Tennis Magazine Signs 9 Girls," *World Tennis* (November 1970); "9 Women Players Draw U.S.L.T.A. Ban," *NYT*, September 26, 1970; King and Chapin, *Billie Jean*, 104–106; Heldman, address, "The Women's Pro Circuit."

15. Heldman, address, "The Women's Pro Circuit"; King and Chapin, *Billie Jean*, 103–105; "Women Net Rebels Planning Own Tour," *NYT*, September 25, 1970.

16. King and Chapin, *Billie Jean*, 105.

17. King and Starr, *We Have Come a Long Way*, 128–31; Neil Amdur, "Women Revolt in Tennis," *NYT*, February 14, 1971, sec. 5, p. 10.

18. King and Chapin, *Billie Jean*, 107.

19. "Women Lobbers," *Newsweek*, May 3, 1971, 90–91; Lichtenstein, *A Long Way Baby*, 200; King and Starr, *We Have Come a Long Way*, 110.

20. "U.S.L.T.A. Agrees to Lift Ban On Dissident Women's Pro Unit," *NYT*, February 12, 1971, 46; Parton Keese, "Women Players Invited to Join $250,000 Grand Prix of Tennis," *NYT*, April 7, 1971.

21. "Mrs. King Posts Earnings Record," *NYT*, October 4, 1971, 58; "Billie Jean King Talks with Nixon," *NYT*, October 5, 1971, 53.

22. Heldman, address, "The Women's Pro Circuit"; Neil Amdur, "U.S.L.T.A. Faults Women's Lob on Fees," *NYT*, January 8, 1972; "Women's Pro Tour Reaches Agreement with U.S.L.T.A.," *NYT*, February 15, 1972, 41.

23. "No, No, Not Suspension Again!" *World Tennis* (November 1972): 11. Heldman even filed a lawsuit against USLTA, charging it with an unlawful and maliciously conceived conspiracy to undermine her tour's arrangements. It was soon dropped. See the *New York Times* for January 27, 1973, and February 27 and 28, 1973.

24. King and Chapin, *Billie Jean*, 109–12; Chris Evert Lloyd with Neil Amdur, *Chrissie; My Own Story*, 59–66; Heldman, address, "The Women's Pro Circuit"; Pete Axthelm, "Tennis: A Triumph for Women's Lob," *Newsweek*, June 26, 1972, 56–63.

25. "World Tennis Body Issues Ultimatum to Women Players," *NYT*, April 16, 1973, 57; Neil Amdur, "Split Killing Women's Tennis," *NYT*, April 15, 1973, sec. 5, p. 4.

26. Lichtenstein, *A Long Way Baby*, 198; Heldman, address, "The Women's Pro Circuit"; King and Starr, *We Have Come a Long Way*, 142; Neil Amdur, "Tennis Near Peace Pact for Women," *NYT*, April 10, 1973, 51.

27. The first year's (1971) total prize money was $309,000; the second, $501,000; the third, $775,000. Lichtenstein, *A Long Way Baby*, 198.

28. King and Starr, *We Have Come a Long Way*, 142: Heldman, address, "The Women's Pro Circuit."

29. King and Starr, *We Have Come a Long Way*, 120; King and Chapin, *Billie Jean*, 100–101; "Women Tennis Stars Threaten Boycott Over Unequal Purses," *NYT*, September 8, 1970, 1. Margaret Court said, "I honestly didn't believe we were entitled to equal prize money" (Margaret Court and George McGann, *Court on Court*, 157–60).

30. "Women's Lob," *Time*, December 7, 1970, 78.

31. Billie Jean King and Frank Deford, *Billie Jean*.

32. Axthelm, "Tennis: A Triumph for Women's Lob," 56–63. And Stan Smith reportedly said, "They should all be home having babies" ("Women Lobbers," *Newsweek*, May 3, 1971, 90–91).

33. Kirkpatrick, "The Ball in Two Different Courts."

34. Axthelm, "Tennis: A Triumph for Women's Lob"; King and Starr, *We Have Come a Long Way*, 120; "Women's Lob," *Time*, December 7, 1970.

35. Durr and Wade both quoted in Axthelm, "Tennis: A Triumph for Women's Lob." See also Margaret Court on the women's tour (Court and McGann, *Court on Court*, 157–60); and for Goolagong, King and Starr, *We Have Come a Long Way*, 132.

36. Anonymous pro quoted in Russell, "Tennis and the Woman Player," 86–87.

37. Quoted in Lichtenstein, *A Long Way Baby*, 86.

38. Quoted in King and Starr, *We Have Come a Long Way*, 128.

39. Quoted in Lichtenstein, *A Long Way Baby*, 137.

40. Quoted in Lichtenstein, *A Long Way Baby*, 86.

41. Evert Lloyd and Amdur, *Chrissie*, 169.

42. Quoted in Lichtenstein, *A Long Way Baby*, 86.

43. Quoted in Vincent Hanna and Julie Heldman, "The Young Champion," *World Tennis* (November 1971): 58; "Chris Evert Tennis Togs: Netting a Bundle at Age 18," *NYT*, January 13, 1973.

44. Billie Jean King, interview by author, December 10, 1988 (telephone); Lichtenstein, *A Long Way Baby*, 151.

45. King, interview.

46. "Scorecard," *Sports Illustrated*, October 5, 1970, 11.

47. Kirkpatrick, "The Ball in Two Different Courts."

48. Parton Keese, "Women Set Up Tennis Tour," *NYT*, October 8, 1970. King recalled, "Gladys used to say, 'Oh we're not women's lib, we're women's lob' because she was trying to lighten it up, you know, we're in the entertainment business folks, lighten up" (King, interview).

49. She said they seemed like liberal Democrats, a category she did not put herself in. King and Chapin, *Billie Jean*, 140–42.

50. To her, women's lib meant every woman ought to be able to pursue whatever career or personal lifestyle she chose as a full and equal member of society without fear of sexual discrimination. King and Chapin, *Billie Jean*, 140–42.

51. King, interview.

52. King and Deford, *Billie Jean*, 127.

53. King and Chapin, *Billie Jean*, 148–60.

54. King and Deford, *Billie Jean*, 127.

55. King believed in the marketing theory that the public won't buy unless they're in their "comfort zone": "Because we are performers and we have to relate to the public, and if the public is uncomfortable with that, then you're hurting your opportunity" (King, interview).

56. Dave Anderson, "Love at Wimbledon," *NYT*, July 7, 1974, sec. 5, p. 5.

57. Dave Anderson, "The Chris and Jimmy Romance Revival," *NYT*, September 6, 1975, 13.

58. Edwin Shrake, "A Long Way, Bébé," *Sports Illustrated*, March 6, 1972, 35–42.

59. Quoted in King and Chapin, *Billie Jean*, 111.

60. King, interview; Edwin Shrake told *Sports Illustrated* readers he asked Françoise Durr about lesbians on the tour (see Shrake, "A Long Way Bébé,").

61. Evert Lloyd and Amdur, *Chrissie*, 168.

62. In retrospect it's clear that Billie Jean King, for one, was romantically involved with a woman at the time (see King and Deford, *Billie Jean*). Although the press did ask a lot of rude questions, certain reporters who regularly followed the tour (such as Neil Amdur, Bud

Collins, and Grace Lichtenstein) had plenty of reason to suspect certain women of being lesbians, but did not give them "bad press" or publish innuendoes. Wanting the tour to succeed and sharing the perception that the tour would be harmed by discussions of lesbianism, I believe they chose to "protect" the players. Grace Lichtenstein, for example (*A Long Way Baby*, 188), published the detail that Marilyn Barnett's attaché case was a gift from her boyfriend. If Barnett told her that to try to mislead her, did she really believe it? Whether she did or not, why print it unless she wanted to imply that Barnett was heterosexual?

63. Many people characterized lesbian-labeling as social control. With regard to the phenomenon in sports, see Guthrie, "Homophobia: Its Impact on Women in Sport," and Roberta S. Bennett et al., "Changing the Rules of the Game," 370–79.

64. See King and Chapin, *Billie Jean*, esp. 6; Robert Lipsyte's column, *NYT*, July 28, 1974, sec. 5, p. 2. After following the tour for a year, Lichtenstein said that male spectators alternately admired the women's shots and remarked about their chromosomes or hen-pecked husbands. The anti-Billie Jean King contingent couldn't decide whether they disliked her more for her abortion or because she was a lesbian, yet they "usually wanted to sleep with her." She claimed that toward King there was a mixture of admiration, hatred, and lust. Lichtenstein, *A Long Way Baby*, 176.

65. Quoted in Axthelm, "Tennis: Triumph for Women's Lob."

66. A photo of the poster is included in Lichtenstein, *A Long Way Baby*.

67. An appendix in Riggs's autobiography is filled with pages of his "tricks." Bobby Riggs with George McGann, *Court Hustler*, appendix.

68. Pete Axthelm, "The Hustler," *Newsweek*, May 28, 1973.

69. King and Chapin, *Billie Jean*, 160–65.

70. The match started sooner than Court expected and although Riggs had warmed up for hours, she had not; and during their brief collective warm-up together, he intentionally did not hit her the sorts of balls she needed. Riggs and McGann, *Court Hustler*, 196.

71. Court and McGann, *Court on Court*, 70.

72. Riggs and McGann, *Court Hustler*, 173.

73. Riggs and McGann, *Court Hustler*, 173–77.

74. Pete Axthelm, "The Battle of the Sexes," *Newsweek*, September 24, 1973, 82–85; "How Bobby Runs and Talks, Talks, Talks," *Time*, September 10, 1973, 54–60; Lichtenstein, *A Long Way Baby*, 29.

75. Lichtenstein, *A Long Way Baby*, 24–29.

76. Pete Axthelm, "The Hustler Outhustled," *Newsweek*, October 1, 1973, 63–64; "How Bobby Runs and Talks, Talks, Talks," *Time*, September 10, 1973; "How King Rained on Riggs' Parade," *Time*, October 1, 1973.

77. Lichtenstein, *A Long Way Baby*, 23, 234; King and Chapin, *Billie Jean*, 177–78.

78. "How King Rained on Riggs' Parade," *Time*, October 1, 1973; King and Deford, *Billie Jean*, 82.

79. During the 1960s the number of recreational players in the United States doubled (for a total of 10.7 million). But in 1974 alone there was a 68 percent increase in the number (for a total of 33.9 million). *NYT*, February 14, 1974.

80. King and Starr, *We Have Come a Long Way*, 143–45; King and Chapin, *Billie Jean*, 170.

81. Parton Keese, "Tennis Decides All Women Are Created Equal, Too," *NYT*, July 20, 1973, 19.

82. "Women Also Consider Boycott of Wimbledon Tourney," *NYT*, June 21, 1973, 47.

83. "Wimbledon Concession Is Small," *NYT*, January 30, 1975.

84. "Women Pros Vote Ban on Wimbledon," *NYT*, February 7, 1975.

85. King and Starr, *We Have Come a Long Way*, 154; "British Pros Set to Defy Mrs. King," *NYT*, November 20 and 21, 1974.

86. Russell, "Tennis and the Woman Player," 103.

87. King and Chapin, *Billie Jean*, 191, 200.

88. Ibid., 197.

89. Evert Lloyd, *Chrissie*, 147–60.

90. Ibid., 147.

91. Heldman estimated she funneled about $100,000 into the tour, especially donating to purses (King and Starr, *We Have Come a Long Way*, 128). Professional tennis has not ever supported itself solely on gate receipts—it is dependent upon corporate sponsorship and television revenues for its continued survival.

7. Equality and/or Difference?

1. The statement in the epigraph is quoted in Cheryl Fields, "Striking a Balance in Women's Sports," *Chronicle of Higher Education* (hereafter, *Chronicle*), January 23, 1978, 5.

2. Even Gwen Gregory, who did most of the drafting of the guidelines, grew impatient with the delay. Her superiors held back from issuing the regulations. *Education Daily*, March 15, 1974 (copy in "Fear of Effect on Athletics Delays Guidelines" file, Box 294, AIAW papers).

3. There the courts held that a school's educational functions included any service, facility, activity, or program which it operated or sponsored, including athletics or other extracurricular activities. The introduction of the regulations cited *Brenden v. Independent School District*, 742, 477 F. 2d 1292 (8th Cir. 1973); in 45 CFR Part 86, *Federal Register* 39 (June 20, 1974): 22228–22240. The HEW also cited another case that implied sports programs ought to be covered, which had declared that federal funds were not to be used to support programs that might be "infected by a discriminatory environment." *Board of Public Instruction of Taylor Co., FL v. Finch*, 414 F. 2d 1068, 1078–79 (5th cir. 1969), in *Federal Register* 39, June 20, 1974.

4. Proposed Sex Discrimination Regulations, *Federal Register* 39 (June 20, 1974): 22228–22240.

5. Eric Wentworth, "HEW Offers 'Nondisruptive' Bans on Sex Bias," *Washington Post*, June 19, 1974, D1.

6. HEW officials said that instead of trying to coerce them, its investigators would take into consideration schools' efforts at voluntary compliance. Wentworth, "HEW Offers 'Nondisruptive' Bans on Sex Bias"; Eric Wentworth, "U.S. Sets Curbs on Sex Bias," *Washington Post*, June 19, 1974, 1.

7. Proposed Sex Discrimination Regulations, *Federal Register* 39 (June 20, 1974): 22228–22240.

8. AIAW Comment to the Director of the Office of Civil Rights (OCR) in the matter of Proposed HEW Title IX Regulations, submitted by Margot Polivy, October 15, 1974 (Box 294, AIAW papers).

9. AIAW liked that the per capita method allowed men's and women's athletic administrators some options about how they spent their money. If women did not want to spend quite as much on recruiting, they could shift the money elsewhere, and if the men's athletic department preferred to spend more on football and ignore wrestling, it could do that.

10. If men's and women's athletic departments merged, they feared, female employees,

who had significant teaching but less coaching experience, would be at a disadvantage. Women who had authority in their own PE department would become subordinate to male heads of athletic departments and lose their influence. Surely, the comment implied, Title IX should not result in women losing control in their own area of expertise. AIAW Comment to Director of OCR, October 15, 1974.

11. NCAA Draft of Comments to the Department of Health, Education, and Welfare on the Proposed Regulations on Nondiscrimination on the Basis of Sex in Education Programs and Activities Receiving Federal Financial Assistance (probably September 1974) (copy in Box 70, AIAW papers).

12. In support of that claim, the NCAA cited statistics about the increase in women's intercollegiate athletic programs since 1966, as if the NCAA had promoted that growth. Speaking for male-run athletic departments, the NCAA argued they deserved no culpability for limiting women in the past and then gave them credit for expanding women's opportunities in the present. The NCAA implied that women previously had not been interested in sports and that therefore male athletic directors owed them little. NCAA Draft of Comments to HEW.

13. NCAA Draft of Comments to HEW.

14. Minutes, NCAA Committee on Women's Athletics, October 10, 1974 (in Appendix to Donna Lopiano Affidavit, Box 70, AIAW papers); Hunt, "Governance," 205.

15. Minutes, NCAA Committee on Women's Athletics, October 10, 1974.

16. Sensing the NCAA might be up to something, AIAW leaders made a number of inquiries to NCAA officials but learned nothing. Then on November 20, a month after the council had met, Carol Gordon (of the NCAA's Committee on Women's Athletics) received word from David Swank. "The Council has agreed we should continue our negotiations," he wrote, "but hope[s] that we can get some matter resolved very promptly so that this is not left without solution. I doubt very much that we will have any opportunity to have the joint committee meet before the January Council meeting." Swank's vague letter did not exactly lie to Gordon, but communicated only part of the truth. It led AIAW to believe that the NCAA had put matters about women's sports on hold. Hunt, "Governance," 204–206; David Swank to Carol Gordon, November 20, 1974 (in Lopiano Affidavit); NCAA Council minutes, October 21–23, 1974 (NCAA, *Annual Reports*, 1973–74).

17. John Fuzak, Report of the Council, NCAA, *Proceedings of the Annual Convention*, January 1975.

18. "NCAA Eyes Women's Sports," *Chronicle*, January 13, 1975, 3.

19. NCAA Council minutes, January 3–7, 1975 (NCAA, *Annual Reports*, 1974–75).

20. Division II Roundtable, NCAA, *Proceedings*, January 1975.

21. Swank explained, "If the NCAA would insist its standards are the best and the women's organization would insist its standards were the best, the institution is caught in a bind [over] which standard shall it comply with. I think this is one of the reasons that the Council feels they ought to proceed in the way they are going." General Roundtable, NCAA, *Proceedings*, January 1975; Gordon S. White, Jr., "Women Are a Problem to N.C.A.A.," January 7, 1975, *NYT*, 39, 41.

22. Pressed by AIAW supporters about why there was so much secrecy surrounding the proposals, an NCAA rep said the timing had prevented NCAA officials from publicizing the matter, but also that the NCAA staff was not obligated to inform either AIAW or even its own Committee on Women's Athletics about its report. Hunt, "Governance," 207–209.

23. "N.C.A.A.'s Plan Draws Criticism," *NYT*, January 8, 1975, 45.

24. Ibid.

25. Hunt, "Governance," 208.

26. Business Session, January 8, 1975 (NCAA, *Proceedings*, January 1975).

27. NCAA, *Proceedings*, January 1975, appendix.

28. "Report of the Council of the NCAA on the Several Issues Involved in the Administration of Women's Intercollegiate Athletics at the National level," April 28, 1975 (copy in Appendix to Lopiano Affidavit).

29. "NCAA Council Report on the Several Issues."

30. "NCAA Council Report on the Several Issues."

31. Leotus Morrison to AIAW Institutional Presidents, January 23, 1975 (in Appendix to Lopiano Affidavit).

32. "Response of the AIAW to the NCAA Report on the Several Issues Involved in the Administration of Women's Intercollegiate Athletics," May 1975 (Lopiano Affidavit).

33. Leotus Morrison to AIAW Voting Representatives, April 29, 1975.

34. Section 431(d) of the General Education Provisions Act, as amended by section 509(a) of P.L. 93–380, signed into law August 21, 1974. See letter from Rep. James O'Hara to Caspar Weinberger, June 16, 1975, included in House Committee on Education and Labor, *Hearings before the Subcommittee on Postsecondary Education on "Sex Discrimination Regulations,"* 94th Cong., 1st sess., June 17–26, 1975.

35. HEW made it clear that it would not be judging athletic departments by their aggregate expenditures on males and females. Nor would it overlook justifiable differences in the needs of particular teams or sports. However, that did not mean HEW would be ignoring financial considerations altogether. Money would be a relevant factor, especially if, for example, men's teams were given greater per diem allowance or travel accommodations, or three sets of uniforms while the women's team got one. In general, male and female athletes and teams had to be treated comparably.

36. Title IX Regulations and HEW's discussion of changes by sections; see esp. paragraphs 86.34, 86.37, and 86.41 (*Federal Register* 40, no. 108 [June 4, 1975]: 24128–24144).

37. *Federal Register* 40, June 4, 1975.

38. Caspar Weinberger testimony, June 26, 1975, *Hearings on "Sex Discrimination Regulations,"* 439.

39. The resolutions were introduced by James Martin (R—N.C.) and James O'Hara (R–Mich.) in the House, and Jesse Helms (R–N.C.) in the Senate. The Senate took no action on Helms's resolution. But in the House, the resolution (H330) was sent to the Committee on Education and Labor. Four different subcommittees shared jurisdiction on the matter, but only the Subcommittee on Postsecondary Education held hearings.

40. Of those sending letters to the subcommittee, 58 percent mentioned sports, and of those, 60 percent mentioned no other part of the guidelines except sports.

41. Groups like NOW, the Women's Equity Action League (WEAL), and the Federation of Organizations for Professional Women joined sportswomen in defending the regulations.

42. Tom Osborne, *Hearings on "Sex Discrimination Regulations,"* 50.

43. In November 1974, two years after passage of the law, Representative Green stated on the floor of the House, "When funds for athletic departments come out of tuition, fees, or tax dollars, women students are to have equal opportunity with men. But intercollegiate sports financed by gate receipts, is an entirely different matter, and was not covered by Title IX." Quoted by John Fuzak, president of the NCAA (*Hearings on "Sex Discrimination Regulations,"* 99).

44. Maxie T. Lambright to Rep. James O'Hara, June 18, 1975, *Hearings on "Sex Discrimination Regulations,"* 626–27.

45. *Hearings on "Sex Discrimination Regulations,"* 59, 49, 114.
46. Bob Blackmun testimony, *Hearings on "Sex Discrimination Regulations,"* 52.
47. *Hearings on "Sex Discrimination Regulations,"* 49.
48. Stanley Marshall testimony, *Hearings on "Sex Discrimination Regulations,"* 106, 52.
49. *Hearings on "Sex Discrimination Regulations,"* 101.
50. Stan Watts to Hon. Allan T. Howe, May 23, 1975, *Hearings on "Sex Discrimination Regulations,"* 611.
51. National Association of Collegiate Directors of Athletics to Rep. James O'Hara, *Hearings on "Sex Discrimination Regulations,"* 610.
52. *Hearings on "Sex Discrimination Regulations,"* 173.
53. This court interpretation was of Title VI (on which Title IX was based) and said that a program could be "infected by a discriminatory environment." *Board of Public Instruction of Taylor Co., FL v. Finch,* 414 F. 2d 1068, 1078–79 (5th cir. 1969).
54. Statement of the Eastern Association for Intercollegiate Athletics for Women, *Hearings on "Sex Discrimination Regulations,"* 521–28.
55. *Hearings on "Sex Discrimination Regulations,"* 168–87.
56. Ibid., 168–87. Many football programs were struggling economically (one report said 100 of 128 Division I football programs were operating in the red), and it was certainly not because athletic departments were spending a lot of money on women.
57. Norma Raffel testimony, *Hearings on "Sex Discrimination Regulations,"* 286.
58. Jean Simmons, *Hearings on "Sex Discrimination Regulations,"* 140.
59. *Hearings on "Sex Discrimination Regulations,"* 125.
60. Ibid., 77–90.
61. "Women are eager for equal opportunities in intercollegiate athletics, but to our mind that does not require that women's programs be a carbon copy of the men's," asserted AIAW's Laurie Mabry. "Women must be permitted to develop and participate in programs designed by them, for their needs and interests. We believe this is the spirit of Title IX, and the regulations promulgated by HEW are a start in that direction." Laurie Mabry, *Hearings on "Sex Discrimination Regulations,"* 127.
62. In the first battle, the Subcommittee on Postsecondary Education reported (11–7) the resolution to disapprove the athletic regulations to the full committee. However, in a close vote, the House Education and Labor Committee postponed the bill (21–18), in effect killing it. Then the bill was sent to a new subcommittee, which unanimously rejected it. By then, even if it had not been rejected, the full Congress would not have had time to disapprove the regulations before the forty-five-day period was up. Another bill to exempt revenue-producing sports from the regulations also failed in July. *Congressional Quarterly Almanac* 31, July 8–9, 1975.
63. Sen. Jesse Helms also proposed legislation that would have prevented federal agencies from enforcing Title IX's athletic regulations, but no action was ever taken on it. The Tower bill, S. 2106, read that Title IX's regulations would "not apply to an intercollegiate athletic activity insofar as such activity provides to the institution gross receipts or donations required by such institution to support that activity."
64. Margot Polivy to AIAW and NAGWS Presidents, August 21, 1975 ("Title IX–Amendment, Tower Bill, S. 2106" file, Box 294, AIAW papers).
65. Sen. Roman L. Hruska testimony, U.S. Senate, Committee on Labor and Public Welfare, *"Prohibition of Sex Discrimination, 1975": Hearings before the Subcommittee on Education on S. 2106 to Amend Title IX,* 94th Cong., 1st sess., September 16 and 18, 1975.

334   Notes

66. Byers dismissed the survey because of its low response rate and its irrelevance to the NCAA's legal obligation. Minutes of Joint meeting, September 24–25, 1975 (in Appendix to Lopiano Affidavit).

67. It appears that, having failed on one front, NCAA officers shifted to another. Published minutes of a Conference Call note that the NCAA Council had approved the move before the convention but delayed the decision "pending completion of the recent Convention." Such phrasing makes one wonder whether it still would have gone ahead with the lawsuit if the convention had agreed to annex women's sports. If it had, the organization would have had more control over the direction and pace of equality and could have protected men's sports from any rule changes. Defensively, the minutes claim that the lawsuit was not related to actions regarding women's championships, but acknowledged that fact would "be misunderstood by many." Minutes of Council Conference Call, January 30, 1976 (NCAA, Annual Reports, 1975–76).

68. John A. Fuzak and Stanley J. Marshall to Chief Executive Officers, Faculty Athletic Representatives, and Directors of Athletics of NCAA Institutions, February 13, 1976 (in Appendix to Lopiano Affidavit).

69. NCAA leaders also appeared hypocritical in their willingness to spend money for litigation against Title IX while refusing to enter a declaratory judgment with AIAW (to look into whether the NCAA actually had to offer women's championships).

70. "Women's Sports Group Enters Sex-Bias Suit," Chronicle, May 31, 1976, 2.

71. Margot Polivy to AIAW-NAGWS, August 21, 1975 ("Title IX–Amendment, Tower Bill S. 2106" file, Box 294, AIAW papers); Polivy to Kay Hutchcraft, August 1, 1977 (Box 294, AIAW papers).

72. In particular, they argued over whether formerly gender-separate physical education departments should be merged (some male athletic directors apparently were using that directive to claim that athletic departments had to be merged), and over a booklet suggesting methods for compliance ("Competitive Athletics: In Search of Equal Opportunity") was written by a feminist, Margaret Dunkle, of the Project on the Status and Education of Women. Series of memos in "Report of AAHPER meeting with HEW/OCR Dir, 5/20/76" file (Box 294, AIAW papers); Cheryl Fields, "July 31: Title IX Deadline," Chronicle, November 14, 1977, 9–11; xerox of NCAA News article (no date), in "Title IX: AAHPER Rep Meeting with HEW/OCR Director" file (Box 294, AIAW papers).

73. Peter E. Holmes, director of the Office of Civil Rights, HEW, to Chief State School Officers, September 1975 (copy in "Title IX: Pamphlets, Qs and As, Statements" file, Box 294, AIAW papers).

74. The statistic on numbers of AIAW members is from 1971–72 to 1974–75. "Response of the AIAW to the NCAA Report on the Several Issues Involved in the Administration of Women's Intercollegiate Athletics," May 1975 (in Appendix to Lopiano Affidavit). See also Jay Searcy, "Big Money Is Pointing More Women Toward Pro Sports," NYT, April 14, 1974, sec. 5, p. 5; Cheryl M. Fields, "Demands of Women Athletes Rivaling Those of Men," Chronicle, May 24, 1976, 7.

75. Dr. George H. Gallup, The Gallup Poll: Public Opinion, 1972–1977, vols. 1 and 2; Stanley M. Elam, ed., A Decade of Gallup Polls Toward Education, 1969–1978.

76. Those exercising especially included young people and professional, college-educated, and upper- and middle-income adults. Gallup, The Gallup Poll; Elam, ed., A Decade of Gallup Polls.

77. Elam, ed., *A Decade of Gallup Polls*. Another way that the times boded well was that people seemed ready for some reform in intercollegiate sports. See Steve Cady, "Educators Prepare for First Major Study of Sports in 45 Years," *NYT*, March 10, 1974, 1, 52; Larry Van Dyne, "NCAA Writes the Rules, Polices 18 College Sports," *Chronicle*, November 26, 1973, 6.

78. "Penn State Grants Women Scholarships," *NYT*, May 25, 1974, 21.

79. Charles Crawford, "Title IX: No Reason for Fright," *NYT*, August 10, 1975, sec. 5, p. 2.

80. Crawford, "Title IX: No Reason for Fright."

81. Jack Scott, "Sport and the Masculine Obsession," *NYT*, July 27, 1975, sec. 5, p. 2.

82. Dan Wakefield, "All Boys Aren't Athletes, and Some Survive," *NYT*, May 11, 1975, sec. 5, p. 2.

83. Nadine Brozan, "Girls on the Athletic Field: Small Gains, Long Way to the Goal," *NYT*, January 12, 1976, 40; Jay Searcy, "Women Are No Longer Fenced In by Tradition of Men and Sports at Yale," *NYT*, August 4, 1974, sec. 5, p. 21.

84. Margaret Dunkle of the Project on the Status and Education of Women, quoted in Brozan, "Girls on the Athletic Field."

85. High school girls flooded colleges with requests, but the demand vastly outnumbered the supply. When the University of Miami announced in 1974 that it would award fifteen scholarships, 400 girls immediately applied; at the University of Chicago there were 250 applicants for only two scholarships. Fields, "Demands of Women Athletes Rivaling Those of Men"; Jill Gerston, "Athletic Grants for Women," *NYT*, February 24, 1974, sec. 5, p. 12.

86. Larry Van Dyne, "Women's Basketball: Too Good to Put Down," *Chronicle*, March 31, 1975, 6.

87. Van Dyne, "Women's Basketball."

88. Brozan, "Girls on the Athletic Field."

89. Ibid. Virtually every college had its blatant discrimination. At Western Michigan the male athletes got three pairs of shoes and the females, one, and "as recently as 1976, more money was spent on men's hockey sticks than on any one women's sport" (Ann Northrop, "A New Generation of Athletes," *Ms.*, September 1979, 56–57). At Michigan State spectators at a men's basketball game could enter a free throw contest to win an Oldsmobile; at the women's game, winning the same contest would win a dollar ("Women's Sports Boom—Too Slow for Some," *U.S. News and World Report*, July 10, 1978, 79–80). The women's hockey team at Cornell—which had no lockers at the ice rink—had to wait patiently in line before every practice to use the one-stall bathroom in order to change into their practice equipment. For more examples see *Hearings on "Sex Discrimination Regulations."*

90. "People in Sports," *NYT*, August 12, 1975, 24.

91. One use of ridicule/humor was a basketball coach's comment that women had been "dipping into my pocket ever since I learned about them on a farm in Indiana." Ellen Gerber et al., *The American Woman in Sport*, 237.

92. Editorial, NCAA *News*, July 15, 1975, 2.

93. Ibid.

94. Ibid.

95. Burns, "Reconstructing Leadership Experiences," 65.

96. At first colleges could issue invitations only to high school teams for auditions. Later, AIAW extended its approval to inviting individual students, and by 1979 the organization permitted colleges to subsidize individuals' campus visits.

97. See reports of AIAW delegate assemblies for yearly changes in regulations, and Joan

Hult, "Recruiting the Female Athlete," *Journal of Health, Physical Education, and Recreation* (October 1978); for an assertion of the AIAW's differing emphasis, see Fields, "NCAA Asked to Withdraw Its Women's Sports Plan," *Chronicle*, May 27, 1975, 8.

98. Kent Hannon, "Too Far, Too Fast," *Sports Illustrated*, March 20, 1978, 34–45; Neil Amdur, "As A.I.A.W. Grows, So Do Its Problems," *NYT*, April 8, 1979, sec. 5, p. 7; Fields, "Striking a Balance in Women's Sports," *Chronicle*, January 23, 1978, 5.

99. USC's (male) athletic director believed AIAW's antiharassment recruiting regulations to be fiscally irresponsible; if the school was spending thousands of dollars, it should be certain it was getting the best, which meant numerous in-depth meetings with athletes. Hannon, "Too Far, Too Fast."

100. Hannon, "Too Far, Too Fast."

101. Since few newspapers or periodicals kept up with developments in women's intercollegiate sports, the fact that three of them had articles about AIAW's problems of growth and recruiting lends credibility to the notion that the practices were spreading. However, there also seemed to be a certain crowing tone among some men—a "we told you so" attitude in response to AIAW's apparently struggling efforts to create an ethically superior model of intercollegiate athletics.

102. I agree with this observation made by Kent Hannon in "Too Far, Too fast."

103. October 1975 interview with Carol Gordon, cited in Hunt, "Governance," 284.

104. Hunt, "Governance," 284.

105. Peggy Burke, an AIAW president, said, "I'm in a quandary because, as a feminist, it does bother me that male students can get their way paid to campus and that male coaches can be paid for recruiting, while the women can't. It bothers me, but there are so many excesses." Quoted in Cheryl Fields, "Rules Violations Grow in Women's Sports," *Chronicle*, May 17, 1976, 7.

106. AIAW guaranteed due process through an appeals system for individual student-athletes; it also believed its judicial process superior because penalties more closely matched the offense (and were more consistent) and because students did not pay for the violations of coaches. The AIAW's revenue distribution plans also differed, with monies distributed more equitably and widely between institutions. See Presentation to American Council on Education's President's Committee on Collegiate Athletics, February 25, 1980 (Box 378, AIAW papers). In fact, the NCAA's enforcement practices were criticized by a congressional subcommittee which looked into the matter.

107. The committee suggested that AIAW adopt the NCAA's five-year eligibility rule, that AIAW adopt the NCAA's transfer rule, and that both set the maximum for athletic financial aid to be tuition and fees. These proposals were not approved. Both organizations did approve a suggested injury "red-shirting" compromise.

108. NCAA Council meeting minutes, October 1978 (NCAA, *Annual Reports*, 1978–79).

109. Besides interviews by journalists, there is a unique resource in the AIAW papers—a report entitled, "The Current State of Affairs—Telephone Conversations with Random Sample of Women's Coordinators or Directors of Athletics from Southern and Southwestern Institutions and Several Student-Athletes, April 3, 1979." This report was confidential. The names of universities were blacked out to protect anonymity. Although sometimes I could read through the blacking out, I chose to ignore the names of the institutions. I don't know how scientific the sampling was—it seemed fairly informal—but regardless, the report is an invaluable indicator of some women's state of mind. There were far more negative comments

included than positive, and I've picked out some representative and striking examples. In "Title IX—Comments of Women—April 3, 1979" file (Box 43, AIAW papers).

110. "The Current State of Affairs."

111. Ibid.

112. Fields, "July 31: Title IX Deadline."

113. "The Current State of Affairs."

114. Ibid.

115. "The Current State of Affairs."

116. Jeanine McHaney to Christine Grant, November 2, 1978 ("Statements on Title IX on Proposed 45 CFR 86 by AIAW, NAGWS, NAIA" file, Box 294, AIAW papers).

117. "The Current State of Affairs."

118. Ibid.

119. Ibid.

120. In July 1978 a jury awarded her $15,000 in damages. See Project on the Status and Education of Women, "On Campus with Women," no. 22 (Winter 1979).

121. "The Current State of Affairs."

122. "Fortunately my administrator stifled him," the quote continued, although the outcome of the situation is not known ("The Current State of Affairs").

123. "The Current State of Affairs."

124. See also the letter from Candace Lyle Hogan to Sen. Jacob Javits (late 1978?), which asserted, "I and others have documented evidence from investigations performed in spring of 1977 as well as in February of this year indicating that athletic personnel in many of our nation's colleges are being muffled in their expression of their thought regarding Title IX by their male superiors. Women are being harassed, threatened with demotion and even fired when they do gather the courage to speak out about disparities within their institutions." Copy in "To the Rescue! Field Reports" file (Box 43, AIAW papers).

There was also an explicit reference to the courage activism required in a letter from one advocate to another: "I would like to thank you for coming to Washington to testify against the Tower Amendment. I know that doing so is something you believe in, but I also know that the line of least resistance would have been for you not to place yourself in that position." Peg Burke, presumably speaking from her own experience, concluded by saying she valued not only Donna Lopiano's ability but her courage. Peggy Burke to Donna Lopiano, September 22, 1975 ("Statements on Title IX on Proposed 45 CFR 86 by AIAW, NAGWS, NAIA" file, Box 294, AIAW papers).

125. Donna Lopiano to SWAIAW Voting Representatives, June 11, 1979 (Title IX briefings, papers, correspondence file, Box 43, AIAW papers).

126. Theoretically, nothing prevented female coaches from expressing their opinions to HEW (on plain white stationary, if necessary), but clearly Brigham Young University's opinion carried more weight than an individual's. The NCAA repeatedly used the term "institutional control" in its Executive Committee and council meetings. See, for example, Executive Committee minutes: "It was noted that AIAW leaders continue to argue that their institutional chief executive officers do not speak for them because the Title IX interpretation is not an institutional matter. It was suggested that some institutions are experiencing difficulties in exercising institutional control in this regard" (NCAA, *Annual Reports*, 1978–79). See also "NCAA Council Report on the Several Issues," April 28, 1975.

127. HEW General Counsel F. Peter Libassi published a memo confirming the applicabil-

ity of Title IX to revenue-producing sports on April 18, 1978. Still, after congressional inquiries, HEW said it was "carefully considering" the exemption of scholarship aid for revenue-producing sports. Margot Polivy, "July 21: Deadline or Dead End?" *NYT*, July 16, 1978, sec. 5, p. 2; see also NCAA Council minutes, October 16, 1978 (NCAA, *Annual Reports*, 1977–78).

128. Califano, quoted in Cheryl Fields, "HEW Policy on Sports Bias Raises New Questions," *Chronicle*, December 18, 1978, 9.

129. A school could be excused from this affirmative action planning requirement if it could show that it already was satisfying women's interests and abilities, show a pattern of increased participation at all levels, or show that the program's growth was typical of the region. Margot Polivy to AIAW Executive Committee, HEW Proposed Policy Interpretation, December 6, 1978 ("Title IX—1981" file, AIAW papers); Gordon S. White, Jr. "Title IX Guidelines Are Issued for Equal Sports Expenditures," *NYT*, December 7, 1978, 19, 21; "Title IX of the Education Amendments of 1972: A [final] Policy Interpretation; Title IX and Intercollegiate Athletics," *Federal Register* 44, no. 239 (December 11, 1979): 71413–71423.

130. AIAW press statement on the proposed guidelines, December 7, 1978 ("Title IX Task Force Draft, November 13, 1978" file, Box 294, AIAW papers). See also Fields, "HEW Policy on Sports Bias Raises New Questions."

131. Holly Knox, director of the Project on Equal Educational Rights of the NOW Legal Defense and Education Fund, quoted in Fields, "HEW Policy on Sports Bias Raises New Questions."

132. Cheryl Fields and Lorenzo Middleton, "Both Sides Criticize Government on Enforcement of Anti-Sex-Bias Law," *Chronicle*, January 15, 1979, 12.

133. Philip B. Brown, General Roundtable, NCAA, *Proceedings*, January 1979.

134. Minutes of General Roundtable, NCAA, *Proceedings*, January 1979.

135. Joseph Califano said he would like documentation of that figure because in the past colleges and universities had displayed "a great tendency to exaggerate" costs of complying with federal requirements. "As Criticism Continues, U.S. Prepares Final Policy on Sex-Bias in Sports," *Chronicle*, March 19, 1979, 4. See also Gordon S. White, Jr., "Colleges Mystified by Title IX Fund Rules," *NYT*, December 15, 1978, 27.

136. Comments from a representative from the Georgia Institute of Technology, Minutes of General Roundtable, NCAA, *Proceedings*, January 1979.

137. During the discussion, some delegates displayed a greater sensitivity to the opinions of female athletic leaders. One man expressed concern that it would be perceived as "an assertion of male dominance over women's athletics." Another said that although it was not one, it would be perceived "by many women as a grab for power." Division III Roundtable, NCAA, *Proceedings*, January 1979.

138. The resolution declared athletic departments already had made massive new allocations for women and that HEW's open-ended provisions created "excessive and unreasonable financial obligations." It attacked HEW for not taking into account the nature of particular sports, as it had been directed by the Javits amendment, especially the different levels of student, alumni, and public interest in certain sports. It also criticized HEW for writing arbitrary and unworkable compliance standards, for going beyond the original regulations, and for intervening in sports programs that were not federally assisted. Resolution No. 133, Appendix, NCAA, *Proceedings*, January 1979.

139. General Roundtable, NCAA, *Proceedings*, January 1979.

140. There were reports, likely true, that the coalition eventually raised much more money. See "News Clips" file (AIAW papers), and Northrop, "A New Generation of Athletes," 56–57.

According to the Women's Sports Foundation, by the summer of 1979 there were at least three hundred colleges in the coalition, and according to the U.S. Commission on Civil Rights, the majority of the schools were Division I (large) universities. See Women's Sports Foundation to "Carole and Bonnie," summer 1979 (in "To the Rescue! Field Reports" file), and U.S. Commission on Civil Rights, Staff Options Paper, both in Box 43, AIAW papers.

141. Terry Sanford to F. Peter Libassi, General Counsel, HEW, May 22, 1979 (copy in "DeHart Associates" file, Box 43, AIAW papers).

142. Holly Knox, Project on Equal Educational Rights of the NOW Legal Defense and Education Fund, quoted in Cheryl Fields, "50 Presidents Ask U.S. to Withdraw Plan to Monitor Sex Bias in Sports," *Chronicle*, June 8, 1979, 12. Subtle language clues also suggested that although the proposal rightfully was labeled a compromise, it had roots in the most moderate of NCAA positions rather than feminist ones. Language like "realism," "legitimate interests," and "justifiable complaints" were subtly encoded clues that set the position apart from feminist proposals.

143. Bonnie Slatton, acting executive director of AIAW, to Sue Garrison, May 2, 1979 ("To the Rescue! Field Reports" file, Box 43, AIAW papers).

144. By summer 1979 the coalition had thirty-three organizations associated with it, including AIAW, NAGWS, the Women's Equity Action League, the National Organization for Women, the American Association of University Women, the National Federation of Business and Professional Women and the Association of Negro Business and Professional Women, the National Council of Jewish Women, the Coalition of Labor Union Women, and the Girl Scouts of America.

145. Donna Lopiano to SWAIAW's Voting Representatives.

146. Not surprisingly, the DeHart Coalition commended the commission's cognizance of football and the NCAA urged it to consider a permanent exclusion of football. U.S. Commission on Civil Rights, "Comments on a Proposed Policy Interpretation of Title IX of the Education Act of 1972" (copy in "U.S. Commission on Civil Rights" file, Box 43, AIAW papers).

147. "Title IX of the Education Amendments of 1972: A Policy Interpretation," *Federal Register* 44, December 11, 1979. Numbers of participants were changing quickly. In December 1979 one article said the ratio was three to one ("Shift Seen on Title IX Fund Rules," *NYT*, December 4, 1979), but in October 1978 AIAW said women made up 30 percent of intercollegiate athletes.

148. Christine Grant testimony to U.S. Commission on Civil Rights, July 9, 1979 (transcript in "U.S. Commission on Civil Rights" file, Box 43, AIAW papers).

149. The Ashbrook amendment was such an attempt, limiting HEW's power over education, and the Walker amendment prohibited federal rules using ratios to determine guidelines.

150. Women's Sports Foundation plans, press release, and late June memo; copy of petition signed by thirty-four golfers in the Ladies Professional Golf Association; letters from college athletes to AIAW; AIAW to coaches (e.g., Bonnie Slatton to Ginny Hunt, May 15, 1979), all in "To the Rescue! Field Reports" file (Box 43, AIAW papers); *NYT*, April 15, 1979, sec. 5, p. 6, and April 22, 1979, sec. 5, p. 5, and April 23, 1979, C3.

151. The commission changed its mind, citing new data that showed that, at Division I

schools, football cost less on a per capita basis than men's basketball did, and that Division I schools not sponsoring football had per capita expenditures not very different from schools that did offer it. The commission had already rejected special consideration for revenue-producing sports simply on the basis that they were revenue-producing. Louis Nuñez, U.S. Commission on Civil Rights, to David Tatel, Director, ocr/hew, Revised Comments on Title IX Policy Interpretation, September 1979 (Staff Options Paper) (copy in "U.S. Commission on Civil Rights" file, Box 43, AIAW papers).

152. Nuñez, U.S. Commission on Civil Rights, Revised Comments on Title IX Policy Interpretation, September 1979.

153. HEW commended the DeHart Coalition for a suggesting an effective process for campuses to follow, but declared it would not turn over to individual institutions its responsibility to define and enforce equal opportunity.

154. "Title IX of the Education Amendments of 1972: A Policy Interpretation," *Federal Register* 44, December 11, 1979. Rev. Theodore Hesburgh, quoted by Donna Lopiano, speech at the ocr Title IX Training Institute, March 4, 1980 ("Title IX—1980" file, Box 43, AIAW papers).

155. Gordon S. White, Jr., "Mrs. Harris Strengthens Title IX Policies," *NYT*, December 5, 1979. See also AIAW press release, "AIAW Applauds Final Title IX Interpretation," December 5, 1979; and Margot Polivy to AIAW Executive Committee, December 6, 1979 ("Title IX—1979" file, Box 43, AIAW papers).

156. Although a federal district court had dismissed the lawsuit against the regulations (because the NCAA lacked standing), the organization had appealed. Anne C. Roark, "Court Rejects NCAA Challenge to Ban on Sex Bias in Sports," *Chronicle*, January 16, 1978, 1, 14.

157. UCLA's estimate came from Chancellor Young at the 1979 NCAA convention. The AIAW estimated compliance would mean that women would receive 21 percent of expenditures at an average large institution. See Title IX Alert, Carole Mushier to AIAW Voting Representatives, April 6, 1979 ("Title IX—1979" file, AIAW papers).

158. For athletic scholarship numbers, see "Women's Sports Boom—Too Slow for Some," *U.S. News and World Report*, July 10, 1978; for numbers of sports offered, see U.S. Commission on Civil Rights, "Comments on a Proposed Policy Interpretation of Title IX"; for percentages of budgets and participants, see figures from the National Coalition for Women and Girls in Education (copy in "Title IX—Hatch—'81" file, Box 43, AIAW papers).

Part IV. Introduction: 1980–1990

1. Schlafly criticized feminists who had a negative "dog-in-the-manger, chip-on-the-shoulder" attitude that being a woman was unfortunate. She believed a "Positive Woman" was the ideal to strive for, which meant recognizing that the "Divine Architect" had given men muscles and women the ability to nurture in ways appropriate since the Stone Age. She said women have a "different kind of strength"—sexual restraint. Phyllis Schlafly, *The Power of the Positive Woman* (New Rochelle, N.Y.: Arlington House, 1977), 14, 12, 20.

2. Schlafly, *The Power of the Positive Woman*, 14.

3. For an assessment of New Right ideology, see Rosalind Pollack Petchesky, "Antiabortion, Antifeminism, and the Rise of the New Right," *Feminist Studies* 7 (Summer 1981): 206–46. Schlafly reserved special antipathy for "absurd" Title IX regulations written by HEW. See Schlafly, *The Power of the Positive Woman*, 21–25.

8. Backsliding, 1980–1988

1. Carole Mushier speech, AIAW Delegate Assembly, January 6, 1980 (Box 269, AIAW papers).

2. The quote is from an interview with a former AIAW president, who remained anonymous as part of Kristin L. Burns's study, "Reconstructing Leadership Experiences."

3. The NCAA decided to create this committee just one week before the final policy interpretation was officially announced.

4. James Frank, chair, Special Committee on NCAA Governance, Organization, and Services, to Chief Executive Officers of NCAA Institutions, January 31, 1980 (copy in Appendix to Donna Lopiano Affidavit, Box 70, AIAW papers).

5. Indeed, recently the NCAA Executive Committee had agreed the finances could be arranged, and other committees had been discussing the matter as though it were not a question of whether, but when (and how) the NCAA would be running some women's sports. See minutes of NCAA Council meetings (especially the report of the Committee on Women's Athletics), August 15–17, and October 16–19, 1979, and Executive Committee minutes, April 21–22, and August 13–14, 1979 (in NCAA, *Annual Reports*, 1978–79). The NCAA staff had already concluded it was feasible in 1975, when it first proposed women's championships. Walter Byers had already been negotiating with NBC for a multiyear television contract for Division I women's basketball championships. Those negotiations demonstrated an amazing boldness, considering that the NCAA did not yet have any women's championships. Testimony of Arthur D. Watson, President, NBC Sports, and Rex Lynford Lardner, NBC Director of Program Planning for Sports Division, *Association for Intercollegiate Athletics for Women v. National Collegiate Athletic Association* (hereafter, AIAW v. NCAA) antitrust lawsuit (copy in Box 70, AIAW papers). See also nn. 62 and 67, below.

6. Plaintiff's (AIAW's) Second Statement of Contention and Proof, May 7, 1982 (AIAW v. NCAA, Box 70, AIAW papers).

7. All but one of over five hundred AIAW delegates voted to oppose the NCAA's actions (see Lopiano Affidavit). For the wording of the resolution, see Cheryl Fields and Lorenzo Middleton, "Women's Sports Group Stunned, Angered by NCAA Vote on Female Championships," *Chronicle of Higher Education* (hereafter, *Chronicle*), January 14, 1980. Commenting that it represented "one organization attempting to dictate the proper decisions of another organization," the NCAA Council sent the resolution to the Division II and III Steering Committees. NCAA Council meeting, minutes, January 4–7, 1980 (NCAA, *Annual Reports*, 1979–80).

8. See Lopiano Affidavit.

9. Proponents made the case that NCAA women's championships were the right thing to do, legally and ethically. The NCAA would be offering schools greater opportunities by sharing its expertise, rules, and benefits with women. For those who wanted to retain differences, the legislation was permissive, so that no women's program would be forced to compete in the NCAA championships. Even if colleges wished to continue in AIAW, however, they should approve the events because some NCAA schools needed them. "Many" NCAA schools did not belong to the AIAW and thus lacked access to women's championships. For the arguments presented, see minutes of Division II and Division III Roundtables, and Report of the Council, NCAA, *Proceedings of the Annual Convention*, January 1980. The NCAA claimed that 17 percent of NCAA Division II and 27 percent of Division III institutions did not also belong to AIAW. Those numbers were deceiving since many of those schools actually had no women's program

at all. Donna Lopiano disputed NCAA statistics that claimed such high percentages of NCAA schools which were not also in AIAW, pointing out that only 11 out of 182 were in that situation in Division II (that is, only 6 percent, not 17 percent), with a similar situation in Division III (that is, actually 10.3 percent, not 26.6 percent).

10. Christine Grant, quoted in Fields and Middleton, "Women's Sports Group Stunned."

11. Fields and Middleton, "Women's Sports Group Stunned."

12. Ibid.; Jane Gross, "Women's Group Set to Combat N.C.A.A.," *NYT*, January 8, 1980, B8.

13. See James Frank to Chief Executive Officers, January 31, 1980; Christine Grant to AIAW Voting Representatives, February 6, 1980; William Flynn and James Frank to Chief Executive Officers, March 7, 1980; AIAW Executive Committee to AIAW Voting Representatives, April 11, 1980; William Flynn and James Frank to Chief Executive Officers, November 5, 1980; AIAW Executive Committee to AIAW Voting Representatives and Coordinators of women's athletic programs, December 3, 1980 (all included in Appendix to Lopiano Affidavit).

14. The format for most committees was to set aside a certain number of seats for women, a certain number (often the same) for men, and a certain number "unallocated" by gender. For example, on the Division I Steering Committee, it was six for women, six for men, and eight unallocated. As the NCAA pointed out, there was no guarantee that unallocated seats would go to men, but everyone assumed they would virtually all the time. There were many other committees, and women's representation on them ranged from 20 to 40 percent. See Proposal No. 51, NCAA, *Proceedings*, January 1981.

15. Frank to CEOs, January 31, 1980; Flynn and Frank to CEOs, November 5, 1980, and December 1, 1980.

16. Flynn and Frank to CEOs, March 7, 1980.

17. Were there women "strongly urging NCAA involvement"? A few—less than twenty, but they were used well by NCAA leaders, especially at the 1981 convention. Three of the most prominent were Ruth Berkey, the woman hired to run the NCAA women's championships; Judith Holland; and Jean Cerra. Why might they have disagreed with the over 90 percent of sportswomen who wanted only AIAW? Some women in the West wanted to recruit more (and therefore wanted less restrictive rules than AIAW had); they also thought their programs had experienced less discrimination and wanted AIAW to spend less time on Title IX. Some schools in the East, including a number of Ivy League universities, wanted to be able to set more restrictive rules, which AIAW did not permit. Finally, a few small schools wanted Division III to be a no-scholarship division rather than permitting 10 percent scholarships. The vast majority of these women were content to fight out these issues within the AIAW, but a few were bitter and/or wanted the benefits they thought would come through the NCAA.

Regardless, the NCAA's statement unfairly dismissed the enormous opposition by suggesting that the fact that some women also supported the move canceled out the opposition. This tactic is similar to what the NCAA did by saying the majority of men and women in education were neither militant feminists nor male chauvinists. Historian William Chafe argues that opponents of desegregation in North Carolina used the same rhetorical device to make it seem as though supporters of integration like the NAACP were "extremists" just as the KKK was. Then they placed themselves—the so-called moderate opponents—firmly in the center of the ideological spectrum, effectively lending legitimacy to their cause and ostracizing civil rights advocates. See Chafe, *Civilities and Civil Rights*, esp. ch. 3.

18. Flynn and Frank to CEOs, March 7, 1980.

19. Ibid.

20. AIAW Executive Committee to AIAW Voting Representatives, April 11, 1980, and December 3, 1980.

21. Ibid.

22. AIAW said it was willing to discuss a single structure for the administration of men's and women's sports provided the following principles were agreed upon: alternatives would be pursued in an atmosphere of mutual respect and cooperation, and there should be equal opportunity for female student-athletes and assured equal decision-making authority for women; assured student-athlete rights; a sound educational philosophy and economically prudent approaches; full involvement of students, coaches, and administrators of men's and women's programs on individual campuses. Christine Grant to AIAW Voting Representatives, February 6, 1980.

23. AIAW Executive Committee to AIAW Voting Representatives, April 11, 1980, and December 3, 1980.

24. According to NCAA minutes, at least thirty-seven women spoke at the 1981 NCAA Convention; a few supported NCAA championships, but the vast majority were AIAW sympathizers. NCAA, *Proceedings*, January 1981.

25. At the Divisional roundtables, AIAW sympathizers were frustrated that other delegates were untroubled by vague answers about the financing of the championships; when asked about constitutional issues, they seemed to accept the NCAA's lawyer's opinion that backed Byers's interpretation (that a majority vote was sufficient, and two-thirds not necessary). At the Division I roundtable, AIAW supporters' requests for a straw vote were refused (straw votes had never been refused, women claimed, until then). See minutes of Division I, II, and III and General Roundtables, NCAA, *Proceedings*, January 1981; and Lopiano Affidavit.

26. Testimony of Sharon Taylor, *AIAW v. NCAA* (in Box 70, AIAW papers).

27. James Frank, for example, claimed "never before in the history of this association has such an effort been made to seek advice from so many different segments of the membership and to disseminate complete information regarding this proposal." Minutes of the General Roundtable, NCAA, *Proceedings*, January 1981.

28. Thomas Blackburn, faculty athletic representative from Swarthmore, pursued a request for an official organizational legal interpretation of the NCAA's constitution and by-laws regarding the proper procedures for adding women's sports. At issue was whether it required a two-thirds' or simple majority vote. Blackburn strongly believed that the NCAA's leadership knowingly made the improper legal interpretation (of what was known as "O.I. 12")—ignoring the context, history, and commonsense meaning of the legislation—so that it would be easier for the women's championships to pass. He also felt the NCAA pushed aside his requests for further explanation and manipulated the rules so that AIAW supporters had very few options, all of which had very slim chances of success (because each required a two-thirds vote). He felt "steam-rollered." See Thomas Blackburn testimony, *AIAW v. NCAA* (Box 70, AIAW papers).

29. The first major vote was about immediately applying NCAA rules to women, a confusing piece of legislation that NCAA leaders opposed (even though they wanted women's championships) and that AIAW supporters favored because it would have eliminated the NCAA's flexibility in rules during a five-year transition period. The AIAW's supporters lost that round. The issue was confusing because if AIAW had succeeded in reordering the agenda, it may have opposed the legislation.

30. Final Business Session, NCAA, *Proceedings*, January 1981.

31. Thomas Blackburn testimony, *AIAW v. NCAA*; Lopiano Affidavit.

32. Walter Byers testimony, *AIAW v. NCAA* (Box 70, AIAW papers). The whole question of NCAA members' motives is probably impossible for me to answer with absolute certainty, since they may have varied widely in such a large group. I can suggest the possible ones: (1) altruism; (2) paternalism; (3) self-interest. In the self-interest category, men might want to protect men's rules, "cap" expenditures for women's sports, or protect NCAA the institution. Women in AIAW thought the NCAA had been influenced by its decades-long battle with the AAU over which organization would control amateur (especially Olympic) athletics. The battle had recently taken a new turn since governance of Olympic sports was now in the hands of "sport governing bodies" which the NCAA and AAU were competing to develop. Some believed that the NCAA's chances of being approved were very slim if it did not offer women's sports (since AAU did). See Lopiano Affidavit.

33. AIAW complained that while members of the NCAA's Committee on Women's Athletics were interested in discussing a study of alternative governance proposals, the NCAA Council would not permit the meetings to proceed in a constructive manner; and even though its reasoning was that the membership had not approved it, it would not put the issue before the convention. The council rebuffed AIAW initiatives in fall 1978 and summer 1979. See Lopiano Affidavit.

34. Then he solicited a legal opinion backing him up from NCAA's attorneys. For the chronology of constitutional issues regarding O.I. 12, see Thomas Blackburn's testimony, *AIAW v. NCAA*.

35. The NCAA *News* printed supposed answers to questions submitted to HEW's Office of Civil Rights, but in fact the NCAA had never submitted the questions and had invented the answers! William Kramer, an NCAA attorney, admitted there had been an "error" and that the answers were those NCAA thought it would get from OCR. See testimony of Cynthia G. Brown (OCR), *AIAW v. NCAA* (Box 70, AIAW papers).

36. Thomas Blackburn testimony, *AIAW v. NCAA*.

37. Candace Lyle Hogan, "Female Athletes: More to Lose Than Just Their Organization," *NYT*, January 25, 1981, sec. 5, p. 2.

38. (Anonymous) AIAW president, quoted in Burns, "Reconstructing Leadership Experiences," 139.

39. Margot Polivy, interview by author, Washington, D.C., March 28, 1989; Lopiano Affidavit; Christine Grant speech, Final Business Session, NCAA, *Proceedings*, January 1981; Thomas Blackburn testimony, *AIAW v. NCAA*; Hogan, "Female Athletes."

40. Holland wrote to ask that her name be taken off a statement signed by all former AIAW presidents. She said she agreed with much of it but disagreed with its tone and approach, and she was not certain that the NCAA's move would destroy the AIAW. She hoped women in AIAW would respect her differing approach. Judith Holland to Christine Grant, August 18, 1980 (in Appendix to Lopiano Affidavit).

41. General Roundtable, NCAA, *Proceedings*, January 1981.

42. Final Business Session, NCAA, *Proceedings*, January 1981.

43. Outgoing president Donna A. Lopiano, presidential address, AIAW Delegate Assembly, January 6, 1982 (Box 269, AIAW papers).

44. Lopiano, presidential address, January 6, 1982; "NCAA Antitrust Action," report for AIAW Delegate Assembly, January 1982 (Box 269, AIAW papers).

45. An additional complicating factor is that after the NCAA voted to offer women's championships, so did NAIA, another athletic governing body previously for men that catered to smaller institutions. It is possible that if NAIA had not existed, the AIAW could have survived

or at least competed with the NCAA for smaller schools that were not interested in high-powered, expensive, commercialized sports. As it was, many colleges (with men's programs) that differed with the NCAA's philosophy already were in NAIA, so AIAW would not be filling a void. Cheryl M. Fields, "Two College Sports Associations Agree to Use Same Rules for Women's Championships," *Chronicle*, April 6, 1981.

46. Lopiano, presidential address, January 6, 1982; "NCAA Antitrust Action," report for AIAW Delegate Assembly, January 1982.

47. Ann Uhlir (AIAW executive director) testimony, *AIAW v. NCAA* (Box 70, AIAW papers); Lopiano, presidential address, January 6, 1982.

48. Text of AIAW statement, press conference, October 10, 1981 (Box 57, AIAW papers); Lopiano, presidential address, January 6, 1982; Cheryl M. Fields, "Women's Sports Group Plans for Possible Dissolution," *Chronicle*, January 20, 1982.

49. Besides the loss of $191,000 in expected income for the current year, NBC's default meant that AIAW's budget would be depleted by half a million dollars more between 1981 and 1983. Lopiano, presidential address, January 6, 1982; Revised Budget, January 5, 1982 (Box 269, AIAW papers).

50. Quoted in Burns, "Reconstructing Leadership Experiences," 54–55.

51. Lopiano, presidential address, January 6, 1982.

52. Incoming president Merrily Dean Baker, president's address, AIAW Delegate Assembly, January 9, 1982 (Box 269, AIAW papers).

53. The same themes run through both Lopiano's and Baker's presidential addresses and Ann Uhlir's Executive Director's Report. The phrase "dream that was AIAW" comes from Ann Uhlir, "Political Victim: The Dream That Was the A.I.A.W.," *NYT*, July 11, 1982, sec. 5, p. 2.

54. The district court judge declared that AIAW had failed to convince him that it was likely to win its lawsuit or that it would suffer irreparable injury by the time the lawsuit was heard.

55. Cheryl M. Fields, "AIAW Lifts Recruiting Rules After Rebuff by Appeals Court," *Chronicle*, March 10, 1982.

56. Minutes of Special Executive Board meeting, April 13–14, 1982 (Box 269, AIAW papers); Paul Desruisseaux, "Women's Sports Unit Expected to Suspend Activity this Week," *Chronicle*, June 2, 1982.

57. AIAW proposed that representatives from men's and women's programs (including faculty and students) and chief executive officers serve as a joint board that would ensure comparability of rules and resolve conflicts arising as an otherwise autonomous NCAA would run men's and AIAW run women's sports. The NCAA said the proposal could not "be considered a realistic or viable approach" because the NCAA already was serving both men and women as directed by its member institutions. AIAW Settlement Proposal, April 5, 1982; William Kramer, NCAA Response to AIAW Settlement Proposal, April 20, 1982; see also AIAW response, April 28, 1982, and NCAA response, May 7, 1982 (all in Box 70, AIAW papers).

58. Plaintiff's (AIAW's) Second Statement of Contention and Proof, May 7, 1982.

59. Koch testified as to possible motives for the NCAA's "predatory pricing," saying, "By controlling women's intercollegiate athletics [the NCAA] can effectively 'cap' expenditures in that burgeoning area." Of these possible motives—profiting from or capping expenditures of women's sports—neither put NCAA leaders in a positive light. See James Koch testimony, *AIAW v. NCAA* (Box 70, AIAW papers).

60. The decreased per diem payments to most men's teams meant that the only way a school could recoup its loss of per diem was to put its women's program into NCAA championships to receive transportation reimbursements.

61. Cheryl M. Fields, "NCAA Officer Foretold Demise of Women's Group," *Chronicle*, November 3, 1982.

62. Plaintiff's Second Statement of Contention and Proof; the argument also was summarized in *Association for Intercollegiate Athletics for Women v. National Collegiate Athletic Association*, 735 F.2d 577 (1984), U.S. Court of Appeals, District of Columbia Circuit, May 18, 1984. See also Cheryl Fields, "NCAA Tried to Drive Women's Association Out of Business, AIAW Backers Tell Court," *Chronicle*, October 27, 1982.

63. Defendant's (NCAA's) Second Statement of Contention and Proof, May 28, 1982 (Box 57, AIAW papers); "Appeals Court Hears Plan to Ban NCAA from Holding Women's Championships," *Chronicle*, March 3, 1982.

64. Fields, "NCAA Tried to Drive Women's Association Out of Business."

65. Testimony of G. Jean Cerra and Nora Lynn Finch (Box 70, AIAW papers).

66. Defendant's Second Statement of Contention and Proof.

67. *Association for Intercollegiate Athletics v. National Collegiate Athletic Association* (558 F. Supp. 487 [1983]), U.S. District Court, District of Columbia, February 28, 1983.

68. *Association for Intercollegiate Athletics v. National Collegiate Athletic Association*, February 28, 1983; Cheryl M. Fields, "Court Rejects Claim of Women's Group that NCAA Violated Antitrust Law," *Chronicle*, March 9, 1983.

69. *Association for Intercollegiate Athletics v. National Collegiate Athletic Association*, February 28, 1983.

70. The appellate court also accepted NCAA leaders' claims that they had expected AIAW to survive and for colleges to have a choice of championships.

71. *AIAW v. NCAA*, U.S. District Court, District of Columbia, February 28, 1983; see also Cheryl M. Fields, "Appeals Court Rejects Charge that NCAA Forced Women's Group Out of Business," *Chronicle*, May 30, 1984.

72. Margot Polivy, interview.

73. Even in a fair democratic vote in the NCAA, women would lose because they were underrepresented among the voters.

74. AIAW could have appealed to the Supreme Court, but chances of overturning the appeals court's decision were slim and very expensive, so for all practical purposes its legal options had been exhausted. Polivy, interview.

75. Quoted in Burns, "Reconstructing Leadership Experiences," 83.

76. AIAW presidents quoted in this paragraph are (in order of appearance) from Burns, "Reconstructing Leadership Experiences," 58, 118–19, 121, 83.

77. Merrily Dean Baker, president's address, January 9, 1982.

78. Margot Polivy to AIAW Executive Committee, March 25, 1980 ("Title IX—1980" file, Box 43, AIAW papers).

79. Cynthia Brown, speech to National Association of Collegiate Directors of Athletics, June 17, 1980 (copy in Box 43, AIAW papers).

80. In part, enforcement would be made more difficult by shifting jurisdiction from the federal to local and state levels and limiting attorney's fees.

81. Polivy to AIAW Executive Committee, March 25, 1980.

82. Ibid.

83. National Coalition for Women and Girls in Education to Department of Education, late July 1981 (Box 43, AIAW papers).

84. Unidentified person's notes ("Title IX—1981" file, Box 43, AIAW papers).

85. Margaret Kohn (National Coalition) to Joan Standlee (OCR), March 16, 1982 (Box 43, AIAW papers); unidentified person's notes ("Title IX—1981" file, Box 43, AIAW papers).

86. "U.S. Begins Deregulation Review on Rights and Ecology Guidelines," *NYT*, August 13, 1981, 1.

87. Janet Hook, "Exemption from Anti-Bias Rules Proposed for Colleges That Don't Get Direct U.S. Aid," *Chronicle*, October 7, 1981; "Justice Department Says Grants to Students, But Not Loans, Subject Colleges to Title IX," *Chronicle*, March 24, 1982; "Title IX Watch," April 21, 1982 (in Box 43, AIAW papers).

88. Sen. Orrin G. Hatch also introduced a bill on June 11, 1981, to narrow Title IX (it would have limited the scope to programs directly receiving federal aid, restricted admissions coverage, and eliminated coverage of employees). It was cosponsored by Dan Quayle, Paula Hawkins, John East, Jeremiah Denton, Jesse Helms, and Jake Garn. Later the next year, the bill was withdrawn. The Department of Education also was trying to be released from enforcement agreements worked out in the Pratt case for resolving discrimination complaints in higher education.

89. Margot Polivy to AIAW Executive Committee, November 13, 1981 (Box 43, AIAW papers).

90. Female students had filed suits at Temple and West Texas State universities. Lorenzo Middleton, "Female Athletes Sue Temple U.," *Chronicle*, April 21, 1981.

91. Its decision on congressional intent was based first on the fact that Congress had rejected numerous attempts to exclude intercollegiate athletics from Title IX. Second, Congress made exceptions for programs like sororities that did not receive federal aid; why would it have exempted them unless they were expected to have been covered in the first place? Temple's athletic department benefits came from the (federal) College Work Study program, which paid the wages of over fifty students employees. In addition, athletes lived in federally financed dormitories. Cheryl M. Fields, "U.S. Anti-Sex-Bias Law Covers College Sports, Federal Judge Rules," *Chronicle*, September 15, 1982.

92. Cheryl M. Fields, "Judge Bars Civil-Rights Probe of Richmond Athletic Department," *Chronicle*, July 21, 1982.

93. As a result of the Richmond decision, the OCR immediately dropped an investigation of William and Mary, even though it was nearing an agreement with the school to increase the coaching, facilities, financial aid, and clerical support to women's athletics. Cheryl M. Fields, "Civil-Rights Office Dropping Sex-Bias Investigation at William and Mary," *Chronicle*, December 15, 1982.

94. For the responses of the U.S. Commission on Civil Rights and the National Coalition, see Cheryl M. Fields, "Ruling Could 'Decimate' Protection Against Sex Bias, Official Says," and Fields, "Administration Won't Appeal Ruling that Limits Sex-Bias Law," *Chronicle*, September 1 and 7, 1982.

95. "Note Pad," *Chronicle*, September 29, 1982.

96. There were four separate opinions written in the case. Justice Lewis Powell joined the majority but in a separate opinion called the case "an unedifying example of overzealousness on the part of the Federal Government" because Grove City College was unique and because there was no charge of discrimination against it. Justice John Paul Stevens, in a fourth opinion, thought the issue of defining "program" should not have been addressed at all in the case. See reprints of the opinions, "Texts of Opinions by Supreme Court in Case of Grove City College v. Bell," *Chronicle*, March 7, 1984.

97. N. Scott Vance, "Sports Scholarships May Still Be Covered by Title IX," *Chronicle*, March 7, 1984; Cheryl M. Fields, "Strong Anti-Sex-Bias Policies of Universities and States Are Seen Dampening the Effect of Grove City Ruling," *Chronicle*, March 14, 1984.

98. One school reduced the number of scholarships for its women's basketball team the day after the decision. Charles S. Farrell, "Many Women Link Anti-Sex-Bias Law to Outstanding Olympic Performances," *Chronicle*, August 29, 1984. Other schools did begin making cuts in their women's programs, but many of them were also cutting men's nonrevenue sports, purportedly to cut expenses. It is impossible to know if any of the cuts would not have been made if Title IX was being strongly enforced. Angus Paul, "Growing Deficits Force Colleges to Eliminate Some Varsity Sports," *Chronicle*, September 15, 1980.

99. All but one of the Education Department's programs distributed earmarked funds, however. Cheryl Fields, "Civil-Rights Offices Told to Trace U.S. Funds to Specific Program Before Most Bias Probes," *Chronicle*, September 12, 1984.

100. No changes, then, were required by law, and since the athletic director disputed the findings, it seemed unlikely that any would occur. Cheryl M. Fields, "U.S. Refuses to Act on Sex-Bias Charges at U. of Maryland," *Chronicle*, March 21, 1984.

101. William H. Thomas (OCR) to Dr. Wilford Bailey (Auburn), August 19, 1983; Harry M. Singleton (OCR) to James M. Walters, Esq. (Auburn), March 6, 1984, in U. S. Congress, *Joint Hearings before the Committee on Education and Labor and the Subcommittee on Civil and Constitutional Rights of the Committee on the Judiciary on H.R. 700*, 99th Cong., 1st sess., March 1985.

102. There were sixty-four cases in all that the OCR narrowed or dropped, twenty-eight which related to intercollegiate athletics. The decision also affected numerous Title IX court cases, such as that of Temple University, which initially had agreed to comply with the Appeals Court's finding, and West Texas State University's case. See National Women's Law Center, "Federal Funding of Discrimination; The Impact of Grove City v. Bell," in Marcia Greenberger's testimony, U.S. Congress, Senate, *Hearings before the Committee on Labor and Human Resources on S. 557*, 100th Cong., 1st sess., March 19 and April 1, 1987.

103. Cheryl M. Fields, "Bill to Reverse High Court Decision Gets Bipartisan Support," *Chronicle*, April 18, 1984.

104. Packwood denied the charges, calling them "smokescreens" by "civil rights opponents." Stacy E. Palmer, "2 House Panels Back Bill That Would Clarify How Civil-Rights Laws Apply on Campuses," *Chronicle*, June 6, 1984.

105. *Congressional Quarterly Almanac* 41 (Washington, D.C.: Congressional Quarterly, 1986); Fields, "Bill to Clarify How Civil-Rights Laws Apply on Campuses Loses Ground in Senate," *Chronicle*, June 20, 1984.

106. Fewer than 1 percent of schools ever saw an investigator and none had its funding cut off, yet virtually all schools had made extensive changes on behalf of women in sports. Cheryl Fields, "Title IX at X," *Chronicle*, June 23, 1982.

107. Quoted in Farrell, "Many Women Link Anti-Sex-Bias Law to Outstanding Olympic Performances."

108. Sandler, director of the Association of American Colleges' Project on the Status and Education of Women, quoted in Fields, "Strong Anti-Sex-Bias Policies of Universities and State Are Seen Dampening the Effect of Grove City Ruling."

109. Proposal No. 64, NCAA, *Proceedings*, January 1985.

110. "Colleges Must Offer Women and Men Some Minimal Number of Teams," *Chronicle*, January 18, 1984.

111. In 1986–87 there were 770 Division I men's championship teams and 471 women's, but only about half as many female athletes. This may have been justified by the fact that there were fewer women participating in intercollegiate sports at colleges—a fact that didn't seem to bother the NCAA and that the organization did nothing to try to alter. See NCAA, *Annual Reports*, 1986–87.

112. Cheryl Fields, "Women's Sports Officials Favor Changes in Recruiting and Tryout Regulations," *Chronicle*, June 13, 1984.

113. Minutes of the Women's Interests Subcommittee, NCAA Council meeting, October 10–12, 1983, NCAA, *Annual Reports*, 1982–83; Fields, "Women's Sports Officials Favor Changes in Recruiting and Tryout Regulations."

114. For example, on the try-out issue, a majority of NCAA women's sport committees favored allowing the practice (as AIAW had), but "an appreciable majority of all the committees combined [that is, men's and women's] had been opposed." As for women's programs that wanted to retain their multidivision status, it was suggested that they "strive to insure that AIAW continues its program," since the prospects for them in the NCAA were slim. See report of the Legislative Review Committee, NCAA Council meeting, April 21–23, 1982 (NCAA, *Annual Reports*, 1981–82); Cheryl Fields, "Women's Athletic Directors Back Civil-Rights Measure," *Chronicle*, June 13, 1984.

115. "Sidelines," *Chronicle*, September 25, 1985.

116. Paid attendance at men's Division I championships was 1,339,276, and at the women's it was 214,681 (see NCAA, *Annual Reports*, 1985–86). For all men's basketball teams for the year, paid attendance was 32,056,673; for all women's, 2,944,485. The best attendance for women's games over the year was at the University of Iowa, which averaged 4,363 people per game (about the same as a decent men's Division II team). "Sidelines," *Chronicle*, September 25, 1985.

117. Basketball coach Marianne Stanley complained about the media's resistance and ignorance. "The line of questioning still runs, 'What size jumper do you wear?' instead of 'How do you shoot the jumper?'" N. Scott Vance, "The Selling of Women's Basketball: It Takes More than Talented Teams," *Chronicle*, February 9, 1983.

118. Anson Dorrance, interview by author, Chapel Hill, N.C., July 11, 1991; Douglas Lederman, "Penn State Coach's Comments About Lesbian Athletes May Be Used to Test University's New Policy on Bias," *Chronicle*, June 5, 1991; Robert Lipsyte, "Center Fielder Turns 'Political,'" *NYT*, June 21, 1991, B12.

119. Sports sociologist Mary Jo Kane has noted this phenomenon among "postfeminist" athletes, and at a talk she gave at Duke University in 1990, I witnessed the same thing. Female athletes saw nothing "wrong" or unfair about Steffi Graf posing like a model in skimpy dresses; many of them resisted feminist analyses of apologetic behavior and clearly did not want to give it up. (A study by Gai I. Berlage showed that 84 percent of female athletes at a major university said it was important to them to be thought of as feminine, but only 14 percent said participating in their sport stamped them as unfeminine. "Sidelines," *Chronicle*, December 11, 1985.) Miller is quoted in Charles S. Farrell, "Southern California's 2-Time Champions Herald a New Era in women's Basketball," *Chronicle*, December 5, 1984.

120. Many of those women coached in traditionally female sports like field hockey and volleyball, so that in sports like basketball there were even more men coaching women. It was not that female coaches were unavailable or not qualified. Studies showed that although female basketball coaches had been coaching a shorter period of time than men (understandably, since there had been so few teams before Title IX), they had more playing experi-

350   **Notes**

ence and better educational backgrounds than males. See R. Vivian Acosta and Linda Jean Carpenter, "Women in Athletics—A Status Report," *Journal of Physical Education, Recreation, and Dance* (August 1985): 30–37; Donna A. Lopiano, "The Certified Coach," ibid., 34–38; Becky L. Sisley and Susan A. Capel, "High School Coaching—Filled with Gender Differences," ibid., 39–43; and "Women and Sports—Facts and Issues," *Journal of Physical Education, Recreation, and Dance* (March 1986): 33; "Sidelines," *Chronicle*, August 1, 1984, 21.

121. Acosta and Carpenter, "Women in Athletics—A Status Report," 30–37.

122. The theory was presented by Todd Crosset at the 1985 meeting of the North American Society for the Sociology of Sport. He believes that the incidence of abusive relationships between male coaches and female athletes could be staggering, and compared it to phenomena like domestic violence and incest. Coercive measures he witnessed ranged from dictating hairstyles, posture, and personal relationships to demanding affection and overt sexual seduction, and the most common was manipulating an athlete's eating patterns. He admits (and I agree) that abusive relationships exist between male coaches and male athletes, and between female coaches and female athletes, but he thinks the dynamic is different between male coaches and female athletes. See "Sidelines," *Chronicle*, November 20, 1985.

123. Quoted in Burns, "Reconstructing Leadership Experiences."

124. The average number of sports for NCAA Division I institutions in 1985–86 was 7.2 for women, and 9.0 for men. See NCAA, *Annual Reports*, 1986–87.

125. That figure is from 1990, although it remained fairly consistent through the 1980s (see Chip Alexander, "A Man's World," *Raleigh News and Observer*, October 6, 1991; Malcolm Moran, "Title IX Is Now an Irresistible Force," *NYT*, June 21, 1992). In 1981–82 Division I institutions spent an average of $1.7 million on men's and $400,000 on women's sports (see Fields, "Title IX at X").

9. A Second Stage: Pro Tennis in the 1980s

1. Martina Navratilova, "Now You Can Quote Me," *World Tennis* (May 1984): 43.

2. "The Split Not Taken," *World Tennis* (February 1981): 50; Susan B. Adams, "Women's Liberation?" *World Tennis* (December 1980): 4; Neil Amdur, "Women End Threat of U.S. Open Boycott," *NYT*, November 13, 1980, B15; Michael Wilbon, "Women Mull Offer to Stage Own Open," *Washington Post*, September 20, 1980, D1, and Wilbon, "WTA Nearer Pullout of U.S. Open," *Washington Post*, September 25, 1980, F1.

3. Wayne Kalyn, "Jerry Diamond Is a Ladies' Man," *World Tennis* (November 1982): 38–42.

4. King and Deford, *Billie Jean*, 159.

5. Male athletes were the norm and were treated as such linguistically: "athlete" without qualifying adjectives referred to men.

6. Deford continued, "You're beautiful when you're angry, baby." *Sports Illustrated* reporters frequently had an aggressive, tell-it-like-it-is, unawed style, but what distinguishes the style in this case was that it was so gendered. Frank Deford, "Of Volleys and Brollies," *Sports Illustrated*, July 7, 1980.

7. Reporters discussed how a woman player looked not just when a low-ranked player tried to grab headlines à la "Gorgeous Gussie" Moran with an outrageous and sexy costume, but also when the regulars did not meet their standards of attractiveness. Forget Chris and Martina, Curry Kirkpatrick told readers, because Anne White's "dazzling, curves-embracing,

fortnight-stopping alabaster body stocking" made men gasp. She showed "some dynamite" body parts. "Wow!" *Sports Illustrated*, July 8, 1985, 22–23.

See also Barry McDermott, "The Smartina Show; Or, Tennis in a Lethal Vein," *Sports Illustrated*, April 4, 1983, 34, who said Sylvia Hanika distinguished herself by playing "in one of the ugliest outfits ever seen on a tennis court." It was supposedly ugly because her "navy blue shorts . . . served to accentuate her powerful thighs."

8. Curry Kirkpatrick, "Round Two Goes to the Kid," *Sports Illustrated*, September 15, 1980, 16–21. In the same vein of apparently trying to "normalize" or "feminize" the athlete, see a photo in *Ebony*, captioned, "With her coach John Wilkerson, [Zina] Garrison shows that she is not always the tomboy" ("A Wimbledon Champ at 17," *Ebony*, October 1981, 42–46).

9. For example, a respectful story on a Navratilova-Austin match declared: "Against any player except Austin, Navratilova would have followed her second serve to the net as well, but she had too much respect for Austin's passing shots to take that chance. Thus, when her first serves failed—she missed on 27 of 66—she was left at the baseline playing the game that Austin owns. Navratilova's other weapon, her mighty forehand, also failed." Sarah Pileggi, "New Avon Lady Came Calling," *Sports Illustrated*, March 31, 1980, 44.

10. Ever the pragmatist, King would have traded some sexist coverage for more regular coverage. Billie Jean King, interview (telephone), December 10, 1988.

11. Sarah Pileggi, "Rolling onto a New Track," *Sports Illustrated*, December 21, 1981, 36–38.

12. Barry Lorge, "The Future Is Now," *World Tennis* (August 1984): 26–33.

13. Karen Stabiner, *Courting Fame: The Perilous Road to Women's Tennis Stardom*, 107.

14. Stabiner, *Courting Fame*, 12.

15. Lorge, "The Future Is Now"; Grace Lichtenstein, "The Teen Pros—Too Much Too Soon," *World Tennis* (January 1984): 28–34.

16. Nancy McShea, tennis mom, admitted that she was living vicariously through her daughter. See Lorge, "The Future Is Now."

17. Lorge, "The Future Is Now."

18. The actual range of estimated costs were $8,000–10,000 for a ten to twelve-year-old; $5,000–7,000 for a teen. Nick Bolletieri, "The Alarming Cost of Raising a Tournament Player," *World Tennis*, March 1984, 26–27.

19. Joy Duckett, "And The Women Shall Lead Them," *World Tennis* (March 1982): 56–59.

20. Duckett, "And The Women Shall Lead Them," 56–59. In 1982 Leslie Allen was ranked 19; Kim Sands, 60; Renee Blount, 82; Andrea Buchanan, 119. Lori McNeil, Zina Garrison, Cheryl Jones, Camille Benjamin, and Michaela Washington were high-ranking amateurs.

21. Stabiner, *Courting Fame*, 107.

22. Ibid., 155.

23. Many tennis observers commented on this phenomenon. See, for example, Evert with Amdur, *Chrissie*, 115–17, 160, 222; Martina Navratilova with George Vecsey, *Martina*, 148; and Stabiner, *Courting Fame*, 68–69.

24. King, interview.

25. Navratilova with Vecsey, *Martina*, 141–43, 148, 226.

26. Evert with Amdur, *Chrissie*, 199–201.

27. Frank Deford, "Love and Love," *Sports Illustrated*, April 27, 1981, 68–84.

28. Deford, "Love and Love."

29. It seems to me that the female pros wanted fan approval more so than male athletes, although that is an observation based on limited research. Their desire for fan appreciation

seems more personalized than that of the male pros. This corresponds with recent post-Carol Gilligan theories on women's psychology (Gilligan, *In a Different Voice*). Compare, for example, the autobiographies of Chris Evert, Billie Jean King, Pam Shriver, Margaret Court, and Helen Wills Moody with those of Arthur Ashe, Bill Tilden, Bobby Riggs, and John McEnroe.

30. Evert with Amdur, *Chrissie*, 224–25. Neil Amdur's introduction to the book declares: "Suzanne Lenglen and Helen Wills brought women's tennis from the social arena to the center stage of sports. Maureen Connolly introduced the youthful spirit, and Billie Jean King proved that women could be winners. Chris Evert proved that winners could be women."

31. King, interview. King also said Evert "made it sound as if every one of us who had ever come before her had been some kind of witch" (King and Deford, *Billie Jean*, 186). See also Evert's comments that at times Martina Navratilova was threatened by her image and her getting endorsements. Amy Rennert, "A Change of Approach," *Women's Sports and Fitness* (June 1985): 28–31, 52–56.

32. Cheryl McCall, "Larry and Billie Jean King Work to Renew Their Marriage—and Put Her Affair Behind Them," *People Weekly*, May 26, 1981, 73–77.

33. King and Deford, *Billie Jean*, 6.

34. Ibid., 212.

35. Ibid., 212, 10.

36. Cheryl McCall, "The Billie Jean King Case: A Friend's Outrage," *Ms.*, July 1981, 100.

37. Cathleen McGuigan, Martin Kasendorf, and David Friendly, "Billie Jean's Odd Match," *Newsweek*, May 11, 1981, 36; for a feminist critique of King's apologetic attitude, see Shelly Roberts, "Bad Form, Billie Jean," *Newsweek*, May 25, 1981, 119. King repeated her plea for compassion and understanding in an interview with *People* magazine (McCall, "Larry and Billie Jean King Work to Renew Their Marriage," 73–77); "Billie Jean Admits Gay Affair," *Chicago Tribune*, May 2, 1981, 1.

38. King and Deford, *Billie Jean*, 189.

39. Ibid., 26–27.

40. "Of all the criticism I've received the one thing that always hurt me the most was this business about me hating men." King explained that she had spent her whole life snuggling up to Larry and her father. King and Deford, *Billie Jean*, 48; see also McGuigan, Kasendorf, and Friendly, "Billie Jean's Odd Match."

41. King seemed genuinely confused by the labeling ("If you have one gay experience, does that mean you're gay?") and the entire experience, which she seems to have dealt with psychologically partly through denial. She explained that she didn't feel any different from before, and that she'd never felt so feminine as with Marilyn. King and Deford, *Billie Jean*, 25–27.

42. George Vecsey, "Athlete as an Idol—and Human Frailty," *NYT*, May 15, 1981, 24; Neil Amdur, "Homosexuality Sets Off Tremors," *NYT*, May 12, 1981, B11; Pete Axthelm, "The Case of Billie Jean King," *Newsweek*, May 18, 1981, 133; Marvin Kitman, "Dirty Linen," *New Leader*, June 15, 1981, 19–20; King and Deford, *Billie Jean*, 187–88; Bob Greene, "An Ace with a Heart—That's Billie Jean," *Chicago Tribune*, May 11, 1981, sec. 3, p. 1; "The Troubles, and Triumphs, of Billie Jean" (editorial), *NYT*, May 6, 1981, 30; Beverly Stephen, "Courage and Controversy," *Los Angeles Times*, May 7, 1981, sec. 5, pp. 14, 28; Jerry Kishenbaum, "Scorecard; Facing Up to Billie Jean's Revelations," *Sports Illustrated*, May 11, 1981, 13–16.

43. *Sports Illustrated* also asserted that homosexual relations among women athletes tended to be "more open, more enduring and, at the top level of certain sports, more widespread than among their male counterparts." It is unlikely that the magazine was basing the

statement about greater incidence among women on any scientific data; rather, it was based on observation. The obvious problem with observation is that, if homosexuality ran counter to the prevailing assumptions about the traditional "masculinity" of male athletes, gay athletes would be all the more likely to remain "closeted" (Kishenbaum, "Scorecard"). For more qualitative evidence, see David Kopay, *The David Kopay Story: An Extraordinary Revelation.* Kopay, a bisexual football player, said the incidence of homosexuality in football was much more widespread than the public imagined. One ironic possible consequence of the unfeminine stereotype of female athletes might be the greater willingness of lesbian athletes to be "out" since everyone thinks that they're gay anyway.

44. Kishenbaum, "Scorecard."

45. Berman E. Deffenbaugh, Jr., and Dr. Paul Cohen, letters to the editor, *World Tennis* (August 1981).

46. King and Deford, *Billie Jean,* 217.

47. Ibid., 212, 217.

48. Ibid., 213.

49. Barry Lorge, "Women's Tennis and the Feminine Mystique," *World Tennis* (January 1982): 43–48, 73.

50. King, interview. A few months after all the publicity, King admitted, "It's been a very hard year for me. I think I'm all right now, but every day I still hold my breath" (Frank Deford, "Jumpin' Jimmyny," *Sports Illustrated,* July 12, 1982, 16–23). And after the court decided that Barnett could be evicted from the Malibu house, King said, "I am relieved and happy that we won, but with all the damage that has been done to Larry and me, to my family, the people around me and the tennis community, I think that is still bothering me quite a bit." Myrna Oliver, "King's Ex-Lover Loses Claim on Malibu House," *Los Angeles Times,* December 12, 1981, sec. 2, p. 1.

51. For the specific numbers, see King and Deford, *Billie Jean,* 213–14. One report said that a drug company dropped King, but the company claimed it had already made the decision before the revelations. Axthelm, "The Case of Billie Jean King."

52. Only one major manufacturer had approached her before Wimbledon, and that with an insulting offer, which she refused. Deford, "Jumpin' Jimmyny."

53. Amdur, "Homosexuality Sets Off Tremors," B11, 15.

54. Stabiner, *Courting Fame,* 156.

55. King and Deford, *Billie Jean,* 11.

56. McGuigan, Kasendorf, and Friendly, "Billie Jean's Odd Match." In the same vein, Evert said, "There are some very close friendships on tour, but unless you've been behind closed doors (and I haven't been) you can't really know whether they are lesbian relationships. If it is going on, the girls are very discreet and I respect their privacy" (Chris Evert Lloyd, "In Defense of Billie Jean," *World Tennis* [July 1981]: 8). See also Neil Amdur, "Mrs. King Offers to Quit as W.T.A. Head, So Not to Hurt Players," *NYT,* May 6, 1981, sec. 2, p. 8.

57. Evert also declared, "We're in no position to judge right and wrong in someone else's private life." Evert Lloyd, "In Defense of Billie Jean."

58. King and Deford, *Billie Jean,* 186.

59. Axthelm, "The Case of Billie Jean King"; Grace Lichtenstein, "Will the Real Women Pros Please Stand Up?" *World Tennis* (January 1985): 88; McGuigan, Kasendorf, and Friendly, "Billie Jean's Odd Match."

60. Axthelm, "The Case of Billie Jean King"; Amdur, "Homosexuality Sets Off Tremors," B15.

61. Although many therapists advise exactly the opposite for one's self-esteem, a number

of sports psychologists advised lesbian pros not to publicly "come out" (see Amdur, "Homosexuality Sets Off Tremors," and Jaime Diaz, "Find the Golf Here?" *Sports Illustrated,* February 13, 1989, 58–64). King said that everywhere players went, they were hassled. Players, officials, and tour followers were besieged with offers (of up to $25,000) to "tell all" about sex on the women's circuit. Navratilova also called it a "gay witch hunt." Ted Green, "Tough Old Lady Serves Notice She's Still Game," *Los Angeles Times,* May 27, 1981, sec. 3, pp. 1, 6.

62. See, for example, Sarah Pileggi, "Martina's Garden," *Sports Illustrated,* April 6, 1981, 63–64; Pileggi, "New Avon Lady Came Calling," 44–49.

63. Stephanie Salter, "Citizen Navratilova: Is She Home at Last?" *World Tennis* (December 1981): 30–35; Navratilova and Vecsey, *Martina,* 195–207.

64. Pete Axthelm, "The Curse of the Unlovable Champs," *Newsweek,* September 24, 1984, 62.

65. Navratilova tried to take such things in stride, believing a small percentage of fans would reject women's tennis because of a lesbian presence there, but that women's tennis did not want those spectators anyway since they probably harbored other prejudices as well. Navratilova with Vecsey, *Martina,* 55.

66. Salter, "Citizen Navratilova."

67. N. I. Richardson, Beverly Lynn Boyarsky, and Thomas M. Maxwell, letters to the editor, *World Tennis* (January and February 1982).

68. Interestingly, she got that reception when she lost rather than won, and as she got older. The most prominent outpouring of support for Navratilova in the early 1980s came during the U.S. Open finals in 1981, when she lost to Austin. In the late 1980s, as she became older and more beatable, more fans rooted for her. Pete Axthelm with Pamela Abramson and Stephanie Russell, "Martina: A Style All Her Own," *Newsweek,* September 6, 1982, 44–48; Navratilova with Vecsey, *Martina,* 219.

69. Navratilova with Vecsey, *Martina,* 211.

70. Ibid., 269–76.

71. Lichtenstein, "Will the Real Women Pros Please Stand Up?" 88.

72. Navratilova with Vecsey, *Martina,* 211.

73. Ibid., 211–12, 214, 53, 79; Axthelm with Abramson and Russell, "Martina: A Style All Her Own," 44–48; Frank Deford, "Another Big Mac Attack," *Sports Illustrated,* September 28, 1981.

74. Blue, *Grace Under Pressure,* 115–16.

75. Regardless of the reasons behind Navratilova's changed image, it seemed to have helped her self-image. "I felt confident and healthy and feminine," she recalled. "When you feel good about yourself, you look better and perform better, too." Navratilova with Vecsey, *Martina,* 215.

76. Barry Lorge, "Chrissie Got the Back of Martina's Hand," *Sports Illustrated,* December 27, 1982–January 3, 1983, 30–31.

77. Frank Deford, "She Put Herself into High Gear and Headed North," *Sports Illustrated,* September 19, 1983, 29–31.

78. Eve E. Ellis, "Girls Get a Mixed Message," *NYT,* December 11, 1983, sec. 5, p. 2.

79. Navratilova with Vecsey, *Martina,* 211, 243, 268.

80. King, interview; King with Starr, *We Have Come a Long Way,* 184. Diamond is quoted in Lorge, "Women's Tennis and the Feminine Mystique."

81. Lindsey Beaven, *Getting Started, 1986: The WTA Guide to Playing Professional Tennis,* 35. The guide was given out to all juniors aspiring to become professionals. It also informed

them that they were more likely to get endorsements if they were "very attractive, i.e. physically marketable."

82. King did declare that while Evert was good for tennis because she was "safe . . . like the girl next door," Navratilova was also good for tennis. She said that at seminars for the players, "We try to explain to them, 'Each of you has something unique.'" On the other hand, she had some very conservative assumptions. She believed marketing research indicated that tennis needed to aim for audiences' "comfort zone." "People have to feel safe. It can't be too radical" (King, interview).

83. King and Deford, *Billie Jean*, 192.

84. Lichtenstein, "Will the Real Women Pros Please Stand Up?" 88.

85. Stabiner, *Courting Fame*, 156; Lichtenstein, "Will the Real Women Pros Please Stand Up?" 88, 156. Ever the pragmatist, King did not object to the calendar. Of it, she said, "I don't mind it. . . . You can be 'exploited' as long as it's mutual. In other words, if Chris Evert likes being in that calendar . . . and the person who's making the calendar likes it, then that's okay—if that's what they want, if they make that decision. That's freedom of choice. See that's just as important as the other side of the coin: if you don't like it, then that's okay" (King, interview). King also tried to distinguish between players "trying to apologize for their muscles" and those "trying to sell themselves commercially." King with Starr, *We Have Come a Long Way*, 184.

86. Pileggi, "Rolling onto a New Track," 36–38.

87. B. J. Phillips, "Not Cinderella—Just the Best," *Time*, September 14, 1981, 77–80.

88. Deford, "Love and Love," 68–84.

89. Quoted in Evert Lloyd, "In Defense of Billie Jean."

90. Besides balancing separate and coed tournaments, a number of pros experimented with an entirely new format designed by Larry and Billie Jean King. Team Tennis was a professional league made up of coed teams playing for a short season.

10. Dreams Deferred: Professional Basketball in the 1980s

1. The quotation by Molly Van Venthuysen Bolin in the epigraph is from Roy S. Johnson, "The Lady Is a Hot Shot," *Sports Illustrated*, April 6, 1981, 33.

2. Most of the elite players and coaches wanted to use men's rules because they did not want to be held back and be at a disadvantage to other countries. Some players, though, did not care so much since they were accustomed to their different game. A few people were strongly opposed to changing the rules, believing the women's game to be appropriately different and more appealing because of that difference. One sponsor, in fact, of a nationally prominent team dropped his sponsorship when the AAU switched to men's rules. See Bishop, "AAU Women's Basketball."

3. Downing, "Women's Basketball."

4. Carol Kleiman, "Women Cagers Dream of Pros," *Chicago Tribune*, January 24, 1983, sec. 4, p. 11.; Sarah Pileggi, "Full of Heart in an Empty House," *Sports Illustrated*, March 10, 1980, 34–38.

5. Margaret Roach, "New 12-Team Pro League Fulfills Basketball Dreams," *NYT*, January 23, 1977, sec. 5, p. 5.

6. Al Harvin, "Female Pros Make History," *NYT*, December 10, 1978, sec. 5, p. 7.

7. Gary Kriss, "Female Stars Seeking Identity," *NYT*, February 4, 1979, sec. 22, pp. 1, 5.

8. Nancy Williamson, "Red Ink, Rosy Future," *Sports Illustrated*, May 14, 1979, 64.

9. Janice Selinger, "Gems Sparkling in Elizabeth," *NYT*, March 11, 1979, sec. 11, p. 11; Grace Lichtenstein, "Women's Pro Basketball League: The New Million-Dollar Baby," *Ms.*, March 1980, 70; Pileggi, "Full of Heart in an Empty House," 34.

10. Robin Herman, "For Female Basketball, A Big Bounce Forward," *NYT*, July 19, 1978, A14.

11. Skip Myslenski, "How Goes the Hustle?" *Chicago Tribune*, January 18, 1981, sec. 9, p. 9.

12. Al Harvin, "Women's Pro Basketball League Passes Its First Test," *NYT*, April 29, 1979, sec. 5, p. 4.

13. Williamson, "Red Ink, Rosy Future," 64.

14. Marquis quoted in Lichtenstein, "WPBL: New Million-Dollar Baby," 72; Skip Myslenski, "Hustle Struggling to Beat Sexism," *Chicago Tribune*, January 14, 1979, sec. 4, p. 1.

15. Herman, "For Female Basketball, a Big Bounce Forward."

16. Lacy J. Banks, "A 'Money' Career for Women in Basketball," *Ebony*, April 1980, 82.

17. Herman, "For Female Basketball, a Big Bounce Forward."

18. Lichtenstein, "WPBL: New Million-Dollar Baby," 72; Myslenski, "Hustle Struggling to Beat Sexism."

19. Harvin, "Female Pros Make History," 7.

20. Robin Herman, "Jersey Gems Lose in Debut," *NYT*, December 18, 1978, C3.

21. Harvin, "WPBL Passes Its First Test."

22. One article put the amount he sold the franchise for at $1 million. See Lichtenstein, "WPBL: New Million-Dollar Baby," 72.

23. Lichtenstein, "WPBL: New Million-Dollar Baby," 72; Harvin, "Female Pros Make History."

24. Williamson, "Red Ink, Rosy Future," 68.

25. Harvin, "WPBL Passes Its First Test."

26. Ibid.

27. Williamson, "Red Ink, Rosy Future," 64.

28. Ibid., 68.

29. Harvin, "WPBL Passes Its First Test."

30. Quoted in Banks, "A 'Money' Career for Women in Basketball," 75.

31. Crevier quoted in Williamson, "Red Ink, Rosy Future," 64.

32. Quoted in Williamson, "Red Ink, Rosy Future," 67; Jane Gross, "First-Place Stars Go Second Class by Pro Standards," *NYT*, December 24, 1979, C1.

33. But the WBL's salaries averaged only about a tenth of those in the NBA. Jane Gross, "Lieberman Makes a Sales Pitch," *NYT*, June 14, 1980, 16.

34. Myslenski, "How Goes the Hustle?" 8.

35. "Watching the Stars," *New Yorker*, February 18, 1980, 28.

36. Williamson, "Red Ink, Rosy Future," 64.

37. Pileggi, "Full of Heart in an Empty House," 38.

38. Jeff Lyon, "The Hustle: A Sparkle of Life Stirs in Only Game That's Left in Town," *Chicago Tribune*, December 18, 1978, sec. 3, p. 1. A male fan in Chicago wrote the *Chicago Tribune* to complain about that very problem, and said that one or two stories would not suffice for him. Letter to the editor, *Chicago Tribune*, January 23, 1979, sec. 3, p. 2.

39. Pileggi, "Full of Heart in an Empty House," 37.

40. Ibid., 37.

41. Quoted in Myslenski, "Hustle Struggling to Beat Sexism."

42. Quoted in Geils, "Making a Dream Come True."

43. Bill Jauss, "Fincher Fights Her Sexy Stereotype with Hustle," *Chicago Tribune*, November 16, 1979, sec. 6, p. 2. Even coaches sometimes patronized players by calling them kids or girls. One refused to call them women even after players repeatedly asked. "This is a business, not a women's lib thing," he replied bluntly. Mariah Burton Nelson, "Personal Fouls: How I Was Slam-Dunked by the Women's Pro Basketball League," *Gay Games IV Official Program*, June 18–25, 1994 (New York: New York in '94, Inc., 1994), 35.

44. Lichtenstein, "WPBL: New Million-Dollar Baby."

45. Outnumbered feminist fans there, appreciating Fincher's defensive skills, countered with their own T-shirts, which read "Shadow." Jauss, "Fincher Fights Her Sexy Stereotype with Hustle."

46. In fact, one male observer of an intrasquad promotional game made that exact comment: "I really thought they were good. They looked like girls, but on the court they also looked like guys—you know what I mean?" Quoted in Kriss, "Female Stars Seeking Identity."

47. Geils, "Making a Dream Come True."

48. Susan Stilton, "How to Be Charming While Dribbling," *Ms.*, October 1980, 25; Nelson, "Personal Fouls," 35.

49. Myslenski, "Hustle Struggling to Beat Sexism."

50. Stilton, "How to Be Charming While Dribbling," 25.

51. Kriss, "Female Stars Seeking Identity"; Les Williams, "Westchester Journal," *NYT*, July 15, 1979.

52. Skip Myslenski, "Pro Is More Than Being Paid," *Chicago Tribune*, January 15, 1979, sec. 5, p. 5; Myslenski, "Hustle Struggling to Beat Sexism," 4.

53. Sharon Farrah, "Finding Anonymity But Also Satisfaction," *NYT*, July 20, 1980, sec. 5, p. 2; for lesbians hiding their sexuality, see Nelson, "Personal Fouls," 34–35.

54. Stilton, "How to Be Charming While Dribbling," 25.

55. Myslenski, "Pro Is More Than Being Paid," 5.

56. Johnson, "The Lady Is a Hot Shot," 34.

57. Carol Kleiman, "Women Are No Longer Stuck with Half a Court," *Chicago Tribune*, January 27, 1980, sec. 12, p. 3; Myslenski, "How Goes the Hustle?" 9.

58. Myslenski, "How Goes the Hustle?" 14, 16.

59. Trish Roberts, interview by author, Chapel Hill, N.C., April 7, 1988.

60. Informal conversations with WBL players, summer 1982.

61. Banks, "A 'Money' Career for Women in Basketball," 75–82.

62. Kriss, "Female Stars Seeking Identity"; Williamson, "Red Ink, Rosy Future," 68.

63. Williams, "Westchester Journal."

64. Sharon Johnson, "Ann Meyers Signs Amid Doubts," *NYT*, September 6, 1979, D15; Jim Naughton, "Pacers Set to Sign Ann Meyers," *NYT*, September 5, 1979, B7.

65. Alex Yannis, "Miss Meyers Agrees to Sign with Gems," *NYT*, November 15, 1979, B22; "WBL Stars, Miss Meyers Unable to Agree to Terms," *NYT*, October 4, 1979, D19.

66. Geils, "Making a Dream Come True."

67. Farrah, "Finding Anonymity But Also Satisfaction," 2.

68. Jane Gross, "Nancy Lieberman No. 1 Pick by Dallas," *NYT*, June 17, 1980, C15.

69. "2 Women's Fives Fold," *NYT*, December 22, 1979; "W.B.L. Reported Running Ailing Philadelphia Club," *NYT*, December 21, 1979; Myslenski, "How Goes the Hustle?" 9.

70. "W.B.L.'s Milwaukee Team Is in Danger of Folding," *NYT*, January 31, 1980, 21.

71. Quoted in Banks "A 'Money' Career for Women in Basketball," 75; see also Myslenski, "How Goes the Hustle?" 9; Nelson, "Personal Fouls," 35.

72. Myslenski, "How Goes the Hustle?" 9.

73. Gross, "Lieberman No. 1 Pick by Dallas."

74. Gross, "First-Place Stars Go Second Class."

75. Gross, "Lieberman No. 1 Pick by Dallas"; Gross, "First-Place Stars Go Second Class."

76. Lichtenstein, "WPBL: New Million-Dollar Baby."

77. Geils, "Making a Dream Come True."

78. Gross, "Lieberman No. 1 Pick by Dallas"; Carrie Seidman, "Another Season, Another Struggle for W.B.L.," NYT, December 7, 1980, sec. 5, p. 9.

79. Myslenski, "How Goes the Hustle?" 9–10; Seidman, "Another Season, Another Struggle for W.B.L."

80. Geils, "Making a Dream Come True."

81. Myslenski, "How Goes the Hustle?" 10–16.

82. Seidman, "Another Season, Another Struggle for W.B.L."

83. Myslenski, "How Goes the Hustle?" 14.

84. Geils, "Making a Dream Come True."

85. "Players' Association Is Formed in W.B.L.," NYT, November 6, 1980, B19.

86. Myslenski, "How Goes the Hustle?" 12; Nelson, "Personal Fouls," 35.

87. Geils, "Making a Dream Come True."

88. Ibid.

89. "W.B.L. Season in Peril, a Club Owner Warns," NYT, October 29, 1981; Thomas Rogers, "Dead or Alive?" NYT, November 23, 1981.

90. Williamson, "Red Ink, Rosy Future," 64–67; Roy S. Johnson, "The Lady Is a Hot Shot," 34.

91. Myslenski, "How Goes the Hustle?" 8–9.

92. Roberts, interview.

93. "We were treated as people, real fair," said one Chicago player after her first year. "A lot of teams weren't like that. A lot used their girls." Myslenski, "How Goes the Hustle?" 9.

94. Geils, "Making a Dream Come True"; Pileggi, "Full of Heart in an Empty House," 38.

95. Kleiman, "Women Cagers Dream of Pros."

96. Robin Herman, "Another 'Pearl' in the Pros," NYT, December 16, 1978, 14.

97. Professional leagues for women existed overseas, but obviously moving there was a risky venture. While they did constitute an opportunity for players, the overseas leagues did nothing to improve the image of women's basketball in the United States, nor to encourage youngsters to aspire, since they were largely unknown.

Epilogue: Women's Sports in the 1990s

1. Valerie Helmbeck, "Mechem, Players Dismiss Comments," USA Today, May 12, 1995, C3.

2. Every March over five thousand lesbians go to the Dinah Shore Golf Tournament in Palm Springs in an annual gay tourist event (Susan Reed, "Someone's on the Fairway with Dinah," Gay Games IV Official Program, June 18–25, 1994 [New York: New York in '94, Inc., 1994], 23). According to gay columnist Deb Price, lesbians also pack galleries at some other LPGA events. She says the LPGA ought to denounce the homophobia out of respect to its loyal fans. Deb Price, "LPGA Lesbians Should Just Come Out Swinging," USA Today, May 19, 1995, C3.

3. Quoted in Jaime Diaz, "Find the Golf Here?" *Sports Illustrated*, February 13, 1989, 59.

4. Volpe quoted in Diaz, "Find the Golf Here?" 64–64.

5. Mark Soltau, "Giving Women's Golf a Makeover," *San Francisco Examiner*, June 5, 1994, D1, 9.

6. Quoted in Robert Cross, "Chipping Away," *Chicago Tribune*, July 12, 1992, sec. 6, p. 3.

7. The growth was averaging over 9 percent a year between 1986 and 1990. Leonard Shapiro, "LPGA Tries to Wedge into Market," *Washington Post*, May 24, 1995, B1, 5.

8. Christine Brennan, "Golfers All of Them, but Not Exactly by Choice," *Washington Post*, June 11, 1993, C6.

9. Although the journalist interviewing Wright had taken careful notes, the interview was not taped. CBS chose to accept Wright's denial and did not punish him. This stood in contrast to other recent events in which television networks had dismissed commentators who made controversial or insulting comments (even one about a golf course). Unfortunately, some no doubt took from the incident the message that it is permissible to insult women and the homosexual community. However, the outcry also suggests that many did not find the comments appropriate. Tony Kornheiser, "Wright and Wrong," *Washington Post*, May 16, 1995, F1; Richard Sandomir, "A 'He Said, She Said' Story with a Twist," *NYT*, May 16, 1995, B1; "She Said, He Said," *Sports Illustrated*, May 22, 1995, 16.

10. Susan Reed, "Unlevel Playing Fields," *Gay Games IV Official Program*, 20.

11. Debra E. Blum, "College Sports' L-Word," *Chronicle of Higher Education* (hereafter, *Chronicle*), March 9, 1994, A35; Helen Thompson, "A Whole New Ball Game," *Texas Monthly*, March 1994, 92–94, 145–46. Off the record, other coaches have told me of a particularly pernicious example of a long list of supposedly lesbian coaches being sent to students. Functioning in a similar way are other coaches who publicly state they will not permit lesbians on their teams. See, for example, the Rene Portland incident at Penn State University. Robert Lipsyte, "Penn State Coach Will Abide by Lesbian Policy, but Won't Discuss It," *NYT*, December 20, 1991, B14.

12. A student at the University of Maryland has sued the field hockey coach for forcing her to keep quiet about being homosexual. The coach allegedly threatened to revoke the student's athletic scholarship if public displays of lesbianism continued. "Athletics Notes," *Chronicle*, February 23, 1994, A43. This phenomenon of coaches insisting that lesbian players remain closeted rarely makes the news but apparently is fairly common.

13. "History of the Gay Games," *The Games Guide* (New York: Gay Games IV, 1994), 38.

14. "Every Athlete Has a Story," *Gay Games IV Official Program*, 50–55, 19.

15. "Scorecard #2," *Gay Games IV Official Program*, 31.

16. Jay Hill, letter to participants, *Gay Games IV Official Program*, 2.

17. "I Feel So Good," *Detroit News*, June 23, 1994, B3.

18. Statistics about bowling are courtesy of the Women's International Bowling Congress (and Alicia Denzer). Those concerned with softball are from the Amateur Softball Association (and Bill Plummer III).

19. *The Bowlers' Almanac* (Greendale, Wis.: American Bowling Congress and Women's International Bowling Congress, 1994).

20. See, for example, Gerald Eskenazi, "U.S. Women Show the Way," *NYT*, February 20, 1992, B9.

21. Merrell Noden, "Dying to Win," *Sports Illustrated*, August 8, 1994, 54.

22. Quote is from William Plummer in Plummer et al, "Dying for a Medal," *People Weekly*, August 22, 1994, 37. Former tennis pro Julie Anthony estimated that 30 percent of women on

the tennis tour have eating problems (see Noden, "Dying to Win"). A Princeton cross-country coach guessed that 70 percent of his athletes had dabbled in anorexic and bulimic behavior. Perhaps coincidentally, one study shows that high school athletes participating in cross-country have more injuries than those in any other sport. Marc Bloom, "Girls' Cross-Country Taking a Heavy Toll, Study Shows," *NYT*, December 3, 1994, 1.

23. Noden, "Dying to Win," 58.

24. Ibid., 60.

25. Quoted in Susan Bickelhaupt, "The Thin Game," *Boston Globe*, January 13, 1989, 73, 80; Carol Krucoff, "Female Athletes at Risk," *Washington Post*, August 25, 1992 (health supplement), 16; Noden, "Dying to Win," 60.

26. Krucoff, "Female Athletes at Risk," 16.

27. Susan Bickelhaupt, "Two Stars Were Afflicted," *Boston Globe*, January 13, 1989, 80; Noden, "Dying to Win, 58.

28. Bickelhaupt, "Two Stars Were Afflicted."

29. Noden, "Dying to Win," 60; Plummer, "Dying for a Medal," 39.

30. Plummer, "Dying for a Medal," 39.

31. Nelson, *The Stronger Women Get, the More Men Love Football*; Robert Lipsyte, "A Fight to Run Their Own Games," *NYT*, March 25, 1994, B10. Denise Klemencic, a former member of Ohio State University's track team, sued the university, claiming she was denied the opportunity to train with the team and help coach because she had rejected the head coach's sexual advances. In 1991 the university reprimanded the coach for misconduct. "Athletics Notes," *Chronicle*, June 1, 1994, A36.

32. Kelli Anderson, "No Room at the Top," *Sports Illustrated*, September 28, 1992, 62; Mary Faber, "Who's Coaching Girls' Sports?" *NEA Today* (February 1994): 6; Vivian Acosta and Linda Jean Carpenter, "As the Years Go By—Coaching Opportunities in the 1990s," *Journal of Health, Physical Education, Recreation, and Dance* (March 1992): 36.

33. Anderson, "No Room at the Top," 62. In 1994 only fourteen of 301 Division I athletic directors were women. At the 106 schools that played I-A football (the most powerful universities), only four women were athletic directors. Staci D. Kramer, "One to Watch," *Sporting News*, September 5, 1994, 32.

34. Mean household income of triathletes in 1994 was $72,500. Eighty-one percent male and very educated, triathletes trained eleven hours a week and spent over $3,000 on sports purchases per year. Survey results from *Inside Triathlon*, courtesy of Triathlon Federation USA.

35. Debra E. Blum, "A Different 'Equity,'" *Chronicle*, May 18, 1994, A35; Blum, "Forum Examines Discrimination Against Black Women in College Sports," *Chronicle*, April 21, 1993, A39. On restrictive golf policies, see, for example, Lynette Holloway, "What? No Husband?" *NYT*, August 16, 1993, B1, 5.

36. Doug Smith, "Last Hurrah," *USA Today*, July 1, 1994, 1.

37. John Young, "Goodbye, Martina," *Washington Times*, November 13, 1994.

38. Paul Attner, "Martina Wins One for the Ages," *Sporting News*, July 16, 1990; Dave Kindred, "Earning a Piece of History," *Sporting News*, July 11, 1994.

39. Linda Castrone, "Court of Last Resort," *Rocky Mountain News*, January 17, 1993.

40. Collins quoted in Young, "Goodbye, Martina." Navratilova herself said the press had been extremely fair to her for the last seven or eight years.

41. One of the major stories actually was about how loud Monica Seles grunted during points, an issue never raised about male players. In another incident, reporters asked Jan

Novotna if her ring was a wedding ring. " 'I'm not married to anybody—and I think it's none of anybody's business,' she answered." George Vecsey, "Next Waves Pounding Navratilova," *NYT*, July 2, 1993, B9.

42. Robin Finn, "For Seles, the Wound Still Hurts," *NYT*, August 27, 1993, B12.

43. *Sports Illustrated* chastised players as being spoiled, selfish, lazy, boring, and unwilling to contribute to their sport. Sally Jenkins, "The Sorry State of Tennis," *Sports Illustrated*, May 9, 1994, 78–86.

44. Critics attacked the WTA for linking sports and smoking, which may be one reason Virginia Slims cigarettes ended its sponsorship. Michael Precker, "Slim Funding," *Dallas Morning News*, December 9, 1992; Billie Jean King, "Women Pros Are Not 'Being Used' to Promote Smoking," letter to the editor, *NYT*, December 2, 1993, A26.

45. Young Venus Williams is one example. See Sally Jenkins, "Venus Rising," *Sports Illustrated*, November 14, 1994, 30, 32.

46. Young, "Goodbye, Martina"; Cart, "Martina's Gone, So Now What?" *Los Angeles Times*, January 12, 1995.

47. The exact number is 397,586 ("1993 Sports Participation Survey," *1993–94 Handbook*, National Federation of State High School Associations, Kansas City, Mo.). Coaches report that only a few really great players used to graduate from high school each year, but today the number is closer to ten or fifteen.

48. Salaries for coaches of women's basketball teams average 59 percent of men's teams, but at a number of top-ranked schools such as Iowa, Virginia, and Stanford they make the same amount as coaches of the men's teams.

49. Jack Craig, "He's Taking Himself Out of the Women's Game," *Boston Globe*, March 17, 1995, 64. Craig said that other women's sports like track and field and figure skating were as exciting or more than men's, but that basketball was a pale imitation because of women's physical limitations. He also admitted he had never watched a women's basketball game in person.

50. Richard Sandomir, "Women's Sports Get a Boost," *NYT*, April 9, 1995, sec. 8, p. 7.

51. In 1994–95 Smith dunked during a game. However, Smith and two teammates regularly excited fans unaccustomed to women playing above the rim by dunking in pregame warmups.

52. Malcolm Moran, "UConn's Women Make a Perfect Season Better," *NYT*, January 17, 1995, A1. For Tennessee attendance figures, see Frederick C. Klein, "Women's Hoops' Hottest Ticket," *Wall Street Journal*, February 27, 1995, A10.

53. Kelly Carter, "Land of Opportunity," *Dallas Morning News*, June 20, 1990.

54. Dona Carter, "A New E.R.A.," *Denver Post*, April 15, 1991, D1, 8; Jena Janovy, "The Spandex League," *NYT*, March 6, 1991, A25.

55. Elizabeth Birge, "No Net Gain," *Chicago Tribune*, May 1, 1994, sec. 5, pp. 1, 5.

56. Theresa Munoz, "Few Fast Breaks," *Los Angeles Times*, July 14, 1991.

57. Continually followed by a Italian fan, Jennifer Azzi recalled crying and wondering, "Why am I doing this?" Alexander Wolff, "The Home Team," *Sports Illustrated*, May 29, 1995, 65.

58. Kelly Carter, "Land of Opportunity." Stanford coach Tara VanDeveer summed it up. "They love basketball, but hate that they have to go away to play it."

59. Wolff, "The Home Team," 66, 69; Debbie Becker, "McClain Puts Team Before Big Money," *USA Today*, May 23, 1995, C3.

60. The study was performed by the Lyndon B. Johnson School of Public Affairs (the quote

is from Debra E. Blum, "Rights Office at Education Department Blasted for Lax Bias Enforcement," *Chronicle*, March 3, 1993, A40). See also Robert McG. Thomas, Jr., "Major Step Against Sex Discrimination," *NYT*, February 27, 1992, B12; Courtney Leatherman, "Congress Overrides President's Veto of Civil-Rights Bill, Countering High Court's 'Grove City' Decision," *Chronicle*, March 30, 1988, A1.

61. Debra E. Blum, "7 Women Sue U. of Texas, Demanding Varsity Teams," *Chronicle*, July 8, 1992, A32; Blum, "New Head of Civil-Rights Office Vows to Get Tough on College Sports," *Chronicle*, September 15, 1993, 1.

62. In fact, it made headlines and was big news when the Big Ten athletic conference announced it would gradually increase the number of females among its athletes to 40 percent. Douglas Lederman, "Plan to Increase Number of Female Athletes Backed by Big Ten's Faculty Representatives," *Chronicle*, May 20, 1992.

63. Douglas Lederman, "Men Outnumber Women and Get Most of Money in Big-Time Sports Programs," *Chronicle*, April 8, 1992, A1, 37; Malcolm Moran, "Title IX Is Now an Irresistible Force," *NYT*, June 21, 1992, sec. 8, p. 1.

64. Malcolm Moran, "Wanted: A Leaner and Lawful Goose," *NYT*, June 25, 1992, B13.

65. At 45 percent of Division I-A schools, football runs at a deficit. However, those universities make up the most powerful and vocal lobby (statistics quoted from Thomas O'Brien letter, "Help Women Athletes by Cutting Coaching Staffs," *Chronicle*, September 15, 1993, B3). *Sports Illustrated* had slightly different statistics—that about one-fifth of the NCAA's 554 football teams pay for themselves, and one-third of Division I-A programs run an annual deficit averaging over $1 million ("The Third Sex," February 6, 1995, 15).

66. Malcolm Moran, "Campus Changes Coming, Like It or Not," *NYT*, June 22, 1992, C1, 2.

67. Douglas Lederman, "NCAA Officials Try to Counter Charges of Sex Bias in Sports," *Chronicle*, April 15, 1992, A43. Fair-minded parents with only ten cookies wouldn't "give eight of them to the son and only two to their daughter," says Kansas coach Marian Washington. Institutions "have both men and women on their campuses and I believe they have an obligation to treat the sons and daughters fairly." Washington quoted in "Women Basketball Coaches: Grooming the Overlooked Stars of the Collegiate Sports World," *Ebony*, April 1994, 122.

68. Rice continued, "It just seems tighter now." Quoted in Moran, "Campus Changes Coming, Like It or Not," C2.

69. A coalition of coaches from nonrevenue-producing sports (field hockey, gymnastics, softball, swimming, track and field, volleyball, and water polo) realizes it is pointless for have-not men to battle have-not women and have begun mobilizing to get the focus put back on football. "The Third Sex," *Sports Illustrated*, February 6, 1995, 15.

70. "Militant women" in an "irrational attack on football" is quoted from Notre Dame's Rev. Edmund P. Joyce. Clemson's football coach declared everyone is taking potshots at football. Debra E. Blum, "Officials of Big-Time Football See Threat in Moves to Cut Costs and Provide Equity for Women," *Chronicle*, June 16, 1993, A35. The "emasculate" quote comes from Thompson, "A Whole New Ball Game."

71. Douglas Lederman, "Men Get 70% of Money Available for Athletic Scholarships at Colleges That Play Big-Time Sports, New Study Finds," *Chronicle*, March 18, 1992, A1, 45–46.

72. Debra E. Blum, "A Quiet NCAA Meeting?" *Chronicle*, December 8, 1993, A37; "N.C.A.A. Will Not Mandate Gender Equity," *NYT*, August 7, 1993, 33; "NCAA Panels to Sponsor Measures on Gender Equity and Cost Cutting," *Chronicle*, September 8, 1993, A36.

73. Douglas Lederman, "Abide by U.S. Sex-Bias Laws, NCAA Panel Urges Colleges," *Chronicle*, May 26, 1993, A31–32.

74. "The main enforcement problem is that the people who are aware of the inequities are afraid to speak because they're afraid of losing their jobs," writes Mariah Burton Nelson, quoted in Laura Mansnerus, "Women Take to the Field," *NYT*, January 5, 1992, sec. 4A, pp. 40–41.

75. Blum, "College Sports' L-Word," A35.

76. In another case, California State University agreed to pay $328,000 to a former sports administrator who claimed she was fired in 1991 because she pushed for gender equity. "Athletics Notes," *Chronicle*, June 1, 1994, A36.

77. "Graduations Surveyed," *NYT*, July 3, 1992, B6.

78. Debra E. Blum, "Backers of Women's Sports Wonder If Following in the Footsteps of Men's Programs Is a Good Idea," *Chronicle*, May 12, 1993, A41–42.

79. Blum, "Backers of Women's Sports Wonder," A42.

Conclusion

1. Billie Jean King has been an active reformer of tennis. Her most ambitious attempt was the creation of World Team Tennis, which did alter some of the game's rules, scoring, and structure.

2. Major innovations include efforts to stress participation (and personal bests) instead of victory, such as through the Special Olympics (for the handicapped) and the Senior Games (for senior citizens). Some women's running events, athletic leagues, and the Gay Games emphasize bringing groups of people together but have somewhat different outlooks. They slightly redefine competition as striving together instead of defeating one's opponent (power with versus power over). "New Games" (which are cooperative, physical group play intended to promote trust) may not fall under the heading of sports at all. Local and community athletic organizations are much more likely to experiment than are the older, more established national organizations.

3. The movement did not seek true integration (as in competing against men) but rather sought separate but equal status.

4. The entertainment strategy had its own problems. Tennis pros still had to please fans, who might want their female athletes to conform to certain standards of femininity, but obviously they enjoyed relative success.

5. Basketball as an aggressive team sport did not have the traditions, reputation, coed history, or class connections of tennis. The WBL's failure also may be because in basketball the male standard (above the rim) is too established and admired, and that because of physiological disadvantages (and socialization) women have not been able to perform at that standard. Or it may be that the extreme popularity of men's basketball and the linking of it with masculinity make male spectators and sportswriters unwilling to give women a chance.

6. Mariah Burton Nelson makes the same argument (*Are We Winning Yet? How Women Are Changing Sports*).

7. The tennis pros continue playing in the coed, USLTA-run U.S. Open for those reasons.

8. Sport has perpetuated many other societal divisions and prejudices, including those based on age, ethnicity, weight, skill level, and physical disability, to mention just a few others.

SELECTED BIBLIOGRAPHY

Primary Sources

Autobiographical Works

Connolly, Maureen and Tom Gwynne. *Forehand Drive*. London: Macgibbon and Kee, 1957.

Court, Margaret and George McGann. *Court on Court*. New York: Cornwall Press, 1975.

Gibson, Althea. *I Always Wanted to Be Somebody*. New York: Harper, 1958.

———. *So Much to Live For*. New York: Putnam's, 1968.

Hart, Doris. *Tennis with Hart*. Philadelphia: Lippincott, 1955.

Heldman, Gladys. "The Women's Pro Circuit in Tennis." Transcript of address to the NAGWS convention (undated, probably 1975), in Association for Intercollegiate Athletics for Women papers, McKeldin Library, University of Maryland, Box 378.

King, Billie Jean and Frank Deford. *Billie Jean*. New York: Viking, 1982.

King, Billie Jean, with Cynthia Starr. *We Have Come a Long Way*. New York: McGraw-Hill, 1988.

King, Billie Jean, with Kim Chapin. *Billie Jean*. New York: Harper and Row, 1974.

Kopay, David. *The David Kopay Story: An Extraordinary Revelation*. New York: D. I. Fine, 1988.

Kramer, Jack, with Frank Deford. *The Game: My Forty Years in Tennis*. New York: Putnam's, 1979.

Lee, Mabel. *Memories Beyond Bloomers, 1924–1954*. Washington, D.C.: American Alliance for Health, Physical Education, and Recreation, 1978.

Lloyd, Chris Evert, with Neil Amdur. *Chrissie: My Own Story*. New York: Simon and Schuster, 1982.

Navratilova, Martina and George Vecsey. *Martina*. New York: Knopf, 1985.

Redin, Harley. *The Queens Fly High*. Plainview (Texas), 1958 (self-published).

Riggs, Bobby, with George McGann. *Court Hustler*. Philadelphia: Lippincott, 1973.

Ulrich, Celeste. "The Woman in Your Life." *The Amy Morris Homans Lecture*. Washington, D.C.: NAPECW, 1975.

Wills, Helen. *Fifty-Thirty: The Story of a Tennis Player.* New York: Scribners, 1937.

Government Documents

Association for Intercollegiate Athletics v. National Collegiate Athletic Association. 558 F. Supp. 487 (1983). U.S. District Court, District of Columbia, February 28, 1983.

Association for Intercollegiate Athletics for Women v. National Collegiate Athletic Association. 735 F.2d 577 (1984). U.S. Court of Appeals, District of Columbia Circuit, May 18, 1984.

Congressional Record. Washington, D.C.: GPO, August 6, 1971; November 4, 1971; February 15, 1972; February 28, 1972; May 22, 1972; May 23, 1972; July 10, 1975; July 15, 1975.

Grove City College v. Bell. 465 U.S. 555 (1984). U.S. Supreme Court, February 28, 1984.

"Nondiscrimination on Basis of Sex in Education Programs and Activities Receiving or Benefiting from Federal Financial Assistance," Rules and Regulations. *Federal Register* 40 (June 4, 1975): 24128–24144.

President's Council on Youth Fitness (PCYF). Workshop Reports, nos. 2, 3, and 4. Washington, D.C.: GPO, 1960.

President's Council on Physical Fitness (PCPF). "Sports for Fitness" (April 13, 1960). Workshop Report, no. 7. Washington, D.C.: GPO, 1961.

———. *Vigor: Complete Exercise Program for Boys 12 to 18.* Washington, D.C.: GPO, 1964.

———. *Vim: Complete Exercise Plan for Girls 12 to 18.* Washington, D.C.: GPO, 1964.

Proposed Policy Interpretation for Title IX and Intercollegiate Athletics. Federal Register 43 (December 11, 1978): 58070–58071.

Proposed Sex Discrimination Regulations. Federal Register 39 (June 20, 1974): 22228–22238.

"Title IX of the Education Amendments of 1972: A Policy Interpretation; Title IX and Intercollegiate Athletics." *Federal Register* 44 (December 11, 1979): 71413–71423.

U.S. Commission on Civil Rights. "Comments on a Proposed Policy Interpretation of Title IX of the Education Act of 1972." Copy in Box 43, AIAW papers.

———. Staff Options Paper. Revised Comments on Title IX Policy Interpretation, September 1979. Copy in Box 43, AIAW papers.

U.S. Congress. *Joint Hearings before the Committee on Education and Labor and the Subcommittee on Civil and Constitutional Rights of the Committee on the Judiciary on H.R. 700.* 99th Cong., 1st sess. March 1985.

U.S. Congress. House. Committee on Education and Labor. *Hearings before the Special Subcommittee on Education on H.R. 32, H.R. 5191, H.R. 5192, H.R. 5193, and H.R. 7248.* 92d Cong., 1st sess. March, April, and July 1971.

———. Committee on Education and Labor. *Hearings before the Special Subcommittee on Education on Sec. 805 of H.R. 16098.* 91st Cong., 2d sess. June and July 1970.

———. Committee on Education and Labor. *Hearings before the Subcommittee on Equal Opportunities on Concurrent Resolution 230 (Title IX Regulations.* 94th Cong., 1st sess. July 14, 1975.

———. Committee on Education and Labor. *Hearings before the Subcommittee on Postsecondary Education on "Sex Discrimination Regulations."* 94th Cong., 1st sess. June 17–26, 1975.

U.S. Congress. Senate. Committee on Labor and Public Welfare. *"Prohibition of Sex Discrimination, 1975": Hearings before the Subcommittee on Education on S. 2106 to Amend Title IX.* 94th Cong., 1st sess. September 16 and 18, 1975.

——. Committee on Labor and Public Welfare. *"Women's Equity Act of 1973": Hearings before the Subcommittee on Education on S. 2518.* 93rd Cong., 1st sess. October 17 and November 9, 1973.

——. *Hearings before the Committee on Labor and Human Resources on S. 557.* 100th Cong., 1st sess. March 19 and April 1, 1987.

——. *"Sports Arbitration Board Report": Hearings before the Committee on Commerce.* 90th Cong., 2d sess. February 1, 1968.

U.S. Olympic Development Committee and the Division for Girls' and Women's Sports. *Proceedings of the National Institutes on Girls' Sports* (Washington, D.C., 1965–1969).

Manuscript Collections

Association for Intercollegiate Athletics for Women (AIAW) papers. Manuscripts Collection, McKeldin Library, University of Maryland, College Park, Maryland.

——. Box 43: Title IX materials, 1979–1982: telephone interviews with women in athletics; position statements; notes of meetings with HEW; monitoring of investigations; DeHart Coalition; U.S. Commission on Civil Rights.

——. Box 57: Trial materials, *AIAW v. NCAA*; AIAW press releases; minutes of AIAW-NCAA meetings.

——. Box 70: Trial materials, *AIAW v. NCAA*: defendants' exhibits and affidavits; Donna Lopiano Affidavit and Appendix.

——. Box 269: Publications and Official Minutes, Executive Board and Delegate Assemblies; Report of 1981 Think Tank; Presidential Addresses.

——. Box 279: Executive Committee files, correspondence, and reports.

——. Box 292: Alternative Ways to Govern Women's Intercollegiate Athletics.

——. Box 294: Title IX materials, 1974–1979: Think Tank, 1974; Comments to and notes from meetings with HEW; Tower Bill materials; National Coalition for Girls and Women in Education materials.

——. Box 378: AIAW newsletters; Study of AIAW member attitudes; Presentation to American Council on Education's President's Committee on Collegiate Athletics.

——. Box 404: Leotus Morrison Presidential papers; Correspondence about NCAA; Monitoring Title IX; *AIAW v. NCAA* legal action chronology; Television committees.

National Association for the Physical Education of College Women (NAPECW) papers. Manuscripts Collection. Jackson Library, University of North Carolina at Greensboro.

National Section on Women's Athletics (NSWA), National Section for Girls' and Women's Sports (NSGWS), Division for Girls' and Women's Sports (DGWS), and Commission on Intercollegiate Athletics (CIAW) papers. American Alliance for Health, Physical Education, and Recreation (AAHPER) archives. Reston, Virginia.

Southern Association of Physical Education for College Women (SAPECW) papers. Manuscripts Collection. Jackson Library, University of North Carolina at Greensboro.

Tuskegee Institute News Clippings File (microfilm edition). Division of Behavioral Research, Carver Research Foundation, Tuskegee Institute, Alabama.

Women's Physical Education Department and Title IX Committee papers. University of North Carolina at Chapel Hill. University of North Carolina Archives, Wilson Library, Chapel Hill, North Carolina.

Oral Histories

Dorrance, Anson. Chapel Hill, North Carolina. July 11, 1991.
Hogan, Frances. Chapel Hill, North Carolina. May 23 and June 23, 1991.
Holland, Mary C. March 16, 1988, and November 5, 1990 (telephone interviews).
Hult, Joan. College Park, Maryland. March 29, 1989.
Hunter, Gail. January 26, 1991 (telephone interview).
King, Billie Jean. December 10, 1988 (telephone interview).
McDermott, Marcia. Chapel Hill, North Carolina. June 27, 1991.
Polivy, Margot. Washington, D.C. March 28, 1989.
Roberts, Trish. Chapel Hill, North Carolina. April 7, 1988.
Stevenson, Karen L. July 15, 1991 (telephone interview).
Stokes, Maura. Chapel Hill, North Carolina. May 25, 1991.
Strange, Kathy. Greensboro, North Carolina. December 10, 1988.
Women's Basketball League players (who prefer anonymity). Chicago, Illinois. June 1984.

Organizational Publications

Amateur Athlete. New York: Amateur Athletic Union of the United States, 1950–1965.
Beaven, Lindsey. *Getting Started, 1986: The* WTA *Guide to Playing Professional Tennis.* St. Petersburg, Fla.: Lipton and the Women's Tennis Association, 1987.
Division for Girls' and Women's Sports (DGWS) and the National Association for the Physical Education of College Women (NAPECW). *Social Change and Sports: National Conference on Social Changes and Implications for Physical Education and Sports Programs.* Washington, D.C.: AAHPER, 1959.
Division for Girls' and Women's Sports National Conference. *Sports Programs for College Women.* Washington, D.C.: AAHPER, 1970.
Geadelmann, Patricia et al. *Equality in Sports for Women.* Washington, D.C.: AAHPER, 1977.
Journal of Health, Physical Education, and Recreation (after 1975, *Journal of Physical Education and Recreation*; after 1981, *Journal of Physical Education, Recreation, and Dance*). Washington, D.C.: AAHPER, 1950–1987.
National Association for Girls and Women's Sports. NAGWS *Research Reports.* Vol. 2. Washington, D.C.: AAHPER, 1977.
National Association for the Physical Education for College Women. NAPECW *Report—1962 and 1964: Biennial Conference.* Washington, D.C.: AAHPER, 1964.
——. *Proceedings of the* NAPECW/NCPEAM *National Conference.* Washington, D.C.: AAHPER, 1976.
National Collegiate Athletic Association (NCAA). *Annual Reports,* 1973–74 to 1986–87. (Library of Congress.)
——. NCAA *News.* Shawnee Mission, Kan.: NCAA, 1972–1984.
——. *Proceedings of the Annual Convention.* January 1975–January 1990. (Library of Congress.)
National Section for Girls' and Women's Sports (NSGWS). *Standards in Sports for Girls and Women: Guiding Principles in the Organization and Administration of Sports Programs.* Washington, D.C.: AAHPER, 1953.
——. *Standards in Sports for Girls and Women; Guiding Principles in the Organization and Administration of Sports Programs.* Washington, D.C.: AAHPER, 1958.

Snell, Catherine, ed. DGWS *Official Basketball and Officials Rating Guide for Girls and Women* (September 1957–58). Washington, D.C.: AAHPER, 1957.

Secondary Works

Adkins, Vivian B. "The Development of Negro Female Athletic Talent." P.E.D. diss., Indiana University, 1967.

Arwe, Karen E. "The Status of Athletics in Relation to Compliance with Title IX at the University of North Carolina at Chapel Hill in 1980–81." Master's thesis, University of North Carolina at Chapel Hill, 1981.

Barrett, Michelle. *Women's Oppression Today: Problems in Marxist Feminist Analysis.* London: NLB, 1980.

Bennett, Roberta S., K. Gail Whitaker, Nina Jo Wooley Smith, and Anne Sablove. "Changing the Rules of the Game: Reflections Toward a Feminist Analysis of Sport." *Women's Studies International Forum* 10, no. 4 (1987): 370–79.

Bishop, Elva Elisabeth. "Amateur Athletic Union Women's Basketball, 1950–1971: The Contributions of Hanes Hosiery, Nashville Business College, and Wayland Baptist College." Master's thesis, University of North Carolina at Chapel Hill, 1984.

Bishop, Elva E. and Katherine Fulton. "Shooting Stars." *Southern Exposure* 7, no. 2 (Fall 1979): 50–56.

Blue, Adrianne. *Grace Under Pressure: The Emergence of Women in Sport.* London: Sidgwick and Jackson, 1987.

Bontemps, Arna. *Famous Negro Athletes.* New York: Dodd Mead, 1964.

Boston Lesbian Psychology Collective, ed. *Lesbian Psychologies: Explorations and Challenges.* Urbana: University of Illinois Press, 1987.

Boutillier, Mary A. and Lucinda SanGiovanni. *The Sporting Woman.* Champaign, Ill.: Human Kinetics, 1983.

Brown, Wendy. "Finding the Man in the State. *Feminist Studies* 18, no. 1 (Spring 1992): 7–34.

Burns, Kristin L. "Reconstructing Leadership Experiences: Toward a Feminist Theory of Leadership." Ph.D. diss., University of Iowa, 1987.

Cahn, Susan. "Coming on Strong: Gender and Sexuality in Women's Sport, 1900–1960." Ph.D. diss., University of Minnesota, 1990.

———. *Coming On Strong: Gender and Sexuality in Twentieth-Century Women's Sport.* New York: Free Press, 1994

———. "From the 'Muscle Moll' to the 'Butch Ballplayer': Changing Meanings of 'Mannishness' in U.S. Women's Sport, 1900–1960." Paper presented at the Berkshire Conference on Women's History, June 1990.

Caso, Constance L. "A History of the Physical Activities Program at the University of North Carolina at Chapel Hill from 1950 to 1983." Master's thesis, University of North Carolina at Chapel Hill, 1988.

Cayleff, Susan. *Babe: The Life and Legend of Babe Didrikson Zaharias.* Champaign, Ill.: University of Illinois Press, 1995.

Chafe, William H. *The American Woman: Her Changing Social, Economic, and Political Roles, 1920–1970.* 2d ed. New York: Oxford University Press, 1974.

———. *Civilities and Civil Rights: Greensboro, North Carolina, and the Black Struggle for Freedom.* Oxford: Oxford University Press, 1980.

——. *The Paradox of Change: American Women in the 20th Century.* New York: Oxford University Press, 1991.

Chodorow, Nancy Julia. "Gender, Relation, and Difference in Psychoanalytic Perspective." In Hester Eisenstein and Alice Jardine, eds., *The Future of Difference.* 2d ed. New Brunswick, N.J.: Rutgers University Press, 1985.

Congressional Quarterly Almanac. Vols. 31 and 41. Washington, D.C.: Congressional Quarterly Inc., 1976 and 1986.

Culler, Jonathan. *On Deconstruction: Theory and Criticism After Structuralism.* Ithaca, N.Y.: Cornell University Press, 1982.

Cummings, Parke. *American Tennis: The Story of a Game and Its People.* Boston: Little, Brown, 1957.

Czikszentimihaly, Mihaly. *Beyond Boredom and Anxiety.* San Francisco: Jossey-Bass, 1975.

Davenport, Joanna. "The History and Interpretation of Amateurism in the United States Lawn Tennis Association." Ph.D. diss., Ohio State University, 1966.

Davis, Marianna W., ed. *Contributions of Black Women to America.* Vol. 1. Columbia, S.C.: Kenday Press, 1982.

Decrow, Karen. *Sexist Justice.* New York: Random House, 1974.

Deem, Rosemary. *All Work and No Play? A Study of Women and Leisure.* Milton Keynes, Eng.: Open University Press, 1986.

Del Rey, Patricia. "The Apologetic and Women in Sport." In Carole Oglesby, ed., *Women and Sport: From Myth to Reality,* 107–11.

D'Emilio, John. *Sexual Politics, Sexual Communities: The Making of a Homosexual Minority in the United States, 1940–1970.* Chicago: University of Chicago Press, 1983.

D'Emilio, John and Estelle B. Freedman. *Intimate Matters: A History of Sexuality in America.* New York: Harper and Row, 1988.

Domer, Thomas M. "Sport in Cold War America, 1953–1963: The Diplomatic and Political Use of Sport in the Eisenhower and Kennedy Administrations." Ph.D. diss., Marquette University, 1976.

Downing, Margaret Ruth. "Women's Basketball: An Historical Overview of Selected Athletic Organizations Which Influenced Its Ascension Toward Advanced Competition in the United States." Ph.D. diss., Texas Woman's University, 1983.

Du Bois, W. E. B. *Souls of Black Folk* (1903). Rpt., New York: Bantam Books, 1989.

Duncan, Margaret M. and Velda P. Cundiff. *Play Days for Girls and Women.* New York: A. S. Barnes, 1929.

Dunkle, Margaret. "Competitive Athletics: In Search of Equal Opportunity." Project on the Status and Education of Women. Washington, D.C.: U.S. Department of Health, Education, and Welfare, 1976.

Ebert, Frances H. and Billye Ann Cheatum. *Basketball.* Philadelphia: W. B. Saunders, 1977.

Edwards, Harry. *Sociology of Sport.* Homewood, Ill.: Dorsey Press, 1973.

Elam, Stanley M., ed. *A Decade of Gallup Polls Toward Education, 1969–1978.* Bloomington, Ind.: Phi Delta Kappa, 1978.

Engelmann, Larry. *The Goddess and the American Girl.* New York: Oxford University Press, 1988.

Evans, Sara M. *Born for Liberty: A History of Women in America.* New York: Free Press, 1989.

Faderman, Lillian. *Odd Girls and Twilight Lovers: A History of Lesbian Life in Twentieth-Century America.* New York: Penguin, 1992.

Felshin, Jan. "The Full Court Press for Women in Athletics." In Barbara J. Hoepner, ed.,

Women's Athletics: Coping with Controversy. Washington, D.C.: DGWS/AAHPER Publications, 1974.

——. "The Social View." In Ellen Gerber et al., *The American Woman in Sport*, 178–279.

——. "The Triple Option . . . for Women in Sport." *Quest* 21 (1974): 36–40.

Filene, Peter G. *Him/Her/Self: Sex Roles in Modern America.* 2d ed. Baltimore: Johns Hopkins University Press, 1986.

Foreman, Ken and Virginia Husted. *Track and Field Techniques for Girls and Women.* Dubuque, Iowa: William C. Brown, 1965.

Gallup, George H. *The Gallup Poll: Public Opinion, 1972–1977.* Vols. 1 and 2. Wilmington, Del.: Scholarly Resources, 1978.

Gerber, Ellen et al. *The American Woman in Sport.* Reading, Mass.: Addison-Wesley, 1974.

Gilligan, Carol. *In a Different Voice: Psychological Theory and Women's Development.* Cambridge: Harvard University Press, 1982.

Guthrie, Sharon Ruth. "Homophobia: Its Impact on Women in Sport and Physical Education." Master's thesis, California State University at Long Beach, 1982.

Guttmann, Allen. *The Games Must Go On: Avery Brundage and the Olympic Movement.* New York: Columbia University Press, 1984.

——. *A Whole New Ball Game: An Interpretation of American Sports.* Chapel Hill: University of North Carolina Press, 1988.

——. *Women's Sports: A History.* New York: Columbia University Press, 1991.

Halsey, Elizabeth. *Women in Physical Education: Their Role in Work, Home, and History.* New York: Putnam's, 1961.

Harris, Dorothy, ed. *Women and Sport: A National Research Conference.* College of Health, Physical Education, and Recreation: Pennsylvania State University, 1972.

Hart, Marie and Susan Birrell. *Sport in the Sociocultural Process.* 3d ed. Dubuque, Iowa: William C. Brown, 1981.

Henderson, Edwin B. *The Negro in Sports.* Washington, D.C.: Associated Publishers, 1939.

——. "The Negro in Tennis." *Negro History Bulletin* 15 (December 1951): 54.

——. "Negro Women in Sports." *Negro History Bulletin* 15 (December 1951): 55.

Himes, Cynthia L. "The Female Athlete in American Society, 1860–1940." Ph.D. diss., University of Pennsylvania, 1986.

Howell, Reet, ed. *Her Story in Sport: A Historical Anthology of Women in Sports.* West Point, N.Y.: Leisure Press, 1982.

Hunt, Virginia. "Governance of Women's Intercollegiate Athletics: An Historical Perspective." Ph.D. diss., University of North Carolina at Greensboro, 1976.

Hurst, Patricia L. "Carolina Women and the Ramifications of Title IX." Honors essay, University of North Carolina at Chapel Hill, 1988.

Kanowitz, Leo. *Sex Roles in Law and Society: Cases and Materials.* Albuquerque: University of New Mexico Press, 1973.

Kaplan, Janice. *Women and Sports.* New York: Viking, 1979.

Kratz, Laura. "A Study of Sports and the Implications of Women's Participation in Them in Modern Society." Ph.D. diss., Ohio State University, 1958.

Kuhn, Annette and AnnMarie Wolpe, eds. *Feminism and Materialism: Women and Modes of Production.* London: Routledge and Paul, 1978.

Leavitt, Norma. "College Physical Education for Women: The Past, the Present, and the Future." *Journal of Health, Physical Education, and Recreation* (October 1960): 78–79.

Lenskyj, Helen. "Female Sexuality and Women's Sport." *Women's Studies International Forum*

10, no. 4 (1987): 381–86.

———. *Out of Bounds: Women, Sport, and Sexuality*. Toronto: Women's Press, 1986.

Lichtenstein, Grace. *A Long Way Baby: Behind the Scenes in Women's Pro Tennis*. New York: Morrow, 1974.

Loulan, JoAnn. *Lesbian Passion*. San Francisco: Spinsters, 1987.

———. *Lesbian Sex*. San Francisco: Spinsters, 1984.

Lumpkin, Angela. *Women's Tennis: A Historical Documentary of the Players and Their Game*. Troy, N.Y.: Whitson, 1981.

MacKinnon, Catherine. *Toward A Feminist Theory of the State*. Cambridge: Harvard University Press, 1989.

Mangan, J. A. and Robert J. Park. *From "Fair Sex" to Feminism: Sport and the Socialization of Women in the Industrial and Post-Industrial Eras*. London: Frank Cass, 1987.

Messner, Michael. "Boyhood, Organized Sports, and the Construction of Masculinity." In Michael Kimmel and Michael Messner, eds., *Men's Lives*, 161–75. New York: Macmillan, 1989.

———. *Sex, Violence, and Power in Sports: Rethinking Masculinity*. Freedom, Calif.: Crossing Press, 1994.

Messner, Michael A. and Don F. Sabo, eds. *Sport, Men, and the Gender Order: Critical Feminist Perspectives*. Champaign, Ill.: Human Kinetics, 1990.

Metheny, Eleanor. "The Women's Look in Sports." In Metheny, *Connotations of Movement in Sport and Dance*, 43–56. Dubuque, Iowa: William C. Brown, 1965.

Michener, James. *Sport in America*. New York: Random House, 1976.

Nadler, Sylvia Faye. "A Developmental History of the Wayland Hutcherson Flying Queens from 1910 to 1979." Ed.D. diss., East Texas State University, 1980.

Neal, Patsy. *Basketball Techniques for Women*. New York: Ronald Press, 1966.

Nelson, Mariah Burton. *Are We Winning Yet? How Women Are Changing Sports*. New York: Random House, 1991.

———. *The Stronger Women Get, the More Men Love Football: Sexism and the American Culture of Sports*. New York: Harcourt Brace, 1994.

Oglesby, Carole A., ed. *Women and Sport: From Myth to Reality*. Philadelphia: Lea and Febiger, 1978.

Oriard, Michael. *Reading Football: How the Popular Press Created an American Spectacle*. Chapel Hill: University of North Carolina Press, 1993.

Parkhouse, Bonnie L. and Jackie Lapin. *The Woman in Athletic Administration*. Santa Monica, Calif.: Goodyear, 1980.

Paterson, Ann, ed. *Team Sports for Girls*. New York: Ronald Press, 1958.

Picker, Jane M. "Law and the Status of Women in the United States." In Columbia Human Rights Law Review, eds., *Law and the Status of Women: An International Symposium*. New York: United Nations Centre for Social Development and Humanitarian Affairs, 1977.

Piven, Frances Fox and Richard Cloward. *Poor Peoples' Movements: Why They Succeed, How They Fail*. New York: Pantheon, 1977.

Postow, Betsy, ed. *Women, Philosophy, and Sport: A Collection of New Essays*. Metuchen, N.J.: Scarecrow Press, 1983.

Pronger, Brian. *The Arena of Masculinity: Sports, Homosexuality, and the Meaning of Sex*. New York: St. Martin's, 1990.

Rabine, Leslie Wahl. "A Feminist Politics of Non-Identity." *Feminist Studies* 14, no. 1 (Spring 1988): 11–39.

Riess, Steven A. "The New Sport History." *Reviews in American History* 18 (1990): 311–25.

Rotundo, E. Anthony. *American Manhood: Transformations in Masculinity from the Revolution to the Modern Era.* New York: Basic Books, 1993.

Rush, Rob. *Sandlot Seasons: Sport in Black Pittsburgh.* Urbana: University of Illinois Press, 1987.

Rohrbaugh, Joanna Bunker. "Femininity on the Line." *Psychology Today* (August 1979): 30–38.

Russell, Jane Ann. "Tennis and the Woman Player: Why the Changes?" Ed.D. diss., University of Georgia, 1981.

Sabo, Don. *Jock: Sports and Male Identity.* Englewood Cliffs, N.J.: Prentice-Hall, 1980.

Sachs, Albie and Joan Hoff Wilson. *Sexism and the Law: A Study of Male Beliefs and Legal Bias in Britain and the United States.* New York: Free Press, 1979.

Scott, Joan. "Deconstructing Equality-versus-Difference: Or, The Uses of Poststructuralist Theory for Feminism." *Feminist Studies* 14, no. 1 (Spring 1988): 33–52.

———. "Gender: A Useful Category of Analysis." *American Historical Review* 91 (December 1986): 1053–75.

Scott, Phebe M. and Virginia R. Crafts. *Track and Field for Girls and Women.* New York: Appleton—Century—Crofts, 1964.

Sophie, Joan. "Internalized Homophobia and Lesbian Identity." *Journal of Homosexuality* 14, nos. 1–2 (1987): 53–65.

Spears, Betty. *History of Sport and Physical Activity in the United States.* 3d ed. Dubuque, Iowa: William C. Brown, 1988.

———. *Leading the Way: Amy Morris Homans and the Beginnings of Professional Education for Women.* New York: Greenwood, 1986.

Spreitzer, Elmer, Eldon Snyder, and Joseph Kivlin. "A Summary of Some Research Studies Concerning the Female Athlete." *Frontiers* 3, no. 1 (1978): 14–19.

Stabiner, Karen. *Courting Fame: The Perilous Road to Women's Tennis Stardom.* New York: Harper and Row, 1986.

St. Clair, Stephen. "The Play Day/Sport Day Movement in Selected Colleges of the South." Ed.D. diss., University of North Carolina-Greensboro, 1984.

Struna, Nancy. "Beyond Mapping Experience: The Need for Understanding in the History of American Sporting Women." *Journal of Sport History* 11, no. 1 (Spring 1984): 120–33.

Thaxton, Nolan A. "A Documentary Analysis of Competitive Track and Field at Tuskegee Institute and Tennessee State University." D.P.E. diss., Springfield College, 1970.

Tygiel, Jules. *Baseball's Great Experiment: Jackie Robinson and His Legacy.* New York: Oxford University Press, 1983.

Wade, Virginia and Jean Rafferty. *Ladies of the Court: A Century of Women at Wimbledon.* New York: Athenaeum, 1984.

Wayand, Alexander M. *Cavalcade of Basketball.* New York: Macmillan, 1960.

Welch, Paula Dee. "The Emergence of American Women in the Summer Olympic Games, 1900–1972." Ed.D. diss., University of North Carolina at Greensboro, 1975.

Williams, Linda D. "An Analysis of American Sportswomen in Two Negro Newspapers: The *Pittsburgh Courier,* 1924–1948, and the *Chicago Defender,* 1932–1948." Ph.D. diss., Ohio State University, 1987.

Williamson, Nancy P. and William O. Johnson. *"Whatta-Gal!" The Babe Didrikson Story.* Boston: Little, Brown, 1979.

Woloch, Nancy. *Women and the American Experience.* 2d ed. New York: McGraw-Hill, 1994.

Zipter, Yvonne. *Diamonds Are a Dyke's Best Friend: Reflections, Reminiscences, and Reports from the Field on the Lesbian National Pastime.* Ithaca, N.Y.: Firebrand, 1988.

INDEX

Amateur Athletic Union (AAU): basketball tournament, 28–30, 35, 249; contrast to physical educators, 9–14, 19, 23–27

American Tennis Association (ATA), 59–60. *See also*
tennis

anorexia nervosa. *See* eating disorders

apologetic behavior, xxii, 45–52, 304*n*96; assessment
of as a strategy, 289; in basketball, 284–85; in
golf, 265–67; in intercollegiate athletics, 223–25;
in tennis, 67–70, 151–56, 234–46; "phoney apologetic," 242, 304*n*96

appearance, importance of: 90–91, 93–94; in basketball, 46–47, 255–56; in intercollegiate athletics,
224; in tennis, 56, 233

Association for Intercollegiate Athletics for Women
(AIAW): *AIAW v. NCAA*, 210–214; as alternative
to the male model, 124–25, 181–84; athletic
scholarships and recruiting, 115–16, 122–25, 181;
delegate assemblies, 125–27, 200–201, 211,
215–16; founding, 110, 122; numbers of members, 122, 126, 171, 178, 210; philosophy, 110,
124–27; relations with NCAA, 117–22, 168–71,
200–209; sex-separate vs. integrated teams,
114–15; and Title IX, 126–27, 131–34, 137–42,
167–68; and the Tower bill, 131–33

"athletes" (versus "sportswomen"), 12–16, 23

athletic scholarships, 98–99, 115–16, 122–25,
179–80, 191, 226–27, 278

basketball, xxii–xxiii, 24, 34; AAU national tournament, 28–30, 35, 49–50; amateur (1950s), 28–52,
249; apologetic behavior in, 49–51, 255–57;
beauty contest, 49–51; blacks in, 33, 41, 257–58;
"girls' rules," 31–32, 52, 95; media coverage,
40–44, 47–49; Olympics, 95, 277; participation
rates, 249; physical educators on, 34–36; professional, 33–34, 249–64, 276–77, 288–89; racial and
class connotations in, 33–36, 257–58, 262–63,
288–89. *See also* Women's Basketball League

Bayh, Sen. Birch (D, Ind.), 111–13, 174

bipolar dualism, 4, 7, 51; tennis players deconstructing, 151

Department of (HEW), 166–68, 171–72, 177–78
Heldman, Gladys, 145–46, 153, 164
Henrich, Christy, xxiii, 271–72
historiography of women's sports, 293n38
homosexuality. *See* lesbianism

individual sports, xxii
inequality. *See* difference; equality; intercollegiate athletics; tennis
intercollegiate athletics, xxviii; attendance at championships, 223, 275–76; campus politics, 184–86; commercialism in, 12–14; corruption in, 12–14, 115–16; gender inequalities in (and compliance), 175, 179–80, 187–91, 226–27, 278–80; participation rates, 285; women's alternative to the male model, 16–17, 26, 97–99, 115–16, 225–27, 281–82. *See also* Association for Intercollegiate Athletics for Women; Commission on Intercollegiate Athletics for Women

Kennedy, John F., administration of, 85–86
Kerrigan, Nancy, xvii–xxiii
King, Billie Jean, 142–43, 149, 162–64, 275; earnings, 147, 239; and equal purses at Wimbledon, 161–62; and Chris Evert, 235; as feminist, 153–54; and lesbianism, 235–40; love of tennis, 142, 162–64; versus Bobby Riggs, 157–60

Lieberman, Nancy, 258–59, 264
lesbian-baiting, 185–86, 267–68
lesbianism, xxvi, 4–6, 23–25, 285, 295n12; in basketball, 44–45, 258; in the Gay Games, 268; in golf, 265–67; and "mannish" reputation of sports, 295n12; in tennis, 155–56, 233–44
Lopiano, Donna, 209, 211, 213, 319n42
Ley, Katherine, 22, 82–83, 110, 136

male coaches/administrators of female sports, 10, 36–37, 121–22, 224–25, 257, 272–73. *See also* National Collegiate Athletic Association
masculinity: masculine reputation of sports,

xxii, 4–7, 21–33, 43–50. *See also* femininity
media coverage: and Cold War shifts, 91–94; of female athletes, xxiv, xxiii, 128; of intercollegiate basketball, 275–76; of pro golf, 266; of tennis, 230–31
Meyers, Ann, 258–59
Moran, Gertrude "Gorgeous Gussie," 65–66

National Association for the Physical Education of College Women (NAPECW), 9, 12, 15–16, 24, 25–27, 80–81
National Coalition for Girls and Women in Education, 189, 216, 219–20
National Collegiate Athletic Association (NCAA): *AIAW v. NCAA*, 210–14; attitude toward AIAW and self-determination for women, 129–31, 180–81; conventions, 121–22 (1972), 122 (1973), 129 (1974), 168–70 (1975), 177 (1976), 187–88 (1979), 200 (1980), 204–207 (1981); interest in sponsoring women's sports, 117–22, 129–31, 168–71, 177, 200–209; legal interpretations and, 118, 168–69; and Title IX, 127–31, 167–68, 171–73, 177, 187–90; and the Tower bill, 131–33, 177; representation of women in, 201–203, 222–23, 280; and revenue-producing sports, 127, 131, 168, 177
National Section for Girls' and Women's Sports (NSGWS; later, Division for Girls' and Women's Sports): equality and, 114–16; 1950s philosophy, 10–27; relationship with AAU, 95–96; relationship with AIAW, 122; shifts in mid-1950s, 79–83, 96–102. *See also* physical educators
Navratilova, Martina, xxiv, 240–43, 274–75
Nineteen-Twenties, the, 12–13, 30, 34

Office of Civil Rights (OCR; Department of Education), 216–17, 278–80
Olympic Games: 11 (1950s), 13 (1928); and the Cold War, 84–97; and physical educators, 79–80, 96–97; and the U.S.

coverage, 217–22. *See also* DeHart
Coalition; National Collegiate Athletic
Association
Tower bill. *See* Association for Intercolle-
giate Athletics for Women; National
Collegiate Athletic Association; revenue-
producing sports
track and field, 24, 86, 99, 273

unfeminine. *See* femininity
United States Lawn Tennis Association
(USLTA), 54–59, 71, 143–46, 229. *See
also* tennis
U.S. Commission on Civil Rights, 189–90

victims, female athletes as, xxiii–xxiv
"Vim" and "Vigor," 90
Virginia Slims (as tennis sponsor), 145–49,
157, 230, 275. *See also* tennis

volleyball, xxii

Wayland Hutcherson Flying Queens, 28–29,
37, 38, 40, 46, 47, 49
Women's Athletic Association (WAA), 17, 22
Women's Basketball League (WBL): apologetic behavior in, 255–58; black players
in, 257–58; collapse of, 262–64; disadvantages of, 253–56, 260, 262–63; first
season (1978–79), 251–52; media coverage, 253–54; origins of, 249–50; second
season, 259–61; stars of, 258–59; third
season, 260–62
Women's Tennis Association, 149, 161, 229,
243, 275. *See also* tennis
Wright, Ben, 265–67

Zaharias, Babe Didrikson. *See* Didrikson,
Babe